MW00759910

SOCIOLOGICAL
METHODOLOGY
❧ 1997 ❧

SOCIOLOGICAL METHODOLOGY 1997

VOLUME 27

EDITOR: Adrian E. Raftery

ADVISORY EDITORS: Gerhard Arminger

Mark P. Becker

Kathleen Mary Carley

Patrick Doreian

Barbara Entwisle

Larry J. Griffin

Nora Cate Schaeffer

Herbert L. Smith

Michael E. Sobel

Yu Xie

Kazuo Yamaguchi

MANAGING EDITOR: Janet Wilt

An official publication by Blackwell Publishers for

THE AMERICAN SOCIOLOGICAL ASSOCIATION

FELICE LEVINE, *Executive Officer*

North Carolina State University
Department of Sociology and Anthropology
Box 8107
Raleigh, North Carolina 27695-8107

Copyright © 1997 by: American Sociological Association
1722 N Street, NW
Washington, DC 20036, USA

Copyright under International, Pan American, and
Universal Copyright Conventions. All rights
reserved. No part of this book may be reproduced
in any form—except for brief quotation (not to
exceed 1,000 words) in a review or professional
work—without permission in writing from the publishers.

Library of Congress Catalog Card Information
Sociological Methodology, 1969–85
San Francisco, Jossey-Bass. 15 v. illus. 24 cm. annual. (Jossey-Bass behavioral science
series)
Editor: 1969, 1970: E. F. Borgatta; 1971, 1972, 1973–74: H. L. Costner;
1975, 1976, 1977: D. R. Heise; 1978, 1979, 1980: K. F. Schuessler;
1981, 1982, 1983–84: S. Leinhardt; 1985: N. B. Tuma

Sociological Methodology, 1986–88
Washington, DC, American Sociological Association. 3 v. illus. 24 cm. annual.
Editor: 1986: N. B. Tuma; 1987, 1988: C. C. Clogg

Sociological Methodology, 1989–1992
Oxford, Basil Blackwell. 4 v. illus. 24 cm. annual.
Editor: 1989, 1990: C. C. Clogg; 1991, 1992: P. V. Marsden
"An official publication of the American Sociological Association."
1. Sociology—Methodology—Year books. I. American Sociological
Association. II. Borgatta, Edgar F., 1924– ed.

HM24.S55   301'.01'8   68-54940
                            rev.
Library of Congress   [r71h2]

British Cataloguing in Publication Data
Sociological Methodology. Vol. 27
7   1. Sociology. Methodology
         301'.01'8

ISBN 0-63120-792-9
ISSN 0081-1750

CONSULTANTS

Paul Allison
Gerhard Arminger
Carl Barden
Mark P. Becker
Maia Berkane
Carlo Berzuini
Kenneth A. Bollen
Kathleen Mary Carley
M.J. Crowder
Sinan Demirel
Patrick Doreian
Barbara Entwisle
Christina Fraley
Roberto Franzosi
Ann Glusker
Larry J. Griffin
Jacques A. Hagenaars
Michael Hannan
David Heise
Michael Hout
Li Hsu
Edgar Kiser
Kenneth Land

Steven Lewis
Time F. Liao
Jun Liu
J. Scott Long
Diane Lye
Michael Macy
Barry Markovsky
Peter McCullagh
Allan L. McCutcheon
Xiao-Li Meng
Robert M. O'Brien
Trond K. Petersen
Cecilia Ridgeway
Donald B. Rubin
Nora Cate Schaeffer
Tore Schweder
Herbert L. Smith
Michael E. Sobel
Judith Tanur
Ross Taplin
Robert Weiss
Yu Xie
Kazuo Yamaguchi

CONTENTS

Consultants	v
Contributors	xi
Information for Authors	xiii
In This Volume	xv

**FORMAL ANALYSIS OF QUALITATIVE DATA:
A SYMPOSIUM**

1. The Niche Hiker's Guide to Population Ecology: 1
   A Logical Reconstruction of Organization Ecology's
   Niche Theory
   Gábor Péli

2. Sequence Comparison Via Alignment and Gibbs   47
   Sampling: A Formal Analysis of the Emergence
   of the Modern Sociological Article
   Andrew Abbott and Emily Barman

3. A Generic Semantic Grammar for Quantitative Text   89
   Analysis: Applications to East and West Berlin Radio
   News Content from 1979
   Carl W. Roberts

Discussion:
     Comment: The Importance of Order   131
        Kathleen M. Carley

Comment: On Ambiguity and Rhetoric   135
in (Social) Science
        Roberto Franzosi
Comment: On Logical Formalization of Theories   145
from Organizational Ecology
        Michael T. Hannan
Comment: Evaluating Qualitative Methodologies   151
        Edgar Kiser

Rejoinders:
Reply: Intuition and the Formal Approaches   159
        Gábor Péli
Reply to Comments   165
        Andrew Abbott and Emily Barman
Reply: The Curse of Chauvin   169
        Carl W. Roberts

SOCIOECONOMIC INDICES
4.   Socioeconomic Indexes for Occupations: A Review, 177
     Update, and Critique
        Robert M. Hauser and
        John Robert Warren

5.   A Dual-Source Indicator of Consumer Confidence   299
        Gordon G. Bechtel

ESTIMATING TREATMENT EFFECTS
6.   Matching with Multiple Controls to Estimate Treatment 325
     Effects in Observational Studies
        Herbert L. Smith

EVENT-HISTORY ANALYSIS
7.   The Neighborhood History Calendar: A Data Collection   355
     Method Designed for Dynamic Multilevel Modeling
        William G. Axinn, Jennifer S. Barber,
        and Dirgha J. Ghimire

8.   Adjusting for Attrition in Event-History Analysis   393
        Daniel H. Hill

9.   Dynamic Discrete-time Duration Models: Estimation   417
     via Markov Chain Monte Carlo
                Ludwig Fahrmeir and
                Leonhard Knorr-Held

LONGITUDINAL AND MULTILEVEL MODELING
10. Latent Variable Modeling of Longitudinal and   453
     Multilevel Data
                Bengt Muthén

     Name Index   481

     Subject Index   489

CONTRIBUTORS

Andrew Abbott, Department of Sociology, University of Chicago

William G. Axinn, Population Research Institute, Department of Sociology, Pennsylvania State University

Jennifer S. Barber, Population Research Institute, Department of Sociology, Pennsylvania State University

Emily Barman, Department of Sociology, University of Chicago

Gordon G. Bechtel, College of Business Administration, University of Florida

Kathleen M. Carley, Department of Social & Decision Science, Carnegie-Mellon University

Ludwig Fahrmeir, Institut für Statistik, Universität München

Roberto Franzosi, University of Oxford, Trinity College

Dirgha J. Ghimire, Tribhuvan University, Nepal

Michael T. Hannan, Graduate School of Business, Stanford University

Robert M. Hauser, Department of Sociology, Center for Demography and Ecology, The University of Wisconsin, Madison

Daniel H. Hill, Survey Research Center, Institute for Social Research, The University of Michigan

Edgar Kiser, Department of Sociology, University of Washington

Leonhard Knorr-Held, Institut für Statistik, Universität München

Bengt Muthén, Graduate School of Education and Information Studies,
    University of California, Los Angeles

Gábor Péli, Faculty of Management and Organization, University
    of Groningen

Carl W. Roberts, Department of Sociology, Iowa State University

Herbert L. Smith, Population Studies Center, University
    of Pennsylvania

INFORMATION FOR AUTHORS

Sociological Methodology is an annual volume on methods of research in the social sciences. Sponsored by the American Sociological Association, its mission is to disseminate material that advances empirical research in sociology and related disciplines. Chapters present original methodological contributions, expository statements on and illustrations of recently developed techniques, and critical discussions of research practice. Further information on recent volumes is available on the Web page http://weber.u.washington.edu/~socmeth2.

Sociological Methodology seeks contributions that address the full range of problems confronted by empirical work in the contemporary social sciences, including conceptualization and modeling, research design, data collection, measurement, and data analysis. Work on the methodological problems involved in any approach to empirical social science is appropriate for *Sociological Methodology*.

The content of each annual volume of *Sociological Methodology* is driven by submissions initiated by authors; the volumes do not have specific themes. Editorial decisions about manuscripts submitted are based on the advice of expert referees. Criteria include originality, breadth of interest and applicability, and expository clarity. Discussions of implications for research practice are vital, and authors are urged to include empirical illustrations of the methods they discuss.

Authors should submit five copies of manuscripts to

> Adrian E. Raftery, Editor
> *Sociological Methodology*
> Department of Sociology
> Box 353340
> University of Washington
> Seattle, WA 98195-3340

Manuscripts should include an informative abstract of not more than one double-spaced page, and should not identify the author within the text. Submission of a manuscript for review by *Sociological Methodology* implies that it has not been published previously and that it is not under review elsewhere.

Inquiries concerning the appropriateness of material and/or other aspects of editorial policies and procedures are welcome. Prospective authors should contact the Editor by E-mail at socmeth@stat.washington.edu, by phone at (206) 685-9325, by fax at (206) 543-2516, or by regular mail at the above address.

IN THIS VOLUME

Sociological Methodology 1997 focuses on advances in three currently active research areas: formal qualitative methods, socioeconomic indices, and event-history analysis. It also includes important contributions to the estimation of treatment effects and to longitudinal and multilevel modeling. Software to implement the methods proposed and the data used is available for many of the chapters, in many cases free of charge by E-mail or over the World Wide Web, enhancing its usefulness to readers and users. Links to the software and data and much other information are available at the *Sociological Methodology* home page http://weber.u.washington.edu/~socmeth2.

The formal analysis of qualitative data has been developing rapidly in the past ten years. Chapters 1–3 present several of the most recent advances: a chapter by Péli on the use of formal logic to develop theories and test them for consistency, one by Abbott and Barman on sequence comparison methods using alignment algorithms and Gibbs sampling, and one by Roberts on semantic grammars for text analysis. Carley, Franzosi, Hannan, and Kiser have written discussions of these papers, and rejoinders by the authors are also included. Together, the ten pieces that make up this symposium provide an overall perspective on the current state of formal qualitative analysis.

The development of socioeconomic indices has been an active area of sociology for 35 years, with renewed attention recently. In Chapter 4, Hauser and Warren present a very important, and perhaps definitive, analysis of the currently available data on socioeconomic indices for occupations. In Chapter 5, Bechtel proposes an index of consumer confidence for the United States that combines several existing indices.

Event-history analysis is important to sociologists, and Chapters 7–9 extend the methods available in three important ways. Axinn, Barber, and Ghimire propose the Neighborhood History Calendar as a way of collecting data for multilevel event-history data. Hill proposes a way of adjusting for attrition in event-history analysis when attrition is related to the event of interest. Fahrmeir and Knorr-Held propose a Bayesian method for estimating time-varying effects in discrete-time event-history analysis.

In Chapter 6, Smith points out that matching can be used as an alternative to regression for estimating treatment effects when the proportion of cases "treated" is small, and can be more efficient. In Chapter 10, Muthén shows how the standard apparatus of structural equation models with latent variables can be used and extended to analyze data that are both longitudinal and multilevel.

One other unifying thread in this volume is the use of Markov Chain Monte Carlo (MCMC) methods, of which Gibbs sampling is a special case, to make inference in models for complex observational data. Researchers in many disciplines have realized recently that these methods can yield solutions to estimation problems that were previously thought to be intractable, and interest in them is intense. Abbott and Barman use MCMC methods to detect recurring regularities in sequences when the regularities are rare and faint, a task that can be compared to "searching for a needle in a haystack." Fahrmeir and Knorr-Held use MCMC methods to estimate complex event-history models with censoring, unobserved components and time-varying coefficients. Both of these chapters contain useful tutorial introductions to MCMC estimation, which seem potentially promising for many other sociological problems. For further information about MCMC methods, I recommend Gilks, Richardson and Spiegelhalter (1996).

THEORY BUILDING VIA FORMAL LOGIC

In Chapter 1, Péli develops methods for the logical formalization of theory. This enables one to assess the internal consistency of the theory and to answer questions such as: where is the theory incomplete? Where do the conclusions not follow from the premises? It also allows one to make additional deductions from the premises. The chapter is built around an in-depth application to the population ecology theory of Hannan and Freeman (1989).

SEQUENCE ANALYSIS

Has the structure of the typical sociological research article become more "rigid" over time? In Chapter 2, Abbott and Barman develop methods for answering this question and similar ones by breaking down an article into a sequence of "elements," and then finding out whether articles in later decades of the *American Journal of Sociology* have a greater commonality of patterns than those in earlier decades. They first review and extend the alignment methods that Abbott and Hrycak (1990) adapted from molecular biology. These consist of determining the "distance" between any two sequences (in terms of the numbers of substitutions, insertions, and deletions required to get from one to the other), and then using cluster analysis to find groups of articles that are "similar." They then introduce a new method, based on Gibbs sampling, also adapted from molecular biology, due to Lawrence et al. (1993). This performs remarkably well: it can find subsequences that are common to several sequences, even when the subsequences are not the same each time (e.g., they can be "corrupted"), and when they are present in only a small proportion of the population of sequences. They find no evidence of rigidification over time in AJS articles, a conclusion that turns out to be controversial in the ensuing discussion.

A SEMANTIC GRAMMAR FOR TEXT ANALYSIS

Standard content analysis proceeds by counting the occurrences of particular words and types of words in a text. In recent years, there have been several efforts to extend this by taking account of context and of syntax, recognizing the fact that context is important for interpreting the occurrence of words, phrases, and clauses and the structure of texts. In Chapter 3, Roberts introduces a generic *semantic* grammar, in which every clause is encoded according to themes and relations between themes reflecting the meanings that clauses were intended to convey within their social context. This work continues and provides alternative directions to an existing thread of research in *Sociological Methodology*. Previous work on "contextual content analysis" includes the map analysis of Carley (1993) and the set theoretic approach of Franzosi (1994).

DISCUSSION OF QUALITATIVE ANALYSIS

Chapters 1–3 all involve formal analysis of qualitative information. Carley, Franzosi, Hannan, and Kiser provide discussions of these chapters and of the area as a whole, and the authors respond. Franzosi and Kiser point out that they all use formal methods to explore the rhetorical structure of texts and are united by a shared faith in the virtues of science, rigor, and formalism. Kiser points out several ways in which the methods introduced in these chapters allow us to see interesting features of texts that would not have been found by other methods, and concludes that formal qualitative analysis has come of age in sociology.

Hannan recalls that in the 1960s, theory formalization was central in sociology, but that it is now peripheral. He ascribes this failure to the fact that the (old) theory formalization methods required too much from the user, including assumptions about functional forms and so on. He says that Péli's approach, which depends on first-order logic and automated theorem provers, is more flexible and so more likely to succeed. Kiser agrees, saying that once the basic method is learned, the costs of applying it are low and the benefits potentially great.

Carley, Franzosi, and Kiser all comment that both the chapters that rely on content coding (Abbott and Barman, and Roberts) are limited by this requirement. Effective coding requires skilled coders and a lot of time, and the issue of inter-coder reliability is always present. They also question Abbott and Barman's conclusion that the structure of sociological articles has not become more rigid, arguing particularly that the *American Journal of Sociology* may not be representative of sociological journals as a whole. Franzosi takes up Roberts's contention that content analysis based on the Subject-Verb-Object (S-V-O) structure does not work well for "unstructured" text, but then claims that the output of Roberts's method is merely an S-V-O structure in disguise. This claim is vigorously disputed by Roberts in his rejoinder.

Kiser reminds us that the majority of qualitative work in sociology is informal rather than formal and gives as an example Sewell (1994), which, like Chapters 1–3, emphasizes the rhetorical structure of texts. The human mind seems rather well adapted to informal qualitative sociological work; formalization can be useful in providing a basis for agreed conclusions from qualitative data, and also for automating the analysis of large numbers of texts. In this way, qualitative sociological analysis may be like other endeavors such as pattern recognition and speech recognition, at which humans are very good and automated computer procedures are not, at least as yet. Formalizing qualitative analysis is an important and difficult research agenda, and all involved in this symposium agree that Chapters 1–3 advance it substantially.

OCCUPATIONAL SOCIOECONOMIC INDICES

In Chapter 4, Hauser and Warren provide an authoritative review of the history of occupational socioeconomic indices, surely one of the most used variables in social research. They review the evidence for their contention that the measurement of someone's social and economic characteristics in terms of the attributes of his or her job has remarkably high reliability and validity. Many sociologists have long adopted this view, but others, including many economists, have preferred to use a person's current income. Hauser and Warren review a plethora of evidence that occupational characteristics are more stable, easier to measure well, and more predictive of important social outcomes than is current income.

They then develop a new set of indices for 1990 Census occupations using data from the 1989 and 1994 General Social Surveys and the 1990 Census, updating the work of Nakao and Treas (1994) in *Sociological Methodology*. Finally, they ask the question of how best to construct a socioeconomic index for use in basic models of occupational stratification, using model fit as the criterion. They conclude that levels of occupational education define the main dimension of occupational persistence and that composite indices are scientifically obsolete.

Even before publication, their results have already been widely used in social research, and are sure to have a major impact on the measurement of socioeconomic status. The Hauser-Warren SEI scores for 1980 and 1990 are available electronically by ftp.

A NEW INDEX OF U.S. CONSUMER CONFIDENCE

In Chapter 5, Bechtel proposes a new index of U.S. consumer confidence that combines the University of Michigan Survey Research Center's Index of Consumer Sentiment with the Conference Board's Consumer Expectation Index. He does this by recasting the responses from the six items that make up the two indices in terms of a factorial layout (time horizon, communal or personal orientation, business or jobs). A Poisson log-nonlinear model is fit to the resulting data, and the parameter estimates provide new indices of aspects of consumer confidence. The 1992 data for which the model is estimated are available on the World Wide Web from StatLib.

ESTIMATING TREATMENT EFFECTS BY MATCHING

The most usual way to estimate a treatment effect from observational data in sociology is via regression or its generalizations. An alternative is to use *matching*, in which each treated case is matched with one or more control cases that have the same values of covariates. This is particularly useful when there are few treated cases and many controls. One limitation of matching is that it will often be impossible to find an exact match for a treated case on all the covariates of interest. Fortunately, for valid results, one needs only to find controls that have the same, or a similar, value of the *propensity score*—i.e., the probability that the case is a treatment rather than a control given the covariates. This is usually possible.

There are two remarkable aspects to the matching approach. One is that it is possible to validly reduce the size of one's data set considerably, particularly when there are few treated cases and when these are mostly unlike the (numerous) controls. The second is that *by reducing the sample in this way, one can reduce the standard error of the treatment effect relative to regression.* In Chapter 6, Smith provides an overview of this approach to the estimation of treatment effects, illustrating it with the estimation of the effects of an organizational innovation on Medicare mortality within hospitals. The approach has many potential sociological applications.

COLLECTING NEIGHBORHOOD EVENT-HISTORY DATA

One of the enduring themes of sociological research is the effort to measure the effect of *contexts* (such as neighborhood, city, or social network) on the behaviors, outcomes, and lives of individuals. Individual-level event-history data collection and analysis is by now well developed and has become a staple of social research. Contexts also experience events: a neighborhood has a new school or a road built, a city acquires a university, and so on. Just as longitudinal data often provide the best basis for detecting and measuring causal effects of variables and changes on the lives of individuals, the same may well be true in the search for contextual effects. To date, however, effective methods for collecting event histories for neighborhoods and other contexts have not been well developed.

In Chapter 7, Axinn, Barber, and Ghimire take a step toward filling this gap. They propose the Neighborhood History Calendar, an extension to neighborhoods of the individual life history calendar proposed in *Sociological Methodology* by Freedman et al. (1988). Using a calendar format, individuals and local officials are interviewed, and archival sources are also used. Geographic Information System (GIS) technology can also be used to refine the spatial aspect of such information, and to link together multiple sources of contextual-history data. The method is illustrated by application to the study of fertility in a rural area of Nepal.

ADJUSTING FOR ATTRITION
IN EVENT-HISTORY ANALYSIS

Suppose you are studying the rate and determinants of an event, such as divorce. Individuals often leave your study shortly before a divorce, and you are unable, by definition, to determine whether they attrited because of the impending divorce or for other reasons. If you estimate divorce rates on the basis of the (censored) data you have using standard life table or event-history methods, you will underestimate divorce rates, perhaps vastly, and produce biased estimates of event-history regression parameters. What can you do? The problem seems almost insoluble, since you have no way of knowing how many of the attrited cases were due to divorce or what their characteristics were.

In Chapter 8, Hill has produced a clever and elegant solution to this problem, using the Shared Unmeasured Risk Factor (SURF) model introduced in *Sociological Methodology* by Hill, Axinn, and Thornton (1993). The basic trick is to observe that, although one does not know which of the attriting individuals actually got divorced soon after attriting, one can estimate which ones were *most at risk* of divorcing. Using the 1986–1988 Survey of Income and Program Participation (SIPP) data, Hill shows that (1) standard methods underestimate divorce rates massively (by about one-half); (2) standard "weighting" methods for correcting this bias do not work; and (3) the SURF approach does correct the bias quite effectively.

DYNAMIC EVENT-HISTORY ANALYSIS
VIA MARKOV CHAIN MONTE CARLO

Consider event-history data where there are several types of possible events, and covariate effects are time-varying rather than constant. This is quite common in practice. In Chapter 9, Fahrmeir and Knorr-Held consider a typical problem of this kind: the effects of unemployment insurance benefits on the hazard of leaving unemployment to full-time work, part-time work, retirement, or non-labor-force activity. It seems reasonable to suppose that these effects (and the effect of other variables such as national origin) vary with duration of unemployment in a reasonably smooth but not necessarily monotonic way.

They propose a full probability model for this situation, and carry out fully Bayesian estimation using MCMC methods. Their chapter also contains a useful tutorial introduction to general MCMC estimation for complex statistical models, complementing the introduction by Abbott and Barman in Chapter 2. They apply the methods to a German data set on unemployment duration, and find several results that would be hard to establish with more standard methods. Their approach can be compared and used in conjunction with the more nonparametric smoothing methods introduced in *Sociological Methodology* by Wu and Tuma (1990).

LONGITUDINAL AND MULTILEVEL MODELING

In Chapter 10, Muthén considers the analysis of data that are both longitudinal *and* multilevel. His example is mathematics achievement at several time points for a sample of students clustered within classrooms, which in turn are clustered within schools. He shows how such data can be modeled using latent variables, and how estimation can be carried out using standard structural equation modeling software such as LISREL or EQS. This chapter develops previous work in *Sociological Methodology* (Muthén and Satorra 1995). Muthén has made software to calculate the necessary sample statistics available over the Web and by E-mail at StatLib.

ACKNOWLEDGMENTS

Forty-six reviewers, whose names are listed on page v, have collaborated with the authors and me in producing this volume. These include the 11 advisory editors, who have made a major contribution to the editorial work. I would like to thank Larry Griffin for helping to put together the symposium on the formal analysis of qualitative data that starts this volume.

Janet Wilt of the University of Washington is the managing editor of *Sociological Methodology*. She has done a wonderful job; without her this volume could not have been produced. At Blackwell Publishers, production was coordinated by Lisa McLaughlin. Stephanie Argeros-Magean copyedited the chapters of *Sociological Methodology 1997*, and Janet Cronin was responsible for proofreading. Clarisa Fauska of the University of Washington maintained the home page.

The American Sociological Association provides the sponsorship and financial support for this publication. The University of Washington has provided me with office space, a reduction in teaching responsibilities, and colleagues who have helped me develop this volume. I am very grateful to all of these individuals and institutions.

Adrian E. Raftery
University of Washington
December 1996

REFERENCES

Abbott, Andrew, and Alexandra Hrycak. 1990. "Measuring Sequence Resemblance." *American Journal of Sociology* 96:144–85.

Carley, Kathleen M. 1993. "Coding Choices for Textual Analysis: A Comparison of Content Analysis and Map Analysis." In *Sociological Methodology 1993*, edited by Peter V. Marsden, 75–125. Cambridge, MA: Blackwell Publishers.

Franzosi, Roberto. 1994. "From Words to Numbers: A Set Theory Framework for the Collection, Organization and Analysis of Narrative Data." In *Sociological Methodology 1994*, edited by Peter V. Marsden, 105–36. Cambridge, MA: Blackwell Publishers.

Freedman, Deborah, Arland Thornton, Donald Camburn, Duane Alwin, and Linda Young-DeMarco. 1988. "The Life History Calendar: A Technique for Collecting Retrospective Data." In *Sociological Methodology 1988*, edited by Clifford C. Clogg, 37–68. Cambridge, MA: Blackwell Publishers.

Gilks, Walter R., Sylvia Richardson, and David J. Spiegelhalter. 1996. *Markov Chain Monte Carlo in Practice*. London: Chapman and Hall.

Hannan, Michael T., and John Freeman 1989. *Organizational Ecology*. Cambridge: Harvard University Press.

Hill, Daniel H., Willian G. Axinn, and Arland Thornton. 1993. "Competing Hazards with Shared Unmeasured Risk Factors." In *Sociological Methodology 1993*, edited by Peter V. Marsden, 245–77. Cambridge, MA: Blackwell Publishers.

Lawrence, C. E., S. F. Altschul, M. S. Boguski, J. S. Liu, A. F. Neuwald, and J. C. Wooten. 1993. "Detecting Subtle Sequence Signals." *Science* 262:208–14.

Muthén, Bengt, and Albert Satorra. 1995. "Complex Sample Data in Structural Equation Modeling." In *Sociological Methodology 1995*, edited by Peter V. Marsden, 267–316. Cambridge, MA: Blackwell Publishers.

Nakao, Keiko, and Judith Treas. 1994. "Updating Occupational Prestige and Socio-economic Scores: How the New Measures Measure Up." In *Sociological Method-*

ology 1994, edited by Peter V. Marsden, 1–72. Cambridge, MA: Blackwell Publishers.

Sewell, William Jr. 1994. *A Rhetoric of Bourgeois Revolution: The Abbé Sieyes and What Is the Third Estate?* Durham, NC: Duke University Press.

Wu, Lawrance L., and Nancy B. Tuma 1990. "Local Hazard Models." In *Sociological Methodology 1990*, edited by Clifford C. Clogg, 141–80. Cambridge, MA: Blackwell Publishers.

☙ 1 ❧

THE NICHE HIKER'S GUIDE TO POPULATION ECOLOGY: A LOGICAL RECONSTRUCTION OF ORGANIZATION ECOLOGY'S NICHE THEORY

Gábor Péli*

Logical formalization is a formal method for the analysis of theoretical arguments in the social sciences. Hannan and Freeman's organizational niche theory (1989) is rebuilt by means of First-Order Logic, and its predictions are derived as theorems. Translation into a formal language makes the theory's inference structure transparent and accessible to discussion, repair, and development. The consistency of the model can be checked by computational means. The logical approach helps to specify niche theory's domain; it points out hidden assumptions, highlights spots where the reasoning has to be modified, and provides solid foundations for further theory building. Moreover, the established premise set also allows for the deduction of some new results. Logical formalization supports empirical research by delineating constraints on and explicit relations between sociological concepts, facilitating their appropriate operationalization.

A substantial part of this research has been carried out in the Center for Computer Science in Organization and Management, University of Amsterdam. I received a grant from the European Union (Cooperation in Science and Technology with Central and Eastern European Countries, ERBCIPACT #922309) in 1993–94. A number of core ideas were developed together with Jeroen Bruggeman. Many improvements were also suggested by David Beaver, John Freeman, Jaap Kamps, László Leirer, Michael Masuch, Breanndán Ó Nualláin, László Pólos, the three anonymous reviewers, and the editor of *Sociological Methodology* on an earlier version of the paper. E-mail: g.peli@bdk.rug.nl
*University of Groningen, The Netherlands

1

1. INTRODUCTION

Logical formalization is a nonmainstream methodological device for the social sciences. This paper focuses on the methodological aspects of the formalization process. I chose organization ecology's niche theory (Hannan and Freeman 1989) to demonstrate the advantages and the limits of the formal logical approach. The basic objective of the paper is to derive Hannan and Freeman's conclusions by logical means from a formula set that represents their main assumptions. The analysis shows that organizational niche theory's main conclusions follow from the sociological premises, provided that some modifications are implemented. Unperceived features of niche theory that help the identification of hidden constraints become visible through the lens of formal logic. By making these constraints explicit, we can better assess the range of applicability of the theory at hand.

Other areas of organizational ecology have been already formalized in recent years (Péli et al. 1994; Péli and Masuch 1997; Bruggeman 1997). The overlap between these formal models can play an important role from the point of view of theory building: It may serve as a foundation for a future unified formal framework of organization ecology.

1.1. Why Logic?

Logic is not a standard part of the methodologist community's knowledge base, as are statistics and infinitesimal calculus; getting familiar with its application requires an investment of energy. So, why logic, if we have mathematics? Because logic may help when mathematics is not easily applicable, especially when the reasoning is qualitative. While most mathematical methods focus on the quantitative or structural aspects of theories, logical modeling sticks to the theory's verbal reasoning, considering the qualitative descriptions as a reservoir of information. The basic presumptions are put into a logical language to see if they support the theory's main conclusions. The advantages and disadvantages are demonstrated in the course of formalization.

Unlike most mathematical derivations that mix formulas with natural language statements, logical deduction is syntactic. In the case of a logical proof, all the applied premises have to be spelled out explicitly. Critical readers can localize the unacceptable spots in the formalization. Since a precisely expressed critique is also easier to reply to, protagonists get a clear-cut view of what to defend or modify. Logic does not provide the proper content of a theory, but it does help to assess the consequences if certain conjectures have been made.

The derivations of the obtained theorems have been checked by the Metafor theorem prover.[1] Automated theorem proving allows us to shift attention from the sophisticated proof sequences to the formalization process itself: Does the logical rendering grasp the essence of the underlying sociological considerations?

Logical inference differs from statistical inference—that is, from drawing conclusions from empirical findings. Statistical inference is crucial in data evaluation, but limited sample sizes and identification problems of concepts in the obtained data set leave uncertainty about the results (Manski 1993; Clogg and Arminger 1993). Logical inference may complement statistical inference; while the latter taps the data base, the former clarifies the information embodied in the conceptual model.

This chapter is organized as follows. Section 2 describes the basics of the logical machinery and gives a brief introduction to niche theory. Section 3 presents the formalization process, the step-by-step translation of natural language arguments to logical formulas. Section 4 provides a discussion assessing the impact on theory building. Relevant technical and epistemic issues are also addressed. The appendix lists the formulas applied for each theorem.

2. THE INPUTS: LOGIC AND NICHE THEORY

2.1. *Logic Machinery*

2.1.1. *Which Logic?*
The word logic is a collective term for an increasing variety of inference systems, different in expressive power and complexity. I apply First-Order Logic (FOL) as the tool of formalization. FOL is one of the oldest of available logics with well-understood properties; it combines considerable expressive power with relatively simple handling. It is also an archetype for more sophisticated (second-order, modal, default, etc.) logics that extend it in different ways. FOL serves as a test case for the study of logic's applicability in the social sciences. The limits of a certain logic can be best learned by doing: appliers should proceed with the formalization until they meet these limits. Actually, none of the obstacles I met during the formal-

---

[1] The Metafor theorem prover has been developed in the Center for Computer Science in Organization and Management, University of Amsterdam (Ó Nualláin 1993). Another prover, Hyperproof, was designed for didactical purposes (Barwise and Etchemendy 1994). Moreover, several public domain theorem provers are available on the Internet; a well-known example is Otter (ftp://info.mcs.anl.gov:/pub/Otter).

ization were due to the chosen formal language; the present work demonstrates that complex arguments can be modeled in First-Order Logic. However, FOL has inherent limits that may require the use of more sophisticated
logical languages. I return to this problem in Section 4.

2.1.2. The Basics of First-Order Logic[2]

First-Order Logic is based on the following classes of symbols:

- *Name constants* that denote individual objects—e.g., *E1* (environment one), *obs* (observation period)
- *Variables* that can be substituted by objects, e.g., *x, y*
- *Quantifiers* that operate on variables: $\forall$ (for all), $\exists$ (there exists). The scope of a quantifier is marked by square brackets, e.g., $\forall x[...]$.
- *Logical connectives* (in order of decreasing binding strength): $\neg$ negation, $\wedge$ (and), $\vee$ (or), $\rightarrow$ (if ..., then ...), $\leftrightarrow$ (if and only if)[3]
- *Predicates* that express properties of and relations between objects, de-noted by capitalized strings—e.g., *Stable*(x), *Holds_in*$(x, E1)$. Some predicates are in infix form: $x > y$, $e1 = e2$. Their prefix denotation could be $>(x, y)$ and $=(e1, e2)$, respectively.
- *Function symbols*—e.g., *outflow*(x, t). To emphasize the distinction be-tween predicates and functions, the latter are denoted by noncapitalized strings.

Logical formalization can go rather close to natural language reasoning
due to the extensible vocabulary of predicates, name constants, and function symbols. For example, the statement that well-argued theories are
more reliable can be put as follows:

$$\forall x1, x2[Theory(x1) \wedge Theory(x2) \wedge Arg(x1) \wedge \neg Arg(x2)$$
$$\rightarrow reliability(x1) > reliability(x2)]$$

Read: "for all *x1, x2*, if *x1* is a theory and *x2* is a theory and *x1* is well
argued and *x2* is not well argued, then the reliability of *x1* is higher than the
reliability of *x2*."

This formula exploits the one-place *Theory*(x) and *Arg*(x) predicates that
denote, respectively, that object *x* is a theory and that *x* is well argued. The
reliability function assigns reliability values to *x1* and *x2*.

---

[2]For interested readers Gamut (1991) provides a nice introduction to logic. But the best way to get a grip on the subject is to follow the translation process from natural language descriptions to formal premises.

[3]For example, $(a \vee b) \rightarrow ((\neg d) \wedge e)$ can be put as: $a \vee b \rightarrow \neg d \wedge e$.

As is the case in mathematics, logical formulas are premises or theorems according to their role in the deduction. Premises of a certain theorem may be theorems themselves. Otherwise, premises are sorted as assumptions, definitions, and meaning postulates.

Assumptions (also called axioms) describe properties of or relations between the concepts of a theory (e.g., "Specialists have narrow niche."). Definitions fix the meaning of concepts in terms of others. It often happens that there is not enough information to delimit a notion. Then, meaning postulates may summarize the known features of the concept at hand. The use of meaning postulates instead of definitions whenever it is possible has an important advantage: theoretical parsimony. A definition of a concept poses stronger constraints on the theory than a partial characterization. Theories often leave the meaning of their notions somewhat unspecified, which means that different mental models may be compatible with the same formal theory (think of probabilistic versus "smeared" particle locations in quantum mechanics). The formalizer may mutilate the theory, cutting down unforeseen outcomes, if using immature definitions when a partial characterization of the notions would suffice (Lakatos 1976).

2.2. Organization Ecology's Niche Theory

Niche theory is about organizations that economize on the trade-off between the scope and the quality of their activities (Freeman and Hannan 1983; Hannan and Freeman 1989; Carroll 1985). Some of them develop superb skills in certain domains but fail outside a specific range of conditions. Others cope with more wide ranging circumstances but without being ideally suited to any of them. Organizational niche theory tells us the payoffs for such choices in different environmental patterns. The core ideas were borrowed from biological niche theory, which was already spelled out in mathematical form (Levins 1968; Roughgarden 1979). The niche of an organization type is constituted by the range of environmental characteristics that this type can cope with.[4]

Specialist and generalist organizations take opposite positions concerning their niche width and fitness. Specialists restrict their internal organization and performance to a limited range of environmental conditions (narrow niche). Generalists can operate under different environmental conditions (broad niche). They develop multiple structure based on routine

---

[4]Note that under this interpretation the niche is not a geographical area that supports the survival of a certain kind of organization (habitat).

sets that can be invoked in response to different needs. Since an organization's adaptive potential is finite, an increase in niche breadth has a negative effect on fitness (other things being equal), lowering the quality of organizational performance.

The trade-off between generalism and specialism depends on the way the environment changes. If a certain outcome prevails (environmental variability is low), then specialization is favored by selection. However, if the observation period is partitioned approximately equally between the occurring environments (variability is high), then success depends on two other variables: dissimilarity and grain. If the occurring environments represent similar resource conditions, then generalists need not establish extra wide niches; as a consequence, they assume a moderate fitness that leads them to dominance. In case of dissimilar and highly variable conditions, the texture of the observation period determines selection preference. If the alternating environments come in short temporal lumps (grain is fine), then specialist organizations survive by consuming spared resources in bad times and finally dominate because of their excellent performance in good times. If the patches are long (grain is coarse), then specialists face enduring bad periods that are too long to be buffered.

The selection process can be seen as a hurdle race between teams of generalists and specialists, where hurdle configurations represent the environmental conditions and the track stands for the observation period. Two kinds of hurdles, E1 and E2, are distributed along the track. Specialists are quite smart in passing E1 hurdles and clumsy in E2-s. Generalists have a mediocre performance in both kinds of hurdles. Organizations that fail an obstacle are eliminated, and the winner is the team with lower losses at the end.

3. LOGICAL FORMALIZATION

Having the logic machinery and the basic sociological ideas in place, the subsequent task is to zoom in on niche theory's key statements and to construct a set of formulas that grasps the intuition. Two phases follow by turns in the formalization process: (1) some focal elements of niche theory are highlighted in natural language, and (2) the argument is summarized by means of logical formulas. If information is missing, then a search is undertaken to bypass the leakage. Model building stops when the formula set represents sufficient information to derive or falsify niche theory's predictions.

Because translation to a logical language involves interpretation, the derived outcomes may be artifacts of inappropriate formalization. There are no formal criteria to decide if a formal rendering grasps the essence of the subject theory. But the formal machinery is transparent, at least in the sense that the derived conclusions can always be traced back to explicit premises. This feature helps to verify the interpretational effects of the translation process.

3.1. *Environment*

Environment in organization ecology is constituted by the configuration of available resources: It is a cluster of closely related resource conditions. Hannan and Freeman (1989) focus on cases when two environments (*E1* and *E2*) alter during the period of observation. Though niche theory can be generalized to more than two resource conditions, the most important trade-offs can be best demonstrated in the dichotomic case. Assumptions 1 and 2 state that *E1* and *E2* are the two environmental outcomes in question. *Env(e)* says that object *e* is an environment.

A1. *E1* and *E2* are the environments that occur.[5]

$$\forall e[Env(e) \rightarrow e = E1 \vee e = E2]$$

(For all *e*, if *e* is an environment, then *e* is identical either with *E1* or with *E2*.)

A2. Environments *E1* and *E2* are different.

$$\neg(E1 = E2)$$

Homogeneous periods for which a certain resource configuration holds are called environmental patches. Each patch lasts until a shift in resource conditions occurs. The observation period comprises a series of patches that feature environments *E1* and *E2* alternately (Figure 1).

3.2. *Niche Width*

The niche of an organizational population comprises all the resource configurations (environments) that sustain the population. The member organizations in the population are adapted to the resource conditions of which

---

[5]Assumptions, definitions, meaning postulates and theorems are recited by their capitalized initials and their serial number.

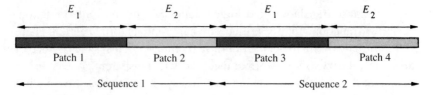

FIGURE 1. The observation period as a series of alternating environments.

the niche is composed. If an organization can operate only in a single environment, then its niche is narrow; if it is adapted to dissimilar circumstances, then its niche is broad (Definitions 1-2). $Org\_type(x)$ and $Adapted(e,x)$ denote that x is an organization type and that x is adapted to environment e; $e1 \approx e2$ claims that $e1$ and $e2$ are similar. The niche(x) function measures the niche breadth of x.

D1. Organization types have narrow niche if and only if they are adapted to a single environment.

$$\forall x[Org\_type(x) \rightarrow (niche(x) = narrow \leftrightarrow$$
$$\forall e1,e2[Env(e1) \wedge Env(e2) \wedge Adapted(e1,x)$$
$$\wedge Adapted(e2,x) \rightarrow e1 = e2])]$$

(For all organization types x, the niche of x is narrow if and only if all environments $e1$ and $e2$ to which x is adapted are identical.)

D2. Organization types have wide niche if and only if they are adapted to dissimilar environments.

$$\forall x[Org\_type(x) \rightarrow (niche(x) = wide \leftrightarrow$$
$$\exists e1,e2[Env(e1) \wedge Env(e2) \wedge \neg(e1 \approx e2)$$
$$\wedge Adapted(e1,x) \wedge Adapted(e2,x)])]$$

(For all organization types x, the niche of x is wide if and only if there are environments $e1$ and $e2$, not similar to each other and to which x is adapted.)

Definition 1 may seem too restrictive associating narrow niche with a single environment. It would be unrealistic to claim that populations cannot tolerate even a tiny drift in resource conditions. However, an environment is not necessarily formed by a single resource configuration; it is rather a grouping of very close ones, represented as a tight cluster of states in a multidimensional resource space (Levins 1968). Thus a narrow niche may also contain a certain range of resource states. Note moreover, that Definitions 1–2 allow for a third case when organizations are adapted to different but similar environments. This case may be said to involve a medium broad niche.

3.3. Fitness

Adaptation to external resource configurations is only a necessary condition of success. Good performance also depends on the structuring and quality of internal organization. The joint effects of external and internal arrangements on performance are summarized by the degree of fitness. Unlike in biology, there are no genes that determine organizational behavior at the level of individuals. Fitness is assessed at the level of the population, through its impact on survival. Therefore a premise is needed to relate mortality and fitness.

Organizational ecology usually addresses disbanding processes by mortality rates. Nonetheless, population losses can be characterized in several other ways (e.g., the number of dissolving organizations per time unit or the intensity of population mass loss). In fact, different mortality measures may be compatible with niche theory. The forthcoming arguments do not exploit any specific features of disbanding processes that would force or even suggest a choice between the potential "measure-candidates," thus indicating that the theory's argumentative structure is not sensitive to the choice of the mortality measure. The logical formalization makes this invariance visible, leaving the testing of different measures to empirical studies.[6] I borrow the neutral term outflow from demography and economics to cover population losses. Readers who prefer concrete measures can instantiate their own candidate in the formulas.

Mathematical niche theory appraises fitness using an interval scale, but its argumentation exploits only a few properties of the real numbers. The formal logical rendering shows that a much weaker structure, a three-element ordering scale, is sufficient to do the same job: organizations may have low, modest or high fitness. Outflow intensity is also measured in an ordering scale (see B5 in 3.5). Assumption 3 connects fitness and outflow. $Period(p)$ states that p is a period, $Holds\_in(p,e)$ means that environment e holds in p; $outflow(x,p)$ measures the losses of x in p, and $fitness(x,e)$ is the fitness of x in e.

---

[6]The invariance of mortality measure cannot be taken for granted in other parts of organizational ecology—for example, in the density dependence model (Hannan and Carroll 1992).

A3. Higher fitness implies lower losses.

$\forall p, e, x[Period(p) \wedge Env(e) \wedge Holds\_in(p,e) \wedge Org\_type(x)$
$$\rightarrow (fitness(x,e) = high \rightarrow outflow(x,p) = very\_low)$$
$$\wedge (fitness(x,e) = modest \rightarrow outflow(x,p) = modest)$$
$$\wedge (fitness(x,e) = low \rightarrow outflow(x,p) = high)]$$

(For all p, e, x, if p is a period and e is an environment and e holds in p and x is an organization type, then high fitness of x in environment e implies very low outflow for x in period p, modest fitness implies modest outflow, and low fitness implies high outflow.)

Note that Assumption 3 is inappropriate in the case of empty organization sets that have zero outflow in spite of their possibly very low fitness. But the essence of niche theory can be demonstrated in cases where generalists and specialists do not die out during the observation period. Therefore we go on with this informal assumption.[7]

Organizations perform poorly in environments to which they are not adapted. They may survive for a while by using their assets, but their populations may face significant losses. Moreover, if bad times last long, then ill-adapted organizations use up their spared resources. At this point, their losses grow dramatically high (Assumption 4). The $dur(p)$ function value measures the duration of p.

A4. Poorly adapted organization types have very high outflow in the short run, and they have extremely high outflow in the long run.

$\forall p, e, x[Period(p) \wedge Env(e) \wedge Holds\_in(p,e) \wedge Org\_type(x)$
$$\wedge \neg Adapted(e,x) \rightarrow$$
$$(\neg(dur(p) = long) \rightarrow outflow(x,p) = very\_high) \wedge$$
$$(dur(p) = long \rightarrow outflow(x,p) = extreme)]$$

(For all p, e, x, if p is a period and e is an environment and e holds in p and x is an organization type that is not adapted to e, then x has a very high outflow in p if p is not long, and x has an extremely high outflow in p if p is long.)

---

[7] A more detailed formalization with a time variable could also handle extinction. This is necessary, for example, when population histories are compared (Péli and Masuch 1997).

3.4. *Principle of Allocation*

Organizations with a broad niche have a structure composed of different routines that can be started and stopped as environments come and go. The development and the maintenance of routines consume time and money. The so-called principle of allocation assumes that organizations have a fixed amount of adaptive capacity (Hannan and Freeman 1989:107). Organizations that establish a broad niche have less energy to improve the quality of their performance, so their routines and procedures stay poorly elaborated. The fitness of organizations with broad niche is not high. Rather, they have a mediocre performance in all the environments to which they are adapted. The next assumption fixes the trade-off between niche breadth and fitness (Levins 1968:15).

A5. Principle of allocation. Wider niche implies lower fitness.

$$\forall e, x1, x2 [Env(e) \wedge Org\_type(x1) \wedge Org\_type(x2)$$
$$\wedge\, Adapted(e, x1) \wedge Adapted(e, x2) \wedge$$
$$niche(x2) > niche(x1) \rightarrow fitness(x1, e) > fitness(x2, e)]$$

(For all e, $x1$, $x2$, if e is an environment and $x1$ and $x2$ are organization types that are adapted to e, and the niche width of $x2$ is bigger than the niche width of $x1$, then the fitness of $x1$ in e is higher than that of $x2$ in e.)

Assumption 5 is only concerned with adapted types. Organizations that are not adapted to the actual environment have poor fitness, regardless of their niche breadth.

The principle of allocation plays a pivotal role in the argumentation, but it considerably confines the theory's domain. In fact, there are organizations with both multiple structure and elaborated routines (*K*-generalism, as discussed in Brittain and Freeman 1980), but these are typically not new organizations. Perhaps the principle of allocation applies mostly to younger organizations and its effects become gradually reduced with age. The justification of this view is beyond the task of logical analysis, so I will keep Assumption 5 for the remainder of this paper. However, it is possible to make room for *K*-generalism in the machinery, provided the required theoretical extension can be precisely stated.

3.5. *Specialists and Generalists*

Specialists aim at good performance and adjust their structure to a single environment (Assumption 6). The name constants S and G denote, respectively, a specialist and a generalist type.

A6. Specialists are adapted to a single environment.

$$\forall e1, e2[Env(e1) \wedge Env(e2) \wedge Adapted(e1, S)$$
$$\wedge Adapted(e2, S) \rightarrow e1 = e2]$$

(For all $e1, e2$, if $e1$ and $e2$ are environments to which specialist type S is adapted, then $e1$ and $e2$ are the same.)

Let the specialists in question be adapted to environment $E1$. Assumption 7 fixes this denotational convention. Generalists are adapted to both $E1$ and $E2$ (Assumption 8).

A7. Specialists are adapted to environment $E1$.

$$Adapted(E1, S)$$

A8. Generalists are adapted to both environments $E1$ and $E2$.

$$Adapted(E1, G) \wedge Adapted(E2, G)$$

Specialists (narrow niche) thus have higher fitness than generalists in $E1$. However, since specialists concentrate their adaptive efforts on $E1$, their performance is poor in $E2$. We are now in the position to derive some simple consequences from the formulas that we have been made. Two theorems concern specialists' losses in good and in bad periods. *Patch*(p) means that p is an environmental patch, a period with nonchanging environmental conditions.

T1. (from D1, A3, A5-7) Specialists have very low outflow in $E1$-patches.

$$\forall p[Patch(p) \wedge Holds\_in(p, E1) \rightarrow outflow(S, p) = very\_low]$$

(For all p, if p is a patch and environment $E1$ holds in p, then specialist type S has very low outflow in p.)

T2. (from A2, A4, A6-7) Specialists have very high outflow in shorter $E2$-patches, and they have extremely high outflow in long ones.

$$\forall p[Patch(p) \wedge Holds\_in(p, E2) \rightarrow$$

$$(\neg(dur(p) = long) \rightarrow outflow(S,p) = very\_high) \wedge$$

$$(dur(p) = long \rightarrow outflow(S,p) = extreme)]$$

(For all p, if p is a patch and environment $E2$ holds in p, then specialist type S has very high outflow in p if p is not long, and has extremely high outflow if p is long.)

Theorems 1–2 are not breathtakingly new. Their role is to serve as building blocks in the derivation of less straightforward consequences. Note that T1–2's derivation requires a number of additional premises that formalize background knowledge. A fully syntactic derivation cannot rely only on common sense, the relevant background information has to be stated explicitly. Hence I present the complete list of the background premises of Theorem 1.

B1. $E1$ and $E2$ are environments. $Env(E1) \wedge Env(E2)$
B2. Patches are time periods. $\forall p[Patch(p) \rightarrow Period(p)]$
B3. Generalists and specialists are organization types.

$$Org\_type(G) \wedge Org\_type(S)$$

B4. Adapted organizations have high, modest or low fitness.

$$\forall x, e[Org\_type(x) \wedge Env(e) \wedge Adapted(e,x) \rightarrow$$

$$fitness(x,e) = high \vee fitness(x,e) = modest$$

$$\vee fitness(x,e) = low]$$

B5. Outflow scale.

$$extreme > very\_high, very\_high > high, high > medium,$$

$$medium > modest, modest > low, low > very\_low$$

B6. Niche width scale. $wide > modest, modest > narrow$
B7. On inequality 1 (transitivity). $\forall x, y, z[x > y \wedge y > z \rightarrow x > z]$
B8. On inequality 2. $\forall x, y[\neg(x > y \wedge x = y) \wedge \neg(x > y \wedge y > x)]$
B9. For environments $E1$ and $E2$, there is an adapted organization type with narrow, modestly wide and wide niche, respectively.

$$\forall e[e = E1 \vee e = E2 \rightarrow \exists x[Org\_type(x) \wedge Adapted(e,x)$$
$$\wedge \; niche(x) = narrow]]$$
$$\forall e[e = E1 \vee e = E2 \rightarrow \exists x[Org\_type(x) \wedge Adapted(e,x)$$
$$\wedge \; niche(x) = modest]]$$
$$\forall e[e = E1 \vee e = E2 \rightarrow \exists x[Org\_type(x) \wedge Adapted(e,x)$$
$$\wedge \; niche(x) = wide]]$$

The distinction between background and foreground is not of a logical nature; it rather reflects the theoretician's focus. Background knowledge may express common sense understanding (e.g., "Identical objects are similar."), or it may describe theoretical considerations taken for granted (e.g., "Generalists and specialists are organization types."). The margin between background and foreground is often vague. However, not to overload this presentation, the main text focuses on the sociologically relevant premises. To preserve formal rigor, the complete premise set is listed for each theorem in the appendix to this chapter.

3.6. *The Pattern of Environmental Change*

The previous sections characterized population losses in a given environment. But environments may alter as time passes. The next step is to depict formally the patterns of change. Niche theory characterizes environmental change by three dichotomic variables: (1) dissimilarity, (2) variability, and (3) grain size. The first measures the similarity between the resource conditions. The second and the third, respectively, reflect the relative and absolute durations of occurance of the resource conditions in the observation period. These variables lead to eight patterns of environmental change. Figure 2 lists the possible value constellations and the corresponding patch configurations in the observation period.

Meaning Postulates 1-2 characterize environmental dissimilarity.[8] *Dissim*(*obs*, *low*) states that dissimilarity is low in observation period *obs*.

M1. If environmental dissimilarity is low in the observation period, then the occurring environments are similar.

$$Dissim(obs, low) \rightarrow E1 \approx E2$$

[8] In mathematical niche theory, low and high environmental dissimilarity are related to convex and concave fitness sets, respectively (Levins 1968:19).

Grain	Variability	Dissimilarity	Corresponding Pattern

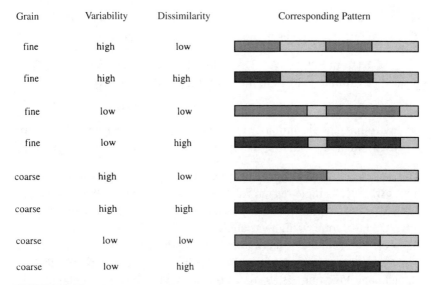

FIGURE 2. The eight patterns of environmental change. The colored blocks stand for environmental patches that constitute the observation period. Differences in tint denote the degree of environmental dissimilarity. Grain size is represented by the average length of the blocks. Variability is low if a certain color dominates, and it is high otherwise.

M2. If environmental dissimilarity is high in the observation period, then the occurring environments are not similar.

$$Dissim(obs, high) \rightarrow \neg(E1 \approx E2)$$

Two intermediate theorems concern generalists' losses in similar and dissimilar environments (Theorems 3–4). Generalists have a medium-wide niche when environmental dissimilarity is low. They assume modest fitness, and modest losses as a consequence. However, if dissimilarity is high, then generalists have to maintain a wide niche, which entails low fitness and high losses.

T3. (from M1, D1-2, A1-3, A5 and A8) Generalists have modest outflow in each environmental patch, if environmental dissimilarity is low.

$$Dissim(obs, low) \rightarrow \forall p[Patch(p) \rightarrow outflow(G, p) = modest]$$

(If environmental dissimilarity is *low* in observation period *obs*, then for all environmental patches *p*, the outflow of generalists is *modest* in *p*.)

T4. (from M2, D2, A1-3, A5 and A8) Generalists have high outflow in each environmental patch, if environmental dissimilarity is high.

$$Dissim(obs, high) \rightarrow \forall p[Patch(p) \rightarrow outflow(G, p) = high]$$

(If environmental dissimilarity is *high* in observation period *obs*, then for all environmental patches *p*, the outflow of generalists is *high* in *p*.)

The second characteristic of environmental change, variability, determines whether a single resource condition prevails during the observation period. In case of low variability, one environment is in place most of the time. On the contrary, high variability means that *E1* and *E2* occupy similar proportions of the observation period. In this case, the chance of being in a certain environment at an arbitrary point of time is approximately 0.5. Hannan and Freeman (1989) focus on cases when environmental change has a roughly cyclical pattern (seasonal changes, business cycles, etc.), as shown in Figure 2. With this constraint in place, high variability means that patches are approximately equal in duration (Meaning Postulate 3).

M3. If environmental variability is high, then patches have the same duration.

$$Var(obs, high) \rightarrow$$
$$\forall p1, p2[Patch(p1) \wedge Patch(p2) \rightarrow dur(p1) = dur(p2)]$$

(If variability is high in observation period *obs*, then for all *p1*, *p2*, if *p1* and *p2* are environmental patches, then their durations are equal.)

Low variability means that there is one dominant resource condition with significantly bigger time-share than the other. If environmental change is cyclical (as it is assumed), then the temporally dominant environment comes in longer patches than the nonprevailing one (Figure 2). *Dom(obs, e)* fixes *e* as the dominant environment in *obs*, $x \gg y$ asserts that *x* is much greater than *y*.

M4. If environmental variability is low, then patches of the dominant environment are much longer than the other patches.

$$Var(obs, low) \rightarrow \forall p1, p2, e[Dom(obs, e) \wedge Patch(p1) \wedge Holds\_in(p1, e)$$
$$\wedge Patch(p2) \wedge \neg Holds\_in(p2, e)$$
$$\rightarrow dur(p1) \gg dur(p2)]$$

(If variability is low in observation period *obs*, then for all *p1*, *p2*, *e*, if *e* is dominant environment in *obs* and *e* holds in patch *p1*, but *e* does not hold in patch *p2*, then *p1* has much longer duration than *p2*.)

The third variable, grain size, is about patch durations. A fine-grained observation period is composed of relatively short patches.

M5. Patches are not long in fine-grained observation periods.

$$Grain(obs, fine) \rightarrow \forall p[Patch(p) \rightarrow \neg(dur(p) = long)]$$

(If observation period *obs* is fine grained, then for all *p*, if *p* is an environmental patch, then its duration is not *long*.)

If grain is coarse, then patches are typically long. This does not imply that all patches are long. What can be claimed is that the dominant environments come in long chunks (Figure 2).

M6. Patches of a dominant environment are long in coarse grained observation periods.[9]

$$Grain(obs, coarse) \rightarrow \forall p, e[Dom(obs, e) \wedge Patch(p)$$
$$\wedge Holds\_in(p, e) \rightarrow dur(p) = long]$$

(If observation period *obs* is coarse grained, then for all *p*, *e*, if *e* is a dominant environment in *obs* and *e* holds in patch *p*, then the duration of *p* is *long*.)

Let *E1* be the dominant environment (Assumption 9). This means that *E1* occurs most of the time if variability is low (and it occurs approximately half of the time if variability is high).

A9. *E1* is a dominant environment in the observation period.

$$Dom(obs, E1)$$

Since Assumption 7 has already declared that specialists adapt to *E1*, Assumption 9 is not only a denotational convention. Postulating that *E1* is

---

[9]M4 and M6 imply a model restriction: the patches of the not dominant environment are not long. If the duration function assigns the "long" value to a period (M6), then shorter periods cannot take the same duration value. Note however, that even the shorter patches can be long if environmental grain is extra coarse, causing hard times for specialists. Technically, these extreme cases can be addressed by using predicates instead of function values for durations: e.g., *Long(p)* can state that *p* is long even if there are much longer patches around.

dominant has theoretical consequences: It zooms in cases where specialists restrict themselves to a frequently occurring resource configuration.
Such outcomes may result simply from chance. Otherwise, specializing to
the right environment assumes knowledge of future conditions—that is,
some predictability.

3.7. *Assumptions on Aggregation*

The main elements of niche theory are now in place as formal premises.
The next step should be to deduce selection preferences, comparing the
population losses in the eight environmental patterns. But, the existing
premises are still insufficient to specify the winner. Theorems 1–4 concern
only population losses in single patches, homogeneous regions in the observation period. However, the observation period is composed of a series
of different environmental patches (Figures 1 and 2). A core element is still
missing: knowledge of the relative magnitudes of benefits and drawbacks
that agents face in different patches. How should the outflows be aggregated to get the overall losses across the whole observation period? For
example, how should high and low outflows be combined if patch durations are similar, and how if they differ?

The necessary information on relative magnitudes is not clearly
stated in the original presentation of niche theory. But if this claim is correct, then where do the theory's conclusions come from? In fact, the predictions of the mathematical rendering are not deduced formally. Hannan
and Freeman specify optimal niche strategies by fitting suitable adaptive
functions to the so-called fitness sets (1989:111–12). The demonstration
goes on graphically, with the outcomes to some extent given qualitatively,
in natural language.

The next paragraphs add some extra premises to the theory that
reflect the underlying arguments of the qualitative descriptions. I cannot
rely directly on the written text at this point. I have to go beyond Hannan
and Freeman's work by finding and formalizing some additional information on outflow aggregation in such a way that niche theory's statements on
selection obtain as theorems. Unlike the earlier formulas, the forthcoming
new premises cannot be considered as straightforward translations of the
authors' arguments. Rather, they embody a kind of interpretation of the
verbal theory or of the implicit assumptions behind it.

The argumentation can be patched up in different ways. The missing data on relative magnitudes could be specified empirically. This would
require ad hoc decisions, since the numerical estimates may vary over

industries. A more general option is to go on without numbers, trying to reduce outflow aggregation to some underlying principles. I opt for the latter. But, before searching for aggregation rules, I spell out a premise that makes the accumulation of losses much simpler. It is superfluous to calculate aggregate outflow for the whole observation period when environmental change has a periodicity like that shown in Figure 1. There, a period composed of an *E1* patch and the subsequent *E2* patch represents the repetitive pattern of the observation period. Call these pairs environmental sequences. Each sequence of the observation period features the same mixture of conditions. Therefore the more successful organization type in an arbitrary sequence is also more successful in the whole observation period (Meaning Postulate 7). *Seq(p)* means that period *p* is an environmental sequence.

M7. Higher outflow in an environmental sequence implies higher outflow in the observation period.

$$\forall x1, x2, p[Org\_type(x1) \land Org\_type(x2) \land Seq(p)$$
$$\land \ outflow(x1,p) > outflow(x2,p)$$
$$\rightarrow outflow(x1,obs) > outflow(x2,obs)]$$

(For all organization types *x1*, *x2* and environmental sequences *p*, if *x1* has higher outflow than *x2* in *p*, then *x1* has higher outflow than *x2* in the observation period, *obs*.)

Meaning Postulate 7 has a distinctive role in the machinery; it is the springboard for jumps between the level of sequences and the level of the observation period. Formalization can go on using sequences, and needs only return to the observation period itself when the main conclusions are derived. The task is reduced to outflow aggregation over pairs of patches that represent the eight environmental patterns. Nevertheless, to specify eight formulas on amalgamation would be tiresome. Fortunately, three extra premises will do the job.

The first aggregation principle says that the composite of strong and weak outflows is medium strong, provided that the component flows hold for similar durations (Assumption 10, Figure 3a). The *union(p1,p2)* function value corresponds to the composite period of *p1* and *p2*.

A10. If two patches with the same duration have very low and very high outflows, respectively, then outflow is medium strong in their union.

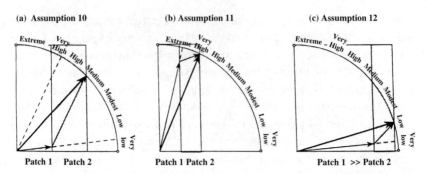

FIGURE 3. Outflow aggregation over patches. Consider outflows as vectors and apply the addition rule of vector calculus. Steepness indicates outflow intensity. The bold arrows denote aggregate outflows over different patches.

$$\forall p1, p2, x[Org\_type(x) \wedge Patch(p1) \wedge Patch(p2) \wedge$$
$$dur(p1) = dur(p2) \wedge outflow(x,p1) = very\_low \wedge$$
$$outflow(x,p2) = very\_high \rightarrow$$
$$outflow(x,union(p1,p2)) = medium]$$

(For all organization types x and patches $p1$, $p2$ of the same duration, if x has *very_low* outflow in $p1$ and x has *very_high* outflow in $p2$, then outflow is *medium* high in their union.)

The second rule characterizes extreme population losses. Such strong outflow occurs when organizations use up their reserves in bad patches and their population collapses. Extreme outflow is difficult to overcome: If it holds at least half of the time, then overall losses are also quite high, as shown in Figure 3(b).

A11. If outflow is extremely strong in a patch, then it is still very high in the union of this patch with another patch that is not longer.

$$\forall p1, p2, x[Org\_type(x) \wedge Patch(p1) \wedge Patch(p2)$$
$$\wedge dur(p1) \geq dur(p2) \wedge outflow(x,p1) = extreme$$
$$\rightarrow outflow(x,union(p1,p2)) \geq very\_high]$$

(For all organization types x, if the duration of patch $p2$ is not longer than that of patch $p1$, and x has extreme outflow in $p1$, then the outflow is at least *very_high* in the union of $p1$ and $p2$.)

The third amalgamation rule aggregates effects across unequal periods, stating that a much longer patch has stronger influence on overall losses, as shown in Figure 3(c). Specifically, if outflow is very low most of the time, then the composite outflow is still low (Assumption 12). There is an exception to this rule: Even a short period of extremely high outflow may raise aggregate losses considerably. So, A12 is restricted to nonextreme cases.

A12. If outflow is very low in a patch, then it is still low in the union of this patch with a much shorter one of nonextreme outflow.

$$\forall \, x, p1, p2[Org\_type(x) \wedge Patch(p1) \wedge Patch(p2)$$
$$\wedge \, dur(p1) \gg dur(p2) \wedge outflow(x,p1) = very\_low$$
$$\wedge \, \neg(outflow(x,p2) = extreme)$$
$$\rightarrow outflow(x, union(p1,p2)) \leq low]$$

(For all organization types x and patches $p1$, $p2$, if $p1$ is much longer than $p2$ and x has $very\_low$ outflow in $p1$ and the outflow of x is not extreme in $p2$, then the outflow is less than or equal to low in the union of $p1$ and $p2$.)

Assumptions 10–12 implicitly pose constraints on the meaning of loosely specified ordinal scale elements like low, high, or extreme. The scaling information they embody leads to a certain interpretation of niche theory (see more on this topic in Section 4).

The last premise we need is about selection preference. Meaning Postulate 8 asserts that selection's favor is with the population of lower losses. $Selection\_favors(x1,x2,p)$ denotes that object $x1$ is favored above object $x2$ in period p.

M8. Selection favors organization types with lower losses.

$$\forall x1, x2, p[Period(p) \wedge Org\_type(x1) \wedge Org\_type(x2)$$
$$\wedge \, outflow(x2,p) > outflow(x1,p)$$
$$\rightarrow Selection\_favors(x1,x2,p)]$$

(For all $x1$, $x2$, p, if p is a period and $x1$ and $x2$ are organization types and $x2$ assumes higher outflow than $x1$ in p, then selection favors $x1$ above $x2$ in p.)

3.8. *Niche Theory's Predictions As Theorems*

This section derives the theory's predictions on selection. Theorem 5 is about cases when environmental variability is low. The prevailing *E1*-patches help specialists to dominance regardless of dissimilarity and grain, as shown in Figure 4(a–b).

T5. (from T1–4, A9, A12, M4–8) Selection favors specialists above generalists, if environmental variability is low.

$$Var(obs, low) \rightarrow Selection\_favors(S, G, ob)$$

Theorem 6 is about highly variable observation periods with coarse grain. *E1* and *E2* patches are similar in length, so specialists experience good and

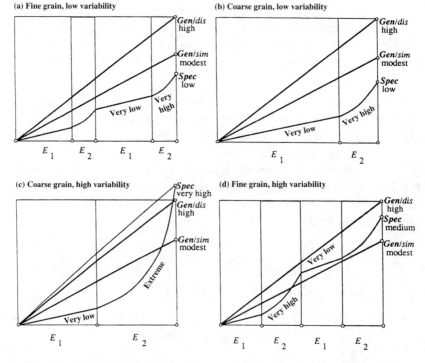

FIGURE 4. Outflows in the eight environmental patterns. *Gen/sim* and *Gen/dis* denote generalists' outflow in case of similar and dissimilar environments respectively. The steepness of the curves represents outflow intensity.

bad conditions for similar durations. Since patches are long, the extreme losses in *E2*-periods bring specialists down. Generalists are favored (Figure 4c).

T6. (from T2-4, A9, A11, M3 and M6-8) Selection favors generalists above specialists in coarse-grained observation periods of high variability.

$$Var(obs, high) \land Grain(obs, coarse) \rightarrow Selection\_favors(G, S, ob)$$

Theorem 7 applies to conditions of high variability, fine grain and low environmental dissimilarity. Patches are short and similar in duration. Bad *E2*-periods are transitory, so specialists' losses do not grow extremely high. But generalists' outflow is not too high either. They assume modest fitness, since modest niche breadth is enough to cope with the similar *E1* and *E2* environments. The question is, which effect is the stronger? Theorem 7 concludes that generalists dominate (Figure 4d).

T7. (from T1–3, A10, M3, M5 and M7–8) Selection favors generalists above specialists in fine-grained observation periods with high variability and similar environmental conditions.

$$Var(obs, high) \land Grain(obs, fine) \land Dissim(low, obs)$$
$$\rightarrow Selection\_favors(G, S, obs)$$

Theorem 8 is about fine-grained observation periods when both variability and dissimilarity are high (Figure 4d). Now, generalists have to maintain broad niche, and this brings selection's favor to specialists.

T8. (from T1–2 and 4, A10, M3, M5 and M7–8) Selection favors specialists above generalists in fine-grained observation periods of high variability and dissimilar environmental conditions.

$$Var(obs, high) \land Grain(obs, fine) \land Dissim(high, obs)$$
$$\rightarrow Selection\_favors(S, G, obs)$$

Figure 5 shows the correspondence between Theorems 5–8 and niche theory's predictions.[10] Hannan and Freeman also mention that under stable

---

[10]Hannan and Freeman (1989:311) mention different predictions in two cases, putting generalists as favored if dissimilarity and variability are low, without respect to grain. These are misprints, as John Freeman informed me. In fact, the correct conclusions follow from the authors' argument (1989:106–12).

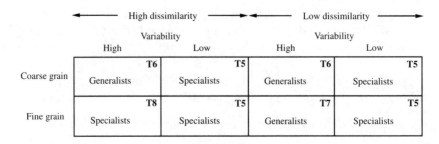

		High dissimilarity		Low dissimilarity	
	Variability			**Variability**	
	High	Low	High	Low	
Coarse grain	**T6** Generalists	**T5** Specialists	**T6** Generalists	**T5** Specialists
Fine grain	**T8** Specialists	**T5** Specialists	**T7** Generalists	**T5** Specialists

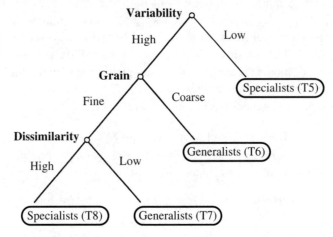

FIGURE 5. Theorems 5–8 and niche theory's predictions.

environmental conditions (i.e., when a single resource configuration holds throughout) selection favors adapted specialists. This corollary follows as a special case of Theorem 5. Consider that stable conditions involve (extra) low environmental variability and (extra) coarse grain (Meaning Postulate 9). *Stable*(*obs*) denotes that environmental conditions are stable during *obs*.

M9. If environmental conditions are stable, then variability is low and grain is coarse.

$$Stable(obs) \rightarrow Var(obs, low) \wedge Grain(obs, coarse)$$

T9. (from M9 and T5) Selection favors specialists above generalists if environmental conditions are stable.

$$Stable(obs) \rightarrow Selection\_favors(S, G, obs)$$

4. DISCUSSION

4.1. *The Niche of Logical Formalization*

Logic cannot replace intuition. It is rather intended to give a decent shape
to theoretical ideas making them accessible to evaluation, refinement, and
empirical justification. Logical formalization preserves much of the flexibility of natural language reasoning. Moreover, it involves the same der-
ivational exactness as mathematics. These properties provide a series of
advantages for theoretical and empirical research, which I will now discuss.

4.1.1. *Consistency*
The consistency of a theory ensures that there is no way to deduce a contradiction from the theory's statements. The consistency of the formula set
that represents the original niche theory can be proven by the Metafor
theorem prover. Testing consistency is important because a contradictory
formula set supports all statements. Technically, the consistency check
means the following: one has to test if the premise set supports an arbitrary
contradictory statement—for example, $A \wedge \neg A$. If the theorem prover fal-
sifies such a conclusion, then the premise set is consistent.

   The consistency check revealed that no contradiction follows from
the presented formal model. Note, however, that this result does not imply
that the original verbal theory is consistent. It demonstrates something less
but still important for theorizing—namely, that the verbal theory has at
least one consistent interpretation. Even reasonable theoretical texts may
have inconsistent readings. The natural language descriptions usually leave
the meaning of key notions and relations somewhat unspecified, and formalizers can easily produce contradictions by playing with these indeter-
minacies. However, the objective is not to create "intelligent misreadings,"
but rather to find consistent and reasonable models for the theory at hand.
A contradiction-free formalization is a useful departure point for further
empirical and theoretical research.

4.1.2. *Transparency of Structure, Remediability*
Logic forces the formalizer to make all the considerations explicit that
play a role in the deduction. Mathematical proofs often fail to do so, being
partially performed in natural language. The specification of the applied
background knowledge helps to ascertain the domain of application of the
theoretical piece at hand. Explicitness supports theory generalization; it

facilitates the removal of unnecessary constraints and the weakening of unnecessarily strong ones. For example, the formalization revealed that besides the death rate several other mortality measures are compatible with niche theory.

Logic is also a device to spot problematic points in the argumentation. If all the premises hold, then the derived conclusions are also warranted. In case of dissatisfaction with unrealistic results, the guilty premise(s) can be traced back and modified. The modular nature of formalization allows for local repairs without destroying the whole construction (cf. Simon's famous example about two watchmakers, 1962). For example, someone may doubt that specialists are preferred to generalists when patches are short, variability is high, and environmental conditions are dissimilar (Theorem 8). Let's say that this person finds Assumption 4 unrealistic and claims that poorly adapted organizations have extreme losses even in the short run. Theorem 8 is not warranted with this modification in place; it would follow that generalists are favored by selection.[11]

4.1.3. Theory Building

When considering how a theory might be extended, one may add new premises to the formula set, allowing the ramifications of the potential extensions to be established precisely. One methodology is to use trial and error to work out the supplementary knowledge from which a certain outcome would follow. What are the consequences if a new assumption is added, and what if its negation is employed? Another way of theory extension is introducing new objects with certain properties and testing if the existing premise set supports theorems about these objects (see E2-specialists in the next subsection). Theory building may also be required by a gap in the original argumentation. For example, without premises on outflow aggregation (A10–12) no selection preference followed.

Another possible application is the compatibility check of different theories. Overlaps can be assessed accurately and connection points become visible, allowing for the construction of a common conceptual framework. The independence of different theories can also be tested. For example, the present formalization does not exploit any considerations of the inertia theory, a central part in organizational ecology (Hannan and

[11]Assumption 4 is a premise of Theorem 8 by Lemma 4 and Theorem 2 (appendix). The reformulated T2 would state that specialists have always extreme outflow in E2-periods. Applying A11, the new L4 would say that specialists' overall outflow is very high (while generalists' outflow is only high, see T4).

Freeman 1989; Péli et al. 1994). That is, niche theory's core arguments also hold with and without the inertia theory.

4.2. *E2-specialists*

Niche theory ignored those specialist organizations that are adapted to the rarely occurring environment (*E2* in the given denotation). The given formal machinery allows for the deduction of selection preferences for "*E2*-specialists" for six environmental patterns of the eight. If environmental variability is high, then *E1*- and *E2*-patches are similar in duration and conditions are similarly good or bad for both *E1*- and *E2*-specialists. Obviously, the "high variability" conclusions (T6-8) also hold for *E2*-specialists. So both kinds of specialists are favored above generalists in highly variable observation periods.

In the low variability cases, *E1* holds most of the time (A9). If grain is coarse, then *E2*-specialists face enduring bad periods, so selection's favor is with the generalists (see Theorem 10 in the appendix to this chapter). Moreover, if *E2*-specialists perform badly in mostly hostile circumstances, then they certainly do not flourish when the beneficial *E2* environment does not occur at all: Stable *E1* conditions favor generalists above *E2*-specialists (see Theorem 11 in the appendix). These new theorems simply claim what common sense predicts. However, the derivation of plausible new results increases the confidence in the presented formalization.

There is not enough information to decide if generalism or *E2*-specialism is favored in the two environmental patterns when low variability combines with fine grain. In these cases, generalists' outflow is high or modest (T3–4). *E2*-specialists suffer heavy losses in the prevailing *E1*-periods, but the short *E2*-patches somewhat diminish their overall outflow. Therefore it is hard to tell which organization type performs better in the long run. Again, knowledge concerning the aggregate effects is missing. Niche theory's predictions were given in the earlier cases, helping the specification of underlying amalgamation principles. Now such guidelines are not available. From this point, empirical research should provide new insights for theory building.

E2-specialism draws attention to some interesting cases where niche theory, in its standard form, does not apply. Some specialist organizations may accumulate enough wealth even in very short beneficial periods to compensate them for longer low seasons. (Anologies can be drawn with hotels in a ski resort.) These organizations are not necessarily inferior to generalists. Niche theory has to be extended to solve this problem: additional effects have to be taken into account that explain the occasional success of *E2*-specialists.

4.3. *Scale Specification*

4.3.1. *Ordinal Scale Engineering*
The formal model represents population losses on an ordinal scale. Three amalgamation premises, Assumptions 10–12, tell us how to calculate outflows in longer periods if losses are known in the component periods. In effect, these premises are scaling assumptions; they implicitly characterize the meaning of ordinal scale elements by establishing relations between them. For example, Assumption 11 suggests that the gap between extremely high and other outflow values is significant.

Shaping the scales means shaping the outcomes. One may specify scaling rules such that the conclusions differ from niche theory's original predictions. However, the goal of the logical approach is formal reconstruction. If some completion is necessary, then the task is to pave the way from underlying considerations to theoretical predictions. In the given case, an appropriate outflow aggregation method was needed. With this in place, the theory's predictions could be warranted. Some readers may not consider such a conclusion important if the premises are tailored to the outcome. But such a view would somewhat miss the point. The specification of missing information may provide even more methodological benefit than the justification of the argumentative structure (Lakatos 1976).

The quest for missing premises exemplifies how a logical approach can support empirical research. The formalization demonstrates that without using interval scales and detailed measure specification, the extra information in A10–12 is sufficient to provide the favored niche strategy in all the cases addressed. The formal model provides guidelines for empirical testing: those metrics that meet the three amalgamation premises may be considered as outflow scale candidates.

By determining what premises could be used to patch up the gaps, the logical model helps to ascertain niche theory's range of applicability. However, the given rendering does not tell us the only conditions when the verbal theory's predictions apply. The formal premises are strong enough to deduce selection preferences, but it is possible that a different, even weaker set could do the same job. That is, the premise set establishes sufficient but maybe not necessary conditions for the validity of the conclusions.

4.3.2. How Many Scale Elements?

Even a change in the number of scale elements may have impact on the theory's interpretation. The outflow scale used has seven degrees (see B5 in Section 3.5), but having exactly seven elements is clearly not a logical necessity. For example, earlier formalization trials showed that the same selection preferences obtained after unifying the very high and high outflow categories. Note that even such a change may have sociological ramifications. With this modification in place, adapted generalists would have the same (high) losses as any nonadapted organizations have under dissimilar conditions in the short run (cf. T4 and A4). This sounds unrealistic, so I kept the distinction between the very high and high categories.

Additional outflow values could also be added by the refinement of the scale. For example, later developments in niche theory may introduce new environmental patterns by identifying new environmental variables. This may require the splitting of some outflow categories into two or more in order to make finer distinctions.

4.4. Directions for Technical Development

4.4.1. Alternative Formalizations

There are always different logical formalizations for the same verbal theory. The differences between alternative representations may arise from several sources.

First, the same theory can be formalized in different logical languages. I return to the problem of language choice in the next subsection.

Second, the formalization can be performed in different "depths." Statements that are assumptions in one theory may be conclusions in another theory on which the first one is built. For example, the principle of allocation (A5) could also be derived as a theorem if formalizing Hannan and Freeman's (1989) descriptions of routine development. There are no strict borderlines to determine which elements should be deduced in a formal model and which can be taken for granted. The given work concentrates on niche theory's conclusions, and therefore the theorems mostly restate its predictions on selection preferences. However, Assumption 5 could be a theorem—for example, in another formalization that focuses on organizational routines.

Third, a theory can be formalized in different "styles." The same reading of a theory can be translated into logic by different sets of predicates, functions and premises.

Fourth, the same verbal theory may have different readings. Even slightly different interpretations may lead to different results. From this point of view, the alternative formalizations may have a similar role to sensitivity analysis in computer simulation.[12] For example, in reconstructing niche theory Bruggeman (1997) assumed that specialist populations do not run out of resources even in enduring bad periods, though they have serious losses. He arrived at the conclusion that with this consideration in place environmental grain does not make difference in the theory. This finding should follow from the formalization presented in this chapter if Bruggeman's assumption is implemented. The proof should require, again, a modification of Assumption 4: now, the outflow of ill-adapted organizations does not become extremely high even in the long run. As a result, Theorem 6 (selection favors generalists if grain is coarse and variability is high) would hold only if environmental dissimilarity is low, and specialists would be favored otherwise (Figure 4c). With this modification in place, grain does not make a difference in the results (Figure 5). This example demonstrates the fruitfulness of having alternative formal interpretations of the same theory. There are industries where specialists suffer extreme losses under enduring hostile conditions, while they mostly survive bad times in other industries. A later, more advanced version of niche theory should account for both cases. I argued in Section 4.1.3 that logical formalization facilitates the unification of different theories. Now, I can add that logical formalization also helps to unify different interpretations of the same theory in a broader framework.

4.4.2. *The Limits of First-Order Logic*

The present formalization shows that First-Order Logic is sufficiently expressive to formalize subtle arguments. However, there are tasks for which some more advanced logics fit better. Unfortunately, the more advanced logics usually combine increased expressive power with poor computational properties.

Second-order logics have the distinctive advantage over FOL that their quantifiers ($\forall$, $\exists$) operate not only over variables but also over predicates and functions. The beneficial effects of this property become obvious—for example, when the model refers not only to function values

---

[12]I borrowed this analogy from an anonymous reviewer of this chapter.

(like the present formalization) but also to the properties of the function itself. A disadvantage of second-order logics is that, technically speaking, the second-order inference relation is not finitely axiomatizable. As a result, it is difficult to develop a clear view on inference, and the automatic theorem checking is limited in application.

Modal logics make available special syntactic operators to express a range of linguistic constructions (intentions, conditionals, temporality, etc.). Such logics can be handy tools to keep the formalization close to the theory's original structure. There is work in progress in this field (Huang, Masuch, and Pólos, 1996).

Default logics represent a relatively new brand of formal languages that give an adequate logical structure for empirical generalizations. Unlike strict rules (usually expressed by universal quantification, $\forall$) empirical generalizations typically allow for exceptions. In a default logic, exceptions from a rule refine, rather than destroy, the formal theory's argumentation (Pólos 1994).

These more advanced logics are all extensions of First-Order Logic. Consequently, formalizations performed in FOL can be easily embedded into a second-order, modal or default logic framework. Work can begin in first-order, and if necessary, it can proceed in a more specific formal language.

Logical languages do not tell the proper content of a theory, but they help to state the chosen content clearly. Logical formalization alone does not disambiguate the applied theoretical concepts, but it helps to see what is ambiguous in them. Has the ambiguity of a notion any affect on the argumentation? If it does, then the vagueness should go. If it does not, then each possible interpretation of the notion can be preserved, and research can continue with a generalized theory.

APPENDIX

Background knowledge assumptions are denoted by B. Lemmas and intermediate theorems are listed as L#.

Lemma 1
A3. *Higher fitness implies lower losses.*
$\forall p,e,x[\text{Org\_type}(x) \wedge \text{Env}(e) \wedge \text{Period}(p) \wedge \text{Holds\_in}(p,e)$
$\quad\quad \rightarrow (\text{fitness}(x,e) = \text{high} \rightarrow \text{outflow}(x,p) = \text{very\_low})$
$\quad\quad \wedge (\text{fitness}(x,e) = \text{modest} \rightarrow \text{outflow}(x,p) = \text{modest})$
$\quad\quad \wedge (\text{fitness}(x,e) = \text{low}) \rightarrow (\text{outflow}(x,p) = \text{high})]$

A5. *Principle of allocation. Wider niche implies lower fitness.*
$\forall$x1,x2,e[Org_type(x1) $\land$ Org_type(x2) $\land$ Env(e) $\land$ Adapted(e,x1)
$\land$ Adapted(e,x2) $\land$ niche(x1) $>$ niche(x2) $\rightarrow$ fitness(x2,e) $>$ fitness(x,e)]
B. *Adapted organizations have high, modest or low fitness.*
$\forall$x,e[Org_type(x) $\land$ Env(e) $\land$ Adapted(e,x) $\rightarrow$ fitness(x,e) $=$ high
$\lor$ fitness(x,e) $=$ modest $\lor$ fitness(x,e) $=$ low]
B. *E1 and E2 are environments.* Env(E1) $\land$ Env(E2)
B. *Outflow scale.* extreme $>$ very_high, very_high $>$ high,
high $>$ medium, medium $>$ modest, modest $>$ low, low $>$ very_low
B. *Niche width scale.* wide $>$ modest, modest $>$ narrow
B. *On inequality 1.* $\forall$x,y,z[x $>$ y $\land$ y $>$ z $\rightarrow$ x $>$ z]
B. *On inequality 2.* $\forall$x,y[$\neg$(x $>$ y $\land$ x $=$ y) $\land$ $\neg$(x $>$ y $\land$ y $>$ x)]
B. *For both environments E1 and E2, there is an organization type adapted to them with narrow, modestly wide and wide niche, respectively.*
$\forall$e[e $=$ E1 $\lor$ e $=$ E2 $\rightarrow$ $\exists$x[Org_type(x) $\land$ Adapted(e,x)
$\qquad\qquad\qquad\qquad\land$ niche(x) $=$ narrow]]
$\forall$e[e $=$ E1 $\lor$ e $=$ E2 $\rightarrow$ $\exists$x[Org_type(x) $\land$ Adapted(e,x)
$\qquad\qquad\qquad\qquad\land$ niche(x) $=$ modest]]
$\forall$e[e $=$ E1 $\lor$ e $=$ E2 $\rightarrow$ $\exists$x[Org_type(x) $\land$ Adapted(e,x)
$\qquad\qquad\qquad\qquad\land$ niche(x) $=$ wide]]
L1. *Organization types which are adapted to environment E1 or E2 have very low, modest or high outflows if their niche is narrow, modestly wide or wide, respectively, in environments.*
$\forall$x,e,p[Org_type(x) $\land$ (e $=$ E1 $\lor$ e $=$ E2) $\land$ Adapted(e,x) $\land$ Period(p) $\land$
Holds_in(p,e) $\rightarrow$ (niche(x) $=$ narrow) $\rightarrow$ outflow(x,p) $=$ very_low)
$\land$ (niche(x) $=$ modest $\rightarrow$ outflow(x,p) $=$ modest)
$\land$ (niche(x) $=$ wide $\rightarrow$ outflow(x,p) $=$ high)]

Theorem 1
L1. *Organization types which are adapted to environment E1 or E2 have very low, modest or high outflows if their niche is narrow, modestly wide or wide, respectively, in environments.*
$\forall$x,e,p[Org_type(x) $\land$ (e $=$ E1 $\lor$ e $=$ E2) $\land$ Adapted(e,x) $\land$ Period(p) $\land$
Holds_in(p,e) $\rightarrow$ (niche(x) $=$ narrow) $\rightarrow$ outflow(x,p) $=$ very_low)
$\land$ (niche(x) $=$ modest $\rightarrow$ outflow(x,p) $=$ modest)
$\land$ (niche(x) $=$ wide $\rightarrow$ outflow(x,p) $=$ high)]
D1. *Organizations have narrow niche if and only if they are adapted to a single environment.*

$\forall$x[Org_type(x) $\rightarrow$ (niche(x)= narrow $\leftrightarrow$
$\forall$e1,e2[Env(e1) $\wedge$ Env(e2) $\wedge$ Adapted(e1,x) $\wedge$ Adapted(e2,x) $\rightarrow$ e1=e2])]
A6. *Specialists are adapted to a single environment.*
$\forall$e1,e2[Env(e1) $\wedge$ Env(e2) $\wedge$ Adapted(e1,S) $\wedge$ Adapted(e2,S) $\rightarrow$ e1 = e2]
A7. *Specialists are adapted to environment E1.* Adapted(E1,S)
B. *E1 and E2 are environments.* Env(E1) $\wedge$ Env(E2)
B. *Patches are time periods.* $\forall$p[Patch(p) $\rightarrow$ Period(p)]
B. *Generalists and specialists are organization types.*
Org_type(G) $\wedge$ Org_type(S)
T1. *Specialists have very low outflow in E1-patches.*
$\forall$p[Patch(p) $\wedge$ Holds_in(p,E1) $\rightarrow$ outflow(S,p) = very_low]

Theorem 2
A2. *Environments E1 and E2 are different.* $\neg$(E1 = E2)
A4. *Poorly adapted organization types have very high outflow in the short
run, and they have extremely high outflow in the long run.*
$\forall$p,e,x[Period(p) $\wedge$ Env(e) $\wedge$ Holds_in(p,e) $\wedge$ Org_type(x) $\wedge$
$\neg$Adapted(e,x) $\rightarrow$ ($\neg$(dur(p) = long) $\rightarrow$ outflow(x,p) = very_high)
$\wedge$ (dur(p) = long $\rightarrow$ outflow(x,p) = extreme)]
A6. *Specialists are adapted to a single environment.*
$\forall$e1,e2[Env(e1) $\wedge$ Env(e2) $\wedge$ Adapted(e1,S) $\wedge$ Adapted(e2,S) $\rightarrow$ e1 = e2]
A7. *Specialists are adapted to environment E1.* Adapted(E1,S)
B. *E1 and E2 are environments.* Env(E1) $\wedge$ Env(E2)
B. *Generalists and specialists are organization types.*
Org_type(G) $\wedge$ Org_type(S)
B. *Patches are time-periods.* $\forall$p[Patch(p) $\rightarrow$ Period(p)]
T2. *Specialists have very high outflow in shorter E2-patches, and they
have extremely high outflow in long ones.*
$\forall$p[Patch(p) $\wedge$ Holds_in(p,E2) $\rightarrow$
($\neg$(dur(p) = long $\rightarrow$ outflow(S,p) = very_high)
$\wedge$ (dur(p) = long $\rightarrow$ outflow(S,p) = extreme)]

Theorem 3
L1. *Organization types which are adapted to environment E1 or E2 have
very low, modest or high outflows if their niche is narrow, modestly wide or
wide, respectively, in environments.*
$\forall$x,e,p[Org_type(x) $\wedge$ (e = E1 $\vee$ e = E2) $\wedge$ Adapted(e,x) $\wedge$ Period(p) $\wedge$
Holds_in(p,e) $\rightarrow$ (niche(x) = narrow) $\rightarrow$ outflow(x,p) = very_low)

$\wedge$ (niche(x) = modest $\rightarrow$ outflow(x,p) = modest)
$\wedge$ (niche(x) = wide $\rightarrow$ outflow(x,p) = high)]

D1. *Organizations have narrow niche if and only if they are adapted to a single environment.*

$\forall$x[Org_type(x) $\rightarrow$ (niche(x) = narrow $\leftrightarrow$
$\forall$e1,e2[Env(e1) $\wedge$ Env(e2) $\wedge$ Adapted(e1,x) $\wedge$ Adapted(e2,x) $\rightarrow$ e1=e2])]

D2. *Organizations have wide niche if and only if they are adapted to dissimilar environments.*

$\forall$x[Org_type(x) $\rightarrow$ (niche(x) = wide $\leftrightarrow$
$\exists$e1,e2[Env(e1) $\wedge$ Env(e2) $\wedge$ Adapted(e1,x) $\wedge$ Adapted(e2,x) $\wedge$
$\neg$(e1 $\approx$ e2)])]

M1. *If environmental dissimilarity is low in ther observation period, then the occurring environments are dissimilar.*

Dissim(obs,low) $\rightarrow$ (E1 $\approx$ E2)

A1. *E1 and E2 are the environments that occur.*

$\forall$e[Env(e) $\rightarrow$ e = E1 $\vee$ e = E2]

A2. *Environments E1 and E2 are different.* $\neg$(E1 = E2)

A8. *Generalists are adapted to environments E1 and E2.*

Adapted(E1,G) $\wedge$ Adapted(E2,G)

B. *Generalists and specialists are organization types.*

Org_type(G) $\wedge$ Org_type(S)

B. *Organizations have narrow, modestly wide or wide niche.*

$\forall$x[Org_type(x) $\rightarrow$
niche(x) = narrow $\vee$ niche(x) = modest $\vee$ niche(x) = wide]

B. *E1 and E2 are environments.* Env(E1) $\wedge$ Env(E2)

B. *In each patch a certain kind of environment holds.*

$\forall$p[Patch(p) $\rightarrow$ $\exists$e[Env(e) $\wedge$ Holds_in(p,e)]]

B. *Equal objects are similar.* $\forall$x[x $\approx$ x]

B. *(Symmetry) If x is similar to y, than y is similar to x.*

$\forall$x,y[x $\approx$ y $\rightarrow$ y $\approx$ x]

T3. *Generalists have modest outflow in each environmental patch if environmental dissimilarity is low.*

Dissim(obs,low) $\rightarrow$ $\forall$p[Patch(p) $\rightarrow$ outflow(G,p) = modest]

Theorem 4

L1. *Organization types which are adapted to environment E1 or E2 have very low, modest, or high outflows if their niche is narrow, modestly wide or wide, respectively, in environments.*

$\forall$x,e,p[Org_type(x) $\wedge$ (e = E1 $\vee$ e = E2) $\wedge$ Adapted(e,x) $\wedge$ Period(p) $\wedge$

Holds_in(p,e) → (niche(x) = narrow) → outflow(x,p) = very_low)

∧ (niche(x) = modest → outflow(x,p) = modest)

∧ (niche(x) = wide → outflow(x,p) = high)]

D2. *Organizations have wide niche if and only if they are adapted to dissimilar environments.*

∀x[Org_type(x) → (niche(x) = wide ↔

∃e1,e2[Env(e1) ∧ Env(e2) ∧ Adapted(e1,x) ∧ Adapted(e2,x) ∧

¬(e1 ≈ e2)])]

M2. *If environmental dissimilarity is high in the observation period, then the occurring environments are not similar.*

Dissim(obs,high) → ¬(E1 ≈ E2)

A1. *E1 and E2 are the environments that occur.*

∀e[Env(e) → e = E1 ∨ e = E2]

A2. *Environments E1 and E2 are different.* ¬(E1 = E2)

A8. *Generalists are adapted to environments E1 and E2.*

Adapted(E1,G) ∧ Adapted(E2,G)

B. *E1 and E2 are environments.* Env(E1) ∧ Env(E2)

B. *Generalists and specialists are organization types.*

Org_type(G) ∧ Org_type(S)

B. *Patches are time-periods.* ∀p[Patch(p) → Period(p)]

B. *In each patch a certain kind of environment holds.*

∀p[Patch(p) → ∃e[Env(e) ∧ Holds_in(p,e)]]

T4. *Generalists have high outflow in each environmental patch if environmental dissimilarity is high.*

Dissim(obs,high) → ∀p[Patch(p) → outflow(G,p) = high]

Lemma 2

T1. *Specialists have very low outflow in E1-patches.*

∀p[Patch(p) ∧ Holds_in(p,E1) → outflow(S,p) = very_low]

T2. *Specialists have very high outflow in shorter E2-patches, and they have extremely high outflow in long ones.*

∀p[Patch(p) ∧ Holds_in(p,E2) →

(¬(dur(p) = long) → outflow(S,p) = very_high)

∧ (dur(p) = long → outflow(S,p) = extreme)]

M4. *If environmental variability is low, then patches of the dominant environment are much longer than the other patches.*

Var(obs,low) → ∀p1,p2,e[Dom(obs,e) ∧ Patch(p1) ∧ Patch(p2) ∧

Holds_in(p1,e) ∧ ¬Holds_in(p2,e) → dur(p1) ≫ dur(p2)]

M5. *Patches are not long in a fine grained observation periods.*
Grain(obs,fine) → ∀p[Patch(p) → ¬(dur(p) = long)]
M6. *Patches of a dominant environment are long in coarse grained obser-*
vation periods.
Grain(obs,coarse) → ∀p,e[Dom(obs,e) ∧ Patch(p) ∧ Holds_in(p,e) →
dur(p) = long]
A9. *E1 is the dominant environment during the observation period.*
Dom(obs,E1)
A12. *If outflow is very low in a patch, then it is still low in the union of this*
patch with a much shorter one of nonextreme outflow.
∀p1,p2,p,x[Org_type(x) ∧ Patch(p1) ∧ Patch(p2) ∧ dur(p1) ≫ dur(p2)
∧ outflow(x,p1) = very_low ∧ ¬(outflow(x,p2) = extreme)
→ outflow(x,union(p1,p2)) ≤ low]
B. *Environmental grain is coarse or fine.*
Grain(obs,coarse) ∨ Grain(obs,fine)
B. *Sequences are unions of an E1 and an E2 patch.* ∀s[Seq(s) →
∃p1,p2[Patch(p1) ∧ Patch(p2) ∧ Holds_in(p1,E1)
∧ Holds_in(p2,E2) ∧ s = union(p1,p2)]]
B. *Generalists and specialists are organization types.*
Org_type(G) ∧ Org_type(S)
B. *Outflow scale.* extreme > very_high, very_high > high,
high > medium, medium > modest, modest > low, low > very_low
B. *On inequality 1.* ∀x,y,z[x > y ∧ y > z → (x > z)]
B. *On inequality 2.* ∀x,y[¬(x > y ∧ x = y) ∧ ¬(x > y ∧ y > x)]
B. *If x is much more bigger than y, then x is also bigger than y.*
∀x,y[x ≫ y → x > y]
L2. *Specialists have low outflow in each sequence of an observation*
periods of low variability.
Var(obs,low) → ∀p[Seq(p) → outflow(S,p) ≤ low]

Theorem 5
T3. *Generalists have modest outflow in each environmental patch if envi-*
ronmental dissimilarity is low.
Dissim(obs,low) → ∀p[Patch(p) → outflow(G,p) = modest]
T4. *Generalists have high outflow in each environmental patch if environ-*
mental dissimilarity is high.
Dissim(obs,high) → ∀p[Patch(p) → outflow(G,p) = high]

L2. *Specialists have very low outflow in each sequence of observation periods of low variability.*
Var(obs,low) → ∀p[Seq(p) → outflow(S,p) = very_low]

M7. *Higher outflow in an environmental sequence implies higher outflow in the observation period.*
∀s,x1,x2[Org_type(x1) ∧ Org_type(x2) ∧ Seq(s)
      ∧ outflow(x1,s) > outflow(x2,s)
      → outflow(x1,obs) > outflow(x2,obs)]

M8. *Selection favors organization types with lower losses.*
∀p,x1,x2[Period(p) ∧ Org_type(x1) ∧
Org_type(x2) ∧ outflow(x2,p) > outflow(x1,p) →
Selection_favors(x1,x2,p)]

B. *Environmental dissimilarity is either high or low.*
Dissim(obs,high) ∨ Dissim(obs,low)

B. *Generalists and specialists are organization types.*
Org_type(G) ∧ Org_type(S)

B. *The observation period is a period.* Period(obS)

B. *Patches are time-periods.* ∀p[Patch(p) → Period(p)]

B. *Sequences are time-periods.* ∀s[Seq(s) → Period(s)]

B. *The observation period has at least one sequence.* ∃s[Seq(s)]

B. *Sequences are unions of an E1 and an E2 patch.* ∀s[Seq(s) →
∃p1,p2[Patch(p1) ∧ Patch(p2) ∧ Holds_in(p1,E1) ∧
Holds_in(p2,E2) ∧ s = union(p1,p2)]]

B. *If outflow is the same in two periods, then this outflow holds in their union.*
∀p1,p2,x[Org_type(x) ∧ Period(p1) ∧ Period(p2) ∧
outflow(x,p1) = outflow(x,p2) →
outflow(x,union(p1,p2)) = outflow(x,p1)]

B. *Outflow scale.* extreme > very_high, very_high > high,
high > medium, medium > modest, modest > low, low > very_low

B. *On inequality 1.* ∀x,y,z[x > y ∧ y > z → (x > z]

B. *On inequality 2.* ∀x,y[¬(x > y ∧ x = y) ∧ ¬(x > y ∧ y > x)]

B. *On "greater or equal to."* ∀x,y[x ≥ y → x > y ∨ x = y]

T5. *Selection favors specialists, above generalists if environmental variability is low.*
Var(obs,low) → Selection_favors(S,G,obs)

Lemma 3

T2. *Specialists have very high outflow in shorter E2-patches, and they have extremely high outflow in long ones.*

∀p[Patch(p) ∧ Holds_in(p,E2) →
(¬(dur(p) = long) → outflow(S,p) = very_high) ∧
(dur(p) = long) → (outflow(S,p) = extreme)]
M3. *If environmental variability is high, then patches have the same duration.*
Var(obs,high) → ∀p1,p2[Patch(p1) ∧ Patch(p2) → dur(p1) = dur(p2)]
M6. *Patches of a dominant environment are long in coarse-grained observation periods.*
Grain(obs,coarse) → ∀p,e[Dom(obs,e) ∧ Patch(p) ∧ Holds_in(p,e)
→ dur(p) = long]
A9. *E1 is the dominant environment during the observation period.*
Dom(obs,E1)
A11. *If outflow is extremely strong in a patch, then it is still very high in the union of this patch with another patch that is not longer.*
∀p1, p2, x[Org_type(x) ∧ Patch(p1) ∧ Patch(p2) ∧ dur(p1) ≥ dur(p2) ∧
outflow(x,p1) = extreme → outflow(x,union(p1,p2)) ≥ very_high]
B. *The union of periods is also a period.*
∀p1,p2[Period(p1) ∧ Period(p2) → Period(union(p1,p2))]
B. *Patches are time-periods.* ∀p[Patch(p) → Period(p)]
B. *Sequences are time-periods.* ∀s[Seq(s) → Period(s)]
B. *Generalists and specialists are organization types.*
Org_type(G) ∧ Org_type(S)
B. *Sequences are unions of an E1 and an E2 patch.* ∀s[Seq(s) →
∃p1,p2[Patch(p1) ∧ Patch(p2) ∧ Holds_in(p1,E1) ∧
Holds_in(p2,E2) ∧ s = union(p1,p2)]]
B. *(Symmetry) If a period is composed of p1 and p2, then it is also composed of p2 and p1.*
∀p1,p2,s[Seq(s) ∧ Period(p1) ∧ Period(p2) ∧ s = union(p1,p2)
→ s = union(p2,p1)]
B. *On "greater or equal to."* ∀x,y[x ≥ y → x > y ∨ x = y]
L3. *Specialists have very high outflow in each sequence of coarse-grained observation periods of high variability.*
Grain(obs,coarse) ∧ Var(obs,high) → ∀p[Seq(p) →
outflow(S,p) ≥ very_high]

Theorem 6

T3. *Generalists have modest outflow in each environmental patch if environmental dissimilarity is low.*
Dissim(obs,low) → ∀p[Patch(p) → outflow(G,p) = modest]

T4. *Generalists have high outflow in each environmental patch if environmental dissimilarity is high.*
Dissim(obs,high) → ∀p[Patch(p) → (outflow(G,p) = high]
L3. *Specialists have very high outflow in each sequence of coarse grained observation periods of high variability.*
Grain(obs,coarse) ∧ Var(obs,high) → ∀p[Seq(p) →
outflow(S,p) ≥ very_high]
M7. *Higher outflow in a sequence implies higher outflow in the observation period.*
∀s,x1,x2[Org_type(x1) ∧ Org_type(x2) ∧ Seq(s)
   ∧ outflow(x1,s) > outflow(x2,s)
   → outflow(x1,obs) > outflow(x2,obs)]
M8. *Selection favors organization types with lower losses.*
∀p,x1,x2[Period(p) ∧ Org_type(x1) ∧ Org_type(x2) ∧
outflow(x2,p) > outflow(x1,p) → Selection_favors(x1,x2,p)]
B. *Environmental dissimilarity is high or low.*
Dissim(obs,high) ∨ Dissim(obs,low)
B. *Generalists and specialists are organization types.*
Org_type(G) ∧ Org_type(S)
B. *The observation period is a period.* Period(obS)
B. *Patches are time-periods.* ∀p[Patch(p) → Period(p)]
B. *Sequences are time-periods.* ∀s[Seq(s) → Period(s)]
B. *The observation period has at least one sequence.* ∃s[Seq(s)]
B. *Sequences are unions of an E1 and an E2 patch.* ∀s[Seq(s) →
∃p1,p2[Patch(p1) ∧ Patch(p2) ∧ Holds_in(p1,E1) ∧ Holds_in(p2,E2) ∧
s = union(p1,p2)]]
B. *If outflow is the same in two periods, then this outflow holds in their union.*
∀p1,p2,x[Org_type(x) ∧ Period(p1) ∧ Period(p2) ∧
outflow(x,p1) = outflow(x,p2)
→ outflow(x,union(p1,p2)) = outflow(x,p1)]
B. *Outflow scale.* extreme > very_high, very_high > high,
high > medium, medium > modest, modest > low, low > very_low
B. *On inequality 1.* ∀x,y,z[x > y ∧ y > z → (x > z]
B. *On inequality 2.* ∀x,y[¬(x > y ∧ x = y) ∧ ¬(x > y ∧ y > x)]
B. *On "greater or equal to."* ∀x,y[x ≥ y → x > y ∨ x = y]
T6. *Selection favors generalists above specialists in coarse-grained observation periods of high variability.*
Grain(obs,coarse) ∧ Var(obs,high) → Selection_favors(G,S,obs)

Lemma 4

T1. *Specialists have very low outflow in E1-patches.*
∀p[Patch(p) ∧ Holds_in(p,E1) → outflow(S,p) = very_low]

T2. *Specialists have very high outflow in shorter E2-patches, and they have extremely high outflow in long ones.*
∀p[Patch(p) ∧ Holds_in(p,E2) → (¬(dur(p) = long) →
outflow(S,p) = very_high ∧ (dur(p) = long → outflow(S,p) = extreme)]

M3. *If environmental variability is high, then patches have the same duration.*
Var(obs,high) → ∀p1,p2[Patch(p1) ∧ Patch(p2) → dur(p1) = dur(p2)]

M5. *Patches are not long in fine grained observation periods.*
Grain(obs,fine) → ∀p[Patch(p) → ¬(dur(p) = long)]

A10. *If two patches with the same duration have very low and very high outflows, respectively, then outflow is medium strong in their union.*
∀p1,p2,x[Org_type(x) ∧ Patch(p1) ∧ Patch(p2) ∧ dur(p1) = dur(p2) ∧
outflow(x,p1) = very_low ∧ outflow(x,p2) = very_high
→ outflow(x,union(p1,p2)) = medium]

B. *Sequences are unions of an E1 and an E2 patch.* ∀s[Seq(s) →
∃p1,p2[Patch(p1) ∧ Patch(p2) ∧ Holds_in(p1,E1) ∧
Holds_in(p2,E2) ∧ s = union(p1,p2)]]

B. *Generalists and specialists are organization types.*
Org_type(G) ∧ Org_type(S)

B. *Sequences are time-periods.* ∀p[Seq(p) → Period(p)]

B. *Patches are time periods.* ∀p[Patch(p) → Period(p)]

L4. *Specialists have medium strong outflow in each sequence of fine grained observation periods of high variability.* Grain(obs,fine) ∧ Var(obs,high)
→ ∀p[Seq(p) → outflow(S,p) = medium]

Theorem 7

L4. *Specialists have medium strong outflow in each sequence of fine-grained observation periods of high variability.* Grain(obs,fine) ∧
Var(obs,high) → ∀p[Seq(p) → outflow(S,p) = medium]

T3. *Generalists have modest outflow in each environmental patch if environmental dissimilarity is low.*
Dissim(obs,low) → ∀p[Patch(p) → outflow(G,p) = modest]

M7. *Higher outflow in a sequence implies higher outflow in the observation period.*
∀x1, x2, p[Org_type(x1) ∧ Org_type(x2) ∧ Seq(p)
        ∧ outflow(x1,p) > outflow(x2,p)
          → outflow(x1,obs) > outflow(x2,obs)]

M8. *Selection favors organization types with lower losses.*
∀p,x1,x2[Period(p) ∧
Org_type(x1) ∧ Org_type(x2) ∧ outflow(x2,p) > outflow(x1,p)
→ Selection_favors(x1,x2,p)]
B. *Generalists and specialists are organization types.*
Org_type(G) ∧ Org_type(S)
B. *The observation period is a period.* Period(ob)
B. *Patches are time-periods.* ∀p[Patch(p) → Period(p)]
B. *Sequences are time-periods.* ∀s[Seq(s) → Period(s)]
B. *The observation period has at least one sequence.* ∃s[Seq(s)]
B. *Sequences are unions of an E1 and an E2 patch.* ∀s[Seq(s) →
∃p1,p2[Patch(p1) ∧ Patch(p2) ∧ Holds_in(p1,E1) ∧
Holds_in(p2,E2) ∧ s = union(p1,p2)]]
B. *If outflow is the same in two periods, then this outflow holds in their union.*
∀p1,p2,x[Org_type(x) ∧ Period(p1) ∧ Period(p2) ∧
outflow(x,p1) = outflow(x,p2) →
outflow(x,union(p1,p2)) = outflow(x,p1)]
B. *Outflow scale.* extreme > very_high, very_high > high,
high > medium, medium > modest, modest > low, low > very_low
B. *On inequality 1.* ∀x,y,z[x > y ∧ y > z → (x > z)]
B. *On inequality 2.* ∀x,y[¬(x > y ∧ x = y) ∧ ¬(x > y ∧ y > x)]
T7. *Selection favors generalists above specialists in fine-grained observation periods with high variability and similar environmental conditions.*
Grain(obs,fine) ∧ Var(obs,high) ∧ Dissim(obs,low)
→ Selection_favors(G,S,obs)

Theorem 8

T4. *Generalists have high outflow in each environmental patch if environmental dissimilarity is high.*
Dissim(obs,high) → ∀p[Patch(p) → (outflow(G,p) = high)]
L4. *Specialists have medium strong outflow in each sequence of fine-grained observation periods of high variability.*
Grain(obs,fine) ∧ Var(obs,high) → ∀p[Seq(p) → outflow(S,p) = medium]
M7. *Higher outflow in a sequence implies higher outflow in the observation period.*

$\forall x1, x2, p[Org\_type(x1) \wedge Org\_type(x2) \wedge Seq(p)$
$\qquad \wedge \, outflow(x1,p) > outflow(x2,p)$
$\qquad \rightarrow outflow(x1,obs) > outflow(x2,obs)]$

M8. *Selection favors organization types with lower losses.*
$\forall p,x1,x2[Period(p) \wedge$
$Org\_type(x1) \wedge Org\_type(x2) \wedge outflow(x2,p) > outflow(x1,p)$
$\rightarrow Selection\_favors(x1,x2,p)]$

B. *Generalists and specialists are organization types.*
$Org\_type(G) \wedge Org\_type(S)$

B. *The observation period is a period.* Period(obs)

B. *Patches are time-periods.* $\forall p[Patch(p) \rightarrow Period(p)]$

B. *Sequences are time-periods.* $\forall s[Seq(s) \rightarrow Period(s)]$

B. *The observation period has at least one sequence.* $\exists s[Seq(s)]$

B. *Sequences are unions of an E1 and an E2 patch.* $\forall s[Seq(s) \rightarrow$
$\exists p1,p2[Patch(p1) \wedge Patch(p2) \wedge Holds\_in(p1,E1) \wedge Holds\_in(p2,E2) \wedge$
$s = union(p1,p2)]]$

B. *If outflow is the same in two periods, then this outflow holds in their union.*
$\forall p1,p2,x[Org\_type(x) \wedge Period(p1) \wedge Period(p2) \wedge$
$outflow(x,p1) = outflow(x,p2) \rightarrow$
$outflow(x,union(p1,p2)) = outflow(x,p1)]$

B. *Outflow scale.* extreme > very_high, very_high > high,
high > medium, medium > modest, modest > low, low > very_low

B. *On inequality 1.* $\forall x,y,z[x > y \wedge y > z \rightarrow x > z]$

B. *On inequality 2.* $\forall x,y[\neg(x > y \wedge x = y) \wedge \neg(x > y \wedge y > x)]$

B. *On "greater or equal to."* $\forall x,y[x \geq y \rightarrow x > y \vee x = y]$

T8. *Selection favors specialists above generalists in fine-grained observation periods of high variability and dissimilar environmental conditions.*
$Grain(obs,fine) \wedge Var(obs,high) \wedge Dissim(obs,high) \rightarrow$
$Selection\_favors(S,G,obs)$

Theorem 9

T5. *Selection favors specialists above generalists if environmental variability is low.*
$Var(obs,low) \rightarrow Selection\_favors(S,G,obs)$

M9. *If environmental conditions are stable, then variability is low and grain is coarse.*
$Stable(obs) \rightarrow Var(obs,low) \wedge Grain(obs,coarse)$

T9. *Selection favors specialists above generalists if environmental conditions are stable.*
$Stable(obs) \rightarrow Selection\_favors(S,G,obs)$

Theorem 10

T3. *Generalists have modest outflow in each environmental patch if environmental dissimilarity is low.*

Dissim(obs,low) → ∀p[Patch(p) → outflow(G,p) = modest]

T4. *Generalists have high outflow in each environmental patch if environmental dissimilarity is high.*

Dissim(obs,high) → ∀p[Patch(p) → outflow(G,p) = high]

L1. *Organization types which are adapted to environment E1 or E2 have very low, modest or high outflows if their niche is narrow, modestly wide or wide, respectively, in environments.*

∀x,e,p[Org_type(x) ∧ (e = E1 ∨ e = E2) ∧ Adapted(e,x) ∧ Period(p) ∧ Holds_in(p,e) → (niche(x) = narrow) → outflow(x,p) = very_low) ∧ (niche(x) = modest → outflow(x,p) = modest) ∧ (niche(x) = wide → outflow(x,p) = high)]

D1. *Organizations have narrow niche if and only if they are adapted to a single environment.*

∀x[Org_type(x) → (niche(x)= narrow ↔ ∀e1,e2[Env(e1) ∧ Env(e2) ∧ Adapted(e1,x) ∧ Adapted(e2,x) → e1 = e2])]

A1. *E1 and E2 are the environments that occur.*

∀e[Env(e) → e = E1 ∨ e = E2]

A2. *E1 and E2 are different.* ¬(E1 = E2)

A4. *Poorly adapted organization types have very high outflow in the short run, and they have extremely high outflow in the long run.*

∀p,e,x[Period(p) ∧ Env(e) ∧ Holds_in(p,e) ∧ Org_type(x) ∧ ¬Adapted(e,x) → (¬(dur(p) = long) → outflow(x,p) = very_high) ∧ (dur(p) = long → outflow(x,p) = extreme)]

A6*. *(E2-)specialists are adapted to a single environment.*[13]

∀e1,e2[Env(e1) ∧ Env(e2) ∧ Adapted(e1,S_{E2}) ∧ Adapted(e2,S_{E2}) → (e1 = e2)]

A9. *E1 is the dominant environment during the observation period.*

Dom(obs,E1)

A11. *If outflow is extremely strong in a patch, then it is still very high in the union of this patch with another patch that is not longer.*

∀p1, p2, x[Org_type(x) ∧ Patch(p1) ∧ Patch(p2) ∧ dur(p1) ≥ dur(p2) ∧ outflow(x,p1) = extreme → outflow(x,union(p1,p2)) ≥ very_high]

M4. *If environmental variability is low, then patches of the dominant environment are much longer than the other patches.* Var(obs,low) →

---

[13]A6* is the version of Assumption 6 for *E2*-specialists.

$\forall$p1,p2,e[Dom(obs,e) $\land$ Patch(p1) $\land$ Patch(p2) $\land$

Holds_in(p1,e) $\land$ ¬Holds_in(p2,e) $\rightarrow$ dur(p1) $\gg$ dur(p2)]

M6. *Patches of dominant a environment are long in coarse grained observation periods.*

Grain(obs,coarse) $\rightarrow$ $\forall$p,e[Dom(obs,e) $\land$ Patch(p) $\land$ Holds_in(p,e)

$\rightarrow$ dur(p) = long]

M7. *Higher outflow in a sequence implies higher outflow in the observation period.*

$\forall$x1, x2, p[Org_type(x1) $\land$ Org_type(x2) $\land$ Seq(p)

$\qquad \land$ outflow(x1,p) > outflow(x2,p)

$\qquad \rightarrow$ outflow(x1,obs) > outflow(x2,obs)]

M8. *Selection favors organizational types with lower losses.*

$\forall$p,x1,x2[Period(p) $\land$ Org_type(x1) $\land$

Org_type(x2) $\land$ outflow(x2,p) > outflow(x1,p)

$\rightarrow$ Selection_favors(x1,x2,p)]

M10. *E2-specialists are adapted to environment E2.*

Adapted(E2,S_{E2})

B. *Environmental dissimilarity is either high or low.*

Dissim(obs,high) $\lor$ Dissim(obs,low)

B. *Generalists and E2-specialists are organization types.*

Org_type(G) $\land$ Org_type(S_{E2})

B. *E1 and E2 are environments.* Env(E1) $\land$ Env(E2)

B. *The observation period is a period.* Period(obs)

B. *Patches are periods.* $\forall$p[Patch(p)$\rightarrow$ Period(p)]

B. *Sequences are time-periods.* $\forall$s[Seq(s) $\rightarrow$ Period(s)]

B. *The observation period has at least one sequence.* $\exists$s[Seq(s)]

B. *Sequences are unions of an E1 and an E2 patch.* $\forall$s[Seq(s) $\rightarrow$

$\exists$p1,p2[Patch(p1) $\land$ Patch(p2) $\land$ Holds_in(p1,E1) $\land$

Holds_in(p2,E2) $\land$ s = union(p1,p2)]]

B. *If outflow is the same in both composite subperiods of a period, then this outflow holds in the whole period.* $\forall$p1,p2,x[Org_type(x) $\land$

Period(p1) $\land$ Period(p2) $\land$ outflow(x,p1) = outflow(x,p2) $\rightarrow$

outflow(x,union(p1,p2)) = outflow(x,p1)]

B. *Outflow scale.* extreme > very_high, very_high > high,

high > medium, medium > modest, modest > low, low > very_low

B. *On inequality 1.* $\forall$x,y,z[x > y $\land$ y > z $\rightarrow$ (x > z]

B. *On inequality 2.* $\forall$x,y[¬(x > y $\land$ x = y) $\land$ ¬(x > y $\land$ y > x)]

B. *On "greater or equal to."* $\forall$x,y[x $\geq$ y $\leftrightarrow$ x > y $\lor$ x = y]

B. *If x is much more bigger than y, then x is bigger than y.*

$\forall$x,y[x $\gg$ y $\rightarrow$ x > y]

T10. *If environmental variability is low and grain is coarse, then selection favors generalists above E2-specialists.*

Var(obs,low) $\wedge$ Grain(obs,coarse) $\rightarrow$ Selection_favors(G,S_{E2},obs)

Theorem 11

T10. *If environmental variability is low and grain is coarse, then selection favors generalists above E2-specialists.*

Var(obs,low) $\wedge$ Grain(obs,coarse) $\rightarrow$ Selection_favors(G,S_{E2},obs)

M9. *If environmental conditions are stable, then variability is low and grain is coarse.*

Stable(obs) $\rightarrow$ Var(obs,low) $\wedge$ Grain(obs,coarse)

T11. *Selection favors generalists above E2-specialists if environmental conditions are stable.*

Stable(obs) $\rightarrow$ Selection_favors(G,S_{E2},obs)

REFERENCES

Adams, Douglas. 1986. *The Hitch Hiker's Guide to the Galaxy. A Trilogy in Four Parts*. London: Heinemann.

Barwise, Jon, and John Etchemendy. 1994. *Hyperproof*. Chicago: Chicago University Press.

Brittain, Jack, and John Freeman. 1980. "Organizational Proliferation and Density Dependent Selection." In *Organizational Life Cycles*, edited by J. R. Kimberly and R. H. Miles, 291–338. San Francisco: Jossey-Bass.

Bruggeman, Jeroen. 1997. "Niche Width Theory Reappraised." *Journal of Mathematical Sociology*. Forthcoming.

Carroll, Glenn R. 1985. "Concentration and Specialization: Dynamics of Niche Width in Populations of Organizations." *American Journal of Sociology* 90: 1262–83.

Clogg, Clifford C., and Gerhardt Arminger. 1993. "On Strategy for Methodological Analysis." *Sociological Methodology*, edited by Peter V. Marsden, 57–74. San Francisco: Jossey-Bass.

Freeman, John, and Michael T. Hannan. 1983. "Niche Width and the Dynamics of Organizational Populations." *American Journal of Sociology* 88: 1116–45.

Gamut, L. T. F. 1991. *Logic, Language and Meaning*. Chicago: Chicago University Press.

Hannan, Michael T., and Glenn R. Carroll. 1992. *The Dynamics of Organizational Populations*. New York: Oxford University Press.

Hannan, Michael T., and John Freeman. 1989. *Organizational Ecology*. Cambridge: Harvard University Press.

Huang, Zhisheng, Michael Masuch, and László Pólos. 1996. "AXL, an Action Logic for Agents with Bounded Rationality." *Artificial Intelligence* 82:75–127.

Kamps, Jaap, and Michael Masuch. 1997. "Partial Deductive Closure: Logical Simulation and Management Science." *Management Science*. Forthcoming.

Lakatos, Imre 1976. *Proofs and Refutations. The Logic of Mathematical Discovery*. Cambridge, England: Cambridge University Press.

Levins, Richard 1968. "Evolution in Changing Environments." Princeton: Princeton University Press.

Manski, Charles F. 1993. "Identification Problems in the Social Sciences." *Sociological Methodology*, edited by Peter V. Marsden, 1–56. San Francisco: Jossey-Bass.

Ó Nualláin, Breanndán. 1993. "Mixing Metafor: A System Description of the Metafor Theorem Prover." CCSOM report. University of Amsterdam.

Péli, Gábor 1994. "Niche Strategists and Propagation Strategists: Unifying Two Subtheories of Organizational Ecology Using First-Order Logic." CCSOM report. University of Amsterdam.

Péli, Gábor, Jeroen Bruggeman, Michael Masuch, and Breanndán Ó Nualláin. 1994. "A Logical Approach to Formalizing Organizational Ecology." *American Sociological Review* 59: 571–93.

Péli, Gábor, and Michael Masuch. 1997. "The Logic of Propagation Strategies: Axiomatizing a Fragment of Organizational Ecology in First-Order Logic." *Organization Science* 8: 310–331.

Pólos, László. 1994. "A Formal Approach to Gallhofer and Saris. Argumentation from the Perspective of Decision Theory." In *Proceedings of the ISSA International Conference in Argumentation*, vol. 3, edited by R. Grootendorst, A. Blair, and C. Willard, 436–449. Amsterdam.

———. 1995. "Towards the Metaphysics of Organizations." CCSOM report. University of Amsterdam.

Roughgarden, Jonathan. 1979. *The Theory of Population Genetics and Evolutionary Ecology: An Introduction*. New York: Macmillan.

Simon, Herbert A. 1962. "The Architecture of Complexity." *Proceedings of the American Philosophical Society* 106: 467–82.

𝄞 2 𝄞

SEQUENCE COMPARISON VIA ALIGNMENT AND GIBBS SAMPLING: A FORMAL ANALYSIS OF THE EMERGENCE OF THE MODERN SOCIOLOGICAL ARTICLE

Andrew Abbott *
Emily Barman *

Various substantive literatures in sociology seek small regularities in sequences: turning points in the life course, catalytic moments in organizational change, sharp turns in occupational trajectories, and the like. Commonly these are turning points, but they may also be simple local patterns. This paper reports a method for discovering such regularities even when they are quite faint, applying that method to rhetorical regularities in sociological articles. The paper begins by analyzing the overall sequence structure of such articles and then gives a basic introduction to Gibbs sampling, one member of the broader class of Markov chain Monte Carlo (MCMC) methods. It then reports an algorithm employing Gibbs sampling to find local sequence regularities and applies that algorithm to demonstrate the subsequence regularities present in sociological articles. Substantively, the paper shows that the rhetorical structure of sociological articles changed from one pattern to another in the period 1895–1965 and that certain faint but standard rhetori-

We would like to thank Steven Altschul for calling this method to our attention. The paper has been considerably improved by comments from Adrian Raftery and the *Sociological Methodology* reviewers, one in particular of whom clarified a number of important points. This work was supported in part by the *American Journal of Sociology* and the University of Chicago Press. E-mail: abbot@cicero.spc.uchicago.edu
*University of Chicago

*cal subsequences became characteristic of articles in the later pe-
riod. Methodologically, it introduces a broad class of methods that
provide effective approaches to a number of previously intractable
statistical questions.*

Sociological analysts often want to detect patterns in sequence data. Life
cycle theories, natural history models, and career concepts all hinge on the
notion of regular patterns in successive events. Methods for analyzing such
data, however, are not widespread. In a set of empirical papers, the senior
author has advocated the use of optimal alignment methods for categori-
zation of sequence regularities (see Abbott 1992, 1995a).

However, alignment methods work poorly with subsequence
problems. If our aim is to find a common short pattern within each version of a longer sequence of events—the kind of pattern suggested by
the idea of "turning points" in careers, for example—global alignment
methods are too unfocused. In this paper we apply a new algorithm
developed for subsequence analysis by Lawrence and others (1993).
The algorithm uses Gibbs sampling, a data resampling strategy in the
tradition of the jackknife, the bootstrap, and other data augmentation
techniques.

At the same time, the paper aims to develop and analyze a particular
empirical question. A recent literature in the sociology of science has examined the rhetorical production of scientific texts. We follow this textual
tradition but apply formal sequence analysis methods to study the rhetorical structure—in simple terms, the fundamental outline—of sociological
articles. The basic questions are whether there have been standard patterns
for articles and whether those patterns have changed.

Our multiple tasks impose a complex structure on the present article. We begin with a necessarily brief discussion of the substantive problem. This leads naturally into a discussion of data, sampling, and coding.
We then introduce optimal alignment as a sequence analysis methodology.
Since this method has been discussed elsewhere, our discussion here merely
recapitulates, laying the groundwork for the later subsequence analysis.
Having presented the basic results of the optimal alignment analysis, we
then examine rhetorical subsequences in articles. Here we introduce Gibbs
sampling, first in general, then as a specific aid in analysis of subsequences.
The paper closes with a brief discussion of subsequence results and the
potentialities of methods presented here.

1. THE RHETORICAL STRUCTURE OF ARTICLES

The first literary analyst of social science, to our knowledge, was Joseph Gusfield, whose literary dissection of studies of alcohol abuse first began appearing in the 1970s. Gusfield's work sprang from that of Kenneth Burke (see Gusfield 1981), emphasizing a broad rhetorical analysis of the strategies of science for representing itself as authoritative. In the years since Gusfield wrote, several others have pursued his lead. McCloskey (1985) has analysed texts in economics. Myers (1990) discussed the rhetorical "taming" of articles in biology. Bazerman (1988) comes closest to the task we undertake here, examining the rhetorical structure imposed on psychology by the APA style manual and the detailed rhetorical patterns of articles in one volume of the *American Political Science Review*.[1]

While the rhetorical tradition has effectively reshaped our thinking about scientific writing, it has not empirically examined long-term changes in rhetorical patterns. Yet what persuades in one generation may not persuade in another. Indeed, the very relation of science to the rest of society has changed during the social sciences' existence, a change that in turn might be expected to change patterns of argument. Moreover, we expect changes in rhetorical patterns as disciplines themselves change and develop, growing now more, now less authoritative relative to competing disciplines.

There is thus a variety of mechanisms predicting changes in the rhetorical patterns of scientific argument. One particular generalization about that change is a common belief among sociologists: that over the years sociological articles have become more and more subject to rigid rhetorical conventions. This common opinion arises in our conceptions about disciplinary history. Most of us believe that the modern quantitative sociological article first appeared with the present tradition of quantitative sociology in the 1930s and that it became a formal, conventional structure by about 1965–1970, complete with theory section, literature review, presentation of data, discussion of methods, recounting of results, and conclusion. But there is little evidence of this trend other than some general

---

[1] O'Neill (1981) contains a good review of rhetorical studies of science as of that date. Kircz (1991) has analyzed article argumentation from the point of view of coding and informational retrieval. Clyne (1987) is an elegant comparison of the internal organization of English as opposed to German academic texts. Connors (1985) offers an actual history of explanatory rhetoric. Mullins et al. (1988) present a general plea for detailed analysis of articles.

statements about personal experience, all of which confound personal with disciplinary aging.[2]

In this paper, we formally evaluate the proposition that sociological articles have become more and more rhetorically fixed. We proceed by developing a lexicon of article elements (short "units" of sociological writing), coding a selected series of articles in terms of those elements, and then analyzing the results using sequence methods. If the "converging rhetoric" generalization is correct, we should find more recent articles to be more narrowly similar in structure at both global and specific levels. The precise nature of that narrow similarity should perhaps be left open. Next to nothing is known about this empirical generalization of convergence, so it would be premature to specify an expectation. But the overall empirical regularity we expect seems clear: convergence on a standard form.

2. DATA, SAMPLING, AND CODING

We propose to examine the question of convergence using a single journal, a stratified sample, and a formal method for coding. In this section we discuss these choices.

[2]This statement is common enough in speech but hard to document on paper. There is much informal data on the disappearance of unusual work from the journals. As one recent member of the AJS editorial staff put it to the senior author, "most of what we publish is extremely competent and extremely boring." Complaints on this score are old. Writing of the ASR, Page (1981) reports "in the fifties, according to many of its critics, the *Review* was theoretically thin, overloaded with small-scale research reports, and neglectful of important social and sociological issues—charges with which I agreed." Page turned to solicitation to get papers from scholars like Bierstedt, Goode, Hughes, Kroeber, Merton, Moore, Parsons, and Riesman.

There is some evidence on changes in methodology. See Smalley (1981), for example, whose data bears also on the trends in section 2.3.3, as well as McCartney (1970) and Bakanic, McPhail, and Simon (1987). Certainly changes in editorial processes might have produced increasing homogenization. Thus, Teevan (1980) had a large panel of blind judges rate published papers and found that ratings vary more within journals than between them, even though he used six general sociology journals with widely varying ratings on the Glenn (1971) prestige scale. This result suggests one dimension of homogenization. Another indication, if not of homogenization then of processes that could easily produce it, is the emergence of the "revise and resubmit" judgment, a judgment that has become very common in sociology journals in recent decades. Bakanic, McPhail, and Simon report 28 percent of articles were given R&R status on first review at ASR in 1977–1982. R&R could easily be a euphemism for a process enforcing standardization, although on another interpretation, the rise of extensive formal revisions would not be producing sterile homogenization, but rather "high standards."

2.1. *Data*

Using a single journal minimizes a variety of random forces that might affect the rhetoric of articles. Different journals have different rhetorical conventions. Some prefer short articles, some long. Some demand many references, some prefer few. Some require particular forms of quantitative analyses, others have broader tastes. All of these differences lead to differences of rhetoric—omitting a literature review or expanding a "data" section or whatever.

Of course, rhetorical patterns change over time, even within a single journal. But by selecting a central disciplinary journal, at the top of a discipline's prestige hierarchy, with purported general interests, we can come as close as possible to a situation in which article rhetoric reflects neither journal differentiation nor particular editors, but rather reflects central disciplinary forces. If the journal has enjoyed such a central position over many years, these forces will play on it in a relatively constant manner. Rhetorical changes will not arise in changes of the journal's status *relative* to other journals.

The *American Journal of Sociology* (AJS) meets these criteria perhaps as well as any journal in social science. It has been central to its discipline for 100 years. Its editors—only ten in that period—all came from the same department, whose relative status in the field changed only marginally over the period. It is true that other sociology journals began to appear after World War I and that the *American Sociological Review* cut seriously into AJS's market after the 1930s. But these new journals did not substantially change AJS's character as a central, high-prestige, general-interest journal. It is also true that sociology was hardly a "scientific" discipline in the early years of the journal, before 1925. But the turning of the discipline toward science is precisely one of the things we hope to investigate and thus this fact is less a disability than an opportunity.[3]

AJS thus stands in a roughly consistent position throughout the period in which the "modern sociological article" supposedly emerged (1900–1960). Its articles form a useful universe for our investigation.

[3] One referee pointed out that the AJS often tried to step outside the normal genres of articles, referring us to editor Charles Bidwell's call for unusual papers in July 1976. Having just completed a monographic history of the AJS, however, the senior author can report that it was precisely the feeling that submissions were homogeneous—intellectually as much as or more than rhetorically—that drove Bidwell, as well as his successors, to take drastic measures to find interesting work.

2.2. Sampling

Our sampling strategy was driven by the need for adequate representation from each time period and by balanced representation of the different types within the general category of empirical articles. The overall time period was set at 1895–1965. By the latter date, as we noted, the current rhetorical format of empirical articles seems by general account to have stabilized. For example, it is around this time that one first sees complaints about the formulaic character of such articles (Abbott 1996a). At the other end of the period, it seemed best to begin with the first years of the journal, even though empirical reports make up a relatively small fraction of its contents at that time; it is crucial to trace the modern rhetoric to its roots.

The 70-year index of the AJS (*American Journal of Sociology* 1966) codes articles into eight types: case analysis, general quantitative, experimental, survey, cross-cultural, methodological, nonquantitative, and theory. The first four of these can be taken as the relevant universe of scientific/ empirical articles, those whose main burden is to present new empirical material.[4]

In order to balance the four specific types within the larger category of empirical articles, we took a stratified quota sample. We aimed at 15 articles per decade, distributed evenly across the four types. Since the experimental articles began only in the journal's fourth decade, this means five each of quantitative, survey, and case analysis articles until that decade, with about four each for the four types thereafter. A number of articles proved unusable for various reasons (extended formats, two-part articles, and the like), and so our eventual sample was 99 (not $7 * 15 = 105$) articles. (The exact numbers of articles per decade were 10, 15, 12, 15, 15, 15, 17.)

---

[4] Some commenters on this paper have wondered about various of these exclusions—why we left out cross-cultural studies, methodological studies, and nonquantitative studies. Our reasons are straightforward. Nonquantitative studies was a residual category, not a positive one. Methodology studies clearly have a different rhetorical structure than "normal research reports," which was the rhetorical form whose emergence we had hypothesized. (Their aim is to introduce new methods, which takes different rhetorical moves.) Finally, cross-cultural studies was also something of a miscellaneous category. We felt that we would increase our likelihood of identifying particular rhetorical structures by focusing on the most likely kinds of papers, understanding that these made up only half of the journal's articles even at the end of the period. Of course, these were not the *only* forms of articles. No such claim is made here.

2.3. Coding

2.3.1. Reasons for Formal Coding

Our third major methodological choice was for a formal coding procedure. There are of course the usual important reasons for coding: consistency across cases, disciplining of reflection, and so on. Thus Bazerman's detailed reading of three political science articles (1988:c. 10), however subtle, is vulnerable to the idiosyncracies of the particular articles chosen and is in many ways more illustrative than definitive. Moreover, since it was a purely cross-sectional analysis devoted to finding "a version of rhetoric," Bazerman's chapter had no need to create an analytic structure that would enable measurement and comparison across time. His equivalent over-time discussion (1988:c. 9) makes length of article its main indicator of rhetoric and contains numerous statements about quantities and proportions of subsections in psychological articles (e.g., 1988:272). But it has no basis in formal measurement, relying rather on the informed judgment of a recollecting reader.[5]

One obvious source for the belief that sociological articles have become more formulaic is change in the proportions of articles using any version of a scientific/empirical format. By the coding used by the AJS indexers in 1965 (*American Journal of Sociology* 1966), the proportion of these articles went from around 15 percent of the total in the first three decades of the journal to 35 percent in the second three decades and to 55 percent by the seventh decade, since which it has steadily increased. Our concern, however, is not with change in the mix of types of articles, although such change undoubtedly reinforces perceptions of change in "the typical article" across the discipline.[6] Rather, we are concerned with change in the rhetorical structure within that group of articles that in particular present some form of systematic empirical information. For it is within such articles that the supposed rhetorical

---

[5]Bazerman's book is meant to open a discussion rather than settle it, and so there was no need—scientific, or, if we wish to follow his discussion, rhetorical—for his interpretations and conclusions to have the support required for one to believe them firmly.

[6]There is good evidence on various changes in topics and areas in sociology journals over time. See Buehler, Hesser, and Weigert (1972), Champion and Morris (1974), Assadi (1987), Kinloch (1988), Murray (1988), and Garnett (1988). See also the various papers in *The American Sociologist*, 11:3, 1976, an entire number devoted to sociological journalism.

straightjacket has emerged.[7] But at a distance, these empirical articles are often indistinguishable. Only by coding them in some detail can we see changes in the nature of their form.[8]

2.3.2. The Coding Procedure

Like most coding schemes, ours went through a number of iterations. Our initial decisions concerned the level at which to code units of argument. We knew from the outset that the different genres (theory, quantitative, etc.) have quite different overall structures. We thus followed Barthes (1974) and began at the lowest level of coding, the sentence. We began building up a simple list of types of statements: introduction of a question, statement of significance, empirical assertion, statement of position, identification of elements of an argument, summary of an argument, and so on.

This sentence-level investigation produced a curious discovery in a number of early articles. Papers in the first two decades of the journal sometimes have mixtures of data, theoretical statements, and policy assertions within the same paragraph. This form of writing is relatively more common in the "social policy" articles, but occasionally appears in the kinds of empirical articles analyzed here. This style may well have emerged from the homiletic style of the time, for which it was a standard rhetorical strategy. (It should be recalled that sociology was considered a

---

[7]Of course, in an ultimate sense, these levels of analysis cannot be firmly distinguished. It is possible that the clarification of the rhetorical form of the empirical article helped lead to the domination of journal's contents by such articles.

[8]Coding was also necessary because of our desire to apply formal methods for comparing the various articles. One *could* pick a sample of early and late articles, compare them hermeneutically, and argue that the obvious differences betrayed a tendency toward rigid form. (This was more or less Bazerman's procedure.) But this would not tell us exactly wherein those differences lay. Nor would it, indeed, tell us that there was movement toward rigidity rather than, for example, change from one rigidity to another. Without a formal method for comparing the articles, such questions could not be precisely answered. There are, to be sure, methods for quantitative comparison that do not involve actually coding the individual steps in each article's argument. For example, one could study length in the belief that shorter articles mean more formulaic rhetoric or study the degree of reference to the work of others, defining citation as an emerging rhetorical device. Both these strategies were used by Bazerman. But length is a very imprecise measure of rhetoric. And citation measures are largely dependent on the numbers of other journals available to cite, on the libraries available to citing authors, and other such environmental factors. (Indeed, citation is even dependent on printing technologies; it has ballooned since the rise of the personal computer.)

religious field at the time.[9]) Fortunately, this style was not common in the more empirical pieces. Otherwise, higher level coding would have been meaningless.

We were interested in higher-level rhetorical structures and hence decided on paragraph coding. Changes in lengths of typical paragraphs over the 70 years investigated led us to also code the data in terms of fractions (quarters) of pages for each type of writing. The two systems produce more or less equivalent results, and we report the page coding here, which we regard as more stable over time. Thus the basic unit of coding is the quarter page. Note that this does not mean grid coding— taking each quarter page and asking what it is that appears there. Rather, we first separated an article into distinguishable elements and then measured the length of each element in quarter pages (or paragraphs, in the other metric). Note that both of these metrics preserve information about the lengths, as well as the order, of elements.

For contents, our initial coding began from the same common-sense understanding of social science articles that is discussed in Bazerman (1988 c. 10). The empirical article is generally made up of introductory material, hypotheses, literature, data and methods, analysis, and concluding material. We initially distinguished 28 subtypes under these general article elements. These are shown in Table 1. They are grouped in categories under the overarching headings just given. The elements are defined verbally in the right column. Each element has a basic ID code, listed at the left. We also give the number of times an element was observed in the complete data set ("Number in state" column). By "number of times" we mean here the number of separate episodes or runs, not the number of individual quarter-page units. (Otherwise length of articles would be the dominating force in these counts.) Thus a run of 30 units of one element in one article counts here as one observation of that element.

In coding, it soon became clear that these elements are often combined. Indeed, sometimes several codes are combined. In Table 2, we list the various combination states. At the left are listed the ID codes of the simple states constituting each combination state. We then list the number

[9]On sociology as a religious field, see Abbott 1996a. (For example, the AJS was regarded by the University of Chicago Press as one of its religious journals.) For the idea that the intermingled style was possibly derivative from sermon-writing, we thank George Levine of Rutgers University and Kirstie McClure of Johns Hopkins, both of whom made this suggestion to us independently.

TABLE 1
Elementary Elements of Articles

State	Number in state	New ID	
A. Introductory			
11	2	1	Topic
12	66	2	State of affairs
13	6	3	Question
14	6	4	Language
15	13	5	Significance of paper
16	11	6	Purpose of paper
17	54	7	Author's theory/assertion
18	9	8	Existing discussion
B. Hypotheses			
21	29	9	Existing theory/hypotheses
22	22	10	Author's hypotheses
C. Literature			
31	2	11	Citation of existing author
32	8	12	Summary of argument
33	11	13	Commentary on existing author/ argument
D. Data and Methods			
41	14	14	Sources of data
42	71	15	Description of research design
43	28	16	Empirical veracity
44	25	17	Methods of analysis of data set
E. Discussion of Data/Analysis			
51	16	18	Presentation of figures
52	5	19	Report of analysis of data set
53	23	20	Summary of findings
54	39	21	Total summary of findings
55	13	22	Relevance for theory/hypotheses
56	16	23	Total relevance for theory/hypotheses
57	11	24	Identification of cause or explanation
58	14	24	Identification of cause or explanation
F. Conclusion Material			
61	3	57	Review of findings
62	18	58	Implications
63	10	59	Prescriptive statements

of times each combination state was observed in the total data set, with the same conventions about runs as in Table 1.

To simplify final data presentation, we assigned new ID codes to all states, simple and combination. These are shown in the third column of each table. Note that the original codes of the simple states were chosen so that their tens digit described their general category and their units digit a specific type. This makes the combination states a little easier to understand. A few complex combinations were observed only once or twice. In the data here these are not reported. In analysis they were lumped under a residual element, new ID 56.

2.3.3. Aggregate Trends in Coded Units

Some comment is necessary on the empirical trends in the elements observed in the 99 articles. First, there were no obvious trends by decade in the total number of counted units per decade, in the relative proportion of combination units, (although there was perhaps a slight tendency to more complex combination units in later years), and in the tendency to use more than one kind of combination unit. Moreover, the median number of units per article is strikingly constant at 10, as are the first and third quartiles of that distribution (at 8 and 13 respectively). The reader should recall that this means *runs* of identical elements, not actual length in numbers of quarter pages; the duration information will be used later in analysis.

The lack of change in combination states argues against one form of rhetorical rigidification: the distillation of article sections into simple, single-purpose units. One possible rhetorical change might have been from the homiletic style (with its melange of facts, analyses, and interpretations) to a style of mixed units and thence to a style marching through rigidly purified sections of theory, methods, data, analysis, interpretation, and conclusion. We do not find evidence consistent with this directional change.

There are minor trends among types of units, which begin to suggest some empirical trends in rhetorical patterns. There is a move from presenting simple numbers and quantities to presenting formal data analysis, signified most clearly by a decline over time in element 40 (presentation of figures plus summary of findings) and a corresponding increase in element 43 (data analysis plus summary of findings). A similar pattern appears for the elements 51 and 53, which are simply elements 40 and 43 plus a "discussion of relevance for theory and hypotheses." Second, there

TABLE 2
Combination Elements of Articles

State	Number in state	NEW ID	
Double States:			
12 17	2	25	State of affairs//Author's theory/assertion
12 51	1	26	State of affairs//Presentation of figures
12 53	2	27	State of affairs//Summary of findings
17 51	4	28	Author's theory/assertion//Presentation of figures
17 53	7	29	Author's theory/assertion//Summary of findings
17 54	10	30	Author's theory/assertion//Total summary of findings
17 55	3	31	Author's theory/assertion//Relevance for theory/hypothesis
17 57	1	32	Author's theory/assertion//Identification of cause or explanation
17 58	1	32	Author's theory/assertion//Identification of cause or explanation
22 32	2	34	Author's hypothesis//Summary of argument
22 55	3	35	Author's hypothesis//Relevance for theory/hypothesis
31 32	15	36	Citation of existing author//Summary of argument
32 33	2	37	Summary of argument//Comment on existing argument
41 51	1	38	Data sources//Presentation of figures
43 51	2	39	Empirical veracity//Presentation of figures

51 53	74	40	Presentation of figures//Summary of findings
51 55	5	41	Presentation of figures//Theory/relevance
51 57	0	42	Presentation of figures//Identification of cause or explanation
52 53	45	43	Data analysis//Summary of findings
53 55	10	44	Summary of findings//Theory/relevance
53 58	2	45	Summary of findings//Identification of cause or explanation
54 55	2	46	Total summary of findings//Theory/relevance
54 56	7	47	Total summary of findings//Total theory/relevance

Triple and Quadruple States

17 51 53	4	48	Author's theory//Presentation of figures//Summary of findings
21 53 55	2	49	Existing theory//Summary of findings//Theory/relevance
22 52 53	1	50	Author's hypothesis//Data analysis//Summary of findings
51 53 55	14	51	Presentation figures//Summary of findings//Theory/relevance
51 53 57	5	52	Presentation figures//Summary of findings//Identification of cause or explanation
52 53 55	16	53	Data analysis//Summary of findings//Theory/relevance
52 53 58	2	54	Data analysis//Summary of findings//Identification of cause or explanation
52 53 55 58	1	55	Data analysis//Summary of findings//Theory/relevance//Identification of cause or explanation

is a substantial increase in general category D (data and methods) elements, specifically in element 15 (description of research design) and element 17 (methods of analysis of data set). As Bazerman notes with respect
to psychology, these sections provide crucial rhetorical anchors in a claim
to scientific authority. The decadal totals for all these elements, shown in
Table 3, suggest that even these trends are not absolutely regular. Nonetheless they do hint at a move from simply reporting numbers to doing
something with them inferentially and date that move pretty clearly to the
fourth and fifth decades of the journal, the period 1925–1945.

3. OPTIMAL ALIGNMENT OF FULL ARTICLES

We now turn to an analysis of the exact rhetorical patterns within articles.
At this point, we reintroduce information on the exact duration of particular sections of articles, which we had removed during the aggregate analysis in order to somewhat standardize for the effects of changes in article
lengths. (That standardization is done differently in the alignment analysis
below.)

A typical data sequence is the following:

1A2   1A9   2A15   20A43   5A21   5A23

The letter A means nothing, but merely separates the number of times an
element is observed sequentially, which precedes the letter, from the identity of the element, which follows it. This sequence thus means that the
article comprises, in the given order:

  1 unit of "state of affairs" followed by
  1 unit of "existing theory and hypotheses" followed by
  2 units of "description of research design" followed by
20 units of data analysis/summary of findings followed by
  5 units of total summary of findings
  5 units of total (overall) discussion of relevance for theory
    and hypotheses

3.1. *Optimal Alignment*

Given such codings for the 99 articles in the sample, we sought sequence
patterns by using optimal alignment methods, which have been described
in detail elsewhere (Abbott and Hrycak 1990; for a general reference see
Sankoff and Kruskal 1983). Alignment methods are simple replacement

TABLE 3

Decadal Observations of Trending Elements

Element	Decade						
	1 1895– 1905	2 1905– 1915	3 1915– 1925	4 1925– 1935	5 1935– 1945	6 1945– 1955	7 1955– 1965
15 Description of research design	5	3	8	12	14	13	16
17 Methods of analysis of dataset	1	1	2	5	7	6	3
40 Presentation of figures//Summary of findings	11	27	12	18	4	1	1
43 Data analysis//Summary of findings			1	1	16	18	9
51 Presentation of figures//Summary of findings// Theoretical relevance		4	3	6	1		
53 Data analysis//Summary of findings// Theoretical relevance				1	6	3	6

61

algebras that compute a distance between any pair of sequences based on the minimum number of replacements and insertions required to transform one of the sequences into the other. For example, it takes two changes to turn the sequence 1A2   1A9   2A15   20A43   5A21   5A23 into the sequence 2A2   1A9   1A10   1A15   20A43   5A21   5A23. These changes are easily seen by aligning the sequences, that is, arraying them so that their similarities are lined up:

1A2	1A9		2A15	20A43	5A21	5A23
2A2	1A9	1A10	1A15	20A43	5A21	5A23

A unit of A2 has been added, and a unit of A15 has been turned into a unit of A10. One can easily imagine a simple metric for assessing distance between pairs of sequences, consisting of the number of such insertions and replacements required for the full transformation. Note that there are other ways to make this change, but they involve more total insertions and replacements. One could insert the A2, then insert an A10, then remove an A15, for example. This would allow alignment with only one elementary operation (insertion/deletion), where we have allowed two (insertion/ deletion plus replacement). But it takes three insertions/deletions where we have used one insertion/deletion and one replacement. (In some circumstances, however, there might be reasons for not allowing replacement as an operation.)

There is a variety of alignment algorithms, depending on what particular kinds of sequence regularities are of interest.[10] The algorithms vary, first, in the elementary operations used (insertions, replacement, swaps, transpositions, and the like) and, second, in the way costs are assigned to those operations. The example just given implicitly assumes that insertion/ deletion "costs" the same thing as replacement and that all replacements "cost" the same. Under some circumstances those assumptions might not be useful. Algorithms may also choose to regard any string of insertions— however long—as having a given, fixed cost.

In the present case, we are agnostic about the kinds of regularities we expect. The regularities could be local patterns—subsections that al-

---

[10]The senior author has briefly noted some of these different algorithms in a comment on a paper in *Sociological Methods and Research* that introduced a variant algorithm as if it were a completely new method (Abbott 1995b). A review of the state of the art in biology (as of 1991) was Gribskov and Devereux (1991) and a more recent (slightly) review is Boguski (1992). Developments in this area, which is force-fed with biotechnology money, are very rapid.

ways come in the same order. They could be "stage" regularities, where certain rhetorical elements are generally early, middle, or late in the article, but the detailed ordering of elements can vary. Where we are so unsure of expected regularities, it makes sense to use a relatively simple algorithm, one with only the two operations of insertion/deletion and replacement and one having fairly simple cost assumptions.

The standard such algorithm is the Needleman-Wunsch (1970) algorithm. It uses the two elementary operations of replacement and insertion. For each, it requires that we assign a "cost" scheme, on the assumption that some replacements and insertion/deletions matter more than others.

Replacement costs have to be set for all pairs among the 59 potential sequence elements listed in Tables 1 and 2. For the "simple" elements (those in Table 1), replacement costs were set at 1.0 for all elements falling under different headings in that table, and at 0.25 for all such units within a given heading. Thus substituting element 15 for element 16 cost only 0.25, but substituting element 15 for element 20 cost 1.0. This ratio (0.25 to 1.0) is somewhat arbitrary; it could easily have been 0.33 to 1.0, for example. But it catches our sense that emphasizing different whole sections of an article is a more drastic rhetorical change than changing the emphasis among ways of writing a particular section.

For the combination elements (elements 25–55, in Table 2), costs were set at the average of replacement costs over all potential pairs of individual elements within the combinations. Thus substituting element 43 (combination of simple elements 52 and 53) for element 26 (combination of simple elements 12 and 51) cost an average of 1.0, 1.0, 0.25, and 0.25, or 0.625. This weighting again made the algorithm tend to emphasize closeness within the element heading types where perfect matches were not possible.

For insertion costs, we chose a uniform but very low value. Many biological alignment algorithms use a fixed "gap penalty" for any insertion plus a much smaller weight linear in the length of the insertion. We chose a uniform insertion cost—that is, an insertion cost scheme with no gap penalty and a fixed insertion/deletion cost linear in the number of inserted elements. We choose this because we feel that the insertion involved in article rhetorics is more a matter of gradual expansion or contraction of subsections than of insertion of new blocks of random length. At the same time we have set the insertion cost quite low. Insertion costs that are high—more than half the largest or even the mean replacement cost—tend to force the alignment to "follow the main diagonal"— that is, to use replacements preferentially, because it takes two insertion/deletions to make one replacement. This in turn makes differences in length unduly important in the alignment, even when, as here, the intersequence distances are all divided by the length of the longer sequence in order to standardize for such differences. An insertion/deletion cost that is low relative to replacement cost makes the algorithm put more emphasis on the order pattern of the elements than on the duration of runs of elements. We have set insertion costs at 0.1 times the largest replacement cost, which means that where replacement costs are high, the algorithm will handle replacements as combinations of insertions. In practice, this means that the algorithm is free to focus on aligning perfectly those parts of the sequences that very closely resemble one another, using insertions more or less as necessary to find these "common locations."[11]

3.2. *Analysis and Results*

Using these parameters, the data were input to an optimal alignment algorithm. The algorithm produces a distance between every pair of articles in the data—$99 * (98/2)$, or 4851 pairs. For a first judgment of the hypothesis

---

[11] All calculations in this paper were done using the program OPTIMIZE. The program (for DOS, Windows, and OS2) is available on the Internet at Web site http://www.cicero.spc.uchicago.edu/usurs/abbot. OPTIMIZE is a simple program for doing optimal alignments following the Needleman-Wunsch algorithm as adapted here. It has two modules, one of which (EXPLORE) permits visual inspection of the actual algorithm pattern between any pair of sequences and allows the investigator to rapidly scan the impact of varying the insertion costs on the actual alignment observed. There are literally dozens of other alignment programs available, most designed for biological applications and input (see Gribskov and Devereux [1991]).

There is at present a small literature on the impact of varying insertion costs, usually in the context of a single-cost replacement model. If one defines a Cartesian space by insertion cost along one axis and replacement cost on another, different points in the space may produce different alignments, in the literal sense of a different sequence of elementary operations (or the same operations at different places), between two given sequences. These changes induce a tessellation of the space, one that becomes even more complicated when we introduce varying replacement costs and with them more dimensions of the space. (See Vingron and Waterman 1994.)

Given the preliminary nature of the formal literature, we must fall back on the test of practice. Forrest and Abbott (1990) present an extended reliability analysis of optimal alignment of coded data, showing that fairly large local differences in coding procedures still produce recognizably similar results because the gross data are constant. In working with various data sets, the senior author has found that placing the insertion cost at 0.1 times the largest replacement cost is usually a good starting point. The aim of alignment is to find patterns of interest. This level seems in practice to produce the best results. It is important, however, to test a variety of values.

of convergence, we calculated means and standard deviations for these distances within and between decades. These are reported in Table 4. (Thus, 0.682 is the mean distance between all pairs of articles such that both were published in the first decade. 0.159 is the standard deviation of this figure.) It is clear by inspection that the data fall into two broad groups: decades 1–4 on the one hand and decades 6 and 7 on the other. Decade 5 is clearly transitional but leans toward the later group. This division into two groups is largely due to the shift from figures to data analysis noted in Table 2. Regardless of this trend, there is no evidence whatever in this table that intradecade distances decrease with time, as would be the case if convergence were occurring.

TABLE 4
Distances Within and Between Decades

A. Mean Distances

| Decade | Decade | | | | | | |
	1 1895– 1905	2 1905– 1915	3 1915– 1925	4 1925– 1935	5 1935– 1945	6 1945– 1955	7 1955– 1965
1 1895–1905	.682						
2 1905–1915	.641	.590					
3 1915–1925	.633	.585	.613				
4 1925–1935	.640	.607	.639	.621			
5 1935–1945	.716	.724	.744	.719	.735		
6 1945–1955	.753	.774	.776	.749	.707	.630	
7 1955–1965	.709	.727	.746	.731	.700	.653	.655

B. Standard Deviations

| Decade | Decade | | | | | | |
	1 1895– 1905	2 1905– 1915	3 1915– 1925	4 1925– 1935	5 1935– 1945	6 1945– 1955	7 1955– 1965
1 1895–1905	.159						
2 1905–1915	.173	.165					
3 1915–1925	.185	.184	.220				
4 1925–1935	.140	.146	.161	.138			
5 1935–1945	.125	.148	.136	.152	.148		
6 1945–1955	.099	.108	.100	.120	.161	.196	
7 1955–1965	.107	.117	.106	.129	.148	.161	.166

These general figures, however, could misrepresent matters if there were multiple forms within particular periods. The earlier period might have been characterized by one form around which there were many minor variants, while the later period might have had two or more forms with much less variation around them. This could produce the distance pattern shown, even though there *had* been convergence. To rule out this possibility, we must consider the data in terms of rhetorical forms themselves.

To search for rhetorical forms, we analyzed the distance data with standard cluster analysis algorithms. In order to avoid the common volatility of cluster analysis results with different algorithms, the sequence distances were analyzed using both single and average linkage. These produced strongly similar results (a somewhat unusual event in our experience). This similarity indicates that the results are fairly robust.[12]

Data for two average-linkage clusters are shown in Table 5. Note that left-right distance has little meaning in this table. We have spread the sequences out to show their alignments most effectively within cluster. (This probably represents that actual alignments used, since insertion/deletion cost was low.) It is clear how the alignment works—picking up

---

[12]Cluster analysis is a general method for producing categorizations of data based on distance metrics. For a general text, see Everitt (1993). As is well known, different algorithms for cluster analysis produce slightly different solutions. We chose both single linkage and average linkage—the first because despite its tendency to stringy clusters it has the advantage of producing the same clustering under any monotonic transformation of the data; the second for its more stable, globular clusters. As noted in the text, stability of clusters across algorithms is good evidence of substantive validity. We report 14 clusters (rather than, say, 3 or 30) because that level of clustering seemed mostly clearly interpretable.

We have not undertaken direct validity measures of these partitions. On the one hand, there were no bases for external validity criteria (no second and uncorrelated types of measurement of resemblance between articles). On the other, internal validity measurement (validity analysis based purely on the proximity matrix itself) is, in the words of Jain and Dubes, more or less a "black art accessible only to those true believers who have experience and great courage" (1988:222). The analysis here produces credible substantive results, showing a clear and plausible relation between rhetorical structure and period of writing. The clusters persist across different clustering algorithms. Any further validity analysis would take us into obscurities that would prevent our getting on to the matter of subsequence analysis.

There is a recent literature on weighting in sequence space prior to analysis. This mainly aims at the problems of redundancy (Henikoff and Henikoff 1994) and direct interdependence (Vingron and Sibbald 1993) among sequences. The second of these is impossible in this data; the structure of one article does not directly coerce another the way an ancestor DNA can coerce its descendant. The first is important, but since our main purpose is to find the major types of articles, weighting in favor of the "rare article type" seems mistaken. For a general review of statistical issues related to sequence analysis, see Karlin et al. (1991).

TABLE 5
Two Clusters of Sequences

Cluster 1															
86	1A6	3A8	1A2	1A8	2A5	2A7	9A19	9A40	9A19	9A40	2A22	18A40	5A21	5A59	
67	1A1	1A7	3A40	2A25		1A17		17A40	1A20	7A40	6A51		3A21	2A17	
			1A2			2A15		19A40	5A24	4A40					
24	2A15	1A4	1A2	1A3				17A40	2A18	5A41	9A40	2A24	2A21	1A7	
52	5A9		9A40	2A7				13A40							
15			1A2			5A15		25A40	1A30	6A40	5A18				
37			1A2			5A15		27A40	1A18						
62			2A2			2A15		28A40	1A58						
36			1A2	2A17		2A15		12A40	2A24	24A40			2A21	2A23	2A59
64			1A2	1A9	1A16	13A15		49A40	9A16						
88				1A14		6A15		49A40					2A7	2A7	
80				2A7		2A14		37A40	2A7	13A40				1A7	
82	6A9		2A2	6A28		2A15		39A40	6A18	7A40	2A5				
81					1A5	5A20	1A17	33A40	1A7	18A40			2A7		
90	1A8	1A9	9A2	9A18				18A40	2A24	48A40	13A46	10A40	2A21	2A7	2A59
95			5A2			6A20		23A40	6A48	23A40	17A48		9A24	30A48	2A24
98			2A2	1A4		6A18		13A40	5A29	26A40					2A56
97			1A2												

Cluster 13															
53	1A6	1A2	9A15	2A12	9A16	5A43	2A17	1A43		1A56	2A54	1A21	5A43	2A43	2A31
16	1A6	1A5	2A15			5A43	2A16	6A43		1A19			1A9	6A16	2A56
40	3A56	3A9	1A15					19A43					1A23		1A53
38	2A12	2A6	2A10	2A4	6A15			16A43				2A21	2A23		1A5
41	1A12	1A13	2A2		6A15			17A43				3A21	3A23		
69	1A2		14A15			5A43	5A56	15A43				5A21		3A7	2A57
32	1A2	2A7	10A15	1A17	1A17	14A43		5A31						2A7	
17	1A2	1A16	1A36		6A15	1A17	1A16	16A43					2A30	1A10	1A58
45	1A2		5A15	1A17	1A20	23A43		1A30					5A16		
49	1A6	1A2	1A9	2A10	2A15	2A39		22A43	1A5				6A23	1A5	
51	1A2	1A34	5A15					31A43				2A21	2A23		
42	2A2		1A15					32A43				2A21			
70	1A2		1A15			21A43	2A21	17A43	2A15			5A21		2A7	1A30
73	6A2		1A15	1A3		21A43		20A43						5A7	
79	1A2	5A17	2A15			10A43		22A43				2A21		1A7	11A43
85	1A5		3A15			15A43	5A56	39A43						1A7	6A2
31	5A43	5A27				12A43	2A24	5A43		6A29	14A43	2A21	1A24		1A58
54	1A2	1A14				2A43	9A24	6A43		1A5	1A14				
25	1A2	1A9	2A15	5A53	5A17	11A43	5A17	2A43						1A58	

67

various parts of various sequences and lining them up. There is a fair amount of minor variation, but in each case the algorithm has found a basic pattern.

Table 6 presents descriptive statistics on the clusters that clearly persist in both clustering methods. For the major clusters, we report their "mean volume year"—that is, the average of the volumes in which the cluster members appeared. We also report the year represented by this volume (always 5 less than the mean volume year because the AJS began publication in 1895) and the standard deviation of that mean.

The principal result is straightforward. The clusters listed in Table 6 are more or less of equal cluster diameter. Most of them are quite clear and distinctive groups. As we might expect, it is at once clear from the standard deviations that article patterns are not randomly distributed through the 70-year period, but rather that certain article patterns are very clearly as-

TABLE 6
Major Sequence Clusters

Cluster Number	Number of Sequences in Cluster[a]	Mean Volume[b] (Year)	SD[c]	Exemplary Sequence[d]
1	17	20 (1915)	9	9A2 9A18 1A5 5A20 33A40 1A7 18A40 2A7
2	9	30 (1925)	12	2A36 2A15 2A16 16A40 2A21 2A57 2A23
5	6	22 (1917)	11	1A2 2A7 1A6 22A40 4A9 2A10 36A51 21A59
7	5	26 (1921)	27	3A2 3A7 2A14 2A16 20A52 2A40 5A21 9A24
9	9	42 (1937)	21	1A13 1A7 5A36 9A56 7A53 1A21
11	6	44 (1939)	22	1A2 1A3 2A9 2A10 2A17 3A53 1A2 1A36 2A7 3A43
12	9	54 (1949)	11	9A36 6A10 2A15 19A53 6A47 2A58
13	19	55 (1950)	9	1A12 1A13 2A2 6A15 17A43 3A21 3A23 3A7 2A57
14	3	64 (1959)	3	6A12 2A10 2A12 5A15 6A43 2A21 2A23

[a]The number of sequences located in the cluster.
[b]The mean of the volume numbers of the volumes in which cluster members appeared.
[c]Standard deviation of the mean volume figure.
[d]A sequence illustrating the characteristic pattern, so far as there is one, of the cluster.

sociated with particular periods. In particular, there appears to be a vocabulary of forms that were used early (clusters 1, 2, 5, and 7), a vocabulary of forms that were used late (clusters 12, 13, and 14), and some patterns that cross much wider periods (clusters 9 and 11). These data, too, are not compatible with the standard hypothesis of increasing concentration on a particular form. Rather these data suggest a move from one set of standard forms to another.

We first discuss clusters 1, 2, 5, and 7, the dominant early forms. Cluster 1 is clearest. It begins with a stage setting description of a state of affairs (element 2) and sometimes has a prefatory section on research design or analysis (element 15 or 17). It continues through a large section mixing numbers and findings (element 40), an interruption or temporary conclusion (variety of elements), and more figures and findings (element 40) to come to a conclusion, either a simple summary (element 21) or the author's theory (element 7). The cluster 2 pattern is much the same, but it lacks the repeated analysis section, more uniformly possesses the research design section, and sometimes has a section before the main analysis that mixes discussion of theory relevance in with the figures and findings (element 51). Cluster 5 moves further in this direction. In it the introductory sections have come apart, and the mixed section (element 51) now dominates the article, although it is sometimes preceded, not followed, by an analysis section with figures and findings but no intermingled discussion of theory relevance (element 40). Cluster 7 has a clear state of affairs introduction (element 2), usually has other introductory material (discussion of author's or others' theories), then moves straight into a short analytic (element 40) midsection, and often concludes with some simple material summarizing findings (element 21).

For the late period, the main forms are shown in clusters 12, 13, and 14. These are distinctive and clear groups. Cluster 12 begins, in six of nine cases, with a literature review—freestanding (element 13) or combined with a summary of the new argument (element 36). There follows a description or methods section (elements 15–17), and a substantial mixed analysis section (element 53). This is followed by a conclusion that is either a restatement of the author's theory (element 7) or a discussion of implications (element 58). This is close to the formulaic pattern described by Bazerman (1988). Note that this cluster marks the first serious appearance of literature reviews as part of consistent style.

Cluster 13 begins with a state of affairs discussion (element 2), followed in most cases by a data/methods setup section (elements 14–17). Most often this is element 15 (description of research design), but to this is often added a specific description of methods (element 17). This material is then followed by the main analytic section (element 43), which is in turn followed by some combination of summary of findings (element 21), relevance of findings for theory and hypotheses (element 23), and author's hypothesis (element 7). Implications discussions (element 58) occur occasionally. This version of the contemporary article is more elaborate than the cluster 12 version, but emphatically lacks the earlier version's focus on the literature.

Finally, cluster 14 with its three late but extremely similar articles, shows a slightly different format. Here, we have a summary of the arguments in the literature (element 12), a research design (element 15), in two cases a discussion of the solidity of the data (element 16), a relatively short mixed analysis section (element 43), in two cases a summary of findings (element 21) and a discussion of relevance of the findings for theory and hypotheses (element 23). This is indeed a formulaic pattern; it is quite extraordinary to find three randomly chosen articles whose patterns match so well.

The two clusters of intermediate date both have large standard deviations, which indicates that their intermediacy does not indicate a "transition form" used in a move from earlier forms to later ones, but rather that they are rhetorical structures that appeared throughout the period studied. The first of these is characterized by a large section of element 56, the residual element, which appears only in scattered places outside this group. Since element 56 can stand for a variety of complex combination states (all of which occur only one or two times apiece), there is no guessing what it stands for. Inspection reveals, however, that group 9 does not in fact have a very clear rhetorical pattern. Cluster 11 does, but it is an odd one. The cluster includes five articles, four of which are characterized by short, choppy sections in no particular order. This is clearly a group of rhetorical failures.

4. RHETORICAL SUBSEQUENCES

Another way of looking at rhetorical change focuses on shorter sequences. Perhaps certain parts of articles always follow in the same order. In particular, it might be helpful to focus on order exclusively, disregarding duration. We can then ask whether rhetorical rigor emerges in the form of a particular sequential armature around which an article must be constructed.

Disregarding duration is not difficult; we simply rewrite the data without allowing any repeats; a run of an element, however long, is represented by one element. But the common subsequence problem itself is more difficult. The technical problem is to find the common subsequences in a sequence data set without knowing ahead of time what those subsequences are, where they start, or how long they are likely to be. Fortunately, a recent iterative algorithm developed by Lawrence et al. (1993; hereafter, LEA) solves this problem.

4.1. *Gibbs Sampling*

The LEA algorithm employs a Gibbs sampler. Before discussing the algorithm, it is important to clarify what Gibbs sampling is and how it works. Tanner (1991) distinguishes statistical methods into "observed data methods," which apply directly to distributions of observed data, and "data augmentation methods," which seek those distributions via more roundabout means. In this view, Gibbs sampling is a data augmentation technique, one that constructs existing probability information into an iterative sampling structure that gives access to distributions that are themselves inaccessible via direct means, either because of analytic intractability or computational inaccessibility.

Put most simply, Gibbs sampling uses conditional information to produce marginal information. For a simple illustration, we apply Gibbs sampling to a two-by-two table. Suppose we have two two-valued variables and the conditional information relating them but do not have the marginal distributions. (We can solve for these directly, of course, but use the Gibbs sampler because the simple example makes it easy to understand.)

Thus we have (1) a row-conditional matrix A showing $\Pr(y|x)$

	$y = 1$	$y = 2$
$x = 1$	.424	.576
$x = 2$	.556	.444

and (2) a column-conditional matrix B showing $\Pr(x|y)$

	$y = 1$	$y = 2$
$x = 1$	.583	.704
$x = 2$	.417	.296

If we start with an arbitrary value for x, we can draw a value for y following the conditionals in the first matrix. We can then use *that* y to draw a value for x following the second matrix. We could then use our new x to draw a value for y following the first matrix and so on. This process will converge, in this case quite quickly, to a random sample on the true x marginals. To see why, consider the following argument.

If we transpose the B matrix, we have a row-conditional matrix with y-defined rows and x-defined columns:

	$x = 1$	$x = 2$
$y = 1$	.583	.417
$y = 2$	.704	.296

Consider the product A times B-transpose: This is a row-stochastic matrix (that is, its rows each sum to one. By elementary algebra the product of any two conformable row-stochastic matrices is also row-stochastic.) Note that this product can be thought of as giving the probability of x given an arbitrary starting x used as a basis to choose a y under the conditionals given in B-transpose and then a new x following those given in A. That is, it gives $Pr(x)$ given an *initial* x and a tour through Y:

	$x = 1$	$x = 2$
$x = 1$	.653	.347
$x = 2$	.637	.363

The square of this matrix is again row-stochastic and describes $Pr(x)$ given an arbitrary start in X and *two* tours through Y:

	$x = 1$	$x = 2$
$x = 1$	.647	.353
$x = 2$	.647	.353

But both rows are the same, which indicates an equilibrium X distribution: in fact, that of the X marginals. The equivalent argument can be made for the Y marginals. This time, we start with B-transpose then move through A. The product B-transpose times A is:

	$y = 1$	$y = 2$
$y = 1$	.479	.521
$y = 2$	.463	.537

And the square of this matrix is:

	$y = 1$	$y = 2$
$y = 1$	.471	.529
$y = 2$	.470	.530

In this case, too, the matrix ends up quickly with identical rows. Reassuringly, the original joint matrix is in fact:

	$y = 1$	$y = 2$
$x = 1$	.275	.373
$x = 2$	.196	.157

which gives exactly these marginals. An equivalent design could be set up for a three-way table for which we possessed the three two-by-two conditional tables specifying the dependence of each variable on particular values of the other two. Indeed, this algorithm applies to larger two-way tables and indeed to any n-way table for which we possess the complete n-1 way conditionals. These conditionals can be used for a direct algebraic calculation of the joint probabilities (and hence the marginals), of course, but the case offers a nice example of Gibbs sampling.

In formal terms, Gibbs sampling defines a transition function on the space of all possible joint values of the variables. Note that all possible joint values could in principle be reached by this function and also that there is no reason to expect the function to get trapped in a particular "cycle" of successive joint values. On these assumptions (irreducibility and aperiodicty) the transition function defines an ergodic Markov chain (see, e.g., Cox and Miller 1965). Since a regular Markov chain has a limiting distribution, it makes no difference what arbitrary values of the variables we start with; the process eventually finds the equilibrium distribution of the variable of interest. Given a system with n variables and sets of complete conditional probabilities describing the probability of particular values of each variable given any possible combination of values of all the others, the basic Gibbs algorithm is as follows:

1. Set all variables at arbitrary initial values.
2. Select a new value for variable 1, given the probabilities of that variable conditional on the current values of all the others, which were fixed in step 1.
3. Accept that value for variable 1 and select a new value for variable 2, given the probabilities of variable 2 conditional on the current fixed values of variables 1 and 3 through n.
4. Repeat step 3 for all variables and then cycle through the variables again and again until convergence.

In cases less simple than that of n-way tables, we often have far less ability to move algebraically from conditional probability to joint or marginal probability. It is in these cases that Gibbs sampling is more necessary. While Gibbs samplers are most commonly used (as here) to develop marginals for intractable distributions, they can also be used for optimization, as in the application given below. Gibbs samplers are part of a larger universe of methods now usually referred to as Markov chain Monte Carlo (MCMC) methods. The oldest of these is the famous Metropolis algorithm for estimating state equations on spaces of individual particles.[13]

4.2. *The LEA Algorithm*

The LEA algorithm uses Gibbs sampling to attack the common subsequence problem. In order to illustrate it, we apply it first to some experimental data with a particularly strong subsequence regularity. The data are twenty random sequences of 50 integers between 1 and 15. At some random point in that sequence, we have overwritten the random digits with the subsequence 8 9 10 X X 13 14 (where X stands for some random number.)

An example is:

11 11 15 9 5 5 12 1 12 13 13 9 7 8 4 10 8 11 14 6 5 5 3 8 9

10 15 14 13 14 11 12 10 12 3 13 4 15 1 1 12 6 7 2 2 3 1 11 8.

The regularity starts at the end of the first line. The data consist of 20 such sequences with their written-in regularities.

The LEA algorithm begins by randomly generating a list of starting points for the common subsection of each data sequence, a procedure that fills a matrix whose rows are the candidates for the common site in each sequence. We shall call this the candidate matrix. (Following the LEA notation, we call this matrix A.[14]). At the start, it is filled with randomly

---

[13]The Metropolis algorithm was set forth in Metropolis and Ulam (1949) and Metropolis et al. (1953). The classic paper redeveloping the algorithm as an optimization technique is Kirkpatrick et al. (1983). Because of the motivation of these methods by analogy with the physical cooling of metals, the technique of combining probabilistic transition with probabilistic acceptance of that transition even if it worsens an objective function is called simulated annealing.

The Gibbs sampler, like MCMC methods more generally, is part of a growth industry in the statistical community today. A straightforward introduction is Casella and George (1992). A more general and analytic exposition is Liu (1991:c. 6), which also makes detailed comparisons with the Metropolis algorithm. An account combining several classic papers with lengthy comments by dozens of statisticians can be found in the *Journal of the Royal Statistical Society*, Series B, (1993), 55:3-102. The name "Gibbs sampling" was coined, and the new generations of such probabilistic optimization begun, by Geman and Geman (1984). The approach was generalized in statistics by the work of Gelfand (Gelfand and Smith [1990], Gelfand et al. [1990]). A related technique of data augmentation is that of Tanner and Wong (1987). A source locating a variety of data augmentation techniques relative to one another is Tanner (1991). A current review of MCMC methods is Gilks et al. (1996).

[14]Our exposition directly follows that of Lawrence et al. (1993). Simulated annealing has also been applied to the global multiple sequence alignment (GMSA) problem (as opposed to its use here for the multiple subsequence alignment problem) by Ishikawa et al. (1993). Other approaches to the GMSA problem are Gotoh (1993) and Gusfield (1993).

chosen subsequences. An example follows. Each row contains the algorithm's first random guess at the regularity in a particular data sequence. We have guessed that the regularity is seven units wide. (In practice, one would not know this and would have to try several widths to find the best result.) Note that the start is not auspicious; pieces of the "real" regularity appear in only three candidates, those for sequences 11, 15, and 19.

The Original A Matrix
Subsequence

		1	2	3	4	5	6	7
	1	9	5	5	12	1	12	13
	2	8	8	7	6	7	5	1
	3	2	3	11	7	6	3	11
	4	12	5	11	4	2	1	5
	5	12	6	7	2	2	3	1
S	6	9	8	15	4	6	6	5
e	7	8	3	4	5	12	1	8
q	8	11	7	13	12	7	2	7
u	9	1	13	12	12	5	7	9
e	10	15	10	8	4	9	12	7
n	11	1	3	7	9	8	9	10
c	12	1	15	2	5	9	8	9
e	13	14	6	2	7	12	6	7
	14	9	1	5	3	5	12	10
	15	6	4	8	9	10	7	7
	16	10	1	9	13	14	14	8
	17	9	11	5	9	9	15	14
	18	1	11	13	8	13	15	8
	19	9	10	12	14	13	14	11
	20	1	1	6	7	6	10	3

We also calculate the background probability of each element over the entire data set. We call this vector P.

The General P Vector
Elements

1	2	3	4	5	6	7	8	9	10	11	12	13	14	15
Pr = .06	.05	.06	.06	.08	.06	.08	.08	.08	.08	.06	.07	.07	.07	.06

Each data sequence of 50 elements will in turn be considered the "focus" sequence. For each focus sequence, we go through two phases of calculation. First, we have a "Q-calculation phase." Ruling out for the moment the focus sequence's row in the candidate matrix, we calculate the probability of each element at each point in the common subsequence. That is, we calculate the probability of each element in any given column of the candidate matrix. These are "location specific probabilities:" the probability of element 1 in the first position, the probability of element 1 in the second position, etc. This will be called matrix Q. The (i,j)-th element of Q is the probability that element j is in the ith position in the subsequence. To deal with the problem that elements can disappear completely from a column of the candidate matrix A, this matrix adds in a Bayesian prior for each element at each position. Thus, while there are no occurrences of elements 3,4,5,7, and 13 in the first column of A, the prior still produces a nonzero probability. This probability is "lost" from the elements that *do* occur. Hence the $Q(1,1)$ element is not $5/19 = 0.26$, as would appear from the five occurrences of element 1 in the first position in the last 19 rows of the A matrix above, but 0.22. (For details, see Lawrence et al. 1993:209 and n. 20).

The Original Q Matrix
Elements

Subsequence Position	1	2	3	4	5	6	7	8	9	10	11	12	13	14	15
1	.22	.05	.01	.01	.01	.05	.01	.10	.23	.06	.05	.10	.01	.06	.05
2	.14	.01	.14	.05	.10	.10	.06	.10	.02	.10	.10	.01	.06	.01	.05
3	.01	.10	.01	.05	.14	.05	.14	.10	.06	.02	.10	.10	.10	.01	.05
4	.01	.05	.05	.14	.10	.05	.14	.06	.14	.02	.01	.14	.06	.06	.01
5	.05	.10	.01	.01	.10	.14	.10	.06	.14	.06	.01	.10	.10	.06	.01
6	.10	.05	.10	.01	.06	.10	.10	.06	.06	.06	.01	.14	.01	.10	.10
7	.10	.01	.05	.01	.10	.01	.19	.14	.10	.10	.10	.01	.06	.06	.01

Next comes what can be called the "sampling phase." Consider the 50-element focus sequence. If the common subsequence is 7 elements long, there are 44 possible choices for candidate site in this sequence. (In general, there are l [= length of sequence] minus w [= width of subsequence] plus one possible choices.) For each of these 44 potential candidates, we calculate its probability given the location-specific element probabilities just derived, and divide this by its probability given the background probabilities. Thus there are 44 possible seven-element subsequences in the first sequence. For each of them, we calculate these two probabilities, simply looking up the relevant values in P and Q and multiplying them out. For each possible subsequence in the focus sequence, the quotient of its probability given Q by its probability given P tells whether that candidate subsequence is "better" in terms of the current list of candidates across all *other* sequences. It is a measure of quality of fit *relative* to the current list.

Now one simply adds these quotients for all the candidate sites across the focus sequence and sets the sum to one, normalizing the quotients and turning them into probability measures. Then one uses *these* probabilities to pick one sample from the candidate sites in the focus sequence and enters that site in the A matrix as the new candidate from the focus sequence.[15]

The iteration consists of repeating the Q-calculation phase and the sample phase for each sequence in turn.[16] After one iteration (Q and sample phases repeated once for each of the twenty sequences), here is the new A matrix.

		Subsequence						
		1	2	3	4	5	6	7
	1	10	10	4	5	8	9	10
	2	14	4	12	6	5	14	10
	3	9	10	9	13	2	3	11
	4	1	8	4	13	9	12	14
	5	11	11	15	6	8	7	11
S	6	9	10	4	8	13	14	11
e	7	1	8	12	13	5	15	8
q	8	15	10	9	14	8	9	10
u	9	4	11	8	3	8	9	10
e	10	10	8	4	9	12	7	14
n	11	9	10	12	5	13	14	8
c	12	9	10	4	5	13	14	12
e	13	1	10	13	10	7	3	8
	14	9	1	5	3	5	12	10
	15	4	8	9	10	7	7	13
	16	9	10	1	9	13	14	14
	17	9	11	5	9	9	15	14
	18	1	11	13	8	13	15	8
	19	9	10	12	14	13	14	11
	20	10	10	15	7	8	9	10

[15] The Gibbs sampler as implemented by LEA differs from simulated annealing (SA) methods. Under an implementation with SA, we would accept the newly "sampled" candidate with probability one if its quality measure was better than that of the current candidate from this focus sequence *and* with some nonzero probability (set by the annealing schedule) even if it were worse. In the typical SA analysis, this probability (analogous with temperature) is set high in the early iterations to avoid trapping in local optima; one accepts a lot of random "worsening." As more iterations are run, the probability falls; one is more certain to have found the global optimum.

[16] We could also do this with random choice (so-called random scan). In the implementation used here, the iteration was for each sequence through the data set (systematic scan). What the methods require is that the scan guarantee that the whole space be visited in finite (although potentially very large) time.

At the third pass,

	Subsequence						
	1	2	3	4	5	6	7
1	10	10	4	5	8	9	10
2	9	10	9	1	13	14	4
3	9	10	9	13	2	3	11
4	1	8	4	13	9	12	14
5	9	10	11	14	13	14	11
S 6	9	10	4	8	13	14	11
e 7	1	8	12	13	5	15	8
q 8	15	10	9	14	8	9	10
u 9	4	11	8	3	8	9	10
e 10	9	5	5	13	8	9	10
n 11	9	10	12	5	13	14	8
c 12	9	10	4	5	13	14	12
e 13	1	10	13	10	7	3	8
14	9	1	5	3	5	12	10
15	9	10	7	7	13	14	1
16	9	10	1	9	13	14	14
17	9	11	5	9	9	15	14
18	9	10	11	11	13	14	8
19	9	10	12	14	13	14	11
20	10	10	15	7	8	9	10

And the fourth,

	Subsequence						
	1	2	3	4	5	6	7
1	8	9	10	13	8	13	14
2	8	9	10	9	1	13	14
3	1	9	10	9	13	2	3
4	6	1	8	4	13	9	12
5	8	9	10	11	14	13	14
S 6	8	9	10	4	8	13	14
e 7	12	1	8	12	13	5	15
q 8	2	15	10	9	14	8	9
u 9	8	9	10	3	11	13	14
e 10	6	9	5	5	13	8	9
n 11	8	9	10	12	5	13	14
c 12	8	9	10	4	5	13	14
e 13	8	9	10	7	13	13	14
14	8	9	10	2	12	13	14
15	8	9	10	7	7	13	14
16	8	9	10	1	9	13	14
17	8	9	10	3	11	13	14
18	8	9	10	11	11	13	14
19	8	9	10	12	14	13	14
20	8	9	10	7	4	13	14

And the final (fifth) A matrix is:

		Subsequence						
		1	2	3	4	5	6	7
	1	8	9	10	13	8	13	14
	2	8	9	10	9	1	13	14
	3	8	9	10	11	11	13	14
	4	8	9	10	8	9	13	14
	5	8	9	10	11	14	13	14
S	6	8	9	10	4	8	13	14
e	7	8	9	10	3	12	13	14
q	8	8	9	10	1	12	13	14
u	9	8	9	10	3	11	13	14
e	10	8	9	10	10	6	13	14
n	11	8	9	10	12	5	13	14
c	12	8	9	10	4	5	13	14
e	13	8	9	10	7	13	13	14
	14	8	9	10	2	12	13	14
	15	8	9	10	7	7	13	14
	16	8	9	10	1	9	13	14
	17	8	9	10	3	11	13	14
	18	8	9	10	11	11	13	14
	19	8	9	10	12	14	13	14
	20	8	9	10	7	4	13	14

Of course, these subsequences start at randomly varying points in the data sequences (which the program records). Note that the algorithm has already closed in on the regularity at the end of the third pass, but it is shifted to the right, missing the 8 that begins the regularity. To speed convergence, the LEA algorithm computes at regular intervals (here, after each pass through the data) a global quality measure for "phase-shifted" A matrices. These are matrices in which the whole array moves to the candidates beginning one or two elements right or left of the current location in each data sequence. These global quality measures are then added and a new A matrix is chosen as in the sampling phase above. (Note that if one candidate is very close to the beginning or the ending of its sequence, this may forbid such phase shifts in one or the other direction.)

This algorithm thus finds what seems like a needle in a haystack. It finds a relatively short regularity, with some noise in the middle, buried at random points in long sequences, without knowing what is in the regularity or where it starts in the different sequences. In fact, experiment shows that the algorithm will successfully find a regularity even if it appears in only a small number of the data sequences and has substantial noise in it.

How does this happen? It happens because of the formal structure of the algorithm. We choose the new candidate from each successive focus sequence by using the conditional likelihood of each possible candidate in that sequence given the current (fixed) values of the candidates from other sequences. By doing this for sequence after sequence, through the whole data set, again and again, we set up a probability process. This process has 44^{20} points in its state space (because the state space is the space of all possible A matrices), making it somewhat intractable to direct analysis. But at any given point in that space, we can always follow the two-phase procedure above to write a current transition rule to choose our next point. And this rule will *always* produce the same probabilities for our next choice of candidate should we accidentally revisit the same point later in the process (that is, should we revisit an earlier version of the A matrix) because that point will produce an identical Q matrix in the Q-calculation phase. Therefore the process we have created is a stationary Markov chain and has a limiting distribution. Moreover, a theorem of Geman and Geman (1984:732, theorem C) guarantees that under any scanning procedure that guarantees a finite recurrence time between successive updates of the entire A matrix, the distribution of any function of that matrix will also approach a limit.

Note that the results depend on the probabilistic nature of the process. The Gibbs sampler rates the changes it could make in a given row of the A matrix and does indeed know the "best way to go uphill in one dimension." But it does not take that direction. Rather it chooses a direction with a probability given by the current conditionals. If the best way were always taken (if the sampling phase followed a simple "take the best" rule, rather than a sampling rule), there would be no guarantee that every possible point in the state space could be visited from every possible beginning, therefore no stationary irreducible Markov chain on the entire state space, and no guarantee that the transition rule's equilibrium distribution would be that of the space. The negative practical result would be the possibility of stopping at some local maximum.[17]

---

[17] All LEA calculations were done by an implementation of the algorithm in QUICKBASIC 4.5 on a 486 clone, written by the senior author. All detailed calculations (Bayesian priors, etc.) are implemented exactly as described in the original LEA paper. Lawrence et al. (1993) report several optimization criteria, of which the information statistic presented in text is the simplest. Note that the algorithm as imple-

The LEA algorithm, like most similar algorithms, wanders through a good deal of the data before converging. However, when random chance throws a few of the true best common subsequences into the candidate matrix, the algorithm focuses effectively. It can converge even in the presence of quite minimal regularities. Convergence is measured in various ways. The algorithm is effectively maximizing the product of the "quality quotients" across the candidates in the A matrix, and Lawrence et al. derive a variety of global statistics related to that product. As their best summary statistic, Lawrence et al. present an "information per bit" statistic, which we report here without discussion. (Higher values are better. Random data has an information statistic around 1.0. Perfect subsequences—replicated exactly in every data sequence—have information statistics around 3.0 in our experience. Unlike other measures discussed by Lawrence et al, the information statistic is not sensitive to subsequence length.)[18]

4.3. Analysis of Article Subsequences

In this application, we consider subsequences only of length two and three. At length four, we are already considering over half of the entire article sequence in one-third of the cases.

Applied to the present data, the LEA algorithm does converge to a best common subsequence. We found the same result in three separate runs of 25 iterations (one iteration uses each of the 99 sequences as focus se-

mented here does not permit insertion. All subsequences are true successive subsequences.

The rate of convergence of the Gibbs sampler is a matter of hot debate and grave concern. For a variety of perspectives, see the comments in the number of the *Journal of the Royal Statistical Society* mentioned in n. 12 above. See also Kong, Liu, and Wong (1994), Liu, Wong, and Kong (1994, 1995). Papers related to the statistical properties of the LEA algorithm are Liu Neuwald, and Lawrence (1995) and Neuwald, Liu, and Lawrence (1995).

In practice, the LEA algorithm converges very fast. One commenter on this exposition pointed out that in fact that the algorithm's developers do not know why it works so quickly; it's a "happy accident."

[18] The discussion of these statistics is found in Lawrence et al. (1993:209–210, 214, fn. 22). The information per bit statistic for the five passes of the example just given are

INFO = .8228551
INFO = .7174581
INFO = .8768407
INFO = 1.457156
INFO = 2.135363.

quence exactly once). That subsequence is 15–43–21 (Description of research design—Data analysis/Summary of findings—Total summary of findings). It appears in six out of the 99 sequences, those six coming from volume years 51, 59, 62, 63, 64, and 66. Thus the single strongest three-element subsequence appears in 2 of 15 articles in the next to last decade and in 4 of 17 articles in the last. Given this result, the algorithm will have found both 15–43 and 43–21 if they exist as two-step subsequences in other data sequences. But they are not particularly common. The first appears twice, in volume years 56 and 67. The second appears four times, in volume years 40, 52, 57, and 59. (Since element 43 is part of this common subsequence and appears seldom before the fifth volume decade, all articles using it are late.)

After we deleted these six sequences from the data set, we ran the LEA algorithm again to see if there was a second best common subsequence, another version of the "rhetorical armature." There is another such common subsequence: 10–15–53 (Author's hypotheses—Description of Research Design—Data analysis/Summary of findings/Discussion of relevance of findings to theory and hypotheses). This appears in four articles, in volumes 44, 49, 62, and 69. Note that element 53 includes element 43 as a subset, and thus that this pattern is close to the first part of the more common 15–43–21 subsequence. In summary, about 10 of the 47 sampled articles in the journal's last three decades follow one of two versions of a common rhetorical subpattern. Both the first and second most common subsequences come from the latter part of the data, even though element 40—the characteristic "analysis" element of the earlier period—is more common than element 43. Indeed, the pattern 10–15–53 appeared only on the third of three runs of 25 iterations, of the reduced data set, the other two being dominated by element 40 in the second or third column in the candidate matrix. But there are not as many common patterns employing element 40 as there are employing 43 and its relative 53, and so repeated iteration ultimately escapes the clutches of element 40.

To test whether these results were due to chance, we performed the following iteration:

1.   Shuffle the elements within each sequence.
2.   Run the LEA algorithm for 25 iterations on the resulting data.

We did steps 1 and 2 100 times to generate a baseline distribution for the information per bit statistic in this data. This can be referred to a standard normal probability table on the assumption that the underlying distribution is normal. (Inspection of normal probability plots for the data verified this assumption. There is also a nonparametric significance test based on the Wilcoxon signed-ranks test; see Neuwald, Liu, and Lawrence 1995 and Liu, Neuwald, and Lawrence 1995.)

For the full data, the resulting information statistic distribution had mean 1.18 and standard deviation 0.16. The unshuffled value was 1.83, a z-value of 4.04. For the data with those articles possessing the most common subsequence deleted, the mean was 1.17 and the standard deviation 0.17. The unshuffled value was 1.74, a z-value of 3.40. In both cases, the results are clearly significant.

The subsequence evidence, therefore, does suggest a slight move toward rhetorical tightness. Nonetheless, it remains clear that the new model was hardly a straightjacket. Most articles did not use it. Even in the final decade, only six articles out of 17 followed one of the common subpatterns.

5. CONCLUSION

Substantively, these analyses show that the evidence for rhetorical rigidification in sociology articles is weak indeed. While there is some evidence of more recent authors' writing to a clearer template (the subsequence evidence), the actual results in both early and late periods remain diverse. It is more likely that there was a change from a fairly clear rhetorical pattern in the 1920s and 1930s to a different clear rhetorical pattern after the war. But even given the clear patterns, authors at both times produced diverse structures indeed. There is no serious evidence here of rising rhetorical hegemony. The rhetorical rigidity seen by analysts like Bazerman in modern social science is probably in the eye of the beholder.

On the methodological side, the LEA algorithm can see broad use in sociology. There are many kinds of data where we are interested in short subpatterns. Sometimes, as in the present case, these are subpatterns in fixed linear orders: rituals, texts, performances and the like. At other times, they will be portions of processes in time, like careers and life cycles. In particular, the concept of "turning point" seems ideally suited to investigation by subsequence methods. Current theory sees turning points in a variety of social processes (see Abbott 1996b for a review). Yet the LEA algorithm can be used to focus directly on such particular, crucial parts of processes, separating them from what may well be extended periods of pure randomness or pure stability that surround them.

More broadly, Gibbs sampling and other MCMC methods will have important uses throughout sociology. Many of these uses will be in improving estimation "behind the scenes" of models that are already widely used in canned programs. But there are important substantive areas that could be revolutionized by such methods. In particular, network analysis seems a likely possibility. Gibbs sampling methods arose within the theory of Markov random fields, within which the Ising model looms large (See Geman and Geman 1984). And the Ising model is the origin of blockmodeling with its emphasis on local correlations (Breiger, personal communication). Having helped transform that area of physics, Gibbs sampling and its relatives will most likely have the same kinds of implications for network analysis. We can look forward to their broad application in sociology.

REFERENCES

Abbott, Andrew. 1992. "From Causes to Events." *Sociological Methods and Research* 20:428–55.

———. 1995a. "Sequence Analysis." *Annual Review of Sociology* 21:93–113.

———. 1995b. "On Dijkstra and Taris: The Scope of Alignment Methods." *Sociological Methods and Research* 24:232–43.

———. 1996a. "AJS: The Growth of an Institution." Unpublished paper, University of Chicago.

———. 1996b. "On the Concept of Turning Point." In *Comparative Social Research*, edited by F. Engelstad et al. Greenwich CN: JAI Press. Forthcoming.

Abbott, Andrew, and Alexandra Hrycak. 1990. "Measuring Sequence Resemblance." *American Journal of Sociology* 96:144–85.

American Journal of Sociology. 1966. *Cumulative Index to the American Journal of Sociology, 1895–1965.* Chicago: University of Chicago Press.

Assadi, B. 1987. "The Social Construction of Knowledge in American Sociology." Ph.D. diss., Howard University.

Bakanic, Von, Clark McPhail, and R. J. Simon. 1987. "The Manuscript Review and Decision-Making Process." *American Sociological Review* 52:631–42.

Barthes, Roland. 1974. *S/Z.* New York: Hill and Wang.

Bazerman, Charles. 1988. *Shaping Written Knowledge.* Madison: University of Wisconsin Press.

Boguski, Mark S. 1992. "Computational Sequence Analysis Revisited." *Journal of Lipid Research* 33:957–74.

Buehler, C., Gary Hesser, and Andrew J. Weigert. 1972. "A Study of Articles on Religion in Major Sociology Journals." *Journal for the Scientific Study of Religion* 11:165–70.

Casella, George, and Edward I. George. 1992. "Explaining the Gibbs Sampler." *American Statistician* 46:167–74.

Champion, D. J., and M. F. Morris. 1974. "A Content Analysis of Book Reviews in AJS, ASR, and Social Forces." *American Journal of Sociology* 78:1256–65.

Clyne, M. 1987. "Cultural Differences in the Organization of Academic Texts." *Journal of Pragmatics* 11:211–47.

Connors, R. J. 1985. "The Rhetoric of Explanation." *Written Communication* 2:49–72.

Cox, D. R., and H. D. Miller. 1965. *The Theory of Stochestic Processes* London: Chapman and Hall.

Everitt, Brian S. 1993. *Cluster Analysis* London: Edwin Arnold.

Forrest, J., and Andrew Abbott. 1990. "The Optimal Matching Method for Studying Anthropological Sequence Data." *Journal of Quantitative Anthropology* 2:151–70.

Garnett, R. A. 1988. "The Study of War." *American Sociologist* 19:270–82.

Gelfand, Alan E., Susan E. Hills, Amy Racine-Poon, and A. F. M. Smith. 1990. "Illustration of Bayesian Inference in Normal Data Models Using Gibbs Sampling." *Journal of the American Statistical Association* 85:972–85.

Gelfand, Alan E., and Adrian F. M. Smith. 1990. "Sampling-based Approaches to Calculating Marginal Densities." *Journal of the American Statistical Association* 85:398–409.

Geman, Stuart, and Donald Geman. 1984. "Stochastic Relaxation, Gibbs Distributions, and Bayesian Restoration of Images." *IEEE Transactions on Pattern Analysis and Machine Intelligence* 6:721–41.

Gilks, Walter R., Sylvia Richardson, and David J. Spiegelhalter, eds. 1996. *Markov Chain Monte Carlo in Practice*. London: Chapman and Hall.

Glenn, Norval D. 1971. "American Sociologists' Evaluations of 63 Journals." *American Sociologist* 6:298–303.

Gotoh, O. 1993. "Optimal Alignment Between Groups of Sequences and Its Application to Multiple Sequence Alignment." *CABIOS* 9:361–70.

Gribskov, Michael R., and John Devereux, eds. 1991. *Sequence Analysis Primer*. New York: Freeman.

Gusfield, D. 1993. "Efficient Algorithms for Multiple Sequence Alignment with Guaranteed Error Bounds." *Bulletin of Mathematical Biology* 55:141–54.

Gusfield, J. 1981. *The Culture of Public Problems*. Chicago: University of Chicago Press.

Henikoff, S., and J. G. Henikoff. 1994. "Position-Based Sequence Weights." *Journal of Molecular Biology* 243:574–78.

Ishikawa, M., T. Toya, M. Hoshida, K. Nitta, A. Ogiwara, and M. Kanehisa. 1993. "Multiple Sequence Alignment by Parallel Simulated Annealing." *CABIOS* 9:267–73.

Jain, Anil K., and Richard C. Dubes. 1988. *Algorithms for Clustering Data* Englewood Cliffs, NJ: Prentice Hall.

Karlin, Samuel, P. Bucher, V. Brendel, and S. F. Altschul. 1991. "Statistical Methods and Insights for Protein and DNA Sequences." *Annual Review of Biophysics and Biophysical Chemistry* 20:175–203.

Kinloch, G. C. 1988. "American Sociology's Changing Interests as Reflected in Two Leading Journals." *American Sociologist* 19:181–94.

Kircz, J. G. 1991. "Rhetorical Structure of Scientific Articles." *Journal of Documentation* 47: 354–472.

Kirkpatrick, S., C. D. Gelatt, and M. P. Vecci. 1983. "Optimization by Simulated Annealing." *Science* 220:671–81.

Kong, Augustine, Jun S. Liu, and Wing H. Wong. 1994. "Sequential Imputations and Bayesian Missing Data Problems." *Journal of the American Statistical Association* 89:278–93.

Lawrence, Charles E., Stephen F. Altschul, Mark S. Boguski, Jun S. Liu, Andrew F. Neuwald, and John C. Wooton. 1993. "Detecting Subtle Sequence Signals." *Science* 262:208–14.

Liu, Jun S. 1991. *Correlation Structure and Convergence Rate of the Gibbs Sampler*. Unpublished Ph.D. diss., University of Chicago.

Liu, Jun S., Andrew F. Neuwald, and Charles E. Lawrence. 1995. "Bayesian Models for Local Sequence Alignment and Gibbs Sampling Strategies." *Journal of the American Statistical Association* 90:1156–70.

Liu, Jun S., W. H. Wong, and A. Kong. 1994. "Covariance Structure of the Gibbs Sampler with Applications to the Comparisons of Estimators and Augmentation Schemes." *Biometrika* 81:27–40.

———. 1995. "Covariance Structure and Convergence Rate of the Gibbs Sampler with Various Scans." *Journal of the Royal Statistical Society*, Series B, 57:157–69.

McCartney, James L. 1970. "On Being Scientific." *American Sociologist* 5:30–35.

McCloskey, Donald. 1985. *The Rhetoric of Economics*. Madison: University of Wisconsin Press.

Metropolis, N., and S. Ulam. 1949. "The Monte Carlo Method." *Journal of the American Statistical Association* 44:335–41.

Metropolis, N., A. W. Rosenbluth, M. N. Rosenbluth, A. H. Teller, and E. Teller. 1953. "Equation of State Calculations by Fast Computing Machines." *Journal of Chemical Physics* 21:1087–92.

Mullins, N., W. Snizek, and K. Oehler. 1988. "The Structural Analysis of a Scientific Paper." *Handbook of Quantitative Studies of Science and Technology*, edited by A. F. I. Raam, 81–105, New York: Elsevier.

Murray, S. O. 1988. "The Reception of Anthropological Work in Sociology Journals, 1922–1951." *Journal of the History of the Behavioral Sciences* 24:135–51.

Myers, G. 1990. *Writing Biology*. Madison: University of Wisconsin Press.

Needleman, S. B., and C. D. Wunsch. 1970. "A General Method Applicable to the Search for Similarities in the Amino-Acid Sequence of Two Proteins." *Journal of Molecular Biology* 48:443–53.

Neuwald, Andrew F., Jun S. Liu, and Charles E. Lawrence. 1995. "Gibbs Motif Sampling." *Protein Science* 4:1618–32.

O'Neill, J. 1981. "The Literary Production of Natural and Social Science Inquiry." *Canadian Journal of Sociology* 6:105–20.

Page, Charles H. 1981. "*The American Sociological Review*, 1958–1960." *American Sociologist* 14:43–47.

Sankoff, D., and Joseph B. Kruskal. 1983. *Time Warps, String Edits, and Macromolecules*. Reading, MA: Addison-Wesley.

Smalley, T. N. 1981. "Trends in Sociology Literature and Research." *Behavioral and Social Sciences Librarian* 2:1–19.

Tanner, Martin A. 1991. *Tools for Statistical Inference*. New York: Springer.

Tanner, Martin A., and Wing H. Wong. 1987. "The Calculation of Posterior Distributions by Data Augmentation." *Journal of the American Statistical Association* 82:528–40.

Teevan, J. J. 1980. "Journal Prestige and Quality of Sociological Articles." *American Sociologist* 15:109–12.

Vingron, Martin, and Michael S. Waterman. 1994. "Sequence Analysis and Penalty Choice." *Journal of Molecular Biology* 235:1–12.

Vingron, Martin, and Peter R. Sibbald. 1993. "Weighting in Sequence Space." *Proceedings of the National Academy of Science* 90:8777–81.

☙ 3 ❧

A GENERIC SEMANTIC GRAMMAR FOR QUANTITATIVE TEXT ANALYSIS: APPLICATIONS TO EAST AND WEST BERLIN RADIO NEWS CONTENT FROM 1979

Carl W. Roberts*

In a semantic text analysis the researcher begins by creating one of two types of semantic grammars, each of which provides one or more templates that specify the ways concepts (or more general themes) may be related. On the one hand, a phenomenal semantic grammar can be created to extract phenomenon-related information from a text population (e.g., "Among the population's grievances [the phenomenon of interest in this case], which were ones for the abolition of taxes?"). On the other hand, a generic semantic grammar may be developed to yield data about the text population itself (e.g., "Among all clauses in the text population, how many were grievances for the abolition of taxes?"). This paper describes a generic semantic grammar that can be used to encode themes and theme relations in every clause within randomly sampled texts. Unlike the surface-grammatical relations mapped by syntax grammars, the theme relations allowed in this grammar only permit unambiguous encoding according to the meanings that clauses were intended to convey within their social context. An application of the grammar provides a concrete illustration of its research potential.

This paper was presented at the American Sociological Association meeting in New York City, August 1996. I am particularly indebted to Albert Baker, whose careful eye added greatly to the rigor and at times to the substance of the formalism developed in this paper, and to Beth Lencowski, whose long hours of coding and analysis were of immeasurable assistance. E-mail: carlos@iastate.edu
*Iowa State University

89

Semantic text analysis is a quantitative text analysis method in which not only themes (or classes of concepts) but also grammatical relations among themes are encoded. The method involves a three-step encoding process. First, the researcher isolates a population of texts germane to the phenomenon under investigation.[1] Second, a semantic grammar must be acquired that specifies the relations that may be encoded among themes in the texts. Finally, the texts' themes are encoded according to the relations specified in the semantic grammar. Encoded interrelations may then be used as indicators of various characteristics of the phenomenon under study.

Consider, for example, the text population of *cahiers de doléances* of 1789 that Markoff, Shapiro, and their colleagues have been analyzing since the mid-1970s (cf. Markoff 1988; Markoff, Shapiro, and Weitman 1974; Shapiro and Markoff, forthcoming). The *cahiers de doléances* are the documents produced by more than 40,000 corporate and territorial entities (e.g., craft guilds, parishes, towns, etc.) in the course of the king's convocation of an Estates-General—documents written as if in response to the open-ended query, "What are your grievances, and what do you propose should be done about them?" The documents were used to generate data on grievances, making grievances the researchers' phenomena of interest and, for the purposes of constructing a data base for these grievances, effectively making "the grievance" the unit of analysis.

In essence, each grievance was encoded according to two syntactic components. (Or, if you prefer, a template with two interrelated fields was used in encoding each grievance.) First, there was the institution or problem area (i.e., the thing being grieved about). These grievances might be about the government, the economy, religion, the constitution, and so on. The second syntactic component of a grievance was the action demanded. These actions were encoded as demands to reestablish, to abolish, to simplify, to modify, to improve, and so on. In brief, the researchers designed a two-place Verb-Object (V-O) semantic grammar for the phenomenon, grievance.[2] The semantic grammar's application to a sample of texts from the *cahiers de doléances* yielded data that have been used to make infer-

---

[1] Throughout this paper I use "the phenomenon under investigation," "the phenomenon under study," "the phenomenon of interest," and "the unit of analysis" interchangeably. All refer to that phenomenon (as defined in the researcher's theory), sampled instances of which correspond to distinct rows in the researcher's data matrix, and measures of which are listed in the columns of this matrix.

[2] For each action (verb) toward a problem area (object), it was uniformly the king and his representatives (subject) who should act. Thus a more detailed Subject-Verb-Object syntax was unnecessary. This discussion presents only a simplified ver-

ences about public opinion on a variety of topics just prior to the French Revolution.

A second illustration can be found with Franzosi's (1994) methodological writings on labor disputes. Applying a more complex semantic grammar to newspaper articles on Italian labor unrest, labor disputes (the phenomena of interest) are conceptualized as clusters of actors' actions toward each other (i.e., of Subject-Verb-Object [S-V-O] tuples). Like Markoff and Shapiro, Franzosi has used texts as a source of historical data. Yet whereas the former researchers commonly found more than one grievance per document (i.e., multiple units of analysis per text block), Franzosi had numerous S-V-O tuples per newspaper article and commonly multiple newspaper articles per labor dispute (i.e., multiple text blocks per unit of analysis). Thus, for Franzosi, the generation of dispute-specific indicators of whether one type of actor acted in a specific way toward another, requires a search for this information among all S-V-O tuples associated with each labor dispute.

1. SEMANTIC GRAMMARS HIGHLIGHT STRUCTURES WITHIN TEXT POPULATIONS

The preceding illustrations demonstrate that in applying a semantic grammar to a sample of texts, the researcher assumes that the texts are structured according to the semantic grammar and that the phenomenon of interest is related to this structure in a specific way. In Franzosi's work, for example, newspaper articles are presumed to contain information on actors' actions toward each other, and labor disputes are portrayed as consisting of clusters of such actions. Thus every semantic text analysis must begin by isolating a population of texts that exhibit the structure assumed in the research at hand.

On the basis of similar observations, Griemas (1984 [1966]) cautioned linguists to assemble a representative, exhaustive, and homogeneous corpus of texts prior to beginning analysis.[3] Even more strongly put, Halliday (1978:32) argued that every utterance (or speech act) must be under-

---

sion of the researchers' semantic grammar. See Markoff, Shapiro, and Weitman (1974) or Shapiro & Markoff (forthcoming) for more detail.

[3] This warning is quite different from that of the statistician who notes that (other things equal) analyses of data from homogeneous populations will afford statistics with small standard errors. Griemas's point is that one must ensure the relevance of one's corpus to one's semantic model: "[A] model can be described only if it is already contained implicitly in the discursive manifestation of a semantic microuniverse" (Griemas 1984[1966]: 163).

stood according to its "context of situation." Moreover, these situational contexts impose structural constraints on what statements are socially appropriate (cf. Lakoff and Johnson 1980:179 on the fit between statement and situation).

Linguists developed semantic grammars (or functional grammars; cf. Halliday 1978, 1994; Propp 1968 [1928]) as a strategy for describing text structure. Application of the strategy begins by identifying speech acts according to how they function within the genre of texts under analysis (e.g., as stating a situation, explaining a problem, responding to the problem, evaluating the response). The genre (e.g., of texts with problem-solution structure; cf. Hoey 1994) is then characterized according to the sequence of functional forms common among its texts. The grammars underlying such sequences have been variously referred to as narrative grammars (Griemas 1984 [1966]), text grammars (van Dijk 1972), and story grammars (Rumelhart 1975).

In fields other than linguistics, social scientists have tended to be less interested in the form than in the content of texts' grammars. In analyses of text sequence, this preference of content to form holds among social scientists who are not primarily linguists but who have orientations both qualitative (Abell 1987; Heise 1991) and quantitative (Namenwirth 1973; Schrodt 1991). In contrast to linguists' objective to reveal text structure as a sequence of distinct forms, in a semantic text analysis one generally presumes a single semantic form with varying content. Whereas linguists typically revise their semantic grammars to fit a relevant corpus, semantic text analysts use fixed semantic grammars to highlight relevant text.

1.1. *Phenomenal Versus Generic Highlighting of Text Structure*

In a semantic text analysis, the researcher encodes only those parts of the text that fit into the syntactic components of the semantic grammar being applied. For example, a preliminary statement in a document from the *cahiers de doléances* that "The members of this guild have always honorably served our King" would quickly be recognized by the coder as not conveying a grievance and would accordingly be ignored. Likewise, Franzosi's semantic grammar does not lend itself readily to evaluative statements (e.g., a reporter's aside that the police had acted inappropriately during a strike). In such cases, the researcher does not experience the linguist's concern that the grammar might not fit the texts but instead notes that the semantic grammar highlights only text structures that fit the grammar (and presumably only those text structures that are relevant to the phenomenon under investigation).

The semantic grammar's highlighting role has methodological advantages when one's research objective is to analyze variations among the aspects of a well-defined phenomenon (e.g., the grievance or the labor dispute). By restricting encoding to text segments with relevance to the phenomenon of interest, such a *phenomenal semantic grammar* will save both time and expense. Yet the highlighting role works poorly when one's research objective requires a more *generic semantic grammar* for investigating the predominance of theme relations within randomly sampled text blocks that themselves do not correspond to specific, highly structured phenomena. In the former case, the researcher encodes only themes that are related according to a semantic grammar; in the latter case, the researcher encodes all data and investigates the conditions under which specific theme relations occur. Research questions posed, for example, in cultural indicators and media research lend themselves more readily to applications of generic than phenomenal semantic grammars: Is government depicted in totalitarian states' news media as the semantic subject (e.g., acting in the people's interests), but in democratic states' news media as the semantic object (e.g., affected by the people's wishes)? On prime-time television, do men utter fewer degrading self-references than women? Here the researcher is not interested in examining only relevant phenomena (be they government depictions or self-references) within a text population but rather in determining whether certain types of content are prevalent relative to all content in a population of texts.

1.2. Surface Grammar's Highlighting of Ambiguous Text Structure

A generic semantic grammar is required to encode interrelations among themes within a domain of relatively unstructured texts (e.g., general content from prime-time television). The most obvious candidate for this semantic grammar is a S-V-O grammar to be applied to each clause in samples of such text.[4] In drawing inferences about the predominance of theme

[4]The reader familiar with literature on semantic grammars will recognize a contradiction in terms when I refer to a clause's surface (or syntax) grammar as a type of semantic grammar. Semantic grammars were developed to map statements' unique meaning-as-intended and in so doing to avoid mapping superficial grammatical relations that could have many intended meanings. I return to this issue in the next section.

relations, the researcher could then treat either the clause or (collapsing data across clauses) the text block as the unit of analysis.

Both Gottschalk (1968, 1995) and Schrodt (1993) developed semantic text analysis methods that incorporate precisely this type of generic S-V-O grammar. Taking advantage of the fact that their methods encode surface-grammatical relations among themes, each has incorporated a parser into his software that identifies which of each clause's themes functions as which of the three syntactic components, subject, verb, and object. The Gottschalk-Gleser content analysis system outputs aggregate scores on individuals' psychological states (e.g., anxiety, hostility, etc.); Schrodt's KEDS program outputs unaggregated S-V-O tuples.[5]

Yet linguists have long argued that texts' intended meanings are not captured solely by their surface grammatical relations. Indeed, it is precisely this realization that led them to develop semantic grammars and to distinguish these grammars from more semantically ambiguous syntax grammars. For example, *He was abandoned* might either refer to a state of affairs (i.e., he was alone) or to a process (i.e., others had abandoned him). *She is a doctor* might be intended as descriptive (implying that she helps sick people) or judgmental (indicating that she is an achiever). In short, semantic grammars require the coder to take clauses' social context into account; syntax grammars do not.

Nonetheless, researchers may have legitimate reasons to base their semantic text analyses on syntax grammar. People often betray their mental states in the ways they phrase their discourse, making the words' surface phrasing more relevant than their intended meanings in making a psychological diagnosis (cf. Gottschalk 1995). On the other hand, if one's analyses are of a sufficiently structured domain of texts (e.g., Reuters news service articles on international conflict), theme relations may follow sufficiently fixed formulae that their surface relations are nearly always unambiguous (cf. Schrodt 1993).

Venturing beyond such cases, one finds syntax grammars fundamentally inadequate for addressing research questions that call for the analysis of words' intended meanings—a central tenet among functional

---

[5] Both Gottschalk and Schrodt take an instrumental approach to text analysis. According to Shapiro (1997) instrumental text analyses treat the text as symptomatic of the phenomenon of interest (for Gottschalk, the individual; for Schrodt, the political event). Because coders are not required to divine clauses' intended meanings, the encoding of theme-relations can be largely automated with the help of parsing software. All other semantic text analysis methods discussed in this paper are what Shapiro refers to as representational. That is, they are text analysis methods in which texts are encoded according to their sources' intended meanings.

linguists such as Halliday (1978:192) and Winter (1994:49). When clauses are embedded in texts that are unstructured enough for identical speech acts to serve different discursive functions (i.e., to have different intended meanings), surface grammatical relations cannot differentiate among these functions and thus cannot specify a clause's intended meaning(s).[6] Inferences about such text populations call for a generic semantic grammar that allows clauses to be encoded according to discursive function.

2. A GENERIC GRAMMAR FOR SEMANTIC TEXT ANALYSIS

It was Gottlob Frege (1959 [1884]), who first noted that the sentence, *x acts*, makes two assertions: "there is an x" and "x acts." That is, sentences of this form simultaneously describe a state of affairs and a process. This dual form is commonly expressed with the following notation:

$$(x)f(x)$$

The first element in the form (namely, "(x)") may be expressed as "There is an x." The second element (namely, "f(x)") is read as "f($\cdot$) is a predicate involving x." If f($\cdot$) predicates acting, f(x) predicates x as acting. As I now formally argue, this rendering is ambiguous as a functional discourse form and as such cannot (without modification) serve as a basis for a generic semantic grammar. Researchers interested in encoding texts according to their intended meanings will have little use for grammars that afford semantically ambiguous mappings from text to meaning. My argument begins with a demonstration that a grammar's functional forms are semantically ambiguous (and thus of little value to these researchers) if they do not have unique semantic opposites.

2.1. *Semantic Opposition in Ordinary Discourse*

This subsection provides the theoretical basis for a generic semantic grammar composed of four unambiguous functional forms (i.e., functional forms having unique semantic opposites). In it, two functional forms for descrip-

---

[6] The assumption here is not that speech acts can serve only a single intended function. On the contrary, speech acts are often intended to affect others in ambivalent ways. The assumption is instead that in natural language each clause is uttered to function in an enumerable number of ways. Thus a coder could in principle apply a semantic grammar to encode the same clause numerous times, each time according to a distinct function that the clause was intended to serve.

tive speech are developed as components in a model of speech acts' intended meanings. The argument here is that in ordinary discourse a speech act's meaning consists of an unintentional, taken-for-granted component plus an intentional, asserted component. The unintentional component is neither denied nor asserted by the source but is simply assumed to be common knowledge. The intentional component's meaning is asserted (and, equivalently, its semantic opposite is denied) in the speech act. The ensuing discussion reveals a structure of linguistic ambiguity within ordinary discourse by showing that descriptive utterances admit of precisely two semantic opposites. This motivates a more formal specification in the next subsection of two unambiguous functional forms for descriptive speech acts. These are then supplemented by another two for judgmental speech acts.

A semantic opposite differs from a logical opposite in that it is the negation of the intended meaning, not the literal formal meaning, of a speech act. For example, consider the sentence, *Jerry went to the store.* Applying the $(x)f(x)$ functional form, and setting x = "Jerry" and $f(\cdot)$ = "went to the store" yields "There is Jerry and Jerry went to the store." In formal Aristotelian logic, the sentence is rendered as follows:

$$\exists(\text{Phenomenon } x) \; \exists(\text{Process } p) \; [p(x) \wedge x = \text{"Jerry"}$$
$$\wedge \; p = \text{"went to the store"}]$$

This statement reads, "There exists a phenomenon, x, such that (sic) there exists a process, p, such that p is predicated of x, x is 'Jerry', and p is 'went to the store'." Note that this statement has the following as its unique logical opposite:

$$\forall(\text{Phenomenon } x) \; \forall(\text{Process } p) \; [\sim p(x) \vee x \neq \text{"Jerry"}$$
$$\vee \; p \neq \text{"went to the store"}]$$

(I.e., for all phenomena, x, such that for all processes, p, p is not predicated of x or x is not "Jerry" or p is not "went to the store.") However, in analyses of ordinary discourse the semantic opposite of the sentence's intended meaning has a much narrower scope.

In ordinary discourse, the efficient functioning of natural language requires that both source and audience take much of the original Aristotelian expression's content for granted. That is to say, most elements of the expression will be assumed semantically invariant and thus superfluous to its intended meaning. There are four such elements.

- $\exists(\text{Phenomenon } x) \; [x = \cdot]$—The speech act mentions physical and symbolic phenomena that are true to the audience's experiences. Thus in ordinary discourse a loyal subject does not intend to communicate that the emperor's clothes exist when making references to their elegance. An emperor without clothes could not occur.

- $\exists$(Process p) [p = ·]—The speech act relates phenomena in ways that are comprehensible to an audience fluent in the language of discourse. Thus in ordinary discourse the source does not intend to communicate the existence of processes such as "going to the store." Discourse will be sidetracked when such processes require definition.

- p(x)—The source genuinely intends to communicate a process predicated on a phenomenon. That is, in ordinary discourse the source does not intend to communicate that a phenomenon and a process are being linked. Were the audience to begin attending to the appropriateness of the p on x link, the source's credibility could be called into question. Accordingly, the statement, "We Grecians offer the citizens of Troy a great wooden horse as a gift," was not understood by Laocoön as intended to describe an event but to link "Grecians" with "gift giving" in the minds of his fellow Trojans.

- $\sim$(x $\neq$ "Jerry" $\wedge$ p $\neq$ "went to the store")—The source intends to communicate relevant information. That is, in ordinary discourse the source does not intend communications that have uninformative semantic opposites. It is for this reason that the following could not be the semantic opposite of "Jodi ran away with a circus":

$$\exists(\text{Phenomenon x}) \; \exists(\text{Process p}) \; [p(x) \wedge x \neq \text{"Jodi"}$$
$$\wedge \; p \neq \text{"ran away with a circus"}]$$

If this were the semantic opposite of the source's intended meaning, "Jodi ran away with a circus" would comprise a denial that "Something 'other than Jodi' did something, which was 'something other than' running away with a circus"—a remarkably uninformative statement. When the audience discovers that such an uninformative denial was intended (e.g., as the source continues, "But the police made her bring it back"), a humorous departure from ordinary discourse results.

Thus, if the audience assumes the truth, comprehensibility, credibility, and relevance of the source's speech acts, the sentence, *Jerry went to the store*, has exactly two semantic opposites:[7]

___

[7]The audience's assumptions of truth, comprehensibility, credibility, and relevance have direct parallels with Habermas's (1979:1–68) discussions of validity claims that in ordinary communication are respectively true, comprehensible, truthful, and right.

$\exists$(Phenomenon x) $\exists$(Process p) [p(x) $\wedge$ x $\neq$ "Jerry"

$\wedge$ p = "went to the store"]

and

$\exists$(Phenomenon x) $\exists$(Process p) [p(x) $\wedge$ x = "Jerry"

$\wedge$ p $\neq$ "went to the store"]

Once the domain of a generic semantic grammar is restricted to ordinary discourse (i.e., to speech acts that the audience assumes true, comprehensible, credible, and relevant), the simpler (x)f(x) notation can be substituted for expressions of Aristotelian logic. Accordingly, the functional forms of the two just-mentioned semantic opposites are as follows:

$$(x)f(\sim x) \quad \text{and} \quad (x)\sim f(x)$$

When applied to the sentence, *Jerry went to the store*, the first form's transformation can be read as, "Something 'other than Jerry' went to the store," whereas the second transformation generates the semantic opposite, "Jerry did 'something other than' go to the store."

It is because of these dual semantic opposites that all sentences fitting the (x)f(x) form are ambiguous. Differently put, the intended meaning of the sentence about Jerry depends on whether its function was to answer the question, "Who or what went to the store?" or "What did Jerry do?"[8] In the former case, the sentence functions to convey a description of a state of affairs; in the latter case, it functions to convey a description of a process.

2.2. *Four Unambiguous Functional Forms*

What this rather lengthy illustration suggests is that a semantic grammar cannot yield unambiguous encoding of texts unless all its functional forms have unique semantic opposites. Let us assume that the discursive function of the sentence, *Jerry went to the store*, was to identify who or what was

[8]Of course, the sentence might instead have been intended to answer the question, "Where did Jerry go?" Or it might have been intended to answer more than one of these questions. The reader is referred to note 6 regarding this latter point. Regarding the former point: In addressing the where-did-Jerry-go question, the sentence would function to convey a description of a state of affairs. Because this function is one of four being suggested in this paper as the basis for a generic semantic grammar, it is a case perfectly consistent with the argument at hand.

storebound. The following functional form provides a syntax for such descriptions of states of affairs:[9]

$$(x)a(x) \quad \text{with semantic opposite} \quad (x)a(\sim x)$$

A fit between sentence and form might be read as, "There was (a storebound) Jerry," with semantic opposite, "There was no (storebound) Jerry."[10] If in a different context the discursive function of the same sentence were to convey a description of a process, the appropriate functional form would be:[11]

$$(x)^i p(x) \quad \text{with semantic opposite} \quad (x)^i \sim p(x), \quad i = 0,1$$

The i-superscript is introduced here to acknowledge the optional role of the semantic subject in passive voice. Accordingly, if the semantic subject, Jerry, had not been named in the sentence being encoded, its rendering might be read as, "The store was gone to," with semantic opposite, " 'Something other than' going to the store happened."

Ambiguity is also present when a clause functions to convey a positive (or negative) judgment of a description's referent. For example, the sentence, *Chris makes charitable contributions*, may function to convey not only a description but also a positive evaluation of Chris (or possibly a positive evaluation of "making charitable contributions," if Chris is one of

---

[9]More formal renderings of $(x)a(x)$ and $(x)a(\sim x)$ are respectively $\exists$(Phenomenon x) $\exists$(Attribute a) $[a(x) \wedge x =$ "Jerry" $\wedge a =$ "storebound"] and $\exists$(Phenomenon x) $\exists$(Attribute a) $[a(x) \wedge x \neq$ "Jerry" $\wedge a =$ "storebound"].

[10]Linguists commonly represent "being" and "becoming" as functions with two arguments, such that the content of one argument can be represented as being or becoming that of the other. Linguistic content analysis (Roberts 1989) uses a functional form that renders descriptions of states of affairs as one of four, two-place predicates ("is an instance of," "becomes," "resembles," or "symbolizes"). When a two-place predicate is used, it is the posterior, not the anterior, argument that is negated in the clause's opposite. For example, it is semantically identical to assert that "Jerry went to the store" (with opposite "Jerry did 'something other than' go to the store") or that "Jerry was an instance of 'a storebound entity' " (with opposite "Jerry was not an instance of 'a storebound entity' "). In both cases, the sentence presumes Jerry's existence while functioning to convey a description of his storebound activity. If one encodes "Jerry" as the posterior argument in the two-place predicate, its rendering (i.e., "The storebound entity was Jerry" with opposite "The storebound entity was not Jerry") not only is semantically distinct from both other renderings but also functions to convey a description of a state of affairs and, identically, the answer to "Who or what went to the store?"

[11]Formal renderings of $(x)p(x)$ and $(x) \sim p(x)$ are respectively $\exists$(Phenomenon x) $\exists$(Process p) $[p(x) \wedge x =$ "Jerry" $\wedge p =$ "went to the store"] and $\exists$(Phenomenon x) $\exists$(Process p) $[p(x) \wedge x =$ "Jerry" $\wedge p \neq$ "went to the store"].

the speaker's heroes). For such cases, a functional form can be introduced that renders a positive judgment of a state of affairs as follows:[12]

$$(x)a(x)Q_a \quad \text{with semantic opposite} \quad (x)a(x)\overline{Q}_a$$

In the former expression x's attribute, a, is assigned the positive qualifier, Q_a. In the latter expression the same attribute is assigned the opposite, negative qualifier, $\overline{Q}_a$. Thus, if the above sentence was solely intended to convey a positive judgment of Chris, its unique semantic opposite could be rendered as "Chris is a bad person (presumably by virtue of the egregious nature of those who contribute to charities)."

A formal representation of a positive judgment of a process can be rendered as follows:[13]

$$(x)^i p(x)Q_p \quad \text{with semantic opposite} \quad (x)^i p(x)\overline{Q}_p, \quad i = 0,1$$

Here the i-superscript acknowledges that a state of affairs need not be explicit in such speech acts. (For example, one may assert, "Dancing on Sunday is immoral," without naming a particular dancer.) In the former expression, the process $p(x)$ is assigned a positive qualifier, Q_p. In the latter expression, the same process is assigned the opposite, negative qualifier, $\overline{Q}_p$. Accordingly, if the sole intention of the speech act about Chris was to convey a positive judgment of his behavior, its unique semantic opposite could be rendered as "Chris's making of charitable contributions is immoral."

Note that in these last two judgmental functional forms, all elements except the quantifiers are semantically invariant. Differently put, in ordinary discourse the extent to which a speech act is intended to positively judge a process (or state of affairs) is the extent to which it is intended to deny a negative judgment of the same process (or state). If a speech act were intended to convey, "Chris is a good person," its intention would not be to deny that someone other than Chris is a good person but

---

[12] Keeping with the earlier illustration, more formal renderings of $(x)a(x)Q_a$ and $(x)a(x)\overline{Q}_a$ are respectively $\exists$(Phenomenon x) $\exists$(Attribute a) $\exists$(EvalFunction e_A) $[a(x) \wedge x = $ "Jerry" $\wedge a = $ "storebound" $\wedge e_A(a)]$ and $\exists$(Phenomenon x) $\exists$(Attribute a) $\exists$(EvalFunction e_A) $[a(x) \wedge x = $ "Jerry" $\wedge a = $ "storebound" $\wedge \bar{e}_A(a)]$. Here the function, e_A, assigns a positive (and $\bar{e}_A$ a negative) judgment to the attribute, a, contained in the set A.

[13] More formal renderings of $(x)^i f(x)Q_p$ and $(x)^i f(x)\overline{Q}_p$ are respectively $\exists$(Phenomenon x) $\exists$(Process p) $\exists$(JustFunction j_P) $[p(x) \wedge x = $ "Jerry" $\wedge p = $ "went to the store" $\wedge j_P(p)]$ and $\exists$(Phenomenon x) $\exists$(Process p) $\exists$(JustFunction j_P) $[p(x) \wedge x = $ "Jerry" $\wedge p = $ "went to the store" $\wedge \bar{j}_P(p)]$. Here the function, j_P, assigns a positive (and $\bar{j}_P$ a negative) judgment to the process, p, contained in the set P.

rather to deny that Chris is a bad person.[14] Likewise, if a speech act were intended to convey, "Dancing on Sunday is immoral," its intention is not to deny that activities other than Sunday dancing are immoral but rather to deny that Sunday dancing is moral.

In summary, when applying a generic semantic grammar to relatively unstructured texts, the coder's task is not one of identifying themes' surface grammatical relations but one of identifying each theme's role within the functional form(s) appropriate to its clause of origin. During the coding process such identifications can, of course, only be made after selecting the appropriate functional form, a selection that requires the coder to look beyond the clause. That is, the selection of functional forms requires that the coder understands both the source's intentions and the social context within which the clause appeared.

2.3. Criteria for Selection Among Functional Forms

Understanding intentions requires coder intuition about the mental process that (by having uttered a clause) the source attempted to initiate in an audience.[15] The preceding discussion hints at four such intended mental processes: the recognition of a state of affairs, a perception or imagination of a process, a positive or negative evaluation of a state of affairs, and a positive or negative judgment (justification?) of a process.[16] Accordingly,

[14]Of course, "Chris is a good person" is a phrase that might be used in an attempt to communicate that someone other than Chris is a bad person (and "Dancing on Sunday is immoral" might be used to suggest that activities other than Sunday dancing are moral). In this, as in other paragraphs, phrases between quotation marks represent intended meanings, not direct quotations.

[15]In different contexts others have also held the premise that speech is motivated by a desire to affect one's audience's mental state: "A good writer or raconteur perhaps has the power to initiate a process very similar to the one that occurs when we are actually perceiving (or imagining) events instead of merely reading or hearing about them" (Johnson-Laird 1970:270). "The production of sound for the purpose of attracting attention *is* language, once we have reason to assert that 'attracting attention' is a meaning that fits in with the functional potential of language" (Halliday, 1978:19).

[16]Rough parallels exist between these four types of intention and the classes some linguists have developed to capture the illocutionary (i.e., intended) force of speech acts (Austin 1975; Searle and Vanderveken 1985) or the structurally apparent features of an aspect grammar (Dowty 1979). For example, among Austin's classes of performative utterances, "exercitives" and "behabitives" respectively function to convey descriptions and judgments of processes. (His "expositives" and "verdictives" have much rougher correspondence to the respective functions of conveying descriptions and judgments of states of affairs.) Dowty's "statives," "activities," "achievements," and "accomplishments" have clear parallels to the respective functions of conveying descriptions of states of affairs, descriptions of processes, judgments of states of affairs, and judgments of processes. Turning to functional linguistics, one

any matching of clause to functional form(s) requires that the coder weigh the relative plausibility of each of these four manners in which the clause may have been intended. By providing a framework for them to make such "judgments of subjective plausibility," the four functional forms provide coders with structure in their strivings to map sources' inherently ambiguous meanings into unambiguous code.

This structuring of the coding process has interesting parallels in Weber's (1973 [1906]:290) recommendation that in their quest for the inherently elusive causes of past events, historical sociologists should guide their analyses by comparing numerous "judgments of objective possibility" (*objektiver Möglichkeitsurteile*). The idea here is that a causal understanding of history requires more than knowing the events that took place; it requires judgments about whether events would have taken place in the presence of various counterfactuals (i.e., "contrary-to-fact historical alternative(s) . . . conceptually and empirically quite close to the 'real past' "; Griffin 1993:1101–102).[17] In his ETHNO program, Heise (1988 1991) provides a structure for such counterfactual inquiry by requiring the user to identify causal links among the actions within a chronology. Similar analytic rigor is gained as coders (possibly under software guidance) are required to identify the functional form(s) judged most appropriate to the clauses in one's texts.

While weighing the relative plausibility of functional forms, the coder may judge the source not to have been sincere but instead to have attempted communication of irony, hyperbole, or understatement.[18] Interestingly, the coder's recognition of such discourse styles can only aid the coding process: Cases of hyperbole and understatement will usually suggest a clause's judgmental rather than descriptive intent. For example, *We have enough food to feed an army* may be used to convey a positive or negative evaluation of the amount of food on hand. Ironic, possibly sarcastic, speech acts must be encoded according to the semantic opposite of the functional form that would apply, were they to have been uttered in

might also draw rough parallels between Winter's (1994) two sets of basic text structures, "situation and evaluation" and "hypothetical and real" and, respectively, my "recognition and evaluation" and, less apparently, "justification and perception."

[17] I am indebted to an anonymous reviewer for bringing the literature on counterfactuals to my attention.

[18] A source's intention to deliberately deceive its audience is unrelated to the coder's selection among functional forms. The semantic grammar proposed here only captures the meanings that sources intend to convey, not the pragmatics of why they opt to convey these meanings. Nonetheless, there is no reason why the coding of particular clauses might not be supplemented with identifiers that indicate the coder's suspicions regarding the genuineness of sources' intentions.

sincerity. For example, when said of a sputtering jalopy, the utterance, *It runs 'beautifully,' doesn't it*, should be encoded as a negative judgment of the jalopy's running (a process).

Finally, applying a semantic grammar requires that speech acts are understood in terms of their respective situational contexts. As always, these situational contexts are those within which the sources believed their speech acts would be interpreted. Invalid code will almost surely result when coders are insufficiently familiar with these contexts. However, even if the coder attained such contextual integrity in apprehending the source's intended meanings, these meanings may not have been those understood by their intended audiences. Little substantive import is likely to be found in an analysis of texts generated by sources who themselves were unable reliably to predict audience reactions (leaving their speech, one might say, little more than sound and fury). Moreover, encoding will be futile if the source's intended meanings (e.g., regarding preferred cookie recipes) are not relevant to the researcher's purposes (e.g., studying political attitudes).[19] Thus the four functional forms are correctly applied within the source's situational context—a context hopefully familiar to both coder and audience, and relevant to both text population and research objectives.

2.4. *The Grammar*

This generic semantic grammar is a model of text (T), according to which text is a sequence of one or more clauses (C) separated by markers (&) that indicate subordination, coordination, and sentence boundaries:

$$T = C(\&C)^n, \quad n \geq 0$$

Each clause in this sequence can be represented within its situational context (SC) according to one or more of the four unambiguous functional forms just introduced. Differently put, intention (I) is a function that maps (→) clause-context pairs into a multiset comprised of subsets having one or more occurrences among recognition (R), perception (P), evaluation

[19] To determine the relevance of texts to a semantic grammar, one may begin by encoding a small representative sample from one's text population. If a phenomenal semantic grammar appears only to highlight a small proportion of the population, it follows that the unhighlighted proportion is not relevant to one's research. Of course, any text with identifiable clauses can be encoded using a generic semantic grammar. Yet, if application of a generic semantic grammar (or, for that matter, of software for representational thematic text analysis; cf. Popping 1997) yields no common vocabulary among large segments of the population, these segments are likely to have little basis of comparison. In such cases, it is reasonable to consider whether one may have selected an inappropriate text population.

(E), and justification (J):

$$I(C_i, SC_{i-1}) \rightarrow MS_{\{R,P,E,J\}},$$

where $MS \neq \{\}$

and $R = (x)a(x)$ with semantic opposite $(x)a(\sim x)$

       $P = (x)p(x)$ with semantic opposite $(x)\sim p(x)$

       $E = (x)a(x)Q_a$ with semantic opposite $(x)a(x)\overline{Q}_a$

       $J = (x)p(x)Q_p$ with semantic opposite $(x)p(x)\overline{Q}_p$

The restriction that this intention function have a single situational context as an argument ensures the common ground (i.e., common assumptions made by the source regarding truth, comprehensibility, credibility, relevance, and evaluation and justification criteria) needed for a one-to-one mapping from clauses' surface representations to their appropriate functional forms.

Finally, situational contexts are continually updated by virtue of successive clauses' intended meanings. If SC_0 is the situational context at the beginning of one's text and SC_i is the situational context after the ith clause, situation (S) can now be introduced as a function that takes the current clause's intention into account in transforming one situational context to the next:

$$S(SC_{i-1}, I(C_i, SC_{i-1})) = SC_i$$

To the extent that situational contexts (and rules for transformations among them) lack formal definition, coders' intuitions regarding these contexts and transformations will be necessary when this generic semantic grammar is used in encoding texts.[20]

---

[20] In practice, applications of this generic semantic grammar will usually call for greater complexity than is provided here. For example, specific types of questions, modality, and clause coordination and subordination may be required. Speaker- and audience-identifiers could be used in encoding direct quotations. Moreover, the grammar contains only Boolean valences and qualifiers, leaving it unable to capture their dimensions of potency and type, as well as that of positive or negative sign. I have refrained from formally specifying these components (and thus from adding to the grammar's complexity), because it would only serve to divert attention from this paper's central contribution to the content analysis literature: The novelty of this paper is its formal specification and illustration of a linguistically grounded semantic grammar for encoding arbitrary clauses according to their sources' intended meanings. In lieu of a formal specification of the additional components just mentioned, these components are given lengthy illustration in the following section (particularly in conjunction with note 27 and Tables 2 and 3). More detail on qualifiers can be found in Section 3.1. The

3. AN APPLICATION OF THE SEMANTIC GRAMMAR

For illustrative purposes, let us consider the population of all clauses uttered during East and West Berlin radio news coverage of two brief military conflicts during the spring of 1979. One of these conflicts, the concluding battles of the Sandinista Revolution (SR) in Nicaragua, was an event widely acclaimed by East Germany and other communist countries, but less enthusiastically received by the West. The other conflict, the Chinese invasion (CI) of Vietnam, was vigorously denounced in East Germany and other Soviet-aligned communist countries, and received more pedestrian treatment in the West. The following is an illustration of one of these news broadcasts:[21]

> Despite their withdrawal-notifications on Monday, Peking's aggression-troops still *provoke* new fighting. Thus, the north Vietnamese provincial capital, Lan Shon, *was* subjected to the Chinese invaders' sporadic artillery fire. According to agency reports, shells *struck* the main streets flagrantly anew. The train station and the provincial hospital *are* said to be completely destroyed. As the station, 'Voice of Vietnam', reported, as yet there *is* still no indication of a real withdrawal of the Peking troops. At a few locations the Chinese *were* said to have removed only certain ranks. In other regions they *were* said still to hold their positions. During their movements the invaders *continued* to commit barbaric crimes. According to statements from the news agency, VNA, China *does* not even resist attacking foreign journalists. Sharpshooters *are* said to have opened fire on a group of correspondents in Lan Shon, whereby they *murdered* Isau Takano, a reporter from Japan's Communist Party's central office. The DDR's demand for the Chinese aggressors' immediate

following section illustrates a more complex generic semantic grammar, built around the one formally presented here and implemented in the computer program Program for Linguistic Content Analysis, or PLCA (MetaText Inc. 1994). PLCA runs under DOS (version 2.2) and Windows 95 (version 3.0), and is available from iec Pro-GAMMA (P.O. Box 841, 9700 AV GRONINGEN, the Netherlands, gamma.post@gamma.rug.nl).

[21] In this English version the phrase, "said to be," is used to translate a German tense (nonexistent in English) that designates the current sentence as a direct quotation from the most recently cited source. An appendix to this chapter gives the original German text of this news report.

unconditional withdrawal from Vietnam *was* affirmed
yesterday in Berlin by Erich Honnecker, General Secre-
tary of the SED's Central Committee and Chairman of
the National Council: "The (East German) Republic
shares the Socialist Republic of Vietnam's government's
opinion that (*indicates*) vigilance *is* still called for, because Peking *has* tied its orders for withdrawal to new
threats against Vietnam." At an inspirational meeting last
night in Helsinki, the Vietnamese Peace Committee's
chairman, Fan An, *made* clear his people's confidence
in victory over the Chinese invaders. "It *grows* from the
fact," he emphasized, "that all peace-loving humanity
stands on our side." (Berliner Rundfunk, 2nd news report, March 9, 1979)

CI coverage began in the sixth report of the January 29 morning
news broadcast from the West Berlin radio station, Sender Freies Berlin
(SFB), with a mention that *Newsweek* reported, "It is not to be ruled out
that China plans a military strike against Vietnam." No references to the
event were made for at least one week after a minor aside on March 28 in
which the East German radio station, Berliner Rundfunk (BR), mentioned
"Peking-expansionists" in conjunction with official UN recognition of the
Pol Pot Regime. In like fashion a continuous period of SR coverage (flanked
by no SR coverage at least one week prior and following) occurred between May 21 and July 20. Two news broadcasts (one each from BR and
SFB) were tape-recorded every morning during the period of study. Transcripts were made of all CI- or SR-related news reports within these broadcasts. Each clause within the reports was then identified by a fluent German
speaker, yielding a total of 1923 clauses.[22] A stratified random sample of

---

[22] "Clause" is referred to here in its usual sense, namely as a sentence or part of
a sentence that contains an inflected verb and, optionally, a subject or object, plus all
modifiers related to this verb, subject, and object. Note that high coder reliability can
be ensured only if coders initially agree on "what counts as a clause." For example,
coders must follow explicit rules regarding cases of ellipsis, as occurs with the omitted
"indicates" parenthetically inserted into the quotation by Erich Honnecker in the twelfth
sentence. Here a coding rule might be established to ensure that constructions of the
form, "the (or a) thought/idea/belief/opinion/etc. that [such-and-such] . . .", should be
encoded as relative clauses with the verb, to indicate, taking the such-and-such clause
as its object (e.g., the belief, that indicates that [vigilance is called for]). A more general
rule was that inflected verbs were not to be treated as clause-identifiers when they
indicated the source of quoted information. Source and audience information were
instead encoded as characteristics of each clause. Thus "reported" (by the 'Voice of

400 clauses was drawn from this total, with 100 clauses being sampled from each station (BR or SFB) by event (CI or SR) combination.

Using key-word-in-context software, the texts of these clauses were scanned for frequently used words and phrases, which were then grouped into a more comprehensive vocabulary consisting of nominal and verbal coding categories. Although specific codes were assigned to some frequently mentioned entities (e.g., VIETNAM, SOMOSA, THE UNITED NATIONS, etc.), most coding categories corresponded to much broader classes (e.g., LATIN AMERICAN COUNTRY, and verbs such as to ENCOURAGE/FACILITATE and to VIOLENTLY ACT). Only very occasionally was vocabulary added once this vocabulary-development stage had been completed.

Two fluent German speakers encoded the sampled clauses directly from the German transcripts. During regular meetings, the coders met to jointly resolve differences in their encodings in the light of an evolving set of consistent coding rules. For example, one coding rule was, " 'Journalist' is to be encoded as 'genitive + noun = MEDIA's PERSON'." Because references to a medium commonly indicated its nation of origin, the rule implies that mention of a Chinese journalist would be encoded as genitive + genitive + noun = CHINA's MEDIA's PERSON. The software used in encoding the news data restricted users to a single genitive for each noun, however.[23] Because the encoding of national affiliation was

Vietnam' in sentence 5) and "emphasized" (by Fan An in sentence 14) did not identify distinct clauses. Applying these coding rules, the above-quoted BR broadcast contains 19 clauses, each identified by its inflected verb (in italics).

[23] This software was PLCA (see note 20 and below). In addition to allowing the encoding of only one genitive per noun, the program only allows the encoding of prepositional phrases when they identify the objects of intransitive verbs (e.g., CHINA VIOLENTLY ACTED toward a PLACE) or of verbs' nominal forms (e.g., VIOLENCE toward a PLACE). PLCA also does not allow arbitrary encoding of adjectival or adverbial modifiers. In principle, there is no reason why in addition to subject-verb-object relations arbitrary sequences of modifiers might not also be encoded, even if only according to the surface grammatical syntax of the original text. Guided on the one hand by the impracticality of assigning unique codes to each word in one's texts and on the other hand by a desire not to gloss over the texts' salient properties, the number of coding categories is in practice usually restricted to a manageable amount. This restriction may involve dropping incidental modifiers from consideration or, when deemed necessary to capture salient properties of the text, incorporating them into the coding through the use of noun modifiers or more specific thematic categories. A case in point is the current illustration in which the need for a distinct coding category is circumvented by encoding *journalist* as the noun, PERSON, supplemented with the genitive, MEDIA (i.e., as MEDIA's PERSON). In contrast, two coding categories were used to distinguish among "subjecting another to artillery fire," "opening fire," "returning to one's barracks," and "eating dinner," despite the fact that all are actions. Within news

TABLE 1
Breakdown of Clauses by Station, Event, and Functional Form

Functional form	Berliner Rundfunk (BR)		Sender Freies Berlin (SFB)		Total
	Chinese Invasion	Sandinista Revolution	Chinese Invasion	Sandinista Revolution	
Recognition	28	34	34	21	117
Perception	67	64	65	79	275
Evaluation	4	2	0	1	7
Justification	1	0	0	0	1
Sampled total	100	100	100	100	400
Population total	403	853	214	453	1923

deemed by the researchers to be of greater theoretical importance than personhood in a study of national alignments in the news, the coding rule was elaborated into the following: "'Journalist' is to be encoded as 'genitive + noun = MEDIA's PERSON', except in cases where the nationality of the journalist's medium (e.g., China) is known. In these cases, 'journalist' is to be encoded as CHINA's MEDIA."

The computer program, PLCA (see note 20), was used in applying vocabulary and coding rules to the sampled clauses. Although coders were blind to clauses' dates and radio stations of origin, they were provided the entire news report within which each sampled clause appeared. Access to entire news reports provided coders with invaluable contextual information needed in determining sampled clauses' intended meanings and corresponding functional forms. After each functional form was selected, PLCA guided coders through a series of prompts for vocabulary being assigned to the various syntactic components (e.g., subject, verb, etc.) within that form's semantic grammar.

Table 1 provides a breakdown of the clauses by stations, events, and functional forms (i.e., recognition, perception, evaluation, and justification). One noteworthy finding in Table 1 is that of the sample's eight judgmental clauses, seven were aired on East German radio. The probability is .035 that sampling error accounts for this finding, namely that positive or negative judgments are more likely to be conveyed in news broadcasts on BR than on SFB. Nonetheless, 98 percent of the sample's clauses were

reports of armed conflict, the violent nature of the former two clearly distinguished them from the latter two phrases. To capture this distinction, thematic categories were created for two classes of verbs, to VIOLENTLY ACT and to ACT.

descriptive of either processes or states of affairs—an understandable fact, given the descriptive nature of news reporting. The following subsection explains how the generic semantic grammar was applied to the sample's 400 clauses. An illustrative log-linear model is then fit to data encoded from the 275 perception-clauses in the sample.

3.1. *Encoding Clauses*

The generic semantic grammar developed in the previous section is at the heart of Roberts's (1989, 1991) quantitative text analysis method, Linguistic Content Analysis (LCA). Given the clause-specific relevance of the grammar, the method must be applied one clause at a time. Let us begin by encoding the first sentence in the BR transcript. In it is described the process of Chinese troops provoking fighting. During the encoding process, words such as "troops," "provoke," and "fighting" are likely to be encoded as falling into more general thematic categories. Classifying "troops" into the thematic category, "MILITARY/WEAPON," "provoke" into the category, "ENCOURAGE/FACILITATE," and "fighting" into the category, "VIOLENCE," and applying the "$(x)f(x)$" functional form appropriate for this *perception*, the sentence might be rendered as "CHINA's MILITARY/WEAPON ENCOURAGE/FACILITATES a VIOLENCE."

The fourth sentence conveys a negative judgment of a Vietnamese train station's and hospital's (viz., two states of affairs') inherent conditions. The syntax for a negatively stated *evaluation* such as this is "$(x)a(x)\overline{Q}_a$", and might be rendered as "VIETNAM's PLACE is pitiful." The fifth sentence is a direct quotation from the radio station, Voice of Vietnam. In it a withdrawal of troops (a state of affairs) is described as absent. If reference here were instead to a withdraw*ing* of troops (a process), the sentence might best be encoded as a perception. Yet given the nominal, nongerund form of withdraw, it is more appropriately encoded as a *recognition*. Applying the corresponding functional form (see note 10), the sentence might be rendered as "VIETNAM's MEDIA said, 'There is not a WITHDRAWAL of a MILITARY/WEAPON.' " The eighth sentence describes the process of the Chinese doing harm (as in answer to the question, "What did they do?"). Yet by applying the abstract judgmental label, "barbaric crimes," to the harm-doing, the sentence also strongly conveys a negative judgment of this process (as in answer to the question, "Is it not terrible what they are doing?"). Thus this coder encoded the sentence twice, once as a perception (rendered, "CHINA harmed.") and once as a *justification* (rendered, "CHINA's doing harm was ethically wrong."). In accordance with the generic semantic grammar, the syntax of this latter rendering is "$(x)f(x)\overline{Q}_p$".

The LCA encoding of judgmental clauses (i.e., evaluations and justifications) is more complex than the encoding of descriptive clauses (i.e., perceptions and recognitions). Research by Thomas and Heise (1995) suggests that culture and gender differences influence the affective meanings that individuals associate with words. Accordingly, coders should be particularly sensitive to the source's world when the source is not of their culture or gender. Likewise, they must strive not to allow their own social biases to color their assignment of codes.

In addition to enhancing coder reflexivity, refinement of the generic semantic grammar's qualifiers adds rigor to the process of coding judgmental clauses. Most text analysis methods provide two dimensions along which to encode affect: positive-negative and strong-weak. For example, the sentence, *The army was great*, appears (assuming lack of sarcasm) intended to convey a strong positive evaluation of the army. However, still unaccounted for is a third dimension, namely the type of evaluation being made. Without more contextual information, it is impossible to determine whether the inherent condition (e.g., health) or the utilitarian value (e.g., destructive capacity) of the army is being evaluated. Likewise, if *The army performed terribly* were intended to negatively judge the process of the army's performing, it would remain unclear if this process were being condemned as inherently unethical, technically flawed, socially inept, or consequently ineffective. Like social historians who are obliged to address counterfactual queries, LCA coders must identify the types as well as the strength and sign of the evaluations and justifications in their texts.

No matter how structured the coding process, some coder disagreement is inevitable. For example, in the fifth sentence *a real withdrawal of the Peking troops* may be thought by some readers to represent a process rather than a state of affairs. As in the eighth sentence, a coder may decide that the clause was intended to have more than one meaning and that it should be encoded more than once.[24] Disagreements among coders are, of course, the makings of poor interrater agreement. However, they are also "grist" in the development of explicit coding rules (for example, "Only noun phrases rendered as gerunds will be considered processes in selections of functional form."). As it turns out, when coding rules have been

---

[24]Multiple coding requires the assignment to each encoding of a weight equivalent to the proportion of its contribution to the clause's overall meaning. To ensure sufficient interrater agreement, assignment will nearly always be of equivalent weights that sum to unity.

conscientiously developed and applied, coders are likely to attain consistently high agreement in LCA encodings (cf. Eltinge and Roberts 1993). One year after the encoding of this study's 400 clauses, 20 of these were selected at random and encoded for a second time. The two encodings identified 11 perceptions and 7 recognitions in common, yielding significant evidence of agreement beyond chance ($\kappa = .79, p < .01$).[25]

3.2. LCA Translation and PLCA 'Retranslation'

Text analysts have frequently depicted their work as a process of translation (Andrén 1981; Franzosi 1994). Yet in making their translations, semantic text analysts will want to avoid both the literal rendering of surface grammar and the paraphrasing of text. For example, when used idiomatically, *I'll stand by you in your misery* should not be encoded according to its surface grammar (i.e., as "I" and "you" having a relation of "standing together"). It would be equally inappropriate to paraphrase the idiom as "I assure you," despite the fact that the sentence is an assurance. In contrast, an LCA translation renders the clause's words according to the syntax of its appropriate functional form (i.e., not as a description of standing—a state of affairs, but as a description of assisting—a process). Thus, in a more accurate translation, the expression "to stand by" would be rendered as "to assist," leaving my relation to you being one of promised future assistance. That is, an acceptable translation would be, "I shall assist you."

The translation metaphor is not only apparent in linguistic content analysis, PLCA literally renders LCA encoding as a translation. The left-hand column in Table 2 provides a PLCA-generated translation of the entire transcript of the March 9 BR news report. By generating ongoing translation of the text being encoded, PLCA affords the coder ready verification that the themes in the original text are related correctly according

[25] In addition, 19 of the 20 clauses (including all 11 clauses jointly identified as perceptions) had sources encoded identically both times. Beyond radio station, event, and source, the only additional variable included in the below statistical analysis (and, thus, for which reliability data need be provided) is the subject of the processes described in the data set's 275 perception clauses. Two minor discrepancies occurred among the subject codes in the 11 clauses jointly identified as perceptions: COMMUNISM's ORGANIZATION versus COMMUNISM's TROOPS and THE ORGANIZATION OF AMERICAN STATES' OFFICIAL versus THE UNITED STATES' OFFICIAL. However, these discrepancies disappear with the collapsing of subject codes prior to analysis (i.e., when both of the former encodings are collapsed into an East-aligned category and both of the latter encodings are collapsed into a non-East-aligned category). Thus, insofar as the subsample of 11 perception clauses can be generalized to the 275 clauses analyzed below, rater agreement was effectively perfect once a clause's functional form was determined.

TABLE 2

LCA (Re)translation and English Rendering of an East Berlin News Report of China's Invasion of Vietnam

LCA Rendering	English Translation from German
CHINA's MILITARY/WEAPON ENCOURAGE/FACILITATES a VIOLENCE.	1 Despite their withdrawal-notifications on Monday, Peking's aggression-troops still provoke new fighting.
CHINA's MILITARY/WEAPON VIOLENTLY ACTED toward VIETNAM's PLACE.	2 Thus the north Vietnamese provincial capital, Lan Shon, was subjected to the Chinese invaders' sporadic artillery fire.
The MEDIA said, "CHINA's MILITARY/WEAPON VIOLENTLY ACTED toward VIETNAM's PLACE.	3 According to agency reports, shells struck the main streets flagrantly anew.
VIETNAM's PLACE is pitiful."	4 The train station and the provincial hospital are said to be completely destroyed.
VIETNAM's MEDIA said, "There is not a WITHDRAWAL of a MILITARY/WEAPON.	5 As the station, "Voice of Vietnam," reported, as yet there is still no indication of a real withdrawal of the Peking troops.
CHINA did somewhat WITHDRAW a MILITARY/WEAPON.	6 At a few locations the Chinese were said to have removed only certain ranks.
There was CHINA's MILITARY/WEAPON."	7 In other regions they were said still to hold their positions.
CHINA harmed.	8(a) During their movements the invaders continued to commit
CHINA's doing harm was ethically wrong.	8(b) barbaric crimes.
VIETNAM's MEDIA said, "CHINA does not DISCOURAGE/IMPEDE a VIOLENCE toward a MEDIA.	9 According to statements from the news agency, VNA, China does not even resist attacking foreign journalists.

CHINA's MILITARY/WEAPON VIOLENTLY ACTED toward a MEDIA's PERSON(S), therefore COMMUNISM's PERSON(S) was harmed."	10 Sharpshooters are said to have opened fire on a group of correspondents in Lan Shon, whereby they murdered Isau Takano, a reporter from Japan's Communist Party's central office.
EAST GERMANY's OFFICIAL DESCRIBED/REPORTED a DEMAND of CHINA.	11 The DDR's demand for the Chinese aggressors' immediate unconditional withdrawal from Vietnam was affirmed yesterday in Berlin by Erich Honnecker, General Secretary of the SED's Central Committee and Chairman of the National Council.
EAST GERMANY's OFFICIAL said, "EAST GERMANY's BELIEF/FAITH is VIETNAM's BELIEF/FAITH (that CONVEYS that [the PERCEPTION/CONSIDERATION is a necessity/certainty, because {according to what CHINA said} the obligation to WITHDRAW LOGICALLY RELATES to a THREAT to VIETNAM])." VIETNAM's OFFICIAL DESCRIBED/REPORTED VIETNAM's BELIEF/FAITH.	12 "The (East German) Republic shares the Socialist Republic of Vietnam's government's opinion that (indicates) vigilance is still called for, because Peking has tied its orders for withdrawal to new threats against Vietnam."
	13 At an inspirational meeting last night in Helsinki, the Vietnamese Peace Committee's chairman, Fan An, made clear his people's confidence in victory over the Chinese invaders.
VIETNAM's OFFICIAL said, "There becomes VIETNAM's BELIEF/FAITH, because VIETNAM's PERSON(S) is good for a good PERSON(S)."	14 "It grows from the fact," he emphasized, "that all peace-loving humanity stands on our side."

Note. This news report was broadcast by the East Berlin radio station, Berliner Rundfunk, on the morning of March 9, 1979. The LCA rendering in this table was generated by PLCA (MetaText, Inc.). The original German version of the news report is in an appendix to this chapter. In the English translation, the phrase, "said to be," is used in translating a German tense (nonexistent in English) that designates the current sentence as a direct quotation from the most recently cited source.

113

to the functional forms appropriate to their respective clauses. Yet the purpose of such semantic encoding is not merely to translate text into a sort of unambiguous pidgin English (a.k.a. LCAese).[26] Like all quantitative text analysis methods, LCA's encoding process is intended to produce a data matrix suitable for statistical analysis.

The translation in Table 2 is in fact a retranslation. That is, it is a direct translation of a data matrix, and only indirectly a translation of the original text. Transparent to the user, the encoding process involves a translation from text to numbers (i.e., to an unambiguous matrix representation). The user is provided the retranslation to make the same kind of verification that developers of machine translation software use to check their routines: After translating the same text from one language to another, the translation is retranslated back to the original. If the retranslation closely resembles the original, the software's functionality is verified.

Unlike translation software, PLCA automates the retranslation but not the translation process. In translating verbatim text into a data matrix, the program's role is one of guiding the user through a sequence of coding decisions. Advances in the fields of linguistics and artificial intelligence remain insufficient to automate the coder's ability to recognize texts' intended meanings (cf. Shapiro 1997). Thus, although potentially supported by various software amenities, the translation from words to numbers requires that coders make considerable use of both their intuition of the source's meanings and their knowledge of the situational context.

The purpose of PLCA's retranslation capability (i.e., from data matrix to LCAese) is to enable coders to verify whether their intuitions are accurately represented in a semantically unambiguous linguistic form that is grounded in the generic semantic grammar described above. LCA encoding requires more of coders than that they merely identify subjects and predicates; they must commit themselves to unambiguous encodings of ofttimes ambiguous linguistic expressions. By comparing original text to LCAese, one is able to evaluate whether the retranslation captures one's intuition that a clause was intended to communicate a description or judgment of a process or state of affairs.

[26] Although PLCA renders linguistic data into a language comprehensible to English speakers, this language is not English but LCAese—a language that unlike English, allows each of a speech act's intended meanings to be expressed in one and only one way. That is, unlike natural languages, LCAese is a language without ambiguity. As a consequence, users cannot legitimately disagree about the meaning of an LCAese expression, only about how well distinct LCAese expressions render the intended meaning(s) of a particular speech act.

Table 3 lists the data matrix from which the retranslation in Table 2 was generated. The first five columns of the matrix give identifying and sequencing information. Missing data are rendered as periods. The first clause (encoded in the first row of the matrix) is a perception (functional form = 1) in present tense (clause tense = 2), that is not a question (question = 0) and that functions to convey a process whereby CHINA's (genitive of subject = 213) MILITARY/WEAPON (subject = 239) ENCOURAGE/ FACILITATES (clause valence = T, main verb = 33) VIOLENCE (object = 50). These codes along with the LCA syntax for a perception comprise sufficient information for LCA software to render the first clause as it appears in Table 2. Other retranslations can be reconstructed via similar comparisons between the two tables.[27]

---

[27] Interpretation of the data in Table 3 will be easier if more code definitions are provided: Identifying information, clause number, and sentence number should be self-explanatory. A main clause has no (i.e., zero) depth in its sentence' syntax tree; a clause subordinate to the main clause has a depth of one; a clause subordinate to this subordinate clause has a depth of two; and so on. There are three forms of subordination. A conjunctive clause is subordinated to a main clause via a conjunction (e.g., T = therefore or 6 = because). The subordination code, OR, identifies a clause that is relative to the object of the previous clause (e.g., "There is a belief *that indicates a need for vigilance*"). The subordination code, OP, identifies an object proxy clause that is itself the object of the previous clause (e.g., "The belief indicates that *vigilance is necessary*"). Valence codes (i.e., indicators of semantic opposition) differ among functional forms. Among perceptions and recognitions, the code, T, identifies a clause that is positively stated. Negation of the main verb in perception and recognition clauses can be identified with NI and SI codes, respectively calling for retranslations in LCAese that include the words *not* (e.g., "There is not a WITHDRAWAL") and *somewhat* (e.g., "CHINA did somewhat WITHDRAW"). In an evaluation of a state of affairs, the valence codes, -- and +, are rendered in LCAese respectively with the predicate adjectives *pitiful* (e.g., "The PLACE is pitiful") and *good* (e.g., "VIETNAM is good"). In a justification of a process, the valence code, E-, is rendered in LCAese using *ethically wrong* (e.g., "CHINA's doing harm was ethically wrong"). Each nominal syntactic component (i.e., audience, source, subject, and object) has a genitive associated with it. When both noun and genitive are phenomena (i.e., having codes > 101), genitives in LCAese take possessive forms such as "CHINA's MILITARY" (genitive = 213, noun = 239) or "VIETNAM's PLACE" (genitive = 214, noun = 120). When the genitive is the nominal form of a verb, in LCAese the noun becomes its object (e.g., "DEMAND of CHINA" [genitive = 28, noun = 213] and "OBLIGATION to WITHDRAW" [genitive = 3, noun = 56]). Whereas clauses 5, 7, 14, and 16 are recognition clauses with main verb codes of 1 (i.e., "is an instance of"), clause 19 is a recognition clause with a main verb code of 2 (i.e., "becomes"). (See footnote 10 for more detail on the four types of recognition clauses.) The three last columns indicate whether clause-weights are fractions of sentence-weights, what the base-weight is for all clauses with the same identifying information, and what the clause-weight is after taking a clause-specific weight and the other weight information into account.

TABLE 3

An LCA Data Matrix Encoded from the East German Broadcast

Field	Record 1	Record 2
Identifying information	ECHINA MAR09	ECHINA MAR09
Clause number	21	2
Sentence number	2	2
Depth in syntax tree (0=main clause, 1=subord. to main, etc.)	1	2
Functional form (P=1, R=2, J=3, or E=4)	0	0
Type of subordination (conjunctive, relative, or proxy)	1	1
Clause tense (1=past, 2=present, 3=future)	0	0
Question? (1=where, 2=when, etc.)	.	.
Clause valence (positive or negative, good or bad)	T	T
Genitive of audience	.	.
Audience	.	.
Genitive of source	.	.
Source	.	.
Genitive of subject	213	213
Subject	239	239
Modal auxiliary verb	33	50
Main verb	.	214
Genitive of object	.	.
Object	50 C	120 C
Weight info.	1.00 / 1.00	1.00 / 1.00

ECHINA	MAR09	3	3	0	1	.	1	0	T	.	.	240	213	239	.	50	214	120	C	1.00	1.00
ECHINA	MAR09	4	4	0	4	.	2	0	–	.	240	214	120	.	.	.	.	239	C	1.00	1.00
ECHINA	MAR09	5	5	0	2	.	2	0	NI	214	240	.	.	213	1	56	239	.	C	1.00	1.00
ECHINA	MAR09	6	6	0	1	.	1	0	SI	214	240	.	213	.	56	.	239	.	C	1.00	1.00
ECHINA	MAR09	7	7	0	2	.	2	0	T	214	240	.	.	213	1	213	239	.	C	1.00	1.00
ECHINA	MAR09	8	8	0	1	.	1	0	E–	.	.	.	213	99	.	.	.	.	C	1.00	0.50
ECHINA	MAR09	9	9	0	3	.	1	0	NI	.	.	.	213	99	.	.	.	.	C	1.00	0.50
ECHINA	MAR09	10	10	0	1	.	2	0	T	214	240	.	213	34	50	240	.	240	C	1.00	1.00
ECHINA	MAR09	11	11	0	1	.	1	0	T	214	240	213	239	50	240	.	200	200	C	1.00	1.00
ECHINA	MAR09	12	11	1	1	T	1	0	T	214	240	.	.	99	116	213	200	.	C	1.00	1.00
ECHINA	MAR09	13	12	0	1	.	1	0	T	.	.	211	201	24	28	213	.	201	C	1.00	1.00
ECHINA	MAR09	14	13	0	2	OR	2	0	T	211	201	211	17	1	214	17	17	.	C	1.00	1.00
ECHINA	MAR09	15	13	1	2	OP	2	0	T	211	201	214	17	20	.	.	.	214	C	1.00	1.00
ECHINA	MAR09	16	13	2	1	6	2	0	T	211	201	.	15	1	.	7	.	201	C	1.00	1.00
ECHINA	MAR09	17	13	3	3	.	2	0	T	.	213	3	56	41	29	214	.	213	C	1.00	1.00
ECHINA	MAR09	18	14	0	1	.	1	0	T	.	.	214	201	24	214	17	214	.	C	1.00	1.00
ECHINA	MAR09	19	15	0	2	.	2	0	T	214	201	214	.	2	214	17	.	214	C	1.00	1.00
ECHINA	MAR09	20	15	1	4	6	2	0	+	214	201	214	200	.	98	200	.	200	C	1.00	1.00

Source: The output in this table was generated by PLCA (MetaText, Inc.).

117

3.3. *A Statistical Analysis of the Encoded Data*

In analyzing LCA data one must be careful not to simultaneously analyze clauses encoded according to distinct functional forms. To do so would be to mix proverbial apples and oranges, leading to not-so-mixed-metaphorical garbage-in, garbage-out consequences. (More on this at the close of the next subsection.) Accordingly, the exploratory analysis in this subsection is restricted to the 275 perception-clauses in the data set. That is, the analysis is of processes described in East and West Berlin radio news coverage of two military conflicts.

To take the structure of the data set into account, terms for radio station (i.e., BR or SFB), event (i.e., CI or SR), and their interaction must be included in the analysis. In addition, let us consider which quoted source (i.e., a person, organization, or anthropomorphized country that is East-aligned, non–East-aligned,[28] or neutral, or the case of no quoted source) describes which subject (i.e., a person, organization, or country that is East-aligned, non–East-aligned, or neutral, or a nonvolitional thing such as a place, or the case of no subject given, as in passive voice) as the initiator of a process. Table 4 lists a series of hierarchical log-linear models in which various joint distributions among these four variables are fit to the LCA data.

The baseline model, Model (4), provides the best fit, given that its BIC statistic is the smallest among Models (1) through (3), in which a single term was added to the baseline model, and Models (5) through (7) in which a single term was dropped.[29] That is, no improvement in fit is gained by adding to this equation terms for QS, SE, or RQE interactions, and that a loss of fit results by removing RS, QE, or RQ from the equation. Model (4) has the following linear form:[30]

[28]Under non–East-aligned fall the non–East-aligned Chinese and the West-aligned Somosan parties to the respective conflicts.

[29]Raftery (1986a, 1986b) has proposed the Bayesian information criterion (or BIC) as an alternative to likelihood ratio tests for selecting among hierarchical log-linear models. The smaller the value of BIC, the better the fit. Although the [RE] interaction affords no improvement in fit, it is retained in all models to ensure that parameter estimates are conditioned for structure in the data resulting from the stratified sampling design.

[30]When a clause was broadcast by BR, $i = 1$, when broadcast by SFB, $i = 2$; when the source of a clause is East-aligned, $j = 1$, when non–East-aligned, $j = 2$, when neutral, $j = 3$, when no source is given, $j = 4$; when the subject of a clause is East-aligned, $k = 1$, when non–East-aligned, $k = 2$, when neutral, $k = 3$, when a thing or place, $k = 4$, when no subject is given, $k = 5$; when a clause is about the Chinese invasion, $l = 1$, when about the Sandinista Revolution, $l = 2$.

TABLE 4
Likelihood-Ratio Chi-Squares (L^2) for Hierarchical Loglinear Models

Model	Marginals Fitted	df	L^2	p	BIC
(1)	[RQ][RS][RE][QS][QE]	47	52.98	.254	−211.01
(2)	[RQ][RS][RE][QE][SE]	55	64.22	.185	−244.70
(3)	[RQE][RS]	57	68.30	.145	−251.86
(4)	[RQ][RS][RE][QE] (baseline)	59	77.21	.056	−254.18
(5)	[RQ][S][RE][QE]	63	101.45	.002	−252.41
(6)	[RQ][RS][RE]	62	101.26	.001	−246.98
(7)	[RS][RE][QE]	62	111.71	<.001	−236.53

Note. R = Radio station, Q = Quoted source, S = Semantic subject, E = Event. The [RE] interaction is included in all models to adjust for the stratified sampling design.

$$\ln(\hat{F}_{ijkl}) = \eta + \lambda_i^R + \lambda_j^Q + \lambda_k^S + \lambda_l^E + \lambda_{ij}^{RQ} + \lambda_{ik}^{RS} + \lambda_{il}^{RE} + \lambda_{jl}^{QE}$$

where i represents the two categories of radio station (R),

j represents the four categories of quoted source (Q),

k represents the five categories of semantic subject (S), and

l represents the two categories of event (E).

Table 5 lists the parameter estimates for Model (4). Significantly nonzero estimates of interactions with radio station yield findings on the rhetoric of political allegiance. For example, the interaction parameter associated with joint occurrences of Berliner Rundfunk radio station and the quotation of an East-aligned source is $\lambda_{ij(11)}^{RQ} = .59$. Conditional on other effects in the model, the log odds are four times this (i.e., 2.36) that a clause broadcast on Berliner Rundfunk mentioned an East-aligned (rather than another or no) person, organization, or country as the source being quoted, or that a clause on Sender Freies Berlin did not (rather than did) mention an East-aligned source. Further restricting this discussion to significant interaction parameters, in Table 5 one also finds the odds to be significantly greater that SFB (and less that BR) mentioned non-East-aligned persons, organizations, and countries either as the source of a quotation or as the initiator of a process. Thus it was in these ways that East and West Berlin radio stations cited and reported on parties with which their nations were politically aligned.

News coverage of the Chinese invasion of Vietnam contained a disproportionately large number of quotations from Eastern sources. That

TABLE 5
Parameter Estimates and Standard Errors for Model 4

Description	Estimate	Standard Error
Marginal Effects		
1. Station effects		
a. Berliner Rundfunk	.027	.124
b. Sender Freies Berlin	−.027	.124
2. Source effects		
a. East-aligned	−.367	.189
b. Non-East-aligned	−.526	.214
c. Neutral	−.573	.184
d. None given	1.466	.117
3. Subject effects		
a. East-aligned	.452	.141
b. Non–East-aligned	.919	.127
c. Neutral	.391	.141
d. Other (e.g., a place or thing)	−1.732	.331
e. None given (i.e., passive voice)	−.031	.159
4. Event effects		
a. Chinese invasion	.093	.087
b. Nicaragua revolution	−.093	.087
Interactions with Station[a]		
5. Station by quoted source effects		
a. Berliner Rundfunk and East-aligned source	.590	.163
b. Berliner Rundfunk and non–East-aligned source	−.950	.211
c. Berliner Rundfunk and neutral source	.257	.179
d. Berliner Rundfunk and no source given	.102	.112
6. Station by semantic subject effects		
a. Berliner Rundfunk and East-aligned subject	.234	.141
b. Berliner Rundfunk and non–East-aligned subject	−.498	.127
c. Berliner Rundfunk and neutral subject	−.032	.141
d. Berliner Rundfunk and other subject	.449	.331
e. Berliner Rundfunk and no subject given	−.153	.159
Interactions with Event[b]		
7. Event by station effects		
a. Chinese invasion and Berliner Rundfunk	.023	.067
b. Chinese invasion and Sender Freies Berlin	−.023	.067
8. Event by quoted source effects		
a. Chinese invasion and East-aligned source	.672	.174
b. Chinese invasion and non–East-aligned source	−.075	.152
c. Chinese invasion and neutral source	−.318	.175
d. Chinese invasion and no source given	−.279	.102

[a]Parameter estimates for interactions with Sender Freies Berlin are the negatives of those with Berliner Rundfunk.

[b]Parameter estimates for interactions with the Sandinista Revolution are the negatives of those with the Chinese invasion of Vietnam.

is, parameter estimates associated with the source-by-event interaction, [QE], show that significantly more clauses on CI than those on SR cited an Eastern source. In place of these Eastern citations, coverage of the Sandinista Revolution (in comparison to CI coverage) simply had more clauses unattributed to any source. Because the Chinese invasion was a communist conflict (i.e., a conflict between communist nations with utopian objectives that are presumably the same), both BR and SFB journalists may have believed Eastern sources were needed to explain this "Eastern event" to their respective audiences.

These are the sorts of inferences afforded when randomly sampled texts are encoded according to a generic semantic grammar. Each of the previous two paragraphs contains assertions (supported at the .05 significance level) about the relative frequencies of various types of clauses among the population of all clauses broadcast in two radio stations' coverage of two military conflicts. Moreover, these types of clauses are defined, in part, according to specific relations among the semantic components of the clauses themselves.

3.4. Inferences from Thematic Versus Semantic Text Analysis

The inferences drawn in the previous subsection are different from those afforded in more traditional thematic text analyses (e.g., Namenwirth 1973; Stone 1997; Stone et al. 1966; Weber 1990). For comparative purposes, the Berlin radio news data are now reanalyzed using traditional coding methods, retaining the clause as unit of analysis, and analyzing the same 275 perception clauses as before. Table 6 presents the data analyzed in the previous subsection; Table 7 provides data on the same clauses but encoded thematically. Both tables indicate how many clauses are associated with each combination of station and event. However, the semantically encoded data specify what the source and subject are for each clause, whereas the thematically encoded data list what combination of East, non-East, and neutral affiliates are mentioned (as audience, source, subject, or object) in each clause. For example, among clauses broadcast on Berliner Rundfunk about the Chinese Invasion, four clauses mentioned no person, organization, or country with any of the three (East, non-East, or neutral) types of alignment; 17 clauses mentioned only East-aligned person(s), organization(s), or country(ies); 11 mentioned both East-aligned and non–

TABLE 6

Cross-Classification of Clauses According to Event, Station, Source, and Subject

Semantic Subject	Source Quoted on Berliner Rundfunk				Source Quoted on Sender Freies Berlin			
	East	Non-East	Neutral	None	East	Non-East	Neutral	None
Chinese Invasion of North Vietnam								
East-aligned	7	0	0	13	2	3	0	5
Non–East-aligned	8	0	1	8	5	8	1	17
Neutral	1	0	2	9	0	1	0	9
Other	2	0	1	2	1	1	0	0
None	6	0	3	4	1	6	1	4
Sandinista Revolution								
East-aligned	0	1	2	20	0	1	2	9
Non–East-aligned	3	3	1	9	1	10	2	29
Neutral	2	0	1	16	1	3	2	11
Other	0	0	0	1	0	0	0	0
None	0	0	2	3	0	1	2	5

TABLE 7

Cross-Classification of Clauses According to Event, Station, and Occurrences of Various Combinations of Eastern, non-Eastern, and Neutral Alignment

			Chinese Invasion		Sandinista Revolution	
Pattern of Occurrences			Berliner Rundfunk	Sender Freies Berlin	Berliner Rundfunk	Sender Freies Berlin
East	non-East	neutral				
	none occurs		4	1	1	3
X			17	6	8	7
	X		4	20	9	26
		X	14	10	15	13
X	X		11	18	6	4
X		X	8	0	14	7
	X	X	4	10	6	18
X	X	X	5	0	4	2

East-aligned but not neutral person(s), organization(s), or country(ies); and so on.

Using the same modeling procedure as in the previous section,[31] the following log-linear model was determined to best fit the data in Table 7:[32]

$$\ln(\hat{F}_{ijklm}) = \eta + \lambda_i^R + \lambda_j^A + \lambda_k^O + \lambda_l^U + \lambda_m^E + \lambda_{ij}^{RA} + \lambda_{ik}^{RO}$$

$$+ \lambda_{im}^{RE} + \lambda_{jk}^{AO} + \lambda_{jl}^{AU} + \lambda_{kl}^{OU} + \lambda_{lm}^{UE}$$

where i represents the two categories of radio station (R),

j represents the two categories of Eastern alignment (A),

k represents the two categories of non–Eastern alignment (O)

l represents the two categories of neutral alignment (U), and

m represents the two categories of event (E).

[31] Tables for this analysis (i.e., ones similar to Tables 4 and 5) are available from the author on request.

[32] When a clause was broadcast by BR, $i = 1$, when broadcast by SFB, $i = 2$; when a clause mentions Eastern alignment, $j = 1$, otherwise $j = 2$; when a clause mentions non–Eastern alignment, $k = 1$, otherwise $k = 2$; when a clause mentions neutral alignment, $l = 1$, otherwise $l = 2$; when a clause is about the Chinese invasion, $m = 1$, when about the Sandinista Revolution, $m = 2$.

A lengthy discussion of this model's parameters is not necessary, given that my purpose in this subsection is solely to distinguish the types of inferences afforded in a thematic versus a semantic text analysis. In fact, a comparison of one parameter from each model will suffice for this purpose.

The $\lambda_{ij(11)}^{RQ}$ parameter from the previous analysis has affinities with the $\lambda_{ij(11)}^{RA}$ parameter in this one. The former statistic allowed the inference that the log odds were 2.36 "that a clause broadcast on BR mentioned an East-aligned (rather than another, or no) person, organization, or country *as the source being quoted*." Given that $\lambda_{ij(11)}^{RQ} = .23$, the thematic text analysis affords the inference that the log odds were .92 "that a clause broadcast on BR mentioned an East-aligned (rather than another, or no) person, organization, or country." The two inferences are substantively identical with the exception of the five words italicized at the end of the former. In brief, thematic text analysis affords inferences about the occurrence of various themes (or concepts) in texts; semantic text analysis affords inferences about how concepts are used within the framework of a (generic or other) semantic grammar.

Finally, it is important to note that in order to make this thematic text analysis comparable to the previous, semantic one, only perception clauses were analyzed. More commonly, all sampled text blocks (here all 400 sampled clauses) would have been scanned for theme occurrences. Changing emphasis for a moment, imagine that all 400 semantically encoded clauses are subjected to a statistical analysis. Superficially such an analysis has appeal because it would allow the addition of functional form to the variables in one's model. Now further imagine that the analysis reveals a relatively large number of BR clauses having an East-aligned subject. The only legitimate interpretation of this finding would be that the East German station (BR) mentioned East-aligned persons, organizations, or countries more often than the West German station (SFB) either as initiators of processes (among perception clauses), as attributes of some object (among recognition clauses), as initiators of positively or negatively judged processes (among justification clauses), or as itself the subject of a positive or negative judgment (among evaluation clauses). Clearly, such an interpretation would afford little more than could have been ascertained from a thematic text analysis. (In fact, less would be gained because only subject segments would have been scanned.) This is why statistical models of LCA data must generally be estimated using data encoded according to a single functional form.

4. CONCLUSION

This paper describes and then applies a text-encoding method for researchers who wish to draw probabilistic inferences about the prominence of semantically related themes within the clauses of a population of texts. Linguists have correctly noted that syntax grammars map themes' surface-grammatical relations and thus afford only ambiguous indicators of texts' intended meanings. In contrast, the generic semantic grammar described here can be used to generate an unambiguous encoding of any clause with identifiable meaning(s). Once the coder has divined a clause's meaning, the clause's themes and theme relations are fit into the functional form appropriate to this meaning. The semantic grammar consists of four such unambiguous functional forms, each of which has a unique semantic opposite. In addition, the semantic grammar affords a sufficiently fine-grained mapping of text that the validity of the encoded data can be evaluated by retranslating them back into a semblance of the original.

The central message of a recent collection on quantitative text analysis methods is that researchers must select the text analysis method that most closely matches the research question at hand (Roberts 1997). If one's objective is to use texts as a source of information about relational characteristics of some well-defined phenomenon (the event, the grievance, etc.), a phenomenal approach to semantic text analysis may be most appropriate (Franzosi 1994; Shapiro and Markoff, forthcoming). If one is primarily concerned with theme occurrences (but not theme relations), thematic text analysis may provide the best match (Stone 1997; Weber 1990). If one's research question requires that text blocks be depicted as sets of interrelated themes, a network text analysis method may be what is needed (Carley 1993; Kleinnijenhuis, de Ridder, and Rietberg 1997). The method presented here is for addressing research questions on how themes are related in relatively unstructured text populations—questions often of interest to students of culture and the media.

APPENDIX

Die Aggressionstruppen Pekings provozieren ungeachtet ihrer Rückzugs-einkündigungen vom Montag, immer neue Kämpfe. So lag die nordvietnamesische Provinzstadt 'Lan Shon' auch gestern unter sporadischem Artilleriefeuer der chinesischen Eindringlinge. Agenturmeldungen zu folge galt der Beschuß offenkundig erneut den Zufahrtsstraßen. Der Bahnhof und das Provinzkrankenhaus seien völlig zerstört. Wie der Sender 'Stimme Vietnams' berichtete, gibt es bisher noch keine Anzeichen für einen wirklichen Abzug der pekinger Truppen. An einigen Orten hätten die Chinesen lediglich bestimmte Mannschaften abgezogen. In anderen Gebieten hielten sie noch immer ihre Stellungen. Während ihrer Bewegungen verübten die Invasoren weiterhin barbarische Verbrechen. Nach Angaben der Nachrichtenagentur VNA sträubt sich China nicht, selbst ausländische Journalisten anzugreifen. Scharfschützen hätten in Lan Shon das Feuer auf eine Korrespondentengruppe eröffnet, wobei sie den Berichterstatter des Zentralorgans der KP Japans, Isau Takano ermordeten. Die Forderung der DDR nach sofortigen bedingungslosen Rückzug der chinesischen Aggressoren aus Vietnam ist gestern in Berlin vom Generalsekretär des ZK der SED und Vorsitzenden des Staatsrates Erich Honnecker bekräftigt worden. Die Republik teile die Meinung der SRV Regierung, daß Wachsamkeit nach wie vor geboten sei, da Peking seinen Rückzugsbefehlen mit neuen Drohungen gegen Vietnam verbunden habe. Die Siegeszuversicht seines Volkes über die chinesischen Eindringlinge verdeutlichte gestern Abend der Vorsitzende des vietnamesischen Friedenskomitees Fan An auf einem eindrucksvollen Meeting in Helsinki. Sie erwachse aus der Tatsache, so betonte er, daß die ganze friedliebende Menschheit an seiner Seite steht. (Berliner Rundfunk, 9. März 1979, 2e Meldung.)

REFERENCES

Abell, Peter. 1987. *The Syntax of Social Life: The Theory and Method of Comparative Narratives*. Oxford, England: Clarendon.

Andrén, Gunnar. 1981. "Reliability and Content Analysis." In *Advances in Content Analysis*, edited by K.E. Rosengren, 43–67. Beverly Hills, CA: Sage.

Austin, John L. 1975. *How to Do Things with Words: The William James Lectures Delivered at Harvard University in 1955*. Cambridge: Harvard University Press.

Carley, Kathleen M. 1993. "Coding Choices for Textual Analysis: A Comparison of Content Analysis and Map Analysis." In *Sociological Methodology, 1993*, edited by P. Marsden, 75–126. Cambridge, MA: Blackwell Publishers.

Dijk, Teun A. van. 1972. *Some Aspects of Text Grammars*. Paris: Mouton.

Dowty, David R. 1979. *Word Meaning and Montague Grammar: The Semantics of Verbs and Times in Generative Semantics and in Montague's PTQ*. Dordrecht, Netherlands: Reidel.

Eltinge, Elizabeth M., and Carl W. Roberts. 1993. "Linguistic Content Analysis: A Method to Measure Science as Inquiry in Textbooks," *Journal of Research in Science Teaching* 30:65–83.

Franzosi, Roberto. 1994. "From Words to Numbers: A Set Theory Framework for the Collection, Organization, and Analysis of Narrative Data." In *Sociological Methodology, 1994*, edited by P. Marsden, 105–36. Cambridge, MA: Blackwell Publishers.

Frege, Gottlob. 1959 [1884]. *The Foundations of Arithmetic: A Logico-Mathematical Enquiry into the Concept of Number*. Oxford: Blackwell Publishers.

Gottschalk, Louis A. 1968. "Some Applications of the Psychoanalytic Concept of Object Relatedness: Preliminary Studies on a Human Relations Scale Applicable to Verbal Samples." *Comprehensive Psychiatry* 9:608–20.

———. 1995. *Content Analysis of Verbal Behavior: New Findings and Computerized Clinical Applications*. Hillsdale, NJ: Lawrence Erlbaum.

Griemas, Algirdas-Julien. 1984 [1966]. *Structural Semantics: An Attempt at a Method*. Lincoln: University of Nebraska Press.

Griffin, Larry J. 1993. "Narrative, Event-Structure Analysis, and Causal Interpretation in Historical Sociology," *American Journal of Sociology* 98:1094–1133.

Habermas, Jürgen. 1979. *Communication and the Evolution of Society*. Boston: Beacon.

Halliday, Michael A. K. 1978. *Language as Social Semiotic*. London: Arnold.

———. 1994. *An Introduction to Functional Grammar*, 2nd ed. London: Arnold.

Heise, David R. 1988. "Computer Analysis of Cultural Structures." *Social Science Computer Review* 6:183–96.

———. 1991. "Event Structure Analysis: A Qualitative Model of Quantitative Research." In *Using Computers in Qualitative Research*, edited by N.G. Fielding and R.M. Lee, 136–63. London: Sage.

Hoey, Michael. 1994. "Signalling in Discourse: A Functional Analysis of a Common Discourse Pattern in Written and Spoken English." In *Advances in Written Text Analysis*, edited by M. Coulthard, 26–45. London: Routledge.

Johnson-Laird, Philip N. 1970. "The Perception and Memory of Sentences." In *New Horizons in Linguistics*, edited by J. Lyons, 261–70. Middlesex, England: Penguin.

Kleinnijenhuis, Jan, Jan A. de Ridder, and Ewald M. Rietberg. 1997. "Reasoning in Economic Discourse: An Application of the Network Approach to the Dutch Press." In *Text Analysis for the Social Sciences: Methods for Drawing Statistical Inferences from Texts and Transcripts*, edited by C.W. Roberts, 191–207. Mahwah, NJ: Lawrence Erlbaum.

Lakoff, George, and Mark Johnson. 1980. *Metaphors We Live By*. Chicago: University of Chicago Press.

Markoff, John. 1988. "Allies and Opponents: Nobility and the Third Estate in the Spring of 1789," *American Sociological Review* 53:477–96.

Markoff, John, Gilbert Shapiro, and Sasha R. Weitman. 1974. "Toward the Integration of Content Analysis and General Methodology." In *Sociological Methodology, 1975*, edited by D.R. Heise, 1–58. San Francisco: Jossey-Bass.

MetaText Inc. 1994. *User's Manual for PLCA (Program for Linguistic Content Analysis)*. MetaText, Inc.

Namenwirth, J. Zvi. 1973. "The Wheels of Time and the Interdependence of Value Change," *Journal of Interdisciplinary History* 3:649–83.

Popping, Roel. 1997. "Computer Programs for the Analysis of Texts and Transcripts." In *Text Analysis for the Social Sciences: Methods for Drawing Statistical Inferences from Texts and Transcripts*, edited by C.W. Roberts, 209–221. Mahwah, NJ: Lawrence Erlbaum.

Propp, Vladimir. 1968 [1928]. *Morphology of the Folktale*, 2nd ed. Austin: University of Texas Press.

Raftery, Adrian E. 1986a. "A Note on Bayes Factors for Log-linear Contingency Table Models with Vague Prior Information," *Journal of the Royal Statistical Society Series B* 48:249–50.

———. 1986b. "Choosing Models for Cross-Classifications," *American Sociological Review* 51:145–46.

Roberts, Carl W. 1989. "Other than Counting Words: A Linguistic Approach to Content Analysis," *Social Forces* 68:147–77.

———. 1991. "Linguistic Content Analysis." In *Verstehen and Pragmatism: Essays on Interpretative Sociology*, edited by H.J. Helle, 283–309. Frankfurt: Peter Lang.

———, ed. 1997. *Text Analysis for the Social Sciences: Methods for Drawing Statistical Inferences from Texts and Transcripts*. Mahwah, NJ: Lawrence Erlbaum.

Rumelhart, David E. 1975. "Notes on a Schema for Stories." In *Representation and Understanding: Studies in Cognitive Science*, edited by D.G. Bobrow and A. Collins, 211–36. New York: Academic.

Schrodt, Philip A. 1991. "Pattern Recognition of International Event Sequences: A Machine Learning Approach." In *Artificial Intelligence and International Politics*, edited by V.M. Hudson, 169–93. Boulder, CO: Westview.

———. 1993. "Machine Coding of Event Data." In *Theory and Management of International Event Data: DDIR Phase II*, edited by R.L. Merritt, R.G. Muncaster, and D.A. Zinnes, 117–40. Ann Arbor: University of Michigan Press.

Searle, John R., and Daniel Vanderveken. 1985. *Foundations of Illocutionary Logic*. Cambridge: Cambridge University Press.

Shapiro, Gilbert. 1997. "The Future of Coders: Human Judgments in a World of Sophisticated Software." In *Text Analysis for the Social Sciences: Methods for Drawing Statistical Inferences from Texts and Transcripts*, edited by C.W. Roberts, 225–238. Mahwah, NJ: Lawrence Erlbaum.

Shapiro, Gilbert, and John Markoff. Forthcoming. *Revolutionary Demands: A Content Analysis of the Cahiers de Doléances of 1789*. Stanford, CA: Stanford University Press.

Stone, Philip J. 1997. "Thematic Text Analysis: New Agendas for Analyzing Text Content." In *Text Analysis for the Social Sciences: Methods for Drawing Statistical Inferences from Texts and Transcripts*, edited by C.W. Roberts, 35–54. Mahwah, NJ: Lawrence Erlbaum.

Stone, Philip J., Dexter C. Dunphy, Marshall S. Smith, and Daniel M. Ogilvie. 1966. *The General Inquirer: A Computer Approach to Content Analysis*. Cambridge: MIT Press.

Thomas, Lisa, and David R. Heise. 1995. "Mining Error Variance and Hitting Pay-Dirt: Discovering Systematic Variation in Social Sentiments," *Sociological Quarterly* 36:425–39.

Weber, Max. 1973 [1906]. "Kritische Studien auf dem Gebiet der Kulturwissenschaftlichen Logik" (Critical Studies in the Logic of the Cultural Sciences). In *Gesammelte Aufsätze zur Wissenschaftslehre* (Collected Essays on the Scientific Method), edited by J. Winckelmann, 215–90. Tübingen, Germany: Mohr.

Weber, Robert P. 1990. *Basic Content Analysis*, 2nd ed. Newbury Park, CA: Sage.

Winter, Eugene. 1994. "Clause Relations as Information Structure: Two Basic Text Structures in English." In *Advances in Written Text Analysis*, edited by M. Coulthard, 46–68. London: Routledge.

COMMENT: THE IMPORTANCE OF ORDER

*Kathleen M. Carley**

Abbott and Barman present and illustrate a technique for locating common sequences. This is an important technique for locating and analyzing order. This technique, and others like it, are very important within sociology because they can be used to empirically locate and determine the significance of potentially illusive patterns. As this paper illustrates, this approach is important in the sociology of science for locating patterns of rhetorical form and changes in those patterns over time. And, as the authors note, this approach can be used with temporal sequences to look at rituals and career paths. But let me suggest a few other areas where this technique could play a vital role: In looking at the impact of technology it could be used to look at whether or how patterns of communication change with technology. Within the field of organizations, it could be used to look at whether there are common patterns of change in organizational structure over time. This technique could also be used to assess the prevalence of common rhetorical forms in reports to stockholders and so assess the nature of organizational accountability.

While the value of this technique is evident, its applicability may be limited. Coding texts at the level of detail undertaken by the authors is a formidable task. Such detailed content analysis is labor intensive and the authors are to be lauded for the detail of their coding. However, issues of inter-rater reliability and distinctiveness of the content categories (which were not addressed in this article) become critical for this level of coding. In general, multiple coders should be used and tests on the difference in the categories should be conducted. For the techniques the authors have proposed to become more commonly used for textual analysis, more automated approaches to coding texts and approaches that minimize issues of inter-rater reliability will be needed. In the final analysis, what sequences are found, and their commonness across texts, is highly dependent on the level of coding and the reliability of the coding. Techniques for coding texts need to become much less researcher intensive if sequence analysis is

*Carnegie-Mellon University. E-mail: Kathleen.Carley@ centro.soar.cs.cmu.edu

to become a more common method in this domain. The field of sociology would benefit if more of our students were trained to perform analyses such as these.

The LEA technique with Gibbs sampling is a stochastic-based search technique and there is no discussion of its convergence properties. That is, the authors do not discuss whether it, like simulated annealing, has been proven to converge on the global optimum; whether the convergence is guaranteed in a reasonable amount of time; and the likelihood that the procedure is converging on a local optimum. Just because the same sequence was found in three trials does not mean that it is necessarily the optimum sequence (i.e., the sequence with the highest frequency), although it is suggestive that this is the case. It may be that this particular problem is small enough, and the search space well enough behaved, that in fact the global optimum is relatively easy to locate. Some research needs to be done on the nature of the space of rhetorical sequences in scientific articles to determine whether in fact this particular technique is the best suited for this particular problem or whether other search techniques, like simulated annealing or genetic algorithms, would be a preferred choice for this particular type of data.

Finally, there are a few issues one can take with the particular data used for illustrating this approach and the analysis of that data. One of them has to do with the generality of the results and the other with the interpretation of those results. First, this analysis may tell us little about sociological writing in general. The authors focused on a single journal where all the editors are drawn from the same department. This discounts the fact that there are styles of research and styles of evaluation that become typical of departments and that are often reinforced through hiring and promotion practices. This limitation of the data makes it unclear whether or not the results will generalize to the wider discipline. Of course, the technique presented by the authors could be used to test whether in fact there is a difference in rhetorical style across the different journals (or between different disciplines). Indeed, the authors' claim that by focusing on one central journal they can locate changes in rhetorical style due to central disciplinary forces can be tested empirically using the techniques they have presented.

Second, Abbot and Barman find that there are more articles with the same rhetorical form in the latter decades than in earlier decades. Indeed, over one-third of the articles in the last decade are of the same form. Moreover, they show that the prevalence of these common forms in later years is significantly greater than that expected by chance. They conclude, however, that there is only weak evidence for rhetorical tightness. This conclusion, however, should be tempered by the fact that although they used a stratified quota sample of empirical articles the number of empirical articles has been increasing dramatically over time. Assuming their sample is representative, then weighting the results by the number of articles of that type suggests that their results are fairly strong evidence for increasing rhetorical rigidity.

The foregoing limitations and difficulties in doing this type of analysis, however, are not the point to focus on. Rather, the point is that Abbott and Barman have presented and clearly illustrated an important technique with many applications within the social sciences for examining the prevalence and importance of order. The use and development of these types of techniques are critical to understanding the processes of change.

COMMENT: ON AMBIGUITY AND RHETORIC IN (SOCIAL) SCIENCE

*Roberto Franzosi**

There is a common thread that runs through Roberts' and Abbott and Barman's articles: an untrammeled faith in the supreme virtues of science, rigor, formalism, hypothesis testing, statistics, particularly new, sophisticated statistical techniques. Expressions that attest to such a view abound in the two papers (e.g., "probabilistic inferences," "unambiguous encoding," "rigor," "new algorithm," "formally evaluate," "formal sequence analysis"). The authors are driven by a common goal of getting away from the murky waters of personal interpretations in the social sciences. They are animated by the firm belief that exact measurements and formal constructs is the way to go.

I am sympathetic to that manifesto. As someone who has been actively involved in the search for solutions to substantive and methodological problems similar to those addressed by these authors, I applaud their "noble dream." I do share the authors' belief that formalism may add precision to our theoretical frameworks, that conceptual rigor is better than muddled argumentation, that counting, whenever possible, is better than guessing. Yet, a close reading of these articles reveals scientific practices that leave me quite skeptical about that optimistic view of science.

I will use Roberts' own concept of ambiguity to highlight the many ambiguities that creep in beneath his method of "unambiguous encoding." Similarly, I will use Abbott and Barman's concept of rhetoric to illustrate the rhetorical devices that the authors use in the construction of their argumentation. Perhaps, there is no way out of ambiguity in science, and, certainly, there is no way out of rhetoric—no matter how we choose to present our points, our presentation will always reflect certain rhetorical practices. But within the infinite ways of writing science, there are ways that are more or less open, more or less transparent about the conditions of their own production (or if you will, that what is shoved under the rug, is

*University of Oxford, Trinity College. E-mail: roberto.franzosi@socres.ox.ac.uk

as visible—well, almost as visible—as what stands on it). So, in the end, read my commentary as just a plea for self-reflectivity in science.

Carl Roberts is driven by the attempt to solve a problem that has long plagued content analysis: that of providing "unambiguous encoding of any clause." According to Roberts, content analysis based on the S-V-O (Subject-Verb-Object) structure works well only when applied to "structured" text. But not all texts are structured, Roberts remarks. Some are "unstructured." And unstructured texts have a different surface representation than structured texts. Content analysis of these texts on the basis of an S-V-O semantic grammar is impossible. In any case, S-V-O structures are semantically ambiguous.

In order to overcome the limitations of semantic grammars based on the S-V-O structure, Roberts sets out to develop a "generic" semantic grammar that could be applied to any kind of text. Roberts proposes a grammar based on unambiguous semantic opposites formally set up with the use of logic. This "generic semantic grammar [Roberts assures us] can be used to generate an unambiguous encoding of any clause." These claims warrant close attention. If Roberts is right, he would have solved a problem that has eluded linguists and philosophers alike (and we should definitely inform both disciplines of this breakthrough coming from sociology).

Roberts's task requires a great deal of linguistic and logical formalism. At the end of these tribulations, I would expect Roberts to emerge victorious with a linguistic structure in hand capable of capturing the complexity of "unstructured" text (and, needless to say, that structure should be *different* from an S-V-O structure). I would also expect Roberts to prove to the reader that his newly found "generic" semantic grammar works well when applied to "unstructured" text. Is this what we get?

What we get is not that easy to grasp. The reader has to weed through the linguistic and logic paraphernalia of speech acts, utterances, ordinary discourse, semantic opposites, predicates, and symbols, to disambiguate a great deal of ambiguous prose, to cut and paste from the abstract, conclusions, footnotes, and examples, to focus on the details of the encoding process. But what we do get, in the end, after our own tribulations, is, *again*, an S-V-O structure in disguise, with the addition of an evaluation of the actors and of the actions. The Recognition, $R = (x)a(x)$, is nothing but the "who," the actor involved; the Perception, $P = (x)p(x)$, is the process, the "what," the action. The Evaluation $E = (x)a(x) \, Q_a$, and Justification, $P = (x)p(x) \, Q_p$, provide a way to code evaluative statements. "Franzosi's semantic grammar—we are told—does not lend itself readily to evaluative statements." Why, do I wonder, could not one rewrite any of the categories in Franzosi's semantic grammar (events, semantic triplets, actors, actions, etc.) with the addition of an evaluative modifier? Be that as it may, what Roberts throws out with grand clamor from the front door (the S-V-O structure) comes back through the back door under a disguised name.

Roberts never clarifies the linguistic differences between "structured" and "unstructured" texts, despite the central position of this distinction in his argument. Roberts is right in claiming that there are texts that conform to the S-V-O structure and texts that do not. Linguists would refer to the first type of text as narrative, where some actors (S), with some characteristics, perform actions (V), again with their characteristics, pro or against some other actors (O). Linguists would also confirm that narrative represents only one type of text genre. Other text genres (e.g., journal articles, to remain in theme) do not conform to the simple noun phrase/verb phrase representation (the S-V-O structure). That hardly makes one text genre structured and another unstructured. Rather, it makes the narrative and nonnarrative texts structured in different ways. Roberts's "generic" semantic grammar would have to capture the greater linguistic complexity of nonnarrative texts. That is not what Roberts delivers.

The LCA data matrix generated by PLCA in output makes explicit the close connection of a "generic" semantic grammar to the S-V-O structure (see the labels Subject, Main verb, and Object). The LCA (re)translation of Roberts' example is in the form S-V-O (e.g., S: China V: encourages O: violence; S: China V: acts violently O: Vietnam). And for good reasons. After all, contrary to expectations, the example that Roberts chooses to elucidate his "generic" grammar is of narrative type, and, therefore, based on an S-V-O structure. In that example, we find actors, such as China, Vietnam, DDR, Japan Communist Party, journalists, sharpshooters, peace committee, and more) performing actions such as provoke fighting, destroy, fire artillery, commit crimes, open fire, etc. We also find implicit and explicit evaluations of actors and situations which Roberts proposes to code. A laudable effort, if an investigator is interested in the ideological aspects of news. But Roberts's "generic" grammar does not provide explicit *linguistic* rules to capture valuative and ideological mechanisms. Typically, valuative statements are disguised by choice of words (some classics: terrorist vs. freedom fighter, entrepreneurial hero vs. robber barron), metaphors (e.g., "time is money"), etc. Much of the moral indignation (negative evaluation) found in Roberts's example comes from the subtle manipulation of language as in "*Despite* their withdrawal notification . . ." "*flagrantly* anew," "*still* no indication of a real withdrawal," "China does *not even* resist attacking." If Roberts's aim is that of eliminating the ambiguity involved in the process of coding, neither his generic semantic grammar nor his example leave me convinced.

Roberts's paper offers readers a roller-coaster ride between ambiguity and disambiguity (the rhetoric of science). Bold statements mix together with cautious ones. Thus we read: "the four functional forms [of his "generic" semantic grammar] provide coders with structure in their strivings to map sources' inherently ambiguous meanings into unambiguous code"; "The theme relations allowed in this grammar only permit unambiguous encoding according to the meanings that clauses were intended to convey within their social context." For all of that, Roberts is well aware that a generic semantic grammar does not rid content analysis of the ambiguities involved in text coding. He is also well aware of "the role of the reader": "The selection of functional forms requires that the coder understands both the source's intentions and the social context within which the clause appeared"; "Applying a semantic grammar requires that speech acts are understood in terms of their respective situational contexts. . . . Invalid code will almost surely result when coders are insufficiently familiar with these contexts"; "Coder's intuition regarding these contexts . . . will be necessary when this generic semantic grammar is used in encoding text"; "The translation from words to numbers requires that coders make considerable use of both their intuition of the source's meanings and their knowledge of the situational context."

As a result of these ambiguities, "some coder disagreement is inevitable"—intercoder reliability, the bane and boon of content analysts. Yet, for Roberts, these problems of understanding can all be solved via the development of the "code book," the talisman of content analysis of old: "when coding rules have been conscientiously developed and applied, coders are likely to attain consistently high agreement in LCA encodings." "Disagreements among coders are, of course, the makings of poor interrater agreement. However, they are also the "grist" in the development of explicit coding rules." And if any difficulties remain: "During regular meetings, the coders met to jointly resolve differences in their encodings in the light of an evolving set of consistent coding rules." In the end, all that ambiguity can be shrugged off: "when coding rules have been conscientiously developed and applied, coders are likely to attain consistently high agreement in LCA codings." "The four functional forms *are correctly* applied within the source's situational context—a context *hopefully* familiar to both coder and audience." And where the code book and the four functional forms do not succeed in stamping out ambiguity, LCA encoding will, because "LCA encoding requires more of coders that they merely identify subjects and predicates; they must commit themselves to unambiguous encodings of often ambiguous linguistic expressions." That is the important thing: that coders should commit themselves to one form of coding or another, regardless of the ambiguities of the text.

Roberts's own ambiguities are clear in the Section *Encoding Clauses*, which describes an example of coding and is filled with verbs that convey doubt and uncertainty: "Words such as . . . *are likely* to be encoded as"; "The sentence *might be* rendered as . . ."; "*Might be* rendered as . . ." (three times). Wasn't this supposed to be an unambiguous process? But at the end of a page filled with such markers of ambiguity, we find the word "rigor." Certainly, Roberts's conclusions contain no trace of ambiguities: "The generic semantic grammar described here can be used to generate an unambiguous encoding of any clause with identifiable meaning(s)." After all, "transparent to the user, the encoding process involves a translation from text to numbers (i.e., to an unambiguous matrix representation)." In the realm of numbers, things are finally *unambiguous*, the ambiguities of the process of generating those numbers forgotten.

And yet, even in that realm, ambiguities do not wither away and keep haunting us. Take the conclusions in Abbott and Barman's paper, for instance: "Substantively, these analyses show that the evidence for rhetorical rigidification in sociology articles is weak indeed." These conclusions are based on numbers and on the statistical analysis of those numbers. Yet, those numbers do not seem to lead us away from ambiguity. The adjective "weak" attached to "evidence of rigidification" underscored by the adverb "indeed" leaves us wondering about the precise level of weakness. The ambiguity of words has crept back in with the interpretation of numbers. Ambiguity in the interpretation of results is further underscored by the sentence that follows in the text. "While there is some evidence of more recent authors' writing to a clearer template (the subsequence evidence), the actual results in both early and late periods remain diverse." The adverbial beginning of the sentence ("while") qualifies the ending of the previous sentence ("weak indeed"). What the authors are saying is that, yes, there is some evidence for rigidification, but that evidence is so weak that we can forget about it and focus on the fact that "the *actual* results in both early and late periods remain diverse" [my emphasis]. I look up the adjective "actual" and obtain the following synonyms: concrete, genuine, real, tangible, accurate, correct, factual, even true appears in the list. Does this mean that the results that were the basis for the conclusions reached in the previous sentences were not concrete, genuine, real, tangible, accurate, correct, factual, or true?

The ambiguity of numbers does not stop there. Abbott and Barman claim that supposedly "most of us" believe that around 1965–1970 the rhetorical structure of sociology journal articles became more rigidified. They repeat their claim several times through such expressions as "most of us believe" or "by general account." Eventually, they use that claim as a basis for the choice of 1965 as the end point of their sample period. The authors provide no evidence and no references to justify their claim. This is quite uncharacteristic for authors who provide pages of references to a statistical method. Even more uncharacteristic for authors who accuse Bazerman of "relying on the *informed* judgment of a *recollecting* reader." How quickly we forget! Such uncharacteristic lack of rigor and validation in the choice of the sample period leaves me wondering whether, in fact, the authors picked their sample period (1895–1965) in order to take advantage of available material from the *American Journal of Sociology* (AJS) cumulative index based on those same years, 1895–1965, and, *then*, tried very hard to find plausible, *substantive* justifications for their choice (quite a common rhetorical device). In fact, moving the end point of the sample period closer to us would have given Abbott and Barman much stronger ammunition for their argument, had they found no evidence of increasing rigidification in recent decades (1965–1995).

Which points to another weakness in the research design: the choice of AJS as source of their data. Again, the authors spend an entire subsection justifying the use of AJS. Methodological choices should be commensurate to one's substantive and theoretical aims. And what is Abbott and Barman's aim? To test the hypothesis of an increased rigidification in the rhetorical formats of sociological articles. But why, then, AJS? AJS is "a central, high-prestige, *general-interest* journal" that provides a forum for a wide and (increasingly) fragmented audience. Consistent with the perceived role and position of the journal in the discipline, AJS editors have taken "drastic measures" to find interesting and *diverse* work, as the authors themselves inform us (footnote 3). In competition with AJS, there has been a great proliferation of disciplinary journals over the years, particularly after World War II, each addressing specialized substantive, theoretical, and methodological interests and concerns. I would expect specialized journals to be more rigid in the rhetorical formats of their articles than general-interest journals. After all, specialized journals address communities likely to share more restricted epistemological assumptions, language conventions, and scientific paradigms. Under these conditions (explicit editorial policies of AJS and proliferation of specialized journals), should anyone be surprised to find a lack of strong evidence in favor of rigidification in AJS? The lack of evidence for rigidification in AJS could hardly be taken as evidence for the lack of rhetorical rigidification in the discipline. I rather like a different type of research design, one based on the worst-case (rather than best-case) scenario. And that scenario would be something like this: (1) let us take a specialized journal, one where we would expect greater rigidification; (2) let us analyze the articles for rhetorical rigidification; (3) if there is no evidence of rigidification there, it is unlikely that it will be elsewhere. I would have found that type of research design more convincing.

Alternatively, the authors could have taken a different line of argumentation. They could have started their argument, as they do, by pointing to the widespread perception that sociological journal production has become more and more rigidified. Then, they could have said: let us take the journal which is more likely to have maintained, in fact, actively fostered intellectual and rhetorical diversity, AJS. The logic being: If we find evidence of rigidification even in that journal, then, there must really be "central disciplinary forces" at work. They could have then used their evidence for some rigidification in the decades after World War II to conclude: Indeed, there appears to be some evidence toward rigidification even in the journal where we are least likely to expect it.

But the logic of that argument would have required a different contextual setting of the authors' work in the "literature." Abbott and Barman do not present a full-blown literature review of rhetoric, just a couple of paragraphs in a section mostly dedicated to issues of research design (after all, this is a method paper). But in their literature review, however short, they set up their work in opposition to that of Bazerman. That is quite a common rhetorical practice: setting up straw "men," real or imaginary windmills, with whom we engage in portentous battles, only to emerge victorious heroes in the end. In fact, perhaps, that practice brings us closest to the Aristotelian meaning of rhetoric as the art of persuasion in the arena of politics (which involves dealing with opponents).

Bazerman is first introduced at the beginning of the paper as someone "who comes closest to the task we undertake here." "Closest" for sure, but not close enough. A formidable opponent but not a serious contender.

After all, "Bazerman's *detailed* reading of *three* political science articles, however *subtle*, is *vulnerable* to the idiosyncrasies of the *particular* articles chosen and is in many ways more *illustrative* than *definitive*." Positive and negative meanings mix together in this sentence to construct an overall negative rhetorical portrait of Bazerman. Bazerman's reading is "detailed" (which is good) but it is based on only "three" articles (which is bad; compare to the 99 that the authors coded). Furthermore, those three articles were too "particular" to be of scientific validity (which, again, is bad; compare to the authors' scientifically drawn stratified sample of articles). Bazerman's analyses, also, are "illustrative" (which is bad; compare to those of the authors which are based on rigorous coding). "Illustrative" is explicitly introduced here in polar opposition to "definitive." Having set up the duality Bazerman versus Abbott-Barman throughout the paper, the authors now introduce another duality ("illustrative" versus "definitive"). In pairing the first terms of the two dualities (Bazerman = illustrative), they leave it to the reader to pair the second terms (Abbott-Barman = definitive).

Bazerman's reading is not only "detailed." It is also "subtle." Now, is that good or bad? Given that this adjective is introduced after the authors tell us that Bazerman only read three articles (which is bad), the "however" between "three" and "subtle" seems to imply that "subtle" is a good thing. Yet, I look up the synonyms of the adjective "subtle:" elusive, implied, indirect, insinuated, astute, cunning, shrewd, sly. The use of this adjective seemingly intended to provide a positive evaluation of Bazerman's analyses (coming after the "however") ultimately leaves the reader with the negative meanings best underscored by the list of synonyms.

Finally, just a few sentences later, Bazerman's work is depicted as having "no basis on formal measurement, relying rather on the informed judgment of a recollecting reader." Again, compare with the authors' approach, where sentences are formally coded and those codes are fed into the computer for statistical analysis. There is no danger here of ever forgetting anything. In fact, all this scientific paraphernalia ultimately produces "serious evidence" (first paragraph of the conclusions). By the end of a paragraph where the adjective "clear" appears four times, the evidence is neither weak nor strong, nor actual; it is simply "serious." So, get serious, Mr. Bazerman! "The rhetorical rigidity seen by analysts like Bazerman in modern social science is probably in the eye of the beholder."

And that, of course, does not go for Bazerman alone. After all, Bazerman is only one of many people who hold false beliefs about the rhetorical rigidification of sociological articles. "Most of us" do, Abbott and Barman assure us. If Bazerman is wrong, then, we are all wrong. This may just be an extreme case of "us versus them," of lining up friends and foes in this rhetorical battle against the windmills. The more, of course, in the enemy camp, the greater the honor that accrues to the hero. It is in the "literature review" section that we line up friends and foes. Abbott and Barman point to the emergence of this rhetorical device in the "modern" journal article, but they do not elaborate upon it. But it is in the literature review section that we set up the terrain for our battles. It is there that we set the context in which to interpret our findings. The main mechanism of those reviews is silence and emphasis, the downplaying and up-playing of argument, authors, theories, methods, data, and findings. Available work on mass media tells us that those same mechanisms of us versus them, of silence and emphasis operate there to produce ideology. But if ideological rhetorical mechanisms underlie both scientific and journalistic production, what does that say about our ideals of science as truth?

So, OK—you may retort—there are some problems in design. The authors may even be guilty, implicitly or explicitly, consciously or unconsciously, of tooting their own horn (but . . . aren't we all?). So what? Since when does rhetoric undermine serious statistical work? Fair enough. So, let us take a closer look at that statistical work. After presenting the first four tables, Abbott and Barman reassure the reader that "the results are fairly robust" (again, more of those nagging qualifiers of those numbers that Roberts finds so unambiguous—that "fairly" attached to "robust," perhaps making those results not so robust, or just somewhat robust). In any case, those results may well be "robust"—this time, in a statistical sense, given that the results presented in the tables are not based on probabilistic assumptions—but they are certainly not "resistant."

The statistical analyses of Tables 1 through 6 are based on the mean and standard deviation applied to seven samples of median size 15. Now, the mean of any sample, but particularly of a sample of size 15, has "an important weakness . . . as a measure of center: it is sensitive to the influence of a few extreme observations." (Moore and McCabe 1993:37). And problems compound with the use of the standard deviation, s, as a measure of spread. "In fact . . . squared deviations [from the mean] renders s even more sensitive to a few extreme observations than is the mean" (Moore and McCabe 1993:49). So, if even introductory statistics textbooks (albeit, of such high caliber as Moore and McCabe's) warn us to stay away from the mean and the standard deviation, particularly when very small samples are involved, why do we still find them in use? How can authors who went through the trouble of applying a "new algorithm" that can find "a needle in a haystack" break such elementary rules of sound statistical analysis? The ill effects on the statistical results due to the use of nonresistant measures of centrality and spread applied to very small samples are likely to be further compounded by the stratified nature of those samples, with four articles per decade within each of four categories: experimental, quantitative, survey, and case analysis articles. Could articles have become rigidified within, rather than across, substantive and methodological subspecialties?

Enough, I will conclude with a quote taken from Abbott and Barman's article. "At a distance these empirical articles [the AJS articles in their sample] are often indistinguishable. Only by coding them in some detail can we see changes in the nature of their form." At a distance, I myself find the articles in this issue of *Sociological Methodology* indistinguishable in their high-trumpeted sales pitch for high tech and formalism. But when I look more closely, beyond the razzle-dazzle of science, I find a strange mixture of rhetorical devices and a great deal of background-ing and foregrounding, of silences and emphases, of ad hoc literature reviews, of elementary problems in the statistical handling of data. For looking closely, Bazerman's tools of in-depth analysis come in handy. And what they reveal, in social science at its best, is not particularly uplifting. And then the problem for me, personally, becomes: can I do better? Would my own work survive Roberto Franzosi's close scrutiny? As the answer to both questions is "no," I am left with the uneasy and pessimistic feelings that come from self-reflecting on the meaning of work we feel so passionately about.

REFERENCE

Moore, David S., and George P. McCabe. 1993. *Introduction to the Practice of Statistics* (2nd ed.), New York: W.H. Freeman.

COMMENT: ON LOGICAL FORMALIZATION OF THEORIES FROM ORGANIZATIONAL ECOLOGY

Michael T. Hannan*

Theory formalization, once positioned at center stage in sociology, currently plays little role in general sociological work. For about a decade beginning in the mid-1960s, the promise was held out that formalization—especially mathematization—would improve the quality of sociological theorizing and promote the development of cumulative theoretical knowledge about general social processes (see, for instance, Coleman 1964; Blalock 1969). Today, formalization lies on the discipline's periphery, as a specialized activity remote from the development and evaluation of sociological theories.[1] This marginalization and devaluation of formalization partly reflects sociology's retreat from general ("ahistorical") formulations. But it also surely reflects an assessment that the payoff to the style of formalization prominent during the heyday of this movement had not met expectations.

This is not the place to attempt a full assessment of what went wrong in sociology's flirtation with formalization.[2] But one thing seems clear: there was a mismatch between theories and formalization tools. The available natural-language theories were—and are—partial and imprecise; use of the formal languages, especially mathematics, demanded closure and extreme (usually metric) precision. Efforts at formalizing sociological theories with classical tools required the analyst to assume too much—e.g., to supply the missing assumptions about metrics, continuity, and differentiability of functions. As a result, the formalizations offered during this period yielded models that failed to resonate closely with the original theories.

Preparation of this comment was supported by a grant from the Alfred P. Sloan Foundation. E-mail: hannan@leland.stanford.edu

*Stanford University

[1] Sørensen (1978) discusses these developments in detail for the enterprise of mathematical sociology.

[2] Patterns of recruitment to the discipline must surely play a role; by any measure, sociology does not fare well in recruiting technically skilled students.

The formalizers tended to blame the theorists for not building sufficiently precise theories, and theorists increasingly stopped paying attention.

The CCSOM project (a collaboration by a group of sociologists, logicians, and computer scientists located primarily at the Center for Computer Science in Organization and Management at the University of Amsterdam) is a notable effort to reassert the importance of formalization for sociological theory by bringing more flexible tools to bear on the problem. Instead of relying on mathematics or the classical propositional logic to represent theoretical structures, this group uses First-Order Logic (FOL) and automated theorem provers. FOL allows natural language statements to be given an expression that is formal (in the sense that it can be used in calculations by a theorem prover) yet remains close to the natural language. The semantic richness of FOL narrows the gap between the theorist's statement and the formalizer's rendition. The power of automated theorem provers, such as OTTER, allows logical assessment of the kind of complex structures that proliferate in sociological theory.

The CCSOM group has demonstrated the value of this kind of formalization largely by seeking to "rationally reconstruct" fragments of organizational ecology. To date, its members have proposed both logical and mathematical formalizations of five strands of theory in organizational ecology: theories of structural inertia (Péli et al. 1994; Kamps and Masuch 1996), life history strategies (Péli and Masuch 1997), density dependence (Péli 1993), niche width (Bruggeman 1997; Péli, this volume), and resource partitioning (Péli 1996). Although the mathematical formalizations follow paths familiar to sociologists, the formalizations in FOL do not. The latter take a theory "fragment" (a reasonably self-contained theory within organizational ecology) expressed in natural language and provide an "interpretation" in FOL. This involves mainly (1) translating the natural language statement into formal definitions, meaning postulates, propositions, and theorems in FOL, (2) supplying statements of the background knowledge needed by the theorem prover, (3) checking the consistency of the resulting structure with a theorem prover, and (4) when the structure is found not to be consistent, constructing a revised interpretation of the natural language theory that fills the gaps, and (5) rechecking for consistency and, if necessary, repeating the cycle, until an interpretation is found to be consistent or the analyst concludes that no such interpretation is consistent with the natural language theory. The strategy is theorist-friendly: When multiple interpretations present themselves, the reconstructors choose those that appear to fit the spirit of the larger theoretical project and that might make the theory consistent. "Even reasonable theoretical texts may have inconsistent readings . . . the objective is not to create 'intelligent misreadings,' but rather to find consistent and reasonable models for the theory at hand" (Péli, this volume).

To my mind, the set of papers formalizing organization ecology in FOL make an impressive contribution, none more so than Péli's paper on niche width theory in this volume. The modesty of its presentation belies its innovation. On a cursory reading (especially one in which attention wanders after the first few definitions and propositions), one might think that the paper marches through the original theory and simply translates from one language to another, much as available software translates uncomplicated prose from, say, German to English. The paper does indeed translate from natural language to FOL. But, the translation is far from mundane; it succeeds brilliantly in capturing what John Freeman and I sought to convey. But, it also goes so far beyond translation and beyond what Freeman and I were able to accomplish that it should be regarded as an important original theoretical statement.

The innovation is especially evident in the material on ordinal scale engineering as a way to make consistent temporal aggregations from sequences of arbitrary length. This improvement of the original theory's dependence on reasoning about "fitness-sets" makes much clearer the scope of the theory's application. It also provides useful guidelines for scaling measurements of "outflows" in empirical research—that is, tests of the theory as reconstructed need distinguish only seven levels of outflow. Moreover, this treatment of scaling also resolves an apparent contradiction between Péli's logic reconstruction and Bruggeman's (1996) mathematical reformulation of the original theory.

What preliminary lessons can be drawn from the logical reconstruction of niche width theory and other theory fragments from organizational ecology? First, even reasonably straightforward natural language formulations prove difficult to render in a form compatible with computer theorem-provers. It is a humbling experience to learn how much of one's formalized arguments in natural language, even when partly formalized, are tacit and incomplete. Unless sociologists can do much better at articulating their theories in natural language, the benefit of and the need for logical reconstructions seem clear.[3]

---

[3] The discussion section of Péli's paper along with the set of other CCSOM papers cited above offer a catalogue of plausible benefits.

Second, partly as a consequence of the first point, logical reconstructions of theory fragments from organizational ecology have been demanding and time-consuming projects. In discussing their effort to reconstruct an evolutionary theory of structural inertia, Péli et al. (1994:587) remark:

> When we began our research, we thought that a superficial knowledge of the theory to be formalized, combined with a sufficient knowledge of the logical formalism, would yield a comprehensive formulation. We discovered that an intimate knowledge of the theory itself is necessary. Our formalization took more than six months.

It is clear that the logical reconstructors have become experts in organizational ecology theory. I suspect that the situation would not be different for efforts to provide logical reconstructions of other kinds of sociological theories.

Finally, as Péli makes clear, logical formalization cannot be considered a panacea. There is nothing automatic in the reconstruction. And, as already noted, useful reconstructions appear to require expert knowledge of the subject matter, technical skill, and good intuition. In short, the talents required for making good logical reconstructions are not very different from those required to build a scientifically useful theory in the first place. In the case at hand, it is hard to separate the effect of the talent of the formalizer from the effect of the tool itself in judging the value of this and the other reconstructions of organizational ecology. Nonetheless, this logical reconstruction of niche-width theory demonstrates that, in the right hands, these new tools can indeed advance theory-building efforts in sociology.

REFERENCES

Blalock, Hubert M., Jr. 1969. *Theory Construction: From Verbal to Mathematical Formulations*. Englewood Cliffs, NJ: Prentice Hall.

Bruggeman, Jeroen. 1997. "Niche Width Theory Reappraised." *Journal of Mathematical Sociology*. Forthcoming.

Coleman, James S. 1964. *Introduction to Mathematical Sociology*. New York: Free Press.

Kamps, Jan, and Michael Masuch. 1997. "Partial Deductive Closure: Logical Simulation and Management Science." *Management Science*. Forthcoming.

Péli, Gábor. 1993. "A Logical Formalization of Population Dynamics: The Density Dependence Model of Organizational Ecology." University of Amsterdam, CCSOM Report.

———. 1996. "Market Partitioning and the Geometry of Resource Space." Unpublished manuscript, University of Groningen.

———. 1997. "The Niche Hikers Guide to Population Ecology: A Logical Reconstruction of Organizational Ecology's Niche Theory." In *Sociological Methodology 1997*, edited by Adrian E. Raftery. Cambridge, MA: Blackwell Publishers.

Péli, Gábor, Jeroen Bruggeman, Michael Masuch, and Breanndán Ó Nualláin. 1994. "A Logical Approach to Organizational Ecology: Formalizing the Inertia-Fragment in First-Order Logic." *American Sociological Review* 59:571–93.

Péli, Gábor, and Michael Masuch. 1997. "The Logic of Propagation Strategies: Axiomatizing a Fragment of Organizational Ecology in First-Order Logic." *Organizational Science*. Forthcoming.

Sørensen, Aage. 1978. "Mathematical Models in Sociology." In *Annual Review of Sociology*, edited by Alex Inkeles, 345–71. Palo Alto, CA: Annual Reviews.

COMMENT: EVALUATING
QUALITATIVE METHODOLOGIES

*Edgar Kiser**

One indication of the dominance of quantitative work in our discipline is the extent to which many sociologists take for granted that it is more systematic, precise, rigorous, and formal than qualitative work, and that it is the only solid foundation for generalization and theory testing. But recent developments in qualitative methodology—for example, Ragin's (1987) qualitative comparative analysis, Heise's (1988) event structure analysis (and its interesting application to historical work by Griffin [1993]), Abbott and Hrycak's (1990) sequence analysis using optimal matching techniques, and Abell's (1987) formal narrative analysis—demonstrate that qualitative work can be just as systematic, formal, rigorous, and precise (see Kiser 1996 for a summary of this work). The three papers published here (Abbott and Barman 1997; Péli 1997; and Roberts 1997) provide further evidence that formal qualitative analysis has come of age in sociology, demonstrating that "both quantitative and qualitative work can be systematic and scientific" (King, Keohane, and Verba 1994:4–5).

Although these three papers initially appear to be quite different, they are all engaged in a similar enterprise. All use formal methods to explore the rhetorical structure of texts. For Abbott and Barman, the focus is on the extent to which the ordering of elements in sociology articles has become more rigid over time; Péli is interested in the logical structure of niche theory; and Roberts uses a new method of content analysis to explore the basic "semantic grammer" of news reports.

My comments focus on one general issue: to what extent do each of these formal qualitative methods allow us to see new and interesting features of texts that would not have been discovered using other methods? In other words, I will judge these methods primarily by the value of their substantive products. After separate analyses of the strengths and weaknesses of each paper, their formal qualitative methods will be evaluated

Thanks to Kathryn Baker for helpful comments.
E-mail: kiser@u.washington.edu
*University of Washington

relative to the more informal type of text analysis that is more common in qualitative sociology.

1. ARE SOCIOLOGY ARTICLES BECOMING MORE RHETORICALLY RIGID?

Abbott and Barman note that many sociologists believe that the rhetorical structure of articles published in major sociology journals has become more rigid over time but that no systematic analysis has been done to test the veracity of this suspicion. They use an innovative combination of sequence methods (optimal alignment and Gibbs sampling) to analyze a sample of papers published in the *American Journal of Sociology* between 1895 and 1965 to discover whether or not their rhetorical structures have become more similar over time.

Abbott and Barman's paper is a great illustration of how formal qualitative methods can produce interesting new findings. They discover first that there have been some important changes over time, including a significant increase in articles using a scientific/empirical format and a "move from presenting simple numbers and quantities to presenting formal data analysis." However, they find no strong evidence of convergence over time on a single rhetorical structure using either optimal alignment or Gibbs sampling methods. The optimal alignment analysis reveals that there have been some standard patterns not just in recent decades but throughout the history of AJS, and the Gibbs sampling results show that patterns never came close to total uniformity (for example, only 6 of 17 articles in the most recent decade used one of the common patterns).

Are Abbott and Barman right to conclude from this that "the evidence for rhetorical rigidification in sociology articles is weak indeed"? As someone who has complained about rigid rhetorical conventions, I must admit that their deft and nuanced analyses have made me much less certain that this griping is justified. However, I am still not totally convinced that the evidence supports their strong conclusion, for two reasons. First, among those who complain about the narrowness of the papers published in the top general sociology journals, *American Sociological Review* and *Social Forces* are usually viewed as the most rigid, whereas AJS is often thought to be open to more varied styles of work. Although I admit I have no evidence supporting that perception, and I realize that using ASR or SF would truncate the historical scope of the analysis, I would be curious to see if their findings held up for these journals. Second, although Abbott and Barman's coverage of 70 years is already quite impressive, their conclusion would be more strongly supported if they included more recent time periods as well. Their argument for stopping at 1965 is that by that time "the current rhetorical format of empirical articles seems by general account to have stabilized." But this seems to assume that the process of rigidification reached a threshold early and did not increase from that point. Perhaps the period between 1945 and 1965 marked the beginning of a process of convergence on a common rhetorical form, and the decades since have seen a deepening of that process. But these are minor complaints about what is overall an innovative and compelling paper.

2. FORMALIZING SOCIOLOGICAL THEORY

One of the most interesting questions Péli raises is why the formalization of data analysis has become so much more widespread than the formalization of theory. Abbott and Barman show that around 1925–1940 there was a shift in most sociology articles from simply presenting numbers to using formal data analysis techniques. Since that time, there has been a proliferation of formal methods for both quantitative and qualitative data analysis, and most would agree that they have often increased the precision and rigor of sociological work. In spite of the fact that prominent sociologists have argued for decades that we could make just as much progress by formalizing our ideas (Merton 1945; Homans 1967; Jasso 1988), the formalization of theory using either logic or mathematics is still a rarity. Journals frequently reject papers because they have failed to use the best formal methods for analyzing data, but they almost never make the formalization of theory a necessary condition for publication. Our graduate students spend years learning formal data analysis, but most do not even spend a day studying formal logic or mathematical theory.

Are the costs of formalizing theory too high, or the benefits too small to justify it? The main costs involve learning the techniques (start-up costs) and costs due to information lost in translating from verbal to formal language (how well does the formalization capture the essential elements of the verbal theory?). The main potential benefits are an increase in precision and clarity (including revealing gaps and inconsistencies in the verbal theory), and, most importantly, the ability to derive new insights that would not be apparent in the verbal exposition.

Péli's paper can help us address these issues: Does it adequately demonstrate the value added from formalizing population ecology's niche theory? First, judging from his paper, the costs of formalization may be quite low. The first-order logic Péli uses is simple and clear; the start-up costs certainly seem no higher than for most data analysis techniques. The information loss in the translation process also seems to be minimal; the formalization clearly captured the main features of the theory. The benefits of formalization in this paper include discovering and filling in important missing information in the theory concerning "outflow aggregation," checking the theory for contradictions (there were none), and deducing new implications of the theory concerning organizations that specialize in rarely occurring environments. My biggest disappointment with the paper was that the new deductions "just claim what common sense predicts." In spite of its limited success in producing results that were both new and interesting, Péli's paper provides some evidence that the costs of formalization are fairly low and the benefits potentially great.

So why has formal theory been so rare in sociology? Perhaps Péli's success has more to do with the particular type of theory he formalized than with the general virtues of formalization. Population ecology theory in its verbal form is already one of the most explicit and precise theories in the discipline. The clarity of the verbal theory may be responsible for the lack of information loss in the translation to formal language. In fact, some threshold of verbal explicitness and clarity may be a necessary condition for successful formal translation. If so, then the lack of formalization could be due to the vagueness of much current verbal theory. The implication is clear: those of us doing verbal theory in sociology need to get beyond ancestor worship and political posturing and begin the hard work of making our ideas clear enough to profit from formalization.

3. QUANTITATIVE CONTENT ANALYSIS

Roberts's paper demonstrates that quantitative content analysis has come a long way since the days of simple word counts. His "generic semantic grammer" codes not only general themes in texts but grammatical relations among themes as well. This facilitates the quantitative measurement of theme relations in relatively unstructured texts, such as news reports. The main limitation of this approach is that it requires coders to have an extraordinary amount of knowledge and skill. In order to adequately code text content using this method, coders need to know the intent of the speaker, characteristics of the audience, and detailed features of the historical, social, political, and intellectual context of the text being coded. Roberts realizes the difficulty of this, as indicated by his use of terms such as "coder intuition," and the need for coders to have "divined" the meaning of a clause. It would be rare indeed to find graduate student research assistants with the talent, knowledge, and intuition necessary to code complex texts using this method. It is perhaps for that reason that Roberts uses fairly simple texts for his illustration, a comparison of radio news broadcasts from East and West Berlin in 1979. The Cold War context made it relatively easy for coders to figure out the historical setting and actors' intentions in these texts. In fact, they could probably have predicted the main findings, "East and West Berlin radio stations cited and reported on parties with which their nations were politically aligned." Although Roberts's method may have promise, it will take more than this substantive illustration to prove that it can uncover new and interesting facts.

4. A CONTRAST CASE: SEWELL'S QUALITATIVE TEXT ANALYSIS

The three papers in this volume illustrate a small and rather unrepresentative subset of contemporary qualitative work—those using formal methods. The extent to which they are outliers is indicated by the fact that none of them fit King, Keohane, and Verba's (1994:4) definition of qualitative research, which they say "has tended to focus on one or a small number of cases, to use in depth interviews or intensive analyses of historical materials, to be discursive in method, and to be concerned with a rounded or comprehensive account of some event or unit." It thus might be instructive to compare these three formal text analysis methods with an exemplary text analysis that illustrates an informal qualitative approach, Sewell's *A Rhetoric of Bourgeois Revolution* (1994).[1] Of course, this is in no way a systematic comparison since both the goals and the objects of analysis are so different, but it may help reveal some of the relative strengths and weaknesses of formal and informal approaches. As with the other three papers, I begin with a short discussion of Sewell's method and then turn to his substantive results.

There were thousands of pamphlets published in the months prior to the French Revolution; by far the most influential was one written by an "obscure ecclesiastic" named Emmanual-Joseph Sieyes called *What Is the Third Estate?* (1). "Sieyes succeeded in scripting both the triumph of the National Assembly on 17 June and its radical abolition of privileges on

---

[1] All of the page references that follow are to this book.

4 August . . . by joining a radical rhetoric of political revolution that pointed toward a seizure of power by the delegates of the Third Estate with a rhetoric of social revolution that inflamed bourgeois resentment against the aristocracy" (185). His success, however, was short-lived, as "the political culture of the revolution developed in directions that Sieyes found antipathetic" (185). Sewell's book is an attempt to discover which aspects of the pamphlet's logical arguments, emotional appeals, and rhetorical devices account for its extraordinary success, but also to uncover the fissures and contradictions in the text that explain its limitations.

Sewell's goals are broad and varied, in a sense combining the orientations of the three papers published here. Like Roberts, he is interested in doing a content analysis of the text that takes its social context into account, and to do this he often pays close attention to the order and sequence of argumentation (as do Abbott and Barman), and must often reconstruct general theoretical models that are used in the text (as does Péli). These wide-ranging goals require a complex mix of methods. Sewell's methodology combines traditional intellectual history focusing on the main themes in the text and their origins in the history of ideas, a deconstructionist emphasis on the importance of studying the gaps and contradictions that exist in all texts, and a "social history of ideas" that stresses the importance of the social context in shaping both the production and reception of texts (xx, 29, 34–37). Sewell's analysis is divided into two main parts. The first half outlines the central argument and main themes of *What Is the Third Estate?*, and the second half probes the ambiguities, incoherences, and contradictions in the text.

Like Abbott and Barman, Sewell is interested in analyzing the overall structure of Sieyes's text. He begins his second chapter with an outline of the pamphlet (41–42), and goes on to discuss the importance of the order of the argument (why his rhetoric of social revolution is a necessary prelude to his arguments for political revolution) (56, 62). Although Sewell makes a compelling case that the sequence of the argument is part of what gives it its rhetorical power, it would be interesting to see if the sequence differs substantially from that of other revolutionary pamphlets. The formal methods used by Abbott and Barman could answer that question, and in that respect could supplement Sewell's analysis.

Sewell's third chapter is a fascinating analysis of the general theoretical foundations of Sieyes's work. The task is roughly analogous to Péli's—both want to extract, complete, and systematize the theories in their texts. For example, Sewell (66–69) shows how Sieyes used Rousseau's version of social contract theory, and how he modifies it significantly to include representative democracy. He goes on to demonstrate the similarities between Sieyes's ideas about political economy and those of Adam Smith (86–102). Could Péli have discovered the same things by applying formal logic to the arguments in Rousseau, Smith, and Sieyes and comparing them? My guess is that the verbal presentations of all of these authors would make translation into formal logic problematic, by making it difficult to arrive at any consensually valid formalization.[2] With texts like these, Sewell's informal analysis is probably preferable to more formal alternatives for uncovering general foundations.

The second half of Sewell's book also illustrates the limitations of formal analyses. All of the formal analyses are oriented primarily toward uncovering the most general features of texts, but they seem to be less well-suited to discovering the minor gaps and contradictions that Sewell unearths from footnotes and passing phrases. For example, Sewell (112–121) uses a close analysis of two footnotes to show that Sieyes does not apply his general condemnation of privilege to the clergy (as the logic of his argument would suggest) but uses subtle word choices and grammatical constructions to appear consistent while criticizing only the privileges of the nobility. He later (146–152) uses an extended analysis of one critical passage to show an even greater contradiction. In spite of the fact that Sieyes argued that only those who do "useful labor" should be considered part of the "nation" (a rhetorical attempt to delegitimate the aristocracy), he suggests later that only members of the Third Estate that had a lot of leisure time should hold political offices! Sewell (152) notes that this contradiction "reveals not only an instability in Sieyes's text but an instability in the Revolution itself," foreshadowing the divisions within the Third Estate that would follow the revolution. It is difficult to imagine that Roberts's formal content analysis, with its focus on quantifying main themes, would have revealed these contradictions buried in small passages. The implication seems to be that when particular infrequently occurring details of texts are important, Sewell's approach is preferable.

5. CONCLUSION

Formal qualitative analysis has developed significantly in recent years, as each of these three papers demonstrates. Yet while formalization improves

---

[2] By a "consensually valid" formalization I mean one that would be accepted by most scholars familiar with these texts.

many aspects of qualitative research, it is far from a panacea. Informal qualitative work will always have an important role. Formal work is not always superior to informal, just as quantitative work is not always better than qualitative. The important questions are: what can each approach contribute, and under what conditions are we better off using one (or one particular combination) rather than another?

REFERENCES

Abell, Peter. 1987. *The Syntax of Social Life*. Oxford: Oxford University Press.

Abbott, Andrew, and Alexandra Hrycak. 1990. "Measuring Resemblance in Sequence Data: An Optimal Matching Analysis of Musicians' Careers." *American Journal of Sociology* 96(1):144–85.

Griffin, Larry. 1993. "Narrative, Event Structure Analysis, and Causal Interpretation in Historical Sociology." *American Journal of Sociology* 98(5):1094–133.

Heise, David. 1988. "Computer Analysis of Cultural Structures." *Social Science Computer Review* 6:183–96.

Homans, George. 1967. *The Nature of Social Science*. New York: Harcourt, Brace, and World.

Jasso, Guillermina. 1988. "Principles of Theoretical Analysis." *Sociological Theory* 6(1):1–20.

King, Gary, Robert Keohane, and Sidney Verba. 1994. *Designing Social Inquiry*. Princeton: Princeton University Press.

Kiser, Edgar. 1996. "The Revival of Narrative in Historical Sociology: What Rational Choice Theory Can Contribute." *Politics and Society* 24(3):249–71.

Merton, Robert. 1945. "Sociological Theory." *American Journal of Sociology* 50:462–73.

Ragin, Charles. 1987. *The Comparative Method: Moving Beyond Qualitative and Quantitative Strategies*. Berkeley: University of California Press.

Sewell, William, Jr. 1994. *A Rhetoric of Bourgeois Revolution: The Abbé Sieyes and What Is the Third Estate?* Durham: Duke University Press.

REPLY: INTUITION AND
THE FORMAL APPROACHES

*Gábor Péli**

> *It's only words.*
> —Bee Gees

So, no formulas in this rejoinder. Franzosi analyzes two other chapters in this volume, but his verdict (worship of formalism) pertains to all three. A conclusion without argument, as far as my work is concerned. *"The authors are driven by a common goal of getting away from the murky waters of personal intuitions in the social sciences,"* he writes. I cannot give an account of the drives in my subconscious, but my ego believes that logic (and other formal tools) cannot replace intuition. In general, I do share Franzosi's doubts about formal fireworks. Flat ideas often use the veil of formulas to look important, and sometimes there is no Salome under the seventh veil. The user of formal methods should be a craftsman rather than a juggler, and the very interest of the guild is to establish standards. Zorros and desperados with analytical skills are needed to hunt down nonsolutions in formal disguise.

Logical formalization can give an inferentially sound shape to theoretical pictures. Theoretical speculation does not seem to follow the ways of Aristotelian logic; it rather proceeds by visualization, analogues, and metaphors. Logic helps to turn insights into arguments, to convert a convincing but somewhat underspecified vision into statements (assumptions, definitions, conclusions, etc.) also establishing an inference structure that connects these statements. Let me mention a few criteria that may help to decide if a logical formalization is correct. The formal representation of a verbal theory can be seen as the metatheory of the original (Pólos 1996). As such it is also subject to falsification by checking if the formalization (1) implies undesirable, empirically false conclusions; (2) is able to reproduce known conclusions of the verbal theory based on sound arguments; (3) mixes together concepts that are clearly distinct in the verbal theory; and (4) produces fake distinctions in the meaning of certain notions. The

Thanks to Charles Carroll, Jaap Kamps, and László Pólos for their helpful comments.

*University of Groningen

list is not complete and the items are not independent. For example, by overlooking the fact that two words stand for the same concept in a text and characterizing them with different formulas, one may block the derivation of some sound conclusions of the verbal theory.

Since I agree with the main lines of Franzosi's argument about the use of formalism, I cannot contradict Hannan's remarks on the role of logical approach in organizational ecology either. Hannan's experience about the *in vivo* use of logic is twofold: first, his works have been the subject of logical formalization; second, he also applies logic to sharpen ideas that further theory specification (Hannan 1996). His works along with those of John Freeman and Glenn Carroll provide the material for most formalizations proposed by my colleagues and myself. We consulted them whenever some conceptual decisions had to be made in the course of logical formalization. Some of our questions triggered answers that had not been verbalized before, bringing the parties closer to a common understanding. These questions also brought unforeseen problems up front, initiating a search for conceptual or empirical solutions. It is often claimed that formalization nails down the theory, ending its existence as a "living," developing entity. Our experience shows that there are counterexamples. Sharply put questions necessitated by the rigor of the formal machinery led to new developments: dead ends have been removed and new paths opened in the verbal theory.

Kiser makes a distinction between the start-up costs (investments to learn a formal technique) and the costs of information lost in the course of processing. He finds these costs quite low in the case of my contribution. Though his conclusion is a good advertisement for the logical approach, let me remark that obtaining formalization skills means more than getting familiar with the applied logic, just like fluency in a language requires more than learning its grammar. It takes some time until the formalizer achieves the experience necessary to exploit the expressive possibilities of first-order logic. I hope that the second cost aspect, information loss due to formalization, is really low. But still, I would encourage the reader to study the appendix of my paper, since the technical-looking background formulas are also potential sources of information loss and so may confine the formalized theory's domain. Please note, that the amount of information loss differs according to which potential interpretation of the text is considered. My goal was to bring close my formulation to the original interpretation of the authors. By tuning the machinery to a certain theory reading, some other potential readings were "closed down." But definitely not forever. The modular nature of formulas helps to identify the crosspoints where the different interpretations separate and other formal models can be developed along the branching. Actually, the more you study a reasonably rich theory, the more interpretations pop up.

Kiser mentions the inconsistency check of verbal theories as a potential benefit of logical formalization. I would like to emphasize the difference between the consistency of a verbally put theory and that of the formula set representing this theory. Since natural language arguments usually use somewhat ambiguous wording, proving the consistency of a verbal theory is just like having a discussion with a person who always changes the subject. The consistency of the formula set guarantees that the verbal theory has at least one consistent interpretation.

Theory development also means formulating new, interesting results, which Kiser misses. In fact, the results in the paper are new findings *about* the theory rather than new findings *from* the theory. However, an appropriately performed formalization also provides a core for the deduction of new theorems. Let me sketch two orientations showing how the search for new results can proceed. The first way is to look for new theorems "by hand." This approach does not require further technical investments, and I suggest that technically interested readers try it. Choose a hypothesis that you feel is related to the theory at hand. Formalize this intuition and check whether it follows from the existing premise set. If it does not, you can add different new assumptions to the model. If the hypothesis finally derives as a theorem, then the additional premises give you a price estimate for the theory extension. Of course, the search can go on to achieve a lower price.

The second way to look for new theorems may also involve automated search. The computer then generates theorem candidates that a theorem prover checks one by one. The original theory may contain overlooked conclusions, so the task is "fishing out the lake." One problem of this approach comes from the nonformalized background knowledge. Assume that there is a statement that could be easily proven by a theoretician, provided that it were known. Assume also that the computer generates a formula that actually stands for this statement. Does this formula follow from the formalized theory? Not necessarily, because some pieces of background information may be missing (like a plus b equals b plus a for real numbers). When proving a theorem, theoreticians mobilize such "trivial" pieces of information even without being aware of it, while theorem prover softwares may get stuck.

However, the main problem of automated theorem generation is not the scarcity but rather the undesirable abundance of deduced items. From a logical point of view, every proven formula is a theorem without respect to its theoretical relevance. Therefore a lot of deduced garbage has to be swept out, like the weakened versions of known theorems (e.g., constrain a known result with an arbitrary predicate), or the conjunctions and disjunctions of known theorems. Kamps and Masuch (1997) reproduced the theorems of an earlier formalization by computer and found some overlooked ones. The formalized fragment was relatively small, with a similar syntactic format for most assumptions and theorems (Péli et al. 1994). This approach was later applied to a more complex formalization of Thompson's classic *Organizations in Action* (Pólos 1995), causing a Big Bang of new logical consequences. The result was several megabytes of new theorems, even though the theorem prover used only a certain part of the premise set. Maybe fascinating results lie in this huge data set, but sorting them out is just like searching on the Internet for persons about whom the only thing we know is that they are "interesting." A central problem of automated theorem finding is that no computer software tells us what makes a theorem relevant, what makes it a scientific result.

Kiser is right that clear-cut, explicit theories are more ready for formalization than opaque ones. However, the explicitness of a theory is not a necessary condition of logical formalization. Vaguely put but insightful theoretical pieces can also be addressed. Then, the rational reconstruction of the text that precedes formalization is much longer, and the unfit interpretations have to be eliminated by the formalizer (maybe for later reuse). When the verbal model is sharply put, formalization proceeds as it does in other cases. Thus, explicitness does really make a difference, but only in the preprocessing phase. The major precondition of formalization is the presence of a vision showing how the described objects relate to each other. In short: the material has to be a theory.

REFERENCES

Hannan, Michael T. 1996. "Selection Mechanism: Organizations and Other Corporate Actors." Paper presented at the Conference on Social Mechanisms, Stockholm, June 6–7.

Kamps, Jaap, and Michael Masuch. 1997. "Partial Deductive Closure: Logical Simulation and Management Science." *Management Science*. Forthcoming.

Péli, Gábor, Jeroen Bruggeman, Michael Masuch, Breanndán Ó Nualláin. 1994. "A Logical Approach to Formalizing Organizational Ecology." *American Sociological Review*, 59: 571–93.

Pólos, László. 1995. *Towards the Metaphysics of Organizations*. CCSOM report. University of Amsterdam.

———. 1996. "Logic and Argumentation: Towards a Theory of Formalization." Lecture delivered at the Belgian Royal Academy of Science, Brussels, May 11. (Available upon request at laszlo@ccsom.uva.nl).

REPLY TO COMMENTS

Andrew Abbott*
Emily Barman*

These comments have one common theme but raise as well a number of minor issues. We shall allow the common theme to emerge from a discussion of the comments in order.

Carley is right that the coding of texts at the level here discussed is "a formidable task." Indeed, it seems unlikely that the methods discussed here will see widespread use in textual analysis except where coding can be routinized.

On her issue of Gibbs sampling versus simulated annealing (SA): there is a large literature on convergence in Gibbs samplers, which can be traced from the papers mentioned in note 17 of our paper. The long-run convergence of Gibbs sampling to the global optimum is guaranteed via fundamental Markov theorems. How long it takes to get there is the matter of contention. It should be remembered that the LEA algorithm could easily incorporate a standard SA acceptance function; one could accept or not accept the new candidate in step 2 of the basic algorithm (as given on page 73) on the basis of an annealing schedule. That makes an SA-Gibbs sampling structure.

We are pleased that Carley thinks our findings stronger than we did, but we aimed to err on the side of caution. Kiser, too, thinks the claims weaker than they need be, referring to the widespread opinion that AJS is more eclectic substantively and stylistically than other leading sociology journals. If AJS shows some minimal degree of rigidification, weren't others probably more rigid? Again, we preferred to err on the side of caution. We should reiterate that we chose to study a single journal to try to "control out" other kinds of variation, and that of course one would have to extend the analysis elsewhere to feel confident about it. Note that Franzosi also chides us for being cautious, which he interprets as being ambiguous. This worry about strength of findings is the common issue, to which we return in a moment.

*University of Chicago

Franzosi is right that stopping in 1965 was in part a data conve-
nience. Had we gone beyond 1965, we would have had to recode all AJS
articles from 1895 to 1995 as being suitable or unsuitable for analysis; we
could not have simply guessed at how the 1965 coders would have viewed
the post-1965 articles and ourselves coded everything from 1965 forward
(not a small job in itself). This total recording was beyond our resources,
given the other things we had to do, and so we stopped in 1965. On the
other hand, having spent several years researching the archives of the AJS
preparatory to writing a now-long-overdue centennial history, the senior
author is convinced that the statement that "the new form of article was
recognized as instituted and rigid by 1965" is in fact empirically correct
(and that therefore it was reasonable, on a first pass, to stop in 1965). Our
caution in making that assertion should be seen as reasonable caution given
the lack of published evidence supporting this judgment.

We are quite persuaded by Franzosi's argument that specialty journals (and, we would imagine, regional journals) are probably more formulaic than central journals. But his analysis presupposes a clear conception
of degrees of rigidification. That several commenters ask whether rigidification was not stronger than we thought indicates the pervasiveness of
the belief in the reality of rigidification. But more important it points to the
paper's lack of a clear conception of what we really mean by degrees of
rigidification. This is in fact a real problem in the paper and makes it
unable to answer effectively the respondents' concerns about whether we
have seen the right amount of rigidification.

Franzosi's analysis of our rhetorical strategies strikes us as amus-
ing, even delightful. However, having at other times published *analyses de
texte* of a fairly detailed sort (e.g., Abbott 1992), we feel that our creden-
tials as residents on both sides of this rhetorical divide free us from the
accusation of killing other people for our own aggrandisement. The rhetorical bullets hit us as well.

On the other hand, we are bewildered by Franzosi's comment that
"the statistical analyses of Tables 1 through 6 are based on the mean and
standard deviation applied to seven samples of median size 15." Tables 1
and 2 are simply coding lists; Table 3 is a frequency listing; Table 5 is a
cluster listing. Only Tables 4 and 6 involve means. Table 4 involves means
and standard deviations of distances, which involve pairs of points. Hence
the denominators of the figures in the tables are quadratic in the number of
cases by decade; they are of order 110 or so. These are quite stable. (If
there is a criticism here, it should be that distance data *a priori* cannot be

normally distributed because of the truncation at zero and that that fact makes means and standard deviations misleading.) Table 6 involves some small numbers, to be sure. It is for that reason that we have not rested much interpretive weight on them.

We are disturbed, finally, by Franzosi's despairing conclusion. He seems to believe in a-rhetorical science, at least that is the implication of his confession that his own work would not pass muster any more than ours. It seems to us that the answer to this despair is that science is ultimately about discovery, not justification, and that the fun in science lies in making discoveries and making up ways to make discoveries. This paper grew out of the latter of these ways of having fun. We are willing to confess that, deep down, there is no profound discovery in our paper. Like the commenters, we were strong believers in the reality of rigidification and had hopes of demonstrating a triumphant rhetorical march that would verify the truly widespread opinion that articles are getting rigid and boring. Unfortunately, we did not find such a clear march. Our results make us suspect that the real explanation of the widespread opinion is not trends in articles but aging effects in scholars who somehow feel their work does not have the excitement of the work that attracted them to the discipline in their late teens and early twenties. Maybe middle age is just like that. Suddenly you realize that what seemed wonderful was in fact pretty pedestrian, indeed that most of science is plodding and boring. It all seemed exciting the first time around. It all seemed exciting when we were not behind the scenes to see the creaking apparatus that put on the show. If that theory holds, it is not the discipline that has a problem, it is us. Maybe there are young people out there who find the current journals exciting beyond belief. Let us hope so.

REFERENCE

Abbott, Andrew. 1992. "What Do Cases Do? In *What Is a Case?*, edited by Charles C. Ragin and Howard S. Becker, 53–82. Cambridge, England: Cambridge University Press.

REPLY: THE CURSE OF CHAUVIN

Carl W. Roberts *

Sociology is dominated by quantitative work, Kiser reports. The three papers in this symposium "are outliers" that "illustrate a small and rather unrepresentative subset of contemporary qualitative work" to "be evaluated relative to the more informal type of text analysis that is more common in qualitative sociology." Kiser then illuminates the limitations of these methods by arguing that they do not allow the researcher to do what more representative qualitative sociologists do. For example, applications of formal logic to eighteenth and nineteenth century figures' writings would be too precise to allow most scholars familiar with these texts to arrive at a consensus. Thus the less formal (less precise?) interpretations of informal qualitative sociologists are to be preferred. I see.

In Kiser's view, the second major limitation of formal text analysis methods is that they "are oriented primarily toward uncovering the most general features of texts, but they seem less well-suited to discovering . . . minor gaps and contradictions." Certainly Kiser does not intend this sentence to apply to Péli's paper, which describes a rigorous method for identifying just such logical gaps and contradictions in texts. However, it does most certainly apply to my method as well as to that of Abbott and Barman. Our statistical methods gloss over many fine distinctions. Franzosi also points to this limitation in his commentary with numerous illustrations of valuational phrases in my radio news data: "flagrantly anew," "not even," etc.[1]

Quantitative methods such as ours require that one begin with a data matrix in which the rich qualities of units of analysis are divided into rather

---

[1] It is curious that after condemning my method for not capturing some of these subtleties, Franzosi closes by acknowledging that his own method can do no better. My argument here is that this is an inevitable aspect of quantitative methods. For the record, Linguistic Content Analysis allows for valuational phrasing in three ways. If the primary intention of a clause is to positively or negatively judge a process and/or state of affairs, the coder can encode the clause according to the justification and/or evaluation functional forms. The coder can also develop finer coding categories to differentiate judgmental (JOE RIDICULED JOHN.) from descriptive (JOE SPOKE TO JOHN.) expressions. Subjects and objects can be modified with genitives that may add valuational content (The DEVIL's PLAYTHING).

*Iowa State University

gross categories. Only once this is done can probabilistic inferences be drawn to the text populations from which our samples have been drawn.[2] The deductive, statistical, and confirmatory qualities of our methods seem to me quite different from the more inductive, nonstatistical, and exploratory nature of the qualitative text analysis methods with which Kiser insists upon comparing them. In fact, are not these disparate qualities the very ones with which qualitative and quantitative methods are distinguished (Berg 1995:2–4)? Moreover, given the long history of quantitative text analysis methods in the works of Lazarsfeld, Berelson, Pool, Stone, Holsti, Krippendorf, Weber, and many others, it is difficult to fathom how anyone might classify such quantitative text analysis methods as methodological outliers for qualitative text analysis. How might such a gross misclassification have occurred?

My best guess is that Kiser's ties to his own methodological perspective have blinded him to noticing that two of the text analysis methods in this symposium are quantitative ones that were crafted to afford statistical inferences about populations of texts. The irony in Kiser's commentary is that quantitative methodologists have traditionally criticized qualitative methods for not affording such inferences, whereas here Kiser critiques quantitative text analysis methods for ignoring infrequently occurring details of texts. Of course, quantitative methods are less appropriate than qualitative methods for investigating the anomalous character of strategically selected case studies (Mitchell 1983). Assertion that they should not be is methodological Chauvinism, not critique.

On a lighter note, allow me to turn to the "main limitation" that Kiser finds in my approach—namely, that "coders need to know the intent of the speaker, characteristics of the audience, and detailed features of the historical, social political, and intellectual context of the text." Yet a mere three paragraphs later we are told that Sewell's exemplary text analysis (presumably devoid of such limitation) "combines traditional intellectual history focusing on the main themes in the text and their origins in the history of ideas . . . and a 'social history of ideas' that stresses the impor-

---

[2]This is why, for example, the finer-grained one's schema for classifying segments of research articles, the less likely one will detect statistically significant temporal differences in occurrences of a specific sequence of even three types of segments. Accordingly, Abbott and Barman's use of 59 segment types in a sample of only 99 articles makes their statistically significant evidence of rhetorical rigidification quite compelling. Could it be that two University of Chicago researchers have confirmed the rhetorical rigidity of the *American Journal of Sociology*? In the silence one senses the spirit of Chauvin.

tance of the social context in shaping both the production and reception of texts." About the only coherent interpretation I can find here is of an assertion that coders should not have expertise, whereas qualitative text analysts should. In reaction, a counterassertion: If the task of the coder is to identify words' intended meanings, then such expertise is required of the coder.[3] More generally, to be worthy of the trust of one's readers any social scientist who professes to understand the meanings of another's words must ensure that such contextual expertise has been applied at every interpretive stage of their work. As a case in point, I now turn to Franzosi's interpretation of my paper.

After a heated critique of my paper and that of Abbott and Barman, Franzosi acknowledges, "I cannot do better." That is, after identifying problems in our methods he notes that these problems are probably intractable for those who do quantitative text analysis. A careful reading of his commentary reveals three such problems: (1) coder intuition is required to divine texts' meanings; (2) due to texts' inherent ambiguity, their encoding is unavoidably problematic; and (3) syntax (i.e., Subject-Verb-Object, or S-V-O) grammars are inadequate for capturing texts' intended meanings.

I agree totally with each of these points, and am surprised to find myself accused by Franzosi of holding views opposed to them. Thus in reacting to this commentary my strategy is to understand why these misinterpretations have occurred and to alert the reader to any vagaries in my writing that might be culpable in such misinterpretation. Allow me to consider each of the three problems in turn.

First, Franzosi accuses me of oversimplifying the coder's interpretive role. He depicts my work as one in which "coders should commit themselves to one form of coding or another, regardless of the ambiguities of the text." Surely Franzosi must have overlooked footnote 6, in which I point out that multiple meanings of ambiguous statements can be encoded using my method, as well as numerous references to functional form(s) or identifiable meaning(s) appropriate to a single clause. He also quotes me: "Transparent to the user, the encoding process involves a translation from text to numbers." Out of context (as it is presented in Franzosi's commen-

---

[3] This assertion might be false at some future date when innovations in linguistics and computer science have developed beyond their current state. Such developments might be based on the sort of "explicit linguistic rules" alluded to by Franzosi for identifying the functional forms appropriate to linguistic expressions. However, at present "working researchers engage in science, not science fiction, and to do such science requires . . . the use of coders" and their interpretive expertise (Shapiro 1997:238).

tary) this sentence might be interpreted as depicting the encoding process as consisting of an automated translation from text to numbers. In fact, the sentence appears while I am describing a computer aid for encoding texts according to the generic semantic grammar. When read in context, it merely describes that the software automatically and internally (i.e., transparent to the user) constructs a data matrix *based on the user's coding judgments*.

Second, Franzosi accuses me of ignoring how texts' inherent ambiguity makes the encoding process unavoidably problematic. I am accused of "shrugging off" problems of linguistic ambiguity, of forgetting "the ambiguities of the process of generating" data, of aiming to eliminate "the ambiguity involved in the process of coding." Finally, we are rhetorically asked, "Wasn't this supposed to be an unambiguous process?" In a word, no.

My argument is that there is a structure to linguistic ambiguity (i.e., that in ordinary discourse every clause has an enumerable number of unambiguous interpretations). Coder judgments are needed to select from among these interpretations. In the paper I assign a unique semantic grammar to each of the four unambiguous ways in which clauses can be interpreted during ordinary discourse. By requiring that coders encode clauses according to these semantic grammars, relations among concepts fit into these grammars are unambiguous. This is why the Subject-Verb-Object (or S-V-O) relations in an LCA data matrix are unambiguous, whereas the S-V-O relations in the original text may not be.

So have I eliminated ambiguity? Of course not. On the contrary, my work is based on a deep respect for linguistic ambiguity. The challenge is to capture in one's data matrix a defensible unambiguous interpretation (what Péli would call a "reading") of the text. There still remains a need to train coders, to develop code books and coding rules, and to evaluate interrater agreement. Yet Franzosi passes off these precautions as immodest claims of having "stamped out ambiguity." One begins to get the impression that nothing could be said to persuade him otherwise.

Finally, Franzosi accuses me of ignoring that S-V-O grammars are inadequate for capturing texts' intended meanings. Although I claim to have a method for providing an unambiguous encoding of any clause, my generic semantic grammar is really an S-V-O grammar "in disguise, with the addition of an evaluation of the actors and of the actions."[4] The clear-

---

[4] Also in this context Franzosi notes that his semantic grammar might fit the bill, if suitably modified with subject and object qualifiers. Although true, this observation begs the issue at hand. My assertion is not that such modifications could not be made, but that if they were, Franzosi's Actor-Action-Object semantic grammar would still not be generic (i.e., it would not lend itself to the encoding of any clause).

est evidence of this, we are told, can be found in the LCA data matrix in my Table 3, because encoded clauses are clearly labeled there as having Subjects, main Verbs, and Objects. On the other hand, "if Roberts is right, he would have solved a problem that has eluded linguists and philosophers alike."

To evaluate this accusation, let us begin by using a S-V-O grammar to encode a simplified version of a relative clause from this last sentence, namely Franzosi's assertion. *Linguists and philosophers have not solved a problem.* In the Subject column of our data matrix, let us place the number 100 (our code for "linguists and philosophers"), in the main Verb column the number 50 (our code for the verb, "to solve"), and in the Object column the number 200 (our code for "problem"). To this we add a 1 (past) in the tense column and NI (negative infinitive) in the valence column.

In contrast, encoding the clause according to my generic semantic grammar requires that the coder judge what Franzosi intended to deny with this assertion. If we assume its truth, comprehensibility, and credibility, the assertion must be a denial of one or more of the following statements:

• Linguists and philosophers have solved a problem.

$$\exists(\text{Phenomenon x}) \exists(\text{Process p}) [p(x) \wedge x = \text{"linguists \& philosophers"}$$
$$\wedge\, p = \text{"solved a problem"}]$$

• Someone other than a linguist or philosopher has solved a problem.

$$\exists(\text{Phenomenon x}) \exists(\text{Process p}) [p(x) \wedge x \neq \text{"linguists \& philosophers"}$$
$$\wedge\, p = \text{"solved a problem"}]$$

• Someone other than a linguist or philosopher has done something other than solving a problem.

$$\exists(\text{Phenomenon x}) \exists(\text{Process p}) [p(x) \wedge x \neq \text{"linguists \& philosophers"}$$
$$\wedge\, p \neq \text{"solved a problem"}]$$

Let us further assume that Franzosi's assertion is in ordinary discourse and that he wishes to communicate relevant information (i.e., that he does not wish to deny the uninformative content of the third statement).

Franzosi's commentary provides considerable context for judging which of the first two statements he intended to deny in the assertion. Of course, Franzosi may have intended to "describe" the process of linguists and philosophers not solving a problem (i.e., a denial of the first statement). The LCA encoding for this "description of a process" would be precisely the one just described for an S-V-O grammar, with the addition of a 1 (perception) code in the column for functional form. However, the assertion was more likely (especially given contextual cues such as "we should definitely inform both disciplines of this breakthrough coming from sociology") intended to describe a state of affairs in which a sociological nonlinguist/nonphilosopher is not a problem solver (i.e., a denial of the second statement). If this were the coder's judgment, the assertion's LCA representation would yield a 2 (recognition) in the functional form column, a -100 (nonlinguist or nonphilosopher) in the subject column, a 1 (to be) in the main verb column, a 50 (solver [of]) in the genitive of object column, and a 200 (problem) in the object column. To this we again add a 1 (past) in the tense column and NI (negative infinitive) in the valence column. Respective LCAese renderings of these two encodings would be as follows:

The LINGUISTS/PHILOSOPHERS
have not SOLVED a PROBLEM.

The NONLINGUIST/NONPHILOSOPHER
was not a SOLVER of a PROBLEM.

Records from an LCA data matrix for both of these renderings of Franzosi's assertion have codes placed in fields for subject, verb, and object. Yet codes placed in these fields may differ among coders, not merely because they misidentify the assertion's surface syntax but because they differ in their interpretations of the assertion's intended meaning. For example, when encoded as a recognition, Franzosi's assertion is rendered with the verb "to be," not with the verb "to solve," as would be the case if mere S-V-O grammatical relations were encoded. In conclusion, this illustration should suffice to show that the subject, verb, and subject fields of an LCA data matrix do not imply, as Franzosi argues, that LCA is a method of encoding texts according to their surface grammar.

Finally, Franzosi notes that "Roberts never clarifies the linguistic differences between 'structured' and 'unstructured' texts, despite the central position of this distinction in his argument." For the record, I define texts' structure as a matter of degree ranging from more structured texts (about which coders are likely to agree regarding clauses' intended meanings) to more unstructured texts (for which linguistic ambiguity and thus interrater disagreement is more prevalent). Thus Franzosi wrongly depicts me as claiming that some texts are unstructured, and that "unstructured texts have different surface representation than structured texts." That said, I must now point out that this structured/unstructured distinction is certainly *not* central to my argument. On the other hand, the distinction is central for Franzosi. In fact, it is by virtue of Franzosi's own, quite different understanding of this distinction that I hope to disentangle Franzosi from his seriously misinformed depiction of my work.

Let me begin by recounting another among an extremely long series of false assertions that Franzosi makes about my paper. Franzosi states, "Roberts is right in claiming that there are texts that conform to the S-V-O structure and texts that do not." Hardly. I define texts as sequences of clauses, each of which has an inflected verb plus optional subject and object. Be that as it may, I cannot help but wonder what Franzosi is referring to when he speaks of texts not structured with subjects, verbs, and objects. As it turns out, the meaning of S-V-O changes in Franzosi's commentary from Subject-Verb-Object to the structure of narrative texts, where S stands for actor, V for action, and O for object. This latter structure is also, not coincidentally, the structure of the semantic grammar Franzosi uses in his research. Because a S-V-O (read Actor-Action-Object) semantic grammar cannot capture the greater linguistic complexity of nonnarrative texts, he argues, my S-V-O (read Subject-Verb-Object) semantic grammar cannot by virtue of the same arguments that delineate the domain of his own method (i.e., it is not that nonnarrative texts are unstructured, they are just structured in ways other than Actor-Action-Object). The curse of Chauvin strikes again.

If anyone should be able to suspend one's perspective and evaluate another's on its own terms, one would expect sociologists to be able to do so.[5] Our literature abounds with references to *Verstehen*, disinterested interest, value neutrality, and the like. Yet when these techniques are not applied in our writings, precious opportunities are lost, leaving authors disentangling their own ideas from those of the commentator rather than

[5] In contrast to some of the commentary in this volume, Roberts (1997) provides a neutral forum in which authors (including two commentators from this symposium) explain their quantitative text analysis methods to the reader, leaving it to the reader (not the authors) to rank the methods. In the collection I have striven to provide much needed relief from the divisive, territorial rhetoric that has unfortunately become commonplace in discourse among text analysts. At issue is not which method is best but "which" is appropriate for "what" research objectives.

grappling with the central issues they have raised. Franzosi rightly accuses me of making bold statements. The boldest of these is my claim that a semantic grammar with four intention-specific forms can be applied to any meaningful clause. If Franzosi or Kiser wished to proffer a serious challenge to this claim, they would need to identify meaningful clauses that were intended to communicate something other than a description or judgment of a process or state of affairs (i.e., that were not perceptions, recognitions, justifications, or evaluations as defined in my paper). It is disappointing that neither faced this challenge.

REFERENCES

Berg, Bruce L. 1995. *Qualitative Research Methods for the Social Sciences*. Boston: Allyn and Bacon.

Mitchell, J. Clyde. 1983. "Case and Situation Analysis." *The Sociological Review* 31: 187–211.

Roberts, Carl W. 1997. *Text Analysis for the Social Sciences: Methods for Drawing Statistical Inferences from Texts and Transcripts*. Mahwah, NJ: Lawrence Erlbaum.

Shapiro, Gilbert. 1997. The Future of Coders: Human Judgments in a World of Sophisticated Software. In *Text Analysis for the Social Sciences: Methods for Drawing Statistical Inferences from Texts and Transcripts*, edited by Carl W. Roberts, 225–38. Mahwah, NJ: Lawrence Erlbaum.

4

SOCIOECONOMIC INDEXES FOR OCCUPATIONS: A REVIEW, UPDATE, AND CRITIQUE

Robert M. Hauser*
John Robert Warren*

Following a review of the history and sources of socioeconomic indexes for occupations, we estimate a new set of indexes for 1990 Census occupation lines, based on relationships between the prestige ratings obtained by Nakao and Treas in the 1989 General Social Survey and characteristics of occupational incumbents in the 1990 Census. We also investigate theoretical and empirical relationships among socioeconomic and prestige indexes, using data from the 1994 General Social Survey. Many common occupations, especially those held by women, do not fit the typical relationships among prestige, education, and earnings. The fit between prestige and socioeconomic characteristics of occupations can be improved by statistical transformation of the variables. However, in rudimentary models of occupational stratification, prestige-validated socioeconomic indexes are of limited value. They give too much weight to occupational earnings, and they ignore intergenerational relationships between occupational education and occupational earnings. Levels of occupational education appear to define the main dimension of occupational persistence across and within generations. We conclude that composite indexes of occupational socioeconomic status are scientifically obsolete.

Support for this research was provided by the National Science Foundation (SBR-9320660), the National Institute on Aging (AG-9775), the Vilas Estate Trust, and the Center for Demography and Ecology at the University of Wisconsin–Madison, which receives core support for Population Research from the National Institute for Child Health and Human Development (P30 HD05876). (*Continues on following page*)
*University of Wisconsin–Madison

1. SOCIOECONOMIC STATUS

Socioeconomic status is typically used as a shorthand expression for variables that characterize the placement of persons, families, households, census tracts, or other aggregates with respect to the capacity to create or consume goods that are valued in our society. Thus socioeconomic status may be indicated by educational attainment, occupational standing, social class, income (or poverty), wealth, and tangible possessions—such as home appliances or libraries, houses, cars, boats, or by degrees from elite colleges and universities. At some times, it has also been taken to include measures of participation in social, cultural, or political life. It is an empirical rather than a conceptual or theoretical question whether we should take socioeconomic status as no more than a convenient shorthand expression for variables like these, or whether such variables, taken collectively, behave as if they formed a unitary construct.[1]

There is a long standing and well-developed methodology for measuring one aspect of socioeconomic status using characteristics of occupations or of their incumbents. This has practical advantages because past as well as current occupations can be ascertained reliably, even by proxy. Occupational status also appears to indicate a reliable and powerful characteristic of persons or households by dint of its temporal stability and substantial correlation with other social and economic variables. At the same time, a scalar measure of occupational standing obviously cannot reflect everything about a job that might be relevant to other social, economic, or psychological variables (Rytina 1992; Hauser and Logan 1992), nor is there a strong theoretical basis for the concept of occupational socioeconomic status (Hodge 1981). Thus, while we both follow and elaborate one tradition of occupation-based socioeconomic measurement in this paper, we caution readers that the product of our work should be used thoughtfully and cautiously. Even the best measure of occupational socioeconomic status cannot stand alone, and some common occupations do not

(*Continued*) We thank Keiko Nakao for providing unpublished data from the 1989 NORC-GSS study of occupational prestige in the United States. We thank John Fox, Harry Ganzeboom, Michael Hout, and Adrian Raftery for helpful advice. The opinions expressed herein are those of the authors. Machine readable versions of the Hauser-Warren 1980-basis and 1990-basis SEI scores and their component data are available online at ftp:\\elaine.ssc.wisc.edu\pub\hauser. Address correspondence to Robert M. Hauser, Department of Sociology, University of Wisconsin–Madison, 1180 Observatory Drive, Madison, Wisconsin 53706 or HAUSER@SSC.WISC.EDU.

[1]For example, see Hauser (1972).

fit typical relationships among socioeconomic characteristics and occupational prestige. Indeed, we hope that our work will help to identify the limits as well as the heuristic value of measures of occupational socioeconomic status.

2. JOBS, OCCUPATIONS, AND OCCUPATIONAL STATUS

In our opinion, the social sciences have recently suffered from a preoccupation with current measures of income or poverty. To some degree, we think this focus is policy and program-driven. In the administration and evaluation of social, economic, and health programs we must necessarily rely upon narrow, temporally specific economic measures of eligibility or of outcome. The focus on strictly economic variables is perhaps also a consequence of the diffusion of economic thinking beyond the disciplinary boundary of economics and into the general population. Whatever its sources, this preoccupation may have diverted us from other major and consequential sources, dimensions, and consequences of social inequality.

There are good reasons to focus more attention on the collection, coding, and scaling of job and occupational data than has recently been the case. First, job-holding is the most important social and economic role held by most adults outside their immediate family or household. When we meet someone new, our first question is often "What do you do?", and that is a very good question. Job-holding defines how we spend much of our time, and it provides strong clues about the activities and circumstances in which that time is spent. Second, job-holding tells us about the technical and social skills that we bring to the labor market, and for most people job-holding delimits current and future economic prospects. Thus, even for persons who are not attached to the labor market, past jobs or the jobs held by other members of the same family or household provide information about economic and social standing. Third, as market labor has become nearly universal among adult women as well as men, it is increasingly possible to characterize individuals in terms of their own current or past jobs. Fourth, once we have a good job description, it is possible to map jobs into a multitude of classifications, scales, and measures, some of which may provide more information about economic standing than we can obtain from the usual questions about income or wealth. Fifth, measurement of jobs and occupations does not entail the same problems of refusal, recall, reliability, and stability as occur in the measurement of income or wealth. While job descriptions—contemporary or retrospective—are imperfect, the reliability and validity of carefully collected occupational data are high enough to support sustained analysis, and there is little tendency for the quality of occupational reports to decay with the passage of time.[2] Thus, even if we are limited to retrospective questions, we can confidently trace occupational trajectories across the adult years. The same cannot be said of earnings trajectories, let alone other components of personal or household income.

2.1. *Conceptual Issues*

It is important to distinguish between jobs and occupations and between establishments and industries. A job is a specific and sometimes unique bundle of activities carried out by a person in the expectation of economic remuneration. An occupation is an abstract category used to group and classify similar jobs. Such abstractions are often heterogeneous and idiosyncratic in construction, but they usually involve determinations of similarity in typical activities, in the sites where work is performed, in the form of job tenure, in the skill requirements of the job, or in the product or service that results from the job. The distinction between establishments and industries parallels that between jobs and occupations. An establishment is a specific geographic location where products or services are made or delivered, while an industry is an abstract category used to group and classify products or services. There are multiple systems for the classification of jobs and establishments and, within them, complex interdependencies between occupational and industrial classifications. Most social scientific uses of occupational data are based on the classification systems of the U.S. Bureau of the Census, which are revised each decade at the time of the decennial census or else on the *Dictionary of Occupational Titles*, which is produced by the Employment and Training Administration of the Department of Labor.

It has recently been proposed that the best way to collect job information may be to ask directly about the conditions of work. Jencks, Perman, and Rainwater (1988) developed a new composite index of the overall

[2]For example, in the Wisconsin Longitudinal Study (WLS), there is virtually no difference between the accuracy of reports of occupations held in 1975, which were reported and coded contemporaneously, and reports of the same occupations that were ascertained and coded independently in 1992–1993 (Hauser, Sewell, and Warren 1994). The WLS is a long-term study of more than 10,000 women and men who graduated from Wisconsin high schools in 1957.

quality of jobs, which they call the index of job desirability. They argue that occupational status measures, like the Duncan Socioeconomic Index (SEI) and occupational prestige, are too distant from the job because they characterize a broad occupational category, while earnings alone fail to capture nonpecuniary job rewards. In a small national telephone sample ($N = 809$), Jencks, Perman, and Rainwater measured the desirability of jobs directly, using a magnitude estimation task.[3] Then, they selected job characteristics that predicted (the natural log of) desirability.[4] Finally, they constructed a composite of those characteristics (the index of job desirability or IJD) and showed that it had high reliability and desirable analytic characteristics relative to conventional measures of occupational standing— e.g., that it reflects gender and experience differences better than the Duncan SEI. Moreover, unlike occupation-based measures of job characteristics, obtained by matching job descriptions or census occupations to lines in the *Dictionary of Occupational Titles*, the IJD pertains directly to individual jobs. Jencks, Perman, and Rainwater argue that it is much easier to ascertain the components of the IJD than to collect and code detailed occupational descriptions, so it is potentially both an economic and powerful measure. The IJD is as yet new and little tried, but we think it is worth careful consideration and evaluation.[5]

From the perspective taken here, some measures of social class reflect job or personal characteristics, while others are strictly occupational. For example, consider two conceptions of "social class," each of which is widely used in international comparative studies of social stratification. Both schemes are shown in Figure 1. Wright's (1985:88) class typology

[3]The question reads, "Now we would like you to rate your job compared to what most people consider an average job. . . . Let's give an average job a rating of 100. Then, if your job is TWICE as good as an average job, you should give it a rating of 200. If it is HALF as good, give it 50, and so on. You can give any number you like. So considering everything . . . if an average job is rated 100, how would you rate your job?"

[4]From 48 job characteristics, Jencks, Perman, and Rainwater selected 14 that significantly predicted job desirability. They narrowed that list to earnings, plus seven other characteristics, which accounted for most of the explained variation. These are educational requirements of the job, hours greater than 35 per week, on-the-job training, dirtiness of the job, frequency of supervision, repetitiveness, and federal employment; dirt, supervision, and repetition were undesirable.

[5]Using Bayesian methods, Hauser (1995) has suggested that earnings and education requirements of the job are the only characteristics whose effects may be large enough to sustain replication. Fortunately, the job desirability item, along with all 14 significant job characteristics, were measured in the Wisconsin Longitudinal Study in 1992–1993, and this will permit a test of the findings of Jencks, Perman, and Rainwater.

Erikson and Goldthorp's Class Schema	Wright's Class Typology
I. Higher-grade Professionals, administrators, and officials; managers in large industrial establishments; large proprietors	Owners: 1. Bourgeoisie 2. Small employers 3. Petty bourgeosie
II. Lower-grade professionals, administrators, and officials; higher-grade technicians; managers in small industrial establishments; supervisors of nonmanual employees	Nonowners: 4. Expert managers 5. Expert supervisors 6. Expert nonmanagers
IIa. Routine nonmanual employees, higher grade (administration and commerce)	7. Semicredentialed managers 8. Semicredentialed supervisors
IIIb. Routine nonmanual employees, lower grade (sales and services)	9. Semicredentialed workers 10. Uncredentialed managers 11. Uncredentialed supervisors 12. Proletarians
IVa. Small proprietors, artisans, etc., with employees	
IVb. Small proprietors, artisans, etc., without employees	
IVc. Farmers and smallholders; other self-employed workers in primary production	
V. Lower-grade technicians; supervisors of manual workers	
VI. Skilled manual workers	
VIIa. Semi- and unskilled manual workers (not in argiculture, etc.)	
VIIb. Agricultural and other workers in primary production	

FIGURE 1. The Erikson-Goldthorpe and Wright social class schemas.

combines concepts of ownership, authority, and expertise. Its measurement requires information about a person's educational attainment as well as ownership, authority, supervision, and occupational classification. On the other hand, although it uses information about employment that is not routinely collected in the course of occupational measurement in the United States, Erikson and Goldthorpe's (1992a:38–39) "class schema," is ultimately a grouping of occupational categories based upon Goldthorpe and Hope's (1974) study of occupational prestige in Great Britain (Goldthorpe 1980).

Each of these schemes is regarded by its authors as a theoretically refined basis for identifying the membership of real and discrete social classes. In Wright's neo-Marxian classification, the aim is to identify modes of labor exploitation in the relations of production. In Erikson and Goldthorpe's neo-Weberian classification, the class categories are designed to identify distinct combinations of occupational function and employment status. Both Wright and Erikson and Goldthorpe vigorously defend their class schemes against suggestions that they are no more than convenient aggregations of constituent variables. For example, Halaby and Weakliem (1993) demonstrated that the variables in Wright's class schema lost some of their power to explain differential earnings when they were combined into his class typology.[6] In reply, Wright (1993:32) declared, "these nominal categories correspond to qualitatively distinct causal mechanisms," and he rejected the empirical evidence of Halaby and Weakliem by arguing that "the choice depends on the questions being asked and the broader theoretical agenda within which a specific analysis is embedded" (p. 34). Similarly, when Hout and Hauser (1992) reported that Erikson and Goldthorpe's (1992a) mobility model vastly understated the explanatory power of the main vertical dimension of their class schema, Erikson and Goldthorpe (1992b:296) rejected their finding because, among other reasons, "In the class structural perspective on mobility that we ourselves adopt, hierarchy need not be specially privileged."[7]

In working with measures of occupational social standing, we emphasize the social and economic grading of the occupational structure, rather than a priori constructions of distinct social classes. Our strong suspicion is that differences between the two class schemes and between them and the measures emphasized in this review lie more in the proximity of constituent variables to jobs and persons than in other theoretical or conceptual distinctions that have been debated by their authors. Other things

[6]See also Halaby (1993).

[7]Hout and Hauser's (1992) model of the mobility table neither accorded the vertical dimension special "privilege" nor denied other social structural effects on mobility. It merely corrected a crude and defective specification of the vertical dimension by Erikson and Goldthorpe (1987).

being equal, we should expect a classification based partly upon personal and job characteristics to be more direct and powerful in its influence than a classification based on occupational characteristics alone. Wright's class typology somewhat resembles Hollingshead's well-known (and too widely used) index of class position in that both combine information about jobs and educational attainment, though in very different ways (Hollingshead 1957; Hollingshead and Redlich 1958). Rather than relying on any precast combination of occupation and other social or economic characteristics, we suggest that, wherever possible, investigators should collect and use data on education and income, as well as on occupational standing.

People are linked to jobs, most often through job-holding, but also through their relationships with other people who hold or have held jobs. Jobs can be mapped into standard occupational classifications, and the categories of those classifications may be linked to occupational characteristics. By working back through this series of linkages, we can describe people in terms of occupational characteristics. Such characteristics will be valid as descriptions of jobs only to the degree that occupations are homogeneous, and the intervening maps and linkages are sound. In our view, the remarkable thing about this way of measuring social and economic characteristics is not that it is error prone, which would seem obvious, but that it has remarkably high reliability and validity. That it does so is a social fact that rests both on skill and care in classification and coding, and also on strong uniformities in social structure.

2.2. *Measurement Issues*

Unlike income, there is little perceived risk to respondents in describing the jobs held by themselves and others they know. Rates of refusal and nonresponse to occupation questions are very low. For example, in the 1994 General Social Survey (GSS), only 139 of 2992 respondents (4.6 percent) could not be classified by the major occupation group of a job that they had held, currently or in the past, and of the unclassifiable cases, all but 13 were persons who had never worked. In the case of family income, 356 respondents (11.9 percent) failed to respond, and about half of the nonresponses were outright refusals. In the case of own income, 865 respondents (28.9 percent) reported that they had no income in the preceding year, and of those with income, 7.9 percent did not report it (Davis and Smith 1994:29–32, 64–65).

Unlike the case of income, respondents usually know enough about their jobs (or those held by other significant persons in their lives) to provide information that can be coded reliably. However, it takes time and care to collect and code occupational data. One way of describing this is to say that the collection of income and other strictly economic data places a large cognitive burden on the respondent, while the collection of occupational data places more of that burden on the collector and coder of the data.

In a complete series of occupation questions, it is necessary to ascertain industry and class of worker as well as occupation; a typical series is shown in Figure 2. These questions would be sufficient to permit coding entries into the classification systems used in any of the U.S. Censuses from 1940 to 1990. The Census revises its classification system decennially, but over the past 50 years there has been a seven-digit coding system, three digits each for occupation and industry and one digit for class of worker. The classification system was relatively stable from 1940 to 1960. There was a minor upgrade in 1970, and in 1980 the system was overhauled completely in order to bring it up to date and render it more comparable to other (including international) classification systems. The 1980 system was carried forward with minor changes in 1990.

It takes time for respondents to answer the five questions in Figure 2, and it takes time to code them. We usually allow about 1.5 minutes

---

1. What kind of work does . . . do? (For example, electrical engineer, stock clerk, typist, farmer)
2. What are . . .'s most important activities or duties at that job? (For example, types, keeps account books, files, sells cars, operates printing press, finishes concrete)
3. What kind of buisness or industry is this? (For example, TV and radio, manufacturing, retail shoe store, State Labor Department, farm)
4. Is this mainly manufacturing, wholesale trade, retail trade, or something else?
5. Is . . . and employee of a private company, business or individual for wages, salary or commission? A federal government employee? A state government employee? Self-employed in own business, professional practice, or farm? (If not farm, ask, "Is the business incorporated?") Working without pay in a family business or farm?

FIGURE 2. Occupation-industry question series.

of telephone or household survey time per occupation-industry entry, and experienced coders can complete about 10 entries per hour. To code occupation and industry, a trained coder must attempt to match text between survey reports and listings in the Census Bureau's alphabetic or classified indexes of industries and occupations.[8] The alphabetic indexes list permissible codes for occupation and industry, based on an alphabetic sort of common responses. The classified index is a reverse listing, in which the same set of entries is sorted by occupation or industry code, thus providing a definition by extension of each line of the classifications.[9] Coders must occasionally refer to other resources, like the *Dictionary of Occupational Titles*, to learn more about specific occupations or to find synonyms for unfamiliar descriptions. Where more than one occupation or industry line may be appropriate, codes can be allocated at random with probabilities determined by the distributions across the candidate lines in the preceding Census—that is, from a cross-classification of detailed occupation by detailed industry. In some surveys, the senior author has trained interviewers as well as coders in occupational classification, and this pays dividends in the quality of industry and occupation reports.

In connection with the 1990 Census, the Bureau of the Census is distributing a VMS software product that can be used to code about half of the typical occupation or industry entries, leaving the remaining half for trained coders. Experienced coders can achieve 85 percent agreement in the classification of three-digit industry and 80 to 85 percent agreement in the classification of three-digit occupation. This level of agreement is sufficient to produce high levels of correlation between independent codings of the same occupational characteristics. For example, Bielby, Hauser, and Featherman (1977:1258, 1262) independently recoded reports of father's occupation and of son's first occupation among 578 white males and

[8] The senior author has often been asked for advice by investigators in *ad hoc* surveys, who have little interest in detailed occupation-industry coding. Often, they have not asked the right questions to begin with, and they are looking for a way of sight-coding one-line descriptions into some scheme like the Hollingshead index. This reflects a casual attitude toward socioeconomic measurement that probably would not be tolerated by the same investigators if it pertained to their major substantive interests. Readers who imagine that detailed occupation-industry coding requires too great an investment might ask themselves about the cognitive demands that are placed on respondents by detailed questions about their incomes and assets.

[9] In the last three decennial Censuses, these references are from the U.S. Bureau of the Census (1971a, 1971b, 1982a, 1982b, 1992a, 1992b). Two recent editions of the *Dictionary of Occupational Titles* are from the U.S. Department of Labor (1977, 1991).

348 black males in the 1973 Occupational Changes in a Generation (OCG) survey. When the codes were mapped into the Duncan SEI, the correlations between recoded occupational statuses were 0.94 for father's occupation and 0.94 for son's first occupation among whites, and the corresponding correlations were 0.88 and 0.93 among blacks.[10]

Occupations can also be reported reliably by respondents, whether the jobs are or were their own or someone else's.[11] Again, using occupations from the 1973 OCG survey that were mapped into the Duncan SEI, Bielby, Hauser, and Featherman (1977) obtained test-retest correlations of 0.64 among black men and 0.87 among white men for father's occupational status over about a three-month period. The corresponding test-retest correlations were 0.77 and 0.87 for men's first, full-time civilian occupations, and they were 0.72 and 0.80 for current occupations.[12] The latter figures may seem low, but they do not measure reliability in the strict sense. They are based on reports of own current occupation in the March 1973 CPS and in a reinterview six months later; thus, the correlation reflects true changes in status as well as reporting error. These correlations of occupational status are somewhat lower than corresponding test-retest correlations of own educational attainment, 0.87 among blacks and 0.92 among whites. In a recent study, Hauser, Sewell, and Warren (1994) obtained correlations between Duncan SEI scores of occupations that were reported contemporaneously by a sample of more than 6000 male and female high school graduates from Wisconsin in 1975, when the sample was about 36 years old, and that were reported again, retrospectively, in

---

[10]A report by Nakao and Treas (1994) of low coding reliability in the NORC General Social Survey seems exceptional. In the 1989 GSS, they found a correlation of only 0.76 between two versions of a 1960-vintage prestige scale for workers' occupations independently coded into the 1970 and 1980 Census occupational classification systems. For further evidence about unreliability of occupational coding in the GSS, see Smith, Crovitz, and Walsh (1988).

[11]Given the likely uses of occupational data, we believe that the reliability and stability of an occupational index, like the Duncan SEI, is more pertinent to an evaluation of the quality of occupational measurement than would be a measure of simple agreement between reports across occasions.

[12]The low reliabilities observed for blacks underscore the need to measure reliability contemporaneously in social surveys. However, the reason for the lower reliabilities was the homogeneity of blacks in occupational standing, not greater reporting error. The standard deviations of errors were barely larger among blacks than among whites, but the standard deviations of true statuses were much smaller among blacks. Since reliability is a ratio of true variance to total variance, reliability was low among blacks (Bielby, et al. 1977: 1258, 1262).

1992–1993. The test-retest correlations over the 17-to-18-year recall period for persons who were employed in 1975 were 0.84 among men and 0.79 among women. Parents' occupations also can be reported reliably by older teenage youth. In a study of sixth, ninth, and twelfth grade boys from Fort Wayne, Indiana, Mason et al. (1976) reported correlations between son's and father's reports of the father's occupational status of 0.80, 0.92, and 0.93 at the sixth, ninth, and twelfth grades among white youth and correlations of 0.39, 0.38, and 0.74 among black youth at the same grade levels.[13]

2.3. Occupational Prestige

What are the relevant status characteristics of occupations? Many discussions of occupations in the stratification system begin with the concept of occupational prestige, the general level of social standing enjoyed by the incumbents of an occupation. There has been great debate about the definition of prestige. For example, should it, as in the classic sociological literature, describe a relationship of deference or derogation between role incumbents, or does it merely pertain to the general desirability or goodness of an occupation? However defined, there is substantial agreement about the properties of occupational prestige.

First, it does not matter much how people are asked to rate occupations. Regardless of the form of the question and the mode of response, essentially the same ranking will be obtained. To take two extreme cases, in an Israeli sample, Kraus, Schild, and Hodge (1978) found that prestige was the main dimension of perceived differences among occupations when respondents were asked to sort pairs of occupation titles into similar groups, without any specification of the kind of similarity that they were to use. Duncan, Featherman, and Duncan (1972:77) estimated a correlation of 0.81 between expert judgments of required occupational intelligence (the Barr scale from the 1920s) and the Duncan SEI for 96 matched 1950-basis Census occupations. For 47 Barr titles that could be matched to a 1964 NORC study of occupational prestige, they found a correlation of 0.91.

Second, it does not matter much who rates the occupations. Even from a small sample, one can obtain a reliable and valid prestige scale by averaging ratings of occupations. There is indirect evidence that prestige ratings of occupations are highly correlated in the United States between

---

[13]The Fort Wayne samples were very small, 80 whites at each grade level and 30 to 50 blacks at each grade level.

the nineteenth and twentieth centuries (Hauser 1982).[14] Between the second major national survey of prestige, carried out in the middle 1960s by the National Opinion Research Center (NORC), and the most recent survey, carried out in 1989 by NORC, the correlation is 0.97 across 160 titles that were rated both in the 1960s and in 1989 (Nakao and Treas 1994). Earlier, Hodge, Siegel, and Rossi (1964) had found a correlation of 0.99 for a smaller set of titles over the 1947–1963 period. Occupational prestige ratings are also highly correlated across countries. Treiman (1975; 1977) assembled a definitive international collection of prestige studies up through the early 1970s, and he found an average intercorrelation of 0.81 across 55 countries. He combined these data to create the Standard International Occupational Prestige Scale (SIOPS), into which one can map from the 1950, 1960, and 1970 U.S. Census classifications and the 1958 and 1969 International Standard Classifications of Occupations (Treiman 1977). Finally, there are scant variations in occupational prestige ratings across populations defined by sex (Bose and Rossi 1983), race (Siegel 1970), or location in the social hierarchy within industrialized nations and most of the nonindustrialized world (Haller and Bills 1979).

In the United States there have been three major national surveys of occupational prestige. The first was carried out at NORC in 1947 by North and Hatt, but its major findings were not reported for more than a decade (Reiss 1961). These ratings covered only 90 titles, and investigators used a variety of questionable methods to fill in the missing lines until Duncan (1961) constructed an approximation to prestige scores for the full 1950 Census classification. The second major U.S. study of prestige was carried out in a series of NORC surveys in the mid-1960s. Siegel (1971) reconciled the ratings from different surveys and directly estimated the prestige of every line in the 1960 Census occupational classification. These ratings were later updated to the 1970 Census classification by Hauser and Featherman (1977) and by Davis and Smith (1994), and Stevens and Hoisington (1987) updated them again to the 1980 Census classification.[15] The third U.S. pres-

---

[14]Hauser's historical data were ratings of occupations by several social historians, each of whom professed great familiarity with the social structure of a nineteenth-century American city and claimed that their ratings would reflect contemporary opinion.

[15]Since there were large changes between the 1960 and 1970 Census classification schemes, the Hauser-Featherman update was carried out by estimating weighted average scores for detailed 1970 Census lines in terms of their 1960 Census components, using a sample of the 1960 population whose jobs had been classified using both systems (U.S. Bureau of the Census 1972). Similarly, Stevens and Hoisington (1987) used a matrix that expressed detailed 1980 Census lines in terms of their 1970 Census

tige study was carried out in conjunction with the 1989 GSS of the National Opinion Research Center (Nakao and Treas 1994). These occupational prestige ratings were initially mapped into categories of the 1980 Census classification, and have been updated to be usable with the 1990 system.

The main problem with occupational prestige ratings is that they lack criterion validity. Prestige is not as highly correlated with other variables as are other measures of occupational social standing—specifically, measures of the socioeconomic status of occupations, as indicated by the average educational attainment and income of occupational incumbents. One well-replicated example of this is intergenerational occupational mobility. In analyses of correlations between the occupational standing of fathers and sons, prestige scales behave roughly as if they were error-ridden measurements of the socioeconomic status of the occupations held by fathers and sons (Featherman et al. 1975; Featherman and Hauser 1976). Indeed, the low criterion validity of occupational prestige is one of the reasons that Treiman found few takers for his Standard International Occupational Prestige Scale.

2.4. Socioeconomic Indexes of Occupational Status

How did we get from occupational prestige to occupational socioeconomic status? While the two more recent prestige surveys obtained ratings for all occupational titles in the then-current Census classification schemes, only 90 titles were rated in the 1947 NORC survey (Reiss 1961:5–6, 261–62). This created a problem for investigators who wanted to "fill in" scores for unrated occupations (Duncan 1961:110–14). Not only did they have to create new scores, but there was no basis for comparability between studies. As part of a project on "Occupational Classification for Vital Statistics Use," Duncan created a set of socioeconomic scores for all occupations, and he transformed these back into the original metric of the NORC prestige scores. First, Duncan matched titles that had been rated in the survey into lines from the 1950 Census; unfortunately, only 45 titles could be matched. Then he regressed the percentage of "good" or "excellent" rat-

components, using a sample of the 1970 population whose jobs had been classified using both systems (U.S. Bureau of the Census 1989). Our guess is that the latter set of scores will not be used widely, for the prestige scores on which it was based date from the 1960s, and the Nakao-Treas prestige scores are now available. Moreover, we might expect the validity of the prestige scores to become attenuated through repeated application of the weighting procedure.

ings on the five-point scale used in the NORC survey on age-adjusted percentages of male occupational incumbents in the 1950 Census who had completed high school or more and who had reported incomes of $3500 or more in 1949. This regression yielded roughly equal weights for the two regressors, and the multiple correlation was 0.91. The socioeconomic index was constructed by applying the regression weights to the age-standardized characteristics of all 1950-basis Census titles (including distinctions by industry and class of worker within large residual groups).[16] Finally, Duncan also reported a transform of the index back to the metric of the original NORC prestige scores, which were the mean ratings of each occupation on the five-point scale, and a set of decile scores, pertaining to the position of each occupation in the ranking of the employed population by values of the socioeconomic index. Most subsequent use of Duncan's work has employed the index, rather than the NORC transform or the decile scores. For example, perhaps the best-known application of the Duncan SEI scale was by Blau and Duncan (1967) in their classic study of social mobility among American men. Unfortunately, because the SEI was initially constructed as a proxy for occupational prestige, some subsequent work has failed to distinguish between the prestige and socioeconomic status of occupations.

The Duncan SEI has been updated or elaborated in several ways, and researchers should be cautious in using the updates because of their potential lack of comparability. Duncan assigned scores to categories of the 1960 Census occupational classification, and these were the scores used in the Blau-Duncan monograph. Hauser and Featherman (1977) updated the 1960-basis SEI scores to occupation lines from the 1970 Census, using the same averaging method described above in relation to the 1960-basis NORC (Siegel) prestige scores.[17] Stevens and Featherman (1981) published a major revision of the SEI. Using the map of Siegel prestige scores into 1970-basis Census occupation lines, they regressed prestige scores for all occupations on measures of the educational attainment and income of all occupational incumbents in 1970; the scale values were the predicted prestige scores in the regressions. In order to meet complaints that the original Duncan SEI ignored women, they produced two versions

---

[16]Unfortunately, neither of the subsequent revisions of the Duncan scale includes these additional distinctions.

[17]The senior author has elaborated the scale scores by class of worker and industry for selected 1970–basis occupation lines. These scores are available by request.

of their new scale, one in which the regressors pertained to the characteristics of male workers (MSEI2) and a second in which the regressors pertained to the characteristics of all workers (TSEI2).

MSEI2 and TSEI2 are entirely new scales. They are not comparable
to the Duncan SEI, even though they were constructed using a similar
methodology. We could compare findings based on those scales to those
based on the SEI by mapping 1970-basis occupations into both systems.
We could compare findings across time using MSEI2 or TSEI2 by project-
ing them back into earlier Census classification systems; to our knowledge, no one has carried out the latter task. Stevens and Cho (1985) carried
the 1970-basis MSEI2 and TSEI2 forward to the 1980 Census classification system using the same methodology as Hauser and Featherman
(1977)—that is, by taking a weighted average of scores for 1980-basis
Census occupation lines in terms of their 1970-basis constituent lines, based
on a sample from the 1970 Census (U.S. Bureau of the Census 1989). This
rendered MSEI2 and TSEI2 as comparable between 1970 and 1980-basis
lines as the Duncan SEI was between 1950 or 1960-basis and 1970-basis
lines.

As part of their update of Siegel's scores, Nakao and Treas (1994)
created socioeconomic scores for 1980-basis Census occupation lines by
regressing their prestige ratings on the characteristics of male and female occupational incumbents in the 1980 Census.[18] The new NORC
prestige scores were collected at the end of the decade (1989), while the
corresponding socioeconomic status scores were based upon characteristics of the work force in 1980. The obvious next step is to create yet
another set of socioeconomic scores, using the 1989 prestige scores as a
criterion, but based upon characteristics of the work force in the 1990
Census. This is one of the analytic tasks that we have undertaken in the
present study.

The revision of indexes of occupational socioeconomic status may
be a good thing, if our focus is on the present day, but it presents great

---

[18]The Nakao-Treas prestige and socioeconomic scores may be obtained in
machine-readable form from Dr. Tom Smith, General Social Survey, National Opinion
Research Center, University of Chicago, Chicago, IL 60637. Unfortunately, Nakao and
Treas (1994:11) present an incorrect version of their SEI prediction equation for all
workers (TSEI). We have verified that the correct equation (excluding three apprenticeship lines), which was earlier presented in a methodological report of the General
Social Survey (Nakao and Treas 1992), is TSEI = 16.896 + 0.620 (Education) +
0.276 (Income).

problems in establishing intertemporal comparability.[19] Findings based on the original Duncan SEI may be compared across occupations coded to the standards of the Censuses of 1950 to 1970. Findings based upon the Stevens-Featherman scales may be compared freely from 1970 to 1990 (for the 1980 and 1990 systems are very close), and those based upon the Nakao-Treas scales are only comparable from 1980 to 1990. Of course, these limits are based on the assumption that occupations have been coded only once, to the standards of a single decennial census. We believe that, given the preservation of original responses in machine-readable form, we shall in years to come be able to code old data to new standards economically. For example, in the 1992–1993 round of the Wisconsin Longitudinal Survey, we have first coded all occupation reports to 1970 standards, in order to preserve comparability with past codes. A next step will be to sort the text entries for each occupation-industry report by the 1970 codes and batch code them into lines in the 1990 classification. This will be both faster and cheaper than an independent recode of the data in multiple systems.

The Duncan SEI and its successors are not the only readily available socioeconomic scores for occupations. The major competitor in this respect is the series of Nam-Powers scores now available for Census occupational classifications from 1940 through 1980 (Stafford and Fossett 1991) using a methodology developed by Nam and Powers (1983). Nam and Powers rate occupations on the basis of the average percentile of their incumbents in the cumulative distribution of workers, when the occupations are ranked by median education and by median income.[20] That is, the Nam-Powers ratings are purely relative measures of standing that have no specific functional relationship to the actual levels of schooling or income in occupations. Depending on one's point of view, this has either the advantage or disadvantage of lacking a criterion to weight the relative importance of occupational education and occupational income; indeed, it suggests that, for some purposes, it might make more sense to use mea-

---

[19]In addition to the aforementioned updates of the Duncan SEI, Fridman, Lee, and Falcon (1987) have used Duncan's methodology to construct socioeconomic scores for occupations in the Census of 1940.

[20]It is not clear why the weights of education and income should be equal. Also, Stafford and Fossett's listing of socioeconomic scores contains serious errors. It lists scores for industries within categories of 1960-basis occupations using 1970-basis, three-digit industry codes. Thus a mechanical recode using their list will generate many erroneous score assignments when data have been coded using 1960-basis occupation and industry codes.

sures both of occupational education and of occupational income and avoid any *a priori* combination of them. One might argue that the Nam-Powers scores are, by construction, comparable across years and occupational classifications. We disagree. First, they will vary across time with changes in the relative standing of occupations. Such changes occur with glacial speed (Duncan 1968), and we do not think that they present a serious problem. Second, and more important, the scores will change over time as the occupational distribution changes, even in the absence of any change in the characteristics of occupational incumbents. We think this is a most undesirable property, and for this reason, we believe that the Nam-Powers scores present serious problems of comparability across time.

Advocates of the Nam-Powers approach have suggested that it yields a purely socioeconomic measure, whereas the Duncan scale (and, presumably, its relatives) is a combination of occupational education, income, and prestige (Haug 1977:3; Powers 1982). There is surely room for confusion about this issue, for Duncan's (1961) text is ambivalent about whether the SEI was a proxy measure of prestige or whether it was a distinct "socioeconomic" measure (Hodge 1981; Stevens and Featherman 1981; Nam and Terrie 1982). While it is possible to argue both about intent and about the accuracy with which the SEI approximates prestige, the fact is that the SEI is simply a weighted average of occupational education and income. Once the weights have been determined, prestige plays no part in the index.[21] Since Duncan's regression analysis gave virtually equal weight to occupational education and income, it is not surprising that the SEI should correlate highly with the Nam-Powers index, despite the nonlinear relationship between the latter and its educational and economic components.[22] Indeed, laying aside the difference between absolute and relative measurement, we would not stray far from the truth in saying that the Duncan SEI and the Nam-Powers index are both equally weighted averages of occupational education and income.

[21] This is patently the case for the vast majority of occupation lines for which no prestige data were obtained in the North-Hatt prestige study. To make the point clearer yet, we might imagine a composite measure of occupational status, constructed as a weighted average of occupational education, income, and prestige. To our knowledge, no one has produced such an index. Unfortunately, Haug's view has recently been taken up by a social historian, Matthew Sobek, who writes of the Duncan SEI that "it can be considered a prestige scale for practical historical purposes" (Sobek 1996).

[22] Beyond this, it is well known that correlations involving linear composites are rather insensitive to differential weighting of the components.

This is not by any means to claim that the SEI or its relatives are better constructions than the Nam-Powers index. For example, there are serious questions about the validity of Duncan's regression estimates. Although Duncan (1961:122–23) listed all of the residuals from his regression, he apparently did not recognize the sensitivity of his estimates to three outlying and influential observations (ministers, railroad engineers, and railroad conductors). Had those observations been deleted, the effect of occupational income would have been more than three times as large as that of occupational education (Fox 1991; Friendly 1991), and the Duncan SEI would have been essentially a measure of occupational income. We might count Duncan's use of all of the observations as a fortunate choice in light of later evidence that the effects of occupational education on prestige are larger than those of occupational income. Siegel (1971) and Stevens and Featherman (1981) have each noted that Duncan's findings were affected by the top-heavy selection of the 45 NORC titles that could be matched to 1950 Census titles. The selection of titles led to an overestimate of the effect of occupational income relative to occupational education, when Duncan's estimates (or similar, contemporaneous estimates based on the same titles) were compared to estimates based on all Census titles in 1970. For example, the effect of occupational education was substantially larger than that of occupational income, both in the male-based scores (MSEI2) and the scores for the total population (TSEI2) that were estimated by Stevens and Featherman (1981:369).[23]

2.5. Other Indexes of Occupational Status

This is perhaps an appropriate point for us to comment on the Hollingshead Index of Social Position, a classification of selected occupational titles into seven occupational grades. There must be something appealing about it, for its use has persisted over more than 30 years, and, as far as we know, it has never been published formally.[24] Perhaps one reason for this is a comparison between the Hollingshead Index and the Duncan SEI by Haug and Sussman (1971), which came out most unfavorably to the SEI. The central finding of the Haug-Sussman paper, on which they base a

----

[23]We shall turn later to methodological problems in the more recent prestige-weighted estimates of occupational socioeconomic status.

[24]The senior author obtained his copy from a colleague at Brown University in the late 1960s.

resounding rejection of the SEI, is a correlation of 0.74 in a national sample between the SEI and Hollingshead's Two Factor Index of Social Position, where both variables were categorized to approximate the marginal distribution of the Hollingshead Index. This "low" correlation, they argue, invalidates the SEI as a measure of "social class." However, as Haug and Sussman note, the Hollingshead Index includes individual variation in education within occupation, while the SEI does not. Moreover, they report in a footnote that in fully disaggregated data, the correlation between the SEI and the Two-Factor Index is 0.82, and it is 0.84 if one uses only the occupational component of the Hollingshead index. It is not clear why one would regard the last correlations as "low," when, for example, Duncan (1961:124) observed correlations of 0.84 and 0.85 between occupational income and prestige and between occupational education and prestige among the 45 titles used in his regression analysis. Indeed, similar correlations are observed between prestige scores and socioeconomic indexes across all occupation lines in the 1990 Census (see Table 3).

In a similar analysis, Haug (1972: 442) reports a correlation of only 0.75 between the Duncan SEI and 1960-basis Census scores for occupational status in a small national sample ($N = 1284$). Recall that the Census (or Nam-Powers) score is an equally weighted composite of the percentile ranks of occupations in the educational and income distributions of the labor force (U.S. Bureau of the Census 1963; Nam and Powers 1983). Noting Gordon's (1969) finding of a correlation of 0.95 between the same two indexes across 91 occupations, Haug attributes the low correlation in her sample to the difference between equal and sample-based weights for the occupations and concludes that the SEI is defective.[25] We were surprised by these discrepant figures, so we estimated the correlation between the Stevens-Featherman MSEI2 and the 1970-basis Census socioeconomic scores in the 1973 Occupational Changes in a Generation sample.[26] Among 26,000 U.S. men aged 25 to 64 in 1973, the correlation between the scores for current occupations was 0.87. The Duncan-type SEI and the Nam-Powers scores are surely not indistinguishable, but neither do they appear as different as Haug suggested.

In an invited commentary on Haug and Sussman's paper, Hollingshead described the development of his occupational "index," which was based on the social standing of occupations in his study of New Haven,

[25]See also Haug (1977:61).
[26]The 1970-basis Census socioeconomic scores were estimated by Stafford and Fossett (1991).

Connecticut. In response to a query about the placement of certain occupations, Hollingshead (1971:566) wrote:

> The problem of allocation of a given individual's occu-
> pation to a particular place on the economic scale is oc-
> casionally difficult. Haug and Sussman puzzle over why
> a correction officer was assigned a rating of 2 while a
> policeman rated 5. This particular correction officer was
> a professional social worker attached to the juvenile court.
> He held a Master of Science degree from a recognized
> school of social work. Policemen were rated 5 because
> they are trained men and were generally regarded in the
> community as skilled municipal employees.

In other words Hollingshead's "index" is a combination of his ratings of
specific individuals in New Haven and of his perception of the general
social standing of occupations. If we were going to use a prestige scale, we
should want to use ratings based on the opinion of more than one individual, and we certainly should not want to rate entire occupational categories
based on the characteristics of a single occupational incumbent.

Ganzeboom, De Graaf, and Treiman (1992) have developed a standard International Socio-Economic Index (ISEI) of occupational status,
which may prove useful in international comparisons. Rather than using
prestige as a criterion, they explicitly constructed a set of scores that best
account for the correlation between occupational education and occupational income. They argue that this construction fits Duncan's (1961:116–
17) rationale for the SEI: "We have, therefore, the following sequence: a
man qualifies himself for occupational life by obtaining an education; as a
consequence of his pursuing his occupation, he obtains income. Occupation, therefore, is the intervening activity linking income to education."
Ganzeboom, De Graaf, and Treiman estimated this model for a pooled
sample of 73,901 full-time employed men from 16 countries for whom
detailed occupational data in the 1968 ISCO classification were available,
and they cross-validated the coefficients using five fresh large national
surveys in countries for which local socioeconomic indexes were available. In the cross-validation, the ISEI performed about as well as locally
constructed indexes. Thus the ISEI would appear to be a valuable tool for
international comparative analyses of the effects of occupational status. Of
course, the weighting scheme used by Ganzeboom, De Graaf, and Treiman,

as well as those based on occupational prestige as a criterion, may not be optimal in other content domains, and a test of those assumptions would be a valuable contribution to our understanding of socioeconomic measurement.

We have argued, thus far, that occupations carry a great deal of information about social standing, that respondents are willing and able to describe occupations, that they can be coded reliably—whether ascertained by self-report or proxy, and that their social standing can be measured by mapping the prestige or socioeconomic status of occupations into detailed occupational classifications. Occupational status also appears to be rather stable across time. For example, observed father-son correlations of occupational socioeconomic status typically range between 0.35 and 0.45. Econometric estimates of intergenerational income persistence approach these magnitudes only with heroic assumptions about unreliability and instability of incomes across time (Solon 1992; Zimmerman 1992). Within individual careers, occupational status correlations are also moderately high. For example, without correction for attenuation, the correlations between the status of a man's first, full-time civilian occupation and that of his current occupation in the Blau-Duncan study ranged only from 0.584 at ages 25 to 34 to 0.513 at ages 55 to 64 in 1962. In the Wisconsin Longitudinal Study, without correction for attenuation, the correlations between Duncan scores of first, full-time civilian occupations and 1992/93 occupations were 0.44 among women and 0.58 among men. The correlations between status scores of contemporaneous reports of current occupations in 1975 and 1992–1993 were 0.57 among women and 0.71 among men. Across the same 17-year span, the correlations of annual earnings were 0.38 among women and 0.51 among men. Findings like these suggest that occupational status may be a better indicator of long-term—or, as economists call it, permanent—income than is income at a single point in time (Goldberger 1989; Zimmerman 1992). Unlike permanent income, occupational status can be measured well at a single point in time. However, as demonstrated below, the persistence of occupational status does not depend on its association with income.

2.6. Gender and Occupational Status

We have thus far ignored relationships between gender and measures of occupational standing. There are scant differences in occupational prestige ratings by men and women (Nakao and Treas 1994); neither do gender specificity in rated occupational titles nor the percentage of women in occupations substantially affect occupational prestige (Fox and Suschnigg 1989). There are, of course, large and persistent differences in occupations held by men and women and in their remuneration. At the same time, depending on the rating or scale used, occupational prestige or status differences favor men, or favor women, or show essentially no differences (Boyd 1986), and the choice of scales also influences gender differentials in the effects of schooling and early occupational experience on the occupational standing of adults (Featherman and Stevens 1982; Warren et al. 1996).

Occupational socioeconomic indexes based on characteristics of male workers are highly correlated with those based on the characteristics of all workers, but recent practice has encouraged the use of the latter scales. First, unlike the Duncan index and its later analog (Stevens and Featherman's MSEI2), the "total" indexes, like Stevens and Featherman's TSEI2, include women in the measurement of occupational status. Second, in both the United States and Canada, the average differences in "total" indexes favor men more than the differences in "male" indexes, and this conforms with widespread beliefs about male-female disparities in occupational standing. Boyd (1986:471) has stated this forcefully: "the scaling of occupations into total scores produces results which are the most consistent with the argument that women in the labor force are disadvantaged relative to men." We do not think this provides sufficient scientific justification for a choice between indexes. There has been relatively little investigation of the specific differences in "male" and "total" indexes that lead to variation in their statistical properties, but see Featherman and Stevens (1982:102–108). Rather, the practice, unfortunate in our opinion, has been to construct "total," "male," and—in some cases "female"—indexes of occupational socioeconomic status in strictly parallel fashion, following Duncan's procedures, and to compare the behavior of the indexes in male or female samples without attempting to solve the puzzle posed by the differential behavior of the indexes.

We suggest the hypothesis that the differential behavior of "male," "total," and "female" indexes of occupational socioeconomic status is in part due to the same difference in male and female work patterns that confounds some other efforts to compare the economic standing of men and women. That is, employed women are more likely to work part-time than men. Both the share of women and the tendency to work part-time vary from occupation to occupation. Thus, when the "economic" status of occupations is indexed by one of the usual functions of the earnings distribution, like the median, mean, or percentage above an arbitrary threshold, the income measure is affected by the extent of part-time work in the occupation.

To our knowledge, none of the several constructions of socioeconomic status indexes has introduced any adjustment for part-time or part-year work. This probably has made little difference in previously constructed indexes for male occupational incumbents, most of whom work full-time and full-year, but it has affected the construction of scores based on the characteristics of women or of all employed persons. Of course, this raises the question whether the status of an occupation is better indexed by the annual pay of its incumbents, regardless of their labor supply, or by something closer to the wage rate. If the wage rate is the key economic variable, the greater external validity of "male-based" occupational status indexes, which has often been observed for women as well as men, becomes understandable.

To test this hypothesis, we need measures of occupational income that standardize for labor supply. One way to accomplish this is to limit the population to full-time, full-year workers of each sex, but this could create selection problems, and it could lead to excessive sampling variability in smaller occupations, especially among women. A preferable course, we think, will be to include all workers, but to adjust earnings for part-time/full-time status and weeks worked.

3. A SOCIOECONOMIC INDEX FOR THE 1990s

We think that it will be useful to base a new socioeconomic index for occupations on characteristics of employed persons that are contemporary to the prestige ratings—that is, those in the 1990 Census. These can easily be mapped into 1980-basis census lines because there were minimal changes in the occupational classification between 1980 and 1990. Finally, they will provide a smoother transition into the future because they will be based on more recent occupational characteristics.

We have made a special extract of occupational education and earnings from the 1990 Census 5 percent public use sample for each state and the District of Columbia. This extract also contains three-digit industry, class of worker, age, sex, race, hours worked per week, and weeks worked per year. In particular, it has enabled us to construct socioeconomic indexes for the total work force and, separately, for men and for women. Our purpose in creating gender-specific indexes has been to compare the behavior of occupational characteristics between men and women, especially in relation to occupational prestige. We do not recommend routine use of the gender-specific indexes in research. As shown below, while the indexes for all workers, men, and women have roughly the same range and are in the same metric, their statistical properties differ. Findings based on the total, male, and female indexes are not strictly comparable (Warren, Sheridan, and Hauser 1996), and, where researchers choose to use a composite socioeconomic index, we recommend the index based on the characteristics of all workers.

3.1. *Data and Variables*

Throughout our analyses, we used the same definition of occupational education as Nakao and Treas (1994)—namely, the percentage of people in an occupation who had completed one or more years of college. We used three alternative definitions of occupational economic standing. First, we selected the employed civilian labor force, eliminated persons without earnings in 1989, and coded earnings as the percentage of workers in an occupation who earned $25,000 or more in 1989. The $25,000 threshold occurs at approximately the same percentile point of the earnings distribution in 1990 as the $15,000 threshold used by Nakao and Treas for 1980 Census data. Second, for the same sample, we coded economic standing as the percentage of workers in an occupation who earned $14.30 per hour or more in 1989. This wage rate yields earnings of $25,000 per year for 35 hours per week of work, 50 weeks per year. To estimate the wage rate, we divided annual earnings by the product of the number of hours worked per week and the number of weeks worked per year. For these two inclusive sampling schemes, 5,559,121 records were selected, and after weighting these cases represented 112,169,744 workers. Third, we selected full-time, full-year workers, those who worked at least 35 hours per week and who worked at least 50 weeks in 1989. In this case, we coded earnings as the percentage of workers in an occupation who earned $25,000 or more in 1989.[27] We selected 3,491,686 records of full-time, year-round workers, which represent 70,517,365 workers after weighting.

Throughout our analyses, we have used occupational earnings (wage and salary earnings, plus farm and nonfarm net business income), rather

[27]We cannot claim that the thresholds of occupational education and occupational income are theoretically equivalent and, thus, that effects of percentage points above or below those thresholds (or transformations of them) are equivalent. However, the use of threshold measures provides a convenient metric, and we doubt that the behavior of these measures differs substantially from that of other potential measures of aggregate occupational standing. In fact, since the Bureau of the Census dropped its years of schooling concept with the 1990 Census, we had little choice but to use a threshold measure of occupational education.

than occupational income. This departs from Duncan's analysis and that of later updates of the SEI, each of which has used occupational income. We have used earnings for several reasons. Earnings is the component of income that is reported best in the Census. It is by far the largest component of most workers' incomes, and it is more closely related to occupational incumbency than other types of income. After experimenting with alternative treatments of earnings, we have constructed the new socioeconomic indexes using occupational wage rates, which should be based solely on earnings.

In previous constructions of socioeconomic indexes for occupations, some researchers have used age-standardized educational attainment and income (Duncan 1961; Nakao and Treas 1994), and others have not adjusted the socioeconomic characteristics by age (Stevens and Featherman 1981). In our analyses, we used three treatments of the data: indirect standardization, direct standardization, and no standardization.

There are 501 occupations in the 1990 Census classification system. Nakao and Treas (1994) were able to assign prestige ratings directly to all but three: Brickmasons' and Stonemasons' Apprentices (564), Carpenter Apprentices (569), and Tool and Die Maker Apprentices (635). These three apprenticeship categories contained no independently rated titles but had merely been assigned the prestige ratings of the corresponding "master" lines. Following Nakao and Treas, we dropped these three cases from our analyses of occupational prestige. Thus our analyses are based on 498 occupation lines.

Like most earlier investigators, we prefer a measure of the percentage of prestige ratings above a fixed threshold as a criterion variable, rather than a weighted average of arbitrarily scored prestige ranks. For example, Duncan (1961:119–20) chose to use the percentage of raters who chose "excellent" or "good" on the 5-point scale offered in the 1947 North-Hatt prestige study, rather than the prestige score.[28] He showed there was an S-shaped relationship between his criterion and the weighted prestige scores and that the percentage criterion varied more in the middle of the prestige hierarchy. In the Stevens-Featherman revision of the SEI, the investigators did not have direct access to percentage ratings. They estimated a cubic equation to describe the relationship between "good" and "excellent" ratings for the 45 titles in the North-Hatt study that were used in Duncan's analysis and the weighted prestige scores estimated by Siegel (1971) for

---

[28]But compare Haug's (1977:60–61) egregious critique of Duncan's (1961) criterion variable.

those same titles (Stevens and Featherman 1981:368). They then constructed a percentage-like dependent variable by using their equation to transform Siegel's prestige scores for all occupations. Nakao and Treas (1994:10) came closer to Duncan's original procedure by analyzing the percentage of raters who chose ranks of 5 or higher on the 9-point scale that was used in the 1989 GSS (as well as in NORC surveys of the 1960s). Our analyses are based upon the same prestige measure used by Nakao and Treas,[29] but we have also analyzed a logistic transformation in order to reduce heteroscedasticity in the residuals from the regression of prestige on occupational earnings and education. That is, where y_i = percentage choosing ranks of 5 or higher for the ith occupation, we analyzed

$$\ln\left(\frac{y_i}{100 - y_i}\right). \tag{1}$$

Another methodological variation is that we have estimated weighted as well as unweighted regressions of the prestige criterion on occupational education and income, where the weights are the population counts in each occupation. To some degree, weighting reduces the influence of outlying observations, in those cases where the outliers are relatively rare occupations, whose unusual characteristics may be consequences of sampling variability. Weighted analyses also approximate the relationships among occupational characteristics that would be estimated in samples of the general population. Finally, chastened and instructed by the example of Fox's (1991) and Friendly's (1991) reanalyses of Duncan's data, we have paid a good deal of attention to issues of fit and functional form.

3.2. Regression Analyses of Occupational Prestige

In preliminary work, we ran 126 regression analyses of occupational prestige on occupational education and earnings. We varied the specification of the models among definitions of samples, variables, and weighting procedures, as described above. That is, half the regressions were weighted by the relevant sample counts (for all workers, men, or women), and half gave equal weight to each occupation line. One-third of the models used total annual earnings of workers; one-third used estimated wage rates; and one-third used total annual earnings of full-time, year-round workers. One-third of the models used weighted prestige scores; one-third used the

[29]The 1989 prestige ratings and 1980-basis occupational characteristics were kindly given to us by Keiko Nakao.

percentage with ranks of five or higher; and one-third used the logit of the percentage with ranks of five or higher. One-third of the models used socioeconomic data for all workers, men, and women, respectively. Finally, we varied the use of raw, indirectly standardized, and directly standardized educational attainment and earnings.[30] Based on comparisons of the fit of these models, we decided to consider further only those weighted models for men, women, and all workers in which no variables were standardized for age, economic standing was indicated by the estimated wage rate, and the dependent variable was the logistic transform of the percentage of ratings of five or higher.

We then turned to a more intensive examination of the socioeconomic and prestige data, and we modified the models in important ways. First, rather than using the simple logistic transformation of prestige, we used a started logit of the percentage of prestige ratings above the threshold (Mosteller and Tukey 1979: 109–15):

$$\ln\left(\frac{y_i + 1}{100 - y_i + 1}\right). \tag{2}$$

This symmetric transformation eliminates the extreme or undefined values of the log transform that would otherwise occur when the observed percentage is at or near 0 or 100. Second, we experimented with corresponding transformations of the measures of occupational education and occupational wage rates. Third, in an additional effort to reduce heteroscedasticity, we estimated the prestige regressions by weighted least squares, using weights, w_{ij}, suggested by Theil (1970):

$$w_{ij} = n_{ij}f_i(1 - f_i), \tag{3}$$

where n_{ij} is the count in occupation i in sample group j (total, men, or women), and f_i is the relative frequency of high prestige ratings in occupation i. Fourth, we used an interactive regression graphics program (R-CODE) to identify influential outlying observations and evidence of nonlinearity (Cook and Weisberg 1994).

It is instructive to display the relationships among the educational and economic characteristics of the occupations of men and women. Linear relationships among these variables would simplify analyses of the

[30]We did not use every possible combination of these several factors. We used direct standardization only in analyses of the characteristics of all workers, male and female.

prestige regressions, and, more important, they would make it easier to comprehend differences in the statistical properties of socioeconomic indexes for women and men. That is, it would be analytically convenient if the standing of men's occupations were a linear transformation of the standing of women's occupations; we could then specify status differences between occupations without reference to gender. Figure 3 shows the bivariate scatterplots of women's and men's occupational education and earnings, where the latter variables are expressed as percentages above the threshold

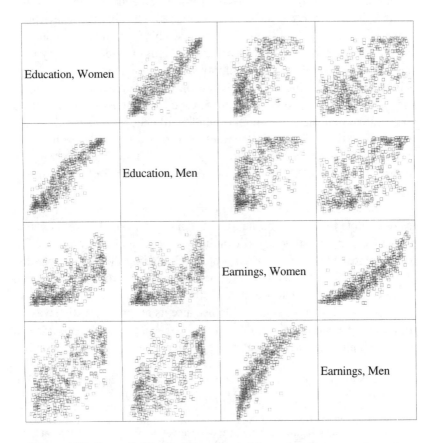

Source: 1990 Census Public Use Files. See text for explanation.

FIGURE 3. Occupational distributions by sex of worker: 1990 Percentages with College Experience and Earnings Above $25,000 in 1989.

levels of one year of college and $25,000, respectively.[31] The relationship
between the occupational education of women and that of men appears to
be linear, but the other five bivariate relationships are far from linear. The
scatterplot of occupational earnings of women by occupational earnings of
men has a crescent moon shape. The scatterplot of women's occupational
earnings by their occupational education is pressed up against the axes,
while the corresponding plot for men shows only a weak relationship. The
shapes of the scatterplots in Figure 3 suggest the desirability of revising or
transforming the variables.

On the hypothesis that part-time work might account for nonlinearity in the relationships, we considered using percentages above a wage-
rate threshold, rather than an earnings threshold. The bivariate scatterplots
of these relationships are shown in Figure 4. This version of the economic
standing measure offered little improvement, thus invalidating our hypothesis that an adjustment for labor supply would eliminate some differences
between socioeconomic indexes based on the characteristics of women
and men. Finally, as shown in Figure 5, we continued to use the estimated
wage rate to indicate the economic standing of occupations, but we transformed both education and wage rates into started logits. These transformations make the bivariate relationships among all four variables roughly
linear, and we have used them in our preferred regression models of occupational prestige.[32]

In the final set of regression analyses, we used several types of
residual plots to identify influential outliers. For example, we looked at
plots of externally studentized residuals by leverage, and we looked at
partial regression (added variable) plots. Guided by these graphical displays, we decided to delete several occupation lines from the regression
analyses used to estimate weights for the socioeconomic scores. We did
not delete an occupation line merely because its observed prestige was far
from the regression line, but only when it appeared that the observation
was also highly leveraged. That is, we deleted an unusual observation if it

---

[31] Five extreme outliers have been eliminated from the scatterplots in Figs. 3, 4,
and 5. They are the occupation lines for natural science teachers, n.e.c. (117), social
work teachers (146), supervisors, brickmasons, stone masons, and tile setters (553),
longshore equipment operators (845), and helpers, extractive occupations (868). In
each of these occupation lines, the number of observations of women, of men, or both,
were very small—that is, no larger than 12.

[32] We have also carried out parallel regression analyses using the percentage-
based measures of occupational education and occupational earnings, and the choice of
regressors does not substantially affect statistical properties of the indexes.

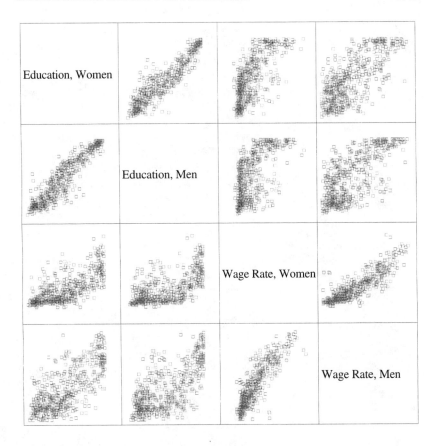

Source: 1990 Census Public Use Files. See text for explanation.

FIGURE 4. Occupational distributions by sex of worker: 1990 Percentages with College Experience and Wage Rate Above $14.30 per hour.

appeared likely to affect the estimated regression coefficients substantially. For example, we did not delete the observation for Sales Occupations, Other Business Service (257), for which the rated titles were Crafting and Moving Estimator and Home Improvement Salesperson (Nakao and Treas 1994:51). Its prestige was much lower than predicted among women, men, and all workers, but because its incumbents have near-average levels of education and earnings, it was not an influential outlier.

Some characteristics of the excluded occupation lines are shown in Table 1. We deleted 7 lines from the regressions for all workers, 10 lines

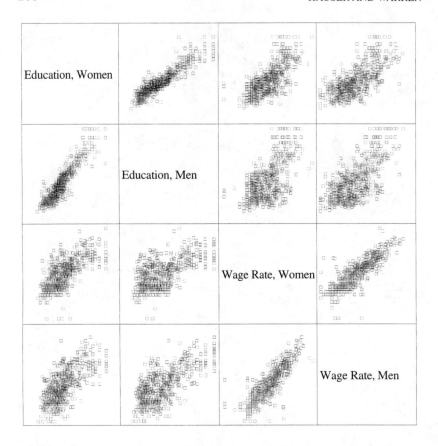

Source: 1990 Census Public Use Files. See text for explanation.

FIGURE 5. Occupational distributions by sex of worker: 1990 Started Logits of College Experience and Wage Rate above $14.30/hour.

from the regressions for men, and 11 lines from the regressions for women. This is a small number of lines, relative to the 498 occupation lines that entered the analyses, but the deleted lines reflect a substantial number of workers. The deletions include 15.9 percent of all workers, 16.4 percent of men, and 30.0 percent of women. Thus we looked closely, both at the characteristics of the deleted lines and at the effects of those deletions on the estimated weights of the socioeconomic scores. Some of the deleted lines contain very small numbers of workers, and it is thus not worthwhile to dwell on their characteristics. These include Longshore Equipment Operators (845), male Natural Science Teachers, n.e.c. (117) and Social Work Teachers (146), and female Supervisors, Brickmasons, Stonemasons, and Tile Setters (553).

The other unusual occupation lines contain many workers, and their behavior is thus important and instructive. Table 1 shows the occupation codes and population estimates of each line, followed by the started logits of education, earnings, and prestige. Columns 6 and 7 display the predicted prestige logits and their residuals—that is, the differences between observed and predicted prestige. The last two columns give the level of earnings that is predicted by education and the residual earnings, net of education.

For example, among all workers, Managers and Administrators, n.e.c., (22) have high levels of education and high wage rates, but their earnings are still high relative to their educational attainment. Their predicted prestige levels fall well below the actual prestige levels of the large number of rated titles for that occupation line in the 1989 GSS (Nakao and Treas 1994:43). This line includes a variety of business owners and managers, as well as bankers and college presidents. About 30 percent of Managers and Administrators, n.e.c, are women, and the patterns of prestige and earnings are similar among men and among women: high wages relative to schooling and high prestige relative to schooling and wage rates.

Truck Drivers (804) also have high earnings among all workers and among men, relative to their low levels of educational attainment. Their prestige ratings are far lower than those of other occupations with similar levels of schooling and wages. Waiters and Waitresses (435) and Janitors and Cleaners (453) are similar to Truck Drivers among all workers, in that their prestige falls well below the level expected from their low educational attainments and wages. However, they are even worse off than Truck Drivers, for their wages also fall below the level expected from their schooling. Note that, while Truck Drivers are mainly men, Janitors and Cleaners are almost evenly divided between men and women, and Waiters and Waitresses are mainly women. Among these three outlying occupation groups, earnings follow gender composition. That is, Waiters and Waitresses are paid least, relative to schooling, and Truck Drivers are paid most, relative to schooling. Even among women workers, Waiters and Waitresses have a prestige deficit relative to their schooling and wage rates, and they are poorly paid, relative to their schooling. Also, among women workers, General Office Clerks (379) follow the same pattern as waiters and waitresses:

TABLE 1
Descriptions and Analyses of Excluded Cases: Regression Analyses of Occupational Prestige

Code	1990 Population	Observed Education	Observed Wage	Started Logit of Prestige			Predicted Wage	Residual Wage	Occupation Title
				Observed	Predicted	Residual			
Total									
22	5,119,742	0.97	0.15	0.91	0.67	0.24	-0.64	0.79	Mngrs./Administrators, n.e.c.
156	2,927,819	2.77	-0.08	1.58	1.39	0.19	0.16	-0.24	Teachers, Elementary School
313	3,783,271	0.20	-2.15	0.22	-0.33	0.55	-0.98	-1.17	Secretaries
435	1,280,050	-0.36	-2.77	-1.38	-0.75	-0.63	-1.23	-1.55	Waiters and Waitresses
453	2,135,885	-1.29	-2.05	-1.53	-0.95	-0.58	-1.64	-0.41	Janitors and Cleaners
804	2,615,667	-1.07	-1.24	-1.16	-0.62	-0.54	-1.55	0.31	Truck Drivers
845	3,831	-1.07	-0.78	-0.78	-0.49	-0.29	-1.54	0.76	Longshore Equipment Operators
Excluded	17,866,265								
Men									
22	3,531,576	1.09	0.56	0.91	0.76	0.15	-0.28	0.84	Mngrs./Administrators, n.e.c.
117	227	3.23	0.30	2.25	1.29	0.96	0.78	-0.47	Natural Science Teachers, n.e.c.
146	18	4.62	4.62	2.25	3.66	-1.41	1.46	3.15	Social Work Teachers
176	279,710	2.22	-1.54	1.54	0.15	1.40	0.28	-1.82	Clergy
453	1,478,275	-1.15	-1.91	-1.53	-1.04	-0.49	-1.38	-0.53	Janitors and Cleaners
473	648,981	-0.69	-1.35	0.24	-0.65	0.88	-1.15	-0.20	Farmers, Except Horticultural
558	587,582	-0.36	-0.20	0.99	-0.02	1.02	-0.99	0.79	Supervisors, Constructing, n.e.c.

210

628	1,030,471	-0.21	-0.07	0.51	0.08	0.44	-0.92	0.84	Supervisors, Production Occupations
804	2,466,768	-1.12	-1.20	-1.16	-0.71	-0.45	-1.36	0.16	Truck Drivers
845	3,805	-1.07	-0.64	-0.78	-0.44	-0.34	-1.34	0.69	Longshore Equipment Operators
Excluded	10,027,413								
Women									
22	1,588,166	0.81	-0.78	0.91	0.46	0.45	-1.48	0.69	Mngrs./Administrators, n.e.c.
23	805,820	1.62	-1.02	1.64	0.77	0.87	-0.99	-0.03	Accountants and Auditors
95	1,734,694	2.76	0.12	1.55	1.59	-0.04	-0.31	0.42	Registered Nurses
156	2,297,247	2.61	-0.24	1.58	1.43	0.15	-0.40	0.16	Teachers, Elementary School
313	3,734,523	0.21	-2.22	0.22	-0.20	0.42	-1.83	-0.39	Secretaries
337	1,609,204	0.13	-2.11	0.26	-0.21	0.46	-1.88	-0.23	Bookkprs., Acc./Audit. Clerks
379	1,114,599	-0.03	-2.34	-0.80	-0.34	-0.46	-1.98	-0.36	General Office Clerks
435	1,022,032	-0.52	-2.97	-1.38	-0.73	-0.64	-2.27	-0.69	Waiters and Waitresses
447	1,417,986	-0.61	-2.34	-0.16	-0.60	0.44	-2.32	-0.01	Nursing Aides, Orderlies, and Attendants
553	96	-4.62	-1.02	0.61	-2.07	2.68	-4.72	3.70	Supervisors, Brickmasons, Stonemasons, and Tile Setters
845	26	-1.30	-1.91	-0.78	-0.80	0.02	-2.73	0.83	Longshore Equipment Operators
Excluded	15,324,393								

low pay relative to schooling and low prestige relative to schooling and wages.

Among all workers, Elementary School Teachers (156) and Secretaries (313) have low wages, relative to their schooling, and their prestige ratings are much higher than would be expected from their schooling and earnings. These two occupation lines mainly include women workers, who account for more than 10 percent of all women workers and almost 40 percent of the women in outlying occupation lines. It would thus be a serious error to identify the socioeconomic status of these (and similar) occupations with their prestige. Note, however, that among women workers, Elementary School Teachers are not underpaid, relative to their schooling.

Among male workers, Clergymen (176) and Farmers (801) are underpaid, relative to their schooling, but they enjoy very high levels of prestige. On the other hand, male Supervisors in Construction (558) and in Production Occupations (628) somewhat resemble Managers and Administrators, though perhaps by virtue of unionization, rather than entrepreneurship. That is, supervisors enjoy high wage rates relative to their schooling and high prestige levels relative to their schooling and wages.

Among the outlying women's occupations, in addition to Managers and Administrators, Elementary School Teachers, and Secretaries, relatively high levels of prestige go to Accountants and Auditors (23), Bookkeepers and Accounting or Audit Clerks (337), and Nursing Aides, Orderlies, and Attendants (447). Registered Nurses (95) are well paid relative to their schooling, but their prestige levels are not out of line with their schooling and wages.

It is striking that several of the largest and most influential exceptions to typical relationships among occupational education, wage rates, and prestige occur in common and visible jobs: business owners, farmers, clergy, secretaries, teachers, waiters and waitresses, janitors, and truck drivers. In each case, it is perhaps easy to rationalize the exceptions. The business of business is making money, and the entrepreneur is an American cultural icon. Farming is as much a way of life as a job; it carries some income in kind; and it, too, is a cultural icon. Religious vocations are a calling. Secretaries and teachers are prototypical women's jobs, paid more in prestige than in dollars. And so on.

There are cautionary messages in these findings. First, the typically strong connections between occupational socioeconomic status and prestige are not simply a product of highly visible relationships across common occupations, but they show up more clearly across a large number of less common or visible jobs. Second, when we think about the relationships among socioeconomic status and prestige, we should be most cautious about thinking of them concretely in relation to common occupations, for they may be exceptions. Third, prestige-validated socioeconomic indexes were initially used as proxies for missing prestige measures. Their greater criterion validity encouraged widespread use, well after prestige scores became available for all occupations. Thus researchers have often glossed over the differences between occupational prestige and socioeconomic status. The present findings remind us that occupational prestige is by no means the same as occupational socioeconomic status, and we should respect both the theoretical and empirical distinctions between them (Hodge 1981; Jencks 1990).

Table 2 shows the estimates from selected regression analyses of occupational prestige on occupational education and earnings or wage rates. The display includes only about one-fifth of the analyses that we examined, but they provide a good indication of the effects of varying specifications. Several important patterns appear. First, regardless of the specification, occupational education and earnings or wage rates account for 70 to 80 percent of the variance in occupational prestige. We note, however, that R^2 is not a particularly good guide to fit in this context, for it sometimes declines when extreme outliers are removed, as in the contrast between models in lines 13 to 15 with those in lines 16 to 18 or between models in lines 19 to 21 with those in lines 22 to 24. This can occur precisely because the outliers are relatively influential observations. Second, as suggested by the contrast between lines 1 to 3 and lines 4 to 6, a better fit is obtained without standardization of education and earnings by age. In the latter models, R^2 is larger, and the standard errors of estimate are smaller. Third, as shown by the contrast between lines 4 to 6 and lines 7 to 9, the fit of weighted regressions is substantially better than that of unweighted regressions. For example, among women workers, comparing lines 6 and 9, weighting increases R^2 by 0.09, from 0.72 to 0.81, and it reduces the standard error of estimate from 12.46 to 9.65. Fourth, regardless of the functional form of the equations—the transformations of the regressors and of prestige—there are consistent variations in the relative effects of education and of earnings or wage rates among men, women, and all workers. Whether we look at regression coefficients or at standardized regression coefficients, among all workers and among women the effects of occupational education are always larger than those of occupational earnings or wage rates. In most cases the education effects are 1.5 to 2.5 times larger

TABLE 2
Specifications, Parameters, and Fit Statistics for SEI Prediction Equations

| | Model Specification | | | | | | SEI Prediction Equation | | | | | | |
| | | | | | | | Metric Coefficients | | | Standardized Coefficients | | | |
Population	Dependent Variable	Independent Variables	Standardization for Age	Sample Weight	Labor Supply Adjustment	Outliers Deleted	Constant	Education	Earnings	Education	Earnings	R^2	Standard Error
1 Total	Percent 5+	Percentages	Indirect	None	No	No	6.340	0.592	0.293	0.680	0.263	0.73	12.18
2 Male	Percent 5+	Percentages	Indirect	None	No	No	1.353	0.492	0.434	0.571	0.342	0.68	13.23
3 Female	Percent 5+	Percentages	Indirect	None	No	No	11.965	0.548	0.350	0.616	0.295	0.70	12.80
4 Total	Percent 5+	Percentages	None	None	No	No	7.926	0.592	0.249	0.695	0.257	0.75	11.58
5 Male	Percent 5+	Percentages	None	None	No	No	5.973	0.511	0.319	0.609	0.327	0.72	12.32
6 Female	Percent 5+	Percentages	None	None	No	No	12.438	0.545	0.313	0.635	0.280	0.72	12.46
7 Total	Percent 5+	Percentages	None	Total	No	No	7.706	0.596	0.278	0.677	0.299	0.80	10.05
8 Male	Percent 5+	Percentages	None	Male	No	No	6.395	0.408	0.439	0.485	0.463	0.78	10.44
9 Female	Percent 5+	Percentages	None	Female	No	No	10.296	0.611	0.315	0.675	0.259	0.81	9.65
10 Total	Percent 5+	Percentages	None	Total	Yes	No	9.238	0.561	0.366	0.638	0.316	0.79	9.24
11 Male	Percent 5+	Percentages	None	Male	Yes	No	9.913	0.363	0.549	0.431	0.504	0.78	10.45
12 Female	Percent 5+	Percentages	None	Female	Yes	No	9.455	0.656	0.278	0.726	0.193	0.80	9.92
13 Total	Started Logit	Percentages	None	WLS, Total	Yes	No	-1.698	0.023	0.016	0.611	0.327	0.74	0.45
14 Male	Started Logit	Percentages	None	WLS, Male	Yes	No	-1.660	0.014	0.024	0.396	0.513	0.72	0.47
15 Female	Started Logit	Percentages	None	WLS, Female	Yes	No	-1.686	0.027	0.014	0.679	0.219	0.75	0.44
16 Total	Started Logit	Percentages	None	WLS, Total	Yes	Yes	-1.692	0.021	0.019	0.558	0.380	0.73	0.45
17 Male	Started Logit	Percentages	None	WLS, Male	Yes	Yes	-1.644	0.013	0.025	0.376	0.535	0.73	0.45
18 Female	Started Logit	Percentages	None	WLS, Female	Yes	Yes	-1.661	0.024	0.016	0.646	0.242	0.71	0.45
19 Total	Started Logit	Started Logits	None	WLS, Total	Yes	No	0.187	0.480	0.268	0.643	0.295	0.74	0.45
20 Male	Started Logit	Started Logits	None	WLS, Male	Yes	No	0.214	0.308	0.481	0.442	0.484	0.74	0.45
21 Female	Started Logit	Started Logits	None	WLS, Female	Yes	No	0.398	0.468	0.280	0.612	0.280	0.74	0.44
22 Total	Started Logit	Started Logits	None	WLS, Total	Yes	Yes	0.205	0.436	0.287	0.605	0.322	0.71	0.45
23 Male	Started Logit	Started Logits	None	WLS, Male	Yes	Yes	0.175	0.303	0.454	0.462	0.466	0.75	0.44
24 Female	Started Logit	Started Logits	None	WLS, Female	Yes	Yes	0.305	0.455	0.270	0.608	0.270	0.70	0.46

Note: Models were estimated using data for a maximum of 497 of the 501 1990-basis occupation lines. Lines 564, 569, and 635, which are apprenticeship occupations, were excluded from all analyses following Nakao and Treas (1994). Line 845, "Longshore Equipment Operators," was also excluded because of the small number of female occupational incumbents. Standardized education and earnings percentages exceeded 100 percent in a small number of lines and were top-coded.

214

than the economic effects. On the other hand, prestige is more sensitive to the earnings of male occupational incumbents. In several specifications, the earning or wage effects are larger than the education effects, and in all cases the earning or wage effects are larger relative to the education effects among men than among women or among all workers. Fifth, as shown by the contrast between lines 7 to 9 and lines 10 to 12, use of the occupational wage rate, rather than occupational earnings has no consistent effect on fit. The standard error of estimate declines in the analysis based on all workers, but it remains stable for men and increases among women. Contrary to our expectation, use of the occupational wage rate increases the gender differential in the relative effects of education and earnings on prestige. That is, in the wage-rate specification, the effect of earnings relative to economic standing increases among men, and it declines among women. Finally, we note the modest effects of the deletion of outliers on the slopes of the prediction equations. These appear in comparisons of lines 13 to 15 with lines 16 to 18 and in comparisons of lines 19 to 21 with lines 22 to 24. Among men and women workers, taken separately, outlier deletion has very little effect on the weights, but among all workers combined, it leads to an increase in the effect of the wage rate relative to educational attainment.

It is less easy to assess the comparative advantages of the started logit specifications relative to those in percentages because there are changes both in the estimation method (to weighted least squares) and a change in the metric of the prestige variable. Moreover, our choice of models has been guided by an interest in consistency in the transformation of variables and by examination of a variety of residual plots, as well as by numeric measures of fit. Our preferred specifications of the prestige equation are those reported in the last three rows of the table (22 to 24), in which the economic indicator is the occupational wage rate, all of the variables have been expressed as started logits, the estimates are obtained by weighted least squares, and outliers have been deleted. In these three models, the estimates for women and for all workers combined are quite similar, and they show larger effects of educational attainment than of occupational wages by a factor of about 1.5. On the other hand, there is an opposite and nearly equal differential in the effects of education and wages among men. Despite the substantial similarity in the started logits of occupational education and occupational wages of men and women, as shown in Figure 5, differences in the estimation equations appear large enough so we might expect to see differences in the statistical properties of the male and the female or total socioeconomic indexes.

3.3. *Socioeconomic Indexes for All Occupations*

Using the estimated parameters of our final preferred models, we computed total-based, male-based, and female-based SEI scores for all occupations.[33] All three sets of scores were transformed to range between 0 and 100; in each case we added 2.08 to the predicted value of the started logit of prestige and multiplied the sum by 17.3. Appendix A presents the 1990-basis and 1980-basis total (TSEI), male (MSEI), and female (FSEI) scores for all occupation lines, the socioeconomic components of those scores, and the 1989 Nakao-Treas prestige scores and ratings.

In Appendix A, a series of flags indicates whether lines have been split, renumbered, renamed, or aggregated. Natural Science Teachers, n.e.c. (117) and Teachers, Postsecondary, n.e.c. (153) have been merged and given the same education, earnings, and SEI scores. The same is true for Longshore Equipment Operators (845) and Miscellaneous Material Moving Equipment Operators (859). By construction, the figures for education and earnings are weighted averages of two lines (117 and 154 in one case, 845 and 859 in the other). In converting from the 1990 Census Occupational Classification System to the 1980 Occupational Classification System, six 1990-basis lines were merged into two 1980-basis lines (017, 021, and 022 into 019; 466, 467, and 468 into 469), and six 1990-basis lines were split into twelve 1980-basis lines (353 into 349 and 353; 368 into 368 and 369; 436 into 436 and 437; 674 into 673 and 674; 795 into 794 and 795; 804 into 804 and 805). When 1990-basis lines were split into multiple 1980-basis lines, the values for education, earnings, and SEI scores were applied to each of the new lines. When 1990-basis lines were merged into a single 1980-basis line, we computed a weighted average of the education and earnings scores (weighted by the number of occupational incumbents), and then recomputed the SEI scores for the new line. Also, many 1990-basis lines were renumbered in the 1980-basis classification, and some lines were renamed.[34]

In several cases, where the three-digit codes for 1990 were heterogeneous and included a large number of individuals, Appendix A provides optional SEI values for splits of the parent line by class of worker and/or

---

[33]Machine-readable versions of the Hauser-Warren 1980-basis and 1990-basis SEI scores and their component data are available on-line at ftp:\\elaine.ssc.wisc.edu\pub\hauser.

[34]See Nakao and Treas (1994:40–41) for details regarding these changes in classification.

industry. This follows the precedent of Duncan's scoring of split lines in the 1950 and 1960 Census classifications. The split 1990-basis lines include Managers, Food Service and Lodging (17); Managers and Administrators, n.e.c. (22); Accountants and Auditors (23); Registered Nurses (95); Supervisors and Proprietors, Sales Occupations (243); Sales Representatives: Mining, Manufacturing, and Wholesale (259); Sales Workers, Other Commodities (274); Cashiers (276); Secretaries (313); Bookkeepers, Accounting and Audit Clerks (337); General Office Clerks (379); Janitors and Cleaners (453); Auto Mechanics, except Apprentices (505); Carpenters, except Apprentices (567); Supervisors, Production Occupations (628); Assemblers (785); Truck Drivers (804); Stock Handlers and Baggers (877); and Laborers, except Construction (889).

Finally, Appendix A lists weighted average values of SEI scores, their components, and NORC prestige scores for major occupation groups. These may be useful in summarizing occupational differences for descriptive purposes or in scoring occupation groups when detailed codes for occupation, industry, and class of worker are not available.

3.4. *Properties of the Socioeconomic Indexes*

Table 3 shows unweighted correlations among the transformed measures of occupational prestige, education, and wage rate; the total, male, and female 1990-basis SEI scores (TSEI, MSEI, and FSEI); and the Nakao-Treas indexes for 1990 Census occupation lines. The correlations of prestige with educational attainment (0.82 to 0.85) are larger than with the wage rate (0.70 to 0.74). In each case, the prestige correlations are slightly lower with the characteristics of female occupational incumbents than with those of male or of all incumbents. The correlations of prestige with the Nakao-Treas indexes and with the corresponding 1990-basis socioeconomic indexes are similar: 0.87 among all workers for both indexes, 0.86 for the 1990-basis MSEI, and 0.84 for the Nakao-Treas MSEI. Also, the correlation between the total and male indexes is the same for the 1990-basis indexes as for the Nakao-Treas indexes, 0.97. However, the 1990-basis indexes are not fully interchangeable with the Nakao-Treas indexes. The correlations are 0.97 for the total indexes and 0.94 for the male indexes.

While the total 1990-basis index is almost equally correlated with the male index and the female index (0.97 and 0.96), the correlation between the new male and female indexes, 0.91, is far from perfect. That is,

TABLE 3

Correlations Among Prestige, Gender-Specific Socioeconomic Characteristics of Occupations, 1990-Basis SEI Scores, and Nakao-Treas SEI Scores: 1990-basis Census Occupation Lines

	(1)	(2)	(3)	(4)	(5)	(6)	(7)	(8)	(9)	(10)	(11)	(12)
1 Prestige 5+ (started logit)	1.00											
2 Total-based education (started logit)	0.85	1.00										
3 Male-based education (started logit)	0.84	0.98	1.00									
4 Female-based education (started logit)	0.82	0.96	0.92	1.00								
5 Total-based wage rate (started logit)	0.71	0.66	0.61	0.64	1.00							
6 Male-based wage rate (started logit)	0.74	0.72	0.70	0.69	0.95	1.00						
7 Female-based wage rate (started logit)	0.70	0.69	0.64	0.70	0.89	0.85	1.00					
8 1990-basis TSEI	0.87	0.97	0.94	0.93	0.83	0.86	0.81	1.00				
9 1990-basis MSEI	0.86	0.93	0.92	0.87	0.85	0.92	0.81	0.97	1.00			
10 1990-basis FSEI	0.84	0.94	0.90	0.98	0.76	0.78	0.84	0.96	0.91	1.00		
11 Nakao-Treas TSEI	0.87	0.95	0.93	0.91	0.78	0.80	0.78	0.97	0.94	0.93	1.00	
12 Nakao-Treas MSEI	0.84	0.94	0.95	0.89	0.72	0.79	0.73	0.94	0.94	0.90	0.97	1.00

Note: Estimates are based on unweighted data for 501 occupation lines.

218

almost 10 percent of the variance in the two indexes is not in common, which is a great deal, if we should like to think that MSEI and FSEI measure the same thing.[35] It is not obvious to what degree this is a consequence of the differential slopes of educational attainment and wage rates in the prediction equations for the two indexes or of the differing socioeconomic characteristics of male and of female occupational incumbents. Both the coefficients and the socioeconomic characteristics differ among the 1990-basis indexes. The coefficient of earnings is about 1.5 times that of education in the male index (MSEI), and the coefficient of education is about 1.5 times that of earnings in the female index (FSEI); its coefficients are similar to those in the total index (TSEI), as shown in lines 22 to 24 of Table 2. At the same time, the occupational socioeconomic characteristics also differ by gender. In Table 3, the correlation between occupational education of men and women workers is 0.92, while that of occupational wage rates is 0.85. Note that the correlation of occupational education between men and women is slightly larger than that between MSEI and FSEI. To identify the source of the imperfect correlations among indexes, we constructed pseudo-indexes for men and women, using the occupational characteristics of the same gender but the regression coefficients for the other gender. The differing coefficients of the male-based and female-based prediction equations had little effect on the correlations. When the coefficients were altered, the correlations between actual and pseudo-indexes were 0.984 among men and 0.983 among women. On the other hand, among combinations of indexes whose socioeconomic components differed, the correlations ranged from 0.90 to 0.92. Almost all of the lack of commonality between MSEI and FSEI can be attributed to differences in the educational attainments and wage rates of male and female occupational incumbents.

Thus, despite our best analytic effort to establish commonality in relationships between the socioeconomic determinants of occupational prestige among American men and women, there remain substantial gender differences among those determinants across occupations. These lead us to doubt the possibility of establishing a metric of occupational socioeconomic status that would be fully and equally valid for male and female workers. Surely, an index based on the characteristics of all workers would be preferable to one based on the characteristics of men alone or of women

[35]That is, the correlation between the two indexes tells us the share of the variance in each that would be explained by a common factor that affected each equally.

alone.[36] The correlations of TSEI with MSEI and FSEI are 0.97 and 0.96, respectively.[37] However, the correlations suggest that the 1990-basis TSEI as common measure is an imperfect substitute for either MSEI or FSEI, while the latter are far from perfect substitutes for one another.

The correlations in Table 3 provide no information about the properties of the old or new socioeconomic indexes in comparisons of mean attainment levels among men and women. Table 4 gives the means and standard deviations of each of the occupational status measures for men and women in the 1990 Census sample and for respondents in the 1994 General Social Survey (GSS) who reported a current or last job or who reported a first, full-time civilian occupation.[38] It is reassuring that the means and standard deviations of the measures for current or last occupations in the GSS look very similar to those of corresponding measures in the 1990 Census. This is important because the GSS, but not the Census, can provide estimates of intergenerational and intragenerational correlations among alternative measures of occupational standing. Whether one indexes occupations with the characteristics of men, of women, or of all workers, women hold jobs with higher average levels of schooling but lower wage rates than men. For example, when occupations are indexed by the started logit of educational attainment for all workers in the 1990 Census, the mean logit is 0.172 for men and 0.449 for women. Obversely, when occupations are indexed by the started logit of the wage rate for all workers in the 1990 Census, the mean logit is -0.878 for men and -1.429 for women.[39] Similar observations hold for current or last jobs in the Census and the GSS and for first civilian occupations in the GSS. Thus use of a composite socioeconomic index will show that women hold better or worse jobs than men, depending on the relative weights given to schooling

[36]We have also experimented with the possibility of constructing an index for all workers that would be based on separate effects on prestige of the occupational education and wage rates of women and men. That is, the prediction equation would be of the form prestige $= f$(male education, female education, male wages, female wages). Such equations provided no predictive advantage over those using the characteristics of all workers combined.

[37]Note that the corresponding correlations are equally large in the case of occupational education: 0.98 and 0.96.

[38]The first-job item was ascertained from a random half of 1994 GSS respondents.

[39]Recall that the education measure refers to the percentage of occupational incumbents with at least one year of post–high school education and that the wage rate measure refers to the percentage of occupational incumbents earning more than $14.30 per hour in 1989.

TABLE 4
Description of Occupational Status Variables, 1990 Census
and 1994 General Social Survey

	Men		Women	
	Mean	(SD)	Mean	(SD)
Current or Last Occupation, 1990 Census	(N = 3,026,651)		(N = 2,532,470)	
Prestige 5+ (started logit)	−0.015	(1.046)	0.028	(1.005)
Total-based Educ. (started logit)	0.172	(1.395)	0.449	(1.303)
Male-based Educ. (started logit)	0.298	(1.473)	0.799	(1.327)
Female-based Educ. (started logit)	0.087	(1.311)	0.310	(1.295)
Total-based Wage (started logit)	−0.878	(0.973)	−1.429	(1.055)
Male-based Wage (started logit)	−0.641	(0.998)	−0.913	(0.989)
Female-based Wage (started logit)	−1.472	(0.908)	−1.779	(0.961)
1990-basis TSEI	36.5	(14.5)	35.8	(14.4)
1990-basis MSEI	35.5	(14.7)	36.0	(13.9)
1990-basis FSEI	35.1	(13.9)	35.4	(14.3)
Nakao-Treas TSEI	48.6	(18.9)	47.8	(18.5)
Nakao-Treas MSEI	48.3	(19.3)	52.3	(16.8)
Current or Last Occupation, 1994 General Social Survey	(N = 1,250)		(N = 1,589)	
Prestige 5+ (started logit)	0.037	(1.042)	−0.019	(1.017)
Total-based Educ. (started logit)	0.172	(1.398)	0.398	(1.313)
Male-based Educ. (started logit)	0.281	(1.472)	0.751	(1.321)
Female-based Educ. (started logit)	0.112	(1.311)	0.262	(1.311)
Total-based Wage (started logit)	−0.816	(0.963)	−1.494	(1.027)
Male-based Wage (started logit)	−0.597	(0.987)	−0.987	(0.971)
Female-based Wage (started logit)	−1.416	(0.921)	1.826	(0.945)
1990-basis TSEI	36.8	(14.4)	35.1	(14.4)
1990-basis MSEI	35.8	(14.5)	35.2	(13.8)
1990-basis FSEI	35.5	(13.9)	34.8	(14.3)
Nakao-Treas TSEI	48.7	(19.2)	46.9	(18.6)
Nakao-Treas MSEI	48.1	(19.5)	51.2	(17.1)
First Occupation, 1994 General Social Survey	(N = 579)		(N = 790)	
Prestige 5+ (started logit)	−0.293	(1.124)	−0.255	(1.009)
Total-based Educ. (started logit)	−0.125	(1.446)	0.129	(1.319)
Male-based Educ. (started logit)	−0.018	(1.535)	0.499	(1.340)
Female-based Educ. (started logit)	−0.163	(1.355)	0.015	(1.317)
Total-based Wage (started logit)	−1.256	(1.076)	−1.802	(0.976)
Male-based Wage (started logit)	−1.062	(1.097)	−1.272	(0.930)
Female-based Wage (started logit)	−1.747	(1.015)	−2.080	(0.938)
1990-basis TSEI	32.3	(15.5)	31.5	(14.4)
1990-basis MSEI	30.6	(15.9)	31.7	(13.7)
1990-basis FSEI	31.8	(14.8)	31.7	(14.5)
Nakao-Treas TSEI	44.2	(19.5)	42.4	(17.6)
Nakao-Treas MSEI	43.5	(19.6)	47.5	(16.3)

and wages (or earnings) in construction of the index. If schooling is given more weight, women will appear to have better jobs than men; if wages or earnings are given more weight, men will appear to have better jobs than women.

Despite this analytic possibility, among the 1990-basis socioeconomic indexes, there are small and generally consistent gender differentials. Excepting the Census estimates based on the 1990-basis MSEI, the occupational status of men slightly exceeds that of women. This occurs because the men in women's most common occupations are relatively high in status. Thus when women are described by the characteristics of men in their occupations, the women appear well off, and this effect overwhelms the greater weight given to wages in the male-based index. However, between Nakao and Treas's two measures, the weights may differ by enough to affect gender comparisons. In the Census and in the GSS, men hold slightly higher status than women on the TSEI, but they hold lower status than women on the MSEI. Of course, the latter gender comparisons are affected by differences in the characteristics of occupational incumbents in the 1980 Census as well as by differences in weights of components of the Nakao-Treas socioeconomic indexes.

Regardless of the comparisons of the indexes in Table 4, it is not clear why one should regard prestige-validated weights—or any other particular set of weights—as uniquely appropriate for gender comparisons. That is, as long as occupation-specific education levels are higher for women than for men, while occupation-specific wages are higher for men than for women, gender comparisons based on a composite socioeconomic index will necessarily hide more than they reveal. It would be more accurate to describe women's and men's occupational standing directly and separately in terms of occupational education and occupational wage rates, rather than to rely on any composite of those two characteristics.

Table 5 shows correlations among corresponding occupational status measures of father's occupation, first occupation, and current occupation for men and women in the 1994 General Social Survey. It provides evidence about the predictive validity of alternative status measures in the context of intergenerational and intragenerational occupational stratification. For example, among men, the correlation between father's occupational standing and the standing of current or last occupation is 0.29 when occupations are indexed by their prestige and 0.38 when occupations are indexed by their average levels of schooling among men. Several striking patterns appear in Table 5. First, among men and women, the correlations

TABLE 5
Correlations Among Status Characteristics of Father's Occupation, First Occupation, and Current or Last Occupation:
Men and Women in the 1994 General Social Survey

	Men			Women		
Occupational Status Measure	Father's Occ. First Occ.	Father's Occ. Current Occ.	First Occ. Current Occ.	Father's Occ. First Occ.	Father's Occ. Current Occ.	First Occ. Current Occ.
Prestige 5+ (started logit)	0.21	0.29	0.59	0.25	0.23	0.63
Total-based Education (started logit)	0.30	0.36	0.72	0.33	0.34	0.71
Male-based Education (started logit)	0.32	0.38	0.72	0.31	0.31	0.69
Female-based Education (started logit)	0.25	0.30	0.70	0.32	0.32	0.72
Total-based Wage (started logit)	0.17	0.21	0.49	0.17	0.23	0.58
Male-based Wage (started logit)	0.22	0.26	0.54	0.20	0.23	0.57
Female-based Wage (started logit)	0.15	0.21	0.51	0.17	0.21	0.65
1990-basis TSEI	0.28	0.34	0.68	0.30	0.33	0.69
1990-basis MSEI	0.29	0.35	0.67	0.28	0.30	0.66
1990-basis FSEI	0.23	0.29	0.67	0.29	0.30	0.72
Nakao-Treas TSEI	0.30	0.35	0.67	0.32	0.32	0.67
Nakao-Treas MSEI	0.34	0.37	0.69	0.31	0.29	0.67

223

based on occupational prestige and occupational wage rates are all substantially lower than corresponding correlations based on occupational
schooling or on any of the socioeconomic indexes. The low prestige correlations confirm many previous findings, but it is striking that in most
cases, the correlations based on wage rates are even lower than those based
on prestige. Thus a purely economic measure of occupational standing
appears no more likely a candidate than occupational prestige to be the
major basis of occupational stratification. Second, the correlations are generally similar for each of the composite socioeconomic measures—that is,
the three 1990-basis SEIs and the two Nakao-Treas indexes. The findings
suggest that gender-specific indexes will yield slightly higher correlations
than total or opposite-gender indexes, but the differences are not large. If
one were to use either of the indexes for all workers, the correlations would
be similar among men and among women. Third, the intergenerational and
intragenerational correlations are as large or larger when the educational
level alone is used to index occupational standing, as when a composite
socioeconomic index is used. For example, among women, the correlation
of father's occupation with first occupation based on the education of all
workers is 0.33, while the largest of the correlations based on a socioeconomic index (the Nakao-Treas TSEI) is 0.32. In fact, if we consider only
gender-specific comparisons—that is, those among the total-based and
male-based education measures with the total-based and male-based socioeconomic indexes—the correlations of occupational education are all
as large or larger than the corresponding SEI correlations.

These findings suggest several interesting questions. Should we
doubt the validity of findings about occupational stratification that have
been based upon existing socioeconomic indexes? Why are occupational
wage rates or earnings not more important in the stratification process? Is
there an alternative scheme for weighting occupational education and wages
or earnings that would yield a more valid socioeconomic composite? Or
would it be better, in future stratification research, to index occupations by
their education levels, rather than by a socioeconomic composite? If education is the preferred indicator of occupational standing for research on
social stratification and mobility, is it also a preferred index in analyses of
political behavior, health and well-being, or any of the research areas in
which measures of occupational status have been used?

The correlations in Table 5 suggest that previous findings about
social stratification would not be changed dramatically if an education-
based index rather than a composite index had been used. Most of the other

questions lie beyond the scope of this paper, but we have looked further at the choice of optimal weights for occupational education and wages or earnings.

4. STRUCTURAL MODELS OF THE SOCIOECONOMIC INDEX

The preceding analyses have demonstrated two potential weaknesses in composite socioeconomic indexes of occupational standing. First, gender differences are manifest both in the relationships between occupational socioeconomic standing and prestige and in the socioeconomic characteristics of occupational incumbents. Second, occupational wage rates appear to be far less highly correlated, both within and across generations, than occupational education. The latter finding leads us to wonder whether the use of prestige-validated socioeconomic indexes may implicitly overestimate the importance of the economic standing of occupations in the stratification process. To investigate this possibility, we have developed structural equation models in which the construction of socioeconomic indexes is embedded in the stratification process.

4.1. Prestige-Validated Models

Figure 6 shows a path model of the relationships among father's occupational status, the status of a man or woman's first occupation, and the status of his or her current or last occupation. In this rudimentary model, we specify that the status of first occupation depends on that of father's occupation, while the status of current or last occupation depends upon father's occupation and first occupation. To be sure, this is scarcely a complete model of the stratification process, but even in the absence of other variables, it is sufficient both to illustrate and to test the prestige-validated concept of occupational socioeconomic status.[40] For each occupation, there are three measures of occupational standing: educational level, wage rate, and prestige. At each of the three stages of the model—father's occupation, first occupation, and current or last occupation—we specify the determination of a socioeconomic status construct following exactly the scheme of prestige validation used in the construction of the Duncan SEI

---

[40]If we added other variables to the model—e.g., the educational attainment or wage rate of the respondent—the model would yield additional overidentifying restrictions and, hence, additional empirical tests of the hypotheses implicit in the construction of prestige-validated socioeconomic indexes.

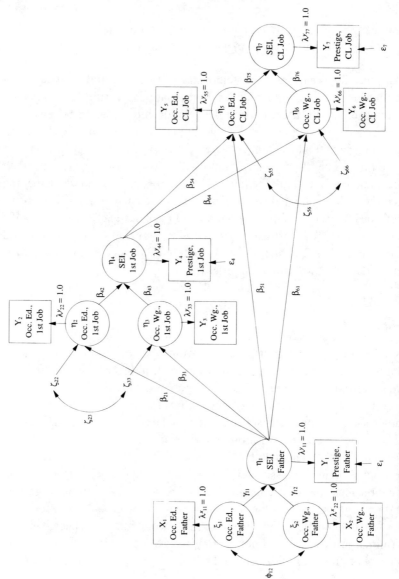

FIGURE 6. A model of intergenerational stratification in occupational status and prestige.

226

and other similar socioeconomic indexes. That is, an SEI composite is completely determined by measures of occupational education and occupational wages, while occupational prestige is affected by those prior variables only through the SEI composite. For example, in the case of father's occupational standing

$$\eta_1 = \gamma_{11}\xi_1 + \gamma_{12}\xi_2$$

$$Y_1 = \lambda_{11}^y \eta_1 + \epsilon_1,$$

(4)

where η_1 = SEI composite, ξ_1 = occupational education, ξ_2 = occupational wage rate, Y_1 = occupational prestige, ϵ_1 = a random error term, γ_{11} and γ_{12} are coefficients to be estimated, and we adopt the normalizing restriction, $\lambda_{11}^y = 1$.[41] In addition, we specify trivial measurement models of occupational education and the occupational wage rate

$$X_1 = \lambda_{11}^x \xi_1$$

$$X_2 = \lambda_{22}^x \xi_2,$$

(5)

where $\lambda_{11}^x = 1$ and $\lambda_{22}^x = 1$. Unlike earlier efforts to express the relationships between occupational socioeconomic status and prestige in a structural model, in which prestige and socioeconomic status were represented as consequences of a common latent factor (Featherman et al. 1975; Featherman and Hauser 1976), we believe the model of Figure 6 accurately expresses the relationships between occupational prestige and socioeconomic variables that are implicit in the construction of occupational socioeconomic indexes.

This first stage of the model in Figure 6 would have the same statistical properties as the previously estimated regressions of prestige on socioeconomic variables, were it not the case that other measured variables occur later in the model. For example, consider the second stage of the model, determination of the status of the first job. Since the educational status (η_2) and wage rate (η_3) pertaining to the first job completely determine the SEI composite for first job (η_4), characteristics of the father's occupation must affect the SEI composite of the first job by way of those components. To be sure, the path diagram shows η_2 and η_3 affected di-

[41]Throughout this discussion, when we refer, for example, to "wage rate of the father's occupation," we mean the wage rate that is typical of the occupation held by the father, not the father's wages.

rectly only by η_1, the SEI composite of father's occupation, but this is only a hypothesis. For example, we could imagine that the components of the SEI of first occupation could be affected directly by corresponding components of the SEI of father's occupation. We might draw a path from ξ_1 to η_2—i.e., from the educational level of the father's occupation to the educational level of the first job—or from ξ_2 to η_3—i.e., from the occupational wage rate of the father's job to the occupational wage rate of the first job. Or we could even suppose that the components of the SEI of first job or its prestige were affected directly by the prestige of the father's occupation.

Moreover, the relationships between the characteristics of father's occupation and those of the first occupation are repeated with respect to the current or last job. If we suppose that the effects of measured aspects of father's occupation (ξ_1 and ξ_2) occur only by way of its SEI composite (η_1), that variable directly or indirectly affects seven subsequent measured variables: prestige of father's occupation (Y_1), educational level of the first occupation (Y_2), wage rate of the first occupation (Y_3), prestige of the first occupation (Y_4), educational level of the current or last occupation (Y_5), wage rate of the current or last occupation (Y_6), and prestige of the current or last occupation (Y_7). Consider the unrestricted reduced-form regressions of the Y_i on ξ_1 and ξ_2, say

$$Y_1 = \pi_{11}\xi_1 + \pi_{12}\xi_2 + \epsilon_1$$
$$Y_2 = \pi_{21}\xi_1 + \pi_{22}\xi_2 + \epsilon_2$$

$$\cdots$$

$$Y_7 = \pi_{71}\xi_1 + \pi_{72}\xi_2 + \epsilon_7. \tag{6}$$

Then, if the model of Figure 6 holds in the population, $\pi_{11} = \gamma_{11}$ and $\pi_{12} = \gamma_{12}$, while $\pi_{21} = \beta_{21}\gamma_{11}$ and $\pi_{12} = \beta_{21}\gamma_{12}$, so

$$\frac{\pi_{11}}{\pi_{12}} = \frac{\pi_{21}}{\pi_{22}} = \frac{\gamma_{11}}{\gamma_{12}}. \tag{7}$$

Equation 7 shows that the model places proportionality constraints on the reduced-form coefficients of ξ_1 and ξ_2. Similar observations hold for the ratios of all seven pairs of reduced form coefficients. Thus, again based on the model of Figure 6, unlike the case of the simple prestige regressions, the ratios of slopes of father's SEI on its components, γ_{11} and γ_{12}, are overidentified. In this way, the model yields testable hypotheses about the relative weights of occupational education and occupational wage rates in the determination of the socioeconomic construct for father's occupation.

Similar observations hold with respect to the effects of the components of the SEI of first job, except there are fewer overidentifying restrictions. In that case, the model provides only four measured variables that depend directly or indirectly on the SEI construct (η_4): prestige of the first job (Y_4), educational level of the current or last job (Y_5), wage rate of the current or last job (Y_6), and prestige of the current or last job (Y_7). The last stage of the model, the determination of the SEI of current or last occupation, provides no additional overidentifying restrictions on the coefficients of the SEI composite because there is only one indicator of η_7—namely, prestige of the current or last job (Y_7). However, one more set of overidentifying restrictions is based upon the measurements at all three stages of the model. That is, if the conventional model holds, by assumption, the same relative weights should apply to the educational level and wage rate of an occupation, regardless of the stage of the model at which it appears. We expressed these constraints by equating effects of occupational education and of occupational wage rates on the socioeconomic composites:

$$\gamma_{11} = \beta_{42} = \beta_{75}$$
$$\gamma_{12} = \beta_{43} = \beta_{76}. \tag{8}$$

In estimating the model of Figure 6, we initially add one other set of restrictions pertaining to similarity in the relationships between occupational socioeconomic status and prestige across the three stages of the model. Although the socioeconomic composites (η_1, η_4, and η_7) are completely determined by their components, there is a disturbance (ϵ_1, ϵ_4, and ϵ_7) in each of the equations for occupational prestige measures (Y_1, Y_4, and Y_7). In each such equation, the variances—for example, $Var[\epsilon_1] = \theta_{11}^\delta$—could be a free parameter, as is the error variance in the previous regressions of occupational prestige on educational levels and wage rates. However, with the idea that the determination of prestige should be the same across all three stages of the model, we add the restriction that

$$\theta_{11}^\epsilon = \theta_{44}^\epsilon = \theta_{77}^\epsilon, \tag{9}$$

that is, the unexplained variance in occupational prestige is invariant.

To summarize, the model of Figure 6 has three important features. First, it embeds the determination of occupational socioeconomic status and prestige within a model of the stratification process. Second, it specifies a set of overidentifying restrictions following from the absence of lagged effects from prestige and from the components of occupational socioeconomic status to variables that appear later in the model. Third, it specifies a set of overidentifying restrictions pertaining to constant relative effects of occupational education and occupational wage rate on the socioeconomic status of occupations. Some of these last restrictions apply to each stage of the model taken separately, while others apply to the constancy of the effects across stages of the model. The satisfaction of all of these overidentifying restrictions is presumed in the usual models of stratification because they assume that a composite socioeconomic index conveys all of the relevant information about the behavior of its components.

Table 6 gives fit statistics for several variants of the model of Figure 6. The vertical panels of the table correspond to variations in the gender of the GSS sample and to the gender basis of the socioeconomic components used in the model. The horizontal panels refer to variations in the specification of the model. Each model has been estimated by maximum likelihood using LISREL 8.12 (Jöreskog and Sörbom 1993). In addition to the degrees of freedom (df), which are the same for entries in the same row, we also show the Bayesian information criterion, BIC $= L^2 - df \times \ln(N)$, where L^2 is the likelihood-ratio chi-square statistic and N is the sample size. BIC is useful in making judgments about model fit when a model would be rejected by conventional statistical tests. That is, in analyses based on large samples, BIC may suggest accepting a model that is rejected by conventional criteria of statistical significance. Positive values of BIC suggest model rejection, while negative values provide evidence in favor of a model. Between two models, a difference of 10 or more in BIC provides strong evidence favoring the model with the lower BIC value (Raftery 1995:25).

The first row of Table 6 gives fit measures for model A, which incorporates all of the overidentifying restrictions discussed earlier. That is, at each stage of the model socioeconomic characteristics affect later variables only through SEI composites, and the effects of the components on the composites are invariant across the three stages of the model. Moreover, the error variance in occupational prestige is invariant across stages of the model. This model—which corresponds to the typical, linear specifications of the stratification process—has 27 overidentifying restrictions, and it fits quite badly. Regardless of the population or the gender-basis of the socioeconomic measures, it would be rejected by conventional statistical criteria. Moreover, with one exception—estimates based on male-based SEI components among GSS women—the values of BIC also lead to rejection of the model.

We next estimated several less restrictive models in order to locate the constraints leading to lack of fit in model A. In model B, we retained the restrictions of model A, but we freed the paths between successive educational components of occupational socioeconomic status. That is, relative to the model in Figure 6, we added paths from ξ_1 to η_2 and from η_2 to η_5. This change dramatically improves model fit. While all of the versions of model B would nominally be rejected at conventional levels of statistical significance, L^2 declines substantially, and BIC is large and negative in each case. Similarly, in model C, we added paths between the successive wage-rate components of socioeconomic status, letting ξ_2 affect η_3 and η_3 affect η_6.[42] In this case, the fit improves substantially for women, both in comparison with the baseline model and model B. However, while model C improves fit for men, relative to model A, the BIC statistics are not impressive, and the fit is worse than that of model B. In model D, we added both the paths between successive educational components and those between successive wage-rate components. Here, the fit was still improved relative to the baseline models for men and for women, but it was not much better than model B for men or model C for women. The implication of these findings is that one source of invalidity in the traditional prestige-validated indexes of socioeconomic status is the failure to observe specific effects of the socioeconomic components. Among men, the traditional model does not fully represent the effects of occupational education, while among women, the traditional model does not fully represent the effects of occupational wage rates. Both among men and among women, the lagged effects of the socioeconomic variables occur mainly between first and current occupations, not between father's occupation and first occupation. The intergenerational effects are small but positive among men and negligible among women.

In model E, we retained the restrictions of model A, except we freed the error variances of the three prestige measures. That is, we permitted the validity of prestige as an indicator of socioeconomic status to vary across the life course by eliminating the restrictions in equation (9). While model E improves fit for men in the analyses based on the total and male SEI, it does not provide satisfactory fit in those cases, nor does it improve fit substantially in the other four analyses.

---

[42]Note that, in each of these cases, we have not added the lag-2 effects of the socioeconomic components—e.g., the path from ξ_1 to η_5 or that from ξ_2 to η_6. We also estimated models incorporating these effects, but the improvement in fit was negligible.

TABLE
Specifications and Fit Statistics for Models of

| | | Men | | | |
| | | Total-based SEI | | Male-based SEI | |
Model specification	df	Chi-sq.	BIC	Chi-sq.	BIC
A. Base model as described in Figure 6.	27	179.8	13.2	191.4	24.8
B. Model A, but free paths between successive occupational education variables.	25	93.8	−60.5	107.7	−46.6
C. Model A, but free paths between successive occupational wage rate variables.	25	151.0	−3.3	163.9	9.6
D. Model A, but free paths between successive occupational education and wage rate variables.	23	92.6	−49.3	105.6	−36.3
E. Model A, but free prestige variances.	25	157.2	2.9	165.7	11.4
F. Model A, but free prestige covariances.	24	156.4	8.3	166.5	18.3
G. Model A, but free covariance between prestige for respondent's first and current or last occupations.	26	158.3	−2.1	169.1	8.7
H. Model A, but free all prestige variances and covariance between prestige for respondent's first and current or last occupations.	24	136.1	−12.1	143.6	−4.5
I. For MEN: Model H, but also free paths between successive occupational education variables.	22	48.0	−87.8	57.4	−78.4
J. For WOMEN: Model H, but also free paths between successive occupational wage rate variables.	22	—	—	—	—
K. Model I or J, but allow effects of occup. education to vary for father's SEI, respondent's first job SEI, and respondent's current or last job SEI.	20	34.8	−88.7	47.4	−76.0
L. Model I or J, but allow effects of occup. wage rate to vary for father's SEI, respondent's first job SEI, and respondent's current or last job SEI.	20	27.0	−96.4	29.4	−94.1
M. Model I or J, but allow effects of occupational education and wage rate to vary for father's SEI, respondent's first job SEI, and respondent's current or last job SEI.	18	26.4	−84.7	27.2	−83.9

In model F, we reinstated the restrictions of equation (9) but freed the three covariances among errors in prestige, θ^{ϵ}_{14}, θ^{ϵ}_{17}, and θ^{ϵ}_{47}. Under this specification, while the prestige scores partly determine the weights of occupational education and occupational wage rates in the socioeconomic

6
Mobility in Occupational Status and Prestige

(N = 479)		Women (N = 622)					
Female-based SEI		Total-based SEI		Male-based SEI		Female-based SEI	
Chi-sq.	BIC	Chi-sq.	BIC	Chi-sq.	BIC	Chi-sq.	BIC
181.6	15.0	178.9	5.2	166.5	−7.2	205.9	32.2
91.6	−62.7	123.3	−37.5	126.3	−34.5	109.6	−51.2
148.1	−6.2	108.4	−52.4	114.1	−46.7	98.0	−62.8
90.3	−51.6	98.0	−50.0	106.2	−41.8	80.7	−67.3
171.9	17.6	169.0	8.2	148.6	−12.3	192.7	31.9
160.1	12.0	123.4	−30.9	111.5	−42.9	153.0	−1.4
162.1	1.6	124.1	−43.1	112.3	−55.0	153.5	−13.7
151.6	3.5	113.8	−40.6	95.5	−58.9	140.1	−14.3
59.0	−76.8	—	—	—	—	—	—
—	—	43.3	−98.2	43.0	−98.5	32.0	−109.5
47.3	−76.1	40.4	−88.3	26.7	−102.0	30.3	−98.3
40.1	−83.4	41.0	−87.7	34.1	−94.6	29.6	−99.1
34.9	−76.2	23.9	−91.9	22.8	−93.0	27.3	−88.5

composites, the determination of prestige by socioeconomic status is no longer required to account for correlation among prestige indicators across the life course. This specification improves fit substantially among women in the GSS but not among men. Inspection of the estimated error covariances showed that one of the three covariances, θ^ϵ_{47}, was large and statistically significant in all six analyses, while the other two error covariances were always very small and nonsignificant. For this reason, we estimated model G, which alters model A only by freeing θ^ϵ_{47} in each analysis. This one specification improves fit substantially in all six analyses, and it moves BIC into the acceptable range in all but two analyses, those based on the male and the female SEI among men. That is, the model of Figure 6 does satisfactorily account for intergenerational persistence in occupational prestige, but it does not account for persistence in occupational prestige from first to current jobs, especially among women. We suspect this is explained by overall stability in occupational careers, magnified by the tendency of women to hold common jobs whose prestige is not determined by occupational education or wage rates.[43]

In model H, we modified model G by freeing the three prestige variances. As indicated by BIC, this improved fit slightly in three of the analyses, but it did not improve fit in the other three cases. We then combined the specifications of model H and model B or model C in models I and J for men and women, respectively. That is, in model I we freed the prestige variances, the covariance between prestige of first and current occupation, and the lagged effects of the occupational education variables; in model J we freed the prestige variances, the covariance between prestige of first and current occupation, and the lagged effects of the occupational wage rate variables. For each of the three sets of socioeconomic components, models I and J fit well, yielding large, negative BIC statistics. Again, the lagged effects of occupational education (among men) and of occupational wage rates (among women) were substantial only in the case of the effect of first occupation on current occupation.

Before settling on models I and J as preferred specifications, we considered relaxing one other set of restrictions—namely, those pertaining to the constant effects of occupational education and occupational wage rate on the socioeconomic composite at each stage of the model. Using models I or J as the new baseline, in model K we released the constraints on γ_{11}, β_{42}, and β_{75} in equation (8). In model L, we released the constraints on γ_{12}, β_{43}, and β_{76} in equation (8). In model M, we released both those sets of constraints. In all of the comparisons of models K, L, or M with models I or J, the contrasts were nominally statistically significant, but BIC either increased or declined slightly. While the evidence is mixed, we

---

[43]Recall the discussion of outliers in Table 1.

have concluded that differentials in effects of occupational education and occupational income across the three stages of the model are not large enough to warrant the specification of differential weights for the components of the socioeconomic composite.

Thus, within the constraints of the traditional, prestige-validated model of occupational socioeconomic status, we prefer the specifications of model I for men and model J for women. While the general structure of models I and J remains similar to the model of Figure 6, there are important differences. First, and most important, there are lagged, intragenerational effects of occupational education (among men) and of occupational wage rates (among women), and these are inconsistent with the implicit assumption that a composite measure of occupational socioeconomic status fully accounts for the effects of its components. Second, the error variance of occupational prestige varies across stages of the model, and this is inconsistent with the implicit assumption that occupational prestige is equally valid across the life course as a measure of socioeconomic status. In our opinion, the violation of this assumption is relatively unimportant, for it may reflect no more than differentials in occupational composition across generations and within the career. However, the finding is cautionary: The usual aggregate regressions of prestige on socioeconomic status do not necessarily tell us the validity of prestige. Third, the traditional socioeconomic model of occupational prestige does not account for the persistence of prestige in individual careers, and this failure of the model is especially striking among women. Even though there is a great deal of evidence that the persistence of occupational prestige is relatively weak, the low level of persistence does not follow from socioeconomic explanations of prestige.

4.2. Modeling Socioeconomic Status without Prestige

Because the initial versions of the model in Figure 6 fit poorly, and because there were so many overidentifying restrictions in that model, we considered the possibility that a socioeconomic model of occupational standing might be identified without recourse to a prestige-validated index. Figure 7 shows a model of this kind. It differs from Figure 6 only by the elimination of measured occupational prestige from all three stages of the stratification process. That is, as in the case of Figure 6, we show three occupational status composites, corresponding to the status of father's occupation, first occupation, and current or last occupation, each fully determined by occupational education and occupational wage rate.

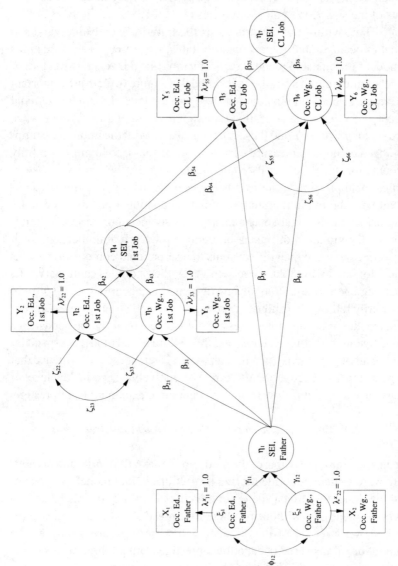

FIGURE 7. A model of intergenerational stratification in occupational socioeconomic status.

If we are willing to make assumptions corresponding to our initial specification of Figure 6 or to models I or J of Table 6, then all of the parameters of the model in Figure 7 are identified, without reference to any prestige measure. For example, any of Y_2, Y_3, Y_5, and Y_6 are sufficient to identify the relative sizes of γ_{11} and γ_{12}, while either of Y_5 and Y_6 are sufficient to identify β_{42} and β_{43}. To be sure, because no variable in the model follows η_7, the coefficients of the final composite, β_{75} and β_{76}, would not be identified in Figure 7, except by the assumption that the corresponding effects are constant across the three stages of the model. However, that assumption is sustained by the findings in Table 6. Moreover, in a more elaborate model of the stratification process—e.g., one that included personal earnings or other job outcomes—those effects would be identified without that type of cross-equation constraint.

In short, the idea that occupational stratification processes can be described adequately by relationships among composite socioeconomic indexes need not depend at all on use of a prestige criterion to determine weights of index components. Indeed, the model of Figure 7 permits us to ask directly whether a prestige criterion yields optimal weights for occupational education and wage rates in analyses of the stratification process.

In each of the models based on Figure 7, we have constrained the weights of the socioeconomic components to be equal across the three stages of the stratification process. Also, because the prestige criterion is no longer available to define a metric for the weights of the socioeconomic components, we have normalized the slopes relative to the effect of occupational education on the socioeconomic composites. That is, we specify

$$\gamma_{11} = \beta_{42} = \beta_{75} = 1, \tag{10}$$

and

$$\gamma_{12} = \beta_{43} = \beta_{76}. \tag{11}$$

Thus, γ_{12}, β_{43}, and β_{76} indicate the relative magnitude of the slopes of occupational wage rate and occupational education in the socioeconomic composites. Since the education and wage rate components are each in the same metric (started logits), this normalization is convenient and appropriate.

Table 7 reports the fit to the 1994 GSS data of alternative specifications of the model in Figure 7. Model A does not fit well. It would be rejected at conventional levels of statistical significance, and the BIC statistics are positive in each combination of gender and occupational measure. Thus use of a prestige criterion alone is not responsible for the

TABLE
Specifications and Fit Statistics for Models of Mobility in

		Men			
		Total-based SEI		Male-based SEI	
Model Specification	df	Chi-sq.	BIC	Chi-sq.	BIC
A. Base model as described in Figure 7.	5	34.3	3.4	37.3	6.4
B. Model A, but free paths between successive occupational education variables.	3	5.8	−12.7	4.7	−13.9
C. Model A, but free paths between successive occupational wage rate variables.	3	2.6	−15.9	2.9	−15.6
D. Model A, but free paths between successive occupational education and wage rate variables.	1	2.2	−4.0	1.4	−4.8
E. Model A, but constrain all free parameters to equal those in the baseline prestige-validated model (Model A in Table 6).	21	90.5	—	89.3	—
F. Model C, but constrain all free parameters to equal those in the gender-specific preferred prestige-validated model (Model I in Table 6 for men and Model J in Table 6 for women).	21	8.2	—	9.2	—

limitations of the traditional socioeconomic model. As shown in models B, C, and D, the lack of fit in model A can be attributed to the absence of lagged effects of socioeconomic components. In model B, we free the paths between successive occupational education variables. This change yields a satisfactory fit among men but not among women. In model C, we free the paths between successive occupational wage rate variables. This specification fits well in all six analyses. None of the chi-square statistics is significant at even the 0.05 level, and the BIC statistics are all negative. In model D, we free the lagged effects of occupational education and of the occupational wage rate. This provides no improvement in fit relative to model C, which becomes our preferred model. That is, the strictly socio-

7

Occupational Education and Occupational Wage Rates

(N = 479)				Women (N = 622)			
Female-based SEI		Total-based SEI		Male-based SEI		Female-based SEI	
Chi-sq.	BIC	Chi-sq.	BIC	Chi-sq.	BIC	Chi-sq.	BIC
44.9	14.0	72.2	40.0	55.3	23.1	112.5	80.3
8.9	−9.6	19.6	0.3	12.7	−6.6	24.9	5.6
7.1	−11.4	4.0	−15.3	1.9	−17.4	3.4	−15.9
6.5	0.3	1.1	−5.3	0.0	−6.4	0.2	−6.2
99.0	—	82.4	—	59.9	—	125.5	—
11.3	—	10.2	—	6.8	—	16.1	—

economic model works well, provided that we specify lagged effects of occupational wage rates among men and among women. Again, the lagged effects occur only from first occupation to current occupation, not from father's occupation to first occupation. The intergenerational effects are small and nonsignificant in each analysis. The lagged intragenerational effects are approximately 0.22 among men and about 0.45 among women, regardless of which socioeconomic measures—total, male, or female— were used. As explained below, while the lagged effects are needed to obtain satisfactory fit, they are not very important substantively.

To what degree does use of the prestige-validated index contribute to lack of fit in the models of Figure 6? We cannot directly compare the fit of models between Table 6 and Table 7 because of the former fit variances and covariances of occupational prestige as well as of the socioeconomic measures. To answer this question, we fitted the variance-covariance matrix of the socioeconomic variables using parameter estimates from model A in Table 6. The chi-square statistics from this exercise are shown in line E of Table 7. Among GSS men, use of the prestige criterion contributes substantially to lack of fit in the baseline model. That is, the chi-square statistics are much larger for the model of Figure 7 when the parameter estimates are borrowed from the model of Figure 6. However, among GSS women, the deterioration of fit is not substantial when parameter estimates are borrowed from the baseline model of Figure 6. That is, prestige-validation of socioeconomic composites is not as serious a threat to the validity of models of the stratification process among women as among men.

In line F of Table 7, we report findings from a similar exercise, based on our preferred specifications of the models of Figure 6 and Figure 7. That is, we fitted the variances and covariances of the socioeconomic variables, using the parameter estimates from model I or model J of Table 6. In this case, none of the test statistics becomes much larger when we borrow parameter estimates from the preferred model of Figure 6. This is further evidence that our modifications of the baseline model of Figure 6 have accounted for its lack of fit to relationships among the socioeconomic variables.

How does prestige-validation affect the relative weights of occupational education and wage rates in models of the stratification process? Table 8 shows these estimates under the baseline and preferred models of Figure 6 and Figure 7. In the first pair of lines, we report the estimates from Figure 6, and in the third pair of lines, we report those from Figure 7. The middle pair of lines renormalizes the estimates from Figure 6 to correspond directly with those from Figure 7. Thus our most important finding stands out in any comparison between the middle two lines and the lowest two lines of Table 8. The occupational wage rate has negligible influence in the process of stratification.

In all of the prestige-validated models the occupational wage rate has a substantial, positive weight, just as it did in the aggregate regressions of Table 2. In the total-based analysis for GSS women, the slope of the wage rate is less than half as large as that of education, but in most analyses, the wage slope is 75 to 90 percent as large as the education slope. The upper panel of Table 8 shows that the slope of the wage rate is always

TABLE 8

Effects of Occupational Education and Occupational Wage Rate on Socioeconomic Composite among Men and Women in the 1994 General Social Survey

Model specification	Men (N = 479)						Women (N = 622)					
	Total-based		Male-based		Female-based		Total-based		Male-based		Female-based	
	Educ.	Wage	Educ.	Wage	Educ.	Wage	Educ.	Wage	Educ.	Wage	Educ.	Wage
Prestige-weighted model (Figure 6)												
Baseline (Model A in Table 6)	0.462 (0.013)	0.333 (0.018)	0.390 (0.013)	0.389 (0.019)	0.470 (0.015)	0.358 (0.021)	0.509 (0.013)	0.236 (0.019)	0.427 (0.014)	0.355 (0.019)	0.445 (0.016)	0.350 (0.022)
Preferred (Model I in Table 6 for men, Model J in Table 6 for women)	0.439 (0.013)	0.375 (0.018)	0.365 (0.013)	0.436 (0.019)	0.441 (0.015)	0.401 (0.021)	0.515 (0.014)	0.223 (0.018)	0.434 (0.013)	0.340 (0.019)	0.451 (0.016)	0.339 (0.022)
Prestige-weighted model (renormalized for comparison with the socioeconomic model)												
Baseline (Model A in Table 6)	1.000	0.721	1.000	0.997	1.000	0.762	1.000	0.464	1.000	0.831	1.000	0.787
Preferred (Model I in Table 6 for men, Model J in Table 6 for women)	1.000	0.854	1.000	1.195	1.000	0.909	1.000	0.433	1.000	0.783	1.000	0.752
Socioeconomic model (Figure 7)												
Baseline (Model A in Table 7)	1.000 (—)	−0.237 (0.072)	1.000 (—)	−0.163 (0.084)	1.000 (—)	−0.266 (0.073)	1.000 (—)	0.009 (0.103)	1.000 (—)	0.353 (0.161)	1.000 (—)	0.017 (0.123)
Preferred (Model C in Table 7 for both men and women)	1.000 (—)	−0.220 (0.072)	1.000 (—)	−0.167 (0.083)	1.000 (—)	−0.241 (0.075)	1.000 (—)	0.089 (0.115)	1.000 (—)	0.349 (0.161)	1.000 (—)	0.066 (0.134)

241

statistically significant in models based on Figure 6. However, in the socioeconomic models of Figure 7, the slope of the wage rate is in every case negative among men, and, while the wage slopes among GSS women are all positive, they are in most cases not statistically significant.

Our reading of these findings is that, in a purely socioeconomic model, the appropriate weight of the wage rate is approximately zero. That is, in the GSS data the process of occupational stratification would best be described by relationships among occupation-based measures of educational attainment, to which the relationships of occupational prestige and occupational wage rates would be merely incidental.[44] While the correlated errors of prestige (in the models of Figure 6) and the lagged effects of occupational wage rates (in the models of Figure 7) show that there are unique aspects of the persistence of occupational prestige and occupational economic standing, our findings from the socioeconomic model point to occupational differentiation by education as the central feature of the stratification process, among the three dimensions considered in the present study.

The estimated slopes from the prestige-validated model also display other interesting features. First, as already noted, they somewhat resemble the weights in the aggregate prestige regressions of Table 2. For example, regardless of the gender of the GSS respondents, educational level carries relatively more weight in the analyses based on the occupational characteristics of all workers and on women workers than in the analyses based on the occupational characteristics of male workers. Second, the relative weights of educational level and wage rate are affected by the gender of the GSS respondent as well as by the gender of the source of the occupational characteristics. In five of six possible comparisons, the relative weight of wages is greater among male than among female GSS respondents. Third, in the preferred models of Table 6 (model I and model J), education always gets a larger weight relative to the wage rate than in the baseline model. That is, as parameters are added to capture the persistence of occupational prestige, the weights shift toward those estimated in the purely socioeconomic model. Finally, in the case of women

---

[44]We hasten to add that it will be desirable to validate these findings in larger bodies of data in which father's occupation, first occupation, and current occupation have been ascertained, such as the two Occupational Changes in a Generation surveys (OCG). However, since those data were coded to standards of the 1960 and/or 1970 Censuses, the exercise depends on the availability of measures of occupational education and earnings from those earlier censuses.

the weights in the prestige-validated models more closely resemble the weights in the socioeconomic models than in the case of men.[45]

Our overall findings about intergenerational and intragenerational persistence in occupational standing are both illustrated and tempered by Table 9, which shows model-based and observed correlations among socioeconomic status and its components. Again, we show correlations separately by the gender of the GSS respondent and by the source of the socioeconomic characteristics of occupations used in the analysis. Since each set of correlations for men or women is based upon the same set of occupational data, differences among the sets must arise from differences in the Census data (for all workers, men, and women), from differences in the weights of educational level and wage rate in the composite indexes, and from other differences in model specification—e.g., lagged effects or correlated errors.

There are several important patterns in Table 9. First, although the differences in specification between the baseline and preferred models of Figure 6 and Figure 7 affect model fit, they have very little influence on the model-based correlations between socioeconomic composites. Whether we consider the prestige-validated or socioeconomic models, there are negligible differences between baseline and preferred models in the correlations among socioeconomic composites. Second, the source of the socioeconomic characteristics of occupational incumbents affects the model-based correlations among composites. This is especially evident among GSS men, for whom female-based occupational indexes yield substantially lower correlations, between and within generations, than total- or male-based occupational indexes. For example, the father-son correlation is 0.225 when women's characteristics are used to construct the index in the baseline model, and it is 0.305 when men's characteristics are used to construct the index in the baseline model. Notice that there is little sign of a corresponding, gender-specific differential on intergenerational correlations among women, but the female-based first-current correlations are slightly larger among women than the male-based first-current correlations. Third, correlations based on the socioeconomic models are always larger than those based on prestige-validated models. The differences are modest, but the sharp differences in weights do make a difference. Notice that the differences in correlation are smaller among women than among

---

[45]This presumably accounts for the smaller contrasts for women than for men between model A and model E in Table 7.

TABLE 9

Correlations among Selected Occupational Variables: Men and Women in the 1994 General Social Survey

Model Specification	Total-based			Male-based			Female-based		
	Father/ First	Father/ Current	First/ Current	Father/ First	Father/ Current	First/ Current	Father/ First	Father/ Current	First/ Current
Men (N = 479)									
Prestige-weighted model (Figure 6)									
Baseline (Model A in Table 6)	0.274	0.336	0.679	0.305	0.365	0.686	0.225	0.282	0.663
Preferred (Model I in Table 6 for men, Model J in Table 6 for women)	0.270	0.332	0.672	0.300	0.361	0.680	0.222	0.281	0.658
Socioeconomic model (Figure 7)									
Baseline (Model A in Table 7)	0.302	0.358	0.720	0.315	0.379	0.725	0.246	0.299	0.704
Preferred (Model C in Table 7 for both men and women)	0.302	0.358	0.721	0.315	0.379	0.725	0.247	0.300	0.705
Occupational education	0.300	0.359	0.718	0.315	0.383	0.725	0.245	0.299	0.701
Occupational wage rate	0.167	0.213	0.495	0.220	0.261	0.542	0.150	0.213	0.507
Women (N = 622)									
Prestige-weighted model (Figure 6)									
Baseline (Model A in Table 6)	0.313	0.336	0.697	0.294	0.309	0.678	0.286	0.300	0.712
Preferred (Model I in Table 6 for men, Model J in Table 6 for women)	0.314	0.336	0.696	0.295	0.309	0.676	0.287	0.299	0.709
Socioeconomic model (Figure 7)									
Baseline (Model A in Table 7)	0.332	0.341	0.710	0.307	0.314	0.688	0.317	0.316	0.722
Preferred (Model C in Table 7 for both men and women)	0.329	0.342	0.709	0.307	0.314	0.689	0.316	0.316	0.722
Occupational education	0.332	0.341	0.710	0.313	0.309	0.689	0.318	0.316	0.722
Occupational wage rate	0.168	0.233	0.579	0.197	0.233	0.573	0.172	0.211	0.655

men; this is consistent with our observation that the differences in weights are smaller among women than among men.

Most important, the observed intergenerational and intragenerational correlations of occupational education are virtually the same as those of indexes based on socioeconomic models. That is, to estimate correlations of occupational status across generations or within the career, we would do quite as well to index occupations by their educational level alone as by some combination of their educational and wage levels. Combining educational levels and wages in an index of occupational status adds nothing to our understanding of occupational stratification; indeed, choice of a substantial positive weight for the wage rate leads to an understatement of occupational persistence. As a corollary to this observation, the last two lines of Table 9 permit us to contrast the correlations of occupational education and occupational wage rates in the GSS data. In every case, the correlations of occupational wage rates are much lower than the correlations of occupational education. Also, as in the case of the composite indexes, there are gender differences in the education correlations, depending on the gender of the population from which the occupational education measures were ascertained.

Early in our review, we noted the observation that occupational status behaved across the life course something like the latent variable of economic theory, permanent income (Goldberger 1989; Zimmerman 1992), but the source of persistent occupational standing appears to be the educational level of occupations rather than their economic compensation.[46] To be sure, if educational level were chosen to index occupational standing, analysts would have to live with the observation that the occupational standing of women typically exceeds that of men, but, unlike a composite socioeconomic index, use of education alone would at least present an unambiguous gender differential.

The specific weights that we obtain for occupational education and occupational wage rates will depend on which other variables are included in or excluded from the model, as well as on our decisions about the measurement of occupational standing. Thus, when we add other educational variables to the rudimentary models of Figure 6 and Figure 7—mother's and father's education as measures of family origin and respondent's ed-

---

[46]Thus, Sobek's (1996) analysis of historical stability in occupational income in the United States justifiably supports the wide use of occupation as an indicator of social standing in historical research, but it appears to have focused on the wrong component of occupational socioeconomic status.

ucational attainment as an additional outcome—the relative weights of occupational education and occupational wage rates change along with the overall effect of the occupational status composite. This occurs partly because the educational variables carry some of the effect of occupational education and partly because respondent's education enters the model as yet another indicator of father's occupational status.[47] The changes are greater in the purely socioeconomic model than in the prestige-validated model. In the socioeconomic model, as one might expect, the relative weight for occupational wage rates increases when parents' educational attainments are added to the model. We think that the findings from the models of Figure 6 and Figure 7 are persuasive about the fundamental role of occupational education in the stratification process. The addition of other variables to the models may help to explain the role of education in the occupational stratification process, but it does not alter our central finding. The sensitivity of the weights of the SEI construct to alternative specifications reminds us that those weights are model-dependent. This is yet another reason why researchers should be cautious in using composite measures of occupational socioeconomic status.

4.3. Occupational Stratification in Education

Our findings suggest an alternative specification of the stratification process, which brings occupational prestige back into the picture, but identifies education as the main dimension of occupational stratification.[48] This idea is illustrated by the path model in Figure 8. We assume that occupational education, wage rate, and prestige are each perfectly measured. Thus the measurement models in those variables are trivial. For example, in the case of father's occupation, we have

$$Y_1 = \eta_1,$$

$$Y_2 = \eta_2, \tag{12}$$

$$Y_3 = \eta_3.$$

---

[47]These findings are available from the authors by request.

[48]Hout (1996) has made a similar proposal, based on multivariate analyses of mobility tables from the General Social Survey.

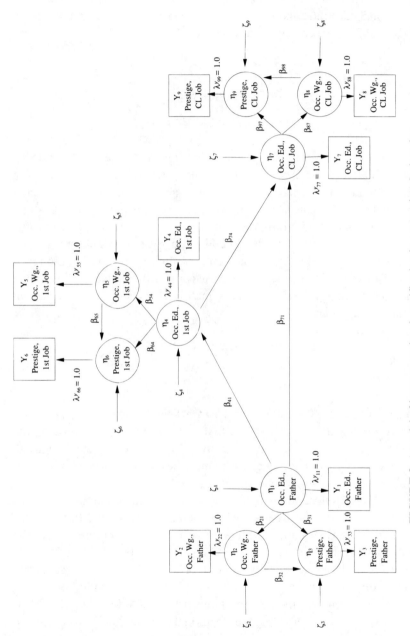

FIGURE 8. A model of intergenerational stratification in occupational education.

247

As in Figure 6, we postulate that occupational prestige depends upon occupational education and wage rates at each stage of the model. Again, in the case of father's occupation, we have

$$\eta_1 = \zeta_1,$$

$$\eta_2 = \beta_{21}\eta_1 + \zeta_2, \tag{13}$$

$$\eta_3 = \beta_{31}\eta_1 + \beta_{32}\eta_2 + \zeta_3.$$

That is, we specify that occupational wage rate and occupational prestige are each affected by occupational education, while occupational prestige also depends upon the occupational wage rate. Thus the equation in occupational prestige is the same as that used in the construction of a prestige-validated socioeconomic index. However, the model specifies that the relationships among occupational education, wage rate, and prestige are incidental to the role of occupational education in the stratification process. The stratification process is specified primarily by relationships among the educational levels of father's occupation, first occupation, and current or last occupation:

$$\eta_4 = \beta_{41}\eta_1 + \zeta_4,$$

$$\eta_7 = \beta_{71}\eta_1 + \beta_{74}\eta_4 + \zeta_7. \tag{14}$$

In addition, as in earlier models, we permit specific relationships between the occupational wage rate of the first and current jobs and between the occupational prestige of first and current jobs. In the model of Figure 8, these are specified in terms of covariances between disturbances in equations: $Cov(\zeta_5,\zeta_8) = \psi_{58}$ and $Cov(\zeta_6,\zeta_9) = \psi_{69}$.

Table 10 gives fit statistics for three versions of the model of Figure 8 for each combination of socioeconomic data from the 1990 Census with the 1994 GSS samples. Model A corresponds to Figure 8, with the addition of the two correlated disturbances, and its fit is excellent. The BIC statistics are large and negative, and in only one case, that of the female socioeconomic characteristics applied to the GSS men, would the model be rejected even with the probability level $\alpha = 0.05$. In model B, we impose six restrictions, equating the slopes in the regressions of wage rate on occupational education and of prestige on wage rate and education at each stage of the model:

TABLE 10
Specifications and Fit Statistics for Models of Stratification in Occupational Education

Model specification	df	Data for All Workers		Data for Men		Data for Women	
		Chi-sq.	BIC	Chi-sq.	BIC	Chi-sq.	BIC
Men (N = 479)							
A. Base model as described in Figure 8.	22	30.7	−105.1	26.8	−109.0	41.4	−94.4
B. Model A, but equate corresponding slopes in measurement model.	28	59.8	−113.0	61.2	−111.6	67.4	−105.5
C. Model B, but equate corresponding error variances in measurement model	32	84.0	−113.5	90.6	−106.9	83.4	−114.1
Women (N = 622)							
A. Base model as described in Figure 8.	22	21.7	−119.8	25.1	−116.4	16.0	−125.5
B. Model A, but equate corresponding slopes in measurement model.	28	80.9	−99.2	53.7	−126.5	50.1	−130.0
C. Model B, but equate corresponding error variances in measurement model	32	124.8	−81.1	98.0	−107.8	140.0	−65.9

$$\beta_{21} = \beta_{54} = \beta_{87},$$
$$\beta_{31} = \beta_{64} = \beta_{97}, \qquad (15)$$
$$\beta_{32} = \beta_{65} = \beta_{98}.$$

Here, the models would in each case be rejected at conventional levels of statistical significance, but the BIC statistics improve substantially (decrease by 10 or more) in three of the six analyses and deteriorate substantially in only one case. Finally, in model C, we impose the additional restrictions that the variances of the disturbances in occupational wage rates are the same at each stage of the model and that the variances of the disturbances in occupational prestige are the same at each stage of the model:

$$\psi_{22} = \psi_{55} = \psi_{88},$$
$$\psi_{33} = \psi_{66} = \psi_{99}. \qquad (16)$$

In this case, the fit is much worse in each of the analyses of GSS women, and the value of BIC improves in only one group of GSS men. For these reasons, we reject model C. While there is some evidence of stability in the slopes of the auxiliary regressions (equation 15) across the three stages of the model, we are inclined to prefer model A, where the fit is good by any standard.

Again, the model of Figure 8 does not specify that occupational education is the sole dimension of occupational persistence, for there are lagged correlations of disturbances in occupational wage rates and prestige. These correlations are moderate, ranging from 0.25 to 0.39 for wage rates and from 0.19 to 0.22 for prestige across the several specifications of model A. However, these correlations are misleadingly high, for the disturbances have been purged of the effects of occupational education and—in the case of prestige—of occupational wage rates. The covariances of the disturbances account for 12 to 19 percent of the total covariances between wage rates of first and current occupations, and they account for only 6 to 10 percent of the total covariances between prestige levels of first and current occupations.

5. DISCUSSION

In this paper, we have carried out three distinct tasks. First, we reviewed the history and properties of occupational prestige and of socioeconomic indexes of occupational status. Second, we constructed new indexes of occupational socioeconomic status for men, women, and all workers, based on the education and income of workers in the 1990 Census and validated against occupational prestige ratings from the 1989 General Social Survey. We believe that the new indexes are not only an update of earlier socioeconomic indexes, but also an improvement, by dint of our changes in variable definition, functional form, and the treatment of outliers. Third, we have embedded the construction of socioeconomic indexes within a rudimentary model of the process of occupational stratification, which we have estimated and tested using data from the 1994 General Social Survey.

Findings from the third part of our analysis lead us to question the value of traditional socioeconomic indexes of occupational standing, including those that we have constructed. If the 1994 GSS data are a reliable guide, we would do better—in studies of the stratification process—to index occupations by their educational level alone than by any of the usual, weighted combinations of educational level and earnings. Similarly, Kalmijn (1994) finds that occupational education is more important than occupational income in assortative mating. However, given the modest sensitivity of occupational status correlations to differences in model specification, we would not suggest any wholesale effort to reevaluate previous findings about levels, trends, and differentials in occupational stratification. It would be sufficient, we think, to suggest that previously estimated levels of correlation are slightly too low. For example, corrections of correlations for simple attenuation would be much larger than corrections for differences in weighting between our prestige-validated and socioeconomic models.

We also think that it would be unwise to overstate the strength of the evidence presented here. We should very much like to see our analyses of the 1994 GSS data cross-validated in larger samples—e.g., the 1986–1988 Surveys of Income and Program Participation or the 1962 or 1973 Occupational Changes in a Generation Surveys. Finally, we would caution that our findings about the relative importance of occupational education and occupational wage rates are specific to models of the stratification process. Just as the relative weights of occupational education and wage rates differ between prestige and socioeconomic outcomes, so they may also differ across other outcomes—e.g., health, well-being, social participation, or political choice. If there is any general conclusion to be drawn from the present analysis, it is that we ought to move toward a more specific and disaggregated appraisal of the effects of occupational characteristics on social, psychological, economic, political, and health outcomes. While composite measures of occupational status may have heuristic uses, the global concept of occupational status is scientifically obsolete.

Appendix
1989 Nakao-Treas Prestige Measures and 1980/1990

							1980/1990-basis		
							Total		
	F	Number of		Nakao-Treas Prestige Scores					
	L	Occup.					Logit	Logit (%	
Census	A	Incumbents	%	Prestige		Logit	(% 1 Yr.	$14.30/	
Code	G	in 1990	Male	Score	%5+	%5+	Col. +)	hour +)	TSEI
ALL OCCUPATIONS									
	–	112,169,744	54.5	43.43	49.64	0.00	0.30	−1.13	36.81
MANAGERIAL AND SPECIALTY OCCUPATIONS									
	8	30,030,911	51.8	59.46	75.27	1.19	1.99	−0.04	55.27
Executive, Administrative, and Managerial Occupations									
	7	14,007,863	58.0	54.74	69.80	0.88	1.23	−0.16	40.22
3.00	1	12,100	61.5	60.92	80.18	1.36	1.68	−0.28	50.86
4.00	1	18,677	73.1	70.45	88.41	1.96	0.61	−0.12	43.51
5.00	1	488,497	54.4	51.23	80.82	1.40	1.41	0.12	50.77
6.00	1	47,609	72.0	53.66	67.24	0.70	0.97	−0.08	46.47
7.00	1	615,979	53.9	58.94	77.59	1.21	1.68	0.28	53.60
8.00	1	266,213	50.8	53.85	72.12	0.93	1.07	−0.04	47.43
9.00	1	116,894	66.2	62.73	84.11	1.62	1.61	0.36	53.45
13.00	1	584,688	68.5	59.46	79.04	1.29	1.76	0.48	55.18
14.00	1	601,728	47.8	63.70	83.33	1.56	1.92	0.04	54.25
15.00	1	225,606	33.5	69.22	87.89	1.91	1.29	−0.28	47.90
16.00	2	384,781	53.9	38.53	45.74	−0.17	0.74	−0.52	42.50
16.00	3	39,647	52.7	52.85	70.65	0.86	0.44	1.18	48.68
17.00	2	39,647	52.7	52.85	70.65	0.86	0.44	1.18	48.68
17.00	5	959,040	55.9	41.00	46.90	−0.12	0.24	−1.51	33.82
17.01	6	201,839	66.3	–	–	–	0.16	−1.68	32.35
17.02	6	129,135	55.1	–	–	–	0.74	−0.61	42.08
17.03	6	628,066	52.7	–	–	–	0.16	−1.07	35.38
18.00	2	45,527	87.8	49.14	65.52	0.63	1.41	−0.48	47.80
18.00	3	384,781	53.9	38.53	45.74	−0.17	0.74	−0.52	42.50
19.00	2	6,465,041	65.9	51.00	66.52	0.67	0.86	−0.11	45.52
19.00	3	45,527	87.8	49.14	65.52	0.63	1.41	−0.48	47.80
21.00	3	386,259	49.7	42.00	46.50	−0.14	1.23	−0.61	45.83
22.00	5	5,119,742	69.0	57.00	71.70	0.91	0.97	0.15	47.60
22.01	6	45,165	64.2	–	–	–	0.78	−0.48	43.05

Hauser–Warren SEIs and Component Data

SEIs and Component Data						
Males			Females			
Logit (% 1 Yr. Col. +)	Logit (% $14.30/ hour +)	MSEI	Logit (% 1 Yr. Col. +)	Logit (% $14.30/ hour +)	FSEI	Occupational Title
0.53	−0.77	36.37	0.19	−1.61	35.83	
2.25	0.35	54.48	1.79	−0.57	53.57	
1.55	0.33	50.64	0.96	−0.90	45.40	
1.76	0.00	48.19	1.68	−0.74	51.05	Legislators
0.61	0.16	43.39	0.52	−0.78	41.71	Chief Executives and General Administrators, Public Administration
1.76	0.69	53.62	1.02	−0.52	46.87	Administrators and Officials, Public Administration
1.29	0.32	48.22	0.36	−1.23	38.30	Administrators, Protective Service
2.46	0.97	59.51	1.07	−0.44	47.66	Financial Managers
1.23	0.36	48.24	0.92	−0.48	46.29	Personnel and Labor Relations Managers
1.84	0.74	54.39	1.12	−0.36	48.45	Purchasing Managers
1.92	0.92	56.30	1.47	−0.32	51.39	Managers, Marketing, Advertising, and Public Relations
2.34	0.69	56.65	1.61	−0.56	51.30	Administrators, Education and Related Fields
1.76	0.44	51.63	1.12	−0.65	47.08	Managers, Medicine and Health
1.02	0.00	44.33	0.44	−1.23	38.95	Managers, Properties and Real Estate
0.92	2.01	59.61	−0.04	0.56	43.58	Postmasters and Mail Superintendents
0.92	2.01	59.61	−0.04	0.56	43.58	Postmasters and Mail Superintendents
0.55	−1.15	32.82	−0.17	−2.11	30.07	Managers, Food Serving and Lodging Establishments
0.32	−0.65	35.55	−0.12	−1.41	33.74	Mngrs., Food Services & Lodging Est. (SE)
1.07	−0.78	38.47	0.32	−1.92	34.77	Mngrs., Food Services & Lodging Est. (NSE, Personal Services)
0.52	−1.47	30.15	−0.28	−2.46	27.58	Mngrs., Food Services & Lodging Est. (NSE, Other)
1.47	−0.40	43.59	0.97	−1.18	43.41	Funeral Directors
1.02	0.00	44.33	0.44	−1.23	38.95	Managers, Properties and Real Estate
1.00	0.27	46.36	0.67	−0.95	42.14	Managers and Administrators, n.e.c.
1.47	−0.40	43.59	0.97	−1.18	43.41	Funeral Directors
1.18	−0.20	43.61	1.29	−1.07	46.41	Managers, Service Organizations, n.e.c.
1.09	0.56	49.08	0.81	−0.78	43.95	Managers and Administrators, n.e.c.
0.88	−0.44	40.13	0.61	−1.68	38.18	Mngrs./Administrators, n.e.c. (NSE, Agr. For., & Fish.)

continued

Census Code	F L A G	Number of Occup. Incumbents in 1990	% Male	Nakao-Treas Prestige Scores			1980/1990-basis Total		
				Prestige Score	%5+	Logit %5+	Logit (% 1 Yr. Col. +)	Logit (% $14.30/ hour +)	TSEI
22.02	6	37,213	86.1	–	–	–	1.07	−0.24	46.45
22.03	6	380,344	84.0	–	–	–	0.74	−0.92	40.51
22.04	6	1,191,124	79.3	–	–	–	1.23	−1.76	40.11
22.05	6	493,873	72.3	–	–	–	0.97	−0.56	44.06
22.06	6	244,606	69.6	–	–	–	0.88	−0.78	42.25
22.07	6	313,761	54.3	–	–	–	0.52	−1.84	34.33
22.08	6	338,765	51.1	–	–	–	1.41	−1.47	42.86
22.09	6	337,648	64.1	–	–	–	0.97	−0.83	42.75
22.10	6	48,567	44.3	–	–	–	0.44	−0.28	41.45
22.11	6	72,370	60.5	–	–	–	1.02	−1.29	40.83
22.12	6	641,209	42.1	–	–	–	1.54	−0.20	50.18
22.13	6	77,312	65.4	–	–	–	1.54	−0.78	47.27
22.14	6	25,338	80.9	–	–	–	0.65	−0.74	40.76
22.15	6	8,408	92.1	–	–	–	0.69	−0.78	40.87
22.16	6	251,147	92.7	–	–	–	0.28	−0.52	39.01
22.17	6	188,109	82.6	–	–	–	0.69	−1.02	39.68
22.18	6	58,050	79.9	–	–	–	0.48	−0.52	40.55
22.19	6	47,026	82.1	–	–	–	1.07	−0.78	43.74
22.20	6	58,970	74.9	–	–	–	0.78	−1.41	38.43
22.21	6	35,654	77.5	–	–	–	1.68	−0.97	47.40
22.22	6	132,976	77.9	–	–	–	0.56	−0.83	39.66
22.23	6	25,338	60.1	–	–	–	0.44	−1.02	37.75
22.24	6	12,427	70.8	–	–	–	0.83	−1.02	40.71
22.25	6	54,342	60.2	–	–	–	1.84	−0.48	51.03

Continued

SEIs and Component Data

Males			Females			
Logit (% 1 Yr. Col. +)	Logit (% $14.30/ hour +)	MSEI	Logit (% 1 Yr. Col. +)	Logit (% $14.30/ hour +)	FSEI	Occupational Title
1.07	1.12	53.42	1.02	−0.61	46.47	Mngrs./Administrators, n.e.c. (NSE, Mining)
0.74	0.48	46.60	0.65	−1.07	41.36	Mngrs./Administrators, n.e.c. (NSE, Construction)
1.35	1.07	54.46	0.83	−0.48	45.54	Mngrs./Administrators, n.e.c. (NSE, Manufacturing)
1.02	0.78	50.47	0.78	−0.24	46.32	Mngrs./Administrators, n.e.c. (NSE, Trans., Comm. & Util.)
0.97	0.44	47.51	0.61	−0.92	41.72	Mngrs./Administrators, n.e.c. (NSE, Wholesale)
0.78	−0.24	41.23	0.24	−1.76	34.91	Mngrs./Administrators, n.e.c. (NSE, Retail)
2.11	1.35	60.63	0.88	−0.56	45.52	Mngrs./Administrators, n.e.c. (NSE, Finance, Insur.)
0.97	0.16	45.30	0.92	−0.78	44.87	Mngrs./Administrators, n.e.c. (NSE, Bus. & Repair Serv.)
0.78	−0.56	38.66	0.16	−1.84	33.91	Mngrs./Administrators, n.e.c. (NSE, Personal Serv.)
1.07	−0.36	41.80	0.92	−1.47	41.64	Mngrs./Administrators, n.e.c. (NSE, Enter. & Rec. Serv.)
2.34	0.83	57.71	1.12	−0.83	46.24	Mngrs./Administrators, n.e.c. (NSE, Prof., Related Serv.)
1.76	0.92	55.43	1.18	−0.28	49.25	Mngrs./Administrators, n.e.c. (NSE, Public Admin.)
0.65	−0.48	38.62	0.78	−1.29	41.39	Mngrs./Administrators, n.e.c. (SE, Agr. For., & Fish.)
0.69	0.20	44.15	0.52	−0.20	44.45	Mngrs./Administrators, n.e.c. (SE, Mining)
0.28	0.04	40.73	0.40	−0.78	40.73	Mngrs./Administrators, n.e.c. (SE, Construction)
0.74	0.24	44.70	0.61	−0.74	42.59	Mngrs./Administrators, n.e.c. (SE, Manufacturing)
0.44	0.08	41.89	0.61	−0.78	42.38	Mngrs./Administrators, n.e.c. (SE, Trans., Comm. & Util.)
1.12	0.78	51.01	0.83	−0.52	45.35	Mngrs./Administrators, n.e.c. (SE, Wholesale)
0.88	0.16	44.80	0.56	−1.02	40.92	Mngrs./Administrators, n.e.c. (SE, Retail)
1.92	0.92	56.30	0.97	−0.52	46.48	Mngrs./Administrators, n.e.c. (SE, Finance, Insur.)
0.52	−0.16	40.48	0.74	−0.78	43.41	Mngrs./Administrators, n.e.c. (SE, Bus. & Repair Serv.)
0.61	−0.44	38.72	0.16	−1.41	35.91	Mngrs./Administrators, n.e.c. (SE, Personal Serv.)
0.97	−0.36	41.28	0.52	−0.97	40.82	Mngrs./Administrators, n.e.c. (SE, Enter. & Rec. Serv.)
2.22	0.56	55.03	1.47	−0.83	49.00	Mngrs./Administrators, n.e.c. (SE, Prof., Related Serv.)

continued

Appendix—

Census Code	F L A G	Number of Occup. Incumbents in 1990	% Male	Nakao-Treas Prestige Scores			1980/1990-basis Total		
				Prestige Score	%5+	Logit %5+	Logit (% 1 Yr. Col. +)	Logit (% $14.30/ hour +)	TSEI
23.00	4	1,535,605	47.5	65.38	84.44	1.64	2.11	−0.34	53.79
23.01	6	386,513	44.9	–	–	–	2.46	−0.83	54.03
23.02	6	990,052	44.7	–	–	–	1.92	0.12	54.64
23.03	6	134,525	77.1	–	–	–	3.20	−0.36	61.92
23.04	6	24,515	41.6	–	–	–	1.84	−0.83	49.30
24.00	1	66,083	31.9	48.40	59.63	0.38	1.07	−0.44	45.45
25.00	1	649,757	48.6	48.40	59.63	0.38	1.47	−0.32	49.09
26.00	1	273,409	66.8	60.65	85.22	1.70	2.22	0.40	58.26
27.00	1	493,886	42.5	43.32	54.32	0.17	1.23	−0.44	46.67
28.00	1	15,811	85.1	41.85	47.32	−0.11	−0.16	−0.78	34.44
29.00	1	217,323	47.0	50.11	69.03	0.78	0.56	−1.02	38.70
33.00	1	236,797	54.8	40.99	52.33	0.09	0.88	−0.56	43.33
34.00	1	33,289	53.7	51.43	64.91	0.60	1.12	−0.65	44.79
35.00	1	62,185	94.1	46.85	47.66	−0.09	0.56	−0.24	42.60
36.00	1	155,122	69.0	50.06	63.64	0.55	1.02	−0.20	46.26
37.00	1	355,609	22.6	48.72	57.39	0.29	0.92	−1.12	40.91
Professional Specialty Occupations									
	7	16,023,048	46.4	63.59	80.05	1.47	2.66	0.06	60.92
43.00	1	152,556	85.2	73.15	93.04	2.47	2.77	0.36	62.25
44.00	1	135,830	91.7	71.60	86.84	1.83	2.97	1.92	71.48
45.00	1	16,994	89.3	60.94	77.88	1.23	2.11	1.02	60.56
46.00	1	5,712	92.9	59.62	72.65	0.95	2.01	0.88	59.09
47.00	1	24,698	93.8	65.85	82.14	1.48	2.46	1.23	64.27
48.00	1	64,448	89.4	73.30	91.82	2.31	2.97	1.61	69.92
49.00	1	10,915	92.0	63.30	80.73	1.39	2.97	1.76	70.66
53.00	1	245,580	93.2	68.81	84.11	1.62	2.61	1.07	64.56
54.00	1	2,408	93.1	59.54	74.56	1.05	1.92	0.83	58.17
55.00	1	455,244	90.4	64.19	85.39	1.71	2.61	1.47	66.55
56.00	1	169,171	85.8	62.26	76.19	1.14	1.92	0.69	57.50
57.00	1	182,075	95.1	64.14	83.33	1.56	2.22	1.23	62.42
58.00	1	13,056	97.1	59.46	76.58	1.16	1.41	0.97	55.01
59.00	1	333,459	89.9	70.69	89.92	2.10	2.61	1.07	64.56
63.00	1	10,242	90.6	51.35	65.77	0.64	2.11	0.04	55.68
64.00	1	462,047	69.1	73.70	91.30	2.25	2.61	0.92	63.81

Continued

SEIs and Component Data

Males			Females			
Logit (% 1 Yr. Col. +)	Logit (% $14.30/ hour +)	MSEI	Logit (% 1 Yr. Col. +)	Logit (% $14.30/ hour +)	FSEI	Occupational Title
3.13	0.32	57.88	1.62	−1.02	49.26	Accountants and Auditors
3.50	0.12	58.23	2.01	−1.02	52.35	Accountants and Auditors (NSE, Prof., Related Serv.)
2.97	0.32	57.00	1.47	−1.02	48.09	Accountants and Auditors (NSE, Other)
3.50	0.78	63.44	2.34	−0.48	57.40	Accountants and Auditors (SE, Prof., Related Serv.)
2.61	−0.08	52.03	1.47	−0.83	49.00	Accountants and Auditors (SE, Other)
2.34	0.40	54.33	0.65	−0.88	42.28	Underwriters
2.34	0.36	54.01	0.92	−1.07	43.52	Other Financial Officers
2.46	0.69	57.32	1.92	−0.12	55.85	Management Analysts
1.29	0.12	46.67	1.12	−0.88	46.03	Personnel, Training, and Labor Relations Specialists
−0.08	−0.61	33.82	−0.61	−1.84	27.90	Purchasing Agents and Buyers, Farm Products
0.74	−0.52	38.76	0.44	−1.61	37.19	Buyers, Wholesale and Retail Trade Except Farm Products
1.07	−0.08	43.98	0.65	−1.23	40.61	Purchasing Agents and Buyers
1.07	−0.28	42.43	1.18	−1.18	45.03	Business and Promotion Agents
0.52	−0.20	40.17	0.65	−1.02	41.60	Construction Inspectors
1.02	0.04	44.64	1.07	−0.83	45.83	Inspectors and Compliance Officers, Except Construction
0.97	−0.24	42.22	0.92	−1.47	41.64	Management Related Occupations, n.e.c.
2.86	0.37	57.84	2.51	−0.28	60.71	
2.77	0.52	57.60	2.97	−0.48	62.36	Architects
3.20	2.01	71.53	2.46	0.83	64.53	Aerospace Engineers
2.11	1.12	58.87	2.61	0.20	62.71	Metallurgical and Materials Engineers
2.01	0.92	56.77	1.35	0.36	53.55	Mining Engineers
2.46	1.29	62.01	1.61	0.44	55.98	Petroleum Engineers
2.97	1.68	67.70	3.20	1.02	71.21	Chemical Engineers
2.97	1.92	69.60	2.11	0.61	60.72	Nuclear Engineers
2.46	1.12	60.71	2.61	0.36	63.46	Civil Engineers
1.84	0.78	54.75	4.62	1.68	85.44	Agricultural Engineers
2.61	1.54	64.72	2.01	0.88	61.21	Electrical and Electronic Engineers
2.01	0.88	56.40	1.47	−0.28	51.58	Industrial Engineers
2.22	1.23	60.28	2.61	0.74	65.23	Mechanical Engineers
1.41	0.97	53.99	1.92	1.47	63.29	Marine Engineers and Naval Architects
2.61	1.18	61.88	2.46	0.32	62.13	Engineers, n.e.c.
2.11	0.08	50.67	1.84	−0.69	52.49	Surveyors and Mapping Scientists
2.77	1.12	62.33	2.34	0.52	62.08	Computer Systems Analysts and Scientists

continued

Appendix—

Census Code	F L A G	Number of Occup. Incumbents in 1990	% Male	Nakao-Treas Prestige Scores			1980/1990-basis Total		
				Prestige Score	%5+	Logit %5+	Logit (% 1 Yr. Col. +)	Logit (% $14.30/ hour +)	TSEI
65.00	1	243,532	56.4	53.04	70.09	0.83	1.92	0.48	56.44
66.00	1	18,844	66.0	44.47	52.63	0.10	3.50	1.18	71.80
67.00	1	30,249	49.3	55.57	73.27	0.99	2.11	−0.04	55.29
68.00	1	5,519	73.7	63.46	77.78	1.22	2.97	1.29	68.34
69.00	1	26,911	86.1	73.48	88.79	2.00	3.20	1.02	68.77
73.00	1	136,111	73.5	73.33	91.50	2.28	2.77	0.36	62.25
74.00	1	8,541	89.1	63.39	83.93	1.60	2.61	0.65	62.45
75.00	1	51,113	84.8	69.75	89.29	2.04	3.50	0.56	68.74
76.00	1	17,967	70.1	73.09	89.83	2.10	2.97	0.16	62.71
77.00	1	32,493	73.9	58.00	75.68	1.11	1.61	−0.48	49.30
78.00	1	59,751	58.0	73.14	90.35	2.15	3.20	−0.24	62.52
79.00	1	33,437	87.0	54.53	71.55	0.90	1.68	−0.36	50.46
83.00	1	26,642	56.3	64.27	80.43	1.38	4.62	0.00	74.40
84.00	1	572,733	79.4	86.05	94.64	2.71	4.62	1.23	80.53
85.00	1	154,158	87.5	71.79	91.74	2.30	3.91	1.61	77.08
86.00	1	48,537	73.3	62.28	79.65	1.33	3.91	0.36	70.86
87.00	1	27,275	84.9	67.16	82.73	1.52	3.91	1.29	75.50
88.00	1	8,159	90.2	64.86	81.98	1.47	3.91	1.18	74.94
89.00	1	43,759	71.2	50.44	61.61	0.46	2.11	0.28	56.86
95.00	4	1,836,802	5.6	66.48	83.19	1.55	2.77	0.12	61.07
95.01	6	1,801,519	5.4	–	–	–	2.77	−2.22	49.46
95.02	6	35,283	13.4	–	–	–	1.76	−0.20	51.83
96.00	1	178,998	63.8	68.32	84.48	1.64	2.77	0.92	65.06
97.00	1	87,492	10.1	55.61	74.77	1.06	0.83	−1.23	39.65
98.00	2	64,345	38.5	62.99	82.52	1.51	2.46	−0.65	54.92
98.00	3	64,345	38.5	62.99	82.52	1.51	2.46	−0.65	54.92
99.00	1	36,446	9.7	55.97	78.89	1.28	2.77	−0.08	60.08
103.00	1	88,286	24.7	61.45	83.19	1.55	2.22	0.20	57.27
104.00	1	65,258	7.9	60.76	75.00	1.07	3.50	0.20	66.92
105.00	1	68,659	27.6	62.36	84.62	1.65	2.01	−1.07	49.42
106.00	1	23,279	52.7	61.20	77.73	1.22	1.41	−0.83	46.07
113.00	1	1,352	61.7	73.51	91.30	2.25	3.91	0.08	69.48
114.00	1	5,892	65.0	73.51	91.30	2.25	4.62	0.48	76.79
115.00	1	4,718	77.9	73.51	91.30	2.25	3.91	0.32	70.66
116.00	1	3,729	88.5	73.51	91.30	2.25	3.50	0.56	68.74
117.00	1	298	76.2	73.51	91.30	2.25	3.20	0.08	64.09
118.00	1	4,320	50.2	73.51	91.30	2.25	3.50	0.32	67.52
119.00	1	3,662	72.8	73.51	91.30	2.25	3.50	0.69	69.39
123.00	1	4,239	75.0	73.51	91.30	2.25	3.91	0.36	70.86
124.00	1	956	66.3	73.51	91.30	2.25	3.50	0.36	67.72
125.00	1	1,503	66.9	73.51	91.30	2.25	2.46	0.74	61.80
126.00	1	780	52.2	73.51	91.30	2.25	4.62	0.48	76.79
127.00	1	7,248	85.6	73.51	91.30	2.25	2.61	0.40	61.20
128.00	1	16,906	62.4	73.51	91.30	2.25	3.50	0.12	66.53
129.00	1	3,785	61.0	73.51	91.30	2.25	2.97	−0.74	58.27

Continued

SEIs and Component Data

Males			Females			
Logit (% 1 Yr. Col. +)	Logit (% $14.30/ hour +)	MSEI	Logit (% 1 Yr. Col. +)	Logit (% $14.30/ hour +)	FSEI	Occupational Title
2.22	0.92	57.84	1.61	0.00	53.93	Operations and Systems Researchers and Analysts
4.62	1.68	76.35	2.46	0.48	62.89	Actuaries
2.77	0.56	57.93	1.68	−0.61	51.67	Statisticians
3.20	1.61	68.36	2.46	0.65	63.69	Mathematical Scientists, n.e.c.
3.50	1.23	66.98	2.46	−0.16	59.92	Physicists and Astronomers
2.77	0.56	57.93	2.97	−0.16	63.87	Chemists, Except Biochemists
2.61	0.83	59.14	2.11	−0.52	55.46	Atmospheric and Space Scientists
3.50	0.65	62.39	3.20	0.04	66.62	Geologists and Geodesists
2.97	0.36	57.32	2.77	−0.20	62.17	Physical Scientists, n.e.c.
1.68	−0.32	45.31	1.61	−1.02	49.16	Agricultural and Food Scientists
3.50	−0.04	57.00	2.97	−0.52	62.17	Biological and Life Scientists
1.68	−0.20	46.25	1.92	−1.35	50.10	Forestry and Conservation Scientists
4.62	0.20	64.71	4.62	−0.24	76.48	Medical Scientists
4.62	1.47	74.72	3.91	0.56	74.69	Physicians
4.62	1.84	77.58	3.50	0.61	71.61	Dentists
4.62	0.65	68.26	3.91	−0.44	70.01	Veterinarians
3.91	1.47	71.04	2.97	0.52	67.04	Optometrists
4.62	1.35	73.75	2.34	−0.20	58.72	Podiatrists
2.97	0.78	60.65	1.02	−0.88	45.21	Health Diagnosing Practitioners, n.e.c.
2.57	0.32	54.94	2.76	0.12	63.57	Registered Nurses
2.61	0.32	55.13	2.77	0.12	63.64	Registered Nurses (NSE)
2.34	0.40	54.33	1.68	−0.36	52.83	Registered Nurses (SE)
3.50	1.18	66.54	2.22	0.56	61.36	Pharmacists
0.28	−1.18	31.19	0.92	−1.23	42.76	Dietitians
2.46	−0.28	49.73	2.34	−0.92	55.33	Inhalation Therapists
2.46	−0.28	49.73	2.34	−0.92	55.33	Respiratory Therapists
1.61	0.04	47.72	3.20	−0.12	65.89	Occupational Therapists
2.46	0.48	55.65	2.11	0.08	58.26	Physical Therapists
3.20	0.69	61.18	3.50	0.16	69.52	Speech Therapists
2.22	−0.78	44.48	1.92	−1.18	50.90	Therapists, n.e.c.
1.76	−0.61	43.44	1.02	−1.12	44.05	Physicians' Assistants
4.62	0.83	69.66	3.20	−1.18	60.93	Earth, Environmental, and Marine Science Teachers
4.62	1.12	71.98	4.62	−0.56	74.96	Biological Science Teachers
3.91	0.44	62.92	3.50	−0.08	68.42	Chemistry Teachers
3.91	0.69	64.92	2.22	−0.40	56.87	Physics Teachers
3.23	0.30	58.27	3.34	−0.30	66.13	Natural Science Teachers, n.e.c.
4.62	1.18	72.41	3.20	−0.44	64.39	Psychology Teachers
3.50	0.78	63.44	3.20	0.52	68.87	Economics Teachers
3.91	0.65	64.57	4.62	−0.44	75.54	History Teachers
4.62	0.74	68.95	2.77	−0.36	61.42	Political Science Teachers
3.20	0.88	62.60	1.61	0.56	56.56	Sociology Teachers
3.91	0.52	63.57	4.62	0.44	79.64	Social Science Teachers, n.e.c.
2.61	0.48	56.41	2.77	−0.04	62.90	Engineering Teachers
3.50	0.40	60.42	3.20	−0.36	64.77	Mathematical Science Teachers
2.77	−0.56	49.09	3.91	−1.02	67.28	Computer Science Teachers

continued

Appendix—

| Census Code | F L A G | Number of Occup. Incumbents in 1990 | % Male | Nakao-Treas Prestige Scores | | | 1980/1990-basis Total | | |
				Prestige Score	%5+	Logit %5+	Logit (% 1 Yr. Col. +)	Logit (% $14.30/ hour +)	TSEI
133.00	1	2,873	75.8	73.51	91.30	2.25	3.91	1.54	76.74
134.00	1	15,271	24.6	73.51	91.30	2.25	2.97	0.32	63.50
135.00	1	4,501	43.6	73.51	91.30	2.25	3.50	0.52	68.54
136.00	1	979	84.4	73.51	91.30	2.25	3.91	0.32	70.66
137.00	1	20,680	46.9	73.51	91.30	2.25	3.20	−0.16	62.92
138.00	1	3,735	42.0	73.51	91.30	2.25	2.77	−0.83	56.36
139.00	1	1,323	55.3	73.51	91.30	2.25	2.77	0.36	62.25
143.00	1	23,221	40.5	73.51	91.30	2.25	3.20	−0.20	62.72
144.00	1	9,876	32.3	73.51	91.30	2.25	3.20	−0.69	60.25
145.00	1	4,786	68.3	73.51	91.30	2.25	3.91	1.68	77.44
146.00	1	267	6.7	73.51	91.30	2.25	4.62	0.74	78.07
147.00	1	2,397	79.9	73.51	91.30	2.25	3.50	−0.20	64.97
148.00	1	1,208	42.5	73.51	91.30	2.25	1.92	0.00	54.06
149.00	1	456	15.1	73.51	91.30	2.25	2.46	0.20	59.12
153.00	1	13,352	64.5	73.51	91.30	2.25	3.20	0.08	64.09
154.00	1	592,095	60.8	73.51	91.30	2.25	3.50	0.16	66.73
155.00	1	248,195	1.8	54.93	71.05	0.88	1.07	−2.34	36.03
156.00	1	2,927,819	21.5	64.08	83.58	1.58	2.77	−0.08	60.08
157.00	1	611,115	43.1	66.37	81.42	1.44	3.20	0.08	64.09
158.00	1	58,459	17.3	65.06	86.32	1.78	1.76	−0.56	50.01
159.00	1	539,519	38.0	45.73	51.64	0.06	1.54	−0.83	47.04
163.00	1	230,797	38.0	56.69	71.18	0.88	2.61	−0.20	58.25
164.00	1	194,054	19.5	54.42	69.91	0.82	1.92	−0.78	50.17
165.00	1	26,250	44.9	52.04	65.38	0.62	1.76	−0.88	48.46
166.00	1	145,546	57.0	62.86	80.00	1.35	3.91	0.28	70.46
167.00	1	187,194	41.4	69.39	86.44	1.79	4.62	0.24	75.58
168.00	1	2,128	50.1	60.75	80.37	1.37	4.62	−0.24	73.23
169.00	1	19,936	52.9	65.02	80.77	1.40	3.91	−0.40	67.12
173.00	1	17,913	67.6	52.32	64.60	0.59	2.77	0.40	62.45
174.00	1	629,824	31.2	51.50	68.52	0.76	1.84	−1.02	48.34
175.00	1	43,365	28.5	38.06	40.54	−0.38	0.74	−2.11	34.60
176.00	1	310,871	90.0	68.96	83.04	1.54	2.11	−1.61	47.50
177.00	1	89,756	43.6	43.55	53.92	0.15	1.54	−1.68	42.81
178.00	1	731,435	75.9	74.77	90.02	2.12	4.62	1.18	80.26
179.00	1	30,195	76.9	71.49	86.84	1.83	2.11	1.02	60.56
183.00	1	96,950	51.4	63.05	81.32	1.43	2.61	−0.40	57.26
184.00	1	73,090	49.7	54.31	73.56	1.00	2.22	0.04	56.49
185.00	1	561,925	45.2	46.53	56.73	0.27	1.07	−0.65	44.40
186.00	1	136,116	66.5	46.56	69.97	0.83	1.18	−0.65	45.20
187.00	1	94,046	60.6	57.62	72.20	0.93	2.11	−0.20	54.51
188.00	1	195,843	47.7	52.38	69.52	0.81	1.35	−1.07	44.39
189.00	1	134,190	70.3	45.11	58.26	0.33	1.07	−0.92	43.04

Continued

SEIs and Component Data						
Males			Females			
Logit (% 1 Yr. Col. +)	Logit (% $14.30/ hour +)	MSEI	Logit (% 1 Yr. Col. +)	Logit (% $14.30/ hour +)	FSEI	Occupational Title
3.91	1.76	73.26	3.91	0.92	76.37	Medical Science Teachers
3.50	0.69	62.74	2.97	0.20	65.52	Health Specialties Teachers
3.91	1.23	69.15	3.20	0.04	66.62	Business, Commerce, and Marketing Teachers
3.91	0.56	63.90	4.62	−1.12	72.33	Agriculture and Forestry Teachers
3.50	0.28	59.47	3.20	−0.56	63.81	Art, Drama, and Music Teachers
2.97	−0.48	50.76	2.61	−1.12	56.53	Physical Education Teachers
2.97	0.78	60.65	2.61	−0.16	61.05	Education Teachers
2.77	0.20	55.05	3.50	−0.48	66.54	English Teachers
3.20	−0.56	51.33	3.20	−0.74	62.99	Foreign Language Teachers
4.62	2.22	80.56	2.97	0.92	68.91	Law Teachers
4.62	4.62	99.34	4.62	0.65	80.62	Social Work Teachers
3.91	0.00	59.48	2.34	−1.02	54.87	Theology Teachers
1.92	0.36	51.86	2.01	−0.24	56.02	Trade and Industrial Teachers
1.84	1.84	63.02	2.61	−0.04	61.61	Home Economics Teachers
3.23	0.30	58.27	3.34	−0.30	66.13	Teachers, Postsecondary, n.e.c.
3.50	0.44	60.74	3.20	−0.32	64.96	Postsecondary Teachers, Subject Not Specified
1.61	−1.41	36.36	1.07	−2.34	38.80	Teachers, Prekindergarten and Kindergarten
3.50	0.40	60.42	2.61	−0.24	60.68	Teachers, Elementary School
3.50	0.36	60.10	2.97	−0.12	64.05	Teachers, Secondary School
2.22	0.00	50.61	1.68	−0.69	51.26	Teachers, Special Education
1.61	−0.40	44.30	1.47	−1.12	47.61	Teachers, n.e.c.
2.77	0.00	53.51	2.61	−0.36	60.12	Counselors, Educational and Vocational
2.77	−0.52	49.43	1.76	−0.88	51.01	Librarians
1.68	−0.61	43.04	1.84	−1.18	50.23	Archivists and Curators
3.91	0.83	65.98	3.91	−0.36	70.39	Economists
4.62	0.48	66.93	4.62	0.04	77.77	Psychologists
4.62	0.20	64.71	4.62	−0.74	74.14	Sociologists
3.91	−0.08	58.87	3.91	−0.78	68.40	Social Scientists, n.e.c.
2.97	0.65	59.61	2.46	−0.12	60.10	Urban Planners
1.92	−0.69	43.63	1.76	−1.23	49.33	Social Workers
1.07	−1.61	31.99	0.61	−2.34	35.12	Recreation Workers
2.22	−1.54	38.54	1.92	−2.01	46.99	Clergy
1.76	−1.41	37.13	1.35	−1.92	42.90	Religious Workers, n.e.c.
4.62	1.41	74.23	4.62	0.69	80.83	Lawyers
2.22	1.35	61.19	1.68	0.12	55.05	Judges
2.61	−0.08	52.03	2.61	−0.74	58.34	Authors
2.34	0.48	54.98	2.11	−0.36	56.23	Technical Writers
1.41	−0.08	45.76	0.83	−1.23	42.02	Designers
0.97	−0.56	39.66	1.61	−0.88	49.84	Musicians and Composers
2.11	−0.08	49.44	2.22	−0.36	57.06	Actors and Directors
1.23	−0.69	40.01	1.41	−1.47	45.48	Painters, Sculptors, Craft–Artists, and Artist Printmakers
1.18	−0.69	39.72	0.74	−1.61	39.55	Photographers

continued

Appendix—

Census Code	F L A G	Number of Occup. Incumbents in 1990	% Male	Nakao-Treas Prestige Scores			1980/1990-basis Total		
				Prestige Score	%5+	Logit %5+	Logit (% 1 Yr. Col. +)	Logit (% $14.30/ hour +)	TSEI
193.00	1	19,628	23.6	53.49	67.31	0.71	0.08	−1.23	33.98
194.00	1	83,993	51.1	35.55	43.89	−0.24	1.02	−0.78	43.35
195.00	1	255,144	49.0	59.75	84.62	1.65	2.34	−0.48	54.79
197.00	1	159,563	41.4	47.52	59.48	0.38	1.92	−0.36	52.29
198.00	1	54,656	79.4	54.81	68.29	0.75	0.92	−1.12	40.91
199.00	1	77,394	72.5	64.66	78.45	1.26	1.12	−1.07	42.69
TECHNICAL, SALES, AND ADMINISTRATIVE SUPPORT OCCUPATIONS									
	8	35,653,850	37.4	41.55	47.99	−0.08	0.35	−1.48	35.45
Technicians and Related Support Occupations									
	7	4,182,414	53.8	54.66	69.60	0.88	1.33	−0.67	47.05
203.00	1	316,659	24.4	68.40	87.78	1.90	1.54	−0.97	46.33
204.00	1	71,755	1.7	52.23	64.29	0.58	3.50	−0.04	65.75
205.00	1	53,072	7.3	52.28	70.43	0.85	0.44	−2.34	31.23
206.00	1	126,098	27.4	58.48	74.11	1.03	1.84	−0.78	49.52
207.00	1	408,301	6.3	59.98	77.98	1.23	0.97	−1.68	38.51
208.00	1	393,899	28.6	56.67	70.14	0.84	0.78	−1.76	36.70
213.00	1	378,966	85.6	59.88	78.13	1.24	1.12	−0.24	46.84
214.00	1	15,038	79.2	39.74	45.83	−0.16	1.07	0.16	48.40
215.00	1	28,098	91.3	54.12	76.14	1.13	1.18	0.56	51.22
216.00	1	225,854	69.8	48.25	60.80	0.43	0.97	−0.61	43.85
217.00	1	308,193	82.1	51.49	65.14	0.61	1.29	−0.56	46.48
218.00	1	85,789	90.6	36.10	40.19	−0.39	0.56	−0.74	40.11
223.00	1	51,982	57.3	32.35	31.96	−0.74	0.48	−1.02	38.07
224.00	1	73,961	75.7	37.61	40.54	−0.38	0.61	−0.20	43.12
225.00	1	70,517	67.1	44.38	54.13	0.16	1.02	−0.74	43.57
226.00	1	106,168	96.5	61.02	75.75	1.11	2.11	0.88	59.83
227.00	1	44,675	77.5	64.76	84.48	1.64	1.02	0.08	47.63
228.00	1	32,347	75.7	42.83	50.43	0.02	0.74	−0.83	40.97
229.00	1	638,438	67.6	60.51	81.82	1.46	2.34	0.28	58.54
233.00	1	3,731	84.2	48.25	62.00	0.48	0.92	0.28	47.86
234.00	1	244,428	23.3	56.53	73.45	0.99	1.23	−1.12	43.26
235.00	1	504,445	71.1	40.85	47.74	−0.09	0.97	−0.56	44.06
Sales Occupations									
	7	13,151,354	52.5	38.35	44.83	−0.23	0.30	−1.24	36.24
243.00	4	3,296,516	65.7	44.15	56.74	0.27	0.40	−0.81	38.51
243.01	6	483,241	83.2	–	–	–	0.61	−1.47	36.78
243.02	6	1,700,902	58.6	–	–	–	0.24	−1.02	36.23
243.03	6	216,255	56.8	–	–	–	1.35	−1.54	42.07

Continued

SEIs and Component Data

Males			Females			
Logit (% 1 Yr. Col. +)	Logit (% $14.30/ hour +)	MSEI	Logit (% 1 Yr. Col. +)	Logit (% $14.30/ hour +)	FSEI	Occupational Title
0.44	−1.02	33.27	−0.04	−1.29	34.92	Dancers
0.88	−0.48	39.81	1.12	−1.07	45.11	Artists, Performers, and Related Workers, n.e.c.
2.61	−0.16	51.42	2.22	−0.78	55.07	Editors and Reporters
1.92	0.12	49.98	1.84	−0.74	52.29	Public Relations Specialists
0.88	−1.12	34.75	1.18	−1.29	44.51	Announcers
1.12	−0.92	37.64	1.12	−1.68	42.26	Athletes
0.71	−0.93	36.04	0.21	−1.89	34.62	
1.43	−0.37	44.35	1.22	−1.11	46.47	
1.61	−0.69	41.98	1.47	−1.07	47.86	Clinical Laboratory Technologists and Technicians
2.34	0.16	52.45	3.50	−0.04	68.60	Dental Hygienists
1.12	−1.76	31.10	0.40	−2.34	33.48	Health Record Technologists and Technicians
1.76	−0.24	46.34	1.84	−1.02	50.96	Radiologic Technicians
1.23	−1.18	36.21	0.92	−1.76	40.32	Licensed Practical Nurses
1.18	−1.12	36.34	0.65	−2.22	36.01	Health Technologists and Technicians, n.e.c.
1.18	−0.12	44.23	0.74	−0.92	42.75	Electrical and Electronic Technicians
1.29	0.44	49.18	0.52	−0.83	41.49	Industrial Engineering Technicians
1.18	0.61	49.91	0.88	0.00	48.15	Mechanical Engineering Technicians
1.07	−0.32	42.12	0.83	−1.54	40.59	Engineering Technicians, n.e.c.
1.29	−0.44	42.31	1.35	−1.23	46.12	Drafting Occupations
0.56	−0.69	36.50	0.74	−1.07	42.06	Surveying and Mapping Technicians
0.44	−0.74	35.49	0.56	−1.47	38.81	Biological Technicians
0.56	−0.04	41.62	0.69	−0.78	43.06	Chemical Technicians
1.07	−0.40	41.49	0.88	−1.54	40.96	Science Technicians, n.e.c.
2.11	0.92	57.29	1.61	−0.16	53.19	Airplane Pilots and Navigators
1.18	0.32	47.63	0.69	−0.78	43.06	Air Traffic Controllers
0.78	−0.65	37.99	0.61	−1.54	38.84	Broadcast Equipment Operators
2.46	0.44	55.33	2.11	0.00	57.89	Computer Programmers
0.97	0.56	48.49	0.52	−1.54	38.17	Tool Programmers, Numerical Control
1.61	−0.65	42.32	1.12	−1.29	44.09	Legal Assistants
0.92	−0.32	41.34	1.07	−1.23	43.94	Technicians, n.e.c.
0.54	−0.83	35.96	0.05	−1.81	33.81	
0.54	−0.46	38.19	0.15	−1.68	34.58	Supervisors and Proprietors, Sales Occupations
0.65	0.04	42.69	0.40	−0.83	40.52	Superv. and Propr., Sales Occs. (NSE, Wholesale)
0.40	−0.92	33.82	0.00	−2.22	30.89	Superv. and Propr., Sales Occs. (NSE, Retail)
1.92	1.12	57.88	0.74	−0.20	46.15	Superv. and Propr., Sales Occs. (NSE, Finance, Insur.)

continued

Appendix—

Census Code	F L A G	Number of Occup. Incumbents in 1990	% Male	Nakao-Treas Prestige Scores			1980/1990-basis		
				Prestige Score	%5+	Logit %5+	Total		
							Logit (% 1 Yr. Col. +)	Logit (% $14.30/ hour +)	TSEI
243.04	6	175,794	69.7	–	–	–	0.56	−0.69	40.33
243.05	6	123,200	87.2	–	–	–	0.52	−1.41	36.45
243.06	6	533,195	68.3	–	–	–	0.28	−0.97	36.78
243.07	6	33,081	79.1	–	–	–	1.54	−0.92	46.58
243.08	6	30,848	73.8	–	–	–	0.44	−2.61	29.88
253.00	1	645,158	65.1	44.85	56.22	0.25	1.18	−0.20	47.45
254.00	1	758,122	49.7	48.82	60.45	0.42	1.29	−0.40	47.30
255.00	1	284,096	72.8	52.80	68.22	0.75	2.01	0.24	55.92
256.00	1	162,252	49.0	39.29	43.81	−0.24	1.35	−0.61	46.71
257.00	1	509,876	64.1	32.32	25.85	−1.03	1.02	−0.36	45.47
258.00	1	42,639	95.4	53.16	74.71	1.06	2.34	0.97	61.99
259.00	4	1,458,256	78.3	48.54	64.50	0.58	0.83	−0.22	44.69
259.01	6	1,263,597	77.4	–	–	–	0.88	−1.76	37.40
259.02	6	194,659	84.3	–	–	–	0.74	−1.68	36.74
263.00	1	326,127	90.4	34.24	36.32	−0.55	0.12	−1.18	34.55
264.00	1	387,126	18.6	30.22	26.82	−0.98	−0.16	−2.34	26.73
265.00	1	100,042	38.2	27.67	21.35	−1.27	−0.32	−2.46	24.89
266.00	1	175,838	56.4	30.62	23.85	−1.13	0.16	−1.41	33.70
267.00	1	154,214	71.6	30.79	26.85	−0.98	0.78	−1.07	40.11
268.00	1	163,478	78.2	31.58	29.46	−0.85	0.00	−1.68	31.16
269.00	1	124,077	90.5	29.93	26.32	−1.01	−0.56	−2.01	25.25
274.00	4	1,660,192	34.1	32.03	39.39	−0.42	−0.04	−1.87	29.96
274.01	6	1,359,306	30.6	–	–	–	−0.12	−2.97	23.90
274.02	6	92,932	40.6	–	–	–	0.48	−2.61	30.19
274.03	6	207,954	54.2	–	–	–	0.24	−2.01	31.30
275.00	1	182,637	35.4	33.60	29.36	−0.86	−0.48	−2.22	24.87
276.00	4	2,362,872	21.6	29.45	27.44	−0.95	−0.69	−2.59	21.41
276.01	6	1,951,798	20.4	–	–	–	−0.78	−2.61	20.65
276.02	6	351,357	25.3	–	–	–	−0.36	−1.84	27.69
276.03	6	59,717	41.3	–	–	–	−0.40	−2.34	24.91

Continued

SEIs and Component Data						
Males			Females			
Logit (% 1 Yr. Col. +)	Logit (% $14.30/ hour +)	MSEI	Logit (% 1 Yr. Col. +)	Logit (% $14.30/ hour +)	FSEI	Occupational Title
0.65	−0.28	40.22	0.44	−1.47	37.82	Superv. and Propr., Sales Occs. (NSE, Other)
0.52	−0.04	41.40	0.48	−1.02	40.26	Superv. and Propr., Sales Occs. (SE, Wholesale)
0.36	−0.69	35.41	0.20	−1.54	35.61	Superv. and Propr., Sales Occs. (SE, Retail)
1.76	0.78	54.33	0.88	−0.69	44.91	Superv. and Propr., Sales Occs. (SE, Finance, Insur.)
0.48	−0.28	39.33	0.28	−1.41	36.84	Superv. and Propr., Sales Occs. (SE, Other)
1.54	0.24	48.90	0.61	−1.07	41.02	Insurance Sales Occupations
1.54	−0.08	46.44	1.02	−0.69	46.06	Real Estate Sales Occupations
2.34	0.56	55.63	1.29	−0.56	48.79	Securities and Financial Services Sales Occupations
1.54	−0.28	44.89	1.18	−0.92	46.23	Advertising and Related Sales Occupations
1.12	−0.04	44.57	0.83	−0.92	43.47	Sales Occupations, Other Business Services
2.34	1.07	59.62	1.84	−0.04	55.55	Sales Engineers
0.92	−0.03	43.62	0.58	−0.97	41.26	Sales Representatives, Mining, Manufacturing, and Wholesale
0.97	−0.04	43.76	0.56	−0.97	41.16	Sales Reps., Mining, Manuf., and Whlsl. (NSE)
0.78	−0.04	42.77	0.52	−0.92	41.05	Sales Reps., Mining, Manuf., and Whlsl. (SE)
0.12	−1.12	30.78	−0.16	−1.92	31.04	Sales Workers, Motor Vehicles and Boats
0.28	−1.61	27.81	−0.24	−2.61	27.22	Sales Workers, Apparel
0.04	−2.11	22.62	−0.56	−2.77	23.87	Sales Workers, Shoes
0.28	−1.12	31.61	0.00	−1.92	32.27	Sales Workers, Furniture and Home Furnishings
0.97	−0.92	36.84	0.40	−1.54	37.19	Sales Workers, Radio, TV, Hi–Fi, and Appliances
0.08	−1.54	27.32	−0.32	−2.61	26.59	Sales Workers, Hardware and Building Supplies
−0.56	−1.92	20.95	−0.65	−2.97	22.30	Sales Workers, Parts
0.39	−1.21	31.54	−0.27	−2.34	28.23	Sales Workers, Other Commodities
0.36	−1.41	29.79	−0.36	−2.61	26.27	Sales Workers, Other Commodities (NSE, Retail)
0.83	−0.88	36.46	0.28	−1.76	35.22	Sales Workers, Other Commodities (NSE, Other)
0.40	−0.74	35.28	0.12	−1.68	34.33	Sales Workers, Other Commodities (SE)
−0.04	−1.61	26.16	−0.74	−2.61	23.27	Sales Counter Clerks
−0.30	−1.99	21.78	−0.83	−2.77	21.76	Cashiers
−0.40	−2.11	20.34	−0.92	−2.97	20.14	Cashiers (NSE, Retail)
0.00	−1.76	25.20	−0.48	−2.61	25.30	Cashiers (NSE, Other)
0.00	−1.02	30.97	−0.65	−2.01	26.74	Cashiers (SE)

continued

Appendix—

| Census
Code | F
L
A
G | Number of
Occup.
Incumbents
in 1990 | %
Male | Nakao-Treas Prestige Scores | | | 1980/1990-basis | | |
				Prestige Score	%5+	Logit %5+	Logit (% 1 Yr. Col. +)	Logit (% $14.30/ hour +)	TSEI
277.00	1	196,182	34.2	22.37	18.02	−1.47	0.28	−1.35	34.90
278.00	1	98,900	60.2	19.38	15.60	−1.64	−0.69	−1.76	25.54
283.00	1	37,478	18.3	32.09	30.91	−0.79	−0.16	−1.35	31.62
284.00	1	7,498	87.2	39.19	41.44	−0.34	−0.20	−0.61	35.02
285.00	1	17,778	50.6	35.58	37.00	−0.52	0.74	−0.92	40.51
Administrative Support Occupations, Including Clerical									
	7	18,320,082	22.8	40.84	45.33	−0.20	0.17	−1.84	32.24
303.00	1	558,659	36.7	50.54	61.89	0.48	0.48	−0.74	39.48
304.00	1	33,013	62.3	53.99	72.41	0.94	1.18	0.16	49.20
305.00	1	107,570	30.7	51.83	64.66	0.59	0.97	−0.48	44.48
306.00	1	4,397	36.7	48.55	58.93	0.35	0.36	−0.40	40.24
307.00	1	188,993	69.7	41.72	44.91	−0.20	0.36	−0.32	40.64
308.00	1	622,778	39.1	50.32	60.68	0.43	0.52	−1.35	36.75
309.00	1	5,650	46.3	40.09	35.14	−0.60	−0.12	−1.76	29.89
313.00	4	3,783,271	1.3	46.08	55.61	0.22	0.20	−2.15	30.30
313.01	6	25,166	0.9	–	–	–	−0.04	−2.01	29.21
313.02	6	22,022	0.3	–	–	–	0.40	−1.68	34.17
313.03	6	134,556	0.9	–	–	–	0.04	−2.22	28.79
313.04	6	428,213	0.8	–	–	–	0.12	−2.61	27.45
313.05	6	157,222	1.5	–	–	–	0.16	−2.11	30.21
313.06	6	159,844	0.9	–	–	–	0.00	−2.22	28.49
313.07	6	170,799	1.4	–	–	–	−0.12	−2.61	25.67
313.08	6	468,431	1.0	–	–	–	0.12	−2.01	30.40
313.09	6	156,225	1.8	–	–	–	0.20	−2.22	29.98
313.10	6	37,394	1.1	–	–	–	0.12	−2.34	28.81
313.11	6	29,547	3.8	–	–	–	0.40	−1.61	34.53
313.12	6	1,565,864	1.4	–	–	–	0.36	−2.46	29.98
313.13	6	303,689	1.7	–	–	–	0.20	−2.22	29.98
313.14	6	124,299	1.9	–	–	–	−0.04	−2.22	28.20
314.00	1	77,834	9.8	46.70	61.82	0.47	0.92	−0.78	42.61
315.00	1	609,800	5.2	40.03	42.78	−0.29	0.16	−2.22	29.68
316.00	1	168,116	22.3	48.79	59.65	0.38	0.44	−2.01	32.82
317.00	1	85,014	28.1	31.93	25.21	−1.06	0.16	−2.77	26.94
318.00	1	254,022	29.4	35.34	33.95	−0.65	0.83	−1.23	39.65
319.00	1	735,421	4.0	39.02	40.00	−0.40	−0.04	−2.77	25.45
323.00	1	158,715	22.0	34.50	33.78	−0.66	0.08	−1.92	30.56
325.00	1	5,184	19.4	30.60	21.90	−1.24	0.12	−1.84	31.28

Continued

SEIs and Component Data						
Males			Females			
Logit (% 1 Yr. Col. +)	Logit (% $14.30/ hour +)	MSEI	Logit (% 1 Yr. Col. +)	Logit (% $14.30/ hour +)	FSEI	Occupational Title
0.52	−0.92	34.47	0.12	−1.68	34.33	Street and Door–To–Door Sales Workers
−0.78	−1.68	21.69	−0.56	−1.92	27.84	News Vendors
0.44	−0.74	35.49	−0.28	−1.47	32.20	Demonstrators, Promoters and Models, Sales
−0.20	−0.48	34.19	−0.36	−1.92	29.47	Auctioneers
0.92	−0.32	41.34	0.56	−1.84	37.11	Sales Support Occupations, n.e.c.
0.66	−1.13	34.22	0.08	−2.13	32.49	
0.83	0.08	43.94	0.32	−1.35	37.45	Supervisors, General Office
1.41	0.52	50.46	0.88	−0.44	46.10	Supervisors, Computer Equipment Operators
2.01	0.61	54.29	0.65	−0.97	41.83	Supervisors, Financial Records Processing
0.78	0.74	48.86	0.16	−1.12	37.24	Chief Communications Operators
0.40	−0.12	40.14	0.28	−0.88	39.35	Supervisors, Distribution, Scheduling, and Adjusting Clerks
1.02	−0.69	38.90	0.24	−2.01	33.71	Computer Operators
0.04	−1.23	29.51	−0.24	−2.46	27.89	Peripheral Equipment Operators
0.74	−1.35	32.33	0.21	−2.22	32.54	Secretaries
0.00	−1.02	30.97	−0.04	−2.61	28.77	Secretaries (NSE, Agr. For., & Fish.)
4.62	−4.62	27.00	0.40	−1.84	35.80	Secretaries (NSE, Mining)
0.61	−1.35	31.57	0.04	−2.34	30.66	Secretaries (NSE, Construction)
0.52	−0.69	36.28	0.12	−2.01	32.78	Secretaries (NSE, Manufacturing)
0.44	−1.12	32.46	0.16	−1.68	34.64	Secretaries (NSE, Trans., Comm. & Util.)
0.28	−1.35	29.85	0.00	−2.22	30.89	Secretaries (NSE, Wholesale)
0.20	−1.61	27.40	−0.12	−2.61	28.15	Secretaries (NSE, Retail)
0.56	−1.35	31.35	0.12	−2.11	32.32	Secretaries (NSE, Finance, Insur.)
0.78	−1.54	31.01	0.20	−2.22	32.44	Secretaries (NSE, Bus. & Repair Serv.)
0.97	−1.29	33.95	0.12	−2.61	30.01	Secretaries (NSE, Personal Serv.)
0.56	−2.22	24.54	0.40	−2.01	34.98	Secretaries (NSE, Enter. & Rec. Serv.)
1.02	−1.54	32.26	0.36	−2.22	33.70	Secretaries (NSE, Prof., Related Serv.)
0.74	−1.23	33.17	0.20	−2.34	31.90	Secretaries (NSE, Public Admin.)
0.40	−0.83	34.57	−0.04	−1.61	33.43	Secretaries (SE)
1.54	0.36	49.85	0.83	−0.92	43.47	Stenographers
0.88	−1.47	32.01	0.12	−2.34	31.28	Typists
1.07	−1.35	34.02	0.28	−2.34	32.53	Interviewers
0.69	−2.46	23.30	−0.04	−2.97	27.10	Hotel Clerks
0.83	−0.56	38.90	0.78	−1.61	39.90	Transportation Ticket and Reservation Agents
0.61	−1.76	28.38	−0.04	−2.77	28.00	Receptionists
0.65	−1.18	33.14	−0.08	−2.22	30.28	Information Clerks, n.e.c.
1.41	−1.18	37.14	−0.16	−2.01	30.61	Classified–Ad Clerks

continued

Appendix—

	F L A G	Number of Occup. Incumbents in 1990	% Male	Nakao-Treas Prestige Scores			1980/1990-basis Total		
Census Code				Prestige Score	%5+	Logit %5+	Logit (% 1 Yr. Col. +)	Logit (% $14.30/ hour +)	TSEI
326.00	1	12,662	15.4	34.86	35.78	−0.57	0.40	−2.01	32.51
327.00	1	213,324	27.8	31.03	31.25	−0.77	0.08	−1.41	33.10
328.00	1	76,710	14.3	36.08	38.68	−0.45	0.24	−1.92	31.75
329.00	1	142,070	20.5	29.28	26.13	−1.02	0.65	−2.61	31.47
335.00	1	228,997	19.3	36.06	38.94	−0.44	−0.16	−2.46	26.09
336.00	1	131,120	21.8	31.49	26.92	−0.98	0.32	−1.76	33.18
337.00	4	1,797,497	10.5	46.64	56.48	0.26	0.20	−2.00	31.06
337.01	6	310,418	7.9	–	–	–	−0.08	−1.54	31.27
337.02	6	323,185	8.9	–	–	–	0.44	−1.54	35.18
337.03	6	980,721	11.8	–	–	–	0.24	−1.35	34.60
337.04	6	39,078	8.1	–	–	–	−0.04	−2.34	27.62
337.05	6	50,468	17.9	–	–	–	0.78	−2.01	35.43
337.06	6	93,627	7.1	–	–	–	0.04	−1.92	30.26
338.00	1	172,056	11.6	41.71	45.79	−0.17	0.12	−1.92	30.85
339.00	1	159,476	9.8	30.89	32.18	−0.73	0.00	−2.34	27.92
343.00	1	70,619	25.8	27.90	24.11	−1.12	0.00	−1.54	31.86
344.00	1	48,821	14.4	34.83	32.04	−0.74	0.04	−2.22	28.79
345.00	1	25,856	48.5	35.34	33.65	−0.66	0.00	−2.22	28.49
346.00	1	5,531	49.4	36.02	33.64	−0.67	−0.74	−1.92	24.39
347.00	1	30,701	36.2	38.51	36.04	−0.56	−0.44	−2.22	25.18
348.00	1	212,956	12.9	39.55	39.66	−0.41	−0.36	−2.01	26.81
349.00	2	–	38.9	39.11	40.27	−0.39	−0.04	−0.97	34.39
353.00	2	–	38.9	39.11	40.27	−0.39	−0.04	−0.97	34.39
353.00	3	9,599	38.9	39.11	40.27	−0.39	−0.04	−0.97	34.39
354.00	1	338,538	55.7	42.20	46.30	−0.15	0.24	0.16	42.08
355.00	1	318,059	73.5	47.04	60.53	0.42	0.20	−0.08	40.61
356.00	1	187,293	50.5	31.94	25.44	−1.05	−0.40	−2.11	26.02
357.00	1	129,674	75.0	22.30	18.01	−1.47	−0.08	−1.54	31.27
359.00	1	192,742	53.2	34.76	28.57	−0.90	−0.12	−1.41	31.62
363.00	1	240,529	53.5	41.81	46.15	−0.15	0.44	−0.69	39.38
364.00	1	596,131	70.9	32.71	26.31	−1.01	−0.65	−1.84	25.48
365.00	1	635,290	63.0	27.43	22.34	−1.21	−0.44	−1.84	27.07
366.00	1	48,131	85.5	34.00	28.04	−0.92	−0.28	−1.12	31.84
368.00	2	–	54.0	31.00	23.79	−1.14	−0.69	−1.54	26.62

Continued

SEIs and Component Data

Males			Females			
Logit (% 1 Yr. Col. +)	Logit (% $14.30/ hour +)	MSEI	Logit (% 1 Yr. Col. +)	Logit (% $14.30/ hour +)	FSEI	Occupational Title
0.92	−0.83	37.32	0.32	−2.46	32.24	Correspondence Clerks
0.32	−0.92	33.40	0.00	−1.68	33.41	Order Clerks
1.12	−0.69	39.44	0.12	−2.34	31.28	Personnel Clerks, Except Payroll and Timekeeping
0.97	−2.46	24.76	0.56	−2.77	32.75	Library Clerks
0.32	−2.01	24.84	−0.28	−2.61	26.90	File Clerks
0.88	−0.88	36.71	0.16	−2.11	32.63	Records Clerks
0.99	−1.17	35.00	0.13	−2.11	32.39	Bookkeepers, Accounting and Auditing Clerks
0.83	−1.68	30.14	−0.16	−2.46	28.51	Bookkprs., Acc./Audit. Clerks (NSE, Retail)
1.29	−1.47	34.19	0.40	−2.22	34.02	Bookkprs., Acc./Audit. Clerks (NSE, Prof., Related Serv.)
0.97	−1.12	35.26	0.12	−2.22	31.82	Bookkprs., Acc./Audit. Clerks (NSE, Other)
0.44	−0.92	34.04	−0.08	−1.54	33.45	Bookkprs., Acc./Audit. Clerks (SE, Retail)
1.35	−0.61	41.30	0.69	−1.54	39.52	Bookkprs., Acc./Audit. Clerks (SE, Prof., Related Serv.)
0.56	−0.56	37.51	0.00	−1.35	34.95	Bookkprs., Acc./Audit. Clerks (SE, Other)
0.56	−0.97	34.31	0.04	−2.11	31.70	Payroll and Timekeeping Clerks
0.65	−1.47	30.83	−0.08	−2.61	28.46	Billing Clerks
0.69	−0.48	38.85	−0.24	−2.11	29.53	Cost and Rate Clerks
0.48	−1.18	32.25	−0.04	−2.61	28.77	Billing, Posting, and Calculating Machine Operators
0.20	−2.01	24.22	−0.20	−2.34	28.80	Duplicating Machine Operators
−0.20	−1.68	24.77	−1.35	−2.34	19.73	Mail Preparing and Paper Handling Machine Operators
−0.08	−1.54	26.49	−0.65	−2.97	22.30	Office Machine Operators, n.e.c.
0.36	−1.29	30.73	−0.48	−2.22	27.12	Telephone Operators
0.28	0.00	40.42	−0.28	−1.92	30.10	Telegraphers
0.28	0.00	40.42	−0.28	−1.92	30.10	Communications Equipment Operators, n.e.c.
0.28	0.00	40.42	−0.28	−1.92	30.10	Communications Equipment Operators, n.e.c.
0.36	0.40	43.96	0.08	−0.08	41.51	Postal Clerks, Exc. Mail Carriers
0.28	0.12	41.35	0.04	−0.69	38.33	Mail Carriers, Postal Service
−0.24	−1.76	23.96	−0.56	−2.61	24.64	Mail Clerks, Exc. Postal Service
−0.04	−1.47	27.22	−0.20	−1.84	31.13	Messengers
−0.12	−0.97	30.74	−0.12	−2.22	29.97	Dispatchers
0.56	−0.16	40.70	0.28	−1.47	36.55	Production Coordinators
−0.65	−1.68	22.39	−0.65	−2.46	24.64	Traffic, Shipping and Receiving Clerks
−0.40	−1.54	24.82	−0.48	−2.46	25.98	Stock and Inventory Clerks
−0.32	−1.07	28.91	−0.12	−1.68	32.48	Meter Readers
−0.74	−1.12	26.29	−0.69	−2.34	24.90	Weighers, Measurers, and Checkers

continued

Appendix—

Census Code	FLAG	Number of Occup. Incumbents in 1990	% Male	Nakao-Treas Prestige Scores			1980/1990-basis Total		
				Prestige Score	%5+	Logit %5+	Logit (% 1 Yr. Col. +)	Logit (% $14.30/ hour +)	TSEI
368.00	3	71,934	54.0	31.00	23.79	−1.14	−0.69	−1.54	26.62
369.00	2	–	54.0	31.00	23.79	−1.14	−0.69	−1.54	26.62
373.00	1	222,150	35.3	42.89	47.37	−0.10	−0.08	−1.92	29.37
374.00	1	31,708	33.5	23.56	20.69	−1.31	−0.20	−1.41	31.02
375.00	1	336,453	29.1	47.27	59.66	0.38	0.74	−1.23	38.96
376.00	1	556,394	25.9	40.36	43.07	−0.27	0.56	−1.61	35.78
377.00	1	47,744	10.1	46.10	51.38	0.05	0.61	−2.34	32.50
378.00	1	151,824	33.8	24.30	20.20	−1.34	0.28	−1.84	32.47
379.00	4	1,352,263	17.6	33.88	30.70	−0.80	0.04	−2.03	29.71
379.01	6	10,899	13.0	–	–	–	0.20	−2.11	30.51
379.02	6	6,007	24.6	–	–	–	0.24	−1.68	32.95
379.03	6	33,518	23.6	–	–	–	−0.08	−2.22	27.90
379.04	6	159,481	18.2	–	–	–	−0.16	−2.61	25.38
379.05	6	126,993	22.3	–	–	–	−0.04	−2.34	27.62
379.06	6	65,401	20.1	–	–	–	−0.24	−2.11	27.23
379.07	6	120,320	15.4	–	–	–	−0.40	−2.61	23.56
379.08	6	186,131	15.2	–	–	–	−0.04	−2.46	26.98
379.09	6	69,324	17.8	–	–	–	0.08	−2.46	27.87
379.10	6	23,014	19.0	–	–	–	−0.24	−2.46	25.49
379.11	6	20,763	29.9	–	–	–	0.00	−2.22	28.49
379.12	6	354,508	15.4	–	–	–	0.40	−2.77	28.75
379.13	6	175,904	18.2	–	–	–	0.12	−2.61	27.45
383.00	1	476,928	9.8	43.28	46.96	−0.12	0.00	−2.97	24.79
384.00	1	28,137	26.5	43.14	51.33	0.05	0.74	−1.68	36.74
385.00	1	580,035	12.9	41.18	50.98	0.04	0.20	−2.46	28.77
386.00	1	137,982	33.3	37.50	38.74	−0.45	0.56	−1.18	37.92
387.00	1	254,548	10.9	43.06	48.89	−0.04	0.16	−2.34	29.11
389.00	1	649,163	28.5	33.03	35.03	−0.60	0.56	−1.35	37.07
SERVICE OCCUPATIONS	8	14,440,230	42.1	32.32	31.25	−0.85	−0.64	−2.21	24.14
Private Household Occupations	7	471,722	4.9	25.41	21.01	−1.31	−1.26	−2.70	16.87
403.00	1	1,610	10.7	23.25	15.79	−1.62	−1.47	−2.34	16.77

Continued

SEIs and Component Data						
Males			Females			
Logit (% 1 Yr. Col. +)	Logit (% $14.30/ hour +)	MSEI	Logit (% 1 Yr. Col. +)	Logit (% $14.30/ hour +)	FSEI	Occupational Title
−0.74	−1.12	26.29	−0.69	−2.34	24.90	Weighers, Measurers, Checkers, and Samplers
−0.74	−1.12	26.29	−0.69	−2.34	24.90	Samplers
0.16	−1.29	29.68	−0.20	−2.46	28.20	Expediters
0.52	−0.40	38.60	−0.52	−2.34	26.25	Material Recording, Scheduling and Distributing Clerks, n.e.c.
1.68	−0.28	45.63	0.44	−1.76	36.50	Insurance Adjusters, Examiners, and Investigators
1.12	−0.69	39.44	0.36	−2.11	34.20	Investigators and Adjusters, Except Insurance
1.84	−1.68	35.43	0.52	−2.46	33.86	Eligibility Clerks, Social Welfare
0.69	−1.23	32.94	0.12	−2.34	31.28	Bill and Account Collectors
0.46	−1.23	31.72	−0.03	−2.34	30.08	General Office Clerks
0.28	−1.68	27.25	0.16	−2.34	31.59	General Office Clerks (Agr. For., & Fish.)
0.36	−1.07	32.44	0.20	−2.01	33.40	General Office Clerks (Mining)
0.28	−0.61	35.67	−0.16	−1.92	31.04	General Office Clerks (Construction)
0.12	−0.74	33.81	−0.24	−2.11	29.53	General Office Clerks (Manufacturing)
0.24	−0.44	36.78	−0.12	−1.68	32.48	General Office Clerks (Trans., Comm. & Util.)
−0.08	−1.29	28.45	−0.28	−2.22	28.72	General Office Clerks (Wholesale)
0.00	−1.76	25.20	−0.48	−2.61	25.30	General Office Clerks (Retail)
0.52	−1.35	31.13	−0.16	−2.34	29.11	General Office Clerks (Finance, Insur.)
0.61	−1.35	31.57	−0.04	−2.11	31.08	General Office Clerks (Bus. & Repair Serv.)
0.16	−1.68	26.62	−0.32	−2.61	26.59	General Office Clerks (Personal Serv.)
0.16	−2.01	24.01	−0.08	−2.46	29.13	General Office Clerks (Enter. & Rec. Serv.)
0.97	−1.84	29.66	0.32	−2.46	32.24	General Office Clerks (Prof., Related Serv.)
0.65	−1.23	32.71	0.04	−2.46	30.06	General Office Clerks (Public Admin.)
0.88	−2.01	27.78	−0.08	−2.97	26.79	Bank Tellers
1.12	−1.18	35.64	0.61	−1.92	37.05	Proofreaders
0.92	−1.54	31.74	0.08	−2.61	29.70	Data–Entry Keyers
1.02	−0.40	41.22	0.36	−1.76	35.86	Statistical Clerks
1.02	−1.68	31.15	0.04	−2.46	30.06	Teachers' Aides
0.88	−0.48	39.81	0.44	−1.84	36.12	Administrative Support Occupations, n.e.c.
−0.38	−1.91	22.42	−0.76	−2.45	24.20	
−0.87	−2.17	17.69	−1.31	−2.72	18.57	
0.08	−0.36	36.59	−1.76	−2.97	13.57	Launderers and Ironers

continued

Appendix—

	F L A G	Number of Occup. Incumbents in 1990	% Male	Nakao-Treas Prestige Scores			1980/1990-basis Total		
Census Code				Prestige Score	%5+	Logit %5+	Logit (% 1 Yr. Col. +)	Logit (% $14.30/ hour +)	TSEI
404.00	1	8,295	11.1	29.98	22.22	−1.22	−1.07	−2.46	19.17
405.00	1	29,572	4.5	33.93	32.97	−0.69	−1.61	−2.61	14.40
406.00	1	131,991	2.7	29.25	25.47	−1.05	−0.56	−2.97	20.53
407.00	1	300,254	5.7	22.77	17.86	−1.48	−1.54	−2.61	14.92
Protective Service Occupations									
	7	1,959,742	84.6	48.67	58.77	0.39	0.44	−0.85	39.29
413.00	1	28,830	98.1	59.87	80.70	1.39	1.12	0.40	49.99
414.00	1	58,604	87.9	61.84	83.19	1.55	1.29	0.56	52.07
415.00	1	43,345	86.0	37.64	45.45	−0.18	0.40	−0.83	38.40
416.00	1	15,753	87.7	60.42	73.15	0.98	0.52	−0.44	41.28
417.00	1	219,013	97.7	52.87	61.47	0.46	0.61	−0.65	40.87
418.00	1	507,533	88.3	59.99	77.08	1.18	1.18	0.04	48.62
423.00	1	118,189	81.5	48.32	58.26	0.33	0.69	−0.74	41.09
424.00	1	176,097	81.5	39.81	43.50	−0.26	0.16	−0.97	35.88
425.00	1	43,652	27.9	32.33	33.62	−0.67	−1.41	−2.01	18.84
426.00	1	702,037	83.7	42.11	49.24	−0.03	−0.08	−1.54	31.27
427.00	1	46,689	52.7	37.16	36.04	−0.56	0.04	−2.46	27.58
Service Occupations, Except Protective and Household									
	7	12,008,766	36.6	29.92	27.16	−1.03	−0.79	−2.42	21.96
433.00	1	256,317	43.2	35.16	35.71	−0.58	−0.24	−2.11	27.23
434.00	1	288,843	51.5	24.53	20.54	−1.32	−0.12	−2.46	26.39
435.00	1	1,280,050	20.2	28.08	19.57	−1.38	−0.36	−2.77	23.05
436.00	2	–	51.6	30.00	26.36	−1.00	−1.23	−2.77	16.42
436.00	3	1,732,977	51.6	30.00	26.36	−1.00	−1.23	−2.77	16.42
437.00	2	–	51.6	30.00	26.36	−1.00	−1.23	−2.77	16.42
438.00	1	185,253	28.3	23.02	17.86	−1.48	−1.12	−2.97	16.29
439.00	1	179,633	24.0	24.08	19.27	−1.39	−1.02	−2.77	18.02
443.00	1	303,420	56.2	21.12	18.97	−1.41	−1.02	−2.77	18.02
444.00	1	594,950	47.0	16.78	12.61	−1.87	−1.35	−2.77	15.54
445.00	1	171,137	2.6	44.56	48.15	−0.07	0.28	−2.61	28.65
446.00	1	206,782	20.3	50.86	65.12	0.61	−0.36	−2.22	25.80
447.00	1	1,628,210	12.9	41.71	45.98	−0.16	−0.48	−2.34	24.29
448.00	1	158,565	71.8	35.62	32.74	−0.70	−0.61	−1.35	28.23
449.00	1	592,010	20.3	20.05	12.61	−1.87	−1.68	−2.61	13.85
453.00	4	2,135,885	69.2	22.33	17.16	−1.53	−1.29	−2.05	19.56

Continued

Males			Females			
Logit (% 1 Yr. Col. +)	Logit (% $14.30/ hour +)	MSEI	Logit (% 1 Yr. Col. +)	Logit (% $14.30/ hour +)	FSEI	Occupational Title
−0.56	−1.76	22.25	−1.18	−2.61	19.80	Cooks, Private Household
−1.18	−1.68	19.62	−1.61	−2.77	15.64	Housekeepers and Butlers
−0.83	−2.22	17.24	−0.56	−2.97	22.97	Child Care Workers, Private Household
−0.88	−2.22	17.00	−1.61	−2.61	16.41	Private Household Cleaners and Servants
0.43	−0.77	35.85	0.41	−1.34	38.92	
1.12	0.40	47.99	1.47	−0.12	52.32	Supervisors, Firefighting and Fire Prevention Occupations
1.35	0.69	51.49	0.78	−0.40	45.57	Supervisors, Police and Detectives
0.44	−0.78	35.14	0.32	−1.18	38.25	Supervisors, Guards
0.56	−0.32	39.45	−0.04	−1.76	32.74	Fire Inspection and Fire Prevention Occupations
0.61	−0.61	37.40	0.88	−1.35	41.85	Firefighting Occupations
1.18	0.12	46.08	1.02	−0.48	47.06	Police and Detectives, Public Service
0.74	−0.65	37.75	0.52	−1.18	39.86	Sheriffs, Bailiffs, and Other Law Enforcement Officers
0.12	−0.92	32.36	0.32	−1.41	37.16	Correctional Institution Officers
−1.29	−1.61	19.60	−1.47	−2.22	19.29	Crossing Guards
−0.12	−1.47	26.80	−0.08	−1.92	31.66	Guards and Police, Exc. Public Service
0.16	−2.22	22.41	−0.08	−2.97	26.79	Protective Service Occupations, n.e.c.
−0.49	−2.09	20.43	−0.94	−2.63	22.01	
0.12	−1.61	26.98	−0.56	−2.61	24.64	Supervisors, Food Preparation and Service Occupations
0.24	−2.11	23.66	−0.48	−2.77	24.53	Bartenders
0.24	−2.34	21.91	−0.52	−2.97	23.31	Waiters and Waitresses
−1.07	−2.61	12.92	−1.47	−2.97	15.80	Cooks, Except Short Order
−1.07	−2.61	12.92	−1.47	−2.97	15.80	Cooks
−1.07	−2.61	12.92	−1.47	−2.97	15.80	Short−Order Cooks
−0.97	−2.77	12.15	−1.18	−3.20	17.04	Food Counter, Fountain and Related Occupations
−0.69	−2.46	16.03	−1.12	−2.97	18.55	Kitchen Workers, Food Preparation
−1.12	−2.77	11.35	−0.92	−2.77	21.04	Waiters'/Waitresses' Assistants
−1.35	−2.77	10.17	−1.35	−2.77	17.68	Miscellaneous Food Preparation Occupations
0.69	−1.41	31.55	0.28	−2.61	31.25	Dental Assistants
0.16	−1.54	27.73	−0.48	−2.46	25.98	Health Aids, Except Nursing
0.16	−1.84	25.39	−0.61	−2.34	25.58	Nursing Aides, Orderlies and Attendants
−0.40	−1.07	28.49	−1.12	−2.61	20.22	Supervisors, Cleaning and Building Service Workers
−1.29	−2.22	14.82	−1.84	−2.77	13.84	Maids and Housemen
−1.15	−1.91	17.96	−1.57	−2.46	17.41	Janitors and Cleaners

continued

Appendix—

| | | | | Nakao-Treas Prestige Scores | | | 1980/1990-basis | | |
| | | | | | | | Total | | |
Census Code	F L A G	Number of Occup. Incumbents in 1990	% Male	Prestige Score	%5+	Logit %5+	Logit (% 1 Yr. Col. +)	Logit (% $14.30/ hour +)	TSEI
453.01	6	248,643	83.2	–	–	–	−1.41	−1.76	20.12
453.02	6	190,080	77.7	–	–	–	−1.47	−1.54	20.72
453.03	6	1,538,563	68.1	–	–	–	−1.29	−1.54	22.10
453.04	6	158,599	48.3	–	–	–	−0.78	−0.97	28.77
454.00	1	9,560	83.5	27.59	17.92	−1.48	−1.18	−1.61	22.61
455.00	1	47,367	94.4	32.34	26.61	−0.99	−0.52	−1.68	27.22
456.00	1	59,495	30.4	36.75	41.43	−0.34	0.20	−1.61	33.01
457.00	1	78,821	80.7	35.71	34.70	−0.62	−0.69	−1.84	25.15
458.00	1	683,099	10.3	36.08	37.11	−0.52	−0.40	−2.11	26.02
459.00	1	114,248	63.0	25.33	20.54	−1.32	−0.20	−1.76	29.30
461.00	3	36,768	46.0	28.63	23.08	−1.17	0.40	−1.84	33.39
462.00	3	24,826	67.7	20.03	17.05	−1.54	−0.32	−2.01	27.12
463.00	2	36,768	46.0	28.63	23.08	−1.17	0.40	−1.84	33.39
463.00	3	100,878	20.2	42.05	48.94	−0.04	1.07	−0.08	47.23
464.00	2	24,826	67.7	20.03	17.05	−1.54	−0.32	−2.01	27.12
464.00	3	35,311	89.8	27.26	19.71	−1.37	−0.12	−1.68	30.27
465.00	2	100,878	20.2	42.05	48.94	−0.04	1.07	−0.08	47.23
465.00	3	42,536	15.9	46.50	52.34	0.09	−0.08	−2.11	28.43
466.00	2	35,311	89.8	27.26	19.71	−1.37	−0.12	−1.68	30.27
466.00	3	386,121	1.4	35.76	30.43	−0.81	−0.40	−2.97	21.79
467.00	2	42,536	15.9	46.50	52.34	0.09	−0.08	−2.11	28.43
467.00	3	291,627	4.2	35.76	30.43	−0.81	−0.16	−2.77	24.56
468.00	2	863,649	4.5	36.00	30.43	−0.81	−0.35	−2.78	23.09
468.00	3	185,901	11.2	35.76	30.43	−0.81	−0.56	−2.46	23.02
469.00	1	198,176	31.7	25.41	23.43	−1.16	−0.32	−2.22	26.10
FARMING, FORESTRY, AND FISHING OCCUPATIONS									
	7,8	2,675,596	85.1	32.97	36.24	−0.62	−0.95	−1.90	23.34
473.00	1	745,055	87.1	40.39	55.98	0.24	−0.65	−1.41	27.60
474.00	1	32,189	90.1	37.39	42.73	−0.29	−0.12	−1.18	32.77
475.00	1	222,741	88.3	47.59	60.53	0.42	−0.48	−1.41	28.88
476.00	1	16,822	75.6	47.59	60.53	0.42	0.20	−1.41	33.99
477.00	1	39,432	86.8	44.17	53.33	0.13	−0.78	−1.54	25.95
479.00	1	612,542	82.7	23.28	18.87	−1.42	−1.54	−2.61	14.92
483.00	1	766	80.5	30.52	26.13	−1.02	−0.97	−2.34	20.57
484.00	1	31,573	52.5	25.83	20.95	−1.29	−1.07	−2.46	19.17
485.00	1	61,938	91.9	36.10	35.51	−0.58	−0.12	−1.47	31.30
486.00	1	600,464	92.7	28.57	22.94	−1.18	−1.02	−2.11	21.30
487.00	1	96,514	36.8	21.16	21.59	−1.26	−0.28	−2.46	25.19

Continued

SEIs and Component Data

Males			Females			
Logit (% 1 Yr. Col. +)	Logit (% $14.30/ hour +)	MSEI	Logit (% 1 Yr. Col. +)	Logit (% $14.30/ hour +)	FSEI	Occupational Title
−1.35	−1.23	22.23	−1.84	−2.22	16.42	Janitors and Cleaners (NSE, Manufacturing)
−1.41	−2.46	12.27	−1.76	−2.77	14.47	Janitors and Cleaners (NSE, Retail)
−1.12	−2.11	16.52	−1.61	−2.61	16.41	Janitors and Cleaners (NSE, Other)
−0.56	−1.12	27.21	−1.07	−1.76	24.61	Janitors and Cleaners (SE)
−1.29	−1.54	20.14	−0.88	−2.11	24.50	Elevator Operators
−0.52	−1.68	23.06	−0.40	−2.46	26.62	Pest Control Occupations
0.36	−1.02	32.84	0.12	−2.01	32.78	Supervisors, Personal Service Occupations
−0.78	−1.68	21.69	−0.36	−2.34	27.54	Barbers
−0.12	−1.35	27.78	−0.40	−2.34	27.22	Hairdressers and Cosmetologists
−0.20	−1.61	25.33	−0.16	−1.92	31.04	Attendants, Amusement and Recreation Facilities
0.36	−1.54	28.77	0.44	−2.11	34.84	Guides
−0.61	−2.01	20.01	0.20	−2.22	32.44	Ushers
0.36	−1.54	28.77	0.44	−2.11	34.84	Guides
0.78	−0.08	42.47	1.18	−0.04	50.36	Public Transportation Attendants
−0.61	−2.01	20.01	0.20	−2.22	32.44	Ushers
−0.12	−1.68	25.18	−0.32	−1.84	30.18	Baggage Porters and Bellhops
0.78	−0.08	42.47	1.18	−0.04	50.36	Public Transportation Attendants
0.65	−1.29	32.26	−0.20	−2.34	28.80	Welfare Service Aides
−0.12	−1.68	25.18	−0.32	−1.84	30.18	Baggage Porters and Bellhops
−0.32	−2.34	19.02	−0.40	−2.97	24.28	Family Child Care Providers
0.65	−1.29	32.26	−0.20	−2.34	28.80	Welfare Service Aides
0.52	−2.01	25.92	−0.20	−2.77	26.76	Early Childhood Teacher's Assistants
0.02	−2.19	21.86	−0.37	−2.78	25.36	Child Care Workers, Except Private Household
−0.08	−2.22	21.17	−0.61	−2.46	24.98	Childcare Workers, n.e.c.
−0.08	−2.01	22.77	−0.44	−2.34	26.90	Personal Service Occupations, n.e.c.
−1.00	−1.86	19.52	−0.62	−2.31	26.05	
−0.69	−1.35	24.76	−0.40	−1.92	29.15	Farmers, Except Horticultural
−0.20	−1.12	29.13	0.28	−2.01	34.02	Horticultural Specialty Farmers
−0.52	−1.35	25.67	−0.24	−1.84	30.81	Managers, Farms, Except Horticultural
0.16	−1.23	30.13	0.40	−2.11	34.52	Managers, Horticultural Specialty Farms
−0.78	−1.47	23.32	−0.74	−2.34	24.55	Supervisors, Farm Workers
−1.61	−2.61	10.10	−1.18	−2.97	18.13	Farm Workers
−1.07	−2.77	11.63	−0.65	−1.41	29.56	Marine Life Cultivation Workers
−1.23	−2.34	14.21	−0.83	−2.77	21.79	Nursery Workers
−0.12	−1.41	27.30	0.04	−2.61	29.39	Supervisors, Related Agricultural Occupations
−1.07	−2.11	16.80	−0.48	−2.22	27.12	Groundskeepers and Gardeners, Except Farm
−0.44	−2.11	20.12	−0.20	−2.77	26.76	Animal Caretakers, Except Farm

continued

Appendix—

	F L A G	Number of Occup. Incumbents in 1990	% Male	Nakao-Treas Prestige Scores			1980/1990-basis		
							Total		
Census Code				Prestige Score	%5+	Logit %5+	Logit (% 1 Yr. Col. +)	Logit (% $14.30/ hour +)	TSEI
488.00	1	35,667	34.3	30.69	25.89	−1.03	−2.01	−2.77	10.51
489.00	1	4,055	55.2	49.45	65.49	0.63	−0.48	−1.76	27.16
494.00	1	11,811	96.2	43.53	51.79	0.07	−0.78	−0.69	30.15
495.00	1	17,453	83.9	38.54	37.96	−0.48	−0.28	−1.68	29.07
496.00	1	95,562	96.8	31.10	26.64	−0.99	−1.54	−1.47	20.55
497.00	1	5,492	95.9	42.63	52.00	0.08	−0.61	−0.32	33.36
498.00	1	43,995	94.3	34.46	37.84	−0.49	−1.02	−1.02	26.72
499.00	1	1,525	82.8	22.78	15.89	−1.62	−0.08	−1.84	29.79
PRECISION PRODUCTION, CRAFT, AND REPAIR OCCUPATIONS									
	7,8	12,811,525	90.6	41.37	46.43	−0.15	−0.63	−0.76	31.51
503.00	1	260,168	91.6	49.82	62.82	0.51	−0.04	0.12	39.80
505.00	4	879,332	98.1	39.64	38.74	−0.45	−0.88	−1.36	26.16
505.01	6	298,570	98.8	–	–	–	−0.78	−2.01	23.59
505.02	6	274,306	98.5	–	–	–	−1.02	−1.68	23.44
505.03	6	139,820	95.1	–	–	–	−0.78	−1.61	25.60
505.04	6	166,636	98.7	–	–	–	−0.97	−1.35	25.46
506.00	1	1,408	97.1	34.05	29.52	−0.85	−0.36	−1.76	28.09
507.00	1	255,257	99.2	43.64	54.46	0.18	−0.97	−1.02	27.09
508.00	1	131,768	96.0	52.86	63.94	0.56	0.36	−0.04	42.01
509.00	1	55,233	98.6	27.75	23.85	−1.13	−0.83	−1.54	25.60
514.00	1	205,087	98.0	31.43	28.04	−0.92	−1.29	−1.23	23.63
515.00	1	31,209	92.9	52.86	63.94	0.56	0.08	−0.08	39.72
516.00	1	148,721	99.1	44.82	53.15	0.12	−0.88	−0.56	30.10
517.00	1	26,552	99.0	36.41	36.52	−0.54	−0.83	−1.84	24.12
518.00	1	318,216	96.1	29.51	27.91	−0.93	−0.83	−0.69	29.81
519.00	1	23,110	96.0	25.88	16.67	−1.56	−1.18	−0.44	28.43
523.00	1	164,872	91.6	38.88	38.53	−0.46	0.28	−0.65	38.38
525.00	1	86,355	86.8	51.43	68.42	0.76	1.23	−0.04	48.65
526.00	1	48,615	96.1	37.61	31.58	−0.76	−0.36	−1.07	31.49
527.00	1	49,629	93.5	41.28	46.79	−0.13	−0.20	0.78	41.91
529.00	1	186,031	85.7	36.38	40.45	−0.38	−0.04	0.52	41.80
533.00	1	65,282	94.9	38.53	37.61	−0.50	−0.08	−0.16	38.14

Continued

SEIs and Component Data						
Males			Females			
Logit (% 1 Yr. Col. +)	Logit (% $14.30/ hour +)	MSEI	Logit (% 1 Yr. Col. +)	Logit (% $14.30/ hour +)	FSEI	Occupational Title
−1.76	−2.46	10.45	−2.22	−2.97	9.94	Graders and Sorters, Agricultural Products
−0.08	−1.47	27.01	−1.07	−2.22	22.45	Inspectors, Agricultural Products
−0.78	−0.69	29.44	−0.08	−1.41	34.05	Supervisors, Forestry and Logging Workers
−0.36	−1.61	24.49	0.16	−2.61	30.32	Forestry Workers, Except Logging
−1.61	−1.47	18.99	−1.18	−2.22	21.62	Timber Cutting and Logging Occupations
−0.69	−0.24	33.49	0.69	−2.97	32.87	Captains and Other Officers, Fishing Vessels
−1.02	−1.02	25.61	−1.07	−1.54	25.62	Fishers
0.08	−1.76	25.61	−0.92	−2.34	23.09	Hunters and Trappers
−0.62	−0.69	30.91	−0.59	−1.41	30.55	
−0.08	0.12	39.49	0.28	0.12	43.99	Supervisors, Mechanics and Repairers
−0.90	−1.36	23.62	−0.78	−1.35	28.83	Automobile Mechanics
−0.78	−1.35	24.29	−0.69	−1.54	28.61	Automobile Mech. (NSE, Retail)
−1.02	−1.76	19.85	−0.61	−1.54	29.29	Automobile Mech. (NSE, Bus. & Repair Serv.)
−0.78	−0.56	30.46	−0.74	−0.97	30.91	Automobile Mech. (NSE, Other)
−0.97	−1.54	21.81	−1.35	−2.01	21.22	Automobile Mech. (SE)
−0.40	−1.68	23.71	0.04	−4.62	20.01	Automobile Mechanic Apprentices
−0.97	−1.02	25.88	−1.07	−0.83	28.95	Bus, Truck, and Stationary Engine Mechanics
0.36	0.00	40.85	0.32	−0.97	39.21	Aircraft Engine Mechanics
−0.83	−1.54	22.56	−0.97	−1.41	27.02	Small Engine Repairers
−1.29	−1.23	22.54	−1.02	−1.68	25.36	Automobile Body and Related Repairers
0.08	0.00	39.39	−0.24	−0.88	35.31	Aircraft Mechanics, Exc. Engine
−0.88	−0.56	29.97	−0.44	−0.88	33.72	Heavy Equipment Mechanics
−0.78	−1.84	20.47	−1.84	−2.46	15.28	Farm Equipment Mechanics
−0.78	−0.69	29.44	−0.97	−1.76	25.40	Industrial Machinery Repairers
−1.23	−0.40	29.40	−0.88	−1.35	28.06	Machinery Maintenance Occupations
0.28	−0.65	35.34	0.36	−0.78	40.41	Electronic Repairers, Communications and Industrial Equipment
1.29	0.08	46.36	0.88	−0.92	43.84	Data Processing Equipment Repairers
−0.36	−1.07	28.70	−0.24	−1.92	30.41	Household Appliance and Power Tool Repairers
−0.20	0.83	44.44	0.08	0.20	42.80	Telephone Line Installers and Repairers
−0.04	0.65	43.86	0.04	−0.20	40.65	Telephone Installers and Repairers
−0.04	−0.08	38.16	−0.56	−1.35	30.52	Miscellaneous Electrical and Electronic Equipment Repairers

continued

Appendix—

Census Code	F L A G	Number of Occup. Incumbents in 1990	% Male	Nakao-Treas Prestige Scores			1980/1990-basis Total		
				Prestige Score	%5+	Logit %5+	Logit (% 1 Yr. Col. +)	Logit (% $14.30/ hour +)	TSEI
534.00	1	178,310	98.8	42.00	44.74	−0.21	−0.44	−0.88	31.85
535.00	1	29,535	88.1	35.49	37.93	−0.48	0.24	−0.97	36.47
536.00	1	25,231	94.0	39.17	43.75	−0.25	−0.40	−1.07	31.18
538.00	1	39,485	95.1	36.57	31.78	−0.75	0.44	−1.02	37.75
539.00	1	19,309	95.6	35.67	31.19	−0.77	−0.56	−0.36	33.48
543.00	1	24,377	98.4	39.02	43.48	−0.26	−0.40	0.78	40.40
544.00	1	88,017	96.8	42.75	44.44	−0.22	−0.74	0.20	34.91
547.00	1	198,110	93.2	31.55	29.78	−0.84	−0.40	−1.02	31.44
549.00	1	462,263	95.9	43.53	50.00	0.00	−0.65	−0.88	30.26
553.00	1	12,035	99.2	50.33	65.18	0.61	−0.92	−0.32	30.96
554.00	1	43,164	99.2	50.33	65.18	0.61	−0.56	−0.16	34.47
555.00	1	70,724	98.0	50.33	65.18	0.61	0.08	0.56	42.90
556.00	1	28,808	95.1	50.33	65.18	0.61	−0.78	−0.74	29.93
557.00	1	18,709	97.7	50.33	65.18	0.61	−0.61	0.04	35.13
558.00	2	604,944	97.1	54.05	73.43	0.99	−0.36	−0.20	35.84
558.00	3	604,944	97.1	54.05	73.43	0.99	−0.36	−0.20	35.84
563.00	1	165,402	98.8	36.08	36.36	−0.55	−1.41	−0.69	25.40
564.00	1	678	92.2	26.08	17.35	−1.52	−0.97	−1.84	23.04
565.00	1	48,551	98.1	31.36	27.68	−0.94	−1.07	−0.78	27.52
566.00	1	97,775	97.8	34.38	25.00	−1.07	−1.23	−1.07	24.86
567.00	4	1,169,156	98.4	38.92	42.15	−0.31	−0.78	−1.07	28.31
567.01	6	834,265	98.2	−	−	−	−0.92	−1.23	26.41
567.02	6	334,891	98.6	−	−	−	−0.52	−2.22	24.55
569.00	1	3,975	93.7	28.92	22.93	−1.18	−0.88	−1.68	24.54
573.00	1	125,815	97.6	34.26	32.14	−0.73	−1.41	−0.92	24.26
575.00	1	586,379	97.5	51.27	66.10	0.65	−0.16	−0.28	36.95
576.00	1	14,390	94.8	40.60	44.76	−0.21	−0.16	−2.22	27.31
577.00	1	116,099	98.5	46.25	51.82	0.07	−0.48	0.48	38.27
579.00	1	464,758	92.5	33.91	31.28	−0.77	−0.92	−1.35	25.83
583.00	1	16,416	74.4	31.14	23.64	−1.14	−0.36	−1.02	31.74
584.00	1	36,327	98.2	34.91	33.62	−0.67	−1.47	−0.78	24.48
585.00	1	440,157	98.7	44.75	53.57	0.14	−0.78	−0.44	31.42
587.00	1	7,191	97.3	35.49	34.48	−0.63	−0.56	−1.84	26.13

Continued

SEIs and Component Data						
Males			Females			
Logit (% 1 Yr. Col. +)	Logit (% $14.30/ hour +)	MSEI	Logit (% 1 Yr. Col. +)	Logit (% $14.30/ hour +)	FSEI	Occupational Title
−0.44	−0.88	29.82	−0.56	−1.61	29.31	Heating, Air Conditioning, and Refrigeration Mechanics
0.24	−0.92	32.98	0.04	−1.54	34.37	Camera, Watch, and Musical Instrument Repairers
−0.36	−1.07	28.70	−0.74	−1.23	29.69	Locksmiths and Safe Repairers
0.44	−0.97	33.66	0.48	−1.68	37.18	Office Machine Repairers
−0.56	−0.32	33.54	−0.65	−0.97	31.61	Mechanical Controls and Valve Repairers
−0.40	0.78	43.03	0.12	−0.20	41.27	Elevator Installers and Repairers
−0.74	0.24	36.96	−1.23	−1.12	26.29	Millwrights
−0.40	−0.97	29.28	−0.65	−1.92	27.16	Specified Mechanics and Repairers, n.e.c.
−0.65	−0.88	28.71	−0.32	−1.41	32.18	Not Specified Mechanics and Repairers
−0.92	−0.32	31.66	−4.62	−1.02	0.16	Supervisors: Brickmasons, Stonemasons, and Title Setters
−0.56	−0.16	34.79	−0.78	−1.12	29.84	Supervisors, Carpenters and Related Work
0.08	0.56	43.80	−0.44	−0.36	36.14	Supervisors, Electricians and Power Transmission Installers
−0.83	−0.69	29.20	0.16	−0.97	37.96	Supervisors: Painters, Paperhangers, and Plasterers
−0.65	0.04	35.88	0.00	−1.02	36.49	Supervisors: Plumbers, Pipefitters, and Steamfitters
−0.36	−0.20	35.57	0.04	−0.88	37.48	Supervisors, n.e.c.
−0.36	−0.20	35.57	0.04	−0.88	37.48	Supervisors, Construction, n.e.c
−1.41	−0.69	26.15	−0.97	−1.54	26.42	Brickmasons and Stonemasons
−1.02	−2.01	17.83	−0.40	−0.40	36.28	Brickmason and Stonemason Apprentices
−1.07	−0.78	27.22	0.08	−1.47	34.99	Tile Setters, Hard and Soft
−1.23	−1.02	24.50	−1.07	−2.77	19.87	Carpet Installers
−0.81	−1.06	26.46	−0.51	−1.61	29.69	Carpenters
−0.92	−1.07	25.73	−0.65	−1.68	28.29	Carpenters (NSE)
−0.56	−1.02	28.02	−0.20	−1.61	32.19	Carpenters (SE)
−0.92	−1.68	20.96	−0.56	−1.54	29.63	Carpenter Apprentices
−1.47	−0.92	24.01	−1.29	−1.76	22.89	Drywall Installers
−0.16	−0.24	36.30	−0.16	−0.83	36.15	Electricians, Except Apprentices
−0.16	−2.11	21.59	0.12	−3.91	23.91	Electrician Apprentices
−0.52	0.52	40.33	−0.40	−0.48	35.89	Electrical Power Installers and Repairers
−0.97	−1.29	23.77	−0.40	−1.92	29.15	Painters, Construction and Maintenance
−0.52	−0.88	29.38	0.12	−1.41	35.60	Paperhangers
−1.47	−0.83	24.75	−0.78	−0.61	32.27	Plasterers
−0.78	−0.44	31.44	−0.56	−0.97	32.29	Plumbers, Pipefitters, and Steamfitters
−0.61	−1.92	20.72	1.12	−0.44	48.07	Plumber, Pipefitter, and Steamfitter Apprentices

continued

Appendix—

							1980/1990-basis		
							Total		
	F	Number of		Nakao-Treas Prestige Scores			Logit	Logit (%	
	L	Occup.					(% 1 Yr.	$14.30/	
Census	A	Incumbents	%	Prestige		Logit			
Code	G	in 1990	Male	Score	%5+	%5+	Col. +)	hour +)	TSEI
588.00	1	61,691	98.8	37.50	33.01	−0.69	−1.54	−0.88	23.52
589.00	1	43,157	94.8	30.26	26.17	−1.01	−0.97	−1.02	27.09
593.00	1	63,348	96.5	32.59	29.06	−0.87	−1.02	−0.83	27.67
594.00	1	9,893	98.6	33.00	35.00	−0.61	−1.61	−1.12	21.76
595.00	1	157,032	98.7	37.16	35.45	−0.59	−1.54	−1.29	21.46
596.00	1	25,994	98.4	35.34	34.48	−0.63	−0.92	−0.74	28.87
597.00	1	61,315	98.0	42.96	52.87	0.11	−0.92	−0.24	31.36
598.00	1	18,414	97.7	39.82	45.13	−0.19	−1.23	−1.07	24.86
599.00	1	151,755	97.1	35.67	33.18	−0.69	−1.18	−1.29	24.19
613.00	1	48,209	96.4	44.07	51.55	0.06	−0.36	0.32	38.39
614.00	1	31,233	98.9	41.50	39.81	−0.41	−1.18	−1.29	24.19
615.00	1	8,167	95.1	37.50	42.31	−0.30	−1.23	−0.78	26.30
616.00	1	56,516	97.2	35.06	31.94	−0.74	−1.29	0.00	29.75
617.00	1	30,366	97.4	28.76	24.78	−1.08	−1.29	−0.48	27.37
628.00	5	1,245,699	82.7	47.07	62.78	0.51	−0.28	−0.26	36.11
628.01	6	1,204,955	82.6	–	–	–	−0.28	−2.46	25.19
628.02	6	40,744	85.8	–	–	–	−0.04	−1.92	29.67
633.00	2	1,245,699	82.7	47.07	62.78	0.51	−0.28	−0.26	36.11
634.00	1	136,947	97.9	42.93	49.49	−0.02	−0.32	0.08	37.51
635.00	1	2,240	93.8	32.93	29.18	−0.87	0.04	−2.34	28.21
636.00	1	38,315	77.2	31.47	26.32	−1.01	−0.88	−0.97	28.07
637.00	1	538,949	95.9	46.93	53.77	0.15	−0.69	−0.74	30.61
639.00	1	1,634	90.6	35.31	29.82	−0.84	0.00	−1.76	30.79
643.00	1	20,791	97.3	39.64	40.00	−0.40	−0.78	−0.16	32.82
644.00	1	21,209	91.8	25.87	18.26	−1.46	−0.92	−0.65	29.31
645.00	1	5,185	92.9	38.41	39.09	−0.43	−0.12	0.48	41.00
646.00	1	16,588	88.2	29.52	22.86	−1.19	−0.65	−1.07	29.28
647.00	1	55,962	67.8	44.55	56.41	0.25	−0.36	−1.41	29.81
649.00	1	16,356	63.7	38.17	40.18	−0.39	−0.44	−1.18	30.35
653.00	1	131,786	94.4	50.33	61.95	0.48	−0.78	−0.61	30.59
654.00	1	853	91.4	37.95	36.36	−0.55	−0.52	−1.61	27.58
655.00	1	2,088	77.3	35.71	40.95	−0.36	−1.68	−1.07	21.47
656.00	1	3,219	91.8	38.66	37.96	−0.48	0.08	0.48	42.49
657.00	1	67,397	93.9	43.81	50.44	0.02	−0.74	−1.54	26.29
658.00	1	30,585	75.3	38.94	40.71	−0.37	−0.83	−1.92	23.70
659.00	1	1,929	82.3	36.31	38.79	−0.45	−0.74	−1.92	24.39
666.00	1	84,275	6.7	36.08	36.79	−0.53	−0.92	−2.46	20.30
667.00	1	51,036	53.2	42.48	44.07	−0.23	−1.29	−1.92	20.20
668.00	1	67,625	76.3	34.75	29.36	−0.86	−1.23	−1.84	21.06

Continued

SEIs and Component Data

Males			Females			
Logit (% 1 Yr. Col. +)	Logit (% $14.30/ hour +)	MSEI	Logit (% 1 Yr. Col. +)	Logit (% $14.30/ hour +)	FSEI	Occupational Title
−1.54	−0.88	24.04	−0.74	−1.02	30.68	Concrete and Terrazzo Finishers
−0.97	−0.97	26.27	−0.56	−2.11	26.96	Glaziers
−1.02	−0.78	27.49	−0.88	−1.54	27.17	Insulation Workers
−1.61	−1.12	21.72	−1.29	−0.65	28.07	Paving, Surfacing, and Tamping Equipment Operators
−1.54	−1.29	20.78	−0.83	−1.35	28.43	Roofers
−0.92	−0.69	28.71	−1.07	−1.84	24.23	Sheetmetal Duct Installers
−0.92	−0.24	32.29	−1.84	−1.41	20.20	Structural Metal Workers
−1.23	−1.07	24.10	−1.92	−1.18	20.61	Drillers, Earth
−1.18	−1.29	22.68	−0.74	−1.47	28.57	Construction Trades, n.e.c.
−0.36	0.36	39.90	0.52	0.04	45.55	Supervisors, Extractive Occupations
−1.18	−1.29	22.68	−1.07	−1.07	33.76	Drillers, Oil Well
−1.23	−0.74	26.73	−1.41	−2.97	16.30	Explosives Workers
−1.29	0.00	32.21	−1.07	−0.16	32.08	Mining Machine Operators
−1.35	−0.48	28.14	−0.97	−0.44	31.56	Mining Occupations, n.e.c.
−0.21	−0.07	37.29	−0.61	−1.35	30.19	Supervisors, Production Occupations
−0.24	−0.08	37.12	−0.61	−1.35	30.18	Supervisors, Production Occupations (NSE)
−0.04	−0.16	37.54	−0.12	−1.23	34.57	Supervisors, Production Occupations (SE)
−0.21	−0.07	37.29	−0.61	−1.35	30.19	Supervisors, Production Occupations
−0.32	0.08	37.93	−0.61	−1.02	31.72	Tool and Die Makers
0.00	−2.61	18.54	0.32	−0.40	41.89	Tool and Die Maker Apprentices
−0.78	−0.74	29.09	−1.35	−1.92	21.65	Precision Assemblers, Metal
−0.65	−0.69	30.14	−1.18	−1.76	23.77	Machinists
0.04	−1.84	24.78	−0.52	−1.02	32.38	Machinist Apprentices
−0.74	−0.12	34.19	−2.01	−0.56	22.77	Boilermakers
−1.02	−0.61	28.87	−0.36	−1.29	32.42	Precision Grinders, Fitters, and Tool Sharpeners
−0.16	0.56	42.57	0.61	−0.69	42.79	Patternmakers and Model Makers, Metal
−0.74	−1.02	27.10	−0.28	−1.47	32.20	Lay−Out Workers
−0.32	−1.12	28.50	−0.44	−2.34	26.90	Precious Stones and Metals Workers
−0.48	−0.83	29.97	−0.36	−2.11	28.58	Engravers, Metal
−0.74	−0.56	30.69	−1.02	−1.12	27.96	Sheet Metal Workers
−0.40	−1.54	24.82	−2.01	−2.01	15.99	Sheet Metal Worker, Apprentices
−1.68	−0.88	23.30	−1.61	−1.84	20.01	Miscellaneous Precision Metal Workers
0.04	0.61	43.93	0.48	−1.35	38.73	Patternmakers and Model Makers, Wood
−0.74	−1.47	23.56	−1.02	−2.46	21.71	Cabinet Makers and Bench Carpenters
−0.74	−1.68	21.93	−1.12	−2.61	20.22	Furniture and Wood Finishers
−0.83	−1.76	20.86	−0.28	−4.62	17.53	Miscellaneous Precision Woodworkers
−1.07	−1.68	20.17	−0.92	−2.61	21.81	Dressmakers
−1.41	−1.41	20.52	−1.18	−2.97	18.13	Tailors
−1.23	−1.68	19.33	−1.29	−2.46	19.59	Upholsterers

continued

Appendix—

							1980/1990-basis		
							Total		
				Nakao-Treas Prestige Scores			Logit	Logit (%	
Census	F L A G	Number of Occup. Incumbents in 1990	% Male	Prestige Score	%5+	Logit %5+	(% 1 Yr. Col. +)	$14.30/ hour +)	TSEI
Code									
669.00	1	26,243	71.1	36.14	32.39	−0.72	−1.29	−1.92	20.20
673.00	2	–	36.7	35.00	32.56	−0.71	−0.69	−1.61	26.28
674.00	2	–	36.7	35.00	32.56	−0.71	−0.69	−1.61	26.28
674.00	3	14,294	36.7	35.00	32.56	−0.71	−0.69	−1.61	26.28
675.00	1	19,000	85.6	32.00	30.28	−0.82	−0.83	−1.23	27.12
676.00	1	20,329	76.0	27.59	21.95	−1.24	−0.08	−0.20	37.94
677.00	1	70,927	44.2	37.73	38.89	−0.44	0.08	−1.61	32.12
678.00	1	54,366	60.0	55.93	70.69	0.86	0.40	−1.12	36.93
679.00	1	27,334	49.2	31.58	27.68	−0.94	−0.97	−1.35	25.46
683.00	1	275,290	33.0	28.16	21.84	−1.24	−1.18	−2.22	19.58
684.00	1	49,944	83.5	30.00	24.55	−1.10	−1.07	−1.47	24.08
686.00	1	252,066	81.4	34.66	35.27	−0.59	−1.35	−1.47	21.99
687.00	1	140,809	55.0	34.86	32.61	−0.71	−0.92	−1.92	22.98
688.00	1	46,919	38.6	29.57	20.87	−1.30	−1.12	−2.34	19.41
689.00	1	122,955	76.6	41.80	43.81	−0.24	−0.16	−0.40	36.35
693.00	1	8,242	72.4	39.64	40.95	−0.36	−0.12	−0.74	34.96
694.00	1	58,623	94.7	38.49	38.60	−0.45	−0.12	−0.97	33.80
695.00	1	37,266	94.5	43.28	41.51	−0.34	0.08	0.88	44.45
696.00	1	154,841	95.7	40.16	41.67	−0.33	0.16	0.20	41.68
699.00	1	51,384	92.5	42.89	44.04	−0.23	−0.32	0.04	37.32
OPERATORS, FABRICATORS, ASSEMBLERS, AND LABORERS									
	8	16,557,632	74.2	31.40	27.37	−0.99	−1.15	−1.54	23.58
Machine Operators, Assemblers, and Inspectors									
	7	7,641,538	61.1	33.54	30.28	−0.84	−1.24	−1.60	22.58
703.00	1	26,972	91.5	41.30	38.24	−0.47	−1.18	−1.12	25.02
704.00	1	34,277	88.2	37.24	37.50	−0.50	−0.97	−1.07	26.84
705.00	1	5,853	84.5	32.03	20.83	−1.30	−0.88	−1.02	27.82
706.00	1	98,621	71.9	34.80	36.04	−0.56	−1.54	−1.29	21.46
707.00	1	12,162	87.1	39.56	38.83	−0.45	−1.47	−0.44	26.19
708.00	1	18,543	79.7	36.95	38.94	−0.44	−1.29	−1.54	22.10
709.00	1	112,542	84.2	22.75	16.47	−1.58	−1.47	−1.23	22.24
713.00	1	16,715	93.3	35.61	33.96	−0.65	−1.47	−0.97	23.54

Continued

SEIs and Component Data

Males			Females			
Logit (% 1 Yr. Col. +)	Logit (% $14.30/ hour +)	MSEI	Logit (% 1 Yr. Col. +)	Logit (% $14.30/ hour +)	FSEI	Occupational Title
−1.12	−1.76	19.30	−1.68	−2.77	15.07	Shoe Repairers
−0.61	−1.02	27.79	−0.78	−2.22	24.73	Apparel and Fabric Patternmakers
−0.61	−1.02	27.79	−0.78	−2.22	24.73	Miscellaneous Precision Apparel and Fabric Workers
−0.61	−1.02	27.79	−0.78	−2.22	24.73	Miscellaneous Precision Apparel and Fabric Workers
−0.83	−1.12	25.82	−0.61	−2.34	25.58	Hand Molders and Shapers, Except Jewelers
−0.20	0.00	37.95	0.32	−0.92	39.44	Patternmakers, Lay–Out Workers, and Cutters
0.24	−0.97	32.60	−0.04	−2.61	28.77	Optical Goods Workers
0.44	−0.69	35.84	0.36	−2.01	34.66	Dental Laboratory and Medical Appliance Technicians
−0.78	−0.78	28.74	−1.18	−2.22	21.62	Bookbinders
−0.74	−1.61	22.50	−1.47	−2.61	17.47	Electrical and Electronic Equipment Assemblers
−0.97	−1.35	23.30	−1.54	−2.46	17.63	Miscellaneous Precision Workers, n.e.c.
−1.29	−1.35	21.63	−1.61	−2.77	15.64	Butchers and Meat Cutters
−0.97	−1.61	21.27	−0.92	−2.61	21.81	Bakers
−1.35	−1.92	16.82	−1.02	−2.77	20.27	Food Batchmakers
0.00	−0.12	38.05	−0.78	−1.54	27.90	Inspectors, Testers, and Graders
0.40	−0.32	38.58	−1.84	−2.61	14.61	Adjusters and Calibrators
−0.12	−0.92	31.12	0.28	−1.47	36.55	Water and Sewage Treatment Plant Operators
0.08	0.92	46.62	0.24	−0.08	42.75	Power Plant Operators
0.12	0.24	41.45	0.32	−0.61	40.92	Stationary Engineers
−0.32	0.08	37.93	−0.32	−0.69	35.53	Miscellaneous Plant and System Operators
−1.08	−1.33	23.34	−1.17	−2.21	22.10	
−1.08	−1.24	24.03	−1.49	−2.40	18.62	
−1.18	−1.02	24.79	−1.68	−2.11	18.15	Lathe and Turning Machine Set–Up Operators
−0.97	−0.97	26.27	−1.07	−1.61	25.30	Lathe and Turning Machine Operators
−0.97	−0.88	27.02	−0.40	−2.22	27.77	Milling and Planing Machine Operators
−1.47	−1.02	23.24	−1.92	−2.22	15.75	Punching and Stamping Press Machine Operators
−1.47	−0.28	29.08	−1.41	−1.84	21.57	Rolling Machine Operators
−1.18	−1.35	22.22	−1.84	−2.61	14.61	Drilling and Boring Machine Operators
−1.41	−1.12	22.76	−1.54	−2.22	18.77	Grinding, Abrading, Buffing, and Polishing Machine Operators
−1.47	−0.88	24.39	−1.02	−2.61	21.04	Forging Machine Operators

continued

Appendix—

Census Code	FLAG	Number of Occup. Incumbents in 1990	% Male	Nakao-Treas Prestige Scores			1980/1990-basis Total		
				Prestige Score	%5+	Logit %5+	Logit (% 1 Yr. Col. +)	Logit (% $14.30/ hour +)	TSEI
714.00	1	1,798	81.5	39.52	34.45	−0.63	−0.52	−0.65	32.35
715.00	1	24,113	82.4	29.17	21.30	−1.27	−1.12	−0.92	26.43
717.00	1	23,581	70.2	37.83	34.78	−0.62	−1.61	−1.54	19.70
719.00	1	80,735	77.7	33.74	32.74	−0.70	−1.23	−1.35	23.48
723.00	1	32,476	87.3	36.20	33.02	−0.69	−1.23	−1.54	22.54
724.00	1	17,381	95.0	39.93	46.30	−0.15	−1.12	−0.61	28.00
725.00	1	16,354	85.3	34.76	32.46	−0.72	−1.41	−1.92	19.29
726.00	1	7,341	87.1	37.02	39.42	−0.42	−1.23	−1.84	21.06
727.00	1	82,238	87.0	33.77	33.65	−0.66	−1.68	−2.22	15.78
728.00	1	4,835	71.9	29.89	21.82	−1.24	−1.84	−2.34	14.02
729.00	1	2,895	67.5	26.74	26.74	−0.98	−1.84	−2.61	12.67
733.00	1	37,173	83.7	22.18	15.32	−1.66	−0.92	−2.22	21.52
734.00	2	335,040	82.4	39.47	38.60	−0.45	−0.69	−1.07	28.95
734.00	3	335,040	82.4	39.47	38.60	−0.45	−0.69	−1.07	28.95
735.00	1	48,271	74.4	39.85	43.53	−0.26	−0.28	−0.36	35.65
736.00	1	69,971	30.3	40.21	42.45	−0.30	0.20	−1.47	33.68
737.00	1	46,202	46.5	37.03	38.68	−0.45	−0.61	−1.92	25.38
738.00	1	63,279	28.6	30.41	27.03	−0.97	−2.01	−2.77	10.51
739.00	1	54,184	34.8	34.50	28.85	−0.88	−1.68	−2.77	13.03
743.00	1	6,689	59.1	28.10	22.22	−1.22	−1.47	−2.46	16.13
744.00	1	675,693	12.2	27.50	20.91	−1.30	−2.01	−2.97	9.56
745.00	1	30,145	31.6	32.57	24.77	−1.08	−2.34	−2.97	7.13
747.00	1	125,310	35.5	28.54	22.12	−1.23	−1.84	−2.46	13.38
748.00	1	188,313	37.2	31.85	33.04	−0.69	−1.41	−2.34	17.25
749.00	1	84,257	60.2	33.29	32.58	−0.71	−1.54	−2.22	16.85
753.00	1	27,712	60.4	35.16	29.46	−0.85	−1.61	−1.68	19.00
754.00	1	227,778	41.8	25.11	19.13	−1.40	−1.54	−2.11	17.38
755.00	1	24,498	85.5	32.09	28.83	−0.88	−1.29	−1.54	22.10
756.00	1	103,077	88.9	25.82	18.45	−1.45	−1.12	−1.23	24.88

Continued

SEIs and Component Data						
Males			Females			
Logit (% 1 Yr. Col. +)	Logit (% $14.30/ hour +)	MSEI	Logit (% 1 Yr. Col. +)	Logit (% $14.30/ hour +)	FSEI	Occupational Title
−0.32	−0.32	34.84	−1.54	−4.62	7.58	Numerical Control Machine Operators
−1.12	−0.69	27.65	−1.29	−2.46	19.59	Misc. Metal, Plastic, Stone, and Glass Working Machine Oper.
−1.54	−1.23	21.23	−1.84	−2.77	13.84	Fabricating Machine Operators, n.e.c.
−1.12	−1.12	24.26	−1.61	−2.61	16.41	Molding and Casting Machine Operators
−1.18	−1.47	21.24	−1.76	−2.22	17.06	Metal Plating Machine Operators
−1.12	−0.52	28.99	−1.54	−2.11	19.27	Heat Treating Equipment Operators
−1.41	−1.76	17.80	−1.47	−3.50	13.32	Miscellaneous Metal and Plastic Processing Machine Operators
−1.18	−1.76	19.02	−1.54	−2.61	16.95	Wood Lathe, Routing and Planing Machine Operators
−1.68	−2.22	12.77	−1.61	−2.77	15.64	Sawing Machine Operators
−1.92	−2.22	11.50	−1.84	−2.77	13.84	Shaping and Joining Machine Operators
−1.76	−2.77	8.03	−2.01	−2.46	13.89	Nailing and Tacking Machine Operators
−0.88	−2.11	17.83	−1.12	−2.97	18.55	Miscellaneous Woodworking Machine Operators
−0.69	−0.92	28.11	−0.74	−2.34	24.55	Printing Machine Operators
−0.69	−0.92	28.11	−0.74	−2.34	24.55	Printing Press Operators
−0.24	0.04	38.05	−0.44	−1.84	29.22	Photoengravers and Lithographers
0.16	−0.74	34.02	0.20	−2.01	33.40	Typesetters and Compositors
−0.48	−1.47	24.91	−0.74	−2.46	23.95	Miscellaneous Printing Machine Operators
−1.68	−1.92	15.09	−2.22	−3.50	7.46	Winding and Twisting Machine Operators
−1.84	−2.46	10.03	−1.68	−2.97	14.17	Knitting, Looping, Taping, and Weaving Machine Operators
−1.41	−2.11	15.02	−1.61	−3.50	12.26	Textile Cutting Machine Operators
−1.76	−2.11	13.20	−2.01	−3.20	10.46	Textile Sewing Machine Operators
−2.01	−2.77	6.69	−2.46	−3.20	6.93	Shoe Machine Operators
−1.54	−1.92	15.83	−2.01	−2.97	11.55	Pressing Machine Operators
−0.88	−1.84	19.98	−1.84	−2.97	12.94	Laundering and Dry Cleaning Machine Operators
−1.35	−2.01	16.11	−1.92	−2.77	13.17	Miscellaneous Textile Machine Operators
−1.35	−1.35	21.32	−2.11	−2.22	14.26	Cementing and Gluing Machine Operators
−1.23	−1.61	19.90	−1.92	−2.61	13.94	Packaging and Filling Machine Operators
−1.23	−1.41	21.45	−1.41	−2.22	19.79	Extruding and Forming Machine Operators
−1.12	−1.18	23.84	−1.07	−1.68	24.96	Mixing and Blending Machine Operators

continued

Appendix—

Census Code	F L A G	Number of Occup. Incumbents in 1990	% Male	Nakao-Treas Prestige Scores			1980/1990-basis		
							Total		
							Logit (% 1 Yr. Col. +)	Logit (% $14.30/ hour +)	TSEI
				Prestige Score	%5+	Logit %5+			
757.00	1	66,169	88.6	29.71	24.77	−1.08	−0.56	−0.04	35.06
758.00	1	20,820	78.1	29.74	29.47	−0.85	−1.35	−1.54	21.66
759.00	1	123,986	85.9	29.83	26.14	−1.01	−1.35	−1.29	22.90
763.00	1	4,453	81.1	22.73	16.36	−1.58	−1.12	−1.61	23.02
764.00	1	8,763	73.0	24.67	19.13	−1.40	−1.54	−1.92	18.32
765.00	1	17,963	36.3	28.09	21.78	−1.25	−1.61	−1.92	17.79
766.00	1	90,147	93.8	40.26	33.65	−0.66	−1.07	−0.52	28.82
768.00	1	38,884	81.4	30.57	26.00	−1.02	−1.61	−1.47	20.03
769.00	1	162,366	72.2	33.61	26.42	−1.00	−1.54	−1.84	18.74
773.00	1	9,454	83.7	37.94	38.60	−0.45	0.32	−0.92	37.32
774.00	1	90,938	48.3	37.98	33.33	−0.68	0.04	−1.84	30.68
777.00	1	550,700	68.5	29.86	25.99	−1.02	−1.23	−1.29	23.77
779.00	1	858,790	70.2	32.84	27.30	−0.96	−1.18	−1.41	23.60
783.00	1	579,843	95.6	41.89	44.80	−0.20	−1.18	−1.02	25.53
784.00	1	24,950	32.7	33.09	29.41	−0.86	−1.61	−2.34	15.75
785.00	4	1,352,911	57.4	35.28	31.96	−0.74	−1.23	−1.48	22.86
785.01	6	1,119,269	56.4	–	–	–	−1.29	−2.46	17.52
785.02	6	199,028	61.6	–	–	–	−1.12	−0.69	27.57
785.03	6	34,614	68.3	–	–	–	−0.24	−1.68	29.38
786.00	1	13,878	65.8	25.56	21.18	−1.28	−1.54	−2.46	15.63
787.00	1	24,452	73.0	33.11	28.83	−0.88	−0.65	−1.23	28.48
789.00	1	41,130	68.2	31.31	27.03	−0.97	−0.61	−1.54	27.28
793.00	1	12,691	57.0	42.13	47.00	−0.12	−0.74	−2.11	23.45
794.00	2	–	65.4	35.00	31.00	−0.78	−1.23	−1.84	21.06
795.00	2	–	65.4	35.00	31.00	−0.78	−1.23	−1.84	21.06
795.00	3	37,243	65.4	35.00	31.00	−0.78	−1.23	−1.84	21.06
796.00	1	569,584	48.3	35.53	33.49	−0.67	−0.78	−1.29	27.19
797.00	1	55,314	66.7	38.38	38.94	−0.44	−0.12	−0.83	34.51
798.00	1	9,587	54.1	41.52	47.62	−0.09	−1.29	−1.92	20.20

Continued

SEIs and Component Data

Males			Females			
Logit (% 1 Yr. Col. +)	Logit (% $14.30/ hour +)	MSEI	Logit (% 1 Yr. Col. +)	Logit (% $14.30/ hour +)	FSEI	Occupational Title
−0.52	0.04	36.55	−0.88	−0.83	30.50	Separating, Filtering, and Clarifying Machine Operators
−1.35	−1.35	21.32	−1.35	−2.61	18.45	Compressing and Compacting Machine Operators
−1.29	−1.23	22.54	−1.47	−2.22	19.29	Painting and Paint Spraying Machine Operators
−1.12	−1.61	20.47	−1.02	−1.68	25.36	Roasting and Baking Machine Operators, Food
−1.47	−1.68	18.07	−1.68	−3.20	13.08	Washing, Cleaning, and Pickling Machine Operators
−1.18	−1.18	23.56	−1.92	−2.77	13.17	Folding Machine Operators
−1.07	−0.44	29.92	−1.18	−1.47	25.10	Furnace, Kiln, and Oven Operators, Except Food
−1.47	−1.35	20.67	−2.22	−2.34	12.88	Crushing and Grinding Machine Operators
−1.47	−1.68	18.07	−1.76	−2.61	15.24	Slicing and Cutting Machine Operators
0.28	−0.83	33.93	0.44	−1.47	37.82	Motion Picture Projectionists
0.24	−1.35	29.64	−0.16	−2.46	28.51	Photographic Process Machine Operators
−1.12	−1.02	25.07	−1.41	−2.34	19.25	Miscellaneous Machine Operators, n.e.c.
−1.07	−1.12	24.54	−1.54	−2.34	18.23	Machine Operators, Not Specified
−1.18	−0.97	25.18	−1.47	−1.92	20.67	Welders and Cutters
−1.18	−1.84	18.39	−1.84	−2.61	14.61	Solderers and Brazers
−1.06	−1.09	24.83	−1.51	−2.22	18.98	Assemblers
−1.12	−0.97	25.46	−1.61	−2.22	18.23	Assemblers (NSE, Manufacturing)
−1.02	−1.68	20.44	−1.23	−2.46	20.04	Assemblers (NSE, Other)
−0.28	−1.41	26.47	−0.20	−1.92	30.73	Assemblers (SE)
−1.41	−2.11	15.02	−1.84	−3.20	11.85	Hand Cutting and Trimming Occupations
−0.69	−0.92	28.11	−0.61	−2.61	24.31	Hand Molding, Casting, and Forming Occupations
−0.65	−1.23	25.90	−0.56	−2.46	25.32	Hand Painting, Coating, and Decorating Occupations
−0.56	−1.92	20.95	−1.02	−2.46	21.71	Hand Engraving and Printing Occupations
−1.23	−1.54	20.44	−1.29	−2.77	18.15	Hand Grinding and Polishing Occupations
−1.23	−1.54	20.44	−1.29	−2.77	18.15	Miscellaneous Hand Working Occupations
−1.23	−1.54	20.44	−1.29	−2.77	18.15	Miscellaneous Hand Working Occupations
−0.28	−0.65	32.44	−1.29	−2.34	20.19	Production Inspectors, Checkers, and Examiners
0.12	−0.44	36.16	−0.61	−1.92	27.50	Production Testers
−1.02	−1.61	21.01	−1.61	−2.34	17.68	Production Samplers and Weighers

continued

Census Code	F L A G	Number of Occup. Incumbents in 1990	% Male	Nakao-Treas Prestige Scores			1980/1990-basis Total		
				Prestige Score	%5+	Logit %5+	Logit (% 1 Yr. Col. +)	Logit (% $14.30/ hour +)	TSEI
799.00	1	109,498	43.7	32.80	25.57	−1.04	−1.41	−2.34	17.25
Transportation and Material Moving Occupations									
	7	4,600,242	90.2	32.25	27.94	−0.96	−1.02	−1.17	26.50
803.00	1	76,814	84.2	37.93	39.66	−0.41	0.08	−0.69	36.66
804.00	2	–	94.3	30.00	23.30	−1.16	−1.07	−1.24	25.27
804.00	5	2,615,667	94.3	30.00	23.30	−1.16	−1.07	−1.24	25.27
804.01	6	45,314	96.2	–	–	–	−1.41	−1.76	20.12
804.02	6	36,232	97.1	–	–	–	−1.61	−1.54	19.70
804.03	6	162,190	97.6	–	–	–	−1.61	−1.76	18.62
804.04	6	294,526	96.1	–	–	–	−1.35	−2.77	15.54
804.05	6	1,165,887	95.0	–	–	–	−1.07	−2.34	19.81
804.06	6	312,352	96.7	–	–	–	−1.07	−2.46	19.17
804.07	6	411,759	91.4	–	–	–	−0.83	−2.77	19.48
804.08	6	5,902	92.6	–	–	–	−0.83	−2.34	21.65
804.09	6	73,508	93.4	–	–	–	−0.97	−2.34	20.57
804.10	6	17,439	89.4	–	–	–	−0.88	−2.34	21.30
804.11	6	5,954	89.0	–	–	–	−0.69	−2.77	20.51
804.12	6	55,488	71.1	–	–	–	−0.61	−2.61	21.98
804.13	6	29,116	91.1	–	–	–	−1.07	−2.77	17.64
805.00	2	–	94.3	30.00	23.30	−1.16	−1.07	−1.24	25.27
806.00	1	133,923	90.5	23.87	17.19	−1.53	−0.52	−1.54	27.92
808.00	1	420,125	51.8	32.07	26.92	−0.98	−0.83	−1.41	26.24
809.00	1	185,204	89.4	28.15	25.22	−1.06	−0.44	−1.68	27.85
813.00	1	40,818	90.0	21.22	16.51	−1.57	−0.65	−2.11	24.11
814.00	1	3,105	94.2	24.89	16.10	−1.60	−1.07	−0.83	27.29
823.00	1	35,514	93.6	42.16	50.00	0.00	−0.44	0.83	40.31
824.00	1	43,746	97.5	41.34	54.88	0.19	−0.40	0.92	41.09
825.00	1	31,007	98.5	40.09	43.24	−0.27	−0.56	0.69	38.69
826.00	1	4,773	94.3	47.01	53.98	0.16	−0.56	0.65	38.48
828.00	1	30,343	96.9	54.48	64.52	0.59	−0.32	−0.32	35.55
829.00	1	20,829	97.0	34.16	38.37	−0.46	−0.88	−0.88	28.55
833.00	1	3,667	98.6	42.61	47.27	−0.11	−0.08	−0.04	38.73
834.00	1	5,929	88.6	27.58	18.56	−1.44	−0.88	−1.12	27.31
843.00	1	21,611	94.0	44.63	50.88	0.03	−0.36	−0.36	35.05
844.00	1	207,638	98.3	50.00	59.26	0.37	−1.29	−0.69	26.31
845.00	1	3,831	99.3	33.62	31.03	−0.78	−1.07	−0.78	27.56
848.00	1	18,516	98.0	36.22	40.82	−0.36	−1.41	−1.18	22.99
849.00	1	76,953	97.4	42.34	46.85	−0.12	−1.35	−0.20	28.33

Continued

SEIs and Component Data

Males			Females			
Logit (% 1 Yr. Col. +)	Logit (% $14.30/ hour +)	MSEI	Logit (% 1 Yr. Col. +)	Logit (% $14.30/ hour +)	FSEI	Occupational Title
−1.02	−1.92	18.55	−1.76	−2.77	14.47	Graders and Sorters, Except Agricultural
−1.04	−1.09	25.49	−0.72	−1.78	27.79	
0.08	−0.61	34.64	0.08	−1.29	35.85	Supervisors, Motor Vehicle Operators
−1.12	−1.20	23.70	−0.66	−1.92	27.11	Truck Drivers, Heavy
−1.12	−1.20	23.70	−0.66	−1.92	27.11	Truck Drivers
−1.41	−1.84	17.17	−0.65	−2.46	24.64	Truck Drivers (Agr. For., & Fish.)
−1.68	−0.97	22.54	−0.36	−0.69	35.22	Truck Drivers (Mining)
−1.61	−1.35	19.96	−1.29	−1.68	23.24	Truck Drivers (Construction)
−1.35	−1.23	22.23	−0.97	−1.76	25.40	Truck Drivers (Manufacturing)
−1.12	−0.88	26.22	−0.52	−1.54	29.96	Truck Drivers (Trans., Comm. & Util.)
−1.07	−1.54	21.28	−0.88	−1.76	26.16	Truck Drivers (Wholesale)
−0.83	−1.84	20.23	−0.65	−2.77	23.20	Truck Drivers (Retail)
−0.83	−1.84	20.23	−0.48	−2.34	26.58	Truck Drivers (Finance, Insur.)
−0.97	−1.84	19.48	−0.69	−2.46	24.30	Truck Drivers (Bus. & Repair Serv.)
−0.83	−1.76	20.86	−1.47	−2.77	16.70	Truck Drivers (Personal Serv.)
−0.74	−1.29	24.99	−0.32	−2.34	27.86	Truck Drivers (Enter. & Rec. Serv.)
−0.56	−1.92	20.95	−0.65	−2.34	25.24	Truck Drivers (Prof., Related Serv.)
−1.18	−1.68	19.62	−0.16	−2.34	29.11	Truck Drivers (Public Admin.)
−1.12	−1.20	23.70	−0.66	−1.92	27.11	Truck Drivers, Light
−0.48	−1.47	24.91	−0.88	−2.34	23.46	Driver–Sales Workers
−0.65	−1.02	27.57	−1.07	−1.92	23.83	Bus Drivers
−0.44	−1.61	24.07	−0.52	−2.34	26.25	Taxicab Drivers and Chauffeurs
−0.69	−2.11	18.78	−0.40	−2.11	28.26	Parking Lot Attendants
−1.07	−0.78	27.22	−0.97	−0.88	29.52	Motor Transportation Occupations, n.e.c.
−0.48	0.97	44.08	0.28	−0.88	39.35	Railroad Conductors and Yardmasters
−0.44	0.97	44.30	0.12	0.00	42.19	Locomotive Operating Occupations
−0.56	0.69	41.46	−0.12	0.16	41.07	Railroad Brake, Signal, and Switch Operators
−0.52	0.69	41.68	−0.78	0.16	35.83	Rail Vehicle Operators, n.e.c.
−0.36	−0.28	34.94	0.20	−0.97	38.27	Ship Captains and Mates, Except Fishing Boats
−0.92	−0.88	27.28	0.24	−1.29	37.09	Sailors and Deckhands
−0.08	−0.04	38.26	−0.12	−0.12	39.78	Marine Engineers
−0.83	−1.02	26.63	−0.97	−1.76	25.40	Bridge, Lock and Lighthouse Tenders
−0.40	−0.36	34.10	0.16	−0.65	39.46	Supervisors, Material Moving Equipment Operators
−1.35	−0.65	26.81	−0.44	−1.18	32.31	Operating Engineers
−1.07	−0.64	28.33	−1.30	−1.91	22.15	Longshore Equipment Operators
−1.41	−1.18	22.34	−0.44	−1.35	31.51	Hoist and Winch Operators
−1.35	−0.20	30.36	−1.02	−0.28	31.93	Crane and Tower Operators

continued

Census Code	FLAG	Number of Occup. Incumbents in 1990	% Male	Nakao-Treas Prestige Scores			1980/1990-basis Total		
				Prestige Score	%5+	Logit %5+	Logit (% 1 Yr. Col. +)	Logit (% $14.30/ hour +)	TSEI
853.00	1	86,712	98.3	37.73	36.70	−0.53	−1.54	−0.78	23.98
855.00	1	54,190	98.9	34.46	33.04	−0.69	−1.76	−1.07	20.90
856.00	1	394,970	93.4	35.16	29.91	−0.83	−1.41	−1.41	21.84
859.00	1	84,357	87.7	26.75	24.30	−1.11	−1.07	−0.78	27.56
Handlers, Equipment Cleaners, Helpers, and Laborers									
	7	4,315,852	80.2	26.70	21.62	−1.30	−1.14	−1.84	22.22
863.00	2	14,111	89.0	26.77	24.53	−1.10	−0.28	−0.61	34.42
864.00	2	17,567	94.6	33.38	32.95	−0.70	−1.29	−1.68	21.40
864.00	3	14,111	89.0	26.77	24.53	−1.10	−0.28	−0.61	34.42
865.00	2	64,946	96.0	29.50	26.32	−1.01	−1.35	−2.01	19.30
865.00	3	17,567	94.6	33.38	32.95	−0.70	−1.29	−1.68	21.40
866.00	2	4,000	87.7	37.86	42.86	−0.28	−0.20	−2.01	28.02
866.00	3	64,946	96.0	29.50	26.32	−1.01	−1.35	−2.01	19.30
867.00	2	2,227	90.1	38.02	32.29	−0.72	−0.83	−0.97	28.42
867.00	3	4,000	87.7	37.86	42.86	−0.28	−0.20	−2.01	28.02
868.00	3	2,227	90.1	38.02	32.29	−0.72	−0.83	−0.97	28.42
869.00	1	892,448	96.5	36.43	33.33	−0.68	−1.12	−1.29	24.60
873.00	2	30,218	77.3	30.80	24.07	−1.12	−1.35	−2.01	19.30
874.00	3	30,218	77.3	30.80	24.07	−1.12	−1.35	−2.01	19.30
875.00	1	52,033	96.7	27.72	28.70	−0.89	−1.61	−1.29	20.94
876.00	1	9,678	97.4	37.26	32.69	−0.71	−0.97	0.61	35.18
877.00	4	867,744	70.1	22.95	16.52	−1.57	−1.02	−2.38	20.00
877.01	6	710,608	71.6	–	–	–	−0.97	−1.29	25.76
877.02	6	157,136	63.4	–	–	–	−1.02	−2.46	19.56
878.00	1	75,240	66.4	36.70	35.45	−0.59	−1.41	−1.84	19.72
883.00	1	493,522	89.1	26.86	19.94	−1.35	−0.88	−1.54	25.25
885.00	1	227,576	89.1	21.44	15.13	−1.67	−1.18	−2.22	19.58
887.00	1	186,810	87.3	19.38	12.89	−1.85	−1.35	−2.22	18.29
888.00	1	291,149	35.3	22.05	13.76	−1.78	−1.47	−2.46	16.13
889.00	4	1,086,583	78.4	23.95	19.74	−1.37	−1.18	−1.78	21.75
889.01	6	30,695	77.9	–	–	–	−1.41	−1.92	19.29
889.02	6	16,665	96.4	–	–	–	−1.41	−2.61	15.90
889.04	6	459,409	73.5	–	–	–	−1.47	−2.77	14.60
889.05	6	115,857	89.9	–	–	–	−0.97	−2.34	20.57

Continued

SEIs and Component Data

Males			Females			
Logit (% 1 Yr. Col. +)	Logit (% $14.30/ hour +)	MSEI	Logit (% 1 Yr. Col. +)	Logit (% $14.30/ hour +)	FSEI	Occupational Title
−1.54	−0.78	24.77	−1.29	−1.18	25.59	Excavating and Loading Machine Operators
−1.76	−1.07	21.36	−1.12	−1.12	27.15	Grader, Dozer, and Scraper Operators
−1.47	−1.41	20.19	−1.18	−1.76	23.77	Industrial Truck and Tractor Equipment Operators
−1.07	−0.64	28.33	−1.30	−1.91	22.15	Miscellaneous Material Moving Equipment Operators
−1.12	−1.74	19.84	−1.09	−2.31	22.22	
−0.32	−0.56	32.90	0.04	−0.92	37.26	Supervisors: Handlers, Equipment Cleaners, and Laborers, n.e.c.
−1.29	−1.76	18.43	−1.02	−1.35	26.91	Helpers, Mechanics and Repairers
−0.32	−0.56	32.90	0.04	−0.92	37.26	Supervisors, Handlers, Equipment Cleaners, and Laborers, n.e.c.
−1.35	−2.01	16.11	−0.97	−2.34	22.70	Helpers, Construction Trades
−1.29	−1.76	18.43	−1.02	−1.35	26.91	Helpers, Mechanics and Repairers
−0.32	−1.92	22.24	0.88	−4.62	26.59	Helpers, Surveyor
−1.35	−2.01	16.11	−0.97	−2.34	22.70	Helpers, Construction Trades
−1.18	−0.92	25.56	2.61	−1.54	54.59	Helpers, Extractive Occupations
−0.32	−1.92	22.24	0.88	−4.62	26.59	Helpers, Surveyor
−1.18	−0.92	25.56	2.61	−1.54	54.59	Helpers, Extractive Occupations
−1.18	−1.29	22.68	−0.74	−1.76	27.24	Construction Laborers
−1.35	−1.84	17.49	−1.41	−2.77	17.20	Production Helpers
−1.35	−1.84	17.49	−1.41	−2.77	17.20	Production Helpers
−1.68	−1.29	20.04	−0.74	−1.41	28.86	Garbage Collectors
−1.02	0.61	38.37	0.44	−0.20	43.79	Stevedores
−0.95	−2.24	16.45	−1.12	−2.77	19.51	Stock Handlers and Baggers
−0.97	−2.46	14.57	−1.07	−2.77	19.87	Stock Handlers and Baggers (Retail)
−0.92	−1.61	21.52	−1.29	−2.61	18.92	Stock Handlers and Baggers (Other)
−1.35	−1.68	18.72	−1.68	−2.46	16.51	Machine Feeders and Offbearers
−0.88	−1.47	22.83	−0.83	−2.01	25.33	Freight, Stock, and Material Movers, Hand, n.e.c.
−1.23	−2.22	15.12	−0.92	−2.46	22.49	Garage and Service Station Related Occupations
−1.35	−2.22	14.51	−1.29	−2.22	20.73	Vehicle Washers and Equipment Cleaners
−1.23	−2.11	15.95	−1.68	−2.77	15.07	Hand Packers and Packagers
−1.15	−1.64	20.08	−1.38	−2.46	18.92	Laborers, Except Construction
−1.41	−2.11	15.02	−1.47	−2.77	16.70	Laborers, Exc. Construction (Agr. For., & Fish.)
−1.41	−0.88	24.72	−1.02	−1.29	27.19	Laborers, Exc. Construction (Mining)
−1.41	−1.54	19.51	−1.68	−2.46	16.51	Laborers, Exc. Construction (Manufacturing)
−0.97	−1.23	24.21	−0.97	−1.92	24.62	Laborers, Exc. Construction (Trans., Comm. & Util.)

continued

Appendix—

| | F
L | Number of
Occup. | | Nakao-Treas Prestige Scores | | | 1980/1990-basis | | |
| | | | | | | | Total | | |
Census Code	A G	Incumbents in 1990	% Male	Prestige Score	%5+	Logit %5+	Logit (% 1 Yr. Col. +)	Logit (% $14.30/ hour +)	TSEI
889.06	6	161,490	84.2	–	–	–	−1.12	−2.46	18.78
889.07	6	140,230	76.5	–	–	–	−0.97	−2.22	21.15
889.08	6	15,317	84.7	–	–	–	−1.07	−2.34	19.81
889.09	6	49,778	82.0	–	–	–	−1.07	−2.46	19.17
889.10	6	14,181	67.9	–	–	–	−1.29	−2.34	18.16
889.11	6	10,824	86.2	–	–	–	−0.88	−1.92	23.34
889.12	6	39,542	67.5	–	–	–	−0.65	−2.01	24.60
889.13	6	32,595	85.0	–	–	–	−0.78	−1.92	24.04

Guide to Using this Appendix

This appendix may be used with the 1980 census occupational classification, the 1990 cation which splits some 1990–basis occupation categories by industry and/or class of worker

	1980 Classification	1990 Classification, No Split Occupation Categories
Flag = 1	Use	Use
Flag = 2	Use	X
Flag = 3	X	Use
Flag = 4	Use	Use
Flag = 5	X	Use
Flag = 6	X	X
Flag = 7	X	X
Flag = 8	X	X

Continued

SEIs and Component Data

Males			Females			
Logit (% 1 Yr. Col. +)	Logit (% $14.30/ hour +)	MSEI	Logit (% 1 Yr. Col. +)	Logit (% $14.30/ hour +)	FSEI	Occupational Title
−1.07	−1.92	18.28	−1.41	−2.61	17.97	Laborers, Exc. Construction (Wholesale)
−0.92	−1.92	19.06	−1.18	−2.77	19.03	Laborers, Exc. Construction (Retail)
−1.18	−1.68	19.62	−0.56	−2.34	25.92	Laborers, Exc. Construction (Finance, Insur.)
−1.07	−2.01	17.56	−0.92	−2.46	22.49	Laborers, Exc. Construction (Bus. & Repair Serv.)
−1.23	−2.34	14.21	−1.35	−2.22	20.27	Laborers, Exc. Construction (Personal Serv.)
−0.92	−1.84	19.73	−0.44	−2.34	26.90	Laborers, Exc. Construction (Enter. & Rec. Serv.)
−0.61	−1.84	21.39	−0.69	−2.46	24.30	Laborers, Exc. Construction (Prof., Related Serv.)
−0.78	−1.92	19.80	−0.61	−2.34	25.58	Laborers, Exc. Construction (Public Admin.)

census occupational classification, or a revised version of the 1990 census occupational classifi-classification.

1990 Classification, With Split Occupation Categories	
Use	Line identical in 1980 and 1990 classifications and not involved in splits.
X	Line unique to 1980 classification and not involved in splits.
Use	Line unique to 1990 classification and not involved in splits.
X	Line identical in 1980 and 1990 classifications; should be omitted if splitting.
X	Line unique to 1990 classification; should be omitted if splitting.
Use	Split category, only to be used with 1990 classification.
X	Major categories of 1990–basis occupations (13 categories)
X	Major categories of 1990–basis occupations (6 categories)

REFERENCES

Bielby, William T., Robert M. Hauser, and David L. Featherman. 1977. "Response Errors of Black and Nonblack Males in Models of the Intergenerational Transmission of Socioeconomic Status." *American Journal of Sociology* 82:1242–88.

Blau, Peter M., and Otis Dudley Duncan. 1967. *The American Occupational Structure.* New York: Wiley.

Bose, Christine E., and Peter H. Rossi. 1983. "Prestige Standings of Occupations as Affected by Gender." *American Sociological Review* 48:316–30.

Boyd, Monica. 1986. "Socioeconomic Indices and Sexual Inequality: A Tale of Scales." *Canadian Review of Sociology and Anthropology* 23:457–80.

Cook, R. Dennis, and Sanford Weisberg. 1994. *An Introduction to Regression Graphics.* New York: Wiley.

Davis, James Allan, and Tom W. Smith. 1994. *General Social Surveys, 1972–1994: Cumulative Codebook.* Chicago: National Opinion Research Center.

Duncan, Otis Dudley. 1961. "A Socioeconomic Index for All Occupations." In *Occupations and Social Status*, edited by Albert J. Reiss, Jr., 109–38. New York: Free Press.

———. 1968. "Social Stratification and Mobility: Problems in the Measurement of Trend." In *Indicators of Social Change*, edited by Eleanor B. Sheldon and Wilbert E. Moore, 675–719. New York: Russell Sage Foundation.

Duncan, Otis Dudley, David L. Featherman, and Beverly Duncan. 1972. *Socioeconomic Background and Achievement.* New York: Seminar Press.

Erikson, Robert, and John H. Goldthorpe. 1987. "Commonality and Variation in Social Fluidity in Industrial Nations. Part I: A Model for Evaluating the FJH Hypothesis." *European Sociological Review* 3:54–77.

———. 1992a. *The Constant Flux: A Study of Class Mobility in Industrial Societies.* Oxford: Clarendon Press.

———. 1992b. "The CASMIN Project and the American Dream." *European Sociological Review* 8:283–305.

Featherman, David L., and Robert M. Hauser. 1976. "Prestige or Socioeconomic Scales in the Study of Occupational Achievement?" *Sociological Methods and Research* 4:403–22.

Featherman, David L., F. Lancaster Jones, and Robert M. Hauser. 1975. "Assumptions of Social Mobility Research in the U.S.: The Case of Occupational Status." *Social Science Research* 4:329–60.

Featherman, David L., and Gillian Stevens. 1982. "A Revised Socioeconomic Index of Occupational Status: Application in Analysis of Sex Differences in Attainment." In *Measures of Socioeconomic Status*, edited by M. Powers, 93–129. Boulder: Westview.

Fox, John. 1991. *Regression Diagnostics*, edited by Michael S. Lewis-Beck. In *Quantitative Applications in the Social Sciences*, Series/Number 07-079. Newbury Park, CA: Sage.

Fox, John, and Carole Suschnigg. 1989. "A Note on Gender and the Prestige of Occupations." *Canadian Journal of Sociology* 14:353–60.

Fridman, Samuel, Sharon Mengchee Lee, and Luis M. Falcon. 1987. "Estimating Income–Dependent Occupational Scores for 1940." *Social Science Research* 16:260–83.

Friendly, Michael. 1991. *SAS System for Statistical Graphics*. In *SAS Series in Statistical Applications*. Cary, NC: SAS Institute.

Ganzeboom, Harry B., Paul M. De Graaf, and Donald J. Treiman. 1992. "A Standard International Socio–Economic Index of Occupational Status." *Social Science Research* 21:1–56.

Goldberger, Arthur S. 1989. "Economic and Mechanical Models of Intergenerational Transmission." *The American Economic Review* 79:504–13.

Goldthorpe, John H. 1980. *Social Mobility and Class Structure in Modern Britain*. Oxford: Clarendon Press.

Goldthorpe, John, and Keith Hope. 1974. *The Social Grading of Occupations: A New Approach and Scale*. Oxford: Clarendon Press.

Gordon, Jerome B. 1969. "Socioeconomic Status: A Re–Examination of Its Dimensions." *Human Resources* 4:343–59.

Halaby, Charles N. 1993. "Reply to Wright." *American Sociological Review* 58:35–36.

Halaby, Charles N., and David L. Weakliem. 1993. "Ownership and Authority in the Earnings Function: Nonnested Tests of Alternative Specifications." *American Sociological Review* 58:16–30.

Haller, Archibald O., and David Bills. 1979. "Occupational Prestige in Comparative Perspective." *Contemporary Sociology* 8:721–34.

Haug, Marie. 1972. "An Assessment of Inequality Measures." In *Social Inequality*, edited by Gerald W. Theilbar and Saul D. Feldman, 429–51. Boston: Little, Brown.

Haug, Marie R. 1977. "Measurement in Social Stratification." In *Annual Review of Sociology*, vol. 3, edited by A. Inkeles, J. Coleman and N. Smelser, 51–77. Palo Alto: Annual Reviews.

Haug, Marie R., and Marvin B. Sussman. 1971. "The Indiscriminate State of Social Class Measurement." *Social Forces* 49:549–63.

Hauser, Robert M. 1972. "Disaggregating a Social–Psychological Model of Educational Attainment." *Social Science Research* 1:159–88.

———. 1982. "Occupational Status in the nineteenth and twentieth Centuries." *Historical Methods* 15:111–26.

———. 1995. "Better Rules for Better Decisions." In *Sociological Methodology 1995* edited by Peter V. Marsden, 175–84. Cambridge: Blackwell Publishers.

Hauser, Robert M., and David L. Featherman. 1977. *The Process of Stratification: Trends and Analyses*. New York: Academic Press.

Hauser, Robert M., and John A. Logan. 1992. "How Not to Measure Intergenerational Occupational Persistence." *American Journal of Sociology* 97:1689–711.

Hauser, Robert M., William H. Sewell, and John Robert Warren. 1994. "Education, Occupation, and Earnings in the Long Run: Men and Women from Adolescence to Midlife." Paper presented at the 1994 Meetings of the American Sociological Association, University of Wisconsin–Madison.

Hodge, Robert W. 1981. "The Measurement of Occupational Status." *Social Science Research* 10:396–415.

Hodge, Robert W., Paul M. Siegel, and Peter H. Rossi. 1964. "Occupational Prestige in the United States, 1925–63." *American Journal of Sociology* 70:286–302.

Hollingshead, August B. 1957. "Two Factor Index of Social Position," Unpublished manuscript. New Haven: Yale University.

———. 1971. "Commentary on 'The Indiscriminate State of Social Class Measurement.'" *Social Forces* 49(4):563–67.

Hollingshead, August B., and F. C. Redlich. 1958. *Social Class and Mental Illness.* New York: Wiley.

Hout, Michael. 1996. "Speed Bumps on the Road to Meritocracy: Occupational Mobility of Women and Men in the United States, 1972–1994." Paper presented at Social Science and Statistics: A Conference in Honor of the Late Clifford C. Clogg. Pennsylvania State University, September.

Hout, Michael, and Robert M. Hauser. 1992. "Symmetry and Hierarchy in Social Mobility: A Methodological Analysis of the CASMIN Model of Social Mobility." *European Sociological Review* 8:239–66.

Jencks, Christopher S. 1990. "What Is the True Rate of Social Mobility?" In *Social Mobility and Social Structure*, edited by Ronald L. Breiger, 103–30. Cambridge: Cambridge University Press.

Jencks, Christopher S., Lauri Perman, and Lee Rainwater. 1988. "What Is a Good Job? A New Measure of Labor Market Success." *American Journal of Sociology* 93:1322–57.

Jöreskog, Karl G., and Dag Sörbom. 1993. *New Features in LISREL 8.* Chicago: Scientific Software International.

Kalmijn, Matthijs. 1994. "Assortative Mating by Cuttural and Economic Occupational Status." *American Journal of Sociology* 100:422–52.

Kraus, Vered, E.O. Schild, and Robert W. Hodge. 1978. "Occupational Prestige in the Collective Conscience." *Social Forces* 56:900–918.

Mason, William, Robert M. Hauser, Alan C. Kerckhoff, Sharon S. Poss, and Kenneth Manton. 1976. "Models of Response Error in Student Reports of Parental Socioeconomic Characteristics." In *Schooling and Achievement in American Society*, edited by William H. Sewell, Robert M. Hauser and David L. Featherman, 443–519. New York: Academic Press.

Mosteller, Frederick, and John W. Tukey. 1979. *Data Analysis and Regression: A Second Course in Statistics.* Reading, MA: Addison–Wesley.

Nakao, Keiko, and Judith Treas. 1992. "The 1989 Socioeconomic Index of Occupations: Construction from the 1989 Occupational Prestige Scores," GSS Methodological Report No. 74. Chicago: National Opinion Research Center.

———. 1994. "Updating Occupational Prestige and Socioeconomic Scores: How the New Measures Measure Up." In *Sociological Methodology 1994*, edited by Peter V. Marsden, 1–72. Cambridge: Blackwell Publishers.

Nam, Charles B., and Mary G. Powers. 1983. *The Socioeconomic Approach to Status Measurement (with a Guide to Occupational and Socioeconomic Status Scores).* Houston: Cap and Gown Press.

Nam, Charles B., and E. Walter Terrie. 1982. "Measurement of Socioeconomic Status from United States Census Data." In *Measures of Socioeconomic Status: Current Issues*, edited by Mary G. Powers, 29–42. Boulder: Westview.

Powers, Mary G. 1982. *Measures of Socioeconomic Status: Current Issues*. Boulder: Westview.

Raftery, Adrian E. 1995. "Bayesian Model Selection in Social Research." In *Sociological Methodology 1995*, edited by Peter V. Marsden, 111–63. Cambridge: Blackwell Publishers.

Reiss, Albert J., Jr. 1961. *Occupations and Social Status*. New York: Free Press of Glencoe.

Rytina, Steve. 1992. "Scaling the Intergenerational Continuity of Occupation: Is Occupational Inheritance Ascriptive After All?" *American Journal of Sociology* 97:1658–88.

Siegel, Paul M. 1970. "Occupational Prestige in the Negro Subculture." *Sociological Inquiry* 40:156–71.

———. 1971. "Prestige in the American Occupational Structure." Ph.D diss., University of Chicago.

Smith, Tom W., Sara P. Crovitz, and Christopher Walsh. 1988. "Measuring Occupation: A Comparison of 1970 and 1980 Occupation Classification Systems of the Bureau of the Census," GSS Methodological Report No. 59, December. Chicago: National Opinion Research Center.

Sobek, Matthew. 1996. "Work, Status, and Income: Men in the American Occupational Structure Since the Late Nineteenth Century." *Social Science History* 20:169–207.

Solon, Gary. 1992. "Intergenerational Income Mobility in the United States." *American Economic Review* 82:393–408.

Stafford, M. Therese, and Mark A. Fossett. 1991. "Measuring Occupational Sex Inequality Over Time Using Nam–Powers SES Scores." Austin: University of Texas at Austin.

Stevens, Gillian, and Joo Hyun Cho. 1985. "Socioeconomic Indexes and the New 1980 Census Occupational Classification Scheme." *Social Science Research* 14:74–168.

Stevens, Gillian, and David L. Featherman. 1981. "A Revised Socioeconomic Index of Occupational Status." *Social Science Research* 10(4):364–95.

Stevens, Gillian, and Elizabeth Hoisington. 1987. "Occupational Prestige and the 1980 U.S. Labor Force." *Social Science Research* 16:74–105.

Theil, Henri. 1970. "On the Estimation of Relationships Involving Qualitative Variables." *American Journal of Sociology* 76:103–54.

Treiman, Donald J. 1975. "Problems of Concept and Measurement in the Comparative Study of Occupational Mobility." *Social Science Research* 4:183–230.

———. 1977. *Occupational Prestige in Comparative Perspective*. New York: Academic Press.

U.S. Bureau of the Census. 1963. *Methodology and Scores of Socioeconomic Status*. Working Paper No. 15. Washington: Government Printing Office.

———. 1971a. *Alphabetic Index of Industries and Occupations*. 1970 Census of Population. Washington: Government Printing Office.

———. 1971b. *Classified Index of Industries and Occupations*. 1970 Census of Population. Washington: Government Printing Office.

———. 1972. *1970 Occupation and Industry Classification Systems in Terms of Their 1960 Occupation and Industry Elements*. Technical Paper 26. Washington: Government Printing Office.

————. 1982a. *Alphabetic Index of Industries and Occupations*. 1980 Census of Population. PHC80–R3. Final edition. Washington: Government Printing Office.

————. 1982b. *Classified Index of Industries and Occupations*. 1980 Census of Population. PHC80–R4. Final edition. Washington: Government Printing Office.

————. 1989. *The Relationship Between the 1970 and 1980 Industry and Occupation Classification Systems*. Technical Paper 59. Washington: Government Printing Office.

————. 1992a. *Alphabetic Index of Industries and Occupations*. 1990 Census of Population and Housing. 1990 CPH–R–3. Washington: Government Printing Office.

————. 1992b. *Classified Index of Industries and Occupations*. 1990 Census of Population and Housing. 1990 CPH–R–4. Washington: Government Printing Office.

U.S. Department of Labor. 1977. *Dictionary of Occupational Titles*, 4th ed. Washington: Government Printing Office.

U.S. Department of Labor, Employment, and Training Administration. 1991. *Dictionary of Occupational Titles*. 4th ed., rev. 1991. Lanham, MD: Bernan Press.

Warren, John Robert, Jennifer T. Sheridan, and Robert M. Hauser. 1996. "How Do Indexes of Occupational Status Affect Analyses of Gender Inequality in Occupational Attainment?" CDE Working Paper 96–10. Madison: Center for Demography and Ecology, University of Wisconsin–Madison.

Wright, Erik Olin. 1985. *Classes*. London: Verso.

————. 1993. "Typologies, Scales, and Class Analysis: A Comment on Halaby and Weakliem's 'Ownership and Authority in the Earnings Function.'" *American Sociological Review* 58:31–34.

Zimmerman, David J. 1992. "Regression Toward Mediocrity in Economic Stature." *American Economic Review* 82:409–29.

5

A DUAL-SOURCE INDICATOR OF CONSUMER CONFIDENCE

Gordon G. Bechtel*

The objective of this paper is to improve the U.S. leading confidence indicator by combining its amended version with the Conference Board's equally well known Consumer Expectation Index. *The resulting dual-source indicator provides a factorial structure in which survey items are nested. The results presented here show that this structure is not well fit by a generalized linear model. Hence a nonlinear model is invoked which provides differential logistic slopes for the survey items. This latter model is based on the work of McCullagh (1980). The effects estimated in this nonlinear structure provide the United States with a potential leading indicator that is richer and more informative than its current* Index of Consumer Expectations. *The suggested indicator prevents the mixed signals and inconsistencies that can occur when separately reporting results from our two most prominent sources of consumer perception.*

1. INTRODUCTION

1.1. *The University of Michigan's Index*

The *Index of Consumer Sentiment*, pioneered by George Katona in 1952 and now used monthly in widely reported American Surveys, is perhaps

The author is indebted to Peter McCullagh who kindly provided the software used in the present study. The Conference Board and the University of Michigan's Survey Research Center provided the data for the present report, and three anonymous reviewers made helpful comments. Special thanks go to Adrian Raftery whose penetrating critique extended and improved this work. The study was supported by a research grant from the University of Florida's College of Business Administration. E-mail: bechtel@nervm.nerdc.ufl.edu

*University of Florida

299

the world's first and best known social indicator (see Katona 1975, chaps. 5–8). Adaptations of this index are also reported in monthly surveys in each nation of the European Union, as well as in Canada, Australia, and Japan. This widespread usage demonstrates that western governments have heeded Katona's (1979) call for a "macropsychology" in which the attitude-behavior link is more demonstrable and lawlike at the aggregate level than it is at the individual level.

Three of Katona's five items, which form Michigan's *Index of Consumer Expectations*, appear in Table 1. These items tap different facets of consumer confidence. The third item addresses pocketbook concerns—i.e., personal well-being and security at the household level. The first and second items embrace the collective interest associated with short- and long-term expectations about the American economy. These two items are "sociotropic" in the sense originally used by Meehl (1977). (See also Bechtel 1991; Bechtel et al. 1993.) That is, they tap expectations about well-being and security through reliance on collective strength, as distinct from altruism (cf. Hardin 1968; Kinder and Kiewiet 1984; Dawes 1991).

The University of Michigan's Survey Research Center has been monitoring the items in Table 1 every month since 1980. A fresh random sample of approximately 800 households is contacted by telephone, and about 500 completed interviews are obtained each month. In January 1989 the U.S. Commerce Department included Michigan's *Index of Consumer Expectations* as one of the 11 components of the revised U.S. leading eco-

TABLE 1
Components of Michigan's Index of Consumer Expectations

Item	Response Categories		
Business conditions in the country during the next 12 months	Bad times	Good and bad	Good times
Continuous good times vs. unemployment or depression in the country during the next 5 years	Bad times	Good and bad	Good times
Financial situation of your household 1 year from now vs. now	Will be worse	Same	Will be better

Source: These items and response categories were drawn from *Surveys of Consumers: Historical Data*, Survey Research Center, The University of Michigan, 1993.

nomic indicators. Figure 1 traces this index for 1992, which was a transitional year for consumer confidence in the United States.

1.2. *The Conference Board's Index*

The Conference Board's equally well known *Consumer Expectation Index* appears in Table 2 (Linden 1982). This index also contains a single personal item, along with two communal items on business conditions and jobs. Since July 1977 the questions in Table 2 have been mailed to a representative panel of 5000 homes every month, with a fresh sample contacted each month. This mail survey is conducted for the Conference Board by National Family Opinion of Toledo, who obtained about a 68 percent response rate in 1992, which is the year analyzed in the present study (see Section 5.1).

Figure 1 tracks the Conference Board's index for 1992, which takes somewhat higher numerical values than the Michigan index. The impor-

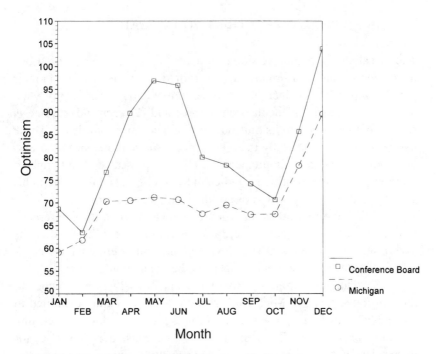

FIGURE 1. The Michigan and Conference Board indexes of consumer expectation for 1992.

TABLE 2
Components of the Conference Board's Consumer Expectation Index

Item	Response Categories		
General business conditions in your area 6 months from now	Worse	Same	Better
Available jobs in your area 6 months from now	Fewer	Same	More
Your total family income 6 months from now	Lower	Same	Higher

Source: These items and response categories were drawn from *The Consumer as Fore-caster*, Consumer Research Center, The Conference Board, 1982.

tant findings in this figure, however, are the mixed signals and inconsistencies in the movements of these two indicators of American consumer confidence. From January to February they move in opposite directions. From March to October the Michigan index is flat, whereas the Conference Board's indicator sharply rises and then plummets.

2. ALIGNING THE TWO INDICATORS

The two above indexes have stood for many years as major contributions to socioeconomic measurement in the United States. However, (1) their monthly reporting is vulnerable to mixed signals about the economy when they show opposite or inconsistent trends, and (2) each index alone is restricted with respect to its time horizon for consumer confidence. These two problems are solved by the creation of a *single* indicator that draws upon both data sources simultaneously. Thus the present study attempts to improve our leading confidence indicator by combining items from Michigan's consumer survey with those of the Conference Board.

This improvement stems from three factors. First, the Conference Board items (Table 2) more explicitly define consumer confidence in terms of jobs and unemployment. The U.S. economy and its employment capability are matters of perennial concern in the population at large.

Second, the Conference Board items in Table 2 will be matched to three *different* items in Michigan's monthly survey that are exhibited in Table 3. That is, in the present study Table 3 replaces Table 1 in defining consumer expectations. The items in Table 3 have also been in service for many years in the Michigan survey. Their substitution here is supported by

TABLE 3
Suggested Michigan Replacement Items

Item	Response Categories		
Business conditions in the country 1 year from now	Worse	Same	Better
Unemployment during the coming 12 months vs. now	More	Same	Less
Your (family) income during the next 12 months vs. the past year	Lower	Same	Higher

Source: These items and response categories were drawn from *Surveys of Consumers: Historical Data*, Survey Research Center, The University of Michigan, 1993.

their more explicit language, which matches them to the Conference Board's items in Table 2.

Finally, the combination of the six-month expectations in Table 2 with the one-year anticipations in Table 3 gives a richer and more informative treatment of consumer confidence. It also limits the present confidence indicator to *short-term expectations* that are more easily defended on psychological grounds. (Adams and Klein 1972; Praet and Vuchelen 1984; Praet 1985; Biart and Praet 1987; Vanden Abeele 1988).

The alignment of the Conference Board and Michigan items in Tables 2 and 3 is accomplished by the nested and crossed factorial layout in Table 4. Here the *six-month* and *one-year* levels of the temporal factor are crossed with the *personal* and *communal* levels of the orientation factor. The six items are then nested within each temporal-orientation combination as shown in the table. The short-term expectations in this layout will be brought together in Section 4 by means of an item response model that scales them jointly in a single indicator.

TABLE 4
Items Nested in Temporal-by-Orientation Combinations

		Communal			Personal		
Six months	γ_{11}	Business Jobs	δ_{111} δ_{112}	γ_{12}	Income	δ_{121}	α_1
One year	γ_{21}	Business Jobs	δ_{211} δ_{212}	γ_{22}	Income	δ_{221}	α_2
		β_1			β_2		

3. SURVEY MODEL SELECTION

3.1. *Single Versus Multiple Month Models*

As indicated above, the dual-source items in Table 4 are presented monthly to national samples. Therefore the first decision in model selection involves the choice between month-specific models and one overarching model that connects successive months. The present approach opts for the former strategy, which analyzes the data for each month separately, using a fresh set of parameters for each time point. The latter strategy, which analyzes all of the data at once with the inclusion of monthly effects, is problematic in survey monitoring for two reasons. First, one model frame requires a reestimation of the past with each new survey. In contrast, each month-specific model estimates the present alone without readjusting previously observed indicators. Second, the large number of parameters in one multiple-month model can present prohibitive computational problems that are averted by separate monthly estimations.

Having settled on successive month-specific models, the present approach finalizes this model selection issue by permitting the data to be tested for various submodel structures at a single point in time. Because these structures are month-specific, it is possible to observe distinct model forms with the passage of time. The important point here is that temporal specificity makes it possible to capture the present with *its* best possible fit.

3.2. *Loglinear Versus Cumulative Logit Models*

This choice between alternative rating-scale models may be posed in terms of one's tendency to focus on the probability *in* an item category rather than the probability *below* that category. This question splits ordinal categorical analysis into two basic types for the aggregate treatment of survey ratings scales. The traditional Thurstonian method of successive intervals models the cumulative probability *below* a given category boundary. In contrast, Rasch methods have modeled the probability *in* a single response category. Recent reviews of these two approaches to polytomous categorical analysis are found in Andrich (1995) and Mellenbergh (1995).

3.2.1. *Probability in a Category*
Let a survey item partition n respondents into $C + 1$ categories, where $c = 0, 1, \ldots, C$, and let ϵ_c be the expected frequency in category c. Also, let

$$\log \epsilon_c = \lambda_c, \tag{1}$$

where λ_c has a specified linear composition for category c. This equation is a log-linear model, and by definition,

$$\epsilon_c = \exp\{\lambda_c\}.$$

The probability in category c is

$$\theta_c = \frac{\epsilon_c}{n},$$

and because $\sum_{c=0}^{C}\theta_c=1$, it follows that

$$\sum_{c=0}^{C} \epsilon_c = n \sum_{c=0}^{C} \theta_c = n,$$

and

$$\theta_c = \frac{\exp\{\lambda_c\}}{\sum_{c=0}^{C} \exp\{\lambda_c\}}. \tag{2}$$

Therefore the multinomial logit model (2) for the probabilities θ_c is equivalent to the log-linear model (1) for the log expected frequencies ϵ_c, where $c = 0, 1, \ldots, C$.

Using a rather general specification for λ_c, a generic model for probabilities *in* nominal or ordinal item categories was derived by Rasch (1961). A specification for λ_c was also presented by Samejima (1972, chap. 4). Subsequent treatments of this model have been given by E. B. Andersen (1977), and Andrich (1978; 1979; 1982) has applied it to rating scales, which are of concern here.

In the context of the present paper, the Rasch rating model produces C thresholds for measuring several item locations on a confidence continuum. This log-linear model utilizes a scoring function, which assigns values $\varphi_0, \varphi_1, \ldots, \varphi_C$ to the item categories *a priori*. The ordinality of the item is captured by the integer scoring function $0, 1, \ldots, C$. J.A. Anderson (1984) generalized this model, keeping the category scores as unknown parameters that, when estimated, *test* the ordinality of item i. He noted the "considerable price to pay in terms of model fitting" with linear φ functions such as the integer scoring function. He also related his "stereotype" model to a more general logistic family and compared it with McCullagh's (1980) formulation, which he termed "the grouped continuous regression model."

3.2.2. Probability Below a Category

Again, let a survey item have categories $c = 0, 1, \ldots, C$. Like the Rasch model, McCullagh's (1980) formulation measures item location against C thresholds. However, now the cumulative probability *below* threshold $c = 1, \ldots, C$ is represented by

$$\pi_c = \frac{\exp\{\lambda_c\}}{1 + \exp\{\lambda_c\}}, \tag{3}$$

where the logit λ_c is a linear or nonlinear function of threshold c.

In his discussion of J.A. Anderson's (1984) paper, McCullagh states that "in the more usual case where the order is important and not in doubt, the grouped continuous models would appear to be preferable because of the ease of parameter interpretation and invariance under combination of adjacent categories" (Anderson 1984:23). Other advantages of the grouped continuous models lie in (1) their guaranteed ordering of thresholds, which can be out of proper order in the Rasch rating model (cf. Andrich 1979) and (2) their avoidance of assigned category scores, which can contribute to lack of model fit (cf. Anderson 1984). These special multinomial response models exploit the *a priori* information in rating scales—i.e., the *order* information in the response categories themselves, by modeling the *cumulative* probabilities along the scale.

Finally, as McCullagh and Nelder (1989:213) note: "Not all log-linear models are equivalent to multinomial response models, and conversely, not all multinomial response models can be generated from log-linear models."

These authors go on to emphasize the fact that cumulative logit models "cannot be derived by conditioning in a log-linear model without extending the accepted definition of a loglinear model." This latter point is implicitly made by Clogg and Shihadeh (1994) who, in their analysis of ordinal variables, clearly separate logit and log-linear models. The latter authors identify log-linear models with the *association* analysis of a multi-dimensional contingency table. In contrast, they identify logit models with *response* analysis in which a particular ordinal variable has been set aside as a dependent variable. Among the several ordinal logit models they consider, Clogg and Shihadeh (1994) exempt the cumulative logit model from log-linear identifications. They point to McCullagh's (1980) analysis of cumulative logits as the most widely used ordinal regression model and regard it as one of the two most interesting ordinal logit models to consider. The present analysis is based on the more general *nonlinear* form of this model given by McCullagh (1980) and discussed again by McCullagh and Nelder (1989). This same nonlinear model has a venerable psychometric history in the area of Thurstonian analysis, where it is called "successive intervals" scaling (cf. Gulliksen 1954; Torgerson 1958; Jones 1960).

4. THE MONTH-SPECIFIC MODEL

4.1. *Cumulative Probabilities*

The layout in Table 4 calls for an analysis-of-variance model in which the dependent variable is an ordered three-category multinomial consisting of pessimistic, neutral, and optimistic response options. Let $i = 1, 2$ represent the two temporal levels in Table 4 and $j = 1, 2$ denote the two orientations. Then the kth item nested within the ij temporal-orientation combination is designated ijk.

For each item ijk there is a response probability in each of its three ordered categories. The sum of these three probabilities is one. Let

$$\pi_{ijk1} = pr \text{ (pessimistic) for item } ijk,$$

$$\pi_{ijk2} = \pi_{ijk1} + pr \text{ (neutral) for item } ijk.$$

Then π_{ijkc} for $c = 1, 2$ is the cumulative probability of responding *below* cutpoint τ_c on the latent confidence scale common to the six items in Table 4. The cutpoints τ_1 and τ_2 are the lower and upper bounds of the neutral zone on this scale.

4.2. *The Nonlinear Logistic Link*

The function that links π_{ijkc} to the cutpoints τ_c and the parameters of the layout in Table 4 is as follows:

$$\log\{\pi_{ijkc}/(1 - \pi_{ijkc})\} = \text{logit}\{\pi_{ijkc}\} = \kappa_{ijk}\{\tau_c - \eta_{ijk}\}, \qquad (4a)$$

where

π_{ijkc} = the probability of a response to item ijk *below* cutpoint c,

κ_{ijk} = item ijk's logistic slope ($\kappa_{ijk} > 0$),

τ_c = cutpoint c's confidence scale location,

η_{ijk} = item ijk's confidence scale location.

The parameters τ_c and η_{ijk} in the linear portion of (4a) are points on the latent confidence scale. The cutpoints τ_1 and τ_2 partition this scale into successive intervals representing *pessimistic*, *neutral*, and *optimistic* respectively.

Using the parameterization in Table 4, model (4a) is completed by the following decomposition of population confidence η_{ijk} for item ijk:

$$\eta_{ijk} = \alpha_i + \beta_j + \gamma_{ij} + \delta_{ijk}, \tag{4b}$$

where

$$\alpha_i = \text{horizon } i\text{'s effect,}$$

$$\beta_j = \text{orientation } j\text{'s effect,}$$

$$\gamma_{ij} = \text{horizon-by-orientation interaction,}$$

$$\delta_{ijk} = \text{item } ijk\text{'s effect.}$$

Model (4b) for the nesting and crossing in Table 4 has also been given by Scheffé (1959:182). The identification of the parameters in model (4) is accomplished by the following side (uniqueness) conditions:

$$\prod_{ijk} \kappa_{ijk} = 1, \tag{5a}$$

$$\alpha_1 + \alpha_2 = 0, \tag{5b}$$

$$\tfrac{2}{3}\beta_1 + \tfrac{1}{3}\beta_2 = 0, \tag{5c}$$

$$\gamma_{11} + \gamma_{21} = 0 = \gamma_{12} + \gamma_{22}, \tag{5d}$$

$$\tfrac{2}{3}\gamma_{11} + \tfrac{1}{3}\gamma_{12} = 0 = \tfrac{2}{3}\gamma_{21} + \tfrac{1}{3}\gamma_{22}, \tag{5e}$$

$$\delta_{111} + \delta_{112} = \delta_{211} + \delta_{212} = \delta_{121} = \delta_{221} = 0. \tag{5f}$$

Condition (5a) sets the unit of the *ratio* scale of the κ_{ijk}. By reciprocation this in turn sets the unit of the *interval* confidence scale inside the brackets on the right of (4a). Equations (5c) and (5e) are weighted side conditions that identify the parameters in model (4) when, as seen in Table 4, two items are nested within first column cells and one item is nested within second column cells (cf. Scheffé 1959). Condition (5f) centers the item main effects in Table 4 within each cell in which they are nested.

4.3. *The Confidence Indicator*

It follows from the side conditions (5) that

$$\sum_i \sum_j \sum_k \eta_{ijk} = 0,$$

which places the origin of the latent confidence scale at the mean of the item values η_{ijk}. In defining an overall confidence indicator, this mean may be measured against the midpoint $\frac{1}{2}(\tau_1 + \tau_2)$ of the neutral interval on the confidence scale. Under this definition the indicator is

$$\mu = 0 - \tfrac{1}{2}(\tau_1 + \tau_2) \tag{6}$$

$$= -\tfrac{1}{2}(\tau_1 + \tau_2),$$

which shifts the scale origin to the midpoint of the neutral zone. Under this calibration, negative values represent pessimism and positive values denote optimism.

4.4. *Model Specification*

Model (4a) has been written for the important case of three-category rating scales, such as those used by the Conference Board and the University of Michigan. In this case the nonlinear parameters κ_{ijk} given by McCullagh (1980) and McCullagh and Nelder (1989) saturate the polytomous response model with common cutpoints τ_c across all items. With more than three categories, ordered polytomous ratings become unsaturated, and it is then possible but not always necessary to employ item-specific cutpoints, as well as differential item slopes, by an extension of McCullagh's nonlinear model. In the present three-category case, however, we are forced to choose between item-specific cutpoints and differential item slopes. The approach here is to opt for the latter type of model specification for three reasons. First, McCullagh's (1980) nonlinear model is itself an update of a long-standing and useful scaling model originally developed by Thurstone (1925). (See also Gulliksen 1954 and Torgerson 1958, chap. 10.) Second, and more important, the κ_{ijk} provide differential logistic slopes in (4a), which are frequently required in fitting survey rating scales. In fact, the results reported in Tables 6 and 7 later in this chapter show these slopes to have strong effects in the present analysis. Third, in the three-category case the substantive interpretation of the common item cutpoints τ_1 and τ_2 is that the neutral zone, which separates the pessimistic and optimistic regions on the confidence scale, remains constant in width over items. This invariance is a weaker, more defensible assumption with three response categories, where there is only *one* closed region, than it is with more rating options that define multiple closed zones.

4.5. *Estimation of Model* (4)

4.5.1. *The Trinomial Likelihood*

Table 5 contains the probabilities and frequencies for the responses *pessimistic*, *neutral*, and *optimistic* for a single item *ijk*. Applying McCullagh's (1980) analysis, the likelihood of this single observation (n_{ijk1}, n_{ijk2}, n_{ijk3}) is reduced to the product of two binomial factors, one unconditional and the other conditional. The initial split observed for *optimistic* versus *not optimistic* depends upon the unconditional binomial expression

$$f_{ijk} = \pi_{ijk2}^{n_{ijk1}+n_{ijk2}}(1 - \pi_{ijk2})^{n_{ijk3}}. \tag{7}$$

Given this first split, the next split observed for *neutral* versus *pessimistic* rests upon the conditional binomial expression

$$g_{ijk} = \left(\frac{\pi_{ijk1}}{\pi_{ijk2}}\right)^{n_{ijk1}} \left(\frac{\pi_{ijk2} - \pi_{ijk1}}{\pi_{ijk2}}\right)^{n_{ijk2}}. \tag{8}$$

The product of (7) and (8) determines the likelihood of the trinomial observation (n_{ijk1}, n_{ijk2}, n_{ijk3}).

Finally, the product of six item likelihoods, three from the Conference Board sample and three from the Michigan sample, generates the overall likelihood of the 6×3 array of marginal frequencies observed in a given month of 1992. This likelihood is

TABLE 5
Probabilities and Frequencies for a Typical Item *ijk*

	Pessimistic	Neutral	Optimistic
Category frequencies	n_{ijk1}	n_{ijk2}	n_{ijk3}
Cumulative frequencies	n_{ijk1}	$n_{ijk1} + n_{ijk2}$	n_{ijk}
Cumulative probabilities	π_{ijk1}	π_{ijk2}	1.00

$$\prod_{ijk} f_{ijk}\, g_{ijk}, \tag{9}$$

where π_{ijkc} for $c = 1, 2$ in (7) and (8) is

$$\pi_{ijkc} = \frac{\exp\{\kappa_{ijk}(\tau_c - \eta_{ijk})\}}{1 + \exp\{\kappa_{ijk}(\tau_c - \eta_{ijk})\}}. \tag{10}$$

Equation (10) is equivalent to (4a), and η_{ijk} in (10) is defined in (4b). Hence, the likelihood (9) is maximized over the choice of the slopes κ_{ijk}, the cutpoints τ_c, and the effects in (4b).

4.5.2. *The Estimation Algorithm*
The likelihood (9) is maximized for model (4) by Newton-Raphson iterations with Fisher scoring. The details of the nonlinear estimation algorithm, which is carried out by iteratively reweighted least squares, are given by McCullagh (1980:119–21, 125–27). Maximum-likelihood estimation by iteratively reweighted least squares is also described for generalized linear models by McCullagh and Nelder (1989:40–43). In the case of the nonlinear model (4), it is the author's experience that with survey-sized samples the algorithm always converges within a few iterations.

4.5.3. *Model Saturation*
The maximization of (9) produces estimates identical to those found by Gulliksen's (1954) nonlinear least-squares solution for (4a). The perfect fit of both solutions stems from the equal number of parameters and observations in the three-category case. That is, the six items here produce 12 cumulative logits. Referring to Table 4 and side conditions (5b) through (5f), we count five independent parameters which is also the number of independent η_{ijk} whose six values sum to zero. Due to (5a), there are also five independent κ_{ijk}. The cutpoints τ_1 and τ_2 then bring the total number of parameters to 12, producing model saturation and identical estimates for both the maximum-likelihood and nonlinear-least-squares solutions.

4.6. *Standard Errors in Correlated Marginal Estimation*

The sixfold product in (9) is based on the assumption of independence among the six multinomials. Therefore (9) should be regarded as an approximation to the overall likelihood because of the unknown associations among the three items administered to the Conference Board sample, as well as the unknown correlations among the other three items answered by the Michigan sample. These within-sample associations must be tolerated in any analysis of marginal archival data where individual responses are not available for the samples being studied (cf. McCullagh and Nelder 1989:175–78).

It is important to consider the standard errors of the estimated effects that are produced by likelihood maximization when the marginal item distributions are not independent. Information on this issue is provided by two datasets recently analyzed by the author. In each of these studies a *marginal* analysis, assuming inter-item independence, was compared with a *criterion* analysis using the same model on the same data. The marginal analysis was carried out with the algorithm described in Section 4.5.2, which was applied to several item frequency counts regarded as multinomial distributions. However, because these items generate repeated responses from the *same* sample, this sample's full data array is a multiway frequency table. It is evident that a marginal analysis leaves out the information contained in the inter-item associations. Disregarding this information misspecifies the covariances among the cumulative marginal logits. In this case parameter estimates are still unbiased, but their standard errors are misstated.

To remedy this problem, it is necessary to move from a generalized-linear-models analysis for marginal item frequencies to a generalized-linear-models analysis that uses *all* of the information in the multiway frequency table. Because maximum-likelihood software for this latter situation is not readily available, the criterion analysis is carried out here by empirically weighted least squares (EWLS) in the CATMOD procedure of SAS (SAS Institute 1989). This procedure, which handles inter-item associations as *nuisance* parameters, constructs cumulative item logits from the response statement CLOGIT. The comparability between the marginal and criterion analyses is maintained by setting the κ slopes to one in each of the following studies. This control produces generalized linear models with equal degrees of freedom for each comparison of estimates and standard errors under marginal and criterion conditions.

In the criterion EWLS analysis a $(C + 1)$-category response variable is measured in the *same* sample over M items, resulting in a cross-classification of possible outcomes (cells) in $(C + 1)^M$ profiles. Here interest is focused on the MC correlated cumulative logits on the M margins of the $(C + 1)^M$ multiway table. For example, the $M = 3$ Conference Board items in the present analysis generate $3^3 = 27$ possible response profiles and $3 \times 2 = 6$ cumulative marginal logits. More generally, let $\boldsymbol{\theta}$ be the vector of (e.g., 27) cellular response probabilities and $\mathbf{f}(\boldsymbol{\theta})$ be its vector of (e.g., 6) cumulative marginal logits. A description of this transformation is found in Landis et al. (1988). Next, let $\mathbf{f} \equiv \mathbf{f}(\mathbf{p})$ be the corresponding vector of *observed* cumulative marginal logits, where $\mathbf{p}$ is the vector of *observed* cellular proportions. Then $\mathbf{f}$ is a consistent estimator of $\mathbf{f}(\boldsymbol{\theta})$, and the asymptotic expectation of $\mathbf{f}$ is

$$\mathbf{f}(\boldsymbol{\theta}) = \mathbf{X}\boldsymbol{\beta}, \tag{11}$$

where $\mathbf{X}$ is a known model matrix and $\boldsymbol{\beta}$ is a vector of unknown parameters (Koch et al. 1977; Stokes et al. 1995). For example, in this section $\boldsymbol{\beta}$ will contain several intercepts (cutpoints τ), along with effects contained in the scale location η.

Koch et al. (1977) give a consistent estimator $\mathbf{V_f}$ for the covariance matrix of $\mathbf{f}$, and $\mathbf{V_f}$ provides the weighting mechanism in the EWLS procedure that carries the information in the inter-item associations. The EWLS estimator of $\boldsymbol{\beta}$

$$\mathbf{b} = (\mathbf{X}'\mathbf{V_f}^{-1}\mathbf{X})^{-1}\mathbf{X}'\mathbf{V_f}^{-1}\mathbf{f} \tag{12}$$

is a linearized minimum modified chi-squared estimator (Neyman 1949) and hence is consistent, efficient, and best asymptotically normal (BAN) (Agresti 1990; Koch et al. 1977; Bhapkar 1966). A consistent estimator for the covariance matrix of $\mathbf{b}$ is given by

$$\mathbf{V_b} = (\mathbf{X}'\mathbf{V_f}^{-1}\mathbf{X})^{-1}. \tag{13}$$

The square roots of the diagonal elements of $\mathbf{V_b}$ give the standard errors of the estimates in the criterion analyses reported in this section.

Finally, the predicted cumulative marginal logits $\hat{\mathbf{f}} = \mathbf{Xb}$ provide the predicted cumulative marginal probabilities that in turn give the marginal probabilities and frequencies that are expected under model (11) for each of the $C + 1$ categories of each of the M items being analyzed.

4.6.1. A Simulation with Three Ordered Categories

The first study used data simulated for three rating categories. Here 2000 response protocols were generated for three items, and the data were then analyzed by the following generalized linear model:

$$\text{logit}\{\pi_{ic}\} = \tau_c - \eta_i, \tag{14}$$

where

π_{ic} = the probability of a response to item i *below* cutpoint c,

τ_c = cutpoint c's scale location ($c = 1, 2$),

η_i = item i's scale location $\left(\sum_i \eta_i = 0 \right)$.

The latent scale is partitioned by τ_1 and τ_2 into three successive intervals representing the three manifest rating categories. The origin of this scale is placed at the mean of the item values η_i. The overall indicator μ is measured against the midpoint of the neutral scale interval, which in this three-category case gives μ from equation (6) in Section 4.3.

In this analysis the general effect μ and two linearly independent item effects η_i were estimated by the marginal procedure described in Section 4.5.2 and the EWLS criterion procedure in PROC CATMOD of SAS— i.e., in the absence and presence of inter-item covariances in the estimation procedure. The three marginal estimates were virtually identical to their criterion counterparts. However, quoted standard errors for both of the marginal item estimates were *greater* than their corresponding criterion standard errors. In contrast, the quoted standard error for the marginal general effect was *less* than its referential standard error. An item standard error was on average 1.66 times its criterion value in this simulated sample. The general-effect standard error was .64 times its referential value in this sample.

4.6.2. Real Data with Five Ordered Categories

The second (unpublished) study bearing on the estimation issue used four items, each with five response categories, taken from the 1993 Picker/Commonwealth National Survey of American patient satisfaction with hospital care. The author is grateful to Paul D. Cleary and the Picker/Commonwealth Program for Patient-Centered Care, who provided the data for this analysis. Here 1880 medical and surgical patients were segmented into subsamples of 658 men and 1222 women, who rated their satisfaction into five categories that ranged from *poor* to *excellent*.

In this analysis the following generalized linear model was invoked with a 2 (male versus female) × 2 (doctors versus nurses) × 2 (helpfulness versus availability) structure:

$$\text{logit}\{\pi_{ijkc}\} = \tau_c - \eta_{ijk}. \tag{15a}$$

The terms on the left and right sides of this equation have definitions similar to those in (4a) and (14), except that here there are four cutpoints τ_1, τ_2, τ_3, and τ_4. The decomposition of satisfaction is given by

$$\eta_{ijk} = \alpha_i + \beta_j + \gamma_k + \delta_{ij} + \rho_{ik} + \lambda_{jk}. \tag{15b}$$

The terms in (15b) are the usual main effects and two-way interactions under the standard (unweighted) side conditions for a three-way analysis of variance (Scheffé 1959:121). These side conditions place the origin of the satisfaction scale at the mean of the gender-item values η_{ijk}. Therefore the overall satisfaction indicator μ is given by the following equation, which measures it against the midpoint of the middle scale zone:

$$\mu = -\tfrac{1}{2}(\tau_2 + \tau_3). \tag{16}$$

The general effect μ and the six effects in (15b) were estimated by the marginal and criterion procedures described above. The seven marginal estimates were all very close to their corresponding criterion estimates. Five of six marginal standard errors for main effects and interactions were on average 1.59 times *greater* than their criterion counterparts, which is very close to the ratio observed with the simulated data. The general effect in the marginal analysis had a quoted standard error which was .64 times that for the general effect in the criterion analysis. This latter ratio is identical to that found in the preceding simulation.

4.6.3. *Summary*

Counting marginal and criterion comparisons in the two preceeding studies, we find that in all 10 instances accurate parameter estimates were produced in the marginal analyses despite their disregard for inter-item association. However, the marginal analyses misstated standard errors in opposite directions for special and general effects in the generalized linear models studied here. Seven of eight comparisons revealed overstated standard errors for item, main, and interaction effects when inter-item associations are not taken in account. On the other hand, the general-effect comparisons in the simulated and real data both showed understated standard errors for marginally estimated general effects.

The analyses in Sections 4.6.1 and 4.6.2 show that with marginal archival data, such as those analyzed in Section 5 below, the significance of general-effect (indicator) comparisons will be overstated, and that of special-effect comparisons will be understated. This situation can be remedied by adjusting test statistics, and it does not effect the results and conclusions reported in Section 5. However, the major emphasis here is *not* on the robustness of marginal estimation but, rather, on model (4) as a mechanism for combining separate national data sources. In fact, estimation of (4) from marginal archival data will be unnecessary in the future if anonymous case-by-case response protocols are made available for consumer confidence monitoring. In that event accurate standard errors can be produced by the EWLS analysis described above, which incorporates inter-item associations into the estimation procedure. This result has already been realized for models like (4) when they are used for national satisfaction measurement (Bechtel 1996).

5. CONFIDENCE MEASUREMENT

5.1. *Time Series and Data Sources*[1]

Model (4) is based upon the indicator structure in Table 4, which has been implicit in our national confidence surveys for many years. This structure will now be used explicitly in constructing a confidence indicator over the 12 months of 1992. This time span is selected because of its recent historical interest as a period of political and economic transition that, among other things, saw a shift in consumer confidence. The first six months of this period led up to the two national party conventions in the summer of 1992. The second six months witnessed these conventions, along with the presidential campaign and election itself.

The 1992 response proportions for the Michigan items in Table 3 were generated by approximately 500 fresh telephone interviews in each month of that year. Proportions for the Conference Board's items in Table 2 were derived from approximately 3400 mail responses per month in 1992. These responses were obtained for the Conference Board by National Family Opinion of Toledo, which contacted an entirely different group of respondents every month.

5.2. *The Proportional Odds Model*

In the present context the proportional odds model is a generalized linear model that is a special case of (4) with $\kappa_{ijk} = 1$. When tested against its nonlinear counterpart (cf. McCullagh and Nelder 1989:151–55), this lin-

---

[1]The 6 (item) $\times$ 3 (category) $\times$ 12 (month) array of marginal frequencies analyzed here for 1992 may be obtained from Statlib at http://lib.stat.cmu.edu/datasets/ confidence, or by sending the e-mail message "send confidence from data" to statlib@ stat.cmu.edu.

ear model is rejected in each of the 12 months of the present study. These initial results are shown in Table 6 by the large deviance values, which are rounded to the nearest integer. These values are interpretable as chi-squares on 5 degrees of freedom, and they are all significant beyond the .000 level.

5.3. *The General Nonlinear Model*

For $\kappa_{ijk} > 0$ the logistic link (4) is a general *nonlinear* model. The results in Table 6 show that this extension of the proportional odds model is required for the layout in Table 4. This layout contains five linearly independent parameters—i.e., α_1, β_1, γ_{11}, δ_{111}, and δ_{211}, each of which is estimated for model (4) on a given survey. The 12 monthly estimates of these parameters are discussed below after a consideration of the overall confidence indicator in (6).

5.3.1. *The Indicator μ*
The vertical axis in Figure 2 calibrates consumer confidence on a scale with the origin set at neutral. Ten monthly values were on the optimism side in 1992, but the μ estimates for January and February were slightly negative. An upward trend began in March, continued through the spring, but was followed by a fallback in the summer and early autumn. Consumer confidence soared again after November's presidential election and anticipated changes in national direction.

The upward trend in consumer confidence in 1992 is, of course, well known from the separate reports by the University of Michigan and the Conference Board that are graphed in Figure 1. The results in Figure 2, however, express this trend for the first time in one voice that does not contain the mixed signals and inconsistencies seen in Figure 1 between the separate Conference Board and Michigan indicators. Moreover, because the indicator μ is model based, it is possible to examine important facets of consumer confidence given in (4b).

5.3.2. *The Components of η_{ijk}*
The estimates of the parameters in (4b) are also given in Table 6. Except for α_1 in January, the corresponding standard errors reveal that all of these estimates are significantly different from zero. Thus, with this one exception, *all* of the α, β, γ, and δ components of (4b) belong in the model for *every* month of 1992.

TABLE 6
Results for 1992

	J	F	M	A	M	J	J	A	S	O	N	D
Monthly Deviances (5 d.f.) for the Proportional Odds Model												
	303	318	342	300	405	226	237	221	309	286	167	210
Estimates for the Nonlinear Model												
α_1	−.03	−.08	−.15	−.19	−.22	−.18	−.15	−.25	−.24	−.28	−.35	−.40
	(.036)	(.038)	(.035)	(.039)	(.039)	(.038)	(.036)	(.036)	(.040)	(.039)	(.037)	(.036)
β_1	−.40	−.40	−.30	−.37	−.29	−.38	−.37	−.36	−.43	−.39	−.37	−.25
	(.028)	(.028)	(.027)	(.032)	(.033)	(.032)	(.029)	(.029)	(.034)	(.031)	(.032)	(.031)
γ_{11}	.28	.30	.24	.36	.30	.35	.28	.26	.32	.31	.33	.25
	(.028)	(.028)	(.027)	(.032)	(.033)	(.032)	(.029)	(.029)	(.034)	(.032)	(.032)	(.031)
δ_{111}	.17	.18	.22	.22	.22	.23	.23	.21	.18	.16	.16	.18
	(.020)	(.019)	(.020)	(.020)	(.020)	(.021)	(.021)	(.021)	(.020)	(.021)	(.021)	(.021)
δ_{211}	.78	.80	.66	.63	.62	.54	.73	.58	.52	.64	.39	.56
	(.073)	(.078)	(.068)	(.070)	(.071)	(.066)	(.071)	(.068)	(.067)	(.072)	(.065)	(.072)

Note: Standard errors are given in parentheses.

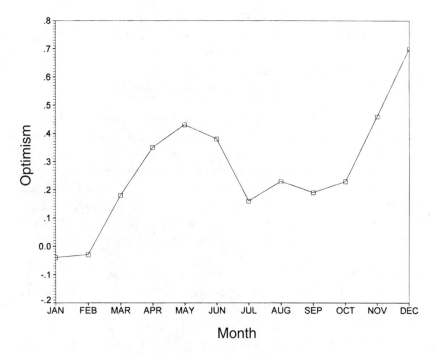

FIGURE 2. The dual-source indicator of consumer confidence for 1992.

Parameter invariance across months may be assessed by a z test. This is illustrated below for adjacent α_i parameters.

Time-Horizon Effects.   Table 6 reveals that six-month consumer optimism α_1 is less than one-year optimism in *all* of the surveys analyzed here. The one-year expectation effects α_2 are found by negating the α_1 values in the table.

Six-month optimism α_1 may also be monitored statistically over time. For example, a z test reveals that the rise in α_1 from June to July was not significant. The subsequent drop from July to August, however, was significant at the nominal .05 level as a comparison planned in July 1992. In view of the results reported in Section 4.6, the significance of this latter main-effect comparison may be regarded as understated.

The other parameters in Table 6 may be monitored similarly. An advantage of the present month-specific model is that parameter comparisons can be planned from one month to the next.

Orientation Effects.   Table 6 shows that communal influence β_1 on consumer confidence is far less than personal influence. The personal effects β_2 are found by negating and doubling the tabled β_1 values. This main effect is also in the same direction over *all* 12 surveys, and it is greater in magnitude than the main effect for time horizon in Table 6.

Temporal-by-Communal Interactions.   The interactions γ_{11} in Table 6 indicate that orientation operates differently over six-month and one-year time horizons. Referring these estimates to γ_{11} in Table 4 we see that under a communal orientation six-month optimism is enhanced by this interaction effect, whereas one-year optimism is depressed. The reverse holds under a personal orientation. Again, the sign of the interaction effects γ_{11} in Table 6 is the same over *all* 12 months studied here. For a given month, the other three interactions are calculated from the side conditions (5d) and (5e).

Six-Month Business Effects.   A valuable property of model (4) is its inclusion of the specific effects of *survey items* that are nested within the four cells in Table 4. Table 6 shows the six-month business item's effects δ_{111}, which display positive values throughout 1992. These values show that six-month employment optimism δ_{112} ($= -\delta_{111}$) was less than six-month optimism about business conditions in *every* month. It would appear from reports in the media that this job insecurity is even more intense now than it was in 1992 (The Economist 1996).

One-Year Business Effects.   Table 6 also reveals that the above discrepancy between business and job perception increases when the time horizon is extended to one year. The one-year business effects δ_{211} are markedly larger than those for six months, especially for January and February of 1992 when, as shown in Figure 2, overall confidence was at its lowest. The one-year job effects are given by $\delta_{212} = -\delta_{211}$.

5.3.3. *The Item Slopes* κ_{ijk}
Table 7 exhibits the slopes κ_{ijk} of the six confidence items in Tables 2 and 3. Due to the side condition (5a) on the κ_{ijk}, the product of the six values in each column of this table is one.

The major finding in Table 7 is the greater discrimination associated with the short time horizon items. Among these three questions, the item addressing expectations about household income has the largest logistic slope in every month of 1992. In contrast, for the longer time horizon

TABLE 7
The Item Slopes κ_{ijk}

Item	J	F	M	A	M	J	J	A	S	O	N	D
Six Months												
Business	1.27	1.32	1.24	1.34	1.36	1.33	1.32	1.30	1.33	1.37	1.23	1.27
Jobs	1.18	1.19	1.12	1.19	1.21	1.13	1.22	1.18	1.23	1.23	1.17	1.16
Income	1.49	1.52	1.51	1.48	1.56	1.34	1.35	1.35	1.45	1.42	1.33	1.41
One Year												
Business	.84	.86	.88	.91	.86	.98	.97	.94	.99	.94	.95	.87
Jobs	.89	.78	.89	.82	.85	.90	.80	.86	.85	.79	.92	.84
Income	.60	.62	.61	.57	.54	.57	.59	.60	.50	.57	.60	.66

Note: The product of the six values in each column (survey) is one.

321

the question about household income stands out in Table 7 as having the least slope. This also holds for every month of 1992. Thus the *relative* discrimination associated with personal versus communal expectation is heavily dependent on time horizon.

The results in Table 7 give a strong substantive justification for using the saturated version of model (4) for the three-category confidence ratings employed by Michigan and the Conference Board (see Sections 4.4 and 4.5.3).

6. IMPACT

The present combination of Michigan and Conference Board items provides the United States with a leading confidence indicator that is richer and more informative than its present *Index of Consumer Expectations* based on the items in Table 1. The indicator derived here matches different expectation items from the Michigan survey (Table 3) to the Conference Board's expectation items already in use (Table 2). This combined item set is arrayed in a nested and crossed structure that produces item effects, time-horizon effects, and orientation effects for short-term expectations. Because it is operationalized in an item response theory, the "proportional odds" version of the proposed indicator may be tested for fit. These model checks (Table 6) are evaded by current American indicators, which are not model-based, as well as by similar measures of consumer confidence used by the European Union. These tests reject the proportional odds model and point to the general *nonlinear* model (4), which requires differential item slopes. The overall confidence indicator produced by this later model is graphed in Figure 2 for 1992. This indicator is a candidate for governmental forecasting studies in which the predictive validity of this new attitude measure may be compared with that of the U.S. Commerce Department's present, and inconsistent, leading indicators (see again Figure 1).

More immediately relevant, however, is the fact that this new indicator is constructed from items that have been in service for many years providing separate sources of information about consumer confidence. The combination of these two item sets into a single confidence measure enables our government to make better use of existing consumer data that are broader than data available in Europe or Japan.

REFERENCES

Adams, F. Gerard, and Lawrence R. Klein. 1972. "Anticipations Variables in Macro-Econometric Models." In *Human Behavior in Economic Affairs*, edited by Burkhard

Strumpel, James N. Morgan, and Ernest Zahn, 289–319. San Francisco: Jossey-Bass.

Agresti, Alan. 1990. *Categorical Data Analysis*. New York: Wiley.

Andersen, Erling B. 1977. "Sufficient Statistics and Latent Trait Models." *Psychometrika* 42:69–81.

Anderson, John A. 1984. "Regression and Ordered Categorical Variables." *Journal of the Royal Statistical Society, Series B* 46:1–30.

Andrich, David. 1978. "A Rating Scale Formulation for Ordered Response Categories." *Psychometrika* 43:561–73.

———. 1979. "A Model for Contingency Tables Having an Ordered Response Classification." *Biometrics* 35:403–15.

———. 1982. "An Extension of the Rasch Model for Ratings Providing Both Location and Dispersion Parameters." *Psychometrika* 47:105–13.

———. 1995. "Distinctive and Incompatible Properties of Two Common Classes of IRT Models for Graded Responses." *Applied Psychological Measurement* 19:101–19.

Bhapkar, Vasant P. 1966. "A Note on the Equivalence of Two Test Criteria for Hypotheses in Categorical Data." *Journal of the American Statistical Association* 61:228–35.

Bechtel, Gordon G. 1991. "Probabilistic Dimensionality: A Study of Confidence and Intention." In *Frontiers of Mathematical Psychology: Essays in Honor of Clyde Coombs*, edited by Donald R. Brown and J. E. Keith Smith, 80–109. New York: Springer-Verlag.

———. 1995. "Quality Control in East and West German Satisfaction Indicators." In *Proceedings of the International Conference on Survey Measurement and Process Quality*, 6–11. Alexandria, VA: American Statistical Association.

———. 1996. "German Life Quality After the Wall: An Application of Categorical Data Analysis." In *Social Science & Statistics: A Conference in Honor of the Late Clifford C. Clogg*, The Pennsylvania State University.

Bechtel, Gordon G., Piet M. Vanden Abeele, and Anne Marie DeMeyer. 1993. "The Sociotropic Aspect of Consumer Confidence." *Journal of Economic Psychology* 14:615–33.

Biart, Michel, and Peter Praet. 1987. "The Contribution of Opinion Surveys in Forecasting Aggregate Demand in the Four Main EC Countries." *Journal of Economic Psychology* 8:409–28.

Clogg, Clifford C., and Edward S. Shihadeh. 1994. *Statistical Models for Ordinal Variables*. Thousand Oaks, CA: Sage.

Dawes, Robyn M. 1991. "Social Dilemmas, Economic Self-Interest, and Evolutionary Theory." In *Frontiers of Mathematical Psychology: Essays in Honor of Clyde Coombs*, edited by Donald R. Brown and J. E. Keith Smith, 53–79. New York: Springer-Verlag.

Gulliksen, Harold. 1954. "A Least Squares Solution for Successive Intervals Assuming Unequal Standard Deviations." *Psychometrika* 19:117–39.

Hardin, Garrett R. 1968. "The Tragedy of the Commons." *Science* 162:1243–48.

Jones, Lyle V. 1960. "Some Invariant Findings Under the Method of Successive Intervals." In *Psychological Scaling: Theory and Applications*, edited by Harold Gulliksen and Samuel Messick, 7–20. New York: Wiley.

Katona, George. 1975. *Psychological Economics*. New York: Elsevier.

———. 1979. "Toward a Macropsychology." *American Psychologist* 34:118–26.

Kinder, Donald R., and D. Roderick Kiewiet. 1984. "Sociotropic Politics: The American Case." In *Controversies in Voting Behavior*, 2nd ed., edited by Richard G. Niemi and Herbert F. Weisberg, 210–38. Washington: Congressional Quarterly.

Koch, Gary G., J. Richard Landis, Jean L. Freeman, Daniel H. Freeman, Jr., and Robert G. Lehnen. 1977. "A General Methodology for the Analysis of Experiments with Repeated Measurement of Categorical Data." *Biometrics* 33:133–58.

Landis, J. Richard, Michael E. Miller, Charles S. Davis, and Gary G. Koch. 1988. "Some General Methods for the Analysis of Categorical Data in Longitudinal Studies." *Statistics in Medicine* 7:109–37.

Linden, Fabian. 1982. "The Consumer as Forecaster." *Public Opinion Quarterly* 46:353–60.

McCullagh, Peter. 1980. "Regression Models for Ordinal Data." *Journal of the Royal Statistical Society, Series B* 42:109–42.

McCullagh, Peter, and John A. Nelder. 1989. *Generalized Linear Models*, 2nd ed. London: Chapman and Hall.

Meehl, Paul E. 1977. "The Selfish Voter Paradox and the Thrown-away Vote Argument." *American Political Science Review* 71:11–30.

Mellenbergh, Gideon J. 1995. "Conceptual Notes on Models for Discrete Polytomous Item Responses." *Applied Psychological Measurement* 19:91–100.

Neyman, Jerzy. 1949. "Contribution to the Theory of the χ^2 Test." In *Proceedings of the Berkeley Symposium on Mathematical Statistics and Probability*, 239–73. Berkeley: University of California Press.

Praet, Peter. 1985. "Endogenizing Consumers' Expectations in Four Major EC Countries." *Journal of Economic Psychology* 6:255–69.

Praet, Peter, and Jozef Vuchelen. 1984. "The Contribution of E. C. Consumer Surveys in Forecasting Consumer Expenditures: An Econometric Analysis for Four Major Countries." *Journal of Economic Psychology* 5:101–24.

Rasch, Georg. 1961. "On General Laws and the Meaning of Measurement in Psychology." In *Proceedings of the Fourth Berkeley Symposium on Mathematical Statistics and Probability, Vol. 4*, 321–33. Berkeley: University of California Press.

Samejima, Fumiko. 1972. "A General Model for Free-Response Data." *Psychometrika Monograph Supplement* 37 (no. 1, part 2).

SAS Institute. 1989. SAS/STAT User's Guide, Version 6, 4th ed., vol. 1. Cary, NC: SAS Institute.

Scheffé, Henry. 1959. *The Analysis of Variance*. New York: Wiley.

Stokes, Maura, W., Charles S. Davis, and Gary G. Koch. 1995. *Categorical Data Analysis Using the SAS System.* Cary, NC: SAS Institute.

The Economist. 1996. "Learning to Cope." *The Economist Newspaper Limited* 339 (no. 7960):13–14.

Thurstone, Louis L. 1925. "A Method of Scaling Psychological and Educational Tests." *The Journal of Educational Psychology* 16:433–51.

Torgerson, Warren S. 1958. *Theory and Methods of Scaling*. New York: Wiley.

Vanden Abeele, Piet M. 1988. "Economic Agents' Expectations in a Psychological Perspective." In *Handbook of Economic Psychology*, edited by W. Fred van Raaij, Gery M. van Veldhoven, and Karl-Erik Warneryd, 478–515. Dordrecht: Kluwer Academic Publishers.

MATCHING WITH MULTIPLE CONTROLS TO ESTIMATE TREATMENT EFFECTS IN OBSERVATIONAL STUDIES

Herbert L. Smith*

Matching to control for covariates in the estimation of treatment effects is not common in sociology, where multivariate data are most often analyzed using multiple regression and its generalizations. Matching can be a useful way to estimate these effects, especially when the treatment condition is comparatively rare in a population, and controls are numerous but mostly unlike the treatment cases. Matching on numerous covariates is abetted by the estimation of propensity scores, or functions of the probability that cases are treatments rather than controls. This procedure is illustrated in the estimation of the effects of an organizational innovation on Medicare mortality within hospitals; the data set is very large, but innovative hospitals few, and many of the remaining hospitals are quite unlike the hospitals constituting the treatment subsample. Results are based on a variance-components model that is extended to consider the effects of an additional covariate. They show effects of the organizational innovation comparable to those estimated via multiple regression models but with substantially reduced standard errors.

This research was supported in part from grants by the Baxter Foundation and the National Institutes of Health (R01 NR02280) (Linda H. Aiken, Principal Investigator). I thank Linda Aiken and Eileen Lake, who proposed the study used here as an example; Debbie McIlvaine, who broached the idea of treating the problem via matching, and who assisted with data manipulation and computation; Tim Cheney, Suzanne Cole, and Linzhu Tian, who also assisted at various stages in this research; and Adrian Raftery, Paul Rosenbaum, and two anonymous reviewers, whose helpful comments are much appreciated. E-mail: hsmith@pop.upenn.edu
*University of Pennsylvania

325

1. INTRODUCTION

Standard discussions of methods of covariate adjustment in observational studies (e.g., Cochran and Rubin 1973; Kish 1987, chap. 4) give a great deal of attention to matching, but in sociology, where observational studies are the norm, matching is little used. This is ironic given that important statistical developments in matching (e.g., Rubin 1973a, 1973b, 1979; Rosenbaum and Rubin 1983, 1984, 1985a, 1985b; Rubin and Thomas 1992a, 1992b, 1996) have a lineal descent from problems in matching raised in sociological studies (Freedman and Hawley 1949, 1950; Freedman 1950; Althauser and Rubin 1970).

Matching can be a very useful method for estimating the effects of factors whose presence is most often found in the "extremes" of a larger population. Sometimes matching is used in such circumstances, but more often multiple regression is applied. Thus Rosenbaum (1986) uses matching to investigate the effects of dropping out of school on test scores for cognitive functioning, but Alwin (1974) uses multiple regression to estimate the effects of attending "prestigious colleges and universities" on occupational status. Both studies have in common large data sets (High School and Beyond, the Wisconsin Longitudinal Study) in which the treatment condition (dropping out of school, attending a prestigious college) is less common than the alternative, and assignment to the treatment rather than control condition is a strong function of other factors (e.g., family background) affecting the outcome of interest (cognitive functioning, occupational status).

The dearth of matching studies involving large data sets is the result not only of the popularity of regression models but of two perceived problems with matching.[1] The first is statistical inefficiency—creating matches for comparatively rare treatments requires "throwing away" a lot of data. However, throwing away irrelevant controls is not necessarily a bad thing. It diminishes bias associated with imbalance between treatments and controls in the distribution of covariates (Rubin 1973a). This imbalance tends to inflate the analysis-of-covariance estimated standard error for the treatment effect (Snedecor and Cochran 1980:368 and 380; Rosenbaum and Rubin 1983:48). Matching, by reducing covariate imbalance and inducing

---

[1]These two problems have been variously labeled "incomplete matching" (Freedman 1950), "attrition" and "incomplete or imperfect matching" (Althauser and Rubin 1970), and "incomplete matching" and "inexact matching" (Rosenbaum and Rubin 1985b).

a correlation between treatments and controls, can result in a lower standard error of the treatment effect, even with a substantial reduction in the number of controls (Rubin and Thomas 1996, sec. 5). Matching also helps to specify the range of covariates, or subpopulation, over which the treatment effect can reasonably be expected to obtain.

The second is the difficulty in finding good matches—as the number of covariates increases linearly, the data demands increase geometrically. Even in a very large data set, it is difficult to find controls with identical or near identical values on more than a small number of variables (Rosenbaum 1996:184–85). However, advances in the statistical theory of matching allow for matching on a scalar summary of a potentially large set of observed covariates. When this matching is exact, it creates equivalence of treatment and control samples with respect to the multivariate distribution of these covariates (Rosenbaum and Rubin 1983, 1985a; Rubin and Thomas 1996).

In this paper, I consider an example of how, when controls are many and treatments are few, matching compares with multivariate regression in the estimation of treatment effects. I show how, when there is more than one control per case, analysis of matched samples can usefully proceed with reference to standard variance-components models (i.e., analysis of variance, analysis of covariance). The analysis presented here differs from other illustrations of matching in its emphasis on the strengths and weaknesses of multiple matching, especially as they relate to the specification of the scalar summary on which treatments and controls are matched.

2. REGRESSION WITH "SKEWED" TREATMENTS

I illustrate the utility of matching, and some problems with multiple regression for "skewed" treatments, with reference to a study by Aiken, Smith, and Lake (1994), which considers the effects of the organization of nursing care within hospitals on inpatient mortality. There are several dozen hospitals that, during the 1980s, were identified as having a variety of desirable organizational characteristics related to nursing. These were (1) a "flat" organization of the nursing department with few supervisors, and a chief nurse executive with a strong position in the bureaucratic hierarchy of the hospital; (2) nurse autonomy to make clinical decisions within their areas of competence and to control their own practice; (3) control over the practice environment, including decentralized decision making at the unit level, a limit to the proportion of nurses who were new graduates, and established mechanisms to facilitate communication between nurses and physicians; (4) organization of nurses' clinical responsibilities at the unit level to promote accountability and continuity of care; and (5) an established culture signifying the importance of nursing in the overall mission of the institution—for example, as reflected, in salaried practice as opposed to hourly wages (Aiken et al. 1994:774).

These hospitals were subsequently dubbed "magnet hospitals," because they were originally identified from among a larger set of hospitals, in competitive labor markets, that were reputed to be good places to practice nursing. In neither the original studies selecting these hospitals nor the subsequent studies identifying their organizational characteristics was there any discussion or measurement of patient outcomes. However, Aiken et al. (1994) argue that there should be a negative relationship between the organizational features of the magnet hospital and a key "output" of hospitals—the mortality of patients. The operant mechanism is a link between the organizational characteristics described above and enhanced professional autonomy, control over practice, and status (relative to physicians) among nurses, all of which are related to timely decision making with respect to patient care.[2]

The analytic problem is that the "effect" of these magnet hospitals is only defined relative to the mortality experience of other hospitals, and there are many hospitals that are not magnet hospitals—a ratio of over 100 to one. In fact, the Health Care Finance Administration (HCFA) data tapes for 1988 contain Medicare mortality data for the 39 magnet hospitals and an additional 5053 hospitals with at least 100 Medicare discharges.[3] The magnet hospitals have a mortality rate (expressed as deaths per thousand) of 105 with a standard deviation (SD) of 21. The other hospitals have a mortality rate of 126 and an SD of 35. The difference between the two (-21) is very large and highly significant ($|Z| = 6.13$, two-sample Z-test).

[2]See Aiken et al. (1994) for further elaboration of this argument, the linchpin of which is that, "Nurses are the only professional caregivers in hospitals who are at the bedside of hospital patients around the clock" (p. 771). The empirical demonstration that the organizational features associated with magnet hospitals do enhance the autonomy, control, and status of nurses relies on data and methods different from those presented here.

[3]The HCFA data for 1988 are relevant because they are bracketed by two years (1986 and 1989) in which the organizational characteristics of the magnet hospitals were studied and redocumented. The use of data for 1988 is arbitrary in the sense that, by the same criterion, data for 1987 would be equally relevant.

This is, however, not a good estimate of the reduction in mortality attributable to being a magnet hospital. The magnet hospitals are not a random subset of all hospitals appearing in the data set, and most of the potential control hospitals are so different from the magnet hospitals as to make suspect their relevance to the estimation of the effect associated with being a magnet hospital. The HCFA tapes contain information on additional organizational variables that have been found to be correlated with mortality, including, for example, hospital ownership (public, private for-profit, or private not-for-profit), whether or not the hospital is a teaching hospital, the hospital's financial status, and the proportion of physicians at the hospital that are board certified (e.g., Hartz et al. 1989; Al-Haider and Wan 1991). The literature on the organizational determinants of inpatient hospital mortality is longer on adumbrations of possible causes of mortality differentials among hospitals than it is on elaborations of the relationship among these predictor variables. It appears, however, that these variables are plausibly antecedent to the organization of nursing, in the sense that they may determine whether or not a hospital has the nursing organizational characteristics represented by a magnet hospital, but not vice versa. (This is most evident for variables such as ownership, hospital size, and size of metropolitan area, but less so for a variable such as physicians' qualifications, which may be jointly determined with the organizational attributes of nursing described above.) Thus, in estimating the effects of magnet hospitals on mortality, we shall need to adjust for the extent that these variables "select" hospitals into the magnet (or nonmagnet) rubric.

In regression I of Table 1, these variables are covariates in a regression of mortality rates on a dummy variable indicating whether a hospital is a magnet hospital or not. With these controls, the estimated reduction in mortality associated with being a magnet hospital is reduced to 7.5 per 1000, and the standard error (5.5) is so large that we have little confidence that there is any real effect.

In addition, differences in mortality rates between hospitals reflect differences in the health of the patients they serve (Silber, Rosenbaum, and Ross 1995). The HCFA data files contain an estimate of predicted mortality, based on the following patient characteristics: age, sex, the presence of four comorbidities (cancer, cardiovascular disease, liver disease, and renal disease), the type and source of admission, and the presence and risk of hospitalizations in the previous six months (Dubois, Brook, and Rogers 1987). It is unclear as to the logical status of this measure of patient

TABLE 1
Regression of Medicare Mortality Rate per Thousand on Magnet Hospital Dichotomy and Covariates, for 5092 Hospitals in 1988 HCFA Data File

Regressors	Regression I		Regression II	
	Coefficient	t-statistic	Coefficient	t-statistic
Magnet hospital	−7.46	−1.36	−4.70	−1.15
Private for-profit hospital	−11.80	−7.13	−5.30	−4.28
Private not-for-profit hospital	−8.50	−7.19	−6.13	−6.94
Teaching hospital	5.14	1.81	3.38	1.59
Average daily census (ADC)	.0778	5.22	.0075	0.67
Hospital beds	−.0679	−5.16	−.0022	−0.22
Medicare discharges (000s)	−.759	−1.41	−.729	−1.81
Payroll (millions of dollars)	.181	2.42	.021	0.38
Occupancy rate (%)	.0651	1.56	−.0422	−1.35
Board-certified physicians (%)	−.0684	−2.67	−.0128	−0.67
Payroll/hospital beds (in $1,000s)	−.0898	−3.78	−.0721	−4.06
High-technology index score	−3.59	−5.50	−0.27	−0.55
Emergency visits/ADC	.0190	5.08	.0097	3.46
Metropolitan size (5 pt. scale)	0.714	2.65	0.533	2.65
Predicted mortality rate[a]			0.958	63.47
Constant	135.00	21.6	12.04	2.38
R^2	.078		.486	
Root mean squared error	33.6		25.1	

[a]This is the mortality rate predicted for the hospital by HCFA on the basis of the demographic and health status characteristics of patients; see text for details. Controlling for this variable is akin to standardizing on patient composition.

characteristics—whether patient characteristics determine some of the organizational features of hospitals, or whether patient populations are determined by the organizational characteristics of hospitals. If the latter, then inclusion of a concomitant variable that has been affected by the "treatments" creates some problems in the interpretation of organizational "effects" (Rosenbaum 1984). With this caveat in mind, regression II of Table 1 adds patient-adjusted predicted mortality as a covariate. The coefficient of determination is far greater than that of regression I, but there are far fewer organizational effects, and the estimated difference in mortality between magnet and other hospitals is now under 5 per 1000, with a t-statistic that is still too low to attach any significance to this effect.

Now let us reconsider these regression estimates of the treatment effect using ideas adapted from Rubin (1973a). Let Y be the response variable (mortality), let S be an indicator variable for whether an observation is a treatment ($S = t$) or not ($S = c$) (magnet hospital or control hospital), and let X be a set of covariates $\{X_1, X_2, \ldots, X_k\}$ with realization x. The "effect" of the treatment condition for a fixed level of X is

$$\tau(x) = E(Y|X = x, S = t) - E(Y|X = x, S = c), \tag{1}$$

where $E(\cdot)$ denotes expectation in the population. There are, in principle, as many observable effects $\tau(x)$ as there are points x with observations on both $E(Y|X = x, S = t)$ and $E(Y|X = x, S = c)$. (Whether these effects are reasonably interpretable as *causal* effects depends on the validity of an additional assumption, to be discussed in the following section.)

A more general treatment effect, or average treatment effect, can be defined as

$$\tau = E_X\{E(Y|X = x, S = t) - E(Y|X = x, S = c)\} = E_X\{\tau(x)\}, \tag{2}$$

where $E_X\{\cdot\}$ is an expectation calculated over the distribution of X. This nonparametric definition of an average treatment effect can create a problem in practice, since, for X of even modest dimensions, only in an imaginary superpopulation will it be the case that both $E(Y|X = x, S = t)$ and $E(Y|X = x, S = c)$ are simultaneously defined. This problem is variously addressed by *smoothing* in nonparametric regression (Härdle 1990, chap. 2), by matching using propensity scores (Rosenbaum and Rubin 1983), and—most commonly—by parametric regression.

Under the multivariate linear model, $E(Y|X = x, S = t) = \alpha_t + x\beta_t$ is the regression of Y on X in the treatment group, and $E(Y|X = x, S = c) =$

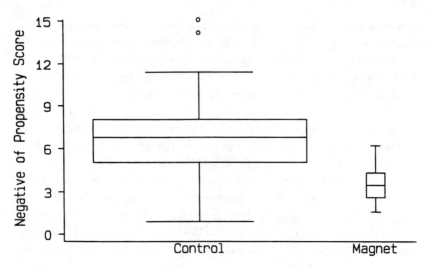

FIGURE 1. Box plot (box width proportional to square root of sample size) showing distribution of a linear composite of covariates (the propensity score) among control and magnet hospitals.

$\alpha_c + x\boldsymbol{\beta}_c$ is the regression of Y on X in the control group. When $\boldsymbol{\beta}_t = \boldsymbol{\beta}_c$ the response surfaces are parallel (Rubin 1973a), which establishes a single treatment effect, $\tau = \tau(x) = \alpha_t - \alpha_c$. It is also obviates the need to consider where in a sample both $E(Y|X = x, S = t)$ and $E(Y|X = x, S = c)$ are defined. When the response surfaces are not parallel, i.e., when $\boldsymbol{\beta}_t = \boldsymbol{\beta}_c$,

$$\tau(x) = (\alpha_t - \alpha_c) + x(\boldsymbol{\beta}_t - \boldsymbol{\beta}_c). \qquad (3)$$

The estimated treatment effect varies as a linear function of x, and the estimation of τ, via equation (2), can depend greatly on the range and density of x used in the definition of $E_X\{\cdot\}$.

In the magnet hospital and similar problems (e.g., Rosenbaum and Rubin 1984), the distribution of treatment cases is strongly skewed relative to the distribution of controls.[4] See Figure 1, a box plot showing the distribution of a linear composite of X for magnet and control hospitals. (The linear composite is a *propensity score*, defined in the next section.) Over half the control cases have composite values of x greater than the highest composite value among magnet hospitals. When the expectation in

[4]This is Althauser and Rubin's (1970) "Situation II"—a smaller treatment sample distributed far in the tail of a larger control sample.

equation (2) is taken over the density of X in the entire sample, or even uniformly over the range of X in the sample, the calculation involves averaging over a potentially large region in which $E(Y|X = x, S = t)$ hence $\tau(x)$ (in the sense of equation (1)), is poorly or not at all defined. When $Pr(S = t) \ll Pr(S = c)$, as in the magnet hospital study, it is difficult to reject $\beta_t = \beta_c$, but this is hardly strong evidence in favor of the assumption of parallel response surfaces. The pooled regression slope is dominated by β_c, which is based in large part on control observations for which there are few or no treatment counterparts. The parallel regression assumption is a particularly strong assumption with skewed treatment variables, since it involves extrapolation where there is very little support (Rubin 1973b, 1979; Rosenbaum and Rubin 1983, sec. 3.2; Manski 1995, chap. 1; see also Snedecor and Cochran 1980:380).

An analogous issue arises when we consider the circumstances under which equation (2) is an average *causal* effect (Holland 1988). This occurs when treatment assignment is *strongly ignorable* (Rosenbaum and Rubin 1983). The assumption of strongly ignorable treatment assignment has two parts. The first is that, conditional on x, assignment of observations to treatment or control status be independent of the *response set*, where, for unit i, the response set is both the observed response given s_i and the counterfactual—the response that would have been observed had s_i taken on the alternative value.[5] Claims of the plausibility of this assumption are legion in sociology, which is overwhelmingly devoted to the study of observational, nonexperimental data. Evaluation of these claims shows up in discussions of specification error, omitted variable bias, and, most subtly, selection effects, which occur when observational units choose treatment or control status on the basis of anticipated unit-specific outcomes.

However, it is the second assumption of strong ignorability that most parallels the issue of support in the estimation of treatment effects. This assumption is that, conditional on x, the probability that a unit receives the treatment is less than unity and greater than zero—i.e., $0 < Pr(S = t|x) < 1$. This is essentially an *existence condition* for the response

---

[5]Adapting slightly the notation of Rosenbaum and Rubin (1983), the ith unit has, in principle, a response r_{ti} under assignment to the treatment condition and r_{ci} under assignment to the control condition. However, only one of the two responses is observable. I am referring to (r_{ti}, r_{ci}) as the response set for the ith unit, and (r_t, r_c) as the response set across all units. The first condition of strongly ignorable treatment assignment stipulates that $(r_t, r_c) \perp s|x$ (where "$\perp$" is the independence operator).

set, since when this condition does not hold, the counterfactual does not exist—not even conceptually. This assumption is given far less consideration by sociologists. One reason for this may be that sociologists tend to make inferences to large, variegated populations where, with sufficient effort, even the oddest combinations of characteristics can be found.[6] The second reason is that acknowledgment of the impossibility of counterfactuals under certain combinations of x is tantamount to acknowledgment of the manipulability criterion for causal inference (Holland 1986). Under this formulation, treatment units that could not possibly be made into control units, and vice versa, can contribute no information regarding the causal effect of the treatment. The manipulability criterion for causal inference has been difficult to assimilate in a discipline that routinely reports measurements of the *causal* effects of sex, race, and age, *inter alia*, on various phenomena (Smith 1990).

Short of the philosophical conundrums raised by this existence condition, I think it does make sense to question whether we wish to define treatment effects using data for which $Pr(S = t|x) \rightarrow 1$ or $Pr(S = t|x) \rightarrow 0$. Restricting estimation to samples in which, for fixed x, there are both treatments and controls has the salutary effect of delimiting the range of our inferences, and specifying the conditions under which manipulation of the treatment will plausibly result in the estimated effect. I do not claim that the necessary restrictions cannot be built into the parametric linear regression model; I claim only that they occur quite naturally in the matching model, to which we now turn.

3. MATCHING VIA PROPENSITY SCORES

When X is multivariate, matching of treatment cases and control cases is abetted by matching on a univariate function of X. This is the *linear propensity score* (Rubin and Thomas 1992b), defined as $Z = f\{Pr(S = t|X)\}$.[7] The probability that each observation is a treatment is not known, but it can be estimated from the data. The two most common models are the linear discriminant function or linear probability model, in which case $f\{\cdot\}$ is the identity link and $\hat{z}$ is a fitted probability; and the logistic regression model, in which case $f\{\cdot\}$ is the logit function and $\hat{z}$ is a fitted logit. Both models

---

[6]As Fienberg (1980:140) observes, just because cross-classified sample data show no Jewish farmers in Iowa does not mean that there are no Jewish farmers in Iowa.

[7]Berk and Newton (1985) provide the first use of propensity scores in sociological research, albeit as a form of analysis of covariance, not matching.

have desirable properties from the standpoint of matching, in the sense that both will lead to "balance" in the distribution of x in the treatment and matched control samples (Rosenbaum and Rubin 1983, 1985a; Rubin and Thomas 1992b, 1996).

Little advice is available regarding which functional form to use. Rosenbaum and Rubin (1985a) match on logits in their example. Rosenbaum (1986) uses a linear probability model to generate propensity scores but notes that "in principle, a method such as logistic regression would have been preferable" (p. 210); see also Rosenbaum (1996:185). Preference for matching on fitted logits presumably derives from the well-known shortcomings of the linear probability model—specifically, the unlikeliness of the functional form when the response variable is highly skewed, and predictions that are outside the 0-1 bounds of probabilities. However, when the purpose of a model is classification, not the estimation of structural coefficients, then it is less clear that these criticisms apply.

More advice is available regarding the inclusion (or exclusion) of covariates in the propensity score model. Rubin and Thomas (1996:253) recommend *against* "trimming" models in the name of parsimony:

> Unless a variable can be excluded because there is a consensus that it is unrelated to the outcome variables or not a proper covariate, it is advisable to include it in the propensity score model even if it is not statistically significant. Excluding potentially relevant variables should be done only when the resultant matched samples are closely balanced with respect to these variables as will typically occur when the treated and full control sample means of the excluded variables are exceptionally close or when the excluded variables are highly correlated with variables already in the propensity score model. Including variables whose treated and control sample means differ only because of sampling variability and not because of substantial differences in their population means contributes only modestly to the difficulty of finding adequate matches on the estimated propensity scores.

By these criteria, there are reasons both for and against the inclusion of all of the covariates appearing in Table 1 (save the patient-adjusted predicted mortality rate) in the equation for estimating the propensity score.[8] All of these variables are known or hypothesized to be associated with the outcome variable, all differ significantly in the treatment and control samples (Aiken et al. 1994, table 2), and some (e.g., measures of the size of the hospital, such as the average daily census) are clearly "proper covariates" in the sense that they may determine the treatment (versus control) status of each hospital. On the other hand, many of these variables are highly correlated with one another. Not only can they thus be removed with little discernible effect on the fit of the prediction model, but the excluded potential predictors are, like the included predictors, balanced in the resultant matched samples.

The first ("additive") model in Table 2 is the logistic regression of the magnet hospital dummy variable on the covariates from regression I in Table 1. The model shows five of the 13 variables with t-statistics in excess of two. This model is not well-specified from the standpoint of hypothesis testing, first, because the number of predictor variables (13) is high relative to the number of magnet hospitals (39); second, because there is high collinearity among several of the predictor variables. However, the goals of both models are prediction (classification) and data reduction, so redundancy and collinearity are of little account (see also Berk and Newton 1985:257–58). Because there are many controls per hospital, the model achieves excellent balance with respect to the various covariates, at least based on the first several matches per treatment hospital.[9]

In the illustrative results that follow, matching is on the propensity score as estimated by the additive logistic response model (i.e., the coefficients in the first column of Table 2).[10] However, it is important to recognize that when the ratio of potential controls to treatments is very high, different models for generating propensity scores can result in great dif-

---

[8]I have omitted the patient-adjusted predicted mortality rate as a predictor in the propensity score model, first, because of its ambiguous causal ordering with respect to the treatment condition (discussed above); and, second, for the didactic purpose of illustrating, below, the regression analysis of matched data.

[9]The issue of balance or its antithesis—bias—is taken up in greater detail below, in the discussion of multiple matching.

[10]In addition to its superiority as a functional form on theoretical grounds, this logistic response model is equal to or better than a corresponding linear probability model on the criteria of sensitivity (percentage of magnet hospitals classified correctly) and specificity (percentage of control hospitals classified correctly) when the classification "cutoff" is .0077, the proportion of magnet hospitals in the full sample. Both models have a sensitivity of 90 percent (35 of the 39 magnet hospitals have predicted probabilities above this value), but the specificity is higher for the logistic model: 78 percent versus 68 percent.

TABLE 2
Logistic Response Models for the Generation of Propensity Scores

Regressors	Additive Model		Trimmed, Quadratic Model	
	Coefficient	t-statistic	Coefficient	t-statistic
Private for-profit hospital	0.511	0.80	—	—
Private not-for-profit hospital	0.397	0.46	—	—
Teaching hospital	0.404	.080	—	—
Average daily census (ADC)	−0.014	−2.19	0.014	3.18
ADC squared	—	—	-1.69×10^{-5}	−2.89
Hospital beds	.0089	2.11	—	—
Medicare discharges (000s)	0.171	1.31	—	—
Payroll (millions of dollars)	.0012	0.09	—	—
Occupancy rate (%)	.0056	2.37	—	—
Board-certified physicians (%)	.0069	0.45	—	—
Payroll/hospital beds (in $1,000s)	.0051	1.21	—	—
High-technology index score	0.454	3.10	0.392	2.98
Emergency visits/ADC	−.0007	0.28	—	—
Metropolitan size (5 pt. scale)	0.284	2.42	1.300	2.04
Metropolitan size squared	—	—	−0.131	−1.67
Constant	−12.64	−5.40	−9.73	−7.47
Pseudo-R^2	.223		.227	
Root mean squared error	.086		.086	
Log-likelihood	−177.78		−176.94	

ferences in which units end up as the control sample. An alternative, parsimonious specification of the propensity score model that emphasizes variable selection (cf. Rosenbaum and Rubin 1984) and nonlinear (in this case, quadratic) response surfaces (Rubin 1973b) is given in the final two columns of Table 2. The propensity scores generated under the two models in Table 2 are highly correlated with one another ($r = .82$). But when each treatment hospital is matched to a single control (in a manner described below), only one of the 39 controls (3 percent) is the same under the two specifications of models for propensity scores. When there are five matches per treatment (195 controls), only 17 percent of the controls are the same across specifications; and it is not until there are 15 matches per treatment (585 controls) that half or more of the controls (52 percent) are chosen by both models. This question of whether—or when—different models for propensity scores will lead to different analytic results is taken up below, in the section on comparative results.

Given estimated propensity scores, magnet hospitals (treatments) are matched to other hospitals (controls) by a *random order, nearest available pair-matching* methods (Rubin 1973a). A set of random numbers is generated, one for each of the cases. Beginning with the lowest random number, and proceeding in random-number size order, each case is matched with the potential control with the nearest propensity score. That control, or "match," is then removed from the sample, so that no observation serves as the control for more than one case. When more than one match per treatment case is desired, the process is repeated, beginning with the generation of a new random number.

Random order, nearest available pair-matching is used because it is conceptually and computationally simple, and it has been shown to work reasonably well in comparison with more complex matching methods (Rosenbaum and Rubin 1985a). Moreover, in studies such as the magnet hospital study, where treatment cases are few, close matches plentiful, and there are few *a priori* reasons for ordering the importance of the matching covariates, it is doubtful whether more complicated matching procedures are necessary. Alternatives include first matching on key covariates, then doing random order, nearest available pair-matching on propensity scores within sets of these matches (Rosenbaum and Rubin 1985a; Rubin and Thomas 1992b), and methods that involve the Mahalanobis metric (Cochran and Rubin 1973; Rubin 1976, 1980), sometimes in combination with propensity scores (Rosenbaum and Rubin 1985a). Matching schemes in which cases serve as controls to more than one treatment are also possible

(Gu and Rosenbaum 1993; Rosenbaum 1995, chap. 9). However, in the balance of the paper, I consider only the issue of multiple controls for each treatment case, not multiple treatments for each control.

Multiple, as opposed to single, matching per treatment case has certain advantages. Multiple matches make more use of the available data and can thereby increase the efficiency of the estimation of differences between treatments and controls (Ury 1975). Multiple matches permit the use of variance-components models in the analysis of these differences, a topic I take up below. Sooner or later, however, all of the really "close" matches will be used up, and differences between cases and controls will reflect the effect not only of the treatment under study but of poorly matched confounds as well. This is the problem of *bias*, or differences between matched treatments and matched controls in the distribution of *x*. Rubin (1973b, 1979) shows how matching with regression can eliminate bias; but when controls are so plentiful it is preferable to be able to conduct analyses without further covariance adjustments for *x*.

Figure 2 shows the bias in from one to 15 matches per treatment in the HCFA data set, along with the increase in the *relative efficiency* of the paired-difference estimator expected as the number of matches per

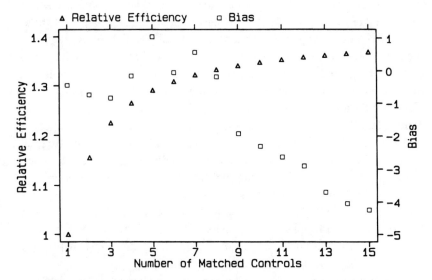

FIGURE 2. Trade-off between relative efficiency and bias with multiple matches per treatment.

treatment increases. Relative efficiency is the ratio of the standard error with one match per case to the standard error with m matches per case. It is calculated as $\sqrt{(m \times 2)/(m + 1)}$, under the (empirically valid) assumption that the standard errors are more or less equal in the treatment and matched control samples (cf. Ury 1975:644–45). Even an infinitely large number of matched controls would increase efficiency by only a factor of $\sqrt{2}$, and over half of the potential increase in efficiency occurs after only three matches, so there is little point in multiple matching once bias is apparent. Bias in Figure 2 is the difference in propensity scores between treatments and matched controls, expressed as a t-statistic for paired data differences $(\overline{\Delta z_i} = \sum_{m=1}^{M} z_{i0} - z_{im})/M$, where z_{i0} is the estimated propensity score for the ith treatment unit, and z_{im} is the estimated propensity score for the mth matched control to the ith treatment unit, and there are M matched controls per treatment. The paired t-statistic is the measure most relevant to the evaluation of bias in the estimate of treatment effects due to insufficiently controlled covariates (Rosenbaum and Rubin 1985a:36). Because this bias measure is an average of the bias across all M matches, the biasing effects of an additional match per treatment must be fairly strong to cause a marked shift in the measure such as that apparent in Figure 2, after the eighth match per case.

The reason for this marked drop-off is a "floor effect": The magnet hospitals are concentrated in the area with the highest propensity scores (or lowest negative propensity scores, to avoid references to ranked values that are all negative). Although there are control hospitals with even lower negative propensity scores than the lowest-ranked magnet hospital, there are not many, and eventually all the potential matches below the lowest treatment cases are exhausted. The matching algorithm then must search for matches above the treatment case only, which thereby leads to bias. This floor effect is evident in Figure 3, which plots the negative propensity score of each treatment hospital against its first, fifth, tenth, and fifteenth match. Fifth matches are as good as first matches. By the tenth match, however, all but one of the treatment hospitals with negative propensity scores below three are matching to controls with propensity scores just under three. By the fifteenth match, all of these treatment cases are matching to controls with negative propensity scores of around 3.5. For the treatment cases most like controls—i.e., the half with negative propensity scores above 3.5—excellent matches are still plentiful.

Examination of individual covariates can be worthwhile if it is essential that one (or more) be finely balanced by the matching procedure.

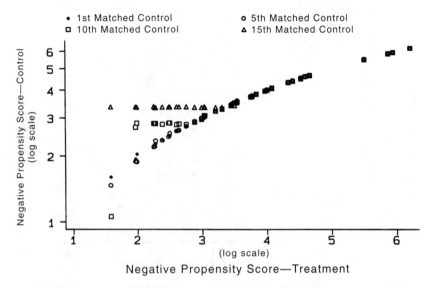

FIGURE 3. "Floor effects" with increasing number of matches are evident for the treatments with the lowest negative propensity scores.

But because the propensity score combines information from a large number of covariates, it is a more reliable measure of bias than individual covariates alone. This is evident in Figure 4, which displays paired t-statistics for cumulative bias in four of the five covariates that were significantly predictive of magnet hospital status in the logistic regression. The signs of the t-statistics have been reversed so that they parallel the t-statistics for the negative propensity scores in Figure 2. Three of the four variables trend downward and are no more biased, in absolute terms, after 12 matches than after the first match. All four variables show more bias on the second match than on the seventh. There is no evidence that bias is worsening substantially after the eighth match (as there is in Figure 2), and none of the 60 t-statistics plotted in this figure approaches 2 in absolute value (i.e., statistical significance).

4. A VARIANCE-COMPONENTS MODEL
FOR DATA WITH MULTIPLE MATCHES

For I treatment cases, each matched to M controls, let y_{im} be the response in the mth match to the ith treatment, $I = 1,\ldots,I$, $m = 1,\ldots,M$. Denote by

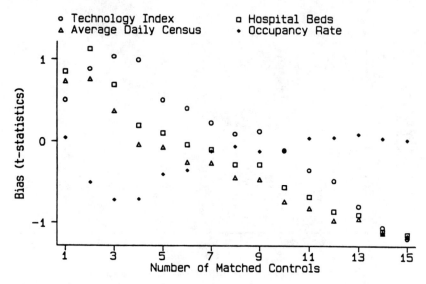

FIGURE 4. None of these four covariates show significant bias through fifteen matches
per treatment.

y_{i0} the response for the ith treatment case. Then there are $I \times M$ differences
between matched cases and controls,

$$\Delta y_{im} = y_{i0} - y_{im}. \tag{4}$$

A variance components model (Snedecor and Cochran 1980, chap. 13;
Bryk and Raudenbush 1992, chap. 3) for the effect of treatment on response is

$$\Delta y_{im} = \beta_{0i} + e_{im}, \tag{5}$$

$$\beta_{0i} = \gamma_{00} + u_{0i}, \tag{6}$$

where $E(e_{im}) = E(u_{0i}) = Cov(e_{im}, u_{0i}) = 0$, $Var(e_{im}) = \sigma^2$, and $Var(u_{0i}) =$
τ_{00}. This model posits an average treatment effect (γ_{00}) across all comparisons, as well as a randomly varying unit treatment effect ($\beta_{0i} = \gamma_{00} + u_{0i}$).
When there are equal numbers of controls matched to each treatment
case, tests of the hypothesis $\gamma_{00} = 0$ are equivalent to t-tests of paired

comparisons of case response with the average response of matched controls.[11]

Then why use the variance-components framework? First, one way to avoid bias, but not throw out "good" matches, is to have a match criterion for differences in propensity scores. If there are varying numbers of matches per treatment case, the paired comparison t-test is no longer equivalent to the random effects analysis-of-variance, and estimates from the latter are, in general, preferable.[12] This said, the differences in estimates according to method are not likely to be large. For example, consider a "very close" matching scheme, with treatments matched only to controls with propensity scores $<|.01|$ logits away, with a maximum of 15 matches per treatment case. The number of matches per treatment is distributed fairly uniformly on the interval 0–15, including three treatments with no matches. (These are the three hospitals with the lowest negative propensity scores.) The estimated mortality differential from the random effects model is -9.46 deaths per thousand, with a standard error (SE) of 3.87; the paired comparison t-test (on average differences) yields an estimate of -8.92, with an SE of 3.64.

Second, the decomposition of variance can be useful analytically. The test of the hypothesis $\tau_{00} = 0$ is the test of the assumption that the treatment effect is constant across all cases. In the magnet hospital study, with $M = 8$, $\hat{\gamma}_{00} = -8.05$ ($SE = 3.14$, $|t| = 2.57$), $\hat{\tau}_{00} = 310.6$, and $\hat{\sigma}^2 = 587.6$.[13] The assumption that magnet hospital effects are equivalent across all such hospitals is unsupported ($\chi^2 = 131$, $1 df$, p $< .0001$)[14]—τ_{00} is clearly greater than zero, and 35 percent ($\hat{\tau}_{00}/[\hat{\tau}_{00} + \hat{\sigma}^2]$) of the variance in the *effect* on mortality lies between blocks of matched mortality rate

---

[11]What the analyst *cannot* do is a t-test for paired differences in the pooled sample of $I \times M$ matches. This is equivalent to setting $u_{0i} = 0$ in equation (6), and ignores the data structure—in particular, the correlation of differences within blocks of matched pairs, where the "blocks" are sets of M matches per treatment. When the design is balanced—a constant number of matches per treatment—the estimated treatment effect will be equal to that obtained under the correct methods (i.e., a t-test for paired differences between the treatment response and the average response of matched controls, or the random effects analysis-of-variance), but the estimated standard error for this effect will be too small, by the factor $\sqrt{1 + (M - 1)\rho}$, where ρ is the intraclass correlation between matched-pair differences.

[12]The two methods are functionally equivalent to, respectively, between-effects and random-effects regression of matched-pair differences on a constant term.

[13]All parameters are estimated using STATA rfreg.ado routine for maximum-likelihood random effects regression.

[14]This is the Breusch and Pagan Lagrangian multiplier test for random effects (Amemiya 1985, sec. 4.5.1), as implemented in the STATA xttest0.ado routine.

differences. When it is meaningful to identify individual analytic units, as in the magnet hospital study, it may be advantageous to examine or highlight between-unit differences in estimated treatment effects. A good estimate of this effect (β_{0i}^*) is obtained by "shrinking back" the treatment-specific control-averaged mortality difference ($\overline{\Delta y}_i = [\sum_{m=1}^{M} \Delta y_{im}]/M$) toward the overall estimated treatment effect ($\hat{\gamma}_{00}$) via

$$\beta_{0i}^* = \lambda \overline{\Delta y}_i + (1 - \lambda)\hat{\gamma}_{00}, \tag{7}$$

where, with balanced data, $\lambda = \tau_{00}/(\tau_{00} + \sigma^2/M)$ is the reliability of the unit-specific treatment effect (Bryk and Raudenbush 1992, chap. 3; see also Searle, Casella, and McCulloch 1992, chap. 7).[15] For $M = 8$, the estimated reliability is .81. For $M = 2, 3, 5,$ and 7, the estimated reliabilities are, respectively, .44, .65, .73, and .80, so several matches are needed to obtain reasonably reliable estimates of hospital-specific treatment effects.

Third, the random effects, analysis of variance model generalizes readily to an analysis of covariance model, for inclusion of additional covariates. Earlier, in the presentation of results from multiple regression, it was noted that patient characteristics, as operationalized in the HCFA data by the regression-estimated predicted mortality rate, account for considerable interhospital variation in mortality, net of organizational covariates. The propensity scores generated in the previous section did not include the effects of predicted mortality. Predicted mortality rates (per thousand) are 112.6 in the magnet hospitals and 122.6 in the remainder of the HCFA sample. Matching on propensity scores eliminates some but not all of the difference in predicted mortality between treatment hospitals and matched controls: The average predicted mortality rates for $M = 1, 2, 5,$ and 8 are, respectively, 117.7, 115.9, 115.9, and 116.6. To adjust for these remaining differences, define x_{ij} as the value of an additional covariate (e.g., predicted mortality) for the mth control matched to the ith treatment, and x_{i0} as the value for the same covariate for the ith treatment case. Set $\Delta x_{im} = x_{i0} - x_{im}$ and $\overline{\Delta x}_i = [\sum_{m=1}^{M} \Delta x_{im}]/M$. Then a random-effects regression of Δy_{im} on within-block (Δx_{im}) and between-block ($\overline{\Delta x}_i$) differences in predicted mortality is (after Bryk and Raudenbush 1992, chap. 5):

$$\Delta y_{im} = \beta_{0i} + \beta_{1i}(\Delta x_{im} - \overline{\Delta x}_i) + e_{im}, \tag{8}$$

$$\beta_{0i} = \gamma_{00} + \gamma_{01}\overline{\Delta x}_i + u_{0i}, \tag{9}$$

$$\beta_{1i} = \gamma_{10} + u_{1i}, \tag{10}$$

---

[15]With unbalanced data—i.e., varying numbers of matches per control M_i—substitute $\lambda_i = \tau_{00}/(\tau_{00} + \sigma^2/M_i)$ for λ in equation (7).

where $E(e_{im}) = E(u_{0i}) = E(u_{1i}) = Cov(e_{im},u_{0i}) = Cov(e_{im},u_{1i}) = 0$, $Var(e_{im}) = \sigma^2$, $Var(u_{0i}) = \tau_{00}$, $Var(u_{i1}) = \tau_{11}$ and $Cov(u_{0i},u_{1i}) = \tau_{01}$. Estimation of this model suggests two empirical regularities in the magnet hospital data: (i) $\gamma_{01} = \gamma_{10} = 1$ and (ii) $\tau_{11} = \tau_{01} = 0$.[16] With these constraints, equations (8)–(10) reduce to a random effects analysis of variance of $\Delta y_{im} - \Delta x_{im}$—that is, the effect of magnet hospitals on *excess mortality*, or observed mortality minus mortality predicted by patient characteristics. Under this model, for $M = 8$, $\hat{\gamma}_{00} = -4.07$ (SE $= 1.94$, $|t| = 2.10$), $\hat{\tau}_{00} = 116.8$, and $\hat{\sigma}^2 = 237.0$. Approximately one-half of the observed mortality difference between magnet and matched control hospitals is attributable to differences in patient characteristics, as the estimate of γ_{00} shrinks from eight to four per thousand. Adjusting between-block differences in mortality by the average within-block difference in predicted mortality (equation [9]) reduces variation in estimated treatment effects by 62 percent (τ_{00} declines from 310.6 to 116.8), but the variance that remains is still significant ($\chi^2 = 119$, $1df$, p $< .0001$). Similarly, three-fifths of the original estimate of variance in estimated treatment effects within blocks of matched hospitals (σ^2) is attributable to uncontrolled differences in patient characteristics. These reductions in the variance components result in a comparable reduction in the estimated SE of $\hat{\gamma}_{00}$: A 95 percent CI for the average effect of magnet hospitals on mortality, with adjustment for hospital-specific predicted mortality, is from 0.3 to 7.9 fewer deaths per thousand.

5. COMPARATIVE RESULTS

Table 3 summarizes estimates of the magnet hospital treatment effect, with and without controls for predicted mortality, for single ($M = 1$) and multiple ($M = 8$ and $M = 15$) matches per treatment, based on propensity scores estimated from the two specifications shown in Table 2 ("additive" and "trimmed, quadratic"). For purposes of further comparison, estimates of the treatment effect from multiple regression models, with and without a control for predicted mortality, are reproduced in the last row of the table. (These estimates are those first shown in Table 1.) Previous investigations of the effect of misspecification of the propensity equation have assumed

[16]For $M = 8$, $\hat{\gamma}_{01} = 1.00$ (SE $= 0.13$), $\hat{\gamma}_{10} = 1.01$ (SE $= 0.05$), $\hat{\tau}_{11} = 0.03$ (SE $= 0.03$) and $\hat{\tau}_{01} = -0.37$ (SE $= 0.66$). Estimation of covariances requires a more general random effects routine, such as *MLn* (Rasbash and Woodhouse 1995). For the joint test of restrictions (i) and (ii), $\chi^2 = 1.94$, $4df$, p $= 0.75$ (Goldstein 1995, sec. 2.11).

TABLE 3

Comparison of Estimates of Magnet Hospital Effects

| | | Specification for Estimation of Propensity Score, and Control for Predicted Mortality[a] | | | |
| | | No control for predicted mortality | | Controlling for predicted mortality | |
Method of Control for Standard Covariates	Sample Size	Additive	Trimmed, quadratic	Additive	Trimmed, quadratic
Matching via propensity scores	39 treatments, 39 controls (M = 1)	−12.23[b] (4.48)[c] 2.73[d]	−4.31 (6.67) 0.65	−7.15 (2.80) 2.56	−4.87 (3.53) 1.38
	39 treatments, 312 controls (M = 8)	−8.05 (3.14) 2.57	−12.34 (4.06) 3.04	−4.07 (1.94) 2.10	−7.18 (2.38) 3.01
	39 treatments, 585 controls (M = 15)	−9.26 (3.06) 3.03	−11.72 (3.62) 3.24	−4.23∙ (2.02) 2.09	−6.10 (2.26) 2.70
Multiple regression	N = 5,092	−7.46 (5.48) 1.36		−4.69 (4.09) 1.15	

[a]Estimation of models with no control for predicted mortality is with respect to equations (5) and (6); estimation of models with a control for predicted mortality is with respect to equations (8)–(10), with restrictions (i) $\gamma_{01} = \gamma_{10} = 0$, with restrictions (i) $\gamma_{01} = \gamma_{10} = 1$ and (ii) $\tau_{11} = \tau_{01} = 0$, except for estimates marked ∙, for which $\gamma_{01} = \gamma_{10} \neq 1$ is substituted for restriction (i)

[b]Treatment effect
[c]Standard error
[d]|t-Statistic|

that the true model is somehow known (e.g., Drake 1993; Rubin and Thomas 1996). In this example, the true model for propensity scores is not known, so the results are better viewed as bearing on the robustness of estimates derived from alternative plausible specifications of the propensity model, for varying numbers of matches per treatment unit.

The first and third columns of data in Table 3 involve matches on the additive specification, and thus extend (to $M = 1$ and $M = 15$) the results reported earlier for $M = 8$ matches per control. The largest estimated treatment effect, with and without a control for predicted mortality, is obtained with a single match per case. The estimated standard errors are larger for one match than for multiple matches, in rough proportion to their theoretical relative efficiency, plotted in Figure 2. Eight matches per treatment is the limit before bias, as measured by treatment-versus-control differences in the estimated propensity score, becomes substantial. So the estimated effects for $M = 8$ are to be preferred to those for $M = 15$, although the latter are somewhat larger and have slightly smaller standard errors.

For $M = 8$, the estimated magnet hospital effect is almost exactly eight per thousand with no control for predicted mortality, and four per thousand with a control.[17] They are very similar to the estimates from multiple regression models, except that the standard errors are substantially reduced, to the point that t-statistics are nearly doubled under the matching procedure. The parallel regression assumption turns out to have little effect on the point estimates of treatment effects; but the unequal variances in the unmatched treatment and control samples lead to less efficient estimation in the regression case. With Medicare mortality rates averaging just over 100 per thousand, these estimated treatment effects correspond to reductions in mortality of nearly 8 percent without controlling for predicted mortality, and over 4 percent with controls. Such potential reductions are of substantive interest, so it is of value to learn that the estimates are statistically significant as well.

When matching takes place on propensity scores estimated using the trimmed set of predictors (the second and fourth data columns of Table 3), estimated standard errors are greater. However, at $M = 8$ and $M = 15$, the estimated treatment effects are larger still, leading to t-statistics that are all in the neighborhood of three (in absolute value). I have no strong advice about which set of propensity scores (additive versus trimmed,

---

[17]Results are very similar for $M = 2$ and $M = 5$ (not shown in Table 3).

quadratic) on which to match. The problems attendant to post hoc "data dredging"—in this case, generating lots of specifications of propensity scores and presenting results from the set of matches that leads to the largest estimate of treatment effects—are well known. On the other hand, there may be several plausible specifications of the propensity score equation. Examining (and presenting) results based on two or more such specifications is a form of sensitivity analysis that can inform analyst and reader alike. In the current case, matching on the scores generated from the additive model seems closer to the theoretical advice offered by Rubin and Thomas (1996); and it is reassuring to note that the estimates of the treatment effect for the preferred number of matches—$M = 8$, the largest number of matches before bias sets in—are very close to the result from the standard analysis of covariance (i.e., multiple regression). Seeing that the estimates are larger (at least at $M = 8$) under matches based on an alternative set of propensity scores (those from the trimmed, quadratic specification) can only buttress our belief that these effects are "real."

When the number of good matches is plentiful, it is preferable to use more than one match per treatment, to "dampen out" the variability in estimated effects that arises not stochastically, but from arbitrary factors such as specification of the model for estimating propensity scores. Thus, in Table 3, treatment effects are more similar across specifications of the propensity score equation when there are multiple matches.[18] Of course, the illustration here is an extreme one, in terms of available controls for each case (cf. Rubin and Thomas 1996:249). When good matches are less prevalent and multiple matching is difficult, differences in the specification of the estimated propensity equation will result in fewer differences in matches between specifications, hence less serendipity in single match estimates of effects.

6. CONCLUSION

Multivariate matching is an area with considerable potential for sociology. In this paper, I have focused on estimation of effects when a treatment condition is comparatively rare, and highly selected with respect to a fairly large number of covariates. The results illustrate that relatively simple matching procedures, using as few as one control unit per treatment, *can*

---

[18]This point also holds for these data for $M = 5$ and even $M = 2$.

result in estimated treatment effects whose standard errors are smaller than those obtained with "full sample" multiple regression analyses—in spite of having dispensed with literally thousands of observations. Previous heuristic arguments concerning this point have focused on the greater efficiency of matched versus random same-size samples in the analysis of covariance (Rosenbaum and Rubin 1983:48), and on the small gains in efficiency attendant to increases in sample size given matched samples (Rosenbaum and Rubin 1985a:33). More recent results, appearing in Rubin and Thomas (1996, esp. sec. 5) give some idea of the factors influencing the comparative efficiency of matching and full-sample regression analysis. That matching will not necessarily lead to gains in efficiency is evident in the first row of Table 3, since for $M = 1$, the estimated standard error for the trimmed, quadratic specification is higher than that obtained from a multiple regression analysis, at least with no control for predicted mortality.

Four other virtues of matching bear at least brief mention. First, by restricting the number of cases under study, matching abets further analyses less often undertaken with large samples. Matching is commonly recommended when observation of the response variable is costly and/or time-consuming and has, at the onset of the study, typically not yet taken place (Rosenbaum and Rubin 1985a). In this sense, the example used here is atypical, since the response variable is obtained from the same secondary data source as the covariates. Yet the same principle applies: The magnet hospital designation is an ambiguous treatment, since it was determined in a manner that does not rule out the possibility that some of the matched control hospitals have organizational characteristics like those of the prototype magnet hospitals (Aiken et al. 1994). If so, then the estimates shown here may be underestimates of the true effect of these organizational factors on rates of in-patient Medicare mortality. A follow-up study of a set of matched control hospitals, although not yet done, is nevertheless far more feasible than a similar study of the several thousand control hospitals in the multivariate analysis of covariance.

Second, by focusing attention on the overlap of treatments and controls with respect to the distribution of covariates, matching effectively delimits the range of causal inference. For example, inference regarding the effects of changing the organization of nursing within hospitals, as operationalized in the magnet hospital designation, should be limited to the population of hospitals that are reasonably like the magnet hospitals. A regression model for predicting propensity scores can be "read backward," in the sense that the complement of specificity provides the percentage of control hospitals whose other observed characteristics on the covariate dimensions of size, ownership, financial consideration, etc., are essentially like those of magnet hospitals. Any attempt to implement the organizational changes in nursing recommended by the magnet hospital studies should focus on the 22 percent of HCFA hospitals with similar characteristics with respect to the observed covariates, since these are the type of hospitals in which the organizational factors associated with the magnet hospital designation have been shown to have their effect.

Third, the 1988 HCFA data are essentially a census, best viewed as a sample from some less time-bounded superpopulation of hospitals and their annual mortality experiences. But many sociological data sets arise from complex multistage samples with both clustering and stratification. In such circumstances, matching can greatly simplify the analysis of data. For example, in his study of the effects of "dropping out" on cognitive ability, Rosenbaum (1986) simplifies analysis in a complex sample by matching students within schools, thereby eliminating "school effects" and between-school components of variability.

Fourth, I raise an issue that works against matching in sociology but may actually be an advantage of the method. Matching assumes an orientation toward analysis that is based on estimating the effects of causes (Holland 1986). The discipline of matching establishes a distinction among variables similar to that outlined by Kish (1987): There are the "explanatory variables," consisting of predictors and predictands, or treatments and response. These "embody the aims of the research" (p. 4). Then there are "extraneous variables," that are variously controlled, randomized, and disturbing. In observational studies, which characterize most of sociology, there is no mechanism to ensure that extraneous variables are randomized, so most of our effort goes into turning potentially disturbing variables into variables that are controlled. This is what occurs in matching studies, where the matching process is our best attempt to control disturbing variables. In many regression studies, however, these distinctions are blurred, especially the distinction between a predictor and a disturbing variable. This is especially true when all antecedent variables are viewed as potential "causes" of the response, as occurs when the orientation toward analysis is one in which the researcher seeks to establish the "causes of effects." Although this is a common orientation in sociology—we are just as likely to ask "What are the causes of y?" as "What is the effect of x on y?"—it is only the latter question that provides a sound epistemological basis for research (Sobel 1996). Matching points us toward asking questions that have answers, and establishing cause-and-effect relations in a meaningful manner.

REFERENCES

Aiken, Linda H., Herbert L. Smith, and Eileen T. Lake. 1994. "Lower Medicare Mortality Among a Set of Hospitals Known for Good Nursing Care." *Medical Care* 32:771–87.

Al-Haider, Abdolmohsin S., and Thomas T. H. Wan. 1991. "Modeling Organizational Determinants of Hospital Mortality." *Health Services Research* 26:303–23.

Althauser, Robert P., and Donald B. Rubin. 1970. "The Computerized Construction of a Matched Sample." *American Journal of Sociology* 76:325–46.

Alwin, Duane F. 1974. "College Effects on Educational and Occupational Attainments." *American Sociological Review* 39:210–23.

Amemiya, Takeshi. 1985. *Advanced Econometrics.* Cambridge: Harvard University Press.

Berk, Richard A., and Phyllis J. Newton. 1985. "Does Arrest Really Deter Wife Battery? An Effort to Replicate the Findings of the Minneapolis Spouse Abuse Experiment." *American Sociological Review* 50:253–62.

Bryk, Anthony S., and Stephen W. Raudenbush. 1992. *Hierarchical Linear Models: Applications and Data Analysis Methods.* Newbury Park, CA: Sage.

Cochran, William G., and Donald B. Rubin. 1973. "Controlling Bias in Observational Studies: A Review." *Sankhyā Series* A 35:417–46.

Drake, Christiana. 1993. "Effects of Misspecification of the Propensity Score on Estimators of Treatment Effect." *Biometrics* 49:1231–36.

Dubois, Robert W., Robert H. Brook, and William H. Rogers. 1987. "Adjusted Hospital Death Rates: A Potential Screen for Quality of Medical Care." *American Journal of Public Health* 77:1162–66.

Fienberg, Stephen E. 1980. *The Analysis of Cross-Classified Categorical Data*, 2nd ed. Cambridge: MIT Press.

Freedman, Ronald. 1950. "Incomplete Matching in Ex Post Facto Studies." *American Journal of Sociology* 55:485–87.

Freedman, Ronald, and Amos H. Hawley. 1949. "Unemployment and Migration in the Depression (1930–1935)." *Journal of the American Statistical Association* 44:260–72.

———. 1950. "Migration and Occupational Mobility in the Depression." *American Journal of Sociology* 56:171–77.

Goldstein, Harvey. 1995. *Multilevel Statistical Models*, 2nd ed. London: Edward Arnold.

Gu, Xing Sam, and Paul R. Rosenbaum. 1993. "Comparison of Multivariate Matching Methods: Structures, Distances, and Algorithms." *Journal of Computational and Graphical Statistics* 2:405–20.

Härdle, Wolfgang. 1990. *Applied Nonparametric Regression.* Cambridge, England: Cambridge University Press.

Hartz, A. J., H. Krakauer, E. M. Kuhn, M. Young, S. J. Jacobsen, G. Gay, L. Muenz, M. Katxoff, R. C. Bailey, and A. A. Rimm. 1989. "Hospital Characteristics and Mortality Rates." *New England Journal of Medicine* 321:1720–25.

Holland, Paul W. 1986. "Statistics and Causal Inference." *Journal of the American Statistical Association* 81:945–60.

———. 1988. "Causal Inference, Path Analysis, and Recursive Structural Equations Models." In *Sociological Methodology 1988*, edited by Clifford C. Clogg, 449–84. Washington: American Sociological Association.

Kish, Leslie. 1987. *Statistical Design for Research.* New York: Wiley.

Manski, Charles F. 1995. *Identification Problems in the Social Sciences.* Cambridge: Harvard University Press.

Rasbash, Jon, and Geoff Woodhouse. 1995. *MLn Command Reference* (Version 1.0). London: Institute of Education, University of London.

Rosenbaum, Paul R. 1984. "The Consequences of Adjustment for a Concomitant Variable That Has Been Affected by the Treatment." *Journal of the Royal Statistical Society, Series A* 147:656–66.

———. 1986. "Dropping Out of High School in the United States: An Observational Study." *Journal of Educational Statistics* 11:207–24.

———. 1995. *Observational Studies.* New York: Springer-Verlag.

———. 1996. "Observational Studies and Nonrandomized Experiments." In *Handbook of Statistics*, vol. 13, edited by S. Ghosh and C. R. Rao, 181–97. Amsterdam: Elsevier Science B.V.

Rosenbaum, Paul R., and Donald B. Rubin. 1983. "The Central Role of the Propensity Score in Observational Studies for Causal Effects." *Biometrika* 70:41–55.

———. 1984. "Reducing Bias in Observational Studies Using Subclassification on the Propensity Score." *Journal of the American Statistical Association* 79:516–24.

———. 1985a. "Constructing a Control Group by Multivariate Matched Sample Methods That Incorporate the Propensity Score." *The American Statistician* 39:33–38.

———. 1985b. "The Bias Due to Incomplete Matching." *Biometrics* 41:103–16.

Rubin, Donald B. 1973a. "Matching to Remove Bias in Observational Studies." *Biometrics* 29:159–83.

———. 1973b. "The Use of Matching and Regression Adjustment to Remove Bias in Observational Studies." *Biometrics* 29:185–203.

———. 1976. "Matching Methods That Are Equal Percent Bias Reducing: Some Examples." *Biometrics* 32:109–20.

———. 1979. "Using Multivariate Matched Sampling and Regression Adjustment to Control Bias in Observational Studies." *Journal of the American Statistical Association* 74:318–28.

———. 1980. "Percent Bias Reduction Using Mahalanobis Metric Matching." *Biometrics* 36:293–98.

Rubin, Donald B., and Neal Thomas. 1992a. "Affinely Invariant Matching Methods with Ellipsoidal Distributions." *Annals of Statistics* 20:1079–93.

———. 1992b. "Characterizing the Effect of Matching Using Linear Propensity Score Methods with Normal Distributions." *Biometrika* 79:797–809.

———. 1996. "Matching Using Estimated Propensity Scores: Relating Theory to Practice." *Biometrics* 52:249–64.

Searle, Shayle R., George Casella, and Charles E. McCulloch. 1992. *Variance Components*. New York: Wiley.

Silber, Jeffrey H., Paul R. Rosenbaum, and Richard N. Ross. 1995. "Comparing the Contributions of Groups of Predictors: Which Outcomes Vary with Hospital Rather Than Patient Characteristics?" *Journal of the American Statistical Association* 90:7–18.

Smith, Herbert L. 1990. "Specification Problems in Experimental and Nonexperimental Social Research." In *Sociological Methodology 1990*, edited by Clifford C. Clogg, 59–91. Cambridge, Mass.: Blackwell Publishers.

Snedecor, George W., and William G. Cochran. 1980. *Statistical Methods*, 7th ed. Ames: Iowa State University Press.

Sobel, Michael. 1996. "An Introduction to Causal Inference." *Sociological Methods and Research* 24:353–79.

Ury, Hans K. 1975. "Efficiency of Case-Control Studies with Multiple Controls per Case: Continuous or Dichotomous Data." *Biometrics* 31:643–49.

7

THE NEIGHBORHOOD HISTORY CALENDAR: A DATA COLLECTION METHOD DESIGNED FOR DYNAMIC MULTILEVEL MODELING

William G. Axinn*
Jennifer S. Barber*
Dirgha J. Ghimire†

This paper presents a new data collection method, called the Neighborhood History Calendar, designed to collect event histories of community-level changes over time. We discuss the need for and the uses of this method. We describe issues related to the design of instruments, collection of data, and data entry. We provide detailed examples from an application of this method to the study of marriage, contraception, and fertility in rural Nepal. The paper addresses applications of this same technique to other settings and research problems. We also extend the technique to collection of other forms of contextual-history data, including school histories and health service histories. Finally, we discuss how Geographic Information System (GIS) technology can be used to link together multiple sources of contextual-history data.

The authors wish to thank the National Institute of Child Health and Human Development (Grant No. R01-HD32912) for their financial support of the research reported here. We also wish to thank the staff of the Population and Ecology Research Laboratory in Nepal for pretesting, refining, and executing the contextual data collection procedures discussed here. The Neighborhood History Calendar design benefited greatly from consultations with Arland Thornton, Tom Fricke, Ganesh Shivakoti, and Daniel Hill. Stephen Matthews provided crucial advice on the use of GPS and GIS. The authors wish to thank Nancy Axinn, as well as three anonymous reviewers and the editor for helpful comments on an earlier draft. (*Continues on following page*)
*Pennsylvania State University
†Tribhuvan University, Nepal

The relationship between macro-level social changes and micro-level individual behaviors has been a focal theme in both classic and modern sociological theory (Alexander 1988; Coleman 1990; Durkheim 1984[1933]; Smith 1989). This theme is not only a theoretical issue, it has practical significance as well. Recent studies indicate that macro-level characteristics play an important role in shaping micro-level behavior in a broad range of substantive areas, including demography, gender relations, child development, criminology, and education (Brooks-Gunn et al. 1993; Entwisle and Mason 1985; Huber 1991; Raudenbush 1988; Rountree et al. 1994). Macro-level characteristics, sometimes called contextual characteristics, do affect individual-level behaviors, and the continued exploration of these effects is likely to be an important area of sociological inquiry for some time to come.

Recent advances in multilevel modeling have dramatically improved efforts to include macro-level contextual characteristics, sometimes called ecological characteristics, in models of individual-level behavior (Bryk and Raudenbush 1992; DiPrete and Forristal 1994; Goldstein 1995; Ringdal 1992). Advances in event-history, or hazard, modeling have also helped researchers formulate increasingly dynamic models of individual behavior (Allison 1984; Petersen 1991; Yamaguchi 1991). However, few researchers have successfully combined multilevel modeling approaches with dynamic models. Some have incorporated static measures of contextual features into dynamic individual-level models (Sastry 1996; Brewster 1994), but incorporation of dynamic measures at both the contextual and individual levels poses many problems. Among them, such models would require data that include dynamic event-history measures of contextual change over time, dynamic measures of individuals' lives, and a detailed migration/ mobility history to link individuals with contexts. Although a great deal of methodological work addresses data collection methods for gathering detailed life histories and migration histories (Freedman et al. 1988; Massey 1987), little work has been done on techniques for gathering standardized, dynamic contextual history data.

In this paper we outline a method for collecting contextual event-history data. Our method integrates reliance on a calendar instrument with a combination of survey and ethnographic techniques for gathering data. The method extends the Life History Calendar technique, which was designed

(*Continued*) Finally, Cassie Johnstonbaugh assisted with the preparation of the manuscript. The authors alone are responsible for any errors or omissions. Please direct correspondence to the first author at 601 Oswald Tower, University Park, PA 16802 or via e-mail at axinn@pop.psu.edu.

to gather individual-level event histories, to data collection at contextual levels (Caspi et al. 1996; Freedman et al. 1988). The method also builds on recent efforts to combine standardized, extensive data collection methods and unstandardized, intensive data collection methods into a single coherent data collection effort (Axinn et al. 1991; Massey 1987). The resulting approach is flexible enough to collect contextual data from a wide range of settings for a broad range of substantive uses. This method has several important advantages, including direct collection of contextual characteristics rather than aggregation of individual-level characteristics; collection of sequences of contextual changes so that researchers can differentiate among contexts that may look the same now but have arrived at that outcome via different paths; documentation of a contextual event history that can be linked to individual life histories to create truly dynamic multilevel models.

1. CONTEXTUAL EVENT-HISTORY DATA

Collection of contextual event-history data poses important obstacles including obtaining accurate information on timing and sequencing of contextual change and measuring the most important contextual changes. The technique we have designed to overcome these obstacles combines the structure of a calendar with a wide open search for data that includes in-depth interviews with key informants, group interviews, and consultation with archival sources.

The methods we describe were designed to meet the specific needs of a particular study, called the Chitwan Valley Family Study (CVFS). The CVFS was designed to measure dynamic changes in the socioeconomic context of 132 neighborhoods in South-Central Nepal and to link these changes to individual-level life histories for the purpose of explaining changes in marriage timing, childbearing, and contraceptive use. Also, because rural Nepal is the setting for the CVFS, the methods were designed to overcome several setting-specific obstacles. However, in the design and implementation of these methods we addressed many issues that will confront any effort to gather standardized dynamic contextual history data, regardless of subject matter or setting. Below we discuss these issues, the design alternatives researchers face, and the specific solutions we chose in the CVFS.

1.1. *The Advantages of a Calendar Format*

An important reason for using a neighborhood (or contextual) history calendar is that it improves respondent recall (Caspi et al. 1996; Freedman et al. 1988). This may be because a calendar instrument allows a respondent to see the sequence of events in his or her life on paper. This inspection helps individuals recall the timing and sequencing of events in their lives. The calendar format also helps respondents use events that are more salient to help them remember the timing of less salient events (Eisenhower et al. 1991). For example, a respondent might use his recall of graduation from college to help recall the timing of a change in living arrangements from a dorm to an apartment. Or, a respondent might use his recall of an important national event, such as a national election, to recall an event in the neighborhood, such as the building of a school nearby.

Calendars also improve data quality by improving interviewing quality. Previous research on the quality of retrospective data collected using calendar instruments indicates no significant differences in data quality when the calendar was administered face-to-face versus a telephone interview (Freedman et al. 1988). This finding suggests that the *interviewer's* inspection of the calendar may be equally important in obtaining complete and accurate data. This may be particularly so in cases with detailed sequences of events, when the calendar technique makes sequences easy to record and overlaps quick to detect. Thus interviewers use the visual calendar display to quickly review a respondent's recall for completeness and accuracy and then probe to improve data quality.

Given the multiple interview approach used in our contextual history data collection, the impact of the calendar format on interviewing quality may be even more important to overall data quality. While measurement errors due to the respondent are likely to occur (Groves 1987), by interviewing multiple respondents about the same events, and cross-checking with archival sources, this method is designed to detect and correct such errors in the field. The calendar format becomes one of the interviewers' most important tools for detecting such errors. So while the calendar format is an aid to a particular respondent during one interview, it is also an aid to the interviewer across multiple interviews regarding the same subject.

1.2. *The Advantages of a Mixed-Method Data Collection Approach*

Mixing structured and unstructured interviewing can help improve individual-level data quality through a number of mechanisms. Recent research documents the benefits of a complete integration of rigorous ethnographic and survey methods throughout every phase of data collection for individual-level data (Axinn et al. 1991). By using a similar mixed-method approach in the collection of contextual data in the CVFS, we also aimed at improving data quality. First, by collecting redundant data from multiple sources, including multiple respondents and available archival sources, we were able to discover discrepancies in the field and resolve them before the data collection was complete. This multiple interview format also allowed us to seek out respondents who were most informed about each specific subject matter. For example, recent in-migrants to a neighborhood usually knew little of early events in the history of the neighborhood. Second, by implementing a high level of supervision and investigator involvement we were able to revise instruments and data collection procedures in the field. We believe this iterative redesign led to the most complete data collection possible as well as to higher data quality. Third, by combining the structure of a calendar with multiple semistructured interviews, we gathered a standardized set of contextual measures while also providing respondents with an opportunity to describe important contextual characteristics or changes that could not be known before visiting the neighborhood. This constituted a useful technique for uncovering important, but localized, contextual changes and events that investigators could not know until the study was underway in the field. Fourth, we were also able to collect information on contextual characteristics which may have been difficult to interpret without ethnographic data. Examples include the aims and activities of local women's groups and government programs.

2. THE NEIGHBORHOOD HISTORY CALENDAR

We designed the CVFS Neighborhood History Calendars to measure contextual changes most relevant to the study's setting and substantive aims. Even so, we faced a variety of issues common to all efforts to collect contextual event-history data. Our discussion of these begins with issues related to the design of the calendar instrument, including the choice of time units, substantive domains, and an accompanying questionnaire.

2.1. *Design of the Instruments*

2.1.1. *Specifying Time Units and Choosing Timing Cues*
As in applications of calendar methods to individual life histories, the choice of time units used in the calendar must depend on both the substantive aims of the study and methodological constraints created by the issues being studied. One might choose days, weeks, months or years.

> The investigator must choose a time unit that is small
> enough to ascertain with adequate precision the sequence
> and temporal interrelation of events. To record events that
> occur fairly frequently or quite close together, it is nec-
> essary to divide time rather finely. At the same time, one
> must consider the respondent's ability to make fine time
> distinctions and the feasibility of fitting the desired time
> unit over the required time span of the study onto a cal-
> endar of manageable size. (Freedman et al. 1988:44)

Although one of our objectives was to determine the order and sequence of
contextual changes over time, the contextual events of interest in the CVFS
did not occur frequently. The study design also required that we collect
histories from a period of 42 years. This reflects the span of time from
when the Chitwan Valley was settled, 1954, to the year the data collection
was completed, 1996. For this combination of reasons we chose years as
the time unit for our Neighborhood History Calendars. Figure 1 presents
an English translation of our Nepalese Neighborhood History Calendar.
The years run across the top row of the calendar and form the column
headings. These year demarcations provide respondents with time references to aid in their recall of the timing and sequencing of changes around
their neighborhood.

Because of the relatively long period of recall, and the fact many
Nepalese do not use calendars to mark timing in their daily lives, we believed additional timing cues would be needed to aid respondents' recall of
event timing. Therefore we created a second row of timing cues, below the
row of years. This row was reserved for major events we believed individuals might find memorable. We chose two types of events to put in this
line. The first type is regional or national events that would have occurred
at the same time for everyone in our study population. It was essential to
our purpose that the timing of these events be quite salient so that respondents could use the timing of these events to help them recall the timing of
neighborhood changes. We conducted semistructured interviews with a
nonsystematic sample of the study population to determine a set of such
events. In this process it is important to interview respondents from several different cohorts since individuals from different cohorts are likely to
remember different important events (Schuman and Scott 1989). The set
of events we chose included earthquakes, floods, national elections, and
the deposition of Nepal's king. These events were printed on the calendar

Neighborhood ID #: 09-15-178   Name of the Neighborhood: Momogau

Year / Event	54	55	56	57	58	59	60	61	62	63	64	65	66	67	68	69	70	71	72	73	74	75	76	77	78	79	80	81	82	83	84	85	86	87	88	89	90	91	92	93	94	95	96	Event
				*															*								*	*								*	*							
1.Electricity																													X															1.Electricity
2.School			3	3																																								2.School
3.Health Service				3	3		2											1																								1		3.Health Service
4.Bus Service-Any Season											2																									1								4.BS-Any
5.Bus Service-Rainy Season											2									1																								5.BS-Rainy

Year / Event	54	55	56	57	58	59	60	61	62	63	64	65	66	67	68	69	70	71	72	73	74	75	76	77	78	79	80	81	82	83	84	85	86	87	88	89	90	91	92	93	94	95	96	Event
				*															*								*	*								*	*							
6.Mill																																		3				2			1			6.Mill
7.Co-operative											3												2					1																7.Co-operative
8.Dairy										2																													1					8.Dairy
9.Market																																										1		9.Market
10.Bank									2															1																				10.Bank

Year / Event	54	55	56	57	58	59	60	61	62	63	64	65	66	67	68	69	70	71	72	73	74	75	76	77	78	79	80	81	82	83	84	85	86	87	88	89	90	91	92	93	94	95	96	Event
				*															*								*	*								*	*							
11.Employment Opp.																1																												11.Empl. Opp.
12.Small Farmers Group								3		2																																		12.Sm. Farmers
13.Women's Group																																												13.Wms. Group
14.Temple																																												14.Temple
15.Police Station																																												15.Police Sta.

Key:

*   National and regional events entered on calendars to aid respondent recall. Examples: First national election, Rapti River flood, Nepal's king resigned.

X   (in Line 1) Indicates the year electricity became available in the neighborhood. A blank line indicates that electricity was still not available at the time of the interview.

1   Respondents were asked, "Where is the nearest _____ (name of service e.g.—bank, school, health service, etc.)?" They, then were asked, "In what year did that open?" Field workers recorded "1" in the column of the year the service first opened.

2   Respondents were asked, "Before _____ (service mentioned in #1) opened, what was the closest one?" and "In what year did that open?" Field workers entered "2" in the column of the year the service first opened.

3   Respondents were asked, "Before _____ (service mentioned in #2) opened, what was the closest one?" and "In what year did that open?" Field workers entered "3" in the column of the year the service first opened.

Blank Lines   Indicate that the service did not exist. (Interviewers were required to respond to opening questions about the existence of each service in the accompanying questionnaire.)

Note: Names and identifiers have been changed to protect the anonymity of the neighborhood.
Nepali years were used in the data collection. Western year 1996 = Nepali year 2052/2053.

FIGURE 1. An example of a completed neighborhood history calendar from the Chitwan Valley Family Study.

361

in the row just below the top row of years (the locations of these events are represented by an asterisk in Figure 1).

The second type of event we chose was neighborhood-specific events that were extremely salient to local residents but were not germane to the study and therefore not included elsewhere on the calendar. For example, in one neighborhood many residents could recall quite clearly the year in which one resident had been mauled by an alligator. Since such neighborhood-specific events did not pertain to the entire population, these events were written on the calendar, in line 2, during the data collection process. We also attempted to put our questions in an order beginning with neighborhood changes that we believed would be quite salient—for example, electrification.

As a result of this strategy, respondents were able to use visual cues on the calendar—years, national events, and local events—to help them recall the timing of local events and changes they found difficult to remember. For example, when faced with the task of recalling an important change in bus service to the neighborhood, from dry season only to year-round, respondents could draw on the calendar years, national events such as elections, or local events that were already recorded on the calendar. This strategy was particularly important among some ethnic groups (Tharu, Kumal, and Derai) who use neither age nor calendar years to mark time.[1] Among these groups the timing of salient local and national events provided the most important cues for the timing of neighborhood changes.

2.1.2. *Choosing Domains*

The choice of domains is also a function of the substantive aims of the study and the setting being studied. For the purposes of the CVFS, we were mainly interested in those neighborhood-level contextual changes that theory suggested should influence marriage timing, childbearing, or contraceptive use. These included changes such as new schooling opportunities, changing employment opportunities, and improvements in the health care infrastructure (Caldwell 1982; Smith 1989). However, we also conducted a series of unstructured interviews with members of the study population to explore the possibility that other local events (either not predicted by theory or unknown outside the study area) might be important deter-

---

[1]These groups typically mark time in terms of personal events, such as marriage, childbirth, or direct experience with disasters (e.g., floods) or rare events (e.g., animal attacks).

minants of these family formation changes. These unstructured interviews helped us develop a list of nearly 50 different types of neighborhood characteristics and changes that residents mentioned when describing their neighborhood. We then worked to reduce this list by focusing on only those characteristics that seemed most likely to influence changes in marriage timing, childbearing, or contraceptive use. Examples of these include changes in agricultural services (mills, cooperatives, and dairies), the formation of local women's groups, the existence of local youth groups, and the introduction of public banks.

One useful consequence of our multiple-interview strategy is that new, locally important domains could be added to the calendar while in the field. In order to accommodate some spontaneous addition of new categories we left a few lines at the bottom of the calendar blank. In practice, the addition of a new domain is useful only if it has been collected from every neighborhood in the study. To accomplish this, we divided our data collection into three stages, or three visits to each neighborhood. None of the second visits were made until all the first visits were complete, none of the third visits were made until all of the second visits were complete, and no new domains were added during the third visit. This strategy gave us the opportunity to discover new domains of questioning during the first and second visits and ensure that they were collected from all the neighborhoods in the second and third visits.

As with Life History Calendars, the substantive areas must be limited in number and precisely defined (Freedman et al. 1988). Collecting history data over a long period of retrospection and over many domains can produce a high respondent burden that may reduce respondent rapport and cooperation. Limiting the number of domains and providing precise definitions helps to reduce the respondent burden. Another useful consequence of our multiple-interview strategy is that this respondent burden can be distributed across multiple respondents during multiple visits.

All domains are not equally likely to generate accurate timing information from the same source. For example, although respondents in the neighborhood were quite able to identify the nearest school to the neighborhood, respondents often said they did not know exactly when the school was first opened or how many teachers worked at the school. Officials at the school, or school records, were much more likely to provide this data. (We provide examples of these discrepancies in Section 3.) Such problems were a major motivation for a mixed data collection strategy that included some interviews in the neighborhood, some interviews with local officials, and as much consultation of written records as possible. However, these issues may also influence the selection of domains included in the Neighborhood History Calendar. This is particularly true in a data collection that includes multiple types of contextual history calendars, such as the CVFS. We used other history calendars, such as school and health service calendars, to supplement our Neighborhood History Calendar (discussed in greater detail below). In general, respondents' inability to provide reliable timing in response to some questions may also influence the choice of domains included in any one particular calendar instrument.

2.1.3. *Designing the Accompanying Questionnaires*

We also designed a questionnaire to accompany the Neighborhood History Calendar. The questionnaires provided a structure of suggested question wordings and standardized probes. Interviewers were not required to follow the question wordings exactly; instead the printed questions constituted a tool interviewers could use during the interview. This tool proved most useful for training the interviewers in appropriate question and probe wordings and sequences. It also provided a crutch to the interviewers in cases where they did not remember the appropriate question sequences or wording.

Accompanying questionnaires also provide greater flexibility for recording information. Although the calendar instruments were designed to record the timing and sequencing of important community events, we used the questionnaire to obtain additional information about community events that could not easily be recorded on the calendar. For example, in the neighborhood histories we asked the location of the nearest school, when it first opened, the location of the nearest school before that one opened, and when this other school opened, for up to three schools. These timing issues were recorded on the calendar. For each school we also asked residents about the availability of bus service to the school, the time to the school by bus and by foot, and the cost of bus service to the school. The responses to these questions were all recorded in the questionnaire.

We used a similar strategy in our histories of other sorts of contexts (discussed in Section 3). For example, when collecting histories of schools and health services, we recorded the timing of changes in the services provided by the specific school or health service on the calendar. In the questionnaire we recorded responses to additional items, such as open-ended questions about how the money to construct the school or health service had been raised. Thus, by using the questionnaire to supplement the calendars we had the flexibility to record a variety of information that was not easily incorporated into the calendar format. This also helped keep the calendar focussed on the timing and sequencing of contextual changes.

2.2. *Data Collection*

Although our data collection procedures included some structure, they were not as structured as many standardized individual-level survey interviews (Kahn and Cannell 1957). The calendar itself provided a good deal of structure, defining both the areas of questioning and a sequence of questions (Freedman et al. 1988). The accompanying questionnaire also provided the structure of suggested question wordings and standardized probes. However, interviewers were not required to ask questions exactly as worded or follow the sequence of questions.

This strategy has both positive and negative consequences. On the negative side, variations in question wording and question order are known to affect responses (Bradburn 1983; Sudman and Bradburn 1974; Biemer et al. 1991). On the positive side, flexibility in the interviewing process can help the interview take on a more natural character that helps the respondent to provide more accurate and detailed information (Briggs 1986; Caldwell et al. 1987; Schaeffer 1991; Suchman and Jordan 1990). We believe our combination of calendar structure, questionnaire wording, and flexible interviewing protocol minimized large sources of response error while allowing the interviewer to interact more naturally with respondents. This style of contextual data collection parallels a flexible style of collecting data on individual-level demographic behavior that has been applied in a number of studies (Axinn et al. 1991; Bach and Stycos 1959; Massey 1987). Note that this flexibility should be accompanied by high levels of interviewer training and supervision in order to produce high-quality data (Fowler 1991).

Our data collection procedures also differed from standardized individual-level surveys because of our multiple-interview format. In each neighborhood we required interviewers to collect contextual data from at least two different sources, and they often consulted three or four. Further, each of these interviews was not constrained to be an individual interview, and group interviews were common. These group interview situations paralleled the Participatory Rural Appraisal technique, encouraging the assembled neighborhood residents to correct each other and come to some collective agreement about the dates of important neighborhood changes

(Chambers 1985). Even when these group interviews were used, we counted the group interview as one source and required interviewers to collect at least one more group interview about the same neighborhood information before leaving the neighborhood. We also cross-checked information provided by neighborhood residents against archival sources whenever possible. In fact this was often possible, and most dates of changes like new schools, health services, electrification, and bus services were cross-checked against archival sources.

2.2.1. *Boundary Issues*

Every effort to collect contextual data faces the issue of defining boundaries for the context. This issue can be particularly difficult in research on neighborhoods, since neighborhoods rarely have well-defined boundaries. In the CVFS a neighborhood was defined as a cluster of 5 to 15 households. This definition fit the settlement pattern in Chitwan. When the valley was deforested in the mid-1950s, the Nepalese government distributed land parcels to settlers systematically around a prepared road grid. The result was that most farmers settled in small clusters of households surrounded by farm lands.[2] Our approach is likely to work well in any setting with a similar settlement pattern. However, by the time of our study some of these settlements had grown large enough so that our upper limit constituted only part of a larger residential community. In fact, our design included sampling eight clusters from a small city in one corner of Chitwan (Barber et al. 1995). This situation was one reason we chose to ask residents about their context without reference to boundaries, as described below. By avoiding the use of boundaries, residents were able to tell us about any aspect of their context they considered relevant to their lives, no matter how distant. Because our approach worked well in this situation, we are confident it can be used to gather data on contextual change over time from many different settings characterized by a wide range of settlement patterns.

Our system for selecting neighborhood clusters was designed to use natural boundaries, such as farm lands, roads, streams, and irrigation canals to identify selected clusters. However, we worked to make our contextual measurements completely independent of our neighborhood boundaries. We accomplished this by visiting each cluster of households and

---

[2]These clusters are called "tols" or "chowks" in Nepalese and each of the clusters in our sample has a unique name, used by the residents to identify their place of residence.

asking residents about their neighborhood context without reference to any boundaries. Our sampling boundaries defined only which residents we asked (although we occasionally spoke with informants who lived nearby our selected households). As we asked about each domain, respondents were free to tell about any aspect of that domain they felt was relevant, and we asked about time and distance to the characteristic in question. For example, within the schools domain, residents were asked about the location of the nearest school and then time and distance to reach that school. No boundaries were used to eliminate some schools. So our neighborhood contextual histories are histories of changes in and around the neighborhood that are salient to residents, not just changes within neighborhood boundaries.

The nature of boundary issues changes for different types of contexts. For example, we also collected histories of schools and health services (discussed in Section 3). When collecting the history of change in a school over time, the boundary was often quite clear: this school, in this building, at this geographic location. However, in a few cases, even these straightforward boundaries introduced problematic issues. Some schools, particularly private schools, changed their geographic location over time. In such a case one is faced with the issue of whether to consider this the same school at two different places or whether to collect two different school histories. In the CVFS we defined schools that moved less than a 10-minute walk as the same school and schools that moved more than a 10-minute walk as different schools (and schools that moved more than 10 minutes received a code to show they were linked). In the CVFS we generally treated 10-minute walks as a negligible difference in exposure or access and in the Chitwan Valley context this definition left us with only 19 schools (out of 146 schools) that moved far enough to be considered two different schools. Thus decisions about boundary definitions must be consistent with both the study aims and the context being studied.

2.2.2. Choosing Respondents
As mentioned above, we interviewed multiple respondents about the same information, sometimes in group interviews. The residents of households located within the selected neighborhoods constituted our set of eligible respondents, but no attempt was made to represent the residents of the neighborhood. Interviewers attempted to vary the respondents they spoke with in each neighborhood, particularly in terms of age, gender, and education. In general, older respondents were particularly helpful since they

tended to be more knowledgeable about early events.[3] More educated respondents also tended to be more knowledgeable about some types of changes, such as schools and health services. Those who traveled often were more knowledgeable about bus services and related transportation issues. Thus interviewing a variety of respondents helped us gather reliable information across a variety of domains.

Interviewers also tried to involve a diverse set of respondents in group interviews.[4] The participants in group interviews were usually self-selected from those hanging around the neighborhood at the time of the interviewer's visit. However, interviewers encouraged women to join the discussion with their husbands, older uneducated residents to join discussions with young educated residents, and residents of Buddhist ethnicities to join discussions with residents of Hindu ethnicities. This diversity of perspectives helped to ensure that group interactions brought together many viewpoints about the same contextual changes. This helped us gain insights into the neighborhood changes, get a more complete record of those changes, and generate reliable estimates of the timing of changes.

2.2.3. Consulting Records

In addition to interviewing, we also consulted archival sources whenever possible. Many features of neighborhood contextual change are recorded in public records, either at the local or regional level. These include features like construction of public schools or health service facilities, electrification, and provision of special economic development programs. Following our general strategy of collecting redundant information, we checked local and regional government agencies for such records even in cases where interviews had already provided the information. This cross-checking helped identify unreliable information on event timing.

Note that whenever redundant information is collected, discrepancies are likely to occur. We found many discrepancies between reports of construction timing from neighborhood residents and reports in official government documents (discussed in detail in Section 2.5). Furthermore, government documents are not necessarily a more accurate source of in-

---

[3] Although not a problem in this part of Nepal, neighborhoods in other settings that are characterized by extremely high levels of migration among residents may prove to be extremely difficult for this type of data collection.

[4] The diversity of respondents was designed to produce disagreements as interviewers worked toward a consensus report from residents. We recorded the consensus value and when there were substantial discrepancies, we recorded the discrepancies as well.

formation. Many government administrators are motivated to misrepresent construction completion dates. Sometimes purely bureaucratic issues create discrepancies. For example, the date a school opens for classes may differ from the date government records show the school opened because of a time lag in registering the school with the government. In general, based on a combination of redundant interviews and record checks, we found local records to be more reliable sources of timing information than regional administrative records. For example, a school's own records often proved to be the most reliable source of information on the date a school opened, as many sources of error intervene between local records and regional sources of information.

2.2.4. *Recording Techniques*

A variety of design features on the neighborhood calendar were created to improve the accuracy of recording. These include repeating both the "year" and local "events" lines multiple times throughout the calendar, shading every other line in the calendar, adding a bold vertical line every ten lines, and repeating the row category in the right-hand margin (see Figure 1). Each of these features was designed to reduce the chance that interviewers would record responses in the wrong row or column of the calendar.

For all the neighborhood-level characteristics, we recorded the beginning date for the nearest facility (1), the beginning date for the nearest facility before that one opened (2), and the beginning date for the nearest facility before that (3). These were identified on the calendar with the numerals 1, 2, and 3 (see Figure 1). Missing data was recorded on the calendar as "NA." Additional information about each of these services (name, time to reach, etc.) was recorded in the accompanying questionnaire. Blank lines on the calendar indicate residents had no access to the service in question. (In addition, interviewers marked that the service did not exist in response to an opening question in the accompanying questionnaire.) We also took complete histories of each of the facilities directly from the facility itself (discussed in Section 3). Each facility was assigned a unique ID number for use in linking data about that facility gathered on different instruments.

In our collection of other contextual histories, we used a broader range of recording devices. For example, in our school and health service history calendars we recorded numbers of staff and numbers of rooms with up to three-digit integers (see Figures 2 and 3 in Section 3). We also recorded the existence of services using X's. We recorded a continuation of the same state with a code in the first and last years of that state, and lines connecting the first and last years. Examples of these recording techniques are provided in Figures 2 and 3.

2.3. *Data Coding and Computer Entry*

As with Life History Calendars, coding, data entry, and data management of Neighborhood History Calendar data can be complex (Freedman et al. 1988). The calendar method produces as many variables as units of time within each substantive domain. As a result, the total number of variables can be as high as the number of time units represented in the entire calendar multiplied by the total number of substantive domains. Within each domain, data can be entered as a new variable for each new time unit or data can be entered as spells. Data entry in spells can reduce the data entry tasks when events (or changes in the coded values) are uncommon in each line. However, data entry in spells increases the data entry tasks when these events are quite common.

For example, in our Neighborhood History Calendar, the nearest school could be entered as a spell of points coded 1 going from the year 1971 to the year 1996 (see Figure 1). This requires entry of both the value of the spell (in this case 1 for nearest school to the neighborhood) and the entry of the time the spell began and the time the spell ended (years in our case). This data entry strategy worked well for our Neighborhood History Calendar, where the number of events per line was quite low.

However, this strategy did not work as well for our School History Calendar (described in detail below). That calendar features a number of substantive domains that change value every year. Examples include the number of teachers, the total number of students, and the number of female students. Since these values change every year, data entry in spells becomes quite cumbersome. When the event values change often, it is much more expedient to set up the data entry as a new variable for each time unit (year) and enter a new variable for each time.

In general we recommend coding and entering the data while in the field. This maximizes the opportunity to reconcile and correct data errors discovered during the coding and entry processes. If coding and data entry take place in the field, when errors or omissions are discovered it is quite straightforward to return to the data source in question to make corrections. Although this slows the data entry process somewhat, the result is a more complete and reliable data set.

2.4. *Examples of Data Gathered with Neighborhood Calendars*

The data from the Neighborhood History Calendar provides a dynamic record of local contextual changes from the neighborhood's point of view. Because these data are collected as independent series of event timings, they can be reorganized into a wide range of useful contextual measures. In this section we review three ways analysts might use these contextual event-history data: (1) as measures of historical change; (2) as measures of exposure to specific characteristics; and (3) as measures of time-varying contextual-level covariates in multilevel hazards models.

2.4.1. *Measures of Historical Change*

The data from these neighborhood histories can easily be aggregated to provide measures of change over time in the geographic unit from which the neighborhoods were selected. In our case, these data provide a historical account of change over time in the Chitwan Valley of southern Nepal. Because our data include timing to the year, we can assemble an annual history of neighborhood changes in the Chitwan Valley. To simplify presentation of this example, however, we have instead assembled a history of decennial changes beginning in 1964. The first example is presented in Table 1.

Table 1 presents the cumulative number of neighborhoods in our sample having any type of school (even if it offers only one year of schooling) within a fifteen minute walk of the neighborhood. The data come from our Neighborhood History Calendar data collection in our sample of 132 neighborhoods. Since our sample is chosen to be representative of all the neighborhoods in Chitwan Valley, these figures give us measures of the change over time in schooling opportunities in the Valley. Only one-third

TABLE 1
Number of Neighborhoods with a School
within a 15-Minute Walk

By	Number	Percent
1964	42	32
1974	86	65
1984	93	70
1994	113	86
1996	119	90

TABLE 2
Number of Neighborhoods with a Health
Service within a 30-Minute Walk

By	Number	Percent
1964	8	6
1974	26	20
1984	39	29
1994	101	76
1996	111	85

of the neighborhoods had a school within a 15-minute walk in 1964, but by 1994 a full 86 percent of the neighborhoods had a school nearby. Note that since we ask for the time to the nearest school, the data could be used to recalibrate these historical change measures for any specific radius, (e.g., 30-minute walk, one-hour walk).

Table 2 presents the cumulative number of neighborhoods that had some type of health service outlet (these range from pharmacies to clinics) within a 30-minute walk. Again the data are presented in decennial increments beginning in the year 1964. Here we see that only 6 percent of the neighborhoods had a health service outlet within a 30-minute walk by 1964. By 1994, however, more than three-quarters of the neighborhoods had nearby health services.

The neighborhood event-history data also allow researchers to reconstruct the sequences of changes across a number of different domains. For example, comparing the data in Table 1 to those in Table 2, it becomes clear that the 1964–1973 decade was a time of dramatic expansion of schooling opportunities in Chitwan, while it is not until the 1984–1993 decade that we see a dramatic expansion in health services. By adding data from our other substantive domains, we could examine the relative timing of the expansion of transportation, employment opportunities, or development programs.

2.4.2. Measures of Exposure
Analysts who are most interested in the impact of a particular neighborhood characteristic on some other outcome may use these data to determine the length of time neighborhoods have been exposed to the characteristic in question. For example, in studies of contraceptive use, researchers might need to know how long neighborhoods have been exposed to the presence

TABLE 3
Years of Exposure to School or Health Service within a 15-Minute Walk

Years of Exposure	School		Health Service	
	Number of Neighborhoods	Percentage of Neighborhoods	Number of Neighborhoods	Percentage of Neighborhoods
31+	42	32	2	1.5
21–30	44	33	11	8.3
11–20	7	5	7	5.3
Less than 10	26	20	51	38.6
None	13	10	61	41.2
Total	132	100	132	100

of a school or health service nearby. Table 3 provides an example reorganizing our neighborhood history data into these types of measures.

For each block of years of exposure, Table 3 indicates the number of neighborhoods associated with that much exposure to schools or health services. Nearly one-third of the neighborhoods in Chitwan have had more than 30 years of exposure to a school within a 15-minute walk. Another third have had 21–30 years of exposure to a nearby school, while only 10 percent have had no exposure to a nearby school. The picture of exposure to health services is quite different. Less than 10 percent of the neighborhoods had more than 20 years of exposure to health services within a 15-minute walk. More than one-third have had less than 10 years of exposure to nearby health services and nearly half have had no exposure to such services.

2.4.3. *Measures of Contextual-Level Time-Varying Covariates*
Perhaps the most exciting potential use of the neighborhood event-history data are as measures of contextual-level time-varying covariates for use in dynamic multilevel models. Consider a multilevel model focusing on a dynamic outcome, such as marriage timing. To estimate a dynamic model of marriage timing examining individual-level covariates (such as educational experience or attitudes) most researchers today would use event-history, or hazards, models (Heaton and Call 1995; Landale 1994; Yamaguchi 1991). Using these techniques one could model the transition to marriage as a dynamic process, also allowing covariates (predictors) to vary with time (Petersen 1991; Xie 1994; Yamaguchi 1991). For example, one could

allow school enrollment to vary month to month in predicting the hazard of marriage (Thornton et al. 1995).

Using neighborhood event-history calendar data, we can take the same dynamic approach in a multilevel model of marriage timing in which the neighborhood is the contextual level being examined. For example, in a discrete-time hazards model of the transition to marriage we could code each of the increments of time with a characteristic of the neighborhood, and allow those characteristics to change over time. So in some periods a neighborhood might be characterized as having no school, in other periods it might be characterized as having only an elementary school, and in still other periods it might be characterized as having both an elementary and a high school. One could then estimate the impact of the different schooling opportunities on the transition to marriage through various periods. Using this time-varying covariates framework, we could also construct measures of the amount of time since any neighborhood change took place. For example, we could estimate the impact of years of exposure to the opportunity to attend high school on the hazard rate of marriage. Thus the combination of detailed dynamic neighborhood history data and the flexibility of event-history or hazards models will allow the construction of dynamic multilevel models.[5]

2.5. Evaluating Data Quality

Evaluation of data quality often depends on the availability of two or more independent sources of information about the same issue or event. Because the CVFS collected data from multiple sources about a number of topics, a good deal of information gathered during the course of the study speaks to the quality of the data. However, it is rare that researchers are in a position to know which of the two or more measures of the same event is, in fact, correct. In some circumstances, when errors are reasonably presumed to be in one direction only (such as underreporting), it is possible to interpret the difference between data collected by two different techniques as a reflection of data quality. Previous work in Nepal indicates that, in these circumstances, ethnographic interviewing generally provides higher-

---

[5]Estimation of dynamic multilevel models with contextual-level time-varying covariates raises some technical obstacles. Although these estimation issues are beyond the scope of this data collection methods paper, recent advances in multilevel modeling of discrete dependent variables suggest that these obstacles can be overcome (Goldstein 1995; Sastry 1995; Wong and Mason 1985).

quality measures of individual behaviors than surveys (Axinn 1989; Stone and Campbell 1984).

Our design of the Neighborhood History Calendar instruments was based on ethnographic interviews and pretests that compared various techniques for collecting information on the timing and sequencing of changes in objective characteristics of community contexts. These comparisons led us to believe that multiple respondent interviews were superior to single respondent interviews because different respondents remembered different changes in the community, and because the conversation among respondents helped them remind each other of the sequences of changes. The comparisons also led us to believe that the calendar instrument provided a critical visual aid giving multiple respondents the means to pool their input. Finally, our comparisons also led us to believe that the structure and visual representation of data inherent in the calendar helped interviewers make fewer errors in recording complex sequences of community change over time.

Our ethnographic work also revealed the limits of the Neighborhood History Calendar method. While neighborhood residents defined broad aspects of the context in which they lived, they were often unable to provide reliable information about specific characteristics of that context. For example, residents of the neighborhood could always identify the nearest school or health service to the neighborhood, but they often had difficulty knowing the date that particular school or health service first opened. Neighborhood residents were generally even less knowledgeable about the timing of changes in more detailed characteristics of the school or health service, such as the number of teachers, class rooms, clinicians, or examining rooms. To measure many of these specific dimensions, we found it necessary to visit the school or health service in question and collect data with a calendar designed especially for the purpose. We describe these procedures in Section 3.

We used our ethnographic interviews, archival data collection, and school (or health service, etc.) specific history information, to create a composite measure of the time each school (or other service) first opened. This process involved comparison of several sources of information regarding the same event and a subjective evaluation of the quality of each source. Investigators made decisions regarding the likely accuracy of each source and then, using all the sources, created a final composite measure. We kept careful records of the information used to reach this subjective evaluation, and we applied the same criteria across the entire sample; how-

TABLE 4

Deviation Between Neighborhood Respondents' Report of School or
Health Service Opening Date and Composite Measure of Opening
Date (Schools and Health Services within a 15-Minute Walk)

Deviation (years)	Schools (%)	Health Services (%)
0	46	20
1–2	25	50
More than 2	29	30
Total	100	100

ever, the judgement regarding quality of source is nonetheless subjective.
We argue that direct involvement of the investigators in the field work and
their participation in the processes of collecting the different reports gives
the investigators the best possible chance of reaching a reasonable judgment about the quality of reports.[6]

Table 4 provides a comparison of our composite measures to the
measures initially provided by neighborhood residents. As shown in
Table 4, our final composite measure, based on multiple sources of information, matches the original report from neighborhood residents to within
the same year in less than half of our neighborhoods. The corresponding
figure dips to a mere 20 percent for health services.[7] In fact, in nearly
one-third of the neighborhoods the neighborhood report of the opening
date differed from the corresponding composite measure by more than two
years (see Table 4). Our initial ethnographic work led us to suspect the
accuracy of residents' reports, and these comparisons support the notion
that our composite measures (compiled from several sources) provide somewhat different information. Note that for some specific analyses researchers may feel that residents' perceptions of the timing of change is more
relevant than the actual timing of change. Because of this possibility, we
chose to preserve both the residents' reports and our composite measures
in the final data.

---

[6]This is similar to the argument many ethnographers might make about the
quality of individual level data (Caldwell 1985; Hammel 1990; Stone and Campbell
1984; Weiss 1994).
[7]Since respondents' knowledge of these events is probably higher for nearby
schools or health services, these comparisons are limited to schools and health services
within a 15-minute walk of the neighborhood.

We found residents' reports of more specific aspects of change over time in local schools, and other infrastructure, even less reliable. We found official government reports at the regional and national levels equally suspect. Officials often had motivation to inflate change in their region. As a result, we turned to written records kept at the specific school (or health service, etc.) and interviews with staff at the school (or other service) to gather accurate measurement of change over time in their specific services. Below we outline the techniques that we used to gather dynamic event histories of changes in schools, health services, and other contextual features. By applying our contextual history calendar methods to other contexts, we were able to both improve the accuracy of our event timing data and refine our measurement of contextual characteristics.

3. OTHER CONTEXTUAL HISTORY CALENDARS

The Neighborhood History Calendar data collection method can easily be adapted for other forms of contextual history data collection. Different substantive aims may lead researchers to apply this technique to a variety of social, economic, or cultural contextual features. As mentioned above, even in the CVFS we found important reasons for expanding our contextual history data collection beyond Neighborhood History Calendars alone. By applying our contextual history calendar methods to other contexts, we were able to both improve the accuracy of our event timing data and refine our measurement of contextual characteristics.

3.1. *School History Calendars*

We used regional government records and local interviews to make a list of every school in our study area.[8] Our data collection at each of these schools was organized around a school history calendar and accompanying questionnaire designed using the same protocols as described above for Neighborhood History Calendars. Figure 2 provides an example of a completed school history calendar from one of the oldest schools in the study area.

As shown in the figure, the design of the school history calendar paralleled the design of our Neighborhood History Calendar. Time units run across the top marking the column headings and substantive domains

---

[8]This included schools in the study area that were not mentioned in neighborhood interviews, and those that were open previously but closed by the time of the data collection.

School ID # 07-06-195   Name of the School: Khaja Secondary School

Top table

Year	54	55	56	57	58	59	60	61	62	63	64	65	66	67	68	69	70	71	72	73	74	75	76	77	78	79	80	81	82	83	84	85	86	87	88	89	90	91	92	93	94	95	96
Event			X0																																	*	*			*		X2	
1. School Location				X1	X2																																						
2. Highest Grade		3		4	5	6	7	8	9	10																												6	1				
3. Lowest Grade		2	1									1		1				6	4																				10				
4. No. of Classrooms		2	3	4	5	6	6	7	8	8	9	10								18																					18		
5. No. of Teachers		1	2	2	3	6	6	7	7	8	8	11	23	23	12	13	15	16	20	19	20	21	20		7	18	22	23	24	18	23		26		30	34			30	34			
6. No. of Students		7	20	60	100	109	123	121	136	189	348	510	565	275	270	265	261	434	464	485	503	579	617	672	618	695	783	838	679	925	974	756	667	708	637	715	1325	994	996	1064	
7. No. of Female Students		5	10	12	14	19	16	24	38	38	74	67	32	34	36	39	77	90	103	133	153	174	194	201	233	237	273	365	349	281	269	265	328	631	477	474	536			

Middle table

Year	54	55	56	57	58	59	60	61	62	63	64	65	66	67	68	69	70	71	72	73	74	75	76	77	78	79	80	81	82	83	84	85	86	87	88	89	90	91	92	93	94	95	96
Event																																											
8. Tuition Grade 1			0							0	1			1																									0			0		
9. Tuition Grade 10		Inap									Inap	10	10.3	10.3	10.5	10.5	11	11					13	13.8	16.3	16.3		20			20		26	26		40			15	15	55	50	
10. Other Fees Grade 1		0								0	Inap					Inap															33								Inap		95	100	45	
11. Other Fees-10		Inap									Inap	5	2.5	2.5			2.5	22	22	35	25	39	22	21.5	18	24	26	53	33					33	52	53		52	95	100	190	175	
12. General Curriculum																										X															X	X	
13. Curriculum Family Plan.																																									X	X	

Bottom table

Year	54	55	56	57	58	59	60	61	62	63	64	65	66	67	68	69	70	71	72	73	74	75	76	77	78	79	80	81	82	83	84	85	86	87	88	89	90	91	92	93	94	95	96
Event																																											
14. No. Students in Hostel		0									0	1	4	4	5	5	7	8					8	9	8	9							9	10							0		
15. No. Fem. Students in Hostel		Inap																																							Inap	0	
16. No. of Graduate Teachers		0									0	1	4	4	5	5	7	8				2	2	2	3	3							9	10							10		
17. Medium		0									0	1	0	1	0	0	1	0			1	2	2	3	3	3	1			2	1	0									0		
18. No. Female Teachers		0								0	0	1	1	2	2	2	0	1			1	2	2	3	3	3	1	1	1	2	1	0	0	2	0	2	0	0	2		2		

Event legend (right margin)

Year	Event
2.	Highest Grade
3.	Lowest Grade
4.	No. of Classrooms
5.	No. of Teachers
6.	No. of Students
7.	No. of Fem. Stdts.
8.	Tuition Grade 1
9.	Tuition Grade 10
10.	Other Fees-1
11.	Other Fees-10
12.	General
13.	Family Plan.
14.	Stdts. Hostel
15.	Fem. Stdts. Hostel
16.	Graduate Tchrs.
17.	Medium
18.	Female Tchrs.

Key:

*   National and regional events entered on calendars to aid respondent recall. Examples: elections, earthquakes, flooding.

X1, X2   (in Line 1—School Location; X1 indicates the years the school was at its first location, X2 indicates the years the school was at its second location, and X3 indicates another location. etc.

Inap   Information not appropriate in this school (e.g. this school had no hostel, so the question about the number of girls in the hostel is inappropriate).

Numbers   (in Lines 8–11) Indicate the number of rupees for tuition or fees.

X   (in Line 12—General Curriculum) Indicates that the standard, government curriculum was followed.

X   (in Line 13—Curriculum Family Plan.) Indicates that the curriculum included some family planning content.

Blanks   (in Lines 12 and 13) Indicate that the standard, government curriculum was not used, or that the curriculum did not include family planning content.

Note: Names and identifiers have been changed to protect the anonymity of the school.
Nepali years were used in the data collection. Western year 1996 = Nepali year 2052/2053.

FIGURE 2. An example of a completed school history calendar from the Chitwan Valley Family Study.

run down the side marking row headings. We began substantive domains with the location of the school, which was recorded on both the calendar and the questionnaire. As mentioned above, some schools changed location, such as the one depicted in Figure 2, so the timing of these changes was recorded on the first line of the calendar. Other lines of the calendar were used to record changes in a variety of important characteristics of schools in Chitwan, including highest grade offered, number of classrooms, number of teachers, number of students, tuition, fees, and curriculum. This information dramatically improved our knowledge of the schooling opportunities available to the residents of each neighborhood, from simply knowing that a school existed to knowing how many grades, classrooms, and teachers were available (as well as other information). These procedures also allowed us to measure much more gradual changes over time in educational opportunities than the neighborhood calendars alone.

At each school we attempted to complete as much of the calendar as possible using data from the school's own records before turning to alternative means to gather missing information. Our first alternative was in-depth interviews with school administrators, and we followed this with in-depth interviews with teachers. In the older schools we often encountered situations in which none of the current administrators or teachers was familiar with the early history of the school. To overcome this problem, we tracked retired administrators and teachers to their homes (usually in Chitwan but occasionally elsewhere), and interviewed them. We also tracked retired administrators and teachers in the few cases where a school existed previously but had closed by the time of our interview.

3.2. Health Service History Calendars

As we did with schools, we used regional government records and local interviews to make a listing of every health service outlet in our study area. These health services included hospitals, clinics, dispensaries, and pharmacies. We used a broad definition of health services because each of these outlets provides access to some types of contraceptive methods and a central aim of the study was to estimate the impact of access to methods on actual use of methods. The type of health service was recorded in questionnaires accompanying the calendars.

Figure 3 provides an example of one of our completed health service history calendars from a clinic in our study area. Again, years and events run across the top forming column headings designed to provide

Health Service ID #: 13-12-176   Name of the Health Service: Khaja Medical Hall

Year	54	55	56	57	58	59	60	61	62	63	64	65	66	67	68	69	70	71	72	73	74	75	76	77	78	79	80	81	82	83	84	85	86	87	88	89	90	91	92	93	94	95	96	
Event				*		*												*		*							*	*								*	*							
1.Open																														X													X	1.Open
2.Service-days/week																														7													7	2.Days/week
3.Service-hours/day																														10		10	12										12	3.Hours/day
4.No. of staff																														1		1	2										2	4.No. of staff
5.Health Workers																																												5.Health Wrkrs.
6.Patient check-up																														X													X	6.Check-up
7.No. of rooms																														1		1	2										2	7.No. of rooms

Year	54	55	56	57	58	59	60	61	62	63	64	65	66	67	68	69	70	71	72	73	74	75	76	77	78	79	80	81	82	83	84	85	86	87	88	89	90	91	92	93	94	95	96	
Event				*		*												*		*							*	*								*	*							
8.Pills																																	2							2	2.5	3	3	8.Pills
9.IUD & Loop																																												9.IUD & Lopp
10.Depoprovera																																												10.Depoprovera
11.Dhal/Condom																																		1.5						1.5	2	2.5	2.5	11.Dhal/Condom
12.Foam																																				3					3		6	12.Foam
13.Laproscopy																																												13.Laproscopy
14.Vasectomy																																												14.Vasectomy
15.Other																																												15.Other

380

Year	54	55	56	57	58	59	60	61	62	63	64	65	66	67	68	69	70	71	72	73	74	75	76	77	78	79	80	81	82	83	84	85	86	87	88	89	90	91	92	93	94	95	96	Event
Event						*													*									*									*							
16.Mobile Camp																																												16.Mobile Camp
17.Motivation																																												17.Motivation
18.Birthing																														X												X		18.Pregnancy
19.Child Vaccin.																																												19.Vaccination
20.Diarrhea																														X												X		20.Diarrhoea
21.Nutrition																														X					X							X		21.Nutrition
22.Prenatal																																												22.Maternity
Year	54	55	56	57	58	59	60	61	62	63	64	65	66	67	68	69	70	71	72	73	74	75	76	77	78	79	80	81	82	83	84	85	86	87	88	89	90	91	92	93	94	95	96	

Key:

*	National and regional events entered on calendars to aid respondent recall. Examples: elections, earthquakes, flooding.
X	(in Line 1—Open) Indicates that the facility was open in that year.
X	(in Line 6—Patient Check-Up) Indicates that the facility provided check-ups in that year..
Numbers	(in Lines 8–15) Indicate the price (in rupees) for each service listed for each year. No number indicates that the service was not available during that year.
Blank Lines	(in Lines 8–15) Blank lines indicate the service did not exist. (Interviewers were required to respond to opening questions about the existence of each service in the accompanying questionnaire.)
X	(in Lines 16–22) Indicates that the service listed was provided in that year.

Note: Names and identifiers have been changed to protect the anonymity of the health service center.
Nepali years were used in the data collection. Western year 1996 = Nepali year 2052/2053.

FIGURE 3. An example of completed health services calendar from the Chitwan Valley Family Study.

cues to aid recall of the timing of service changes. Substantive domains run down the side forming row headings. The first row of the calendar specifies the years in which the health service in question was open to the public. Exact dates were recorded in the accompanying questionnaire. The domains on the calendar include days and hours of operation, numbers of staff, aspects of the physical facility, types of contraceptive methods available, and the cost of each service (in rupees per unit). Blank lines indicate the service was not available, and "NA" indicates the interviewers were unable to ascertain whether the service was offered or its cost.[9]

As with schools, data collection was conducted by visiting each health service, gaining permission to consult the outlet's records, and interviewing administrators and health workers to fill gaps in the records. Also similar to schools, a variety of recording techniques were used on the health service calendars. The recording techniques are explained in Figure 3.

3.3. *Other Extensions*

The contextual history calendar method proved flexible enough to be used in a wide array of substantive applications. For example, we used the technique to gather histories of transportation changes in our study area. We designed a calendar to correspond to each road route (or bus route) in the Valley. The calendars were designed to record the type of vehicles used for public transportation on the route across time, such as tractors, jeeps, buses, and motorized rickshaws. The calendars were also designed to record the time to traverse the route and the cost of traveling the route in different periods. Data collection was conducted by going directly to the owners of vehicles used for public transportation on the route and to long-time residents who lived at important stops along each route.

In another example, we used the contextual history calendar method to collect data on changes in banking services. Bank records and bank administrators were consulted to provide a history of changes in loan programs, interest rates, savings levels, and special outreach programs. We used a similar strategy to apply the calendar technique to the collection of histories of government programs in the study area. By working with local program authorities and using their records we collected histories of changes

---

[9]Note that for each domain on the calendar, interviewers were required to check off the response to an opening question in order to indicate that questions about each domain had been asked and answered.

in program participation, program activities, program objectives, etc. These data provide rich measurement of the socioeconomic context within which our study population has spent their lives.

Overall, the history calendar techniques proved to be a useful method for piecing together data from multiple sources to collect a complete, dynamic record of changes over time in a wide range of infrastructure in our study area. The resulting data are quite flexible. The measures we gathered can be used to assemble a complete history of the many different types of services available, or a history of the quality of the different services available. For example, one might create dynamic measures of changes over time in teacher to student ratios or student to classroom ratios. Or, one could create dynamic measures of the availability of contraceptive distribution outlets in the valley. In addition, by recording the location of each service one can construct summary measures of the quality or availability of services within a particular radius of each neighborhood in the study area, or for that matter, each household in the study area. Techniques for accomplishing this are discussed in detail in Section 4. Once such summary measures are created, they can easily be incorporated in multilevel models of individual level outcomes that quality of schooling opportunities are believed to affect, such as educational attainment.

4. USING GEOGRAPHIC INFORMATION SYSTEM TECHNOLOGY TO ENHANCE CONTEXTUAL DATA

Not only do neighborhood residents find it difficult to report on specific characteristics of services near their neighborhood, they also find it difficult to report on all the different services that shape their context. Residents of the 132 neighborhoods we sampled were able to tell us about the two or three schools nearest their neighborhood, or most salient to them, but reporting on all the different educational opportunities within a reasonable bicycling distance (say, one hour each way) proved too demanding a task. Yet Chitwan valley is only 25 kilometers long and 20 kilometers wide, so the combination of all the schooling opportunities nearby constitutes an important element of the context within which these people live. The same is true for other services, such as health care services and government programs. The multiple calendar strategy, described above, gave us the means to collect detailed information about the changes over time in all the aspects of services and infrastructure in Chitwan. But in order to use the full breadth of this information to create measures of the context, these data must be linked to specific neighborhoods and a means must be devised to distinguish those services near each specific neighborhood from services which are further away.

Geographic Information System (GIS) technology provides the tools to solve this problem. GIS is a collection of software and hardware tools designed to create, enter, manage, and analyze data on spatial relationships (Burrough 1986; Maguire et al. 1991). The Global Positioning System (GPS) is a GIS tool specifically designed to measure the spatial location of points on the earth's surface in terms of their longitude, latitude, and altitude.[10] Other tools, such as digitizers, can be used to enter existing spatial data, such as maps, into a GIS. GIS software can then be used to organize multiple sources of spatial data and calculate distances between points. Although GIS technology is primarily used by geographers, it has many potential applications in the social sciences (Heywood 1990; Martin 1996). Our main interest here is in the tremendous potential of these tools to contribute to the creation of contextual summary measures for use in models of individual behavior. For example, using these tools we can create measures of distance between each neighborhood and all the schools in Chitwan and summary measures of educational context within any particular distance of each specific neighborhood.

In the CVFS, GPS devices are being used to record the location of each of the neighborhoods in our study area. These devices will then be used to measure the location of each of the contextual features of interest in the study, including schools, health service outlets, banks, and government programs. This location data can then be appended to the corresponding history calendar data. When the location data are entered into a GIS, the GIS can generate distance measures—for example, between a neighborhood and each of the schools in the study area. Using these distances, it is also possible to identify each of the schools within a certain distance of each neighborhood. Thus we can construct measures of the distance to all the schooling opportunities in the study area, or measures of all those schools within a specific distance. These measures can then be linked to measures of the characteristics of the schools, so that we can estimate the quality of schooling opportunities to which residents have access. Given the temporal dimension in our measures of quality of

[10]GPS handheld roving units use satellite readings to provide location measures.

schooling opportunities, such measures can also be created for each specific point in time.

Data from other sources can also be input into the GIS in order to construct new access variables. For example, one can digitize maps of physical features or road networks into the GIS. In the CVFS we used aerial photographs of the study area to make maps of the road network that can be digitized into the GIS. By linking specific roads with our bus service history calendar data, we can develop measures of the location of various transportation services relative both to residents' households and to specific services. Since the bus service calendars include time to traverse the route, and our neighborhood data includes time to reach the nearest bus stop, we can use the GIS to create measures of the time to travel (or cost to travel) from each neighborhood to any specific service (such as a health clinic) in the study area. In fact, GIS technology can use these variables to calculate the shortest route to nearby health clinics (e.g., Entwisle et al.1996).

By using these GIS technologies to link our neighborhood history data together in space, we add an important new component to the array of measures possible from these data collection procedures. Now measures of historical change (Section 2.4.1) or measures of exposure to change (Section 2.4.2) can be ordered in space. From the perspective of each specific neighborhood, measures of exposure to changes can be constructed to indicate whether the change is nearby, far away, or in between. These measures make it possible to test spatial hypotheses regarding the effects of context, such as the hypothesis that school opportunities near a family's household have more impact on that family's behavior than schooling opportunities far from the family's household. Even in a multilevel hazards modeling framework (Section 2.4.3) these spatial data allow researchers to add measures of distance to contextual-level time-varying covariates. This addition provides the means to test the impact of variations in distance to contextual changes on individual-level outcomes.

The spatial measures created with GIS have other uses as well. Residents' perceptions of access to contextual features are always likely to be an important aspect of evaluating the impact of context on individual behavior. However, independent information on spatial location provides an important advantage. Respondents' reports of distance and time to nearby services are known to be characterized by measurement error. Use of GIS technology to obtain an independent set of distance measures provides a means of correcting for this measurement error.

5. DISCUSSION

The Neighborhood History Calendar data collection method outlined here is designed to collect a record of community-level change over time for use in dynamic multilevel models. The method is based on Life History Calendar techniques which were designed to collect a dynamic event history of individual life-courses (Caspi et al. 1996; Freedman et al. 1988). The Neighborhood History Calendar method combines the structure of a calendar and accompanying questionnaires with a wide-open data collection strategy born out of recent efforts to combine structured and unstructured data collection methods (Axinn et al.1991; Massey 1987). The result is a standardized technique for collecting measures of community change over time flexible enough to be adapted to many different settings and a wide range of substantive aims. In fact, we found that the technique worked equally well for measurement of changes over time in neighborhoods, schools, health services, transportation, banks, and government programs. Our success with the method across these many different contexts and among a multiethnic, multilingual study population is consistent with the conclusion that this history calendar technique provides a reliable means of gathering contextual event-history data for many substantive purposes.

The calendar methods described in this paper were primarily designed to measure change over time in social and economic infrastructure, not the spread of ideational phenomena. If the spread of new ideas can be operationalized as change over time in an observable contextual characteristic, such as the spread of radios and televisions, changes in media programs, the creation of movie theaters, or the distribution of written media, then the calendar methods can be adapted for this purpose. When such changes are conceptualized as the spread of new ideas among individuals, then individual-level data collection strategies are more appropriate.

Nevertheless, the method reported here generates data with three important advantages over contextual data from other sources that are commonly used in multilevel models. First, current multilevel modeling efforts tend to rely on static measures of context, taken at one or two points in time. Thus individuals are assigned contextual characteristics that correspond only to the point in time at which they were measured. However, contexts are continually changing. For example, a neighborhood that had a school in 1990 may not have one by 1991. This issue is particularly problematic when comparing multiple contexts. Consider two neighborhoods (A and B) which both had health clinics in 1990 while neither had a clinic in 1980. Suppose the clinic in neighborhood A opened in 1981 while the clinic in neighborhood B opened in 1989. Contextual data from two points in time (1980 and 1990) will indicate the same health care contexts in these two neighborhoods even though individuals in neighborhood A have had a much different history of health care from those in neighborhood B. However, our complete neighborhood event-history measurement will demonstrate that these two contexts are quite different. This continuous record of contextual dynamics is an important advantage over static measurement (Rossi et al. 1980).

Second, our method also allows examination of the sequence of contextual change, so that even when neighborhoods (or other contexts) have experienced multiple changes we can decipher which came first. For instance, in neighborhoods with both bus service and a school, we can determine whether the neighborhood first had bus service, and then a school was built, or a school was built and then bus service began. This is an important advantage because community differences are often characterized by variations in more than one factor, and the order of changes allows researchers to differentiate among contexts (Casterline 1985). For instance, discovering that a respondent who lives in a neighborhood with both bus service and a school is more likely to use contraception than a respondent who lives in a neighborhood without either is difficult to interpret because it is unclear whether the effect is due to the presence of the bus service or the presence of the school.

Third, our approach provides direct measures of contextual features rather than secondary measures generated by aggregating individual-level measures. For example, using the Neighborhood History Calendar we collected changes over time in the location of the nearest school and aspects of that school to measure the neighborhood's educational context rather than using the average level of individual educational attainment in the neighborhood. Many multilevel modeling efforts use contextual measures constructed by aggregating individual-level characteristics (Blalock 1985; Brewster 1994; Brooks-Gunn et al. 1993; Casterline 1985; Hirschman and Guest 1990). Using our method, the researcher collects data on contextual features rather than aggregating individual-level characteristics. This approach avoids some of the pitfalls involved with multilevel modeling using aggregated data (Blalock 1985), and instead focuses attention on contextual characteristics which cannot be disaggregated to the individual level.

Of course, as mentioned in the introduction, the Neighborhood History Calendar method does not solve all the problems involved in creating completely dynamic multilevel models. One problem facing all multilevel analysis efforts is the mobility of individuals. When contextual data are linked to individual-level data, it is usually assumed that individuals have lived in that context for a long period, even their entire lives. When individuals move, this assumption is untenable. Those who have moved have been exposed to other contextual characteristics besides those measured in the analysis. Depending on the length of time lived in other contexts, and the number of different contexts experienced, the mobile individual's cumulative contextual experience may be quite different than that of a lifetime resident. Unfortunately the collection of dynamic contextual event histories is not a solution to this problem.

A variety of solutions to this problem may be possible. Migration histories administered at the individual level could be used to identify the location of previous residences. With this information, researchers could visit each previous residence of a respondent and gather contextual data from those neighborhoods. However, this strategy is likely to prove cumbersome in a highly mobile population. Both the number of moves and the distance between residences will dramatically increase data collection costs.

A second solution may be to ask respondents about their exposure to contextual characteristics of interest in an individual-level questionnaire. This strategy has the advantage of matching the contextual data collection directly to the individual's residence history. However, individuals may find it difficult to recall contextual characteristics from earlier in their lives. This problem may be exacerbated among individuals who have migrated often and have lived in many different contexts. This approach may also restrict the precision with which contextual characteristics can be measured. Individuals are unlikely to be able to recall many specific aspects of contextual features from their previous residences.

Though perfect solutions to this problem are not obvious, individual-level mobility histories give researchers a tool to examine the plausibility of their assumptions about mobility. Life histories designed for use in multilevel models should always include mobility histories. By combining such life histories with dynamic histories of contextual change, researchers will be able to construct dynamic multilevel models that match dynamic reality.

Given the broad interest in contextual effects across many substantive areas of social science inquiry, it is quite likely that multilevel modeling efforts will become more common in the future (Bryk and Raudenbush 1992; DiPrete and Forristal 1994; Goldstein 1995; Ringdal 1992). Furthermore, dynamic event-history models have many advantages to offer in modeling the individual-level outcomes of interest to multilevel research-ers (Petersen 1991; Yamaguchi 1991). Thus it seems likely that future multilevel modeling efforts will take on an increasingly dynamic nature. Unfortunately, limitations of the contextual measurements currently avail-able to researchers create an important obstacle to the development and application of truly dynamic multilevel models. The data collection method described here was designed to overcome that obstacle and provide the means to gather a complete event-history record of contextual-level change.

REFERENCES

Alexander, Jeffrey C. 1988. *Action and Its Environments: Toward a New Synthesis.* New York: Columbia University Press.

Allison, Paul D. 1984. *Event History Analysis.* Newbury Park, CA: Sage.

Axinn, William G. 1989. "Interviewers and Data Quality in a Less Developed Setting." *Journal of Official Statistics* 5:265–80.

Axinn, William G., Thomas E. Fricke and Arland Thornton. 1991. "The Microdemo-graphic Community-Study Approach: Improving Survey Data by Integrating the Ethnographic Method." *Sociological Methods and Research* 20:187–217.

Back, Kurt W., and J. Mayone Stycos. 1959. "The Survey Under Unusual Conditions: Methodological Facets of the Jamaican Human Fertility Investigation." *Applied Anthropology* 1–50.

Barber, Jennifer, Ganesh Shivakoti, William G. Axinn, and Kishore Gajurel. 1995. "Sampling Strategies for Less Developed Settings: A Detailed Example from Rural Nepal." Paper presented at the annual meeting of the Population Association of America, April 11–14, 1995, in San Francisco.

Biemer, Paul P., Robert M. Groves, Lars E. Lyberg, Nancy A. Mathiowetz, and Sey-mour Sudman, eds. 1991. *Measurement Errors in Surveys.* New York: Wiley.

Blalock, Hubert M. 1985. "Cross-Level Analysis." In *The Collection and Analysis of Community Data*, edited by John B. Casterline, 187–206. Voorburg, Netherlands: International Statistical Institute.

Bradburn, Norman M. 1983. "Response Effects." In *Handbook of Survey Research,* edited by Peter Rossi, James Wright, and Andy Anderson, 289–328. New York: Academic Press.

Brewster, Karin. 1994. "Race Differences in Sexual Activity Among Adolescent Women: The Role of Neighborhood Characteristics." *American Sociological Review* 59:408–424.

Briggs, Charles L. 1986. *Learning How to Ask: A Sociolinguistic Appraisal of the Role of the Interview in Social Science Research.* New York: Cambridge University Press.

Brooks-Gunn, Jeanne, Greg J. Duncan, Pamela Kato Klebanov, and Naomi Sealand. 1993. "Do Neighborhoods Influence Child and Adolescent Development?" *American Journal of Sociology* 99:353–95.

Bryk, Anthony S. and Stephen W. Raudenbush. 1992. *Hierarchical Linear Models: Applications and Data Analysis Methods.* Newbury Park, CA: Sage.

Burrough, P. 1986. *Principles of Geographical Information Systems for Land Resource Assessment*. Oxford: Clarendon Press.

Caldwell, John C. 1982. *Theory of Fertility Decline*. New York: Academic Press.

―――. 1985. "Strengths and Limitations of the Survey Approach for Measuring and Understanding Fertility Change: Alternative Possibilities." In *Reproductive Change in Developing Countries: Insights from the World Fertility Survey*, edited by John Cleland and John Hobcraft, 45–63. Oxford, England: Oxford University Press.

Caldwell, John C., Pat Caldwell, and Bruce Caldwell. 1987. "Anthropology and Demography: The Mutual Reinforcement of Speculation and Research." *Current Anthropology* 28:25–43.

Caspi, Avshalom, Terrie E. Moffitt, Arland Thornton, Deborah Freedman, James W. Amell, Honalee Harrington, Judith Smeijers, and Phil A. Silva. 1996. "The Life History Calendar: A Research and Clinical Assessment Method for Collecting Retrospective Event-History Data." *International Journal of Methods in Psychiatric Research* 6:101–14.

Casterline, John B., ed. 1985. *The Collection and Analysis of Community Data*. Voorburg, Netherlands: International Statistical Institute.

Chambers, Robert. 1985. "Rapid Rural Appraisal: Rationale and Repertoire." In *Putting People First: Sociological Variables in Rural Development*, edited by M. M. Cernea, 399–415. London: Oxford University Press.

Coleman, James S. 1990. *Foundations of Social Theory*. Cambridge: Harvard University Press.

DiPrete, Thomas A., and Jerry D. Forristal. 1994. "Multilevel Models: Methods and Substance." *Annual Review of Sociology* 20:331–357.

Durkheim, Emile. 1984 [1933]. *The Division of Labor in Society*. New York: Free Press.

Eisenhower, Donna, Nancy A. Mathiowetz, and David Morganstein. 1991. "Recall Error: Sources and Bias Reduction Techniques." In *Measurement Errors in Surveys*, edited by Paul P. Biemer, Robert M. Groves, Lars E. Lyberg, Nancy A. Mathiowetz, and Seymour Sudman, 128–144. New York: Wiley.

Entwisle, Barbara, and William Mason. 1985. "The Multilevel Effects of Socioeconomic Development and Family Planning Programs on Children Ever Born." *American Journal of Sociology* 91:616–49.

Entwisle, Barbara, Ronald R. Rindfuss, David K. Guilkey, Aphichat Chamratrithirong, Sara R. Curran, and Yothin Sawangdee. 1996. "Community and Contraceptive Choice in Rural Thailand: A Case Study of Nang Rong." *Demography* 33:1–11.

Fowler, Floyd J., Jr. 1991. "Reducing Interviewer-Related Error Through Interviewer Training, Supervision, and Other Means." In *Measurement Errors in Surveys*, edited by Paul P. Biemer, Robert M. Groves, Lars E. Lyberg, Nancy A. Mathiowetz, and Seymour Sudman, 259–78. New York: Wiley.

Freedman, Deborah, Arland Thornton, Donald Camburn, Duane Alwin, and Linda Young-DeMarco. 1988. "The Life History Calendar: A Technique for Collecting Retrospective Data." In *Sociological Methodology 1988*, edited by Clifford C. Clogg, 37–68. Washington: American Sociological Association.

Goldstein, Harvey. 1995. *Multilevel Statistical Models*. New York: Halsted Press.

Groves, Robert M. 1987. "Research on Survey Data Quality." *Public Opinion Quarterly* 50th Anniversary Supplement:s156–72.

Hammel, Eugene. 1990. "A Theory of Culture for Demography." *Population and Development Review* 16:455–85.

Heaton, Tim B., and Vaughn R. Call. 1995. "Modeling Family Dynamics with Event History Techniques." *Journal Marriage and the Family* 57:1078–90.

Heywood, I. 1990. "Geographic Information Systems in the Social Sciences." *Environment and Planning* 22:849–54.

Hirschman, Charles, and Philip Guest. 1990. "Multilevel Models of Fertility Determination in Four Southeast Asian Countries: 1970 and 1980." *Demography* 27:369–96.

Huber, Joan, ed. 1991. *Macro-micro Linkages in Sociology*. Newbury Park, CA: Sage.

Kahn, Robert L., and C. F. Cannell. 1957. *The Dynamics of Interviewing*. New York: Wiley.

Landale, Nancy. 1994. "Migration and the Latino Family: The Union Formation Behavior of Puerto Rican Women." *Demography* 31:133–57.

Maguire, D. J., Michael F. Goodchild, and David Rhind. 1991. *Geographical Information Systems. Vol. 1, Principles; Vol. 2, Applications*. London: Longmans.

Martin, David. 1996. *Geographic Information Systems and Their Socioeconomic Applications*. London: Routledge.

Massey, Douglas S. 1987. "The Ethnosurvey in Theory and Practice." *International Migration Review* 21:1498–522.

Petersen, Trond. 1991. "The Statistical Analysis of Event Histories." *Sociological Methods and Research* 19:270–323.

Raudenbush, Stephen W. 1988. "Educational Applications of Hierarchical Linear Models: A Review." *Journal of Educational Statistics* 13:85–116.

Ringdal, Kristen. 1992. "Recent Developments in Methods for Multilevel Analysis." *Acta Sociologica* 35:235–43.

Rossi, Peter H., Robert A. Berk, and K. J. Lenihan. 1980. *Money, Work and Crime: Some Experimental Results*. New York: Academic Press.

Rountree, Pamela Wilcox, Kenneth C. Land, and Terance D. Miethe. 1994. "Macro-micro Integration in the Study of Victimization: A Hierarchical Logistic Model Analysis Across Seattle Neighborhoods." *Criminology* 32:387–413.

Sastry, Narayan. 1995. "A Multilevel Hazards Model for Hierarchically Clustered Data: Model Estimation and an Application to the Study of Child Survival in Northeast Brazil." RAND Working Paper 95–115.

———. 1996. "Community Characteristics, Individual and Household Attributes, and Child Survival in Brazil." *Demography* 33:211–29.

Schaeffer, Nora Cate. 1991. "Conversation with a Purpose—Or Conversation? Interaction in the Standardized Interview." In *Measurement Errors in Surveys*, edited by Paul P. Biemer, Robert M. Groves, Lars E. Lyberg, Nancy A. Mathiowetz, and Seymour Sudman, 367–91. New York: Wiley.

Schuman, Howard, and Jacqueline Scott. 1989. "Generations and Collective Memories." *American Sociological Review* 54:359–81.

Smith, Herbert L. 1989. "Integrating Theory and Research on the Institutional Determinants of Fertility." *Demography* 26:171–84.

Stone, Linda, and Jeffrey G. Campbell. 1984. "The Use and Misuse of Surveys in International Development: An Experiment from Nepal." *Human Organization* 43:27–37.

Suchman, L., and B. Jordan. 1990. "Interactional Troubles in Face-to-Face Survey Interviews." *Journal of the American Statistical Association* 85:232–41.

Sudman, Seymore, and Norman M. Bradburn. 1974. *Response Effects in Surveys*. Chicago: Aldine.

Thornton, Arland, William G. Axinn, and Jay Teachman. 1995. "The Influence of Educational Experiences on Cohabitation and Marriage in Early Adulthood." *American Sociological Review* 60:762–74.

Weiss, Robert S. 1994. *Learning from Strangers: the Art and Method of Qualitative Interview Studies*. New York: Free Press.

Wong, George Y., and William M. Mason. 1985. "The Hierarchical Logistic Regression Model for Multilevel Analysis." *Journal of the American Statistical Association* 80:513–24.

Xie, Yu. 1994. "Log-Multiplicative Models for Discrete-Time, Discrete-Covariate Event-History Data." In *Sociological Methodology 1994*, edited by Peter V. Marsden, 301–40. Cambridge, MA: Blackwell Publishers.

Yamaguchi, Kazuo. 1991. *Event History Analysis*. Newbury Park, CA: Sage.

8

ADJUSTING FOR ATTRITION IN EVENT-HISTORY ANALYSIS

Daniel H. Hill*

The sensitivity of parameter estimates of event-history models to alternative methods of correcting for panel attrition is not well understood. This paper will investigate the issue of weighting for panel attrition in event-history models by comparing alternative treatments of sampling weights in a divorce model for members of the 1986 Survey of Income and Program Participation (SIPP). Three distinct weighting procedures are compared. These are based on (1) the initial selection probability weights; (2) the 1986 SIPP panel weights; and (3) the monthly attrition-adjusted weights. The paper also compares these weighted estimates with the estimates of a structural model in which attrition is treated as an error-correlated competing alternative to divorce. Although it is impossible to identify a "best" procedure without accurate external data, significant differences in the estimates for the various procedures are indicative of significant attrition related problems in event-history models. None of the weighting adjustments are found to have any appreciable effect on the estimates of the divorce hazard model examined. The reason is that all of the weighting procedures are based on the assumption of independent censoring. The competing hazards structural model relaxes this assumption and finds evidence of significant correlated unmeasured heterogeneity. Once

The research reported in this paper was conducted under contract for the WESTAT Corporation (subcontract no. 5-YABC-2-66025) with funding originating from the U.S. Bureau of the Census. The author would like to thank Pat Doyle and Keith Rust of the American Statistical Association—Census Bureau Survey Methods Division SIPP Working Group, Adrian Raftery, and two anonymous referees for their helpful comments on an earlier version of this paper. The findings, opinions, and conclusions are those of the author, as is the responsibility for any errors. E-mail: dhhill@isr. umich.edu

*The University of Michigan

393

corrections for this are made, the net divorce hazards are seen to increase by more than one-half. This suggests that in many instances divorces in the SIPP end up being recorded as attrition.

1. INTRODUCTION

One of the major strengths of panel data is that change measures are derived from current reports rather than from recollected statuses. This removes recall error as a source of bias affecting parameter estimates of event-history and other dynamic models. Unfortunately, another characteristic of panel data is that respondents tend to drop out or attrite as the panel progresses. This introduces a different potential source of bias in event-history models. Which of these biases is most important (and implicitly, whether panel data is superior to retrospective data) is a complicated question—the answer to which probably varies from one substantive application and set of surveys to another.

The seriousness of the biases introduced to event-history models by panel attrition will depend, for example, on the amount of attrition and on the relationship between two propensities: the propensity to leave the sample and the propensity to undergo the substantive change being analyzed. If these propensities are related, then the seriousness of the bias will depend on whether the relationship is confined to the covariates included in the event-history model specification and weight adjustment procedures or whether there are excluded, or even unmeasured, factors that affect both propensities. If the covariates do fully account for the relationship between the propensity to change and the propensity to attrite, then the parameter estimates of the substantive model will be unaffected by attrition. If, on the other hand, there is a residual relationship, then explicit corrections for attrition will be required to obtain unbiased estimates.

This paper investigates two alternative strategies for correcting for this type of nonignorable attrition in event-history models. The first strategy explored is the use of attrition-adjusted sampling weights in the event-history model. The purpose of these weights in panel surveys is to bring the panel back in line with the intended population of inference with respect to the distributions of key variables. Application of such weights is currently the most commonly recommended method of adjusting for attrition in event-history analysis. The second strategy investigated is modeling attrition and the substantive change of interest as correlated competing hazards (i.e., competing hazards with correlated unmeasured heterogeneity). The estimated *net* survival function for the substantive change is interpretable as the one we would obtain if attrition were eliminated.

The context of these investigations is divorce (or separation) in the 1986 Panel of the Survey of Income and Program Participation (SIPP). Although the SIPP appears to remain roughly representative of marital statuses once adjustments for attrition are made (e.g., see Singh 1988), there is concern that it seriously underrepresents *change* in marital status, particularly divorces, over the panel period (e.g., see M. Hill 1987; D. Hill 1993). Since divorce is rare, both absolutely and relative to attrition, the parameter estimates from event-history models of it are especially vulnerable to attrition bias. Divorce is also important substantively. Not only is it of interest to behavioral scientists in its own right, but it is also an important determinant of family income, program participation, and economic well-being. Furthering our understanding of these conditions in the population is a fundamental reason for conducting the survey.

Section 2 provides background on the SIPP and defines some key concepts and procedures used in the remainder of the paper. Section 3 develops a simple event-history model of divorce and presents the results obtained using alternative weighting schemes in its estimation. Section 4 models and presents the results of the model-based alternative to weighting. The conclusions and recommendations for future research are presented in Section 5.

2. BACKGROUND AND CONVENTIONS

2.1. *Background*

The SIPP—a large panel survey of individuals in the United States—has been in operation since 1984 (see Jabine et al. [1990] for a detailed description of the SIPP). The survey is comprised of a set of panels that are fresh cross-sections introduced annually. The members of each panel are interviewed every four months for roughly two and one-half years, and retrospective information on income, employment, program participation, and family composition is obtained for each month of the four-month reference period.

Although SIPP study procedures call for following and interviewing all panel members when they leave the original sample of households, this is not always possible. In the 1986 panel just under one-fourth of the individuals originally in interviewed households became nonrespondents at some point in the panel period and two-thirds of these individuals were never successfully recontacted (i.e., they attrited). Early on in the survey the concern was raised that attrition was particularly problematic when individuals experienced a marital status change. The reason for this concern is apparent in Table 1, which presents the attrition and marital status patterns for husbands and wives in the 1986 SIPP panel. The sample consists of all couples who were married at some point in the panel period. In the vast majority (6,333 + 130) of these couples, neither spouse attrited. The 24-month divorce/separation rate among these panel members was just over 2 percent. This rate is in sharp contrast to the 60 percent (= 92/(92 + 64)) divorce/separation rate among those couples in which one or the other (but not both) partners attrited. The more common situation in which both partners attrite is even more problematic when it comes to estimating marital status change. The reason is that we do not know how many of the 1004 couples who were still married at the time of their last interview, divorced or separated subsequent to (or concurrently with) their last interview.

The original concern over the effects of differential attrition was heightened when initial analysis of the first three waves of the 1984 panel indicated that estimated divorce rates were only some 60 percent as high as other data sets indicated they should be (see Table 2). More recent analysis confirms this initial finding and shows that the problem persists in more recent panels (Hill 1993). Among those couples who eventually attrited from the 1986 SIPP panel, the hazard of divorce prior to attrition was some 60 percent higher than among those individuals who responded throughout the panel period. Since it is quite possible that much of the divorce

TABLE 1
Last Observed Marital Status of Couple by Number of Spouses
Attriting (Initially Married Couples: 1986 SIPP)

	Married	Divorced
Neither spouse attriting	6,333	130
	98%	2%
One spouse attriting	64	92
	41%	59%
Both spouses attriting	1,004	9
	99%	1%

TABLE 2
Annual Divorce and Separation Rates: 1986 SIPP Versus Benchmarks

Population and type of disruption	Vital Statistics	Panel Study of Income Dynamics	1986 SIPP
Persons over 14 years old:			
Divorce	1.3%	—	0.7%
Divorce/separation	—	1.8%	1.0%
Married women aged 18–44:			
Divorce	3.0%	—	1.2%

Source: Hill 1987.

among attritors occurred concurrently with, or just subsequent to, their leaving the study (and therefore their divorces are unrecorded in the study), the divorce hazard may be underestimated.

Partly in light of this concern about differential attrition among marital status changers, a series of sampling weight adjustments was developed. Most of these adjustments take the form of poststratification adjustments, which have the effect of forcing survey estimates to correspond to outside information on the distributions of key variables including census region, age, race, ethnicity, and other demographic factors (see Jabine et al. [1990:85–88] for a detailed discussion of these adjustments). An additional adjustment, the family composition adjustment, was also developed to adjust for the double selection probabilities for families formed when an original sample member marries someone who was not part of the original sample (but who had a positive *ex ante* chance of having been selected).

With these adjustments to the weights, the SIPP sample appears to be roughly representative of the entire population with respect to the proportions of adults married, single, divorced, or widowed (see McMillen 1989). This is not the same thing, however, as the survey being representative of marital status changes since it is always possible to have good estimates of the numbers of individuals in particular states (i.e., stocks) at each point in time without having good representation of the flows of individuals between those states. With rare events such as divorce, such stock-flow imbalances can persist well beyond the length of the panel period.

2.2. *Conventions*

Since the SIPP is a survey of individuals while the appropriate unit of analysis for divorce is the married couple, some conventions need to be adopted to deal with the situation that arises when one marital partner exhibits a different pattern of marital status change or attrition than the other. This would occur, for instance, if one spouse drops out of the study while the other remains in and reports being divorced. Since divorce is of more substantive interest than attrition, we will apply the following priority coding scheme to conflicting spousal reports: (1) divorced; (2) separated; (3) married; and (4) nonresponse. Those couples who remain married but live separately are treated, here, as married. This means that if only one spouse is responding and providing a marital status report, then the couple will be given that status. Only if neither spouse is responding will the couple be considered as having attrited.

The fact that two individuals are involved also raises the question of whose weight should be used in the weighted analysis.[1] For those couples beginning the sample period married, the differences in the initial weights are relatively minor and, as a practical matter, it does not matter whose weight is used. However, when one respondent leaves the study or when an individual from outside the original sample marries a sample member, then the weight of the nonsample member will be zero. This means the weights for spouses can be quite different. The following convention will be used in this paper:

1.   If both spouses are responding and are still married to each other, then the average of their weights will be used.
2.   If only one spouse is responding, then the larger of the two weights will be used.

This weighting convention is an example of what Kalton and Brick (1994) term a "multiplicity approach" in which the selection probability of the nonoriginal sample individual is assumed to equal that of their sample spouse. It is similar to the procedures used in the Panel Study of Income

---

[1] A weight is a multiplicative factor assigned to each observation in a sample whose members were selected with nonequal probabilities of selection in order to allow unbiased inference to the entire population. The base weight is generally the inverse of the selection probability most often adjusted for differential nonresponse and other factors that affect inference.

Dynamics (PSID) in assigning family weights to families composed of a mix of sample and nonsample spouses.

2.3. *Weighting Schemes Investigated*

As in most panel surveys, a variety of sampling weights are provided for the SIPP. The Longitudinal Research File, upon which I rely most heavily, contains three weights: (1) the "panel" weight, (2) the 1986 calendar year weight, and (3) the 1987 calendar year weight. Each of these weights is intended to allow inference to the entire population from that portion of the sample that responded to each interview in the reference period. The reference period for the "panel" weight is the entire 28-month period covered by the 1986 panel, while for the 1986 and 1987 calendar year weights, it is the 12-month period from January through December of the respective years. These weights are zero for individuals who were nonrespondents at any time during the respective reference period.

Since the divorce history model I will investigate in Section 3 deals with the hazard of divorce over the entire panel period, the first weighting scheme investigated will be that based on the panel weight from the 1986 Full Panel Longitudinal Research File.

In addition to the weights provided on the Longitudinal Research File, the Census Bureau provides a series of monthly weights for SIPP individuals which were merged from the individual wave files to the Longitudinal Research File. The existence of these monthly weights allows the application of two additional weighting schemes to the divorce history analysis. The first scheme is to use the initial month weights for the divorce model. The advantage of this is that the initial weights reflect all the differences in selection probabilities from the original sample design with a minimum of adjustments for sample attrition. The estimates from this weighting procedure are potentially useful as a benchmark in evaluating the efficacy of the attrition adjustments in the other weighting schemes.

The final weighting scheme investigated uses the monthly weights as the basis of a time-varying weighting adjustment in the divorce history model. This weighting scheme is somewhat unusual in that there is a different weight for each couple for each time period. The rationale here is that since each monthly weight has been adjusted for attrition to bring the sample in line with the population during that month, use of these weights brings the total number of individuals at risk of divorce in each month in line with total number at risk in the population. Similarly, to the extent that the attrition adjustments are effective, the monthly estimates of numbers of couples experiencing divorce should also be representative of the corresponding number in the population. Since the estimated divorce risk is the ratio of the number of divorces to the number of couples at risk, application of these weights might be thought to yield unbiased estimates.

2.4. *Sample and Construction of Married Couple Records*

Two related samples are used in the analysis. The first sample is composed of marriage spells for couples in the 1986 SIPP Panel who married during the observation period. Such spells will be referred to as non–left-censored (NLC) spells. In all there are 1,090 such marriage spells in the 1986 SIPP panel.

The second sample consists of *all* spells in which two individuals in the 1986 SIPP panel lived together as a married couple—including those in which marriage began prior to the observation period. This later group of spells is left-censored (LC) and is only useful in constant hazard models.

The first stage of constructing the married couple pair data consisted of eliminating from the entire sample of 35,792 individuals those individuals for whom none of the 28 marital status variables equaled 1 (married spouse present). The resulting 15,608 individuals were then matched on the basis of sample unit, household, and person number of spouse ID variables. In all, there were 7821 marriage spells (there were 34 cases of multiple marriages during the 24-month panel period).[2] Of the 7821 marriage spells, 189 ended in widowhood and were eliminated from the analysis. Of the remaining 7632 marriage spells, 231 ended in divorce or separation and 6397 remained intact. Both spouses attrited in the residual 1004 cases.

The final stage of data management was to subset the 7632 marriage spells into those which were not left censored. This yielded the 1090 spells mentioned above, with 45 ending in divorce or separation, 817 remaining intact, and 228 attriting.

3. THE EFFECTS OF WEIGHTING

As noted in the introduction, applying attrition-adjusted sampling weights in estimation of event-history models is the most commonly recommended

---

[2]For rotation groups 2–4, there were actually 28 months in the panel reference period. The first four of these months, however, do not contain direct measures of marital status and were removed from consideration. Rotation group 1 was interviewed only six times and provides only 20 months of measured marital status.

method of dealing with attrition in panel surveys. This is true not just for the SIPP but for other panels including the PSID and the National Longitudinal Surveys (NLS). This section explores the effects of such weighting using the SIPP as the example.

3.1. A Simple Divorce Model

The divorce model I use is a very simple one which assumes that for each married couple (i) there is, at each time period (t), a latent underlying divorce propensity D_{it}^*. This propensity is assumed to be a scalar value that reflects the net effect of all factors affecting marital instability. If this propensity at any point in time is greater than some threshold (τ), the marriage will end in divorce at that time. Furthermore, the model assumes that the divorce propensity can be decomposed into systematic and random components according to

$$D_{ti}^* = \alpha + \beta' X_{ti} + \epsilon_{ti}, \tag{1}$$

where the systematic portion is composed of: X_{ti}—a vector of covariates; β—a vector of parameters relating these covariates to the divorce propensity; and α—a constant. ϵ_{ti} is a random disturbance representing the net effects of all excluded factors on the divorce propensity. In this specification the ϵ_{ti} are assumed to be identically and independently distributed. Following Allison (1982), I assume that the ϵ are distributed according to the probability density function (pdf) which, when integrated, yields the logistic *cumulative* density function (cdf). The pdf which yields the logistic cdf is known as the hyperbolic secant-square distribution. In this case, the probability of the marriage surviving up to period t, and then ending in divorce during time period t, is

$Prob(D_{ti}^* > \tau | D_{k<ti}^* \leq \tau)$

$$= \exp(\alpha - \tau + \beta' X_{ti})^{w_t} \prod_{j=1}^{t} [1 + \exp(\alpha - \tau + \beta' X_{ji})]^{-w_j}, \tag{2}$$

where w_j is the appropriate sampling weight for period j and where the expression $D_{k<ti}^* < \tau$ simply means that divorce has not occurred in any prior time period k.

The covariates that I will use in the, admittedly simplistic, illustrative example that follows consist of four time-invariant characteristics (age at the beginning of the panel period, whether the couple received government food stamps, whether they owned, or were buying, their home at the beginning of the panel, and whether the original sample member was not employed at that time). I chose these covariates in part because they are plausibly related to divorce propensities but also because some have been found elsewhere to be systematically related to attrition in the SIPP (Rizzo et al. 1994).

In addition to the time-invariant covariates, time itself is a potentially important determinant of divorce propensities. It is well established that the divorce hazards start out low and then increase for a few years after marriage. Later still they begin declining again. Thus prior analysis suggests the need for a time-varying hazard model in which both rising and subsequently declining hazards are allowed. With such a model, the only spells that are fully informative are those observed from the beginning of the marriage—the NLC spells. With SIPP's short panel length, however, the question is whether the limited duration of the panel provides enough of these spells (especially enough completed NLC spells) to support the estimation of such a model. If it does not, a second question arises: Is information on duration effects in the 6542 LC cases sufficient to make divorce analysis using the SIPP a useful example for illustrative purposes? These are, in part, empirical questions.

3.2. Duration Dependent Divorce Hazards in the SIPP

Table 3 presents the maximum likelihood estimates of the parameters of equation (1). The first column of numbers represents the results from the time-varying specification in which time and its square are included as covariates and where attention is confined to the 1090 NLC marriage spells. While food stamp recipiency and age (and its square) are seen to have significant effects on the divorce hazards, and while the point estimates for duration and its square are reasonable, the duration effects are completely insignificant. The reason for this is not that there are not enough spells for which we observe the beginning (i.e., newlyweds) but that the period of observation is too short for enough of these marriages to end in divorce. There were only 35 such disruptions observed among 1090 new marriages during the 24-month measurement period.

The inability of the SIPP to support this type of analysis in a fully satisfactory manner is one of the reasons it has been redesigned with a longer panel period—48 months. With appropriate changes in other procedures, this should double the effective observation period. The redesigned SIPP began in January 1996 but will not provide data for analysis until

TABLE 3
Divorce Hazard Model Estimates by Left-Censor Status of Spells

	Non–Left-censored	Left-censored	All
Constant	−11.59**	−7.34**	−7.44**
	(2.98)	(.90)	(.79)
Age (years)	.33[+]	.06	.07[+]
	(.18)	(.04)	(.04)
Age squared	−.0053*	−.0013**	−.0014**
	(.0026)	(.0005)	(.0005)
Duration (months)	.17	.13**	.14**
	(.12)	(.04)	(.04)
Duration squared	−.0064	−.0052**	−.0055**
	(.0053)	(.0016)	(.0015)
Home owner	−.42	−.51**	−.52**
	(.41)	(.15)	(.14)
Food stamp recipient	1.41*	1.47**	1.44**
	(.62)	(.21)	(.18)
Unemployed at start	.04	−.36*	−.32*
	(.35)	(.15)	(.13)
Log-likelihood (n)	−209.2	−1,417.2	−1,629.0
	(1,090)	(6,542)	(7,632)

[+] Significant at the .90 level.
*Significant at the .95 level.
**Significant at the .99 level.

sometime in 2001. When these data are ready, the question of how to adjust for attrition in event-history analyses will be even more critical since, with the longer panel period, there will be more of it. Since it would be good to learn about this in the meantime, we need to ask whether there is anything we can do with the existing data. This question turns on whether there is sufficient information on duration effects in the more numerous left-censored cases.

Column 2 of Table 3 presents the results of the estimation performed on the LC spells. These results are surprisingly similar to those for the spells of newly married couples in column 1. The "duration" measure used in this analysis is not the duration of the marriage but rather the length of observation of the intact marriage in the SIPP. The pattern of effects of this duration measure is quite similar to that observed among the NLC spells. Divorce hazards at first increase with time and then begin to decline. The coefficient of .13 on duration combined with the coefficient of

−.0052 on its square suggest that divorce hazards increase for the first year before leveling out and then declining.[3] This is virtually the same result seen for the NLC observations in column 1. While the shape of the duration-divorce hazards for both groups of spells is consistent with the literature, the placement of the deflection point is not—the divorce hazards should rise for several years of marriage. This anomaly is not likely, however, to be an artifact of either measurement error in the SIPP or of our treatment of left-censoring. It is most likely a reflection of unmeasured heterogeneity.

A formal test of the proposition that the LC divorce spells in the SIPP are structurally similar to the NLC spells can be constructed by re-estimating the model on the pooled sample (column 3) and examining the log-likelihood functions from three samples. Under the null hypothesis that all apparent differences between the coefficients in column 1 and column 2 are due to chance, twice the difference between the log-likelihood from the pooled sample and the sum of the log-likelihoods from the separate subsamples has, asymptotically, a χ^2 distribution with degrees of freedom equaling the number of parameters estimated. In the present case this "likelihood-ratio" test statistic is 5.2 with 8 degrees of freedom. This is well below the critical χ^2 of 15.5, so we cannot reject the hypothesis of structural homogeneity of left-censored and non–left-censored marriage spells in the SIPP.

In sum, although there is evidence that divorce hazards in the SIPP vary systematically and significantly with duration, there is no evidence that left censoring has any effect on the estimates—even of the duration effects. Since the purpose here is to illustrate the effects of attrition on event-history models and not to provide a definitive analysis of divorce, all the examples that follow are based on the methods of column 3 in Table 3—i.e., they will examine all marriages spells and will include a truncated measure of duration for the left-censored spells. The reader should be aware that the interpretation of the duration dependence results is nonstandard.

3.3. *Weighting Corrections for Attrition*

Although application of attrition-adjusted sampling weights to equation (2) is the most widely recommended method of dealing with attrition in event-history models, the use of such weights at all in model estimation is

---

[3]With the quadratic $y = \beta_1 x + \beta_2 x^2$, an extreme is obtained where $dy/dx = 0$. That is, where $\beta_1 + 2\beta_2 x = 0$ or where $x = -\beta_1/2\beta_2$.

TABLE 4
Divorce Hazard Model Estimates Under Three Weighting Schemes

	Initial Weight	Panel Weight	Monthly Weight
Constant	−7.39**	−8.04**	−7.44**
	(.70)	(.75)	(.79)
Age (years)	.05[+]	.06	.08*
	(.03)	(.04)	(.04)
Age squared	−.0012*	−.0013**	−.0015**
	(.0005)	(.0005)	(.0002)
Truncated duration	.20**	.19**	.20**
(months)	(.04)	(.05)	(.04)
Truncated duration	−.0075**	−.0069**	−.0076**
squared	(.0016)	(.0018)	(.0015)
Home owner	−.51**	−.45**	−.47**
	(.12)	(.14)	(.12)
Food stamp recipient	1.45**	1.32**	1.62**
	(.17)	(.19)	(.15)
Unemployed at start	−.33**	−.30*	−.46**
	(.13)	(.14)	(.12)
Log-likelihood (n)	−1,782.5	−1,369.5	−1,825.5
	(7,632)	(5,809)	(7,632)
ρ^2	6.6%	5.2%	6.7%

*Significant at the .95 level.
**Significant at the .99 level.

a controversial issue. Their intended function is to remove potential biases in the β's that might result from differential effective sampling rates.[4] In the present case, there are two sources of such differentials—initial differences in sampling rates and differences in subsequent nonresponse rates.

Table 4 presents the parameter estimates obtained for the divorce event-history model using each of the three weighting schemes introduced in Section 2. Perhaps the most remarkable thing to note about these estimates is their similarity across the various weighting schemes as well as their similarity to the results presented in the last column of Table 3. All

[4]Those arguing against weighting note that differential selection probabilities can only introduce bias if the model is improperly specified. In this case, it does not really matter if the parameter estimates are biased since, because of the misspecification, they are not the desired parameters in the first place. Furthermore, if the model is properly specified, then the only effect of weighting is to reduce the efficiency of the estimates by introducing weight variance.

three treatments of the weights yield strong (and highly significant) non-linear age effects with the divorce hazard increasing with age up to the mid to upper twenties and then declining thereafter. The convexity of the age divorce profile is somewhat stronger for the specification using the monthly weights than for the other specifications, but the overall effects of age on the divorce propensity are similar. Similarly the effects of food stamp recipiency, home ownership and employment status are highly similar regardless of the weighting scheme employed.

With respect to the goodness of fit, the specification using the monthly weights yields the highest likelihood ratio index (a.k.a. pseudo R^2) of 6.9 percent, while the specification using the panel weight yields the lowest at 5.2 percent. This result is important. Virtually all panel surveys include a weight like the panel weight, which adjusts for attrition by bringing the distributions of nonattriting cases at the end of the panel in line with the population. Such panel weights are often touted as *the* method of choice for correcting model estimates for attrition. Yet in the context of event-history models such as ours, they can yield the least efficient estimates. The reason is that these weighting procedures generally assign a weight of zero to any nonrespondent regardless of when the case stopped responding. Thus all the information on the divorce propensity prior to attrition is lost for any cases ever attriting. If the case divorced prior to a subsequent attrition, the entire completed spell is lost. If the case is lost before a divorce occurs, the information implicit in right-censored cases is lost.

The impression that the event-history model parameter estimates in Table 4 are insensitive to the treatment of attrition-adjusted sampling weights is borne out when we examine the cumulative hazard functions they imply. These estimated hazards were obtained by means of sample enumeration simulations—i.e., the parameter estimates were applied to the actual values of the covariates for a random sample of cases and the estimates were averaged.[5] The results of these simulations are that even after 24 months of allowing the differences in hazards to accumulate, there is hardly any discernable difference between the variously weighted and unweighted estimates. The only exception is that the simulated cumulative hazards implied by the panel-weighted estimates were substantially *lower* (2.6 percent) than all the other estimates (3.3 percent). This is ironic; the panel weight is the one specifically designed for longitudinal estimation, yet it is the only weight that yields substantially worse estimates. The

---

[5]See Train (1986) for an explanation of the advantages of sample enumeration in interpreting results of discrete state models; see Hill, Axinn, and Thornton (1993) for an explanation of crude and net hazards and survival functions.

reason is that the panel weight is designed to bring the sample of individuals responding in each wave of the survey in line with the entire population. But this sample excludes individuals who ever attrite, and these persons are more likely to have experienced a marital disruption during the panel period. Unless the weight is designed explicitly to bring the sample in line with the population with respect to *change* in the substantive variable of interest (e.g., divorce), it will result in underestimates of these changes.

4. ATTRITION AND DIVORCE AS CORRELATED COMPETING HAZARDS

The robustness of the parameter estimates of the divorce event-history model to the various weighting schemes would be encouraging were it not for the fact that, judging from vital statistics data, all of the estimates obtained imply divorce hazards that are far too low. Weighting, at least of the sort used in most panel surveys, is not the solution.[6] An alternative is to model attrition and divorce as potentially correlated competing hazards. This way, the effects of attrition on the estimated divorce hazards can be removed by examining the net hazard function for divorce. The major deficiency of the weighting approaches examined in Section 3 is that they all implicitly assumed independent censoring—i.e., that attritors behaved the same way after their last interview as before. It is quite likely, however, that divorce and attrition are both symptoms of what might be called marital distress—a shared unmeasured risk factor. Thus individuals in distressed marriages are more likely both to divorce and to attrite than are people in happier marriages. The precise timing of the SIPP interview relative to the timing of a marital disruption is certainly unimportant to these people. It is, of course, crucial to the divorce analyst using SIPP data.

4.1. *The SURF Model*

Most competing hazards models also assume independent censoring and, as a result, are not likely to be any more successful in removing bias than the weighting approaches. An exception is the Shared Unmeasured Risk Factor (SURF) model of Hill, Axinn, and Thornton (1993). As with the

---

[6]At the 1994 American Statistical Association meetings in Toronto, an entire session was devoted to improved weighting in panel surveys. Researchers from WESTAT, RTI, and Iowa State reported on extensive research sponsored by the Census Bureau to improve the SIPP weights. None of the proposed techniques were able to eliminate known biases in the survey (see Rizzo et al. 1994; Folsom and Witt 1994; and An, Breidt, and Fuller 1994).

simple divorce model presented in Section 3, it is most useful to formulate this model in terms of the propensities to divorce (D_{ti}^*) and to leave the sample via attrition (A_{ti}^*). These propensities are the net effects of all factors influencing marital stability and respondent cooperation, respectively, and can be represented according to

$$D_{ti}^* = \alpha_D + \beta_D' X_{Dti} + \epsilon_{Dti}$$

$$A_{ti}^* = \alpha_A + \beta_A' X_{Ati} + \epsilon_{Ati} , \qquad (3)$$

where the first equation is the same divorce propensity equation as used in Section 3 and the second represents the corresponding attrition propensity. The covariate vectors $(X_{Dt}$ and $X_{Ati})$ may or may not have common elements and there may or may not be constraints imposed across the coefficient vectors.[7] The dynamic mechanism assumed is that couples remain in the base state (married and responding) until such time that *either* D_{ti}^* or A_{ti}^* exceeds some threshold τ. At this time, the couple moves to whichever competing state has the highest propensity score. One might think that it would be difficult to identify this model, but Heckman and Honore (1989) have shown that identification requires only one significant continuous covariate.

Unlike most competing hazards models, the SURF model assumes that the random components of the competing propensities are related via

$$F(\epsilon_{Dti}, \epsilon_{Ati}) = \exp(-[\exp(-\epsilon_{Dti}/\rho_t) + \exp(-\epsilon_{Ati}/\rho_t)]^{\rho_t}), \qquad (4)$$

where ρ_t, known as the index of dissimilarity, is confined to the half-open interval $(0,1]$. This distribution is known as Gumbel's Type B bivariate extreme-value distribution.[8] The correlation of the ϵ's can be shown to be

$$r_{\epsilon_{Dti}, \epsilon_{Ati}} = 1 - \rho_t^2. \qquad (5)$$

In the special case where $\rho_t = 1$, the correlation is zero and the SURF model reduces to the ordinary discrete-time competing hazards model with independent censoring discussed by Allison (1982). This special case

[7]If constraints are imposed across the parameter vectors, or if the stochastic components of equation (3) are correlated, then it is necessary to analyze the competing hazards explicitly. Otherwise, it is sufficient to treat one alternative as a form of right censoring in analyzing the other alternative (see Petersen 1991).

[8]There are a number of bivariate distributions we could use in place of Gumbel's. I have done some experimental work, for instance, using the bivariate normal. Gumbel's distribution is quite useful, however, because (1) it allows for correlations in the ϵ's and (2) it has a closed form cdf.

is sufficiently important that I will devote some time to it in Section 4.2, below. First, however, I need to complete the development of the general SURF model.

With equation (4) the hazard of divorcing, conditional on the individual (1) having remained married and responding up to time $t - 1$ (i.e., $D^*_{j<ti} < \tau$ and $A^*_{j<ti} < \tau$); and (2) either divorcing or leaving the sample via attrition during period t (i.e., $D^*_{ti} > \tau$ or $A^*_{ti} > \tau$, becomes

$$Pr(D^*_{ti} > \tau | D^*_{ti} > \tau \cup A^*_{ti} > \tau; D^*_{j<ti} < \tau \wedge A^*_{j<ti} < \tau)$$

$$= \frac{\exp(\beta'_D X_{Dti}/\rho_t)}{S_t \exp(\beta'_A X_{Ati}/\rho_t) + \exp(\beta'_D X_{Dti}/\rho_t)}, \tag{6}$$

where the constant terms $\alpha_A - \tau$ and $\alpha_D - \tau$ are suppressed for clarity and where S_{ti} is a dummy variable equaling 1 if it is possible for attrition to occur in month t and 0 if it is not. Many panel surveys, like the SIPP, have an interviewing interval longer than the time unit of measurement. In the case of the SIPP, the interviewing interval is every four months whereas the basic time unit of measurement is the month. With such a design, measured attrition will be confined to the first month of the reference period—the so-called "seam" month.

The hazard of exiting at time t (given survival through period $t - 1$) via either divorce or attrition is

$$Pr(D_{ti} \cup A_{ti} | T_i \geq t_i) = \frac{[\exp(\beta'_D X_{Dti}/\rho_t) + S_{ti} \exp(\beta'_A X_{Ati}/\rho_t)]^{\rho_t}}{1 + [\exp(\beta'_D X_{Dti}/\rho_t) + S_{ti} \exp(\beta'_A X_{Ati}/\rho_t)]^{\rho_t}}$$

$$= \frac{\exp(\rho_t \ln(I_{ti}))}{1 + \exp(\rho_t \ln(I_{ti}))} = \frac{I^{\rho_t}_{ti}}{1 + I^{\rho_t}_{ti}}, \tag{7}$$

where $I^{\rho_t} = [\exp(\beta'_D X_{Dti}/\rho_t) + S_{ti} \exp(\beta'_A X_{Ati}/\rho_t)]^{\rho_t}$ can be defined as the "inclusive" exit propensity.

The likelihood function for a sample of n couples can be expressed as

$$L = \prod_{i=1}^{n} \left[\prod_{j=D}^{A} \left[\frac{\exp(\beta'_j X_{jti}/\rho_t)}{I_{ti}} I^{\rho_t}_{ti} \right]^{\delta_{ji}} \prod_{k=1}^{t_i} \frac{1}{1 + I^{\rho_t}_k} \right], \tag{8}$$

where $\delta_{ji} = 1$ if, and only if, couple i ultimately exits the base state to state j $(= D$ or $A)$. Otherwise, $\delta_{ji} = 0$. Maximum likelihood estimates of the parameters of the SURF model can be obtained by maximizing (8) with respect to the α's, the β's, and ρ_t.[9]

While fully efficient estimates of these parameters require direct maximization of equation (8), consistent estimates can be obtained using the two-step procedure and ordinary logit packaged programs (see, Hill, Axinn, and Thornton 1993, appendix B). If one does have the capability of direct maximum likelihood estimation,[10] then estimation of more elaborate specifications becomes possible. For instance, we may want to allow the correlation of the unmeasured heterogeneity components to vary systematically either with time or with other characteristics. This is easily accomplished with direct maximization but not with the two-step procedure.

4.2. Independence of Irrelevant Alternatives

As noted above, the special case in which ρ_t of equation (4) is 1 is sufficiently important as to deserve some discussion. It is also important enough to have been given a special name in the discrete choice literature: the Independence of Irrelevant Alternatives (IIA) condition or—since it is most often a *maintained* hypothesis—assumption. The reason for this name can be seen by examining the probability of leaving the base state to one alternative relative to the probability of remaining in the base state. This relative probability for divorce is

$$\frac{P_{Dti}}{(1 - (P_{Dti} + P_{Ati}))} = \exp(\beta_D' X_{Dti}) I^{\rho_t - 1}. \tag{9}$$

If $\rho_t = 1$, then the level of the propensity to attrite rather than divorce is completely irrelevant. This propensity affects the ratio only via the inclusive value I,[11] which drops out when $\rho_t = 1$. This implies that if all the individuals who left the sample via attrition were somehow interviewed, they would be found to be distributed across divorce and marriage in ex-

---

[9]Hill, Axinn, and Thornton (1993) also present a two-step procedure to obtain consistent estimates of these parameters using the ordinary logit algorithm. Because the parameters estimated directly via maximizing equation (8) are more efficient, this method was used in obtaining the parameter estimates presented in this paper.

[10]An example of the complete program employed in the present analysis has been placed in Statlib (http://lib.stat.cmu.edu). The program requires access to a Turbo Pascal compiler (version 4.0 or higher) and a DOS–based computer with a mathematical coprocessor.

[11]If there are parameter constraints imposed across β_D and β_A, then the factors affecting the attrition propensity will also affect the ratio. Most competing hazards specifications assume no such constraints (see Allison 1982; Petersen 1991; Yamaguchi 1991:169–71).

actly the same proportion as the rest of the sample. Only if $\rho_t < 1$ will the attrition propensity (and the factors affecting it uniquely) affect the relative hazards of divorce.

4.3. The Role of Duration in the SURF Model

Duration can affect the attrition/divorce process in the SURF model in three distinct ways: (1) through the attrition propensity; (2) through the divorce propensity; and (3) though the correlation of the stochastic portions of the divorce and attrition propensities. I have already discussed the form of duration dependence in the divorce portion of the model.

In the attrition portion the appropriate metric for duration is not panel month but panel wave. In most panel surveys attrition tends to decrease with wave in a rather uneven manner. For this reason it is most appropriate to control for duration in the attrition propensity by means of including a set of dummy variables defined on the basis of panel wave.

With respect to the duration dependence of the correlation of errors, there is very little *a priori* knowledge. With time, ρ_t may increase or decrease, and it may do so nonlinearly. For this reason ρ_t will be specified as a quadratic of time.

4.4. SURF Model Estimates of Divorce and Attrition Hazards

Table 5 presents the parameter estimates obtained when equation (8) is maximized with respect to the parameters $\alpha - \tau, \beta,$ and ρ_t. The covariates included in the attrition portion of the model consist of the union of those factors found by Rizzo et al. (1994) to be important correlates of attrition (age, home ownership, food stamp recipiency, unemployment, education, and number of Wave 1 imputations) and the covariates included in the marriage propensity specification. The first two columns of the table present the results obtained when the IIA assumption is imposed. It is no coincidence that the estimates for the marriage portion of this IIA model, presented in column 2, are virtually identical to those of the simple divorce hazards model presented in Table 3 (column 3) above. Indeed, it can be shown that competing hazards models that assume IIA are mathematically equivalent to single hazard models that treat exits to alternatives as an independent form of right-censoring (see Petersen 1991). The only reason the estimates are not *exactly* the same is that the maximum likelihood optimization algorithm is subject to a small amount of cumulative round-

TABLE 5
Structural Model of Attrition and Divorce

	IIA		Surf	
	Attrition	Divorce	Attrition	Divorce
Constant	−3.12**	−7.44**	−3.32**	−6.45**
	(.40)	(.72)	(.36)	(.48)
Age	.02	.07*	.02	.06$^+$
	(.01)	(.03)	(.01)	(.03)
Age squared	−.0001	−.0014**	−.0001	−.0010*
	(.0001)	(.0004)	(.0001)	(.0003)
Truncated duration		.13**		.05$^+$
		(.03)		(.03)
Truncated duration-squared		−.0055**		−.0033**
		(.0011)		(.0012)
Home owner	−.37**	−.53**	−.40**	−.30**
	(.07)	(.13)	(.08)	(.09)
Food stamp recipient	−.57**	1.44**	−.46**	1.10**
	(.21)	(.18)	(.18)	(.15)
Not employed	.15*	−.34*	.15*	−.25**
	(.07)	(.13)	(.07)	(.08)
Education	−.65**	—	−.64**	—
	(.11)		(.12)	
Number of Wave 1	.73**	—	.72**	—
imputations	(.09)		(.10)	
Wave 2	−.57**	—	−.59**	—
	(.11)		(.12)	
Wave 3	.65**	—	.64**	—
	(.11)		(.12)	
Wave 4	.24*	—	.26*	—
	(.09)		(.13)	
Wave 5	.27*	—	.22$^+$	—
	(.11)		(.12)	
ρ_0 ρ_1	$\rho_0 = 1.0$	$\rho_1 = 0.0$	$\rho_0 = .36$**	$\rho_1 = .008$**
			(.001)	(.0001)
LN(L), Pseudo R^2	−7,828.3	3.1%	−6,793.2	15.9%

$^+$Significant at the .90 level.
*Significant at the .95 level.
**Significant at the .99 level.

off error. The only advantage of using the competing hazards framework when the independence assumption is made is that it is, at least theoretically, possible to impose and test cross-alternative restrictions on the coefficient vectors β_D and β_A,

The parameter estimates in the attrition portion of the model are similar to those found by others in the SIPP (e.g., see Rizzo et al. 1994). Home owners, food stamp recipients, and the highly educated are less likely to attrite from the SIPP, whereas the unemployed are more likely to do so. The most powerful single predictor of attrition is the number of imputations required to complete the Wave 1 data record. These imputations are made to compensate for respondents' refusals to provide answers to specific questions. The more this happens in Wave 1, the more likely the respondent is to refuse or otherwise drop out of the study in subsequent waves. This same pattern has been found in other panel surveys including the health and retirement survey. The effects of duration are captured in the attrition portion of the model by inclusion of wave-specific dummy variables. These, as a set, are highly significant. The pattern, at first, looks somewhat peculiar. The reference group for these wave dummies is the end of the survey (Waves 6–8). The coefficient of $-.57$ for the Wave 2 dummy suggests that couples are more likely to attrite at the end of the survey than in the second wave. This, however, is an artifact of our sample definition—given SIPP procedures, the only couples at risk of divorce are those in which at least one spouse is responding in panel month 5 and our sample is confined to such couples. The highest attrition propensities are observed in Wave 3 of the panel and then decline gradually thereafter—a pattern common to most panels.

Columns 3 and 4 of Table 5 present the results obtained when the independence assumption is relaxed. The evidence against independent censoring is overwhelming. Relaxing the independence assumption and allowing ρ to vary with time results in an increase in the log-likelihood value of 1,035.1. This implies a likelihood ratio test statistic for the null hypothesis of IIA of 2,070.2 with 2 degrees of freedom. Similarly, the pseudo-R^2 increases more than fivefold when the independence assumption is relaxed. The estimated index of dissimilarity (the next to bottom row of the table) starts out at a value of .36 and increases at a rate of .08 each month of the panel. Throughout the range it is significantly less than 1.0 and implies a correlation between the random portions of the divorce and attrition propensities of roughly .91 at the beginning of the panel and .73 at the end. Relaxing the IIA assumption also has the effect of reducing the estimated effects of duration, home ownership, food stamp recipiency, and unemployment. Evidently, while they remain important and significant, part of the apparent effect of these factors in the independent specification was due to their effects on attrition propensities. This, of course, is an almost unavoidable consequence of the survey design in which interviews are attempted only periodically; unless at least one of the ex-spouses of a new divorce remains reachable until the next SIPP interview, the case will be recorded as attrition.

Unlike the results of the alternative weighting procedures, the effects of correcting for attrition using the SURF model are readily apparent in the estimated cumulative divorce hazards functions. Figure 1 presents the cumulative net and crude (of attrition) hazard functions implied by the coefficients presented in Table 1. In the competing hazard framework, the net hazard is the probability of exiting at a point in time given having not exited to any of the alternatives prior to that time. This hazard corresponds closely to what is actually observed in the sample. The net hazard, however, is a counterfactual concept—being the hazard of exiting to one alternative if the other alternatives were eliminated. The net hazard is conceptually just what we need in correcting our estimates of substantive transitions (e.g., divorce) for the effects of attrition.

In Figure 1 it is clear that relaxing the independence assumption substantially increases both the crude and net cumulative divorce hazards. Indeed, both the net and crude divorce hazards from the SURF model

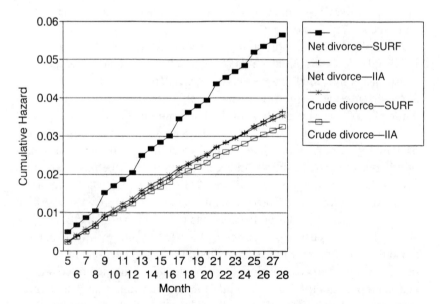

FIGURE 1. Cumulative net and crude divorce hazard for dependent and independent censoring.

exceed the net hazard estimates obtained under the IIA assumption, not to mention the IIA crude hazard estimates. Interestingly, the cumulative net hazard of divorce when independence is not imposed is, after 24 months, 5.9 percent—almost exactly the same as the vital statistics benchmark value presented in Table 2.

5. CONCLUSIONS AND RECOMMENDATIONS FOR FUTURE RESEARCH

This paper has examined the effectiveness of two methods of adjusting for attrition in event-history models. Because there was some evidence that attrition in the SIPP had a significant impact on the observed divorce rates, divorce was chosen as the substantive example. The first method of adjusting for attrition consisted of using attrition-adjusted sampling weights in the likelihood function of the event-history model. This method was found to have virtually no effect on the model estimates. The second method involved modeling attrition as a competing alternative means of exiting the base state (married and responding). When the stochastic portion of the propensity to attrite was allowed to be correlated with the corresponding random component of the propensity to divorce, the estimated cumulative hazard for 24 months was found to increase significantly from roughly 4.2 percent to one of over 5.9 percent. This increase in implied divorce rates brings the SIPP estimates almost in line with those from other data sources.

The results suggest that attrition and divorce are intimately related in that there are shared, or at least correlated, unmeasured risk factors affecting each. This results in a significant stochastic dependence between them that violates the underlying assumption of independent censoring upon which the weighting adjustments are based. Only when this dependency is explicitly recognized and corrected do the estimates change appreciably. While the results of the SURF competing hazards model are encouraging as a means of correcting event-history model estimates for attrition, additional research is needed. First, the method needs to be applied to the wider variety of substantive events tracked by SIPP. This includes poverty transitions and movements onto and off of means-tested public assistance programs. In addition, the technique should be tested on data from other panel surveys such as the PSID. Finally, the model needs to be generalized to distributions other than Gumbel's Type B, and the results need to be compared with those from new weighting schemes which incorporate change in state explicitly in the attrition adjustment procedures.

REFERENCES

Allison, Paul D. 1982. "Discrete-Time Methods for the Analysis of Event Histories." In *Sociological Methodology 1982*, edited by S. Leinhardt, 61–98. San Francisco: Jossey-Bass.

An, A.B., F. J. Breidt, and Wayne A. Fuller. 1994. "Regression Weighting Methods for SIPP Data." Proceedings of the Section on Survey Research Methods of the 1994 American Statistical Association, Toronto, 434–39.

Bureau of the Census. 1990. "Survey of Income and Program Participation (SIPP) 1986 Full Panel Microdata Research File." Washington: Bureau of the Census.

Folsom, R.E., and M.B. Witt. 1994. "Testing a New Attrition Nonresponse Adjustment Method for SIPP." Proceedings of the Section on Survey Research Methods of the 1994 American Statistical Association, Toronto, 428–33.

Heckman, James, and Bo E. Honore. 1989. "The Identifiability of the Competing Risks Model." *Biometrika* 76(2):325–30.

Hill, Daniel H. 1993. "An Investigation of "Under" Estimates in the SIPP." Toledo: Survey Research Institute.

Hill, Daniel, William G. Axinn, and Arland Thornton. 1993. "Competing Hazards with Shared Unmeasured Risk Factors." In *Sociological Methodology 1993*, edited by Peter V. Marsden, 245–77. Cambridge, MA: Blackwell Publishers.

Hill, M. 1987. "Marital Status and Changes Therein in SIPP." Internal Census Bureau Memorandum to Census Staff, February 20, 1987.

Jabine, Thomas B., K. King, and R. Petroni. 1990. "Quality Profile." In *Survey of Income and Program Participation*. Washington: Bureau of the Census.

Kalton, Graham, and J. Brick. 1994. *Weighting Schemes for Household Panel Surveys*. Rockville, MD: Westat.

McMillen, D. 1989. "The Measurement of Demographic Transitions in the Survey of Income and Program Participation." Proceedings of the Social Statistics Section of the American Statistical Association.

Petersen, Trond K. 1991. "The Statistical Analysis of Event Histories." *Sociological Methods and Research* 19:270–323.

Press, W., B. Flannery, S. Teukolsky, and W. Vetterling. 1986. *Numerical Recipes*. Cambridge, England: Cambridge University Press.

Rizzo, Louis, G. Kalton, M. Brick, and R. Petroni. 1994. "Adjusting for Panel Non-response in the Survey of Income and Program Participation." Proceedings of the Section on Survey Research Methods of the 1994 American Statistical Association, Toronto, 422–27.

Singh, R. 1988. "SIPP Estimates of Number of Persons Marrying Per Year." Internal Census Bureau Memorandum to Gary M. Shapiro, February 1, 1988.

Train, K. 1986. *Qualitative Choice Analysis*. Cambridge: MIT Press.

Yamaguchi, Kazuo. 1991. *Event History Analysis*. Applied Research Methods Monograph No. 28. Newbury Park, CA: Sage, 169–71.

9

DYNAMIC DISCRETE-TIME DURATION MODELS: ESTIMATION VIA MARKOV CHAIN MONTE CARLO

*Ludwig Fahrmeir**
*Leonhard Knorr-Held**

Discrete-time or grouped duration data, with one or multiple types of terminating events, are often observed in social sciences or economics. In this paper we suggest and discuss dynamic models for flexible Bayesian nonparametric analysis of such data. These models allow simultaneous incorporation and estimation of baseline hazards and time-varying covariate effects, without imposing particular parametric forms. Methods for exploring the possibility of time-varying effects, as for example the impact of nationality or unemployment insurance benefits on the probability of reemployment, have recently gained increasing interest. Our modeling and estimation approach is fully Bayesian and makes use of Markov Chain Monte Carlo (MCMC) simulation techniques. A detailed analysis of unemployment duration data, with full-time job, part-time job and other causes as terminating events, illustrates our methods and shows how they can be used to obtain refined results and interpretations.

1. INTRODUCTION

Regression models for duration data are an important and widely used tool for statistical analysis of life or event histories. Many well-known models

We thank the referees and the editor for valuable comments and suggestions that led to a substantial improvement of this article. Our thanks also go to Stefan Lang for computational assistance and to the German National Science Foundation (DFG) for financial support. E-mail: fahrmeir@stat.uni-muenchen.de
*Universität München, Institut für Statistik

are based on the assumption that duration, the time until some event occurs, is a continuous variable (for example, see Cox 1972; Kalbfleisch and
Prentice 1980; Blossfeld, Hamerle, and Mayer 1989; Lancaster 1990;
Andersen et. al. 1993). However, in many applications—in particular in
the social sciences—time is often measured as a discrete variable. Discrete-
time models are more appropriate in this case, although the applicability of
continuous-time methods to discrete time data is possible in some situations (Petersen 1991).

Table 1 shows a small sample from data on duration of unemployment, taken from the German socioeconomic panel GSOEP. Duration of
unemployment is discrete and measured in months. Also there are several
alternative types of terminating events or destination states, and we may
distinguish between full-time jobs, part-time jobs and other causes which
end unemployment. Typical questions that arise here are: What is the influence of the covariates (e.g., sex) on the probability of leaving the state
of unemployment? Does the effect of covariates change over duration time?
What does the shape of hazard and survival functions look like in the
presence of such time-varying effects? Is it necessary to distinguish between different types of terminating events?

Conventional duration models with time-constant parameters are
not flexible enough to answer questions of this type. Instead, both baseline
hazards and at least some covariate effects have to be considered as func-

TABLE 1

Some Typical Observations from the Unemployment Duration Data

Terminating Event	Duration of Unemployment (months)	Sex	Nationality	Age	Unemployment Insurance Benefits Received
Full-time job	16	Male	Non-German	21	Yes
Full-time job	3	Female	Non-German	23	Yes
Full-time job	4	Male	Non-German	25	Yes
Housewife	3	Female	Non-German	29	Yes
(Censored)	36	Male	German	30	Until month 6
Househusband	6	Male	German	32	Yes
Full-time job	2	Male	German	36	Yes
Housewife	11	Female	German	30	Yes
(Censored)	4	Female	Non-German	22	Yes
Part-time job	4	Female	German	27	Yes

tions of time—for example, γ_t and β_t, $t = 1, 2, \ldots, q$. Even for a moderate number q of intervals, unrestricted modeling and fitting of $\{\gamma_t\}$ and $\{\beta_t\}$ will cause severe problems: Due to the large number of parameters involved, this will often lead to nonexistence and divergence of ML estimates. These difficulties increase in situations with many intervals—but not enough to apply models for continuous time—and with multiple terminating events. We may try to avoid such problems by a more parsimonious parameterization, using piecewise polynomials or other parametric forms for hazard functions or varying effects (Yamaguchi 1993). Multiphase models may also be considered (Portugal and Addison 1995). However, by imposing such parametric forms we may overlook unexpected patterns like peaks, bumps, or seasonal effects. In this situation, non- or semiparametric approaches are useful for detecting and exploring such unknown patterns. Appropriate parametric models may then be developed in a second step.

In this paper we propose dynamic discrete-time duration models as a flexible nonparametric Bayesian approach, which makes simultaneous modeling and smoothing of hazard functions and covariate effects possible. Dynamic models are regarded as nonparametric, since no particular functional form is specified for the dependence of the parameters on time. Instead only some smoothness is imposed in the form of a prior stochastic process. No approximations based on asymptotic normality assumptions have to be made for statistical inference, and estimation of unknown smoothness or variance parameters is automatically incorporated. Thus the proposed nonparametric Bayesian framework is a promising alternative to more traditional nonparametric methods like spline smoothing (Hastie and Tibshirani 1993), local likelihood estimation (Wu and Tuma 1990; Tutz 1995), discrete kernel smoothing (Fahrmeir and Tutz 1994, chap. 9) or approaches based on counting processes (Aalen 1989, 1993; Huffer and McKeague 1991).

The models are obtained by adopting dynamic or state space models for categorical data to discrete-time duration data, similarly to Gamerman (1991) for a dynamic version of the piecewise exponential model, and Fahrmeir (1994) and Fahrmeir and Wagenpfeil (1996), sec. 2. In contrast to the latter papers, inference is fully Bayesian using Markov chain Monte Carlo (MCMC) methods, based on ideas and suggestions of Knorr-Held (1995, 1996) (sec. 3). Other Bayesian nonparametric approaches based on MCMC simulation have recently been suggested by Arjas and Liu (1995) for continuous-time duration data and by Berzuini and Larizza (1996) for joint modeling of time series and failure time data. MCMC techniques allow flexible and sophisticated inference: pointwise and simultaneous credible regions for covariate effects, predictive survival functions, and other characteristics can be calculated based on posterior samples. We illustrate our approach in Section 4 with a detailed study of unemployment duration data, taken from the German socioeconomic panel GSOEP. In a first analysis, only the terminating event "end of unemployment" regardless of a specific cause, is considered. Based on this nonparametric analysis, we also fit parametric models and compare results. In a second refined analysis we distinguish between three terminating events: employment in a full-time job, employment in a part-time job, and other causes. The analysis shows that it is important to differentiate between alternative terminating events in order to obtain correct interpretations and conclusions. The results suggest that some effects of covariates, characterizing individuals, change through time, whereas the impact of unemployment benefits is more or less constant. This is in contrast to findings of Narendranathan and Stewart (1993) for data from the British labor market. Section 5 concludes with a discussion of other estimation approaches, extensions to multiple time scales, the role of unobserved heterogeneity, and some other comments.

Formal definitions of dynamic models in Section 2 rely on basic concepts for discrete duration data. For easier reference, we give a short review. Let time be divided into intervals $[a_0 = 0, a_1), [a_1, a_2), \ldots, [a_{q-1}, a_q)$ and $[a_q, \infty)$. Without loss of generality, we assume that a_q denotes the end of the observation period. Often the intervals $[a_0, a_1), \ldots, [a_{q-1}, a_q)$ are of equal length but this is not an essential requirement. Instead of a continuous duration time, the discrete duration time $T \in \{1, \ldots, q+1\}$ is observed, where $T = t$ denotes end of duration within the interval $[a_{t-1}, a_t)$. In addition to duration T, a sequence of possibly time-varying covariate vectors $x_t = (x_{t1}, \ldots, x_{tp}), t = 1, 2, \ldots$, is observed. Let $x(t) = (x_1, \ldots, x_t)$ denote the history of covariates up to interval $[a_{t-1}, a_t)$. If there is only one type of terminating event, the discrete hazard function is given by

$$\lambda(t|x(t)) = \mathrm{pr}(T = t | T \geq t, x(t)), \qquad t = 1, \ldots q,$$

which is the conditional probability of the end of duration in interval $[a_{t-1}, a_t)$, given that the interval is reached and the history of the covariates. The discrete survival function

$$S(t|x(t)) = \mathrm{pr}(T > t | x(t)) = \prod_{s=1}^{t} (1 - \lambda(s|x(s))) \qquad (1)$$

is the probability of surviving the interval $[a_{t-1}, a_t)$. A common specification for the hazard function is a binary logit model of the form

$$\lambda(t|x(t)) = \frac{\exp(\gamma_t + z_t'\beta)}{1 + \exp(\gamma_t + z_t'\beta)} \tag{2}$$

(e.g., see Thompson 1977 or Arjas and Haara 1987). The parameter γ_t represents a time-varying baseline effect and the design vector z_t is some function of $x(t)$, often simply $z_t = x_t$. Finally, β is the corresponding vector of fixed covariate effects. A slightly different specification is the grouped proportional hazards or Cox model $\lambda(t|x(t)) = 1 - \exp(-\exp(\gamma_t + z_t'\beta))$ (see Cox 1972; Kalbfleisch and Prentice 1980). This model can be derived by assuming a latent proportional hazards model for durations on a continuous time scale, but durations are observed only in terms of whole time intervals, such as weeks or months. If intervals are short compared to the observation period, the models are similar, as has been shown by Thompson (1977). A detailed survey on discrete-time duration data can be found in Hamerle and Tutz (1989) and a shorter introduction in Fahrmeir and Tutz (1994, chap 9). For several, say m, alternative types of terminating events, causes or destinations, let $R \in \{1, \ldots, m\}$ denote the distinct event. The basic quantities characterizing the duration process are now event-specific hazard functions

$$\lambda_r(t|x(t)) = \text{pr}(T = t, R = r | T \geq t, x(t)), \tag{3}$$

$r = 1, \ldots, m, t = 1, \ldots, q$. Models for multicategorical responses can be used to model event-specific hazard functions. A common candidate for unordered events is the multinomial logit model (e.g., Allison 1982)

$$\lambda_r(t|x(t)) = \frac{\exp(\gamma_{tr} + z_t'\beta_r)}{1 + \sum_{j=1}^{m} \exp(\gamma_{tj} + z_t'\beta_j)}, \tag{4}$$

where γ_{tr} and β_r are event-specific baseline and covariate effects, respectively. A cause-specific generalization of the grouped Cox model is given, for example, in Fahrmeir and Tutz (1994, chap 9). Other discrete choice models like a probit or a nested multinomial logit model (Hill, Axinn, and Thornton 1993) may also be considered.

Event-specific duration models are sometimes also based on the classical "competing risks" model assumption of latent duration times $T_1, \ldots, T_m$, one for each terminating event. The observed duration time can then be defined as $T = \min(T_1, \ldots, T_m)$ and the terminating event as $R = r$

if $T = T_r$, but this approach in general requires untestable assumptions on the independence of latent duration times. Therefore we use event-specific hazard functions (3) as the basic characteristics for duration models, following Prentice et al. (1978), Kalbfleisch and Prentice (1980), and Lancaster (1990:99).

2. DYNAMIC MODELS FOR DISCRETE-TIME DURATION DATA

For individual units $i = 1,\ldots,n$, let T_i denote duration times and U_i right-censoring times. Duration data with multiple terminating events are usually given by $(t_i, \delta_i, r_i, x_i(t_i))$, where $t_i = \min(T_i, U_i)$ is the observed discrete duration time, δ_i is the censoring indicator,

$$\delta_i = \begin{cases} 1, & T_i < U_i \\ 0, & T_i \geq U_i \end{cases},$$

$r_i \in \{1,\ldots,m\}$ indicates the terminating event, and $x_i(t_i) = \{x_{it}, t = 1,\ldots,t_i\}$ is the sequence of observed covariates. We rewrite the data in terms of stochastic processes: Let R_t denote the risk set—i.e., the set of units at risk in $[a_{t-1}, a_t)$. Censoring is assumed to occur at the end of the interval, so that the risk set R_t includes all individuals who are censored in $[a_{t-1}, a_t)$. We define event indicators $y_{it} \in \{0,1,\ldots,m\}$, $i \in R_t$, $t = 1,\ldots,t_i$, by

$$y_{it} = \begin{cases} r, & \text{event of type } r \text{ occurs in } [a_{t-1}, a_t), \quad r = 1,\ldots,m \\ 0, & \text{no event occurs in } [a_{t-1}, a_t) \end{cases}.$$

Then, from a dynamic point of view, duration can be interpreted as a stochastic process of multicategorical decisions between $y_{it} = 0$ and $y_{it} = r$,—i.e., end of duration due to event $r \in \{1,\ldots,m\}$. Similarly, it is convenient to introduce censoring processes by

$$c_{it} = \begin{cases} 1, & U_i \geq a_t, \text{ i.e. } i \text{ not censored up to } [a_{t-1}, a_t) \\ 0, & U_i < a_t, \text{ i.e. } i \text{ censored in } [a_{t-1}, a_t) \text{ or earlier} \end{cases}.$$

We collect covariates, event, and censoring indicators of time interval t—that is, $[a_{t-1}, a_t)$, in the column vectors

$$x_t = (x_{it}, i \in R_t), \qquad y_t = (y_{it}, i \in R_t), \qquad c_t = (c_{it}, i \in R_t)$$

and denote histories up to t by

$$x_t^* = (x_1,\ldots,x_t), \qquad y_t^* = (y_1,\ldots,y_t), \qquad c_t^* = (c_1,\ldots,c_t).$$

Dynamic discrete duration models are defined hierarchically by an observation model, given the unknown baseline and covariate effects, a latent stochastic transition model for these possibly time-varying effects, and priors for unknown hyperparameters of the transition model. The model specification is completed by several conditional independence assumptions.

2.1. Observation Model

The duration process of each unit is viewed as a sequence of multicategorical decisions between remaining in the transient state $y_{it} = 0$—i.e., no event occurs or leaving for one of the absorbing states $y_{it} = r, r = 1,\ldots,m$— i.e., end of duration at t due to terminating event of type r. Individual response probabilities for $y_{it} = r$ are modeled using categorical response models. For the special case of only one type of terminating event $(m = 1)$, we assume for $i \in R_t$ that conditional on parameters γ_t, β_t, and the covariate x_{it}, response probabilities for $y_{it} = 1$ are in the form

$$\mathrm{pr}(y_{it} = 1 | x_{it}, \gamma_t, \beta_t) = h(\eta_{it}) \tag{5}$$

with linear predictor

$$\eta_{it} = \gamma_t + z_{it}' \beta_t \tag{6}$$

and link function $h: \mathbf{R} \mapsto (0,1)$—for example, one of the common link functions for the logit or grouped Cox model. In (6), the design vector z_{it} is some appropriate function of the covariates x_{it}. The observation model can be extended to incorporate the history y_{t-1}^* of past event indicators into z_{it}, a suggestion made by Prentice et al. (1978). However, we do not make use of this possibility here. We assume that the censoring process is conditionally independent of y_{it}, given x_{it}, γ_t and β_t, so that z_{it} does not depend on c_t^*.

For multiple terminating events $(m > 1)$, we assume for $r = 1,\ldots,m$

$$\mathrm{pr}(y_{it} = r | x_{it}, \gamma_t, \beta_t) = h_r(\eta_{it}), \tag{7}$$

with link function $h_r: \mathbf{R}^m \mapsto (0,1)$, and linear predictor vector $\eta_{it} = (\eta_{it1},\ldots,\eta_{itm})$. For the multinomial logit model (4), we have

$$h_r(\eta_{it}) = \frac{\exp(\eta_{itr})}{1 + \displaystyle\sum_{j=1}^{m} \exp(\eta_{itj})} \tag{8}$$

with $\eta_{itr} = \gamma_{tr} + z'_{it}\beta_{tr}$. Other multicategorical response models can also be written in the general form (7). Again, the design vector may be an appropriate function of covariates x_{it} but not of c_t^*.

2.2. Transition Model

Let α_t denote the state vector of unknown time-dependent parameters. Prior specifications for stochastic variation of $\{\alpha_t\}$ are in common linear Gaussian and Markovian form as for linear dynamic or state space models. The simplest model is a random walk of first-order $\alpha_t = \alpha_{t-1} + u_t$, $u_t \sim N(0,Q)$; here $\alpha_t = (\gamma_{t1},\ldots,\gamma_{tm},\beta'_{t1},\ldots,\beta'_{tm})'$. An alternative approach is to take the process α_t to be the superposition of a first-order random walk and a local linear trend component with unknown time-changing slope τ_t, the local linear trend model (e.g., Fahrmeir and Tutz 1994, chap 8). An intermediate strategy is proposed in Berzuini and Larizza (1996), where the slope τ is assumed to be time-constant. Informative priors on τ can be used to incorporate prior beliefs that, say, a specific covariate effect is linear declining with time. Other interesting transition models are second-order random walks and seasonal models.

In general, we admit a multivariate Gaussian autoregressive model of order k for α_t, $t \geq k$:

$$\alpha_t = \sum_{l=1}^{k} F_l\alpha_{t-l} + u_t, \qquad u_t \sim N(0,Q_t). \tag{9}$$

The error variables u_t are assumed to be mutually independent and independent of initial values α_t, for which diffuse priors $\alpha_t \propto \mathrm{const}$, $t = 1,\ldots,k$, are assumed. The matrices $F_1,\ldots,F_k$ are known. If time intervals $[a_{t-1},a_t)$ are of the same length, we set $Q_t = Q$, otherwise $Q_t = h_t Q$, where h_t is the length of $[a_{t-1},a_t)$. Usually Q is unknown and is considered as a hyperparameter. In a full Bayesian setting, a prior specification for Q completes the transition model. Inverse Wishart distributions or products of inverse gamma distributions are the usual choice.

For full Bayesian inference, the joint distribution of $y = (y_1,\ldots,y_q)$, $x = (x_1,\ldots,x_q)$, $c = (c_1,\ldots,c_q)$, $\alpha = (\alpha_1,\ldots,\alpha_q)$, where q is the number of intervals, and Q has to be completely defined. This is achieved by adding a number of conditional independence assumptions. To see what assumptions are useful and how they can be interpreted, we recursively factorize the joint distribution. Let

$$L_t = \mathrm{p}(y_t^*,x_t^*,c_t^*,\alpha_t^*,Q), \qquad t = 1,\ldots,q,$$

denote the joint distribution up to the interval $[a_{t-1}, a_t)$. By repeated conditioning, we get the factorization

$$L_t = L_{t-1} p(y_t | \cdot) p(\alpha_t | \cdot) p(x_t, c_t | \cdot)$$

with

$$p(y_t | \cdot) = p(y_t | y_{t-1}^*, x_t^*, c_t^*, \alpha_t^*, Q),$$

$$p(\alpha_t | \cdot) = p(\alpha_t | \alpha_{t-1}^*, y_{t-1}^*, x_t^*, c_t^*, Q),$$

$$\text{and } p(x_t, c_t | \cdot) = p(x_t, c_t | y_{t-1}^*, x_{t-1}^*, c_{t-1}^*, \alpha_{t-1}^*, Q).$$

We now make the following conditional independence assumptions:

A1 Conditional on x_{it} and α_t, individual event indicators y_{it} are independent of α_{t-1}^* and Q, i.e.

$$p(y_{it} | y_{t-1}^*, x_t^*, c_t^*, \alpha_t^*, Q) = p(y_{it} | x_{it}, \alpha_t).$$

A2 Given $y_{t-1}^*, x_t^*, c_t^*, \alpha_t^*$ and Q, individual event indicators y_{it}, $i \in R_t$ are conditionally independent, i.e.

$$p(y_t | y_{t-1}^*, x_t^*, c_t^*, \alpha_t^*, Q) = \prod_{i \in R_t} p(y_{it} | y_{t-1}^*, x_t^*, c_t^*, \alpha_t^*, Q).$$

A3 The sequence α_t is Markovian of order k, i.e.

$$p(\alpha_t | \alpha_{t-1}^*, y_{t-1}^*, x_t^*, c_t^*, Q) = \begin{cases} p(\alpha_t | \alpha_{t-1}, \ldots, \alpha_{t-k}, Q) & t > k \\ p(\alpha_t) & t = 1, \ldots, k \end{cases}.$$

A4 Given y_{t-1}^*, x_{t-1}^*, c_{t-1}^*, covariates x_t and censoring indicator c_t are independent of α_{t-1}^* and Q.

A5 Initial values $\alpha_1, \ldots, \alpha_k$, x_1, c_1 and Q are mutually independent.

Assumption (**A1**), which is implicitly assumed in the observation model, is common for dynamic or state space modeling. It says that conditional information of α_t^* on y_t is already contained in α_t, and is usually not stated for fixed parameters. Since only individuals i in the risk set R_t contribute likelihood information in time period t—i.e., $c_{it} = 1$ if $i \in R_t$ c_t^* can be omitted on the right-hand side of (**A1**). Note that the covariates x_{it} may contain information on covariate values of other individuals or from the past. As stated above, we do not include the history y_{t-1}^* of failure indicators in the form of covariates. The conditional independence assumption (**A2**) is weaker than the usual unconditional independence assumptions among units, since it allows for interaction via common history, and it is likely to hold if a common cause for failures is incorporated in the covariate process. For fixed parameters, (**A2**) corresponds to Assumption 2 of Arjas and Haara (1987). Assumption (**A3**) is already implied by the transition model (13). Assumption (**A4**) corresponds to Assumption 1 of Arjas and Haara. It will generally hold for noninformative censoring and external or time independent covariates. It may not hold for internal covariates. Independence of initial values $\alpha_1, \ldots, \alpha_k$ in (**A5**) has already been stated in the transition model and is supplemented by the additional independence assumption on x_1, c_1, and Q. Summarizing (**A1**) and (**A2**), we get

$$p(y_t|y_{t-1}^*, x_t^*, c_t^*, \alpha_t^*, Q) = \prod_{i \in R_t} p(y_{it}|x_{it}, \alpha_t).$$

Under assumptions (**A1**)–(**A5**), the joint distribution of y, x, c, α, and Q is now proportional to a product of individual conditional likelihood contributions, defined by the observation model, a smoothness prior for α as a product of transition densities by (13), and the prior for Q:

$$p(y, x, c, \alpha, Q) \propto \left\{ \prod_t \prod_{i \in R_t} p(y_{it}|x_{it}, \alpha_t) \right\}$$

$$\times \left\{ \prod_{t>k} p(\alpha_t|\alpha_{t-1}, \ldots, \alpha_{t-k}, Q) \right\} \times p(Q). \qquad (10)$$

A graphical representation of this model is shown in Figure 1. Individual densities in the first factor are given by the observation model (5) or (7), implying they are independent of the right-censoring mechanism c_t^*, and transition densities in the second factor are given by

$$p(\alpha_t|\alpha_{t-1}, \ldots, \alpha_{t-k}, Q) \sim N\left(\sum_{l=1}^{k} F_l \alpha_{t-l}, Q_t \right). \qquad (11)$$

3. ESTIMATING HAZARD FUNCTIONS AND COVARIATE EFFECTS BY MCMC SIMULATION

Smoothing time-varying parameters—i.e., estimation of the sequence $\alpha = \{\alpha_t\}$ given the data y, x, c—is of prime interest. Full Bayesian inference will be based on the posteriors $p(\alpha|y, x, c)$ or $p(\alpha_t|y, x, c)$, which are proportional to the right hand side of (10). Since the normalizing factor has rather complex structure, direct approaches using numerical integration or ordinary static Monte Carlo methods are computationally infeasible.

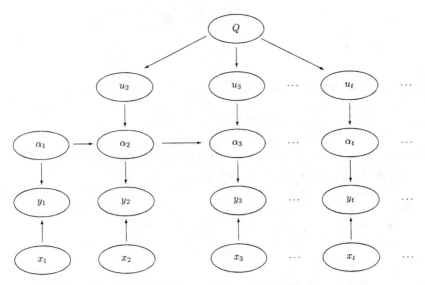

FIGURE 1. Directed graphical representation of a dynamic model with lag $k = 1$.

We suggest a Markov Chain Monte Carlo (MCMC) sampling scheme, that allows us to draw samples from posteriors of time-varying parameters, hazard functions, and similar quantities of interest, thus making full Bayesian inference possible. We start this section with a short review, since some of the readers might not be so familiar with MCMC. The reader is also referred to the tutorial expositions of Casella and George (1992), Chib and Greenberg (1995) and Gilks, Richardson, and Spiegelhalter (1996). A more theoretical study of MCMC techniques can be found in Tierney (1994).

3.1. *Basic Ideas of MCMC*

MCMC techniques have revolutionized general Bayesian inference in the last few years. Bayesian inference starts with a prior distribution $p(\theta)$ for an unknown parameter vector θ. In our context, the unknown parameters are $\alpha_1, \ldots, \alpha_q$ and Q and the corresponding prior distribution is

$$\left\{ \prod_{t>k} p(\alpha_t | \alpha_{t-1}, \ldots, \alpha_{t-k}, Q) \right\} \times p(Q).$$

Having observed data D, Bayes' theorem tells us, that the posterior distribution, conditioning on D, is given by

$$p(\theta|D) = \frac{p(D|\theta)p(\theta)}{\int p(D|\theta)p(\theta)d\theta}. \tag{12}$$

Here $p(D|\theta)$ is the likelihood, in our case equal to

$$\left\{ \prod_t \prod_{i \in R_t} p(y_{it}|x_{it}, \alpha_t) \right\}.$$

The right-hand side of equation (10) corresponds to the nominator $p(D, \theta) = p(D|\theta)p(\theta)$ in (12).

The posterior distribution contains all the information Bayesian inference is based on. Typically, summary characteristics of the posterior, such as the posterior mean

$$E(\theta|D) = \frac{\int \theta p(D|\theta)p(\theta)d\theta}{\int p(D|\theta)p(\theta)d\theta}$$

are of primary interest. However, computation of such expectations involves integrations, which can be very hard to solve, especially if θ is of high dimension. Therefore classical Bayesian inference was restricted to rather simple models, where analytic computation of characteristics of the posterior distribution is possible. Accurate approximations by numerical techniques are available only for problems, where the dimension of the parameter vector is not greater than, say, 10 or 20. However, for a lot of applied problems, the posterior is analytically and numerically intractable. Monte Carlo methods circumvent the integration problem by generating samples from the posterior distribution. However, ordinary Monte Carlo methods, such as importance sampling, are often computationally infeasible for complex, highly structured models. Here MCMC methods are more appropriate.

In this subsection let $p(\theta)$ be the posterior distribution of a random vector θ, suppressing the conditioning on the data D. The basic idea of MCMC is to generate a sample $\theta^{(k)}$, $k = 1, 2, \ldots$, by a Markov transition function $Z(\theta^{(k)} \to \theta^{(k+1)})$ such that $p(\theta)$ is the stationary distribution of the Markov chain Θ. Thus, after a sufficiently long "burn-in phase" of length m, the generated states $\theta^{(k)}, k = m + 1, \ldots, n$ are dependent samples from the posterior. For example, the posterior mean can now be estimated by the arithmetic average

$$\frac{1}{n-m} \sum_{k=m+1}^{n} \theta^{(k)}.$$

Other quantities of interest can also be estimated by the appropriate empirical versions.

For construction of such a Markov chain, it is necessary to find a suitable transition function $Z(\theta^{(k)} \to \theta^{(k+1)})$, such that the posterior distribution $p(\theta)$ is the stationary distribution of Θ. There are surprisingly many different choices of Z for a given distribution $p(\theta)$, but most of them, including the Gibbs sampler, are special cases of the Hastings (1970) algorithm. Most methods split up θ into components $\theta_1, \ldots, \theta_T, \ldots, \theta_H$ of possibly differing dimension. In our context, these components could be chosen as $\alpha_1, \ldots, \alpha_q$ and Q, leading to a so-called single-move updating scheme. These components are updated one by one using the Hastings algorithm. The posterior distribution $p(\theta)$, typically high dimensional and rather complicated, is not needed; only so-called *full conditional distributions* enter in the Hastings algorithm. A full conditional distribution, which we will call *full conditional* for short, is the distribution of one component, conditioning on all the remaining components, such as $p(\theta_T | \theta_1, \ldots, \theta_{T-1}, \theta_{T+1}, \ldots, \theta_H)$. Besag (1974) showed that $p(\theta)$ is uniquely determined by the set of its full conditional distributions. This gives an intuitive justification for the fact that only full conditional distributions and not the posterior itself are needed for MCMC simulation. In hierarchical models, defined by conditional independence assumptions, these full conditionals often have a much simpler structure than the posterior itself. This provides an important computational advantage.

The Gibbs sampling algorithm, probably the most prominent member of MCMC algorithms, iteratively updates all components by samples from their full conditionals. Markov chain theory shows that under very general conditions the sequence of random numbers generated in this way converges to the posterior. However, often these full conditionals are themselves still quite complex, so generation of the required random numbers might be a difficult task. Relief lies in the fact that it is not necessary to sample from the full conditionals; a member of the much more general class of Hastings algorithms can be used to update the full conditionals. Such a Hastings step is typically easier to implement and often makes a MCMC algorithm more efficient in terms of CPU time. A Hastings step proposes a new value for a given component and accepts it with a certain probability. A Gibbs step (i.e., a sample from a full conditional) turns out to be a special case where the proposal is always accepted.

Let $p(\theta_T|\theta_{-T})$ be the full conditional of a component θ_T of θ, given the rest of the components, denoted by θ_{-T}. To update $\theta_T = \theta_T^{(k)}$ in iteration step k, it is sufficient to generate a proposal θ_T' from an arbitrarily chosen transition kernel $P(\theta_T \to \theta_T'; \theta_{-T})$ and accept the generated proposal with probability

$$\delta = \min\left\{1, \frac{p(\theta_T'|\theta_{-T})P(\theta_T' \to \theta_T; \theta_{-T})}{p(\theta_T|\theta_{-T})P(\theta_T \to \theta_T'; \theta_{-T})}\right\};$$

otherwise leave θ_T unchanged. This is the Hastings algorithm used for updating full conditionals. Only a ratio of the full conditional of θ_T enters in δ, so $p(\theta_T|\theta_{-T})$ needs to be known only up to a multiplicative constant and does not need to be normalized, a very convenient fact for implementation. Note that both the current state θ_T and the proposed new state θ_T' as well as the current states of the other components θ_{-T} affect δ.

Gibbs sampling corresponds to the specific choice

$$P(\theta_T \to \theta_T'; \theta_{-T}) = p(\theta_T'|\theta_{-T}),$$

so that δ becomes 1 and therefore all proposals are accepted. Here the current state of θ_T does not affect the new one θ_T'.

There is a great flexibility in the choice of the transition kernel P. Common choices are random walk Metropolis proposals and (conditional) independence proposals (Tierney 1994).

Random walk Metropolis proposals are generated from a distribution, that is symmetric about the current value θ_T. Often used are Gaussian or rectangular distributions. In contrast, conditional independence proposals do not depend on the current state of θ_T; they may however depend on the current values of θ_{-T}. As we have seen above, the Gibbs sampling kernel is a specific conditional independence proposal. However, it is crucial that for a chosen P, the acceptance probability δ not be too small (in average) and that both convergence and mixing behavior of the whole simulated Markov chain be satisfactory. A well-mixing Markov chain is moving rapidly throughout the support of the stationary distribution $p(\theta)$.

Somewhat surprising is the fact that one is allowed to use hybrid procedures—that is, to use different versions of Hastings proposals for updating different components of θ. One strategy is to sample from the full conditionals, that is a "Gibbs step," as long as this is easy and fast. If not, a specific Hastings step with a simple proposal distribution mostly works faster in CPU time. As long as all components are updated in a deterministic or even random order (which may ensure better mixing of the chain), the chain converges to the posterior.

3.2. *MCMC Simulation in Dynamic Discrete Time Duration Models*

In this subsection we propose a hybrid MCMC procedure for simulating the (unnormalized) posterior (10). Time-varying parameters $\alpha_t, t = 1,\ldots,q$ are updated using specific conditional independence proposals, while a Gibbs step is used for updating Q. Consider the full conditional

$$p(\alpha_t | \alpha_{s \neq t}, Q, y, x, c) \propto \prod_{i \in R_t} p(y_{it} | x_{it}, \alpha_t) \times p(\alpha_t | \alpha_{s \neq t}, Q). \qquad (13)$$

While the first factor corresponds to the observation model at time t, the second reflects the dependence of underlying parameters through the transition model and does not depend on the data y, x, and c.

This second factor, the conditional distribution $p(\alpha_t | \alpha_{s \neq t}, Q)$, can be derived from (9). It is Gaussian $N(\mu_t, \Sigma_t)$, where the mean μ_t and covariance matrix Σ_t depend on the current values of Q and of neighboring parameters $\alpha_{s \neq t}$. Different transition models result in different formulas for μ_t and Σ_t. For example, a random walk of first-order $\alpha_t = \alpha_{t-1} + u_t, u_t \sim N(0, Q)$ has conditional distribution

$$N(\mu_t, \Sigma_t) = \begin{cases} N(\alpha_{t+1}, Q) & (t = 1) \\ N(\frac{1}{2}\alpha_{t-1} + \frac{1}{2}\alpha_{t+1}, \frac{1}{2}Q) & (t = 2,\ldots,q-1) \\ N(\alpha_{t-1}, Q) & (t = q) \end{cases} \qquad (14)$$

We use a specific conditional independence proposal—namely, a sample from the conditional distribution $p(\alpha_t | \alpha_{s \neq t}, Q)$, to update α_t via a Hastings step. The acceptance probability simplifies in this case to

$$\delta = \min\left\{ 1, \frac{p(y_t | \alpha_t')}{p(y_t | \alpha_t)} \right\},$$

with

$$p(y_t | \alpha_t) := \prod_{i \in R_t} p(y_{it} | x_{it}, \alpha_t)$$

as the conditional likelihood of objects under risk in interval t, defined by the observation model. Such a proposal has a natural interpretation due to the hierarchical structure of the model: α_t' is drawn independently of the observation model and just reflects the specific autoregressive prior specification. It is therefore called a conditional prior proposal (Knorr-Held 1996). If it produces improvement in the likelihood at time t, it will always be accepted; if it is not, the acceptance probability is equal to the likelihood ratio. This algorithm shows good performance for duration data with an acceptance rate ranging from 0.3 to 0.9. We also experienced with a slightly different MCMC sampling scheme, where blocks $\alpha_a, \ldots, \alpha_b$ are updated simultaneously rather than updating each α_t one at a time. Such a blocking strategy often improves mixing and convergence considerably. Conditional prior proposals can be generalized to this case conveniently.

Sampling from the full conditional

$$p(Q|\alpha, y, x, c) \sim p(Q|\alpha)$$

is straightforward for conjugate priors like inverse gamma or inverted Wishart distributions. If Q is assumed to be diagonal, an inverse gamma prior $Q_{jj} \sim IG(a, b)$ for the j-th diagonal entry in Q is computationally convenient, since the resulting full conditional is still inverse gamma with parameters $a + (q - k)/2$ and $b + \sum u_{tj}^2/2$. Note the transformation from α to u_t, $t = k + 1, \ldots, q$ via the transition model (9). The inverse gamma distribution has density

$$p(Q_{jj}) \propto Q_{jj}^{-a-1} \exp(-b/Q_{jj})$$

and has a unique mode at $b/(a + 1)$. In all our examples we start with the values $a = 1$ and $b = 0.005$, so that $p(Q_{jj})$ is highly dispersed but still proper. This choice reflects sufficient prior ignorance about Q but avoids problems arising with improper priors (see Raftery and Banfield 1991). We then add a sensitivity analysis and rerun the algorithm with different choices for b, such as 0.05 or 0.0005. The parameter b determines, how close to zero the variances are allowed to be *a priori*. Note that the inverse gamma distribution has no expectation for $a = 1$, so our prior guess is rather diffuse for every value of b.

It is very important to carefully check convergence and mixing behavior of any MCMC algorithm. Theoretical considerations are typically limited to rather simple models; therefore empirical output analysis is more practical. This is still an active research area (Raftery and Lewis 1996; Gelman 1996; Cowles and Carlin 1996; and the relevant parts of Gilks, Richardson, and Spiegelhalter 1996). We always look at several plots such as time series plots of the sampled values and routinely calculate autocorrelation functions for every parameter. Figure 2 shows the time series plot of a specific parameter of our first analysis ($m = 1$, Section 4). The figure presents the stored values of the hundredth parameter in our model, the effect of nationality at time $t = 28$. Low values of the autocorrelation function indicate good mixing. Plots for other parameters look quite similar.

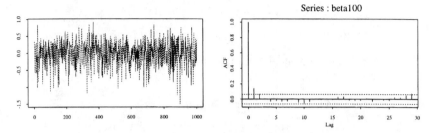

FIGURE 2. Time series plot and estimated autocorrelation function of a selected parameter.

After convergence, the simulated random numbers are samples from the marginal distributions $p(\alpha|y,x,c)$ and $p(Q|y,x,c)$ and are used to estimate characteristics of the posterior distribution. Note that for a given covariate sequence $x_i(t)$ of a specific unit i, samples from its hazard function are calculated by plugging in the samples from $p(\alpha|y,x,c)$ in (5) or (7). Even samples from the survivor function can be obtained by using the samples from the hazard function in the dynamic version of (1). Furthermore it is possible to construct simultaneous credible regions for covariate effects, hazard or survival functions by using the method described in Besag et al. (1995).

4. APPLICATIONS TO DURATION OF UNEMPLOYMENT

4.1 *Data Description and a First Nonparametric Analysis*

We analyze data on duration of unemployment of 1416 persons, older than 16 years and living in West Germany, which are observed from January 1983 until December 1993 in the German socioeconomic panel GSOEP. Only persons with single spells of unemployment are considered. Duration of unemployment is measured in months, and 296 observations are censored. Only a small fraction of persons are unemployed for more than three years, so that there is very little information on such long-term unemployment. Therefore only durations up to 36 months are considered and longer durations are considered as censored. In total, 49 out of the 54 persons, still unemployed in month 36, are censored. Based on previous analysis with time-constant effects (Fahrmeir and Tutz 1994, chap 9), we include the covariates sex, age, and nationality, coded as follows:

Sex S : $S = 1$ for males, $S = 0$ for females;

Nationality N : $N = 1$ for German, $N = 0$ for foreigner;

Age at the beginning of unemployment, grouped in four categories and coded by 0–1 dummies:

$A1 = 1$ for "age ≤ 30 years," 0 else;

$A2 = 1$ for "$41 \leq$ age ≤ 50 years," 0 else;

$A3 = 1$ for "age ≥ 51 years," 0 else;

with reference category "$31 \leq$ age ≤ 40 years" coded by $(A1, A2, A3) = (0,0,0)$. The observed frequency counts for these covariates are 56 %, 64 %, 50 %, 15% and 18 % for S, N, $A1$, $A2$ and $A3$, respectively.

Most often covariates are expected to have much the same impact over the course of unemployment. We let the data decide whether this is really so and admit that the effects of these covariates may vary over time. In particular, we are able to check if unemployment benefits have effects that vary or erode over time. Results of Narendranathan and Stewart (1993) and Portugal and Addison (1995) based on British Labor market data, provide empirical evidence for declining effects of unemployment benefits. In Germany there are two major types of unemployment benefits: unemployment insurance (*Arbeitslosengeld*) and unemployment assistance (*Arbeitslosenhilfe*). Unemployment insurance regularly pays a certain proportion of last income for a first period of unemployment, with receipt of benefits depending on how much has been contributed to the system beforehand. After this period, unemployment assistance is paid, but the amount of support is considerably less. Under certain circumstances, there may be no financial support at all. For more details on unemployment compensation in Germany, see Zimmermann (1993). In our sample, there are only a few persons with no financial support during a particular time. Therefore we collapse the categories "unemployment assistance" and "no financial support" and include the time-varying binary variable

B_t : Unemployment insurance benefit in month t received ($B_t = 1$)

or not ($B_t = 0$) as a further regressor.

In a first analysis, only the terminating event "end of unemployment," regardless of a specific cause is considered. We apply a dynamic binary logit model

$$\lambda(t|x(t)) = \frac{\exp(\gamma_t + z_{it}'\beta_t)}{1 + \exp(\gamma_t + z_{it}'\beta_t)},$$

where $z_{it}' = (S_i, N_i, S_i N_i, A1_i, A2_i, A3_i, B_{it})$ contains the fixed or time-varying covariates above, and $S_i N_i$ is an interaction effect between sex and nationality, with $S_i N_i = 1$ for German males (34 percent observed frequency), $S_i N_i = 0$ else. The baseline-effect γ_t and time-varying covariate effects β_t are modeled by first-order random walks, which we prefer for the following reasons: Although estimates tend to be less smooth than with second-order random walks, they react more flexibly in the presence of unexpected peaks or other dynamic patterns. Furthermore, first-order random walk models reduce to traditional models with constant parameters, if corresponding error variances tend to zero. Thus smoothness priors defined by first-order random walks are in favor of horizontal lines. Our analysis is based on a final run of 41,000 iterations with a burn-in period of 1000. We stored every fortieth sample.

Figure 3(a) shows the estimated baseline effect γ_t. It corresponds to the hazard function for foreign females, between 31 and 40 years old and receiving no unemployment insurance benefit. Apart from a peak at about one year of unemployment, the baseline effect is declining until month 30. The subsequent increase should not be overinterpreted: data becomes sparse at that observation period, and also censoring due to unemployment spells of more than 36 months may introduce some bias. The effects of sex and nationality in Figures 3(b) and 3(c) have to be interpreted together with the interaction effect of sex and nationality in Figure 3(d). Figure 3(c) shows that German females have generally better chances of leaving the state of unemployment than foreign females, but this effect seems to vanish over time. Employment chances are further enhanced for German men during the first year of unemployment as shown in Figure 3(d). However, this effect also seems to vanish later on. This may partly be explained by the fact that Germans with good chances in the labor market have already obtained a job earlier, while many of the remaining Germans are long-term unemployment persons.

Parts (e)–(g) displays the effect of age. As one might expect, younger individuals (age ≤ 30) have better chances of getting a job compared to the reference group (age from 31 to 40), especially for the first 15 months, but this effect vanishes later on. The effect of age between 41 and 50 is negative and almost constant. More surprising is the ef-

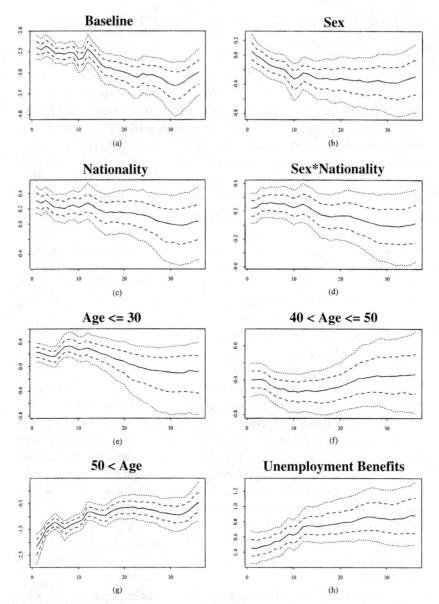

FIGURE 3. Time-varying effects of several covariates. The posterior median (-) within 50 percent and 80 percent pointwise credible regions is shown.

fect of age > 50: It is negative at the beginning but increases distinctly toward zero with duration of unemployment. How can this be interpreted? Perhaps even more surprising is the effect of unemployment benefits: It is positive throughout and even increasing with duration of unemployment. This is in contrast to speculations that unemployment benefits foster apathy in leaving the state of unemployment. As we will see, this effect and other questions—for example, the peak at about month 12 in the baseline effect—can be better interpreted and answered by a refined analysis that distinguishes between different types of terminating events.

Figure 4 shows Bayesian pointwise credible regions for the hazard function and simultaneous credible regions for the survival function. Considered are persons between 31 and 40 years old who receive unemployment insurance benefits. All calculations are based on posterior samples from the corresponding quantities. We see that German men are likely to have a higher hazard in the first month of unemployment than German women. However, we observe the inverse trend for the second and third year, where the hazard for women seems to be even slightly higher. Consequently, the survival function is steeper for men than for women. Note that for foreign men and women hazard and survival functions are much more similar.

We explored the dependence of our conclusions upon prior specifications by a sensitivity analysis, as discussed in Section 3.2. We rerun our algorithm with the value of b changed to 0.0005 for all eight variances. The results can be summarized as follows: In general, all estimated effects show a very similar pattern as for $b = 0.005$ (Figure 3). Both point and interval estimates are visually indistinguishable for parameters with a relatively high temporal variation such as the baseline effect or the effect of age > 50. The new parameter b mainly changes a lower limit for the variances, which is much smaller than the estimated variances anyway. Covariates with less temporal variation show a slightly smoother pattern with smaller variance estimates. The corresponding credible regions are slightly narrower, mainly for $t > 24$. This can be explained by the fact that the data tend to be sparse toward the end of the observation period, so prior assumptions are still inherent in the posterior. Smaller variances therefore cause smaller credible bands. For $b = 0.05$, the patterns are now rougher for covariates with low temporal variation such as the effect of nationality.

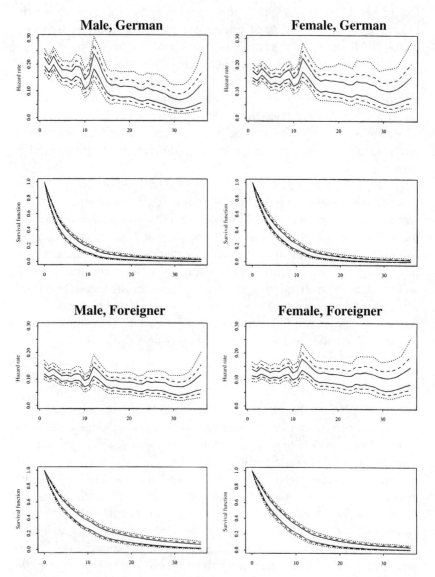

FIGURE 4. Hazard and survival functions for several covariate combinations. The
data are for persons between 31 and 40 who received unemployment insurance benefits. Pointwise (hazard) and simultaneous (survival) credible
regions of 50, 80 and 95 percent are shown.

4.2. A Comparison with a Parametric Model

To compare results obtained from our Bayesian nonparametric approach, we now reanalyze the data with a more conventional parametric model. Based on the estimated effects and associated credible regions displayed in Figure 3, we model the baseline effect and the effects of sex, age ≤ 30, age > 50, and unemployment benefits as simple functions of time, whereas the remaining effects are assumed to be constant over time. It should be noted that specification of appropriate functional forms for time-varying effects will generally be a rather difficult task without exploring patterns nonparametrically in advance.

For the baseline effect, we assume a cubic polynomial

$$\gamma_t = \gamma_0 + \gamma_1 t + \gamma_2 t^2 + \gamma_3 t^3.$$

A look at the credible regions in Figure 3(h) suggests that a simple linear trend function

$$\beta_t^B = \beta_0^B + \beta_1^B t$$

is appropriate for the effect β_t^B of unemployment benefits. The effects β_t^S of sex and $\beta_t^{age\,>50}$ show more variation during the first 12 months of unemployment than later on. Therefore we model them by a simple regression spline, consisting of a cubic polynomial up to the cutpoint $t = 12$ and a linear trend for $t > 12$; i.e., we assume

$$\beta_t^S = \beta_0^S + \beta_1^S t + \beta_2^S \min(0, t - 12)^2 + \beta_3^S \min(0, t - 12)^3$$

for the effect of sex, and an analogous model for the effect of age > 50. Since there is less time-variation for the effect of age ≤ 30, we choose a piecewise constant function with a jump at $t = 12$:

$$\beta^{age \leq 30} = \begin{cases} \beta_1 & \text{for } t \leq 12 \\ \beta_2 & \text{for } t > 12 \end{cases}.$$

Using the relation between discrete-time duration models and sequential binary models (see Allison 1982; Fahrmeir and Tutz 1994, chap. 9), maximum-likelihood estimation can be carried out with standard software for generalized linear models. Figure 5 shows the estimated effects of baseline, sex, age > 50, and unemployment benefits. The overall shape of the baseline effect in Figure 5(a) reflects the nonparametric estimate in Fig-

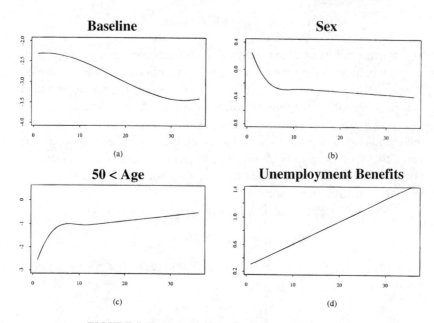

FIGURE 5. Estimated effects for the parametric model.

ure 3(a), but obviously peculiarities like the peak around $t = 12$ cannot be detected by a cubic polynomial. Detailed modeling of this peak will require a more complex but less parsimonious parametric specification. The effect of unemployment benefits in Figure 5(d) is quite close to the estimate obtained from the dynamic model for the first year. Later on, the increase of this effect is less distinct for the nonparametric fit. This can be explained as follows: A large number of observations has duration less than about one year, while data become sparse toward the end of the observation period. The fit of the global parametric linear trend model is influenced to a large extent by the majority of observations with shorter durations. On the other hand, with a dynamic model the influence of these observations on the fit is declining as time increases. Similar considerations have also to be taken into account when comparing the effects of sex and age > 50. The effect of age > 50 in Figure 5(c) is quite similar in shape to that in Figure 3(g), whereas the effect of sex differs a little bit from that of Figure 3(b) but is still in agreement with credible regions.

Table 2 shows all parameter estimates, together with corresponding standard errors and 95 percent confidence intervals. Time variation of the

TABLE 2
Parameter Estimates for the Parametric Model

	Estimate	Std. Err.	95% CI	
γ_0	−2.3271	0.2209	−2.7601	−1.894
γ_1	0.0187	0.0431	−0.0658	0.1033
γ_2	−0.0044	0.0032	−0.0108	0.0020
γ_3	0.00008	0.00006	−0.00005	0.00021
age ≤ 30 years, $t \leq 12$	0.2173	0.0893	0.0422	0.3924
age ≤ 30 years, $t > 12$	−0.0075	0.2431	−0.4839	0.4688
$41 \leq$ age ≤ 50 years	−0.4623	0.1147	−0.6871	−0.2375
$\beta_0^{age>50}$	−1.3354	0.4014	−2.1222	−0.5486
$\beta_1^{age>50}$	0.0230	0.0224	−0.0209	0.0669
$\beta_2^{age>50}$	0.0198	0.0184	−0.0162	0.0560
$\beta_3^{age>50}$	0.0027	0.0016	−0.0005	0.0059
β_0^S	−0.2329	0.3331	−0.8858	0.4200
β_1^S	−0.0043	0.0197	−0.0430	0.0342
β_2^S	−0.0050	0.0099	−0.0245	0.0145
β_3^S	−0.0008	0.0007	−0.0023	0.0006
Nationality	0.2536	0.1078	0.0424	0.4649
Sex*Nationality	0.2421	0.1410	−0.0343	0.5186
β_0^B	0.2733	0.1617	−0.0437	0.5903
β_1^B	0.0331	0.0139	0.0058	0.0603

effect of age ≤ 30 and unemployment benefits is immediate from these estimates: The effect of age ≤ 30 is significantly positive for $t \leq 12$, and the slope parameter for the linear trend effect of unemployment benefits is significantly positive. Evidence for time-variation of effects modeled by (piecewise) polynomials is not so easily seen from Table 2. For example, estimates for γ_2 and γ_3 provide evidence for a nonlinear time-varying baseline effect, although they are only on the borderline to individual significance. A formal test would have to consider all parameters $\gamma_1, \ldots, \gamma_3$ jointly. Also, we have to keep in mind that the cubic polynomial is not able to fit the peak around $t = 12$ adequately, so that significance is confounded by some kind of model misspecification. Similar remarks apply to the effects of age > 50 and sex. The remaining effects, assumed to be time-constant, are in quite reasonable agreement with the estimates in Figure 3.

As shown by this example, conventional parametric modeling of dynamic effects is possible and can be useful as a second step after having explored time-varying structures with nonparametric approaches in a first analysis. Without the first step, however, it will generally be quite difficult or even hopeless to specify appropriate but still parsimonious functional forms and to obtain adequate conclusions.

4.3 Distinguishing Between Several Causes of Leaving Unemployment

In our second analysis we now distinguish between three terminating events:

1. Employment in a full-time job
2. Employment in a part-time job
3. Further causes like retraining or going to university, completing military or civil service, retiring, working as a housewife/househusband, and others.

To study event-specific differences in hazard rates and covariate effects, we apply a multinomial dynamic logit model, with $m = 3$ categories defined by cause 1 (full-time job), 2 (part-time job) and 3 (others). Thus the observation model is

$$h_r(t|x_i) = \frac{\exp(\eta_{itr})}{1 + \sum_{j=1}^{3} \exp(\eta_{itj})}, \qquad r = 1,2,3,$$

with event-specific predictors $\eta_{itr} = \gamma_{tr} + z'_{it}\beta_{tr}$. Covariate vectors z_{it} are the same as in the first analysis. Event-specific baseline effects γ_{tr} and covariate effects β_{tr}, $r = 1,2,3$ are again modeled by first-order random walks.

The baseline effect for transitions to a full-time or a part-time job show the typical smooth decreasing pattern often observed with unemployment data (Figure 6). The peak at month 12 appears only in the baseline effect for transitions to other causes. A closer look at the data shows that transitions "to retirement," "housewife/househusband," and "other reasons" are mainly responsible for this peak. A possible explanation may be that these individuals would lose unemployment insurance benefits after one year and prefer, for example, to retire. A second reason may be due to the specific kind of questions on employment status in GSOEP: Participants of the panel fill out questionnaires for every year and have to give

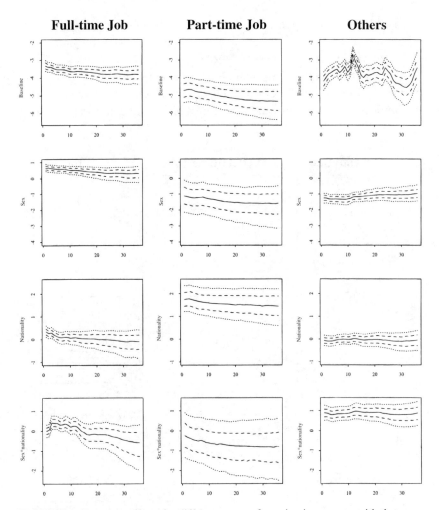

FIGURE 6. Covariate effects for different types of terminating events, with the same credible regions shown in Figure 3.

answers on employment status retrospectively for each month. This group tends not to name a certain month but instead simply names the beginning or end of a year as the time of leaving the status of unemployment. The effects of sex and nationality are also now much better to interpret. For example, there is a distinct positive effect for transitions to a full-time job for men, but also a distinct negative effect for transitions to a part-time job.

The nationality effect provides clear evidence that German females have highly increased chances of getting a part-time job; maybe they are much more interested in getting part-time jobs.

Also the effects of age can be better explained now (Figure 7). In particular, looking at the effects of age > 50, we see that chances for getting full-time and part-time jobs are significantly deteriorated and do

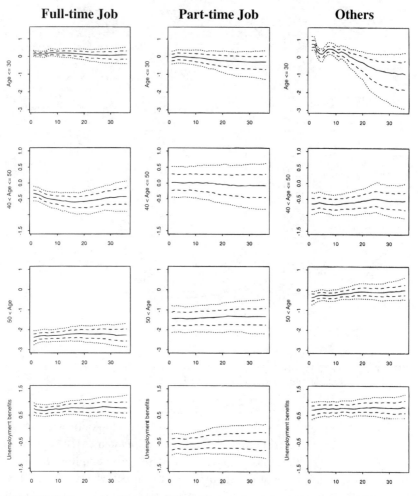

FIGURE 7. Covariate effects for different types of terminating events, with the same credible regions shown in Figure 3.

not improve with increasing duration of unemployment. However, the effect of transitions to other causes is near zero and even slightly increasing. This supports presumptions that older individuals prefer to retire, to become housewife/househusband or to leave the unemployment register for other reasons. We also see that the time-varying effect of age > 50 in Figure 3(g) is largely caused by confounding the effect of the three types of transitions into the effect of only one terminating cause. Also, the effects of unemployment insurance benefits can now be interpreted correctly: The effect is constantly positive for transitions to a full-time job, presumably since individuals with unemployment insurance benefits had regular jobs earlier and thus get offers for a new full-time job more easily. On the other side, the effect is clearly negative for transitions to part-time jobs. A possible explanation is that some individuals with good financial support from unemployment insurance are less motivated to get a part-time job.

For a parametric reanalysis, we first fitted a model with baseline effects specified as low-order polynomials but kept all covariate effects time-constant. The shape of the estimated baseline effects was in agreement with our nonparametric analysis, although the peaks in the baseline effect for "others" could not be reproduced. Attempts to model time-varying structures in more detail by inclusion of time-varying effects led to divergence of ML estimates due to the large number of parameters involved. This illustrates that nonparametric approaches, imposing appropriate smoothness restrictions, are useful tools for refined and flexible analyses.

5. CONCLUSIONS

We conclude with some discussion of topics not treated in detail in the main text—e.g., computational issues, other alternative estimation approaches, multiple time scales, and unobserved heterogeneity.

The MCMC algorithms described in Section 3.2 have been implemented in C++ as part of a broader family of MCMC methods for Bayesian analysis of non-Gaussian cross-sectional, time series and longitudinal data. This development is a subproject of the "Statistische Analyse diskreter Strukturen," a research project supported by the German National Science Foundation (SFB 386). Software is available from the authors.

In this paper, we propose a certain type of Metropolis-Hastings algorithm. In our context, it has distinct advantages compared to a Gibbs step combined with rejection sampling based on knowledge of envelope functions and log-concavity of conditionals (e.g., Gilks and Wild 1992). An attractive feature of the proposed methodology is that implementation of additional observation models concerns only likelihoods appearing in the full conditional, without the necessity to provide score functions and information matrices. Our approach is derivative-free and therefore very flexible for specifying different models. This feature becomes even more important for multivariate observation models, as in Section 4.3.

As for any MCMC approach, computational difficulties may arise if convergence and mixing behavior of the simulated Markov chain is not satisfactory. Now strategies for improving MCMC, such as the block-move, have to be considered. In our view, the additional effort is rewarded by a rich output that can be used for substantially more comprehensive inference than provided by conventional methods.

Other MCMC sampling schemes for dynamic models have been suggested by Gamerman (1995) and Shephard and Pitt (1995), but they require distinctly more computation time per iteration. The multimove schemes of Carter and Kohn (1994) and Frühwirth-Schnatter (1994), designed for observation models with errors from normal, or mixtures of normals, cannot be extended to discrete observation models.

As a conceptually simpler alternative that avoids MCMC at all, posterior mode estimation—obtained by maximizing the unnormalized posterior—has been considered in Fahrmeir (1994, for $m = 1$) and Fahrmeir and Wagenpfeil (1996). This approach can be viewed as an empirical Bayes method, since the matrix Q is treated as fixed and unknown, not as a random variable with some prior distribution. Posterior mode estimation has also a non-Bayesian interpretation, being equivalent to maximization of a penalized likelihood. Efficient estimation can be carried out by iterative Kalman filtering and smoothing. We calculated posterior mode estimators for the models in Section 4, which were in close agreement with the MCMC results.

However, posterior mode estimation suffers from some disadvantages: Duration data usually becomes sparse toward the end of the observation period, so inference based on approximate posterior normality will be questionable. Also, as for any empirical Bayes approach, the uncertainty associated with estimates of $\{\alpha_t\}$ is underestimated, since no allowance is made for the uncertainty associated with Q. Furthermore, estimation of functionals of α, such as hazard or survival functions, has to be based on further approximations like the delta method. Posterior mode estimation is, nevertheless, useful as an ingredient of a fully Bayesian approach: It provides an initial solution for a refined analysis and can be used to check convergence behavior of simulation-based Monte Carlo methods.

Our concepts as well as our applications focused on one time dimension—i.e., that of duration in a certain state—regarding other time scales such as calendar time, age, or cohort as methodologically secondary. Although the models of this paper allow the inclusion of other time scales through covariates, they are not built to deal with multiple time scales in a symmetric way. Here we outline how this could be achieved. For simplicity, let us only consider the case of two time scales: duration time t and calendar time u, with one terminating event. The hazard function, now depending on t, u, and covariates, may be modeled by

$$\lambda(t,u|x) = h(\gamma_t + \vartheta_u + \vartheta_u^s + x'\beta_t),$$

where x is a possibly time-dependent, covariate vector, γ_t is the baseline effect for duration time t, ϑ_u is a trend component in calendar time— e.g., a random walk of first order—and ϑ_u^s may be a monthly seasonal component—e.g., $\vartheta_u^s + \cdots + \vartheta_{u-11}^s = v_u \sim N(0,\sigma_u^2)$, in calendar time. Multiple time scales models require appropriate conditional independence assumptions leading to modified full conditionals for MCMC simulation. In principle real-time effects ϑ_u, ϑ_u^s can be updated using additional Metropolis-Hastings steps analogous to those in Section 3. However, the simple structure of the full conditionals is destroyed, leading to a considerably increasing amount of implementation and computation requirements. We plan to consider dynamic models for multiple time scales and to develop efficient MCMC methods for such models in future research. Close in spirit is the work by Berzuini and Clayton (1994), who discuss survival models with multiple time scales and time-constant covariate effects.

Our dynamic model specifications in Section 2 allow rather flexible modeling of time-varying hazards and covariate effects. However, they do not explicitly take into account unobserved heterogeneity or frailty. For example, differences between short- and long-term unemployment might be considered as a potential source of unobserved heterogeneity that is not or is insufficiently explained by observed variables. The effect of neglected heterogeneity on estimation of hazards and covariate effects in duration models with fixed parameters has been studied by a number of authors, among them Vaupel and Yashin (1985) or Lancaster (1990). The most important consequence of neglecting unobserved heterogeneity is that it may appear as spurious duration dependence.

The conventional procedure to account for heterogeneity is to introduce unit-specific parameters, say ϑ_i, in the linear predictor and to assume that they are random effects, distributed according to some mixing distribution f_ϑ. Two main approaches to the modeling of this mixing distribution have been proposed. The first assumes a parametric form—e.g., a log-Gamma or a normal density—for f_ϑ. For discrete-time duration models with fixed effects and a single terminating event ($m = 1$), one treatment is to extend the linear predictor η_{it} additively to

$$\tilde{\eta}_{it} = \eta_{it} + \vartheta_i, \qquad \vartheta_i \quad \text{i.i.d} \sim N(0, \sigma^2),$$

and to carry out inference by MCMC, see Raftery, Lewis and Aghajanian (1995). Clayton (1991) uses a log-Gamma distribution instead in so-called frailty models. This approach can be combined with dynamic models by extending the linear predictor to

$$\eta_{it} = \alpha_t + x'_{it}\beta_t + \vartheta_i, \qquad \vartheta_i \quad \text{i.i.d} \sim N(0, \sigma^2)$$

and to add a further full conditional for ϑ_i in the MCMC updating steps. For panel data with many repeated events, such mixed dynamic models have been successfully implemented and applied by Knorr-Held (1995). For duration models, without repeated events, there is some evidence given in the literature that estimates can be very sensitive to the choice of the mixing distribution (Meyer 1990). The likelihood of observations becomes rather flat, so that the prior has much influence on the posterior. This is also to be expected for the second approach, where a discrete distribution, typically with small number of mass points, is chosen for f_ϑ (Heckman and Singer 1984). In addition, the effect of heterogeneity decreases with flexible models for baseline hazards (Narendranathan and Stewart 1993) and may be even less serious if time-varying covariate effects are introduced. For duration models with several terminating events ($m > 1$), these problems become even more evident, since the extension to this case is accompanied by additional prior assumptions. Thus misspecification of the mixing distribution can be worse than omitting heterogeneity. Therefore, and since our interest here lies in allowing flexibility in the form of time-varying effects of duration dependence, we have restricted attention to models without heterogeneity. This has to be kept in mind for a careful interpretation of the results in Section 4. For example, the time-varying effect of nationality in Figure 3(c) reflects differences in short-term and long-term unemployment between Germans and non-Germans. Concerning short unemployment, Germans have better chances for leaving unemployment, but this effect vanishes for long-term unemployment. Thus time-varying effects may be interpreted as caused by unobserved heterogeneity.

Other interesting extensions where our approach should be useful are dynamic continuous-time duration models—e.g., the dynamic piecewise exponential model development by Gamerman (1991), with an application to unemployment data in Gamerman and West (1987), and event-history models for multiple cycles and states—for example, semi-Markov models.

Obviously, a large number of possible models raise questions about model determination and validation that are beyond the scope of this paper. Bayesian model choice via MCMC is currently an intensive research area; promising solutions are based on Bayes factors (Lewis and Raftery 1994; Raftery 1996) or on predictive distributions (Gelfand 1996).

A further point of interest and of future research might be a careful comparison of our dynamic modeling approach with non-Bayesian semiparametric methods such as penalized or local likelihood estimation, taking into account theoretical, computational, and empirical aspects.

REFERENCES

Aalen, Odd O. 1989. "A Linear Regression Model for the Analysis of Life-Times." *Statistics in Medicine 8*:907–25.

———. 1993. "Further Results on the Nonparametric Linear Regression Model in Survival Analysis." *Statistics in Medicine 12*:1569–88.

Allison, Paul D. 1982. "Discrete-Time Methods for the Analysis of Event Histories." In *Sociological Methodology 1982*, edited by S. Leinhardt, 61–89. San Francisco: Jossey-Bass.

Andersen, Per Kragh, Ornulf Borgan, Richard D. Gill, and Niels Keiding. 1993. *Statistical Models Based on Counting Processes*. New York: Springer-Verlag.

Arjas, Elja, and P. Haara. 1987. "A Logistic Regression Model for Hazard: Asymptotic Results." *Scandinavian Journal of Statistics 14*:1–18.

Arjas, Elja, and Liping Liu. 1995. "Assessing the Losses Caused by an Intervention: A Hierarchical Bayesian Approach." *Applied Statistics 44*:357-68.

Berzuini, Carlo, and David Clayton. 1994. "Bayesian Analysis of Survival on Multiple Time Scales." *Statistics in Medicine 13*:823–38.

Berzuini, Carlo, and Christiana Larizza. 1996. "A Unified Approach for Modelling Longitudinal and Failure Time Data, with Application in Medical Monitoring." *IEEE Transactions on Pattern Analysis and Machine Intelligence 18*:109–23.

Besag, Julian E. 1974. "Spatial Interaction and the Statistical Analysis of Lattice Systems." *Journal of the Royal Statistical Society B 36*:192–236.

Besag, Julian E., Peter J. Green, David Higdon, and Kerrie Mengersen. 1995. "Bayesian Computation and Stochastic Systems (with discussion)." *Statistical Science 10*:3–66.

Blossfeld, Hans-Peter, Alfred Hamerle, and Karl Ulrich Mayer. 1989. *Event History Analysis.* Hillsdale, NJ.: Lawrence Erlbaum.

Carter, Christopher K., and Robert Kohn. 1994. "On Gibbs Sampling for State Space Models." *Biometrika 81*:541–53.

Casella, George, and Edward I. George. 1992. "Explaining the Gibbs Sampler." *The American Statistician 46*:167–74.

Chib, Siddharta, and Edward Greenberg. 1995. "Understanding the Metropolis-Hastings Algorithm." *The American Statistician 49*:327–35.

Clayton, David G. 1991. "A Monte Carlo Method for Bayesian Inference in Frailty Models." *Biometrics 47*:467–85.

Cowles, Mary Kathryn, and Bradley P. Carlin. 1996. "Markov Chain Monte Carlo Convergence Diagnostics: A Comparative Review." *Journal of the American Statistical Association 91*:883–904.

Cox, David R. 1972. "Regression Models and Life Tables (with discussion)." *Journal of the Royal Statistical Society B 34*:187–220.

Fahrmeir, Ludwig. 1994. "Dynamic Modelling and Penalized Likelihood Estimation for Discrete Time Survival Data." *Biometrika 81*:317–30.

Fahrmeir, Ludwig, and Gerhard Tutz. 1994. *Multivariate Statistical Modelling Based on Generalized Linear Models.* New York: Springer-Verlag.

Fahrmeir, Ludwig, and Stefan Wagenpfeil. 1996. "Smoothing Hazard Functions and Time-Varying Effects in Discrete Duration and Competing Risks Models." *Journal of the American Statistical Association*, 91:1584–94.

Frühwirth-Schnatter, Sylvia. 1994. "Data Augmentation and Dynamic Linear Models." *Journal of Time Series Analysis 15*:183–202.

Gamerman, Dani. 1991. "Dynamic Bayesian Models for Survival Data." *Applied Statistics 40*:63–79.

———. 1995. "Monte Carlo Markov Chains for Dynamic Generalized Linear Models." Unpublished manuscript. Instituto de Matematica, Universidade Federal do Rio de Janerio.

Gamerman, Dani, and Mike West. 1987. "An Application of Dynamic Survival Models in Unemployment Studies." *The Statistician 36*:269–74.

Gelfand, Alan E. 1996. "Model Determination Using Sampling-Based Methods." In *Markov Chain Monte Carlo in Practice*, edited by W. R. Gilks, S. Richardson and D. J. Spiegelhalter, 145–161. London: Chapman and Hall.

Gelman, Andrew. 1996. "Inference and Monitoring Convergence." In *Markov Chain Monte Carlo in Practice*, edited by W. R. Gilks, S. Richardson, and D. J. Spiegelhalter, 131–143. London: Chapman and Hall.

Gilks, Walter R., Sylvia Richardson, and David J. Spiegelhalter. 1996. "Introducing

Markov Chain Monte Carlo." In *Markov Chain Monte Carlo in Practice*, edited by W. R. Gilks, S. Richardson and D. J. Spiegelhalter, 1–19. London: Chapman & Hall.

Gilks, Walter R., and P. Wild. 1992. "Adaptive Rejection Sampling for Gibbs Sampling." *Applied Statistics 41*:337–48.

Hamerle, Alfred, and Gerhard Tutz. 1989. *Diskrete Modelle zur Analyse von Verweildauern und Lebenszeiten.* New York: Campus.

Hastie, Trevor, and Robert Tibshirani. 1993. "Varying-Coefficient Models." *Journal of the Royal Statistical Society B 55*:757–96.

Hastings, W. K. 1970. "Monte Carlo Sampling Methods Using Markov Chains and Their Applications." *Biometrika 57*:97–109.

Heckman, James J., and Burton L. Singer. 1984. "Econometric Duration Analysis." *Journal of Econometrics 24*:63–132.

Hill, Daniel H., William G. Axinn, and Arland Thornton. 1993. "Competing Hazards with Shared Unmeasured Risk Factors." In *Sociological Methodology 1993*, edited by P. V. Marsden, 245–77. Cambridge, MA: Blackwell Publishers.

Huffer, Fred, and Ian W. McKeague. 1991. "Weighted Least Squares Estimation for Aalen's Additive Risk Model." *Journal of the American Statistical Association 86*:114–29.

Kalbfleisch, John D., and Ross L. Prentice. 1980. *The Statistical Analysis of Failure Time Data.* New York: Wiley.

Knorr-Held, Leonhard. 1995. "Markov Chain Monte Carlo Simulation in Dynamic Generalized Linear Mixed Models." Discussion paper No. 8, Sonderforschungsbereich 386, Universität München. Also available under http://www.stat.uni-muenchen.de/sfb386/publikation.html.

———. 1996. "Conditional Prior Proposals in Dynamic Models." *Scandinavian Journal of Statistics*, submitted. Also available under http://www.stat.uni-muenchen.de/sfb386/publikation.html.

Lancaster, Tony 1990. *The Econometric Analysis of Transition Data.* Cambridge, England: Cambridge University Press.

Lewis, Steven M., and Adrian E. Raftery. 1994. "Estimating Bayes Factors via Posterior Simulation with the Laplace-Metropolis Estimator." Technical Report, University of Washington.

Meyer, Bruce. 1990. "Unemployment Insurance and Unemployment Spells." *Econometrica 58*:757–82.

Narendranathan, Wiji, and Mark B. Stewart. 1993. "Modelling the Probability of Leaving Unemployment: Competing Risks Models with Flexible Base-Line Hazards." *Applied Statistics 42*:63–83.

Petersen, Trond. 1991. "The Statistical Analysis of Event Histories." *Sociological Methods and Research 19*:270–323.

Portugal, Pedro, and John T. Addison. 1995. "Short- and Long-Term Unemployment: A Parametric Model with Time-Varying Effects." *Oxford Bulletin of Economics and Statistics 57*:205–27.

Prentice, R. L., John D. Kalbfleisch, Arthur V. Peterson, Jr., Nancy Flournoy, V. T. Farewell, and N. E. Breslow. 1978. "The Analysis of Failure Times in the Presence of Competing Risks." *Biometrics 34*:541–54.

Raftery, Adrian E. 1996. "Hypothesis Testing and Model Selection." In *Markov Chain*

Monte Carlo in Practice, edited by W. R. Gilks, S. Richardson and D. J. Spiegelhalter, 163–87. London: Chapman and Hall.

Raftery, Adrian E., and Jeffrey D. Banfield. 1991. "Stopping the Gibbs Sampler, the Use of Morphology, and Other Issues in Spatial Statistics." *Annals of the Institute of Statistical Mathematics:* *43*:32–43.

Raftery, Adrian E., and Steven M. Lewis. 1996. "Implementing MCMC." In *Markov Chain Monte Carlo in Practice*, edited by W. R. Gilks, S. Richardson and D. J. Spiegelhalter, 115–30. London: Chapman and Hall.

Raftery, Adrian E., Steven M. Lewis, and Akbar Aghajanian. 1995. "Demand or Ideation? Evidence from the Iranian Marital Fertility Decline." *Demography 32*:159–82.

Shephard, Neil, and Michael K. Pitt. 1995. "Parameter-Driven Exponential Family Models." Unpublished manuscript, Nuffield College, Oxford, England.

Thompson, W. A., Jr. 1977. "On the Treatment of Grouped Observations in Life Studies." *Biometrics 33*:463–70.

Tierney, Luke. 1994. "Markov Chains for Exploring Posterior Distributions (with discussion)." *Annals of Statistics 22*:1701–62.

Tutz, Gerhard. 1995. "Dynamic Modeling of Discrete Duration Data: A Local Likelihood Approach." Report 95-15, Tech. Univ. Berlin, Institut für Quantitative Methoden.

Vaupel, James W., Anatoli Yashin. 1985. "Heterogeneity's Ruses: Some Surprising Effects of Selection on Population Dynamics." *The American Statistician 39*:176–85.

Wu, Lawrence L., and Nancy Brandon Tuma. 1990. "Local Hazard Models." In *Sociological Methodology 1990*, edited by C. C. Clogg, 141–180. Cambridge, MA: Blackwell Publishers.

Yamaguchi, Kazuo. 1993. "Modeling Time-Varying Effects of Covariates in Event-History Analysis Using Statistics from the Saturated Hazard Rate Model." In *Sociological Methodology 1993*, edited by P. V. Marsden, 279–317. Cambridge, MA: Blackwell Publishers.

Zimmermann, Klaus F. 1993. "Labor Responses to Taxes and Benefits in Germany." In *Incentives, A North European Perspective*, edited by A. B. Atkinson and G. V. Mogenson, 192–240, Oxford, England: Clarendon Press.

10

LATENT VARIABLE MODELING OF LONGITUDINAL AND MULTILEVEL DATA

Bengt Muthén*

An overview is given of modeling of longitudinal and multilevel data using a latent variable framework. Particular emphasis is placed on growth modeling. A latent variable model is presented for three-level data, where the modeling of the longitudinal part of the data imposes both a covariance and a mean structure. Examples are discussed where repeated observations are made on students sampled within classrooms and schools.

1. INTRODUCTION

The concept of a latent variable is a convenient way to represent statistical variation not only in conventional psychometric terms with respect to constructs measured with error, but also in the context of models with random coefficients and variance components. These features will be studied in this paper. The random coefficient feature is shown to present a useful way to study change and growth over time. The variance component feature is shown to reflect correctly common cluster sampling procedures.

This paper was presented at the annual meeting of the American Sociological Association, Section on Methodology, Showcase Session, August 1994, Los Angeles. The research was supported by a grant from the Office of Educational Research and Improvement, Department of Education to the National Center for Research on Evaluation, Standards, and Student Testing (CRESST), grant AA 08651-01 from NIAAA, grant 40859 from NIMH, and grant K02 AA 00230-01 from NIAAA. I thank Ginger Nelson Goff and Siek-Toon Khoo for expert assistance. E-mail: bmuthen@ucla.edu
*University of California, Los Angeles

This paper gives an overview of some aspects of latent variable modeling in the context of growth and clustered data. A new multilevel latent variable model is presented which not only has a covariance structure but also a mean structure, where the mean structure arises naturally from the growth perspective. Emphasis is placed on the benefits that can be gained from multilevel as opposed to conventional modeling, which ignores the multilevel data structure. Data from large-scale educational surveys are used to illustrate the points.

The paper is organized as follows. Sections 2–6 discuss theory and Sections 7 and 8 applications. Section 2 discusses aggregated versus disaggregated modeling and Section 3 intraclass correlations and design effects in the context of a two-level latent variable model. In Section 4, a two-level latent variable model and its estimation for continuous-normal data will be presented as a basis for analyses. Section 5 shows how a three-level model can be applied to growth modeling and how it can be reformulated as a two-level model. Section 6 shows how this modeling can be fit into the two-level latent variable framework and how the estimation can be carried out by conventional structural equation modeling software. The remaining sections present applications. Section 7 uses two-wave data on mathematics achievement for students sampled within classrooms. Section 7.1 discusses measurement error when data have both within- and between-group variation and gives an example of estimating reliability for multiple indicators of a latent variable. Section 7.2 uses the same example to discuss change over time in within- and between-group variation taking unreliability into account. Section 8 takes the discussion of change over time further using a four-wave data set on students sampled within schools. Here, a growth model is formulated for the relationships between socio-economic status, attitude toward math, and mathematics achievement. Issues related to the assessment of stability and cross-lagged effects are also discussed.

2. AGGREGATED VERSUS DISAGGREGATED MODELING

Consider the following two-level, hierarchical data structure. Let $u_{gi} = (u_{gi1} \ u_{gi2} \ldots u_{gip})'$ denote a p-dimensional vector for randomly sampled groups ($g = 1, 2, \ldots, G$) and randomly sampled individuals within each such group ($i = 1, 2, \ldots, N_g$). We may write the corresponding (total) covariance matrix as a sum of a between- and a within-group part,

$$\Sigma_T = \Sigma_B + \Sigma_W. \tag{1}$$

In a typical educational example, Σ_W refers to student-level variation and Σ_B refers to class-level or school-level variation. In line with Muthén and Satorra (1995; see also Skinner, Holt, and Smith 1989) we will use the term "aggregated modeling" when the usual sample covariance matrix S_T is analyzed with respect to parameters of Σ_T and "disaggregated modeling" when the analysis refers to parameters of Σ_W and Σ_B. In our terms, a multilevel model is a disaggregated model for multilevel data. Such data can, however, also be analyzed by an aggregated model—i.e., a model for the total covariance matrix Σ_T.

In terms of conventional maximum-likelihood covariance structure analysis (e.g., see Bollen 1989) for estimating Σ_T parameters and drawing inferences, multilevel data present complications of correlated observations due to cluster sampling. Special procedures are needed to properly compute standard errors of estimates and chi-square tests of model fit. Effects of ignoring the multilevel structure and using conventional procedures for simple random sampling are illustrated in the next section in the context of a latent variable model. The model is that of a conventional analysis in that the usual set of latent variable parameters is involved.

In a disaggregated (or multilevel) model, the parameters themselves change from those of the conventional analysis. A much richer model with both within and between parameters is used to describe both individual- and group-level phenomena.

It is of interest to compare Σ_T analysis and Σ_W analysis with respect to the magnitude of estimates. This comparison has a strong practical flavor because if the differences are small, the multilevel aspects of the data can be ignored apart from perhaps small corrections of standard errors and chi square. This is frequently the case. Even in such cases, however, there may be information in the data that can be described in interesting ways by parameters of Σ_B. In other words, a frequent shortcoming when ignoring the multilevel structure of the data is not what is misestimated but what is not learned.

3. DESIGN EFFECTS

Drawing on Muthén and Satorra (1995), this section gives a brief overview of effects of the cluster sampling in multilevel data on the standard errors and test of model fit used in conventional covariance structure analysis assuming simple random sampling.

Consider the well-known design effect (deff) formula for the variance estimate of a mean with cluster size c and intraclass correlation ρ,

$$V_C/V_{SRS} = 1 + (c - 1)\rho, \qquad (2)$$

where V_C is the (true) variance of the estimator under cluster sampling and V_{SRS} is the corresponding (incorrect) variance assuming simple random sampling (Cochran 1977). The intraclass correlation is defined as the amount of between-group variation divided by the total amount of variation (between plus within). This formula points out that the common underestimation of standard errors when incorrectly assuming SRS is due to the combined effects of group size (c) and intraclass correlations (ρ's). Given that educational data often have large group sizes in the range of 20–60, even a rather small intraclass correlation value of 0.10 can have huge effects. However, it is not clear how much guidance, if any, this formula gives in terms of multivariate analysis and the fitting of latent variable models (see also Skinner, Holt, and Smith 1989). Muthén and Satorra (1995) carried out a Monte Carlo study to shed some light on the magnitude of these effects.

In our experience with survey data, common values for the intraclass correlations range from 0.00 to 0.50 where the higher range values have been observed for educational achievement test scores and the lower range for attitudinal measurements and health-related measures. Both the way the groups are formed and the content of the variables have major effects on the intraclass correlations. Groups formed as geographical segments in alcohol use surveys indicated intraclass correlations in the range of 0.02 to 0.07 for amount of drinking, alcohol dependence, and alcohol abuse. Equally low values have been observed in educational surveys when it comes to attitudinal variables related to career interests of students sampled within schools. In contrast, mathematics achievement scores for U.S. eighth graders show proportions of variance due to class components of around 0.30–0.40 and due to school components of around 0.15–0.20.

Muthén and Satorra (1995) generated data according to a ten-variable multilevel latent variable model with a two-factor simple structure. This is a disaggregated model of the kind described above. In this case, the loading matrices are equal across the two levels, which means that the same covariance structure model holds on all three levels: within, between, and total. Conventional analysis of the total matrix can then be studied in a case where the model is correct, but standard errors and test of model fit are not. Data were generated as 200 randomly generated groups and group sizes (total sample size) 7 (1400), 15 (3000), 30 (6000), and 60 (12000). These are common values in educational achievement surveys. One thousand replications were used.

Table 1 gives chi-square test statistics for a conventional analysis incorrectly assuming simple random sampling. The model has 34 degrees of freedom. Using the terms above, this is an analysis of an aggregated model using the usual sample covariance matrix S_T. The within and between parameters are not separately estimated; only the parameters of the total matrix are. It is seen that an inflation in chi-square values is obtained by increasing both group size and intraclass correlations, implying that models would be unnecessarily rejected. Only for small values of the intraclass correlations and the group size might the distortion be ignorable— for example, for the combinations (0.05, 7), (0.05, 15), and (0.10, 7). Judging from this table it seems that even for a rather small intraclass

TABLE 1
Chi-Square Testing with Cluster Data

	Group Size			
Intraclass Correlation	7	15	30	60
0.05				
Chi-square				
Mean	35	36	38	41
Var	68	72	80	96
5%[a]	5.6	7.6	10.6	20.4
1%	1.4	1.6	2.8	7.7
0.10				
Chi-square				
Mean	36	40	46	58
Var	75	89	117	189
5%	8.5	16.0	37.6	73.6
1%	1.0	5.2	17.6	52.1
0.20				
Chi-square				
Mean	42	52	73	114
Var	100	152	302	734
5%	23.5	57.7	93.1	99.9
1%	8.6	35.0	83.1	99.4

[a]Percentage of replications where model was rejected at 5-percent level.

correlation of 0.10, the distortions may be large if the group size exceeds 15. The standard errors of the estimates show an analogous pattern in terms of deflated values. Muthén and Satorra (1995) go on to show how standard errors and chi-square tests of fit can be corrected by taking the clustering into account. They also show that the ML estimator of the disaggregated, multilevel model performs well, but the estimator does have problems of convergence at small intraclass correlation values and small group sizes and is also sensitive to deviations from normality. In the normal case with intraclass correlations of 0.10 and groups sizes ranging from 7 to 60, the multilevel ML estimator also performs well when the number of groups is reduced from 200 to 50. In our experience, when the number of groups is much less than 50, this estimator does not give trustworthy results.

We conclude from these simulations that ignoring the multilevel nature of the data and carrying out a conventional covariance structure analysis may very well lead to serious distortions of conventional chi-square tests of model fit and standard errors of estimates.

4. A TWO-LEVEL (DISAGGREGATED) MODEL

This section briefly reviews the theory for two-level modeling and estimation. Specific latent variable models are not discussed here. The specific latent variable model used in growth modeling is given in the next section, where it is shown how it fits into the framework given in the present section.

In line with McDonald and Goldstein (1989) and Muthén (1989, 1990), suppose that there are G groups, of which group g has N_g members $(g = 1, 2, \ldots, G)$. Let $\mathbf{z}_g$ be a vector of length r containing the values of group-level variables for group g and let $\mathbf{u}_{gi}$ be a vector of length p containing the values of individual-level variables for the ith individual in group g. Arrange the data vector for which independent observations are obtained as

$$\mathbf{d}'_g = (\mathbf{z}'_g, \mathbf{u}'_{g1}, \mathbf{u}'_{g2}, \ldots, \mathbf{u}'_{gN_g}), \tag{3}$$

where we note that the length of $\mathbf{d}_g$ varies across groups. The mean vector and covariance matrix are

$$\mu'_{d_g} = [\mu'_z, \mathbf{1}'_{N_g} \otimes \mu'_u] \tag{4}$$

$$\Sigma_{d_g} = \begin{pmatrix} \Sigma_{zz} & \text{symmetric} \\ \mathbf{1}_{N_g} \otimes \Sigma_{uz} & \mathbf{I}_{N_g} \otimes \Sigma_W + \mathbf{1}_{N_g}\mathbf{1}'_{N_g} \otimes \Sigma_B \end{pmatrix}. \tag{5}$$

Here, the symbol $\otimes$ denotes a Kronecker product defined as follows. For an $m \times n$ matrix A and an $s \times t$ matrix B, $A \otimes B$ is the $ms \times nt$ matrix

$$A \otimes B = \begin{pmatrix} a_{11}B & \cdots & a_{1n}B \\ \vdots & \cdots & \vdots \\ a_{m1}B & \cdots & a_{mn}B \end{pmatrix}. \tag{6}$$

Σ_W and Σ_B are $p \times p$ within-group and between-group covariance matrices for the u variables. Muthén (1994a: 378–82) discusses the above covariance structure and contrasts it with that of conventional covariance structure analysis.

The elements of μ_z, μ_u, Σ_{zz}, Σ_{uz}, Σ_W, and Σ_B are functions of the parameters of the model. Assuming multivariate normality of $\mathbf{d}_g$, the ML estimator minimizes the function

$$F = \sum_{g=1}^{G} \{\log|\Sigma_{d_g}| + (\mathbf{d}_g - \mu_{d_g})'\Sigma_{d_g}^{-1}(\mathbf{d}_g - \mu_{d_g})\} \tag{7}$$

with respect to the parameters of the model. Here, the sizes of the arrays involving u variables are determined by the product $N_g \times p$, which is large if there are many individuals per group. A remarkable fact is that the likelihood can be expressed in a form that reduces the sizes of the arrays involving u variables to depend only on p (cf. McDonald and Goldstein 1989; Muthén 1989, 1990),

$$F = \sum_{d=1}^{D} G_d\{\ln|\Sigma_{B_d}| + tr[\Sigma_{B_d}^{-1}(S_{B_d} + N_d(t_d - \mu)(t_d - \mu)')]\}$$
$$+ (N - G)\{\ln|\Sigma_W| + tr[\Sigma_W^{-1} S_{PW}]\}, \tag{8}$$

where

$$\Sigma_{B_d} = \begin{pmatrix} N_d\Sigma_{zz} & \text{symmetric} \\ N_d\Sigma_{yz} & \Sigma_W + N_d\Sigma_B \end{pmatrix},$$

$$S_{B_d} = N_d G_d^{-1} \sum_{k=1}^{G_d} \begin{pmatrix} z_{dk} - \bar{z}_d \\ \bar{u}_{dk} - \bar{u}_d \end{pmatrix} [(z_{dk} - \bar{z}_d)'(\bar{u}_{dk} - \bar{u}_d)'],$$

$$t_d - \mu = \begin{pmatrix} \bar{z}_d - \mu_z \\ \bar{u}_d - \mu_u \end{pmatrix},$$

$$S_{PW} = (N - G)^{-1} \sum_{g=1}^{G} \sum_{i=1}^{N_g} (u_{gi} - \bar{u}_g)(u_{gi} - \bar{u}_g)'.$$

Here, D denotes the number of groups of a distinct size, d is an index denoting a distinct group size category with group size N_d, G_d denotes the number of groups of that size, S_{B_d} denotes a between-group sample covariance matrix, and S_{PW} is the usual pooled-within sample covariance matrix.

Muthén (1989,1990) pointed out that the minimization of the ML fitting function defined by equation (8) can be carried out by conventional structural equation modeling software, apart from a slight modification due to the possibility of singular sample covariance matrices for groups with small G_d values. A multiple-group analysis is carried out for $D + 1$ groups, the first D groups having sample size G_d and the last group having sample size $N - G$. Equality constraints are imposed across the groups for the elements of the parameter arrays μ, Σ_{zz}, Σ_{uz}, Σ_B, and Σ_W (see Muthén 1990 for details).

Muthén (1989, 1990) also suggested an ad hoc estimator that considered only two groups,

$$F' = G\{\ln|\Sigma_{B_c}| + tr[\Sigma_{B_c}^{-1}(S_B + c(t - \mu)(t - \mu)')]\}$$

$$+ (N - G)\{\ln|\Sigma_W| + tr[\Sigma_W^{-1} S_{PW}]\}, \tag{9}$$

where the definition of the terms simplifies relative to Equation (8) due to ignoring the variation in group size, dropping the d subscript, and using $D = 1$, $G_d = G$, and $N_d = c$, where c is the average group size (see Muthén 1990 for details). When data are balanced—i.e., when the group size is constant for all groups—the ML estimator will be obtained. Experience with the ad hoc estimator for covariance structure models with unbalanced data indicates that the estimates, and also the standard errors and chi-square test of model fit, are quite close to those obtained by the true ML estimator. This observation has also been made for growth models where a mean structure is added to the covariance structure, see Muthén (1994b).

In Section 6 we will return to the specifics of how the mean and covariance structures of equations (8) and (9) can be represented in conventional structural equation modeling software for the case of growth modeling. The growth model will be presented next.

5. A THREE-LEVEL HIERARCHICAL MODEL

Random coefficient growth modeling (e.g., see Laird and Ware 1982), or multilevel modeling (e.g., see Bock 1989), describes individual differences in growth. In this way, it goes beyond conventional structural equation modeling of longitudinal data and its focus on autoregressive models (e.g., see Jöreskog and Sörbom 1977; Wheaton et al. 1977). Random-coefficient modeling for three-level data has been described (e.g., see Goldstein [1987]; Bock [1989]; Bryk and Raudenbush [1992]) as follows.

Consider the three-level data

Group : $g = 1,2,\ldots,G$
(school, class)
Individual : $i = 1,2,\ldots,n$
Time : $t = 1,2,\ldots,T$
y_{git} : individual-level, outcome variable
x_{it} : individual-level, time-related variable (age, grade)
w_{git} : individual-level, time-varying covariate
w_{gi} : individual-level, time-invariant covariate
z_g : group-level variable

and the growth equation,

$$y_{git} = \alpha_{gi} + \beta_{gi}x_{it} + \gamma_{git}w_{git} + \zeta_{git}. \tag{10}$$

An important special case that will be the focus of this paper is where the time-related variable $x_{it} = x_t$. This means that for the tth occasion, all individuals have the same x_t value. An example of this is educational achievement studies where t corresponds to grade. The x_t values are, for example, $0,1,2,\ldots,T-1$ for linear growth. We will also restrict attention to the case of $\gamma_{git} = \gamma_t$. Both restrictions are necessary in order to fit the model into currently available software and estimation techniques for the latent variable framework to be discussed in the next section.

The three levels of the growth model are then

$$y_{git} = \alpha_{gi} + x_t\beta_{gi} + \gamma_t w_{git} + \zeta_{git}, \tag{11}$$

$$\begin{cases} \alpha_{gi} = \alpha_g + \pi_\alpha w_{gi} + \delta_{\alpha_{gi}} \\ \beta_{gi} = \beta_g + \pi_\beta w_{gi} + \delta_{\beta_{gi}}, \end{cases} \tag{12}$$

$$\begin{cases} \alpha_g = \alpha + \kappa_\alpha z_g + \delta_{\alpha_g} \\ \beta_g = \beta + \kappa_\beta z_g + \delta_{\beta_g}. \end{cases} \tag{13}$$

In the case of growth modeling using a simple random sample of individuals, it is possible to translate the growth model from a two-level model to a one-level model by considering a $T \times 1$ vector of outcome variables y for each individual. Analogously, we may reduce the three-level model to two levels. For example, in a model without covariates and group-level variables,

$$\mathbf{y}_{gi} = \begin{pmatrix} y_{gi1} \\ \vdots \\ y_{giT} \end{pmatrix} = [1\mathbf{x}] \begin{pmatrix} \alpha_{gi} \\ \beta_{gi} \end{pmatrix} + \zeta_{gi}, \tag{14}$$

which may be expressed as the sum of a between- and a within-group component,

$$\mathbf{y}_{gi} = y_g^* + y_{gi}^*, \tag{15}$$

where

$$y_g^* = [1\mathbf{x}] \begin{pmatrix} \alpha_g \\ \beta_g \end{pmatrix} + \zeta_g^* \tag{16}$$

and

$$y_{gi}^* = [1\mathbf{x}] \begin{pmatrix} \delta_{\alpha gi} \\ \delta_{\beta gi} \end{pmatrix} + \zeta_{gi}^*, \tag{17}$$

where ζ_{gi} is the sum of the two uncorrelated components ζ_g^* and ζ_{gi}^*. Equations (16) and (17) will be further discussed from a latent variable perspective in the next section.

6. LATENT VARIABLE FORMULATION

For the case of simple random sampling of individuals, Meredith and Tisak (1984, 1990) have shown that the random coefficient model of the previous section can be formulated as a latent variable model (for applications in psychology, see McArdle and Epstein [1987]; for applications in education, see Muthén [1993] and Willett and Sayer [1993]; for applications in mental health, see Muthén [1983, 1991]). The latent variable formulation can be directly extended to the three-level data case. The basic idea can be simply described as follows. In the example of equation (16), α_g and β_g are latent variables varying across individuals and the coefficient matrix $[1\mathbf{x}]$ corresponds to a factor analysis loading matrix relating the response variables to the latent variables. In equation (17) the corresponding latent variables are $\delta_{\alpha_{gi}}$ and $\delta_{\beta_{gi}}$, whereas the loading matrix is the same. We find that

$$E(\mathbf{y}_{gi}) = E(y_g^*) + E(y_{gi}^*) = [1\mathbf{x}] \begin{pmatrix} \alpha \\ \beta \end{pmatrix} + 0, \qquad (18)$$

$$V(\mathbf{y}_{gi}) = V(y_g^*) + V(y_{gi}^*) = \Sigma_B + \Sigma_W, \qquad (19)$$

$$\Sigma_B = [1\mathbf{x}]V\begin{pmatrix} \delta_{\alpha g} \\ \delta_{\beta g} \end{pmatrix} [1\mathbf{x}]' + V(\zeta_g^*), \qquad (20)$$

$$\Sigma_W = [1\mathbf{x}]V\begin{pmatrix} \delta_{\alpha gi} \\ \delta_{\beta gi} \end{pmatrix} [1\mathbf{x}]' + V(\zeta_{gi}^*), \qquad (21)$$

so that the parameters of this latent variable model are α, β, and the elements of the covariance matrices in equations (20) and (21). This example fits into the framework of Section 4 by noting that here

$$\mathbf{u} = \mathbf{y}, \qquad (22)$$

where $\mathbf{y}$ is the $T \times 1$ vector of equation (14).

Muthén (1989, 1990) showed how the multilevel fitting functions F and F' of equations (8) and (9) could be implemented in existing structural equation modeling software using multiple-group analysis. Equation (8) shows that there are D such groups that involve between-level parameters and one group that involves within-level parameters. We will focus on how to implement the D mean and covariance structures of equation (8) for the example we are considering, where the mean structure appears in the expression

$$N_d(t_d - \mu)(t_d - \mu)' = N_d(\bar{u}_d - \mu_u)(\bar{u}_d - \mu_u)', \qquad (23)$$

and the covariance structure in the expression

$$\Sigma_{B_d} = \Sigma_W + N_d\Sigma_B. \qquad (24)$$

Figure 1 shows a path diagram that is useful in describing this mean and covariance structure. The figure again corresponds to the case of no covariates w, or group-level variables z. Here, $T = 3$. Figure 1 shows the implementation of the model structure in the example of equations (18)–(21). The top part of the figure introduces the mean structure and the between-level covariance structure of the model by using the latent variables y_g^* of equation (16) premultiplied by the square root of N_d to match

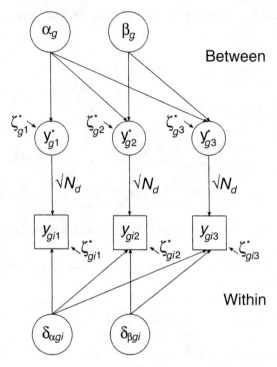

FIGURE 1. Latent variable growth model formulation for two-level, three-wave data.

equations (23) and (24). The bottom part of the figure introduces the within-level covariance structure. On the within side, we note that in our example, the $\delta_{\alpha_{gi}}$ factor influences the y's with coefficients 1 at all time points. The influence of the $\delta_{\beta_{gi}}$ factor on the y variables is captured by the constants of x_t. This makes it clear that nonlinear growth can be accommodated by estimating the x_t coefficients—e.g., holding the first two values fixed at 0 and 1, respectively, for identification purposes. The between-level α_g and β_g factors influence the between-level y_g^* variables with the same coefficients as on the within side; the factor loading matrices are the same and only the factor and residual covariance matrices differ. A strength of the latent variable approach is that this loading matrix equality assumption can easily be relaxed. For example, it may not be necessary to include between-group variation in the growth rate so that the between-level variation is represented by only one factor.

A special feature of the growth model is the mean structure imposed on μ in the ML fitting function of equation (8), where μ represents the means of group- and individual-level variables. In the specific growth model shown in Figure 1, the mean structure arises from the three observed y variable means being expressed as functions of the means of the α_g and β_g factors. Equation (8) indicates that the means need to be included on the between side of Figure 1, while the means on the within side are fixed at zero. This implies that dummy zero means are entered for the within group. The number of degrees of freedom for the chi-square test of model fit obtained in conventional software then needs to be reduced by the number of individual-level variables.

The latent between-level variables may also be related to observed between-level variables z, as in Section 4 and Section 5. Furthermore, it is straightforward to add individual-level covariates such as the w variables in equations (10)–(13), defining

$$\mathbf{u}' = (\mathbf{y}' \quad \mathbf{w}'), \tag{25}$$

where $\mathbf{w}$ is a vector of all time-invariant and time-varying covariates. While z only contributes between-group variability, $\mathbf{u}$ contributes both between-group and within-group variability, as seen in equation (6).

The model in Figure 1 can also be generalized to applications with multiple indicators of latent variable constructs instead of single outcome measurements y at each time point. The covariates may also be latent variables with multiple indicators. Furthermore, estimates may be obtained for the individual growth curves by estimating the individual values of the intercept and slope factors α and β. This relates to empirical Bayes estimation in the conventional growth literature (e.g., see Bock 1989).

The determination of model identifiability can draw on regular latent variable modeling rules by observing in equation (8) that it is sufficient that the individual-level parameters can be identified from the within-group covariance matrix and that the group-level parameters (and the means) can be identified from the between-group covariance matrix (and the means).

Further details and references on latent variable modeling with two-level data are given in Muthén (1994a), where suggestions for analysis strategies are also given. Software for calculating the necessary sample statistics, including intraclass correlations, is available from Statlib at *http: //lib.stat.cmu.edu/general/latent.2level* or by sending the E-mail message "send latent.2level from general" to *statlib@stat.cmu.edu*.

7. ANALYSIS OF TWO-WAVE ACHIEVEMENT DATA

We will first consider data from the Second International Mathematics Study (SIMS) drawing on analyses presented in Muthén (1991b, 1992). Here, a national probability sample of school districts was selected proportional to size; a probability sample of schools was selected proportional to size within school district, and two classes were randomly drawn within each school. The data consist of 3724 students observed in 197 classes from 113 schools; the class sizes varied from 2 to 38, with a typical value of around 20. Eight variables are considered corresponding to various areas of eighth-grade mathematics. The same set of items was administered as a pretest in the fall of eighth grade and again as a posttest in the spring.

Muthén (1991b: 341) poses the following questions:

> The substantive questions of interest in this article are the variance decomposition of the subscores with respect to within-class student variation and between-class variation and the change of this decomposition from pretest to posttest. In the SIMS . . . such variance decomposition relates to the effects of tracking and differential curricula in eighth-grade math. On the one hand, one may hypothesize that effects of selection and instruction tend to increase between-class variation relative to within-class variation, assuming that the classes are homogeneous, have different performance levels to begin with, and show faster growth for higher initial performance level. On the other hand, one may hypothesize that eighth-grade exposure to new topics will increase individual differences among students within each class so that posttest within-class variation will be sizable relative to posttest between-class variation.

7.1. Measurement Error and Reliability of Multiple Indicators

Analyses addressing the above questions can be done for overall math performance, but it is also of interest to study if the differences vary from more basic to more advanced math topics. For example, one may ask if the differences are more marked for more advanced topics. When focusing on specific subsets of math topics, the resulting variables consist of a sum of rather few items and therefore contain large amounts of measurement error. At grade eight, the math knowledge is not extensively differentiated and a unidimensional latent variable model may be formulated to estimate the reliabilities for a set of such variables. Muthén (1991b) formulated a multilevel factor analysis model for the two-wave data. Given that the amount of across-school variation was small relative to the across-classroom variation, the school distinction was ignored and the data analyzed as a two-level structure. At each time point, unidimensionality was specified for both within- and between-class variation, letting factors and measurement errors correlate across time on each level. Table 2 presents estimates from both the multilevel factor analysis (MFA) model (see the within and between columns) and a conventional analysis (see the total columns). Reliability is estimated from the factor model as the proportion of variance in the indicator accounted for by the factor. As is seen from Table 2, the estimated student-level (within) reliabilities are considerably lower than reliabilities obtained from a total analysis.

In psychometrics it is well-known that reliabilities are lower in more homogeneous groups (Lord and Novick 1968). Here, however, it seems important to make the distinction shown in Figure 2.

Figure 2 (a) corresponds directly to the Lord and Novick case. The three line segments may be seen as representing three different classrooms

TABLE 2
The Second International Mathematics Study:
Reliabilities of Math Achievement at Two Time Points

Variables	Number of Items	Pretest			Posttest		
			MFA			MFA	
		Total	Within	Between	Total	Within	Between
RPP	8	.61	.44	.96	.68	.52	.97
FRACT	8	.60	.38	.97	.68	.49	.98
EQ EXP	6	.36	.18	.83	.55	.32	.92
INTNUM	2	.34	.18	.81	.43	.25	.88
STESTI	5	.44	.25	.86	.52	.34	.89
AREAVOL	2	.29	.18	.82	.38	.23	.84
COORVIS	3	.34	.18	.92	.42	.26	.80
PFIGURE	5	.32	.17	.78	.46	.31	.77

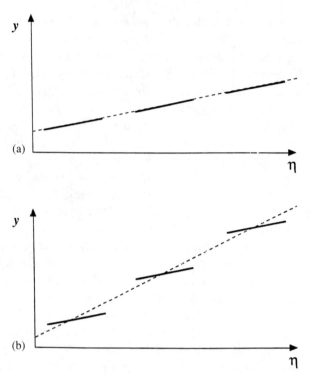

FIGURE 2. Regression of an indicator on its latent variable.

with different student factor values η and student test score values y. The regression line for all classrooms is given as a broken line. All classrooms have the same intercept and slope. For any given classroom, the range of the factor is restricted and due to this restriction in range the reliability is attenuated relative to that of all classrooms.

Figure 2 (b) probably corresponds more closely to the situation at hand. Here, the three classrooms have the same slopes but different intercepts. The regression for the total analysis is marked as a broken line. It gives a steeper slope and a higher reliability than for any of the classrooms. One can argue, however, that the higher reliability is incorrectly obtained by analyzing a set of heterogeneous subpopulations as if they were one single population (cf. Muthén 1989). In contrast, the multilevel model captures the varying intercepts feature and reveals the lower within-classroom reliability that holds for each classroom.

The Table 2 between-classroom reliabilities are considerably higher than the within-classroom values. These between coefficients concern reliable variation across classrooms and therefore have another interpretation than the student-level reliabilities. The results indicate that what distinguishes classrooms with respect to math performance is largely explained by a single dimension—i.e., a total score—and that on the whole the topics measure this dimension rather similarly.

7.2. Attenuation of Intraclass Correlations by Measurement Error

We will consider the size of the intraclass correlations as indicators of school heterogeneity. This can be seen as a function of social stratification giving across-school differences in student "intake," as well as differences in the teaching and what schools do with a varied student intake. The U.S. math curriculum in grades 7–10 is very varied with large differences in emphasis on more basic topics such as arithmetic and more advanced topics such as geometry and algebra. Ability groupings ("tracking") is often used. In some other countries, however, a more egalitarian teaching approach is taken, the curriculum is more homogeneous, and the social stratification less strong. In international studies the relative sizes of variance components for student, class, and school are used to describe such differences (e.g., see Schmidt, Wolfe, and Kifer 1993).

Table 3 gives conventional variance component results from nested, random-effects ANOVA in the form of the proportion of variance between classrooms relative to the total variance. This is the same as the intraclass correlation measure. It is seen that the intraclass correlations increase from pretest to posttest. The problem with these values is, however, that they are likely to be attenuated by the influence of measurement error. This is because student-level measurement error adds to the within-part of the total variance—i.e., the denominator of the intraclass correlation. The distortion is made worse by the fact that the student-level measurement error is likely to decrease from pretest to posttest due to more familiarity with the topics tested.

The MFA columns of Table 3 give the multilevel factor analysis assessment of intraclass correlations using the one-factor model in the previous subsection. Here, the intraclass correlations are computed using the between and within variances for the factor variable, not including measurement error variance. It is seen that these intraclass correlations are considerably higher and indicate a slight decrease over time. This is a

TABLE 3
The Second International Mathematics Study:
Intraclass Correlations (proportion between classroom
variance) of Math Achievement at Two Time Points

Variables	Number of Items	ANOVA		MFA	
		Pretest	Posttest	Pretest	Posttest
RPP	8	.34	.38	.54	.52
FRACT	8	.38	.41	.60	.58
EQ EXP	6	.27	.39	.65	.64
INTNUM	2	.29	.31	.63	.61
STESTI	5	.33	.34	.58	.56
AREAVOL	2	.17	.24	.54	.52
COORVIS	3	.21	.32	.57	.55
PFIGURE	5	.23	.33	.60	.54

change in the opposite direction from the ANOVA results. Results from ANOVA would therefore give misleading evidence for answering the questions posed in Muthén (1991b).

8. ANALYSIS OF FOUR-WAVE DATA BY GROWTH MODELING

The Longitudinal Study of American Youth (LSAY) is a national study of performance in and attitudes toward science and mathematics. It is conducted as a longitudinal survey of two cohorts spanning grades 7 to 12. LSAY uses a national probability sample of about 50 public schools, testing an average of about 50 students per school every fall starting in 1987. Data from four time points, grades 7–10, and one cohort will be used to illustrate the methodology for analysis of individual differences in growth.

In this analysis, mathematics achievement and attitudes toward math will be related to each other and to the socioeconomic status of the family. The data to be analyzed consists of a total sample of 1869 students in 50 schools with complete data on all variables in the analysis. Mathematics achievement is quantified as a latent variable (theta) score obtained by IRT techniques using multiple test forms and a large number of items including arithmetic, geometry, and algebra. The intraclass correlations for the math achievement variable for the four grades are estimated as 0.18, 0.13, 0.15,

0.14, indicating a noteworthy degree of across-school variation in achievement. Attitude toward math was measured by a summed score using items having to do with how hard the student finds math, whether math makes the student anxious, whether the student finds math important, etc. As expected, the intraclass correlations for the attitude variable are considerably lower than for achievement. They are estimated as 0.05, 0.06, 0.04, and 0.02. The Pearson product-moment correlations between achievement and attitude are estimated as 0.4–0.6 for each of the four time points. The measure of socioeconomic status pertains to parents' educational levels, occupational status, and the report of some resources in the home. It has an intraclass correlation of 0.17.

For simplicity in the analyses to be presented, the two-group ad hoc estimator discussed in Section 4 will be used, not the full-information maximum-likelihood estimator. This means that the standard errors and chi-square tests of model fit are not exact but are approximations; given our experience, they are presumably quite reasonable ones. Nevertheless, statements about significance and model fit should not be interpreted in exact terms.

8.1. *Two-Level Modeling*

In this section, two-level modeling of the LSAY data will be outlined, both in terms of the growth model and, as a contrast, in terms of a conventional autoregressive model. The primary analysis considers a growth model that extends the single-variable, two-level growth model of Figure 1 to a simultaneous model of the growth process for both achievement and attitude. SES will be used as a student-level, time-invariant covariate, explaining part of the variation in these two growth processes. No observed variables on the school level will be used in this case, but school-level variables can be easily incorporated in the general model. The model is described graphically in Figure 3.

Let the top row of observed variables (squares) represent achievement at each of the four time points and the bottom row the corresponding attitudes. The SES covariate is the observed variable to the left in the figure.

Consider first the student- (within-)level part of Figure 3. The latent variable (circle) to the right of the observed variable of SES is hypothesized to influence four latent variables, the intercept (initial status) factor and slope (growth rate) factor for achievement (the top two latent vari-

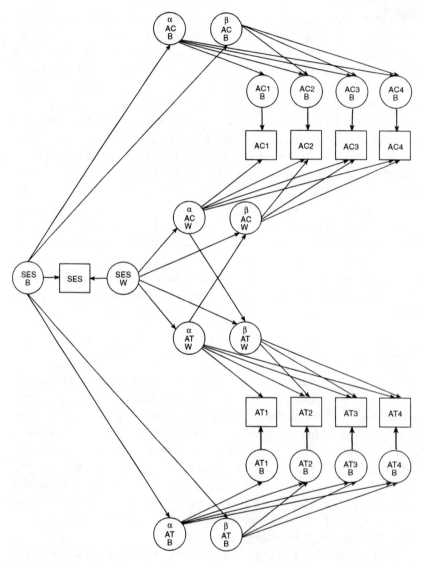

FIGURE 3. Two-level, four-wave growth model for achievement and attitude related to socioeconomic status.

ables) and the intercept and slope factors for attitude (the bottom two latent variables). The intercept for each growth process is hypothesized to have a positive influence on the slope of the other growth process. In order not to clutter the picture, residuals and their correlations are not drawn in the figure, but a residual correlation is included for the intercepts as well as the slopes. For each growth process, the model is as discussed in connection with Figure 1. Preliminary analyses suggest that nonlinear growth for achievement should be allowed for by estimating the growth steps from grade 8 to 9 and from grade 9 to 10, while for attitude a linear process is sufficient. In fact, for attitude, a slight decline is observed over time. The reason for this is not clear, but does perhaps reflect that among a sizable part of the student population there is an initial positive attitude about math that wears off over the grades either because math gets harder or because they stop taking math. For each growth process, correlations are allowed for among residuals at adjacent time points. Residual correlations are also allowed for across processes at each time point. Cross-lagged effects between the outcome variables are allowed for but not shown in the figure. It should be noted that even without cross-lagged effects the model postulates that achievement and attitude do influence each other via their growth intercepts and slopes. For example, if the initial status factor for attitude has a positive influence on the growth rate factor for achievement, initial attitude has a positive influence on later achievement scores.

The hierarchical nature of the data is taken into account by inclusion of the between- (school-)level part of the model. The between-level part of Figure 3 is similar to the within-level part. Starting with the SES variable to the left in the figure, it is seen that the variation in this variable is decomposed into two latent variables, one for the within variation and one for the between variation (the between factor is to the left of the SES square). At the top and the bottom of the figure are given the between-level intercept and slope factors for achievement and attitude, respectively. As in Figure 1, the influence of these factors on achievement/attitude is specified to have the same structure and parameter values as for the within part of the model. A minor difference here is that the intercept for one process is not specified to influence the slope of the other process, but all four intercept and slope factor residuals are instead allowed to be freely correlated. Also, on the between side, correlations among adjacent residuals over time are not included in the model.

As a comparison to the above growth model, a more conventional autoregressive, cross-lagged model will also be analyzed. This is shown in Figure 4 in its two-level form. On the within level, the figure shows a lag-one autoregressive process for both achievement and attitude with lag-one cross-lagged effects, where SES is allowed to influence the outcomes at each time point. The between-level part of the model is here not given a

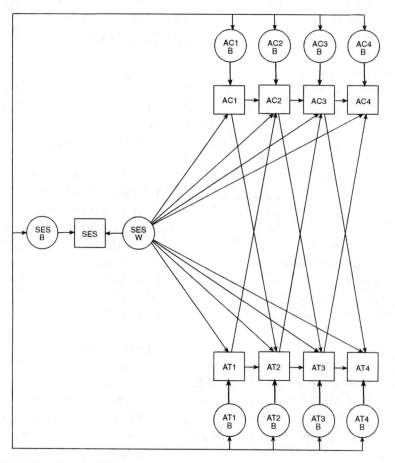

FIGURE 4. Two-level, four-wave autoregressive model for achievement and attitude
related to socioeconomic status.

specific structure but the between-level covariance matrix is made unrestricted by allowing all between-level factors to freely correlate.

8.2. Analyses

The results of the model testing are summarized in Table 4. This table
also includes BIC values for evaluating model fit, comparing the model in
question against the unrestricted model (see Raftery 1993, 1995). It is of
interest to first ignore the hierarchical nature of the data and to give the
incorrect tests of fit for the single-level analogs of the autoregressive and

TABLE 4
Model Testing for LSAY Data ($n = 1,869$)

Model	Chi-square	Degrees of Freedom	BIC
	Autoregressive Model		
	Ignoring the two-level structure (chi-square values incorrect)		
Model 1: Lag-one	534.7	12	418
Model 2: Lag-three	22.3	6	−36
	Two-level analysis		
Model 3: Lag-one	518.8	12	402
Model 4: Lag-three	28.1	6	−30
	Growth Model		
	Ignoring the two-level structure (chi-square value incorrect)		
Model 5: Growth model	44.0	8	−34
	Two-level analysis		
Model 6: Growth model	68.4	30	−152

growth models. To this aim, the conventional maximum-likelihood fitting function is used. The lag-one autoregressive model did not fit well at all. To improve fit it was necessary to include a lag-three model for the autoregressive part. The correct two-level tests of fit using the lag-one model of Figure 4 resulted in a clear rejection of the model, while a two-level, lag-three model gave a reasonable fit. The BIC values agree with this conclusion. The degrees of freedom are the same for the single-level and two-level models because the two-level model doubles the number of parameters as well as the number of sample variances and covariances that are analyzed (a mean structure is not involved in this model). The two-level, lag-three model shows positive and significant student-level cross-lagged effects of achievement and attitude on each other. The lag-three autoregressive structure of the model, however, makes it a rather complex and inelegant representation of the data.

Turning to the growth model, Table 4 gives test results for the single-level model, which ignores the hierarchical nature of the data, and for the two-level model. As indicated by its BIC value, the two-level growth model is clearly preferred over the unrestricted model as well as the other models in Table 4. The estimates of this model are shown in Table 5. What is

TABLE 5
Results from the Two-Level Random Coefficient Growth Model

$n = 1869$
$\chi^2(30) = 68.38$

	Within		Between	
	Parameter Estimates	t-Values	Parameter Estimates	t-Values
Cross-lags				
Achievement → Attitude				
Grade 7 → Grade 8	−0.001	−0.08		
Grade 8 → Grade 9	−0.01	−0.79		
Grade 9 → Grade 10	−0.01	−0.45		
Attitude → Achievement				
Grade 7 → Grade 8	0.04	0.54		
Grade 8 → Grade 9	−0.15	−1.74		
Grade 9 → Grade 10	−0.15	−0.85		
Growth Model				
Achievement initial status → Attitude growth rate	0.003	0.39		
Attitude initial status → Achievement growth rate	0.23	1.29		
Effects of SES on				
Achievement				
Initial status	2.93	10.21	7.96	5.24
Growth rate	0.16	1.84	0.91	3.31
Attitude				
Initial status	0.29	3.54	0.31	0.91
Growth rate	−0.08	−2.31	0.12	0.93

Factor Residual (Co)Variances

Achievement

Initial status	57.84	14.50
Growth rate	1.16	2.17
Initial status, growth rate	1.57	1.16

Attitude

Initial status	4.24	1.33
Growth rate	0.71	0.67
Initial status, growth rate	-0.80	-0.50

Achievement, attitude

Initial status	4.38	6.71
Growth rate	0.28	1.06

Initial Status Intercept

Achievement	52.47	117.38
Attitude	11.36	117.85

Growth Curve

Achievement

Grade 7	0*	
Grade 8	1*	
Grade 9	2.60	12.81
Grade 10	3.85	11.86

Attitude

Grade 7	0*
Grade 8	1*
Grade 9	2*
Grade 10	3*

Growth Rate Intercept

Achievement	2.37	9.82
Attitude	-0.32	-9.10

Factor Residual (Co)Variances

Achievement

Initial status	6.11	3.38
Growth rate	0.08	1.26
Initial status, growth rate	0.15	0.64

Attitude

Initial status	0.19	1.18
Growth rate	0.02	0.66
Initial status, growth rate	-0.03	-0.48

Achievement, Attitude

Initial status	0.65	2.09
Growth rate	-0.02	-1.20
Initial status, growth rate	-0.06	-0.58
Growth rate, initial status	-0.08	-1.50

*Parameter is fixed in this model.

477

particularly interesting about the two-level growth model is that in contrast to the autoregressive model, none of the student-level cross-lagged effects are significantly different from zero. This makes for a very parsimonious model where the achievement and attitude processes are instead correlated via the correlations among their intercept and slope factors. The correlation between the intercept factors (not shown in the table) is positive (0.27) while the slope factor correlation is ignorable (0.08). The influences from the intercepts to the slopes turn out to be not significant.

The student-level influence from SES is significantly positive for both the achievement and attitude intercepts. It is insignificant for the achievement slope and significantly negative for the attitude slope. It is not clear what the negative effect represents, but this effect would be seen if students from high SES homes have a strong initial positive attitude that later becomes less positive. SES explains 12 percent of the student variation in the achievement intercept while it explains only 1 percent of the student variation in the attitude intercept. In terms of the achievement growth, the estimates indicate that relative to the positive growth from grade 7 to 8, the growth is accelerated in later grades. For attitude, linear growth is maintained.

In the school-level part of the model, the correlation between achievement and attitude intercepts (not shown in the table) obtains a rather high value, 0.61 (the student-level value is 0.27). On the school level it is seen that SES does not have a significant influence on the attitude intercept or slope factors. The influence on the achievement intercept and slope is, however, significantly positive. This reflects across-school heterogeneity in neighborhood resources so that schools with higher SES families have both higher initial achievement and stronger growth over grades. It is interesting to note that significant *student*-level influence of SES on the student-level achievement growth rate was not seen, while strongly significant *school*-level influence of SES is seen on the school-level achievement growth rate. This is an example of a difference in between-school and within-school model structure. The latent variable approach readily accommodates such model features.

9. CONCLUSIONS

This paper has presented a general model for latent variable growth analysis that takes into account cluster sampling. The model is of interest from two methodological perspectives. First, it represents a multilevel latent variable model that has not only a covariance structure but also a mean structure. Second, it represents a new latent growth model that has two levels. The latent variable formulation combines these two perspectives and makes for a very general modeling framework. The model has the advantage that it can be analyzed with existing structural equation modeling software.

It is clear from the real data analyses that much can be gained in terms of understanding the data if the multilevel analysis is used not only to compute correct standard errors and chi-square tests of model fit with nonindependent observations but also to interpret the parameters that capture the nonindependence of the observations. The examples showed that different interpretations were obtained for parameters on the between-group level than on the within-group level.

The complexity of the models calls for sound modeling strategies, but these are difficult to formulate in general. Muthén (1994a) discusses latent variable modeling steps that are relevant for two-level data. The examples in the present paper illustrate the wide applicability of the new methodology. It is clear, however, that many other special types of multi-level growth models can be formulated and it will be interesting to have researchers from many fields explore these new possibilities. Further methodological research is also needed, such as regarding restricted maximum-likelihood estimation (REML) and robustness of inference in situations with small sample sizes and data that deviate from normality.

REFERENCES

Bock, R. Darrell. 1989. *Multilevel Analysis of Educational Data*. San Diego: Academic Press.

Bollen, Ken A. 1989. *Structural Equations with Latent Variables*. New York: Wiley.

Bryk, Anthony S., and Stephen W. Raudenbush. 1992. *Hierarchical Linear Models: Applications and Data Analysis Methods*. Newbury Park, CA: Sage.

Cochran, William G. 1977. *Sampling Techniques*, 3rd ed. New York: Wiley.

Goldstein, Harvey I. 1987. *Multilevel Models in Educational and Social Research*. London: Oxford University Press.

Jöreskog, Karl G., and Dag Sörbom. 1977. "Statistical Models and Methods for Analysis of Longitudinal Data." In *Latent Variables in Socio-Economic Models*, edited by D. J. Aigner and A. S. Goldberger, 285–325. Amsterdam: North-Holland.

Laird, Nan M., and James H. Ware. 1982. "Random-Effects Models for Longitudinal Data." *Biometrics* 38:963–74.

Lord, Frederic M., and Melvin R. Novick. 1968. *Statistical Theories of Mental Test Scores*. Reading, MA: Addison-Wesley.

McArdle, Jack J., and David Epstein. 1987. "Latent Growth Curves Within Developmental Structural Equation Models." *Child Development* 58:110–33.

McDonald, Rod, and Harvey Goldstein. 1989. "Balanced Versus Unbalanced Designs for Linear Structural Relations in Two-Level Data." *British Journal of Mathematical and Statistical Psychology* 42:215–32.

Meredith, William, and John Tisak. 1984. "Tuckerizing Curves." Paper presented at the Psychometric Society annual meetings, Santa Barbara, CA.

———. 1989. "Latent Variable Modeling in Heterogeneous Populations." *Psychometrika* 54:557–85.

Muthén, Bengt. 1983. "Latent Variable Structural Equation Modeling with Categorical Data." *Journal of Econometrics* 22:43–65.

———. 1990. "Latent Curve Analysis." *Psychometrika* 55:107–122.

———. 1990. "Mean and Covariance Structure Analysis of Hierarchical Data." Paper presented at the Psychometric Society meeting in Princeton, New Jersey. UCLA Statistics Series #62, August 1990.

———. 1991a. "Analysis of Longitudinal Data Using Latent Variable Models with Varying Parameters." In *Best Methods for the Analysis of Change. Recent Advances, Unanswered Questions, Future Directions*, edited by L. Collins and J. Horn, 1–17. Washington: American Psychological Association.

———. 1991b. "Multilevel Factor Analysis of Class and Student Achievement Components." *Journal of Educational Measurement* 28:338–54.

———. 1993. "Latent Variable Modeling of Growth with Missing Data and Multilevel Data." In *Multivariate Analysis: Future Directions 2*, edited by C. R. Rao and C. M. Cuadras, 199–210. Amsterdam: North-Holland.

———. 1994a. "Multilevel Covariance Structure Analysis." *Sociological Methods and Research* 22:376–98.

———. 1994b. "Latent Variable Growth Modeling with Multilevel Data." Paper presented at the UCLA conference Latent Variable Modeling with Applications to Causality. March, 1994. To appear in *Latent Variable Modeling with Applications to Causality*, edited by Maia Berkane. Cambridge, MA: Springer-Verlag.

Muthén, Bengt, and Albert Satorra. 1995. "Complex Sample Data in Structural Equation Modeling." In *Sociological Methodology* 1995, edited by Peter V. Marsden, 267–316. Cambridge, MA: Blackwell.

Raftery, Adrian E. 1993. "Bayesian Model Selection in Structural Equation Models." In *Testing Structural Equation Models*, edited by Kenneth Bollen and J. Scott Long, 163–80. Newbury Park, CA: Sage.

———. 1995. "Bayesian Model Selection in Social Research." In *Sociological Methodology* 1995, edited by Peter V. Marsden, 111–63. Cambridge, MA: Blackwell.

Schmidt, W., R. G. Wolfe, and E. Kifer. (in press). "The Identification and Description of Student Growth in Mathematics Achievement." In L. Burstein (Ed.), *The IEA Study of Mathematics III: Student Growth and Classroom Processes*. Edited by L. Burstein. London: Pergamon.

Skinner, C. J., D. Holt, and T. M. F. Smith. 1989. *Analysis of Complex Surveys*. Chichester, England: Wiley.

Wheaton, Blair, Bengt Muthén, Duane Alwin, and Gene Summers. 1977. "Assessing Reliability and Stability in Panel Models." In *Sociological Methodology 1977*, edited by D. R. Heise, 84–136. San Francisco: Jossey-Bass.

Willett, John B., and Alice G. Sayer. 1993. "Using Covariance Structure Analysis to Detect Correlates and Predictors of Individual Change over Time." *Psychological Bulletin* 116:368–81.

NAME INDEX

Aalen, O. O., 419
Abbott, A., 47–84, 48, 52, 55n9, 60,
    62n10, 64n11, 83, 131–3, 139–44,
    151–3, 156, 165–7, 169, 170n2,
    171
Abell, P., 92, 151
Adams, D., 45
Adams, F. G., 303
Addison, J. T., 419, 434
Aghajanian, A., 448
Agresti, A., 313
Aiken, L. H., 327, 328, 328n2, 336, 349
Alexander, J. C., 356
Al-Haider, A. S., 329
Allison, P. D., 356, 401, 408–9, 410n11,
    421, 439
Althauser, R. P., 326, 326n1, 332n4
Altschul, S. F., 48, 66n12, 71, 74n14, 76,
    80–1n17, 81
Alwin, D. F., 326, 356–8, 360, 363, 365,
    370, 386, 461
Amell, J. W., 356–8, 386
Amemiya, T., 343n14
An, A. B., 407n6
An, F., 106–7n22
Andersen, E. B., 305
Andersen, P. K., 418
Anderson, J. A., 305, 306
Andrén, G., 111
Andrich, D., 304, 305, 306
Arjas, E., 419–20, 421, 426

Arminger, G., 3
Assadi, B., 53n6
Austin, J. L., 101n16
Axinn, W. G., 355–89, 357, 358–9, 365,
    366, 373–5, 386, 406n5, 407–8,
    410, 410n9, 421

Back, K. W., 365
Bailey, R. C., 329
Bakanic, V., 50n2
Baker, K., 151
Banfield, J. D., 432
Barber, J. S., 355–89, 366
Barman, E., 47–84, 131, 132, 139–44,
    151–3, 156, 165–7, 169, 170n2,
    171
Barthes, R., 54
Barwise, J., 3n1
Bazerman, C., 49, 53, 53n5, 54n8, 55,
    60, 69, 83
Bechtel, G. G., 299–322, 300, 316
Berg, B. L., 170
Berk, R. A., 334n7, 336, 387
Berzuini, C., 419–20, 447
Besag, J. E., 429, 433
Bhapkar, V., 313
Biart, M., 303
Bidwell, C., 51n3
Bielby, W. T., 186–7, 187n12
Biemer, P. P., 365
Bills, D., 189

Blalock, H. M., 145, 387
Blau, P. M., 191
Blossfeld, H.-P., 418
Bock, R. D., 460–1, 465
Boguski, M. S., 48, 62n10, 71, 74n14,
    76, 80–1n17, 81
Bollen, K. A., 455
Borgan, O., 418
Bose, C. E., 189
Boyd, M., 199
Bradburn, N. M., 365
Breidt, F. J., 407n6
Brendel, V., 66n12
Breslow, N. E., 422, 423
Brewster, K., 356, 387
Brick, J., 398–9
Brick, M., 401–2, 407n6, 411, 413
Briggs, Charles L., 365
Brittain, J., 11
Brook, R. H., 329
Bruggeman, J., 2, 26–7, 30, 146, 147,
    148, 162
Bryk, A. S., 342, 344, 356, 388, 461
Bucher, P., 66n12
Buehler, C., 53n6
Burke, K., 49
Burrough, P., 384

Caldwell, B., 365
Caldwell, J. C., 362, 365, 376n6
Caldwell, P., 365
Call, V. R., 373
Camburn, D., 356–8, 360, 363, 365,
    370, 386
Campbell, J. G., 374–5, 376n6
Cannell, C. F., 365
Carley, K. M., 125, 131–3, 165
Carlin, B. P., 432
Carroll, C., 159n
Carroll, G., 160
Carroll, G. R., 5, 9n6
Carter, C. K., 446
Casella, G., 74n13, 344, 427
Caspi, A., 356–8, 386

Casterline, J. B., 387
Chambers, R., 365–6
Champion, D. J., 53n6
Chamratrithirong, A., 385
Chauvin, N., 169–76
Chib, S., 427
Cho, J. H., 192
Clayton, D., 447
Clayton, D. G., 448
Cleary, P. D., 314
Clogg, C. C., 3, 306
Clyne, M., 49n1
Cochran, W. G., 326, 333, 338, 342, 456
Coleman, J. S., 145, 356
Connors, R. J., 49n1
Cook, R. D., 204
Cowles, M. K., 432
Cox, D. R., 73
Cox, David R., 418, 421
Crovitz, S. P., 187n10
Curran, S. R., 385

Davis, C. S., 313
Davis, J. A., 184, 189
Dawes, R. M., 300
De Graaf, P. M., 197–8
DeMeyer, A. M., 300
de Ridder, J. A., 125
Devereux, J., 62n10, 64n11
DiPrete, T. A., 356, 388
Dowty, D. R., 101–2n16
Drake, C., 347
Dubes, R. C., 66n12
Dubois, R. W., 329
Duncan, B., 188
Duncan, G. J., 356
Duncan, O. D., 188, 189, 190–1,
    191n16, 194–7, 202, 202n28
Dunphy, Dexter C., 121
Durkheim, E., 356

Eisenhower, D., 358
Eltinge, E. M., 111
Entwisle, B., 356, 385

Epstein, D., 462
Erikson, R., 183, 183n7
Etchemendy, J., 3n1
Everitt, B. S., 66n12

Fahrmeir, L., 417–49, 419, 421, 424, 433–4, 439, 446
Falcon, L. M., 19n19
Farewell, V. T., 422, 423
Featherman, D. L., 186–7, 187n12, 188, 189, 189n15, 190, 191, 192–3, 194, 195, 196, 199, 202–3, 227
Fienberg, S. E., 334n6
Flournoy, N., 422, 423
Folsom, R. E., 407n6
Forrest, J., 64n11
Forristal, J. D., 356, 388
Fossett, M. A., 193, 193n20, 196n26
Fowler, F. J., Jr, 365
Fox, J., 195, 199, 203
Franzosi, R., 91, 92, 111, 125, 135–44, 159–60, 165–7, 169n1, 171n3, 171–6, 172n4
Freedman, D., 356–8, 360, 363, 365, 370, 386
Freedman, R., 326, 326n1
Freeman, D. H., Jr., 313
Freeman, J., 2, 5, 7, 11, 16, 18, 23n10, 23–4, 24, 26–7, 29, 147, 160
Freeman, J. L., 313
Frege, G., 95
Fricke, T. E., 357, 358–9, 365, 386
Fridman, S., 193n19
Friendly, M., 195, 203
Frühwirth-Schnatter, S., 446
Fuller, W. A., 407n6

Gajurel, K., 366
Gamerman, D., 419, 446, 449
Gamut, L. T. F., 4n2
Ganzeboom, H. B., 197–8
Garnett, R. A., 53n6
Gay, G., 329
Gelatt, C. D., 74n13

Gelfand, A. E., 74n13, 449
Gelman, A., 432
Geman, D., 74n13, 80, 84
Geman, S., 74n13, 80, 84
George, E. I., 74n13, 427
Ghimire, D. J., 355–89
Gilks, W. R., 74n13, 427, 432, 445–6
Gill, R. D., 418
Glenn, N. D., 50n2
Goldberger, A. S., 198, 245
Goldstein, H., 345n16, 356, 374n5, 388, 458–9
Goldstein, H. I., 461
Goldthorpe, J., 183
Goldthorpe, J. H., 183, 183n7
Goodchild, M. F., 384
Gordon, J. B., 196
Gotoh, O., 74n14
Gottschalk, L. A., 94, 94n5
Green, P. J., 433
Greenberg, E., 427
Gribskov, M. R., 62n10, 64n11
Griemas, A.-J., 91, 91n3, 92
Griffin, L., 151
Griffin, L. J., 102
Groves, R. M., 358, 365
Gu, X. S., 338–9
Guest, P., 387
Guilkey, D. K., 385
Gulliksen, H., 307, 309, 311
Gusfield, D., 74n14
Gusfield, J., 49

Haara, P., 421, 426
Habermas, J., 97n7
Halaby, C. N., 183, 183n6
Haller, A. O., 189
Halliday, M. A. K., 91, 92, 95, 101n15
Hamerle, A., 418, 421
Hammel, E., 376n6
Hannan, M. T., 2, 5, 7, 9n6, 11, 16, 18, 23, 23n10, 24, 26–7, 29, 145–8, 160
Hardin, G. R., 300

Härdle, W., 331
Harrington, H., 356–8, 386
Hartz, A. J., 329
Hastie, T., 419
Hastings, W. K., 429–31
Haug, M. R., 194, 194n21, 195–6,
    196n25, 197, 202n28
Hauser, R. M., 177–293, 178, 178n1,
    180n2, 181n5, 183, 183n7, 186–7,
    187n12, 188, 189, 189n14–15,
    190, 191, 192, 199, 201, 216n33,
    227
Hawley, A. H., 326
Heaton, T. B., 373
Heckman, J., 408
Heckman, J. J., 448
Heise, D. R., 92, 102, 110, 151
Henikoff, J. G., 66n12
Henikoff, S., 66n12
Hesser, G., 53n6
Heywood, I., 384
Higdon, D., 433
Hill, D., 406n5, 407–8, 410, 410n9
Hill, D. H., 393–415, 395, 396, 421
Hill, M., 395
Hills, S. E., 74n13
Hirschman, C., 387
Hodge, R. W., 178, 188, 189, 194, 213
Hoey, M., 92
Hoisington, E., 189–90n15
Holland, P. W., 333, 334, 350
Hollingshead, A. B., 184, 186n8,
    195–8
Holt, D., 455, 456
Homans, G., 153
Honnecker, E., 106–7n22
Honore, B. E., 408
Hope, K., 183
Hoshida, M., 74n14
Hout, M., 183, 183n7, 246n48
Hrycak, A., 60, 151
Huang, Z., 31
Huber, J., 356
Huffer, F., 419

Ishikawa, M., 74n14

Jabine, T. B., 395, 397
Jacobsen, S. J., 329
Jain, A. K., 66n12
Jasso, G., 153
Jencks, C. S., 180–1, 181n4–5, 213
Johnson, M., 92
Johnson-Laird, P. N., 101n15
Jones, F. L., 190, 227
Jones, L. V., 307
Jordan, B., 365
Jöreskog, K. G., 230, 461

Kahn, R. L., 365
Kalbfleisch, J. D., 418, 421, 422, 423
Kalmijn, M., 251
Kalton, G., 398–9, 401–2, 407n6, 411,
    413
Kamps, J., 146, 162
Kanehisa, M., 74n14
Karlin, S., 66n12
Katona, G., 299–300
Katxoff, M., 329
Keiding, N., 418
Keohane, R., 151, 155
Kerckhoff, A. C., 188
Kiewiet, D. R., 300
Kifer, E., 469
Kinder, D. R., 300
King, G., 151, 155
King, K., 395, 397
Kinloch, G. C., 53n6
Kircz, J. G., 49n1
Kirkpatrick, S., 74n13
Kiser, E., 151–8, 160–1, 162, 165,
    169–70, 176
Kish, L., 326, 350
Klebanov, P. K., 356
Klein, L. R., 303
Kleinnijenhuis, J., 125
Knorr-Held, L., 417–49, 419, 431–2,
    448
Koch, G. G., 313

Kohn, R., 446
Kong, A., 81n17
Krakauer, H., 329
Kraus, V., 188
Kruskal, J. B., 60
Kuhn, E. M., 329

Laird, N. M., 460–1
Lakatos, I., 5, 28
Lake, E. T., 327, 328, 328n2, 336, 349
Lakoff, G., 92
Lancaster, T., 418, 422, 448
Land, K. C., 356
Landale, N., 373
Landis, J. R., 313
Larizza, C., 419–20
Lawrence, C. E., 48, 71, 74n13, 76,
    80–1n17, 81, 83
Lee, S. M., 193n19
Lehnen, R. G., 313
Lenihan, K. J., 387
Levine, G., 55n9
Levins, R., 5, 8, 11, 14n8
Lewis, S. M., 432, 448, 449
Linden, F., 301
Liu, J. S., 48, 71, 74n13–14, 76,
    80–1n17, 81, 81n17, 83
Liu, L., 419–20
Logan, J. A., 178
Lord, F. M., 467–8
Lyberg, L. E., 365

Maguire, D. J., 384
Manski, C. F., 3, 333
Manton, K., 188
Markoff, J., 90–1n2, 91, 125
Martin, D., 384
Mason, W., 188, 356
Mason, W. M., 374n5
Massey, D. S., 356–7, 365, 386
Masuch, M., 2, 10n7, 26–7, 31, 146,
    148, 162
Mathiowetz, N. A., 358, 365
Mayer, K. U., 418

McArdle, J. J., 462
McCabe, G. P., 143–4
McCartney, J. L., 50n2
McCloskey, D., 49
McClure, K., 55n9
McCullagh, P., 299, 305–7, 309, 310,
    311–12, 316–17
McCulloch, C. E., 344
McDonald, R., 458–9
McKeague, I. W., 419
McMillen, D., 397
McPhail, C., 50n2
Meehl, P. E., 300
Mellenbergh, G. J., 304
Mengersen, K., 433
Meredith, W., 462
Merton, R., 153
Metropolis, N., 74n13
Meyer, B., 448
Miethe, T. D., 356
Miller, H. D., 73
Miller, M. E., 313
Mitchell, J. C., 170
Moffitt, T. E., 356–8, 386
Moore, D. S., 143–4
Morganstein, D., 358
Morris, M. F., 53n6
Mosteller, F., 204
Muenz, L., 329
Mullins, N., 49n1
Murray, S. O., 53n6
Muthén, B., 453–79, 455–60, 461, 462,
    463, 465–7, 468, 469–70, 479
Myers, G., 49

Nakao, K., 177, 187n10, 189–90, 189–
    90n15, 192n18, 192–3, 198–9,
    201–3, 203n29, 207, 209, 216n34
Nam, C. B., 193, 194–5, 196
Namenwirth, J. Z., 92, 121
Narendranathan, W., 420, 434, 448
Needleman, S. B., 63, 64n11
Nelder, J. A., 306, 307, 309, 311–12,
    316–17

Neuwald, A. F., 48, 71, 74n14, 76,
    80–1n17, 81, 83
Newton, P. J., 334n7, 336
Neyman, J., 313
Nitta, K., 74n14
Novick, M. R., 467–8

Oehler, K., 49n1
Ogilvie, D. M., 121
Ogiwara, A., 74n14
O'Neill, J., 49n1

Nualláin, B., 2, 3n1, 26–7, 146, 148, 162

Page, C. H., 50n2
Péli, G., 1–31, 2, 10n7, 26–7, 146–7,
    147n3, 148, 151, 153–4, 156,
    159–62
Perman, L., 180–1, 181n4–5
Petersen, T., 356, 373, 388, 418
Petersen, T. K., 408n7, 410n11, 411
Peterson, A. V., Jr., 422, 423
Petroni, R., 395, 397, 401–2, 407n6,
    411, 413
Pitt, M. K., 446
Pólos, L., 31, 159, 159n, 162
Popping, R., 103n19
Portugal, P., 419, 434
Poss, S. S., 188
Powers, M. G., 193, 194–5, 196
Praet, P., 303
Prentice, R. L., 418, 421, 422, 423
Propp, V., 92

Racine-Poon, A., 74n13
Raftery, A. E., 118n29, 230, 432, 448,
    449, 474
Ragin, C., 151
Rainwater, L., 180–1, 181n4–5
Rasbash, J., 345n16
Rasch, G., 305–6
Raudenbush, S. W., 342, 344, 356, 388,
    461
Redlich, F. C., 184
Reiss, A. J., Jr., 189, 190

Reitberg, E. M., 125
Rhind, D., 384
Richardson, S., 74n13, 427, 432
Rimm, A. A., 329
Rindfuss, R. R., 385
Ringdal, K., 356, 388
Rizzo, L., 401–2, 407n6, 411, 413
Roberts, C. W., 89–126, 99n10, 109,
    111, 125, 135–9, 151, 154–5, 156,
    157, 169–76, 175n5
Rogers, W. H., 329
Rosenbaum, P. R., 326, 326n1, 327, 329,
    331, 332, 333, 333n5, 335, 338–9,
    340, 349, 350
Rosenbluth, M. N., 74n13
Rosenbluth, W., 74n13
Ross, R. N., 329
Rossi, P. H., 189, 387
Roughgarden, J., 5
Rountree, P. W., 356
Rubin, D. B., 326, 326n1, 327, 331, 332,
    332n4, 333, 333n5, 334, 335, 338,
    339, 340, 347–9
Rumelhart, D. E., 92
Rytina, S., 178

Samejima, F., 305
Sankoff, D., 60
Sastry, N., 356, 374n5
Satorra, A., 455–8
Sawangdee, Y., 385
Sayer, A. G., 462
Schaeffer, N. C., 365
Scheffé, H., 308, 315
Schild, E. O., 188
Schmidt, W., 469
Schrodt, P. A., 92, 94, 94n5
Schuman, H., 360
Scott, J., 360
Sealand, N., 356
Searle, J. R., 101n16
Searle, S. R., 344
Sewell, W. H., 180n2, 187
Sewell, W., Jr., 155–7, 170

Shapiro, G., 90–1n2, 91, 94n5, 114, 125, 171n3
Shephard, N., 446
Sheridan, J. T., 199, 201
Shihadeh, E. S., 306
Shivakoti, G., 366
Sibbald, P. R., 66n12
Siegel, P. M., 189, 191–2, 195, 202–3
Sieyes, E.-J., 155–7
Silber, J. H., 329
Silva, P. A., 356–8, 386
Simon, H. A., 26
Simon, R. J., 50n2
Singer, B. L., 448
Singh, R., 395
Skinner, C. J., 455, 456
Smalley, T. N., 50n2
Smeijers, J., 356–8, 386
Smith, A., 157
Smith, A. F. M., 74n13
Smith, H. L., 325–51, 327, 328, 328n2, 334, 336, 349, 356, 362
Smith, M. S., 121
Smith, T. M. F., 455, 456
Smith, T. W., 184, 187n10, 189, 192n18
Snedecor, G. W., 326, 333, 342
Snizek, W., 49n1
Sobek, M., 194n21, 245n46
Sobel, M., 350–1
Solon, G., 198
Sörbom, D., 230, 461
Sørenson, A., 145n1
Spiegelhalter, D. J., 74n13, 427, 432
Stafford, M. T., 193, 193n20, 196n26
Stevens, G., 189–90n15, 191, 192–3, 194, 195, 196, 199, 202–3
Stewart, M. B., 420, 434, 448
Stokes, M. W., 313
Stone, L., 374–5, 376n6
Stone, P. J., 121, 125
Stycos, J. M., 365
Suchman, L., 365
Sudman, S., 365
Summers, G., 461

Suschnigg, C., 199
Sussman, M. B., 195–6, 197

Tanner, M. A., 71, 74n13
Teachman, J,, 373–4
Teevan, J. J., 50n2
Terrie, E. W., 194
Theil, H., 204
Thomas, L., 110
Thomas, N., 326, 327, 334, 335, 338, 347–9
Thompson, W. A., Jr., 421
Thornton, A., 356–60, 363, 365, 370, 373–4, 386, 406n5, 407–8, 410, 410n9, 421
Thurstone, L. L., 309
Tibshirani, R., 419
Tierney, L., 430
Tisak, J., 462
Torgerson, W. S., 308, 309
Toya, T., 74n14
Train, K., 406n5
Treas, J., 177, 187n10, 189–90, 189–90n15, 192n18, 192–3, 198–9, 201–3, 207, 209, 216n34
Treiman, D. J., 189, 197–8
Tukey, J. W., 204
Tuma, N. B., 419
Tutz, G., 419, 421, 424, 433–4, 439

Ulam, S., 74n13
Ury, H. K., 339, 340

Vanden Abeele, P. M., 300, 303
Vanderveken, D., 101n16
van Dijk, T. A., 92
Vaupel, J. W., 448
Vecci, M. P., 74n13
Verba, S., 151, 155
Vingron, M., 64n11, 66n12
Vuchelen, J., 303

Wagenpfeil, S., 419, 446
Walsh, C., 187n10
Wan, T. T. H., 329

Ware, J. H., 460–1
Warren, J. R., 177–293, 180n2, 187, 199, 201, 216n33
Waterman, M. S., 64n11
Weakliem, D. L., 183
Weber, M., 102
Weber, R. P., 121, 125
Weigert, A. J., 53n6
Weisberg, S., 204
Weiss, R. S., 376n6
Weitman, S. R., 90–1n2
West, M., 449
Wheaton, B., 461
Wild, P., 445–6
Willett, J. B., 462
Winter, E., 95, 101–2n16
Witt, M. B., 407n6
Wolfe, R. G., 469
Wong, G. Y., 374n5

Wong, W. H., 74n13, 81n17
Woodhouse, G., 345n16
Wooton, J. C., 48, 71, 74n14, 76, 80–1n17, 81
Wright, E. O., 181–2, 183, 184
Wu, L. L., 419
Wunsch, C. D., 63, 64n11

Xie, Y., 373

Yamaguchi, K., 356, 373, 388, 410n11, 419
Yashin, A., 448
Young, M., 329
Young-DeMarco, L., 356–8, 360, 363, 365, 370, 386

Zimmerman, D. J., 198, 245
Zimmermann, K. F., 434

SUBJECT INDEX

ability groupings, 460
academic texts, language variation and, 49n
accumulation, niche theory and, 19
actual, defined, 139–40
adaption of organizations, outflow and, 10
adaptive capacity, in allocation principle, 11
additive logistic response model, 336
age factor, for unemployment duration study, 433, *436, 438*
aggregated modeling *versus* disaggregated modeling, 454–5
aggregation
    in coded articles, 57–60
    niche theory and, 18–21
    See also outflow aggregation
alcohol abuse studies, 49, 456
alignment algorithms, described, 62–4
alignment methods
    described, 60–2
    subsequence problems and, 48
allocation principle, niche theory and, 11, 29
amalgamation rules, niche theory and, 19–21, 28
    See also assumptions (A); lemmas (L)
ambiguity
    functional forms and, 95–8, 99
    in magnet hospital designation, 348

in social science, 135–44, 172
    surface phrasing and, 94
American Journal of Sociology (AJS), 50n, 51, 51n, 68, 165–6
    index for, 52, 53, 140
American Political Science Review, 49
American Sociological Review (ASR), 50n, 51, 152
aperiodicty, Gibbs sampling and, 73
Aristotelian logic
    rhetoric meaning of, 141
    speech acts and, 96
    theoretical speculation and, 159
articles analysis, 49n
    coding procedures and, *56, 58–9*
    four categories of, 144
    types of, in sociology journals, 52, 139
aspect grammar, 101n
assumptions (A)
    on aggregation, 18–21, *20*
    described, 5, 7n
    niche theory and, 7, 10, 12, 17, 19–21
    niche theory and, detailed, 31–2, 35–6, 37–8, 40
    See also lemmas (L)
attrition, 326n
    in event history models, 394–415
autoregressive models, 424, 461, 473, 474–8, *475*
axioms. *See* assumptions (A)

background knowledge *versus* foreground knowledge, 14
background premises of theorems (B)
niche theory and, 13–14, 31
background probability, in random sequences, 75, 76
Barr scale, 188
Bayesian information criterion (BIC statistic)
in growth modeling, 474–5
in structural equations models, 230, 231, 237, 248–50
text analysis and, 118, 118n, *119*
Bayesian methods
dynamic discrete time duration models and, 419, 424, 426–8, 437, 446
job characteristics and, 181n
Bayesian prior, subsequence analysis and, 76
best asymptotically normal (BAN)
standard errors and, 313
bias
multiple matching and, 339–40, *342*
panel data and, 394, 407, 407n
BIC statistic. *See* Bayesian information criterion
biology
computer software for, 64n
niche theory and, 5
studies of articles on, 49, 62n
blocking strategy, in duration models, 432, 446
blockmodeling, 84
boundary issues, history calendar and, 366–7
broad niche, described, 5
business effects, in confidence models, 320

cahiers de doléances
See under text population studies
calendar format, advantages of, 357–8
career concepts, 48, 83
career turning points as patterns, 48

categorical analysis, 304–7
causal effects, 331, 333–4, 349
unemployment duration study and, 442–5, *444*
CCSOM project, 146, 147n
censoring processes, in divorce rate analysis, 400, 402, *403*, 404, 411, *414*, 415, 422–6, 433
census. *See* U.S. Bureau of the Census
chi-square statistics
aggregated modeling and, 455, *457*, 458, 471
in mobility models, 240
standard errors and, 313
See also likelihood ratio chi-square statistics
Chitwan Valley Family Study (CVFS), 357–85*passim*
calendars from, *361, 378, 380–1*
class schema, *182*, 183
class typology, *182*, 183
clauses in semantic grammars, 93–5, 99n, 139
application of, 105, 109–11, 115n
cross classification of, *122, 123*
as unit of analysis, 121
See also verb-object; subject-verb-object
clusters
history calendar and, 366n, 366–7
rhetorical forms and, 66–70, *67, 68*
in text population studies, 91
variance components and, 453–4, 455–8, *457*
coding methods
article elements used in, 55, *56, 58–9*
book for, 138, 172
clause analysis and, 110–11, 172
clause decisions and, 106–7n, 109–11, 171–2
for history calendar, 370
for occupational classification, 184–6
for semantic text analysis, 90, 95n, 101–3, 102n, 131, 135

for sequence comparisons, 53–60
common sequences technique, 131
competing risks model, latent duration times and, 421–2
comprehensibility, assumption of, 97n, 98
computer software
  for biology, 64n
  ETHNO program, 102
  EWLS and CLOGIT, 312
  for growth modeling, 460
  for latent variable modeling (Statlib), 465
  MCMC algorithms, 445
  for occupation coding, 186
  OPTIMIZE program, 64n
  for parsing, 94n
  Program for Linguistic Content Analysis (PLCA), 105n, 107n, 108, 114
  QuickBasic, 80n
  for random effects regression, 343n
  regression graphics program (R-CODE), 204
  SAS CATMOD procedure, 312, 314
  for SURF model, 410n
  for text analysis, 103n
  See also theorem provers
conditional independence proposals, 430, 431
conditional information, Gibbs sampling and, 71, 73
conditional likelihood
  duration models and, 426, 431
  LEA algorithm and, 80
conditional prior proposals, 431–2
Conference Board
  1992 confidence measurement of, 316–22
  expectation index of, 299–303, 322
  three category rating scales and, 309
confidence measurement model, 316–22
confidence scale
  cumulative probabilities and, 307–8, 309, 310

consistency
  coding procedures and, 53
  estimation and, 313
  niche theory and, 25
  theories and, 146, 161
Consumer Expectation Index (Conference Board), 301
consumer expectation indexes, 299–302, 300, 301, 302
content analysis, 131, 151
  See also text analysis
context of situation
  speech acts and, 103–4
  text populations and, 91–2
contextual event history data collection, 356–7, 360, 363–5, 382–3
contextual level time varying covariates measurement, 373–4, 374n
contingency tables, association analysis and, 306
conventions in divorce rate analysis, 398–9
convergence hypothesis
  for article pairs, 64–5, 71, 73, 81n
  LEA algorithm and, 81, 132
convergence rate
  in duration models, 432
  Gibbs sampler and, 81n
converging rhetoric theory, 50
correlated competing hazards, attrition modeling and, 394–5
costs, in alignment algorithms, 62
counterfactuals, 102
counting processes method, 419
covariance structure analysis, 455, 459, 463
credibility, assumption of, 97n, 98
cultural differences, 52, 52n
  word meaning and, 110
cumulative density function, in divorce model, 401–2
CVFS. See Chitwan Valley Family Study
cyclical patterns, environmental change and, 16

dampening out, 348
data analysis techniques, 153, 173
data augmentation, 74n
data collection
    contextual event history, 356–7
    mixed method of, 358–9
    quality of, 374–7
data dredging, 348
data information
    for article pairs, 64–5
    for sequence comparisons, 51
    for unemployment duration study,
        433–8
default logics, 31
definitions (D), 8
degrees of freedom
    divorce analysis and, 404, 413
    in latent variable modeling, 457, *475*
    in structural equations models, 230
density dependence model, 146
    mortality measurement and, 9n
density functions, in divorce model,
    401–2
descriptions of processes, 101n
descriptions of states of affairs, 101n
descriptive clauses, 110
design effect formula, 456
Dictionary of Occupational Titles, 180,
    181, 186
disaggregated models, 454–5, 456
    See also multilevel modeling
discrete kernel smoothing method, 419
discrete time competing hazards model,
    408, 410–11
discrete time duration data models,
    422–6
discursive functions of sentences, 98
dissimilarity, niche theory and, 6,
    14–16, *15*
distance metrics, cluster analysis and,
    66n
distance pattern, 66
divorce rate analysis, 395–7, *397*
    conventions used in, 398–9

model for, 401–2
    weighting schemes and, 399–400
domains in history calendar, 362–4, 367,
    368, 379
dualism in article analysis, 142
    See also ambiguity
duration dependence in divorce model,
    402–4, 411
duration function, niche theory and, 17n
duration models, for unemployement,
    418–20, 446, 448
duration of article sections, 60, 70
dynamic discrete time duration models,
    417–49, *427*

earnings measurement, 181
    See also income levels
economic status, 179
    See also socioeconomic status
education attainment measurement,
    181–2, 194–5
    latent variable modeling and, 456
    socioeconomic indexes and, 201–2
education levels
    intergenerational stratification model
        in, *247*
    regression analysis and, 201–
        46*passim,* 206n, 246–50, *249*
    respondent choice and, 367, 383
e-mail addresses. See *first page of each
        chapter;* Internet addresses
empirically weighted least squares
        (EWLS)
    in generalized linear model analysis,
        312–16
    See also under computer software
environmental change, 14–18, *15,* 19,
    22, 27, 29
environmental conditions, 5, 7, 24
    See also meaning postulates (M)
environmental patches, niche theory
        and, 7, 14–18, *15, 23*
Erikson and Goldthorp class schema,
    182

error detection, calendar format and, 358, 374
establishments, defined, 180
establishments *versus* industries, 180
evaluation, clause coding and, 109, 136
  See also under text structures
event history analysis, 356, 389
  attrition adjustment and, 393–415
  for calendars, 360–2, 373
  of divorce rates, 395–7
  duration models and, 422
event structure analysis, 151, 425
EWLS. *See* empirically weighted least squares
existence condition, in treatment effects, 333–4
explanatory variables, 350
explicitness, theory generalization and, 25–6
expression, elements of, 96–7
extinction, mortality measurement and, 10n
extraneous variables, 350

failure time modeling, 420, 425–6
First-Order Logic (FOL), 154
  formalization and, 30–1, 146
  introduced, 3–5
Fisher scoring, 311
fitness
  grammar and text structures and, 92–3
  versus niche breadth, 11
  occupational prestige and, 203
fitness sets, niche theory and, 14n, 18, 147
floor effects, multiple matching and, 340, *341*
focus sequences, in random sequences, 75–7
FOL. *See* First-Order Logic
formalization process
  logics and, 31
  methodological aspects of, 2, 153

modular structure of, 26
niche theory and, 25–6, 29
frailty models, 448
full conditional distributions, 429–30
functional forms, 101–3, *108*
  occupational prestige and, 203
  unambiguous, 98–101
functional grammars, 92
  See also semantic grammars
function symbols, described, 4

gap penalty, insertion costs and, 63
Gaussian autoregressive model, 424
Gaussian distributions, 430, 431
Geman and Geman theorem, 80
gender factor
  occupational prestige and, 189, 198–200, *218*
  prestige scores and, 191–2
  respondent choice and, 367
  socioeconomic indexes and, 200–25
  unemployment duration and, 418, 433, *436, 438*
  word meaning and, 110
generalism *versus* specialism, 6, 151
  environmental patterns and, 27
generalists, 12–14, 22–3
  high environmental dissimilarity and, 16
  low environmental dissimilarity and, 15
  versus specialists, mortality measurement and, 10
  wide niche, fitness and, 12, *22*
  See also specialists; theorems (T)
general nonlinear confidence model, 317–22
General Social Survey (GSS), 220, 251
  cross-validation and, 251
  education and income factors in, *241*
  gender factors in, *244*
  occupational prestige ratings in, 190, 203, 209

occupational status variables of, *221, 223*
rates of refusal in, 184
Geographic Information System (GIS), 383–5
German National Science Foundation, 445
German socioeconomic panel GSOEP, 418, 420, 433, 442
Gibbs sampling
    convergence rate and, 81n
    discussed, 48, 74n, 84, 165
    duration models and, 429–30, 431
    in rhetorical subsequences, 71–4, 152
GIS. *See* Geographic Information System
global alignment methods, patterns and, 48, 79
global multiple sequence aligment problem (GMSA), 74n
global optimum, content analysis and, 132
Global Positioning System (GPS), 384, 384n
GMSA. *See* global multiple sequence aligment problem
GPS. *See* Global Positioning System
grain size
    niche theory and, 6, 14, *15*, 17–18, *22*, 30
    patch durations and, 17, 23
grievance analysis *(cahiers de doléances)*, 90, 92
grouped continuous regression model, 305
grouped Cox model, 421, 423
grouped proportional hazards model, 421
growth modeling, 460–2, 465, 470–8
GSS. *See* General Social Survey; National Opinion Research Center
Gumbel's Type B bivariate extreme value distribution, 408, 415

Hastings algorithm, 429–30, 431
hazard modeling
    discrete time competing, 408, 410–11
    discussed, 356, 373–4
    in divorce rate analysis, 400, 402–4, 406, 407–15, 447
    unemployment duration study and, 420–1, *438*
HCFA. *See* Health Care Finance Administration
Health Care Finance Administration (HCFA), 328n, 328–9, *330,* 350
health service history calendars, 379–82
hermenuetic comparisons of articles, 54n
High School and Beyond study, 326
history calendars, 377–83, *378, 380–1*
homiletic style, in sociology journals, 57
hospitals
    magnet, 328–9
    nursing organizational characteristics in, 327–8
    patient satisfaction with, 314
hurdle configurations, niche theory and, 6
hyperbole, in functional forms, 102
hyperbolic secant-square distribution in divorce model, 401–2
Hyperproof theorem prover, 3n

identity link, in linear probability model, 334
IJD. *See* index of job desirability
illustrative *versus* definitive analysis, 142
imagination of process, functional forms and, 101
income levels
    occupational classification schemes and, 180, 184–5, 194, 198
    regression analysis and, 201–50*passim,* 206n
    socioeconomic indexes and, 201–2, 245n

incomplete matching, 326n
independence of irrelevant alternatives (IIA), 410–11, *412*, 413–15
independence proposals, 430, 431
index of class position, 184
Index of Consumer Expectations (University of Michigan), 300, 322
Index of Consumer Sentiment (Katona), 299
index of dissimilarity, 408
index of job desirability (IJD), 181
index of social position, two factor, 195–8
industries
    coding and, 185–6, 186n
    defined, 180
    question series for, *185*
    See also establishments
inertia theory, in organizational ecology, 26–7
inexact matching, 326n
information statistic, subsequence length and, 81
insertion costs, in aligment algorithms, 63–4
intelligent misreadings, niche theory and, 25
intentional components, of speech acts, 96, 101n
International Standard Classifications of Occupations, 189
Internet addresses
    for marginal frequencies analysis (Statlib), 316n
    OPTIMIZE program, 64n
    for PLCA, 105n
    SEI scores, 178n
    for SURF model (Statlib), 410n
    See also computer software
inter-rater reliability, 131
interval scale
    niche theory and, 9
    unemployment duration study and, 421

interviews
    calendar format and, 358, 364–5, 374–7
    event history analysis and, 395–7, 407
inverse gamma distributions, 432, 448
inverse Wishart distributions, 424
irony, in functional forms, 102
irreducibility, Gibbs sampling and, 73, 80
IRT techniqies, 470
Ising model, 84
item slopes, 307, 309, 311, 320–2, *321*

job descriptions, 179
job-holding, 179, 184
jobs, defined, 180
    See also occupations
Journal of the Royal Statistical Society, 74n, 81n
judgements, functional forms and, 101–2, 110
judgements of processes, 101n
judgements of states of affairs, 101n
justification, clause coding and, 109, 136, 140
    See also under text structures

key variables, in marital status analysis, 397
key words, in text analysis, 107
K-generalism, 11
Kronecker product, in two-level disaggregated model, 459

labor market
    in Britain, 420, 434
    in hospitals, 328
    methodological studies of, 91
    social standing and, 179
    See also unemployment duration study
Lagrangian multiplier test, 343n
language use
    in academic texts, 49n

logics and, 31
qualitative reasoning and, 2, 18, 25
speech acts and, 96–7
See also natural language theories;
    semantic grammars; verbal theory
latent variable modeling, 462–6, *464,*
    470–8
statistical variation and, 453
LCA. See linguistic content analysis
LEA algorithm
    calculations for, 80–1n
    discussed, 71, 83–4
    Gibbs sampling and, 74–81, 132, 165
    subsequence analysis and, 82
left censored spells (LC), 400, 402, *403,*
    404
lemmas (L), niche theory and, 29, 31–2,
    35–6, 37–8, 40
    See also assumptions (A)
lexicon of article elements, 50, *56, 58–9*
life cycle theories, 48, 83
life history calendar technique, 356–7,
    363
life history strategies, 146
likelihood ratio chi-square statistics
    linguistic content analysis and, *119*
    in structural equations models, 230
likelihood ratio test statistic, divorce
    analysis and, 404, 406
linear composite of covariates, *332*
    See also propensity score
linear discriminant function, 334
linear dynamic models, 424
linear probability model, 334–5, 336n
linear propensity score, defined, 334
linguistic content analysis (LCA), 109–
    18, 169n, 173–4
    data matrix table of, *116–17*
    functional forms and, 99n
    semantic grammar and, 137–9
    translation table of, *112–13*
linguists
    semantic grammars *versus* syntax
        grammars, 94

versus social scientists, 92
text analysis and, 125, 137
    See also semantic grammars; syntax
        grammars
LISREL, 230
literary analysis, sociological articles
    and, 49–50
local likelihood estimation, 419
local linear trend model, 424
logical connectives, described, 4
logical formalization
    discussed, 2–4, 145, 159–60
    niche theory and, 6–24, 25–7, 30
logical inference *versus* statistical
    inference, 3
logical opposites, in semantic text
    analysis, 96
logic *versus* intuition, 25
logic *versus* mathematics, 2–3
logistic cumulative density function,
    401–2
logistic regression model, 334–5
logistic response model, 336, 336n, *337*
logistic transformations, occupational
    prestige and, 203
logit function
    in logistic regression model, 334
    parameter estimates and, 410n
logit matching, 335
logit models, 421, 434, 442
loglinear models
    versus cumulative logit models,
        304–7
    linguistic content analysis and, *119*
    thematic text analysis and, 123–4
longitudinal data, latent variable
    modeling and, 453–79
Longitudinal Research File, 399
Longitudinal Study of American Youth
    (LSAY), 470, 471
loss accumulation, niche theory
    and, 19
LSAY. See Longitudinal Study of
    American Youth

macro-level characteristics in social
    changes, 356
macropsychology, 300
magnet hospitals, 328–9, 345, *346*
magnitude estimation, job desirability
    and, 181
marginal analysis, 312–15
marginal information, Gibbs sampling
    and, 71
marital status studies, 395–7, *396*
    See also divorce rate analysis
Markov chain
    Gibbs sampling and, 73, 165
    LEA algorithm and, 80
Markov chain Monte Carlo methods
    (MCMC), 73–4, 84
    dynamic discrete time duration
        models and, 419, 426–49
Markov variations, 424–5
marriage spells, weighting and, 400–5
marriage timing model, 373–4
matching
    of logits, 335
    problems with, 326–7
    statistical developments in, 326
mathematics issues, 145, 146, 454, 456,
    466–7, 469–70
maximum likelihood estimations
    cluster sampling and, 455, 458
    duration models and, 419, 445
    for generalized linear models, 311
    growth model and, 465
    software for, 312, 343n
    structural equations models and, 230
    SURF model and, 409–10, 411
MCMC. *See* Markov chain Monte Carlo
    methods
mean deviation analysis
    optimal alignment algorithm and,
        64–5, *65*
    semantic grammar and, *108, 112–13,
        116–17, 119, 120, 122,* 143
meaning postulates (M)
    introduced, 5, 7n

niche theory and, 14–17, 19, 21, 24
meanings in text and speech, 94–5
mean structure, of multilevel latent
    variable model, 454
measure candidates, fitness and, 9
measurement errors, intraclass correla-
    tions and, 469–70, *470*
Medicare mortality data, 328, *330,* 347
mental processes, intentions and, 101–3
Metafor theorem prover, 3, 3n, 25
Metropolis algorithm, 73–4, 74n, 430
Metropolis-Hastings algoritm, 445–6
micro-level characteristics in individual
    behavior, 356
ML estimations. *See* maximum likeli-
    hood estimations
mobility models, 388
    multivariate analyses of, 246n
    occupational classification schemes
        and, 183, 183n, *232–3, 238–9*
modal logics, 31
model trimming, 335
month-specific model, expectation index
    and, 304, 307–16
mortality measures
    fitness and, 9
    niche theory and, 26
multilevel factor analysis model, 467,
    469, *470*
multilevel latent variable model, 454,
    456, 463
multilevel modeling, 356, 387–8, 478–9
    for calendars, 362–4, 365, 373–4, 384
    latent variable modeling and, 453–79
multiple matching, *339,* 339–41
    strengths and weaknesses of, 327
    See also matching
multiple month models
    expectation index and, 304, 317–22
    unemployment duration study,
        433–45, 447
multiple regression methods, 326, 349
multivariate analysis, latent variable
    modeling and, 456

multivariate distribution, matching and, 327
multivariate linear model
    duration models and, 424
    for treatment effects, 331–2

name constants, described, 4
narrative analysis, 151
narrative grammars, 92
narrow niche, described, 5
National Family Opinion of Toledo, 316
National Longitudinal Surveys (NLS), 401
National Opinion Research Center studies (NORC)
    General Social Survey (1989), 187n, 189
    occupational prestige and (1964), 188, 189, 192
    occupational titles survey (1947), 190
    socioeconomic index and, 191
natural history models, 48
natural language theories, 145–7, 161
    descriptions, niche theory and, 25
    efficiency and, 96
    semantic grammars and, 95n
    See also language use; semantic grammars; verbal theory
Needleman-Wunsch algorithm, 63, 64n
neighborhood history calendar, 359–77, 361, 386–9
Nepalese neighborhood history calendar, 360
nested multinomial logit model, 421
neutral response option
    in analysis of variance model, 307, 310
Newton-Raphson iterations, 311
niche theory
    described, 5–6
    formalization process for, 6–24
    logic formalization and, 25–31, 151
    sociological premises and, 2
niche width theory, 7–9, 146, 147, 148

structure of routines and, 11
NLS. See National Longitudinal Surveys
non-left censored spells (NLC), 400, 402, 404
nonparametric modeling, unemployment duration study and, 439, 445
nonparametric regression, in treatment effects, 331
nonparametric significance test, 83
NORC. See National Opinion Research Center
normal distribution, in subsequence analysis, 82–3
nuisance parameters, 312
nursing organizational characteristics, 327–8, 328n

observational studies, 326
observation period, 8
    environmental patches and, 18
    niche theory and, 7
    population losses in, 18
observed data methods, Gibbs sampling and, 71
Occupational Changes in a Generation Survey (OCG), 187–8, 242n, 251
occupational classifications, 188–200
    See also socioeconomic indexes
occupational prestige, 181, 188–90, 198
occupational social standing measurement, 183–4
    intergenerational stratification model and, 236
occupational status measurement, 181–3, 190–8
    intergenerational stratification model and, 226
occupations, 180, 185
    See also jobs
OCG survey. See Occupational Changes in a Generation Survey
optimal alignment, 152
    article coding and, 60–70
    reliability analysis of, 64n

optimistic response option, in variance
   analysis, 307, 310, *319*
optimization techniques, Metropolis
   algorithm as, 74n
ordered three-category multinomial, 307
order patterns technique, 131–3
ordinal categorical analysis, 304–6
ordinal regression models, 306–7
ordinal scale engineering, niche theory
   and, 28–9, 147
organizational ecology, 145–8
   disbanding process of, 9
   five strands of theory in, 146
   intertia theory and, 26–7
   niche theory of, 2
Organizations in Action (Pólos), 162
organization types, niche width and,
   7–9
orientation effects, in confidence
   models, 320
Otter theorem prover, 3n, 146
outflow, 12, 20
   versus fitness, 10, 147
outflow aggregation, in niche theory,
   18–19, *20,* 28–9

page coding procedure, sequence
   comparison and, 55
paired *t*-statistic, multiple matching and,
   340–1, *342*
Panel Study of Income Dynamics
   (PSID), 398–9, 401, 415
panel surveys, 394, 406
paragraph coding procedure, 55
parallel regression assumption, 333
parameter estimates
   duration models and, 419, *441*
   linguistic content analysis and, *120,*
     121
   in mobility models, 240
   in panel data, 394, 405n, 406, 413
   standard errors and, 312
parametric modeling, 439–45, *440*
parametric regression, 331

parsing software, 94n
   See also under computer software
participatory rural appraisal technique,
   365
patch durations, grain size and, 17,
   23
patches, 12–13
   See also environmental patches;
     theorems (T)
patient mortality, 328
   See also mortality measures
patient satisfaction with hospital care
   survey, 314
pattern location technique, 131
patterns in sequence data, 48, 60
Pearson product moment correlations,
   471
perception, clause coding and, 109, 115,
   136
   See also under text structures
perception of process, functional forms
   and, 101, 103–4
performance utterances classes, 101n
pessimistic response option, 307, 310
phenomenal semantic grammar, 93
Picker/Commonwealth National Survey
   (1993), 314
PLCA (Program for Linguistic Content
   Analysis). *See under* computer
   software
polytomous categorical analysis, 304,
   309
pooled regression slope, 333
population ecology theory, 154
   See also organizational ecology
population losses, 9, 10
   in eight environmental patterns, 18
poststratification adjustments, 397
predicates, 30
   described, 4
   in linguistic content analysis, 99n
   in semantic text analysis, 95
predictions
   niche theory and, 22–4, 23n, *24*

unemployment duration study and,
    448
predictions equations for socioeconomic
    index, *214*
predictor variables, mortality rates and,
    329, 336, 336n, 347
premise sorting, 5, 26
    See also background premises of
        theorems (B)
probability density function, 401–2
probability process
    consumer confidence and, 304–7
    LEA algorithm and, 80
    skewed response variables and, 335
probit model, 421
propensities in panel data, 394, 401
propensity score model, *332,* 334n, 347,
    408
    matching via, 334–41, *337, 341*
    See also linear composite of
        covariates
proportional odds confidence model,
    316–17, *318*
PSID. *See* Panel Study of Income
    Dynamics
psychology
    article studies of, 49, 60
    consumer confidence and, 303
    latent variable modeling and, 462

Q-calculation phase, subsequence
    analysis and, 76–7, 80
qualitative analysis, 151, 152, 155
qualitative comparative analysis, 151
qualitative methodologies, evaluation
    of, 151–8, 155
qualitative reasoning, logical modeling
    and, 2
qualitative text analysis, 155–7
quality quotients, in LEA algorithm, 81
quantifiers, 4, 30
quantitative content analysis, 154–5
quantitative sociology, rhetorical con-
    ventions in, 49, 51

quantitative text analysis
    discussed, 90, 169–71
    semantic grammar for, 89–176*passim*
questionnaire design, for history calen-
    dar, 364–5

racial factor
    occupational prestige and, 189
    socioeconomic indexes and, 200
random coefficient growth modeling,
    460–1
random effects ANOVA, 469–70, *470*
random effects tests, 343n, 344–5,
    345n
random numbers
    duration models and, 429
    propensity scores and, 338, 401
random order, nearest available pair
    matching methods, 338
random samples
    latent variable modeling and, 453,
        454–6, 462
    semantic grammars and, 93, 121
random sequences
    LEA algorithm and, 74–5, 77n
    in variance components model, 343
random walk Metropolis proposals, 430,
    431, 435
Rasch rating method, probability models
    and, 304–6
ratings scales, probability and, 304–5
recognition, clause coding and, 109,
    136
    See also under text structures
recording techniques, for history calen-
    dar, 369–70, 379, 382, 383–5
regression analysis
    consumer confidence and, 305–6
    discrete time duration models and,
        417–18
    latent variables and, *468*
    mortality rates and, 344, 349
    of occupational prestige, 203–15,
        210–11

popularity of, 326
skewed treatments and, 327–34
regularities, in alignment algorithms,
62–3, 79–80
relative efficiency, multiple matching
and, *339, 339*–40
relevance
assumption of, 97n, 98
of texts to semantic grammar, 103n
remediability, logic formalization and,
25–6
replacement costs, in alignment
algorithms, 63
repsonse probabilities, 307
residual correlation, in growth
modeling, 473
residual plots, regression analysis and,
206–7
resource conditions, niche theory and,
7–8, 14
resource configurations, degree of
fitness and, 9–10, 24
resource partitioning, 146
respondents
choice of, 367–8, 368n
panel data and, 394, 395–7
recall of, in studies, 357–8, 363,
376
response set, in treatment effects, 333,
333n
retranslation, verification of data and,
114
rhetorical patterns
in social science, 135–44, 152–3
in sociological articles, 49, 51, 53–4,
57, 60, 66, 70
rhetorical structure of articles
ambiguity and, 140
sequence comparisons and, 49–50,
53–4, 63, 83, 132, 151
rhetorical subsequences, in sociological
articles, 70–83
A Rhetoric of Bourgeois Revolution
(Sewell), 155

routines maintenance, niche theory and,
11
routines of organizations, 11
row-stochastic matrix, Gibbs sampling
and, 72, 132

SA. *See* simulated annealing
sampling information, for sequence
comparisons, 52, 76
sarcasm, in functional forms, 102
scale element quantity, niche theory and,
20
scale specifications, niche theory and,
28–9
scatterplots
regression, and occupational prestige,
205–6
regression analysis, *205, 207, 208*
school districts study, 466, *467, 470*
school history calendars, 377–9
science strategies studies, 49, 49n
Second International Mathematics Study
(SIMS), 466, *467, 470*
second order logics, 30–1
SEI. *See* socioeconomic indexes
selection preference, niche theory and,
21–2, 28–9
selection probability, weighting conventions and, 398–9, 405n
semantic grammars
application of, 105–24
for quantitative text analysis,
89–176*passim*
unambiguous coding and, 136–7
semantic opposition
in ordinary discourse, 95–8
in semantic text analysis, 96–8,
99–100, 102
See also ambiguity
semantic text analysis
described, 90, 125
generic grammar for, 95–104
See also text analysis
sequence analysis methods

discrete time duration model and, 422
discussed, 66n, 131–2
optimal matching techniques and, 151
patterns in sociological articles and, 48
sequence patterns, described, 60–2
SES covariate, 471–8, *472, 474*
Shared Unmeasured Risk Factor model
  (SURF), 407–14
Siegel prestige scores, 191–2, 203
SIMS. *See* Second International
  Mathematics Study
simulated annealing (SA), 74n, 77n,
  132, 165
SIOPS. *See* Standard International
  Occupational Prestige Scale
SIPP. *See* Survey of Income and
  Program Participation
situational context
  in speech acts, 103–4
  text populations and, 91–2
skewed treatments
  regression analysis and, 327–34
smoothing methods, 419, 446
  in nonparametric regression, 331
social biases, coding and, 110
social class schemas, 181–3, *182,* 195
social contact theory, 157
Social Forces, 152
social sciences
  versus linguistics, 92
  time measurement and, 418
socioeconomic indexes (SEI)
  Duncan, 181, 187, 188, 190–9, 202–3
  FSEI (female), 216–20
  Hauser-Featherman, 192
  Hauser-Warren, 200–25, *252–93*
  ISEI (international), 197
  MSEI (male), 192, 196, 216–24
  Nakao-Treas, *192,* 193, 201, 217,
    252–93
  for occupations, 177–251, *252–93*
  Stevens-Cho, 192
  Stevens-Featherman, 191–3, 196,
    202–3

structural models of, 225–50
  TSEI (total), 192, 216–24
socioeconomic measurement, expectation indexes and, 302
socioeconomic status, 178–9, 470,
  471–8
Sociological Methodology, 144
Sociological Methods and Research, 62n
sociological regularities in sequences,
  47
sociology
  matching studies in, 326
  as religious field, 54–5, 55n
sociology journals
  discussion of, 50–3, 53n, 132, 140–1,
    152, 165–7
  See also *Individual journal titles*
sociotropic expectations, 300
software. *See* computer software
specialists, 12–14, 22–3, 26n
  grain size and, 17n
  narrow niche, fitness and, 12
  niche theory and, 27–8
  resource configurations and, 18, 22
  See also generalists; theorems (T)
speech acts
  expression elements of, 96–7
  illocutionary force of, 101–2n
  meanings of, 95–6
  situational contexts and, 103–4
  state of affairs in, 100
spline smoothing method, 419
standard deviation analysis
  mortality rates and, 328
  of occupational prestige, 204, 213
  optimal alignment algorithm and,
    64–5, *65,* 68, 70
  semantic grammar and, *108, 112–13,
    116–17, 119, 120, 122,* 143
standard errors
  aggregated modeling and, 455, 456,
    458, 471
  in correlated marginal estimation,
    311–15

linguistic content analysis and, *120*
matching and, 326–7
multiple matching and, 340, 343n
racial factor and, 187n
in structural equations models, 230
Standard International Occupational
    Prestige Scale (SIOPS), 189, 190
started logits, occupational prestige
    analysis and, 204, *208, 218,* 220,
    237
statement mapping, 93n
states of affairs
    evaluation of, 101, 109
    in linguistic content analysis, 99n
    in semantic text analysis, 95, 99–100
state space
    duration models and, 419, 424
    LEA algorithm and, 80
statistical inefficiency in matching,
    326
statistical inference *versus* logical infer-
    ence, 3
story grammars, 92
stratification process, structural equation
    models and, 225–50, *249*
strongly ignorable treatment, 333, 333n
structural inertia theories, 146
structures of articles
    coding procedures and, 54–7
    complexity and, 136–7
subjective plausibility, in functional
    forms, 102
subject-verb-object semantic grammar
    content analysis and, 136–7, 171–5
    in labor disputes analysis, 90n, 91
subordination, in clause coding, 115n
subsequence analysis
    alignment methods and, 48
    of articles, 81–3
    LEA algorithm and, 74
    rhetorical change and, 70–83
subtle, defined, 142
successive intervals method (Thurston),
    304

SURF. *See* Shared Unmeasured Risk
    Factor
surface grammars, 93n, 94
Survey of Income and Program Partici-
    pation (SIPP)
    (1986), 395–400, 402–4, 407, 409,
        413–14
    (1986–1988), 251
survey ratings scales, probability and,
    304–5
survival functions
    attrition modeling and, 394–5
    unemployment duration study and,
        420–1, 433, *438*
synctactic components, in grievance
    analysis, 90
syntax grammars, 93n, 94, 171

temporal by communal interactions,
    320
text analysis, 152, 170
    ambiguity and, 101–3
    instrumental approach to, 94n
    political literature and, 155–7
    See also Linguistic Content Analysis
    See also semantic text analysis;
        thematic text analysis
    See also speech acts
text grammars, 92
text population studies
    cahiers de doléances, 90, 92
    of labor disputes, 91
    structures within, 91–5
text structures, 102n, 104
    highlighting of, 93–5
thematic text analysis *versus* semantic
    text analysis, 121–4, 125
theorem provers, 3, 3n, 25, 146, 162
theorems (T), 7n
    niche theory and, 12–13, 15–16, 22–4
    niche theory and, detailed, 32–5,
        36–7, 38–45
theoretical arguments, logical formaliza-
    tion and, 1, 2, 161

theoretical parsimony, 5
theory building, niche theory and, 26–7,
    29–30
theory formalization, 145, 161
theory relevance, cluster analysis and,
    69
theory testing, logic formalization and,
    26
three element ordering scale, 9
three-level growth model, 460–2
Thurston rating method, 304, 309
time horizon effects, in confidence
    models, 319
time series modeling, 420, 432, *433,
    436,* 461
time varying weighting adjustments, in
    divorce rate analysis, 399–400,
    401–2
transition kernels, 430
transition rule, LEA algorithm and, 80
translation considerations, logical
    formalization and, 7
translation metaphor, in linguistic
    content analysis, 111
transparency of structures, logic formal-
    ization and, 25–6
trending elements, decadal observations
    of, *61*
truth, assumption of, 97n, 98
t-tests, multiple matching and, 343,
    343n
    See also paired *t*-statistic
turning point concept, LEA algorithm
    and, 83
two-level disaggregated model, 458–60
two-level random coefficient growth
    model, *476–7,* 478
two-level socioeconomic status
    modeling, 471–8

unambiguity, in functional forms,
    99–101
understatement, in functional forms,
    102

unemployment duration study, *418,* 420,
    433–45
unintentional components of speech
    acts, 96
University of Michigan
    expectation index of, 299–303, 322
    Survey Research Center of, 300
    three category rating scales and, 309
U.S. Bureau of the Census, 180, 220,
    251, 407n
    classification systems of, 185–6,
    189
    event history analysis and, 399
    occupational status variables of, *221*
U.S. Department of Labor, Employment
    and Training Administration of,
    180

validity analysis, 66n
variability, niche theory and, 4, 14, *15,
    16–17*
variables
    environmental change and, 14, *15*
    matching of, 350
variance components, 453
variance components model
    multiple matching and, 341–5
verbal theory, 159–60, 173
    niche theory and, 25, 28, 30
    See also language use; natural
    language theories; semantic
    grammars
verb-object semantic grammar
    in grievance analysis, 90
vocabulary of forms, cluster analysis
    and, 69

wage rates. *See* income levels
weighted least squares, occupational
    prestige analysis and, 204
weighting schemes, 398n, 399–400,
    405, 405n
    effects of, 400–7

What Is the Third Estate? (Sieyes), 155
Wilcoxon signed-ranks test, 83
Wisconsin Longitudinal Study (WLS),
    180n, 181n, 193, 198, 326
women
    occupations of, 179
    prestige scores and, 191–2, 198

unemployment duration study and,
    433, *436, 438*
word logic, described, 3
World Wide Web. *See* Internet addresses
Wright class typology, *182*

x and *x acts,* discussed, 95